A Guide to English Language Usage
for non-native speakers

Peter Harvey

Illustrations by Alison Litherland

Lavengro Books

English language usage made plain

This book is published by
Lavengro Books
Gomis 43, 1-6
Barcelona
Spain

http://www.lavengrobooks.com
books@lavengrobooks.com
A Guide to English Language Usage for non-native speakers
ISBN 978-84-617-7939-0
Spanish legal deposit B 2082-2017
Text © Peter Harvey
Line drawings © Alison Litherland.
The maze on page xii is from Wikimedia Commons:
http://commons.wikimedia.org/wiki/File:Labirinto_003.svg,
where it is marked as being in the public domain (accessed 11 November 2016).
Cover by Peter Harvey following a design by Joan Quintana.

All rights reserved. No part of this publication may be reproduced, stored in a retrieval system, or transmitted, in any form or by any means, electronic, magnetic tape, electrostatic, photocopying, recording, mechanical, or otherwise, without the prior permission of the publisher in writing.

Intellectual property rights are protected under Articles 270ff of the Spanish criminal code and legislation in other countries. Legal action may be taken to defend the author's rights.

Requests to photocopy or scan any part of this book should be addressed to the Spanish reprographic rights organisation CEDRO at www.conlicencia.com.

GELU 4.1 CS July 2018

contents

about the author	xiii
introductory notes	xiv
note for history articles	xv
main changes in edition 3 (January 2011)	xvi
main changes in edition 4 (February 2017)	xvi
main changes in edition 4.1 (February 2017)	xvi
acknowledgements	xviii

A	**1**
a, A /eɪ/	1
a- adjectives	1
a & an	2
abbreviations	2
-able and -ible	7
abortion & miscarriage	8
above & over	8
abroad & foreign	8
accents and diacritic marks	8
accommodation	8
ache, pain & sore	9
acronyms	9
actual	9
AD and BC	9
adapt & adopt	9
adjective not adverb	9
adjectives	9
adjectives, comparison	10
adjectives, order	12
adjectives, use of *and* between adjectives	12
adjectives with -ly	12
adjectives without nouns	12
adverbs, comparison	13
adverbs, formation	13
adverbs, order	13
adverbs, position	13
adverbs without -ly	16
advertise	16
advice	16
aerial & antenna	16
affect & effect	16
Africa	16
ago, since & for	17
aid, aide & AIDS	17
ain't	17
air-conditioned	17
aisle	17
ale and beer	17
alive, life & live	17
all & everybody/everything	18
all, both & most	18
alliance	19
almost + negative	19
alone, by oneself, on one's own & lonely	19
along, up and down the road	19
already, all ready etc.	19
already, yet & still	19
alternate & alternative	20
although & despite	21
although etc.	21
aluminium	21
always + continuous aspect	21
amen	21
America	21
American English	21
amid(st), among(st), while (whilst) & again(st)	24
among & between	24
analyser & analyst	24
ancient, antique & elderly	24
anger, surprise, insults and taboo words	25
Anglican	29
Anglo-	29
angry	30
animals	30
another	31
anticipate & expect	31
any- & some-	31
appointment, date & rendezvous	33
approve (of)	33
Arabic numerals	33
-arian	33
armistice poppies	33
arrive	34
articles	34
artist & artiste	37
arts and sciences	37
as	37
ascend & ascent	38
assassin	38
assure etc.	38
asterisk	39
at & to	39
attach & enclose	39
audience, onlookers, spectators & viewers	39
autarchy & autarky	39
auxiliary and main verbs have the same form	39
aware	39
away & out	40
axe, axis & axle	40
aye and nay	40

B	**41**
b, B /biː/	41
back-formation	41
backside	41
bald & bold	41
ball	41
bank	41
bar	41
bare etc.	42
bass	42
bath & bathe	42
BBC	42
BBC English	42
beach, coast & shore	42

contents

beans	43	can, can't, cannot & cant	54
bear, bore, born(e)	43	capital letters	54
been & gone	43	car	56
before & in front of	43	care	56
begin & start	43	caricature	57
behave	44	carnival	57
belief	44	carry & fetch	57
belly	44	case	57
below & under	44	case, grammatical	57
bench	44	cast	58
beside & besides	44	caste	58
better	45	catholic	59
bi-	45	cease etc.	59
biannual & biennial	45	-cede & -ceed	60
Bible, books of	45	Celts and Celtic	60
bicycle	45	censor, censure & censer	61
big & large	45	centre & middle	61
bind & bound	46	certain(ly) & sure(ly)	62
bio-	47	-cester	62
biscuit	47	chap	62
bite & sting	47	character, personality & personage	63
bleed & blood	47	cheap(ly)	63
blend	47	cheer	63
blink & wink	47	chemist	63
board	47	chess	63
boat & ship	48	chest	63
bookmaker	48	child	64
bookshop & library	48	childish	64
bourgeois	48	chip	64
bow	48	choler(a)	64
bowdlerise	49	choral & coral	64
bowls & bowling	49	chord & cord	64
boyfriend and girlfriend	49	Christ and Christian	65
brand, logo & trade mark	49	Christmas and New Year	65
bread	49	Church of England	66
breast	50	Church of Scotland	67
bride and bridegroom	50	circuit	67
brief	50	City of London	67
bring & take	50	city, town & village	67
Brit	51	civil service	67
Britain, British etc.	51	classic & classical	68
broad & wide	51	clause	68
broke	52	cleave	68
brow & eyebrow	52	cleft sentences	68
brunch	52	clerk	69
business	52	clever etc.	69
but	52	client & customer	70
by	52	clock & watch	70
by-	52	cloth(s), clothes etc.	70
C	**53**	club	71
c, C /siː/	53	cockney	71
cab and taxi	53	cognate	71
cacao, cocoa & coconut	53	college	72
caesium	53	colours	72
calendar	53	coma & comma	72
call & call on	54	come & go	72
calque	54	Commonwealth	72
camping	54	company	73
		comparatives and superlatives	73

contents

compare	73
compass(es)	73
competence & competition	73
complacent & complaisant	74
complement & compliment	74
complement (grammatical)	74
compound nouns	74
comrade	74
conditional sentences	75
conductor	76
conjunctions	76
conjuror, magician & wizard	77
Conservative Party	77
constitution and government	77
contamination & pollution	79
continuous & continual	79
continuous aspect	80
contractions	80
control	81
cook(er)	81
corn	81
corps & corpse	81
could	82
council & counsel	82
counties	82
countries and nationalities	82
county & country	88
couple & pair	88
cricket	88
crucifixion	89
cry	89
culinary terms	89
current(ly) & present(ly)	89
curriculum & syllabus	90
custom, customer, customs & costume	90
cut	90
Cymru	90
D	**91**
d, D /diː/	91
dairy, diary & daily	91
damage & damages	91
dare say	91
dark	91
dates	91
days and months	92
death	93
debt	93
deduce & deduct	93
defender & defendant	93
demagogy	93
dependant & dependent	94
desert & dessert	94
despite	94
determiners	94
deviant spelling	94
devil & evil	95
dictionaries	95
dictionary words	95
die	95
die & dye	96
different	96
direct speech	96
discover, uncover & invent	96
discreet & discrete	96
disease & illness	96
dismiss, fire (out) & sack	96
Dissenter and Nonconformist	97
do & make	97
dog collar	98
doom, fate, destiny & destination	98
double consonants	98
doublets	101
doubt	101
down/uphill etc.	101
dozen	101
draw	101
drop & fall	102
dumb	102
dynamic and stative	103
E	**104**
e, E /iː/	104
each & every	104
each other & themselves	105
earth, land & soil	105
ease & easy	105
East, Far East, Middle East & Near East	105
economic(al) and economics	106
ecstasy	106
-ed and -es, pronunciation	106
Edinburgh	106
educated	107
-ee	107
e.g. & i.e.	107
either and neither	107
elder and eldest	108
elections	108
ellipsis	109
else	109
email	109
emergence & emergency	109
employ & use	109
-en adjective suffix	109
engage	110
England, a brief history	110
English language, a brief history	112
enjoy	112
enterprise	112
entrance & entry	112
-en verb suffix	113
envy & jealousy	113
epithets	113
eponyms	113
(e)special	113
espresso	113
estate	113
Estuary English	114

contents

etcetera	114
etymology	114
even	115
ever	115
ever & always	115
everyday & every day	116
examination & test	116
excuse	116
executor, executioner & executive	116
expect, hope & wait for	116
experience	117
extend & extent	117
F	**118**
f, F /ef/	118
faction	118
false friends	118
familiar	118
family relationships	118
fare	119
farther & further	119
fast	119
feed & food	120
fellow	120
female & feminine; male, masculine & macho	120
few	120
fiancé(e)	120
find, found, founder & foundry	120
fingers & toes	121
fisher & fisherman	121
flags	121
flammable	122
Fleet Street	122
flesh & meat	122
folk	122
football	122
fore-	123
forego & forgo	123
foreign	123
Foreign Office	123
foreign words and names	123
forget	124
forgive & pardon	124
former and latter	124
forth & fourth	124
fortnight	124
four-letter words	124
frankfurter	124
freedom & liberty	124
friend	125
fronting	125
fruit(s)	125
-ful and -less	125
fumes, smoke, steam & vapour	126
fun and funny	126
future (verb forms)	126
G	**130**
g, G /dʒiː/	130
gain, earn & win	130
games and sports	131
Gandhi	131
garage	131
-gate	131
gay	131
gender	131
gender & sex	132
gentle, genteel & Gentile	132
geographical location	132
German & german	132
gerund	133
get	133
ghost	134
ghost, phantom & spook	134
-ght and -gth	134
girl	134
glass & glasses	135
God & god	135
golf club	135
go + -ing	135
grammar	135
grammar school	136
grapefruit	136
grass & lawn	136
gray & grey	136
Greek alphabet	136
greetings	137
group nouns	137
grow	137
guerrilla	137
gulf	138
gun	138
guts	138
Guy Fawkes night	138
gypsy	138
H	**139**
h, H /eɪtʃ/	139
hamburger	139
Handel	139
happen	139
hard & hardly	139
have	139
haven & heaven	140
healthy, sane, & sanitary	140
hear & listen	141
heaven & sky	141
hello	141
help	141
hence	141
here-, there- and where- with prepositions	141
heroin & heroine	142
highbrow	142
high(ly)	142
high street	142
hijack	143
hire, rent & let	143
historic & historical	143
hit etc.	143

contents

holidays	148
Home Office	149
homonym	149
honours and titles	149
hot	150
hour	150
house & home	150
human etc.	150
hybrid compounds	150
hyper- & hypo-	151
hypocrisy	151
I	**152**
i, I /aɪ/	152
-ic and -ical	152
-ics	153
idioms and metaphors	153
-iety	153
if & whether	153
ill	154
illegible & unreadable	154
imply & infer	155
in & on (including at)	155
in case	156
inclusive language	156
India & Hindu	158
indirect (reported) speech	158
Indo-European languages	159
inferior and superior	160
infinitive	160
infinitive or -ing?	161
information	165
-ing form	165
inner, interior & internal	165
in order to	165
instead of	166
insulate & isolate	166
interest	166
internet	166
intoxication & poisoning	166
intransitive and transitive verbs	167
invalid	167
inversion	167
investigation and research	168
Ireland, a brief history	168
irregular verbs	171
-ise and -ize	174
-ish	175
Islam	175
island	175
it to postpone a subject	175
its & it's	176
J	**177**
j, J /dʒeɪ/	177
Jacobean etc.	177
jam & marmalade	177
jeans	177
Jew, Judaism, Hebrew, Israel and Israeli	177
John Bull	177
judgement	177
jump	178
just	179
K	**181**
k, K /keɪ/	181
Keats and Yeats	181
Keynes	181
kill	181
kith and kin	181
know	181
L	**182**
l, L /el/	182
Labour Party	182
lama & llama	183
languages	183
language skills	183
late, latest & last	183
lavatory	183
law	184
lead	185
lecture(r)	185
left and right	185
legal, legitimate, lawful & licit	185
lemming	185
-let	185
letters	185
Liberal Democrat Party	186
licence & license	187
lie & lay	187
lighting, lightning & lightening	188
like	188
likely	188
lime	189
liquor & liqueur	189
little & small	189
loathe, loath	189
loch	190
lollipop lady/man	190
long	190
longitude	190
lose, loose & loss	191
lot	191
M	**192**
m, M /em/	192
Magdalen(e)	192
maid and maiden	192
major	192
make love	192
manuscript	193
marriage & wedding	193
master and mistress	193
mate	194
material	194
mathematical terms	194
matter & mind	196
maybe	197
meals	197
means	197

contents

media	197	oil	227
meter & metre	198	OK	227
MI5 and MI6	198	on and upon	227
middle age & Middle Ages	198	one, number not article	228
military ranks	199	one representing a noun	228
minister & ministry	199	only (positions)	228
minute	199	onomatopoeia	229
minutes	199	open	229
miscarriage	199	opposite & in front of	229
modal auxiliary verbs	199	-or & -our	230
money	206	order	230
-monger	207	other	231
Mongol	207	*-our* words with suffixes	231
moral & morale	207	out of & outside	231
morning, afternoon & evening	207	overlook, overview, oversee & oversight	231
motion verbs	207	overseas	231
mould	207	**P**	**232**
moustache, sideboards and whiskers	208	p, P /piː/	232
mow	208	Pacific & peaceful	232
Mr etc.	208	palace	232
multi-word verbs	209	palindromes	232
mummy	213	pane of glass	232
musical instruments	213	pantomime	232
musical notation and terminology	214	parallel	233
N	**216**	parking	233
n, N /en/	216	parson	233
naive	216	partial	233
native	216	participle clauses	233
-nce, -ncy and -nt	216	partner	233
needn't have & didn't need to	216	party	233
negation of verbs	216	passed & past	234
negative-only words	218	passive voice	234
news	218	past participle	236
niggardly	219	past simple	236
nightmare	219	past simple & past continuous	236
-(n)naire	219	past simple & present perfect	237
no, none, not one & no-one	219	pay	238
Nobel & noble	220	pedagogy	238
non-British English	220	pence & pennies	238
nouns	220	pepper	238
nouns as adjectives	221	percentages	238
nowadays	221	perfect aspect	239
numbers	221	perforate, pierce, prick & punch	240
number with *be*	223	personal & personnel	240
nut	223	personal names	240
O	**224**	person and people	244
o, O /əʊ/	224	phonetic symbols	244
oar & row	224	physician & physicist	246
objects, direct and indirect	224	pigeons	246
o'clock	225	pineapple	246
odd	225	place names	246
of & off	226	planets	247
official & officious	226	playing cards	247
of for have	227	play (noun)	247
offshore	227	playwright	247
offspring	227	plenty	247
oft	227	plural consistency	247
often	227	plural forms	247

contents

police	250
policy & politics etc.	251
poll	252
pool	252
poorly	252
popular	252
port	253
portend & portent	253
posh	253
possessive	253
pound	255
practice & practise	255
pray, praise & prey	255
precedent & president	255
prefer	255
prefixes	255
premiss & premises	257
prepositions	258
prepositions at the end (deferred prepositions)	259
present & presently	260
present tenses	260
pressure & -pression	261
pretend	261
pretty	262
priceless	262
priestess	262
primate	262
prize	262
produce	262
programme	262
progressive	263
Prohibition	263
pronounce and pronunciation	263
pronouns, personal	263
pronunciation	264
propaganda	265
proper terms	265
prophecy & prophesy	266
propose	266
Protestant	266
prove	266
proverbs	266
publicly	267
public schools and public companies	267
punctuation	268
pundit	273
Q	**274**
q, Q /kjuː/	274
quantifiers	274
quarter, term & trimester	274
queer	274
questions	274
quick	275
quiet & quite	275
quite	275
R	**277**
r, R /ɑː/	277
radio, radium & radius	277
rather	277
receipt	278
received pronunciation	278
recessive accent	279
redoubt	279
reduplicated words	279
reflect & reflex	279
reflexive verbs	280
Reformation	280
refuse	280
regional names	280
register	280
relation, relationship & relative	280
relative clauses	281
religion	283
rely & trust	283
remember & remind	283
repetition of subject	284
replace & substitute	284
resources, recourse & resort	284
rest	285
right and wrong	285
right(ly)	285
rise & arise	286
road	286
rob & steal	287
rogue	287
Roman	287
Roman influence in Britain	287
rouse & arouse	287
row	288
Rowling	288
rule	288
Ruritania	288
Russian	288
S	**289**
s, S /es/	289
safe & save	290
safety & security	290
sail	290
salary & wage	290
same, very & -self (reflexive pronouns)	290
sanction	291
sans	291
SAS	291
saw & see-saw	291
say etc.	291
-scape	293
schedule	293
schism	293
schwa	293
score	294
Scotch, Scots & Scottish	294
Scotland, a brief history	294
search (for)	296
see	296
seem	297
semantic change	297

contents

semester	298
seminar & seminary	298
sense verbs	298
sensible & sensitive	298
sentence	299
sever & several	299
shade & shadow	299
Shakespeare	300
shew	300
shine etc.	301
ship	302
short	302
short answers	302
short questions	303
sibilant sounds	303
sibling	303
similes	303
since	303
sing & song	303
single etc.	303
singular and plural	304
singular verb with quantities	304
ski	304
skirt	304
slang	304
smog	305
so & such	305
so-called	305
solder & weld	305
solidarity	305
south & southern	305
spake	305
spam	305
spectacle(s)	305
spelling	305
split infinitive	306
sport	307
spot	307
stairs & steps	307
stationary & stationery	307
sterling	307
stile, style & stylus	307
story & storey	307
straight & strait	308
stress differences	308
strip	309
strong verbs	309
studio & study	309
subject	309
subjunctive	310
subtle	311
success	311
suit & suite	312
sulfur and sulphur	312
summons	312
supposed to	312
surgery	312
swine & pig	312
syllables	312
sympathetic	312
synonyms	313
syringe	313
T	**314**
t, T /tiː/	314
tag questions	314
talisman	316
Taoiseach	316
tasty & tasteful	316
tax	316
tea	316
teenager	316
telephone language	316
temperature	318
tense & time	318
terror	319
text	319
thanking	319
that (omission of conjunction)	319
that (pronunciation)	319
the	319
theatre	320
their, there & they're	320
there is	320
the … the …	321
thing	321
thing & think	321
think	321
this & these	321
thou etc.	321
three & tree	321
through & until	321
thug	322
tilde	322
time	322
-tion & -xion	323
titles of films etc.	323
to with -ing	323
to & towards	323
tongue-twisters	323
to, too & two	324
touristic	324
travel etc.	324
travesty & transvestite	324
treason	324
Treasury	325
treat and treatment	325
trek	325
troop & troupe	325
try	325
tummy	325
-ture	325
two	325
U	**326**
u, U /juː/	326
U and non-U	326
Uncle Sam	326
underground railways	326

contents

undertaking & undertaker	326
universities	326
up	327
use	327
used to, would & accustomed to	328
V	**329**
v, V /viː/	329
vacation & vacancy	329
vain, vein & vane	329
venal & venial	329
verbal & oral	329
visa	329
voiced and unvoiced consonants	330
W	**331**
w, W /ˈdʌbljuː/	331
wait	331
waive & wave	331
wake etc.	331
Wales, a brief history	332
want	333
-wards	333
wash	333
way	333
wear	334
Wednesday	334
weekend	334
weigh & weight	334
weights and measures	334
well	335
Welsh	335
wet	336
what & which	336
what is … like? & how is …?	336
while = although	336
whisky	337
who and whom	337
whodunnit	337
who's & whose	337
wh- questions	337
widget	337
wish	337
without	338
won't & wont	338
work	338
worth, worthwhile & worthy	338
-worthy	339
write	339
wrong(ly)	339
X	**340**
x, X /eks/	340
X-ray	340
Y	**341**
y, Y /waɪ/	341
-y	341
Yank and Yankee	341
ye	341
yeah	341
youth	341
Z	**342**
z, Z /zed/ (American /ziː/)	342
zodiac	342
index	343

This is a book of answers.
I dedicate it to my students who asked the questions.

Language is a labyrinth of paths. You approach from *one* side and know your way about; you approach the same place from another side and no longer know your way about.

Ludwig Wittgenstein

about the author

Peter Harvey was educated at Merchant Taylors' School Crosby and Queens' College Cambridge, which gave him a good early grounding in the use of the apostrophe. He has a Postgraduate Certificate in Education specialising in the teaching of English as a foreign language (EFL) from the University of Wales. He taught English in Germany, Zambia and Saudi Arabia before moving to Barcelona in 1984. He specialises in teaching English to advanced students and is an oral examiner for the Cambridge EFL examinations.

For further information go to http://www.lavengrobooks.com.

introductory notes

This Guide is intended for all advanced users of the English language. My students include not only people studying for examinations such as the Cambridge Certificate of Proficiency in English but also people who are working in an environment in which using English is an essential part of professional life, and these are the people that I have had in mind while writing it. It is intended as a complement to the bilingual dictionary that is an essential part of so many workplaces around the world; it is for those people who not only need to use English but who want to be confident that they are doing so correctly.

Language usage changes over time. This book describes Standard English as it is used by careful native speakers at the time of writing, including some common variant forms. While starting from this descriptive approach, it nevertheless recognises the very natural desire of non-native speakers to have clear guidelines for speaking and writing English in a way that will seem natural to native speakers that they deal with. The question of prescriptive grammar is discussed further in the articles *grammar* and *right and wrong*.

The purpose of this book is to provide language information, where appropriate in a cultural context; it is not intended as a general guide to British culture.

I live in Spain and most of my teaching experience has been here. Nevertheless, this book is and always has been intended for users worldwide; it is not especially directed towards speakers of Spanish, Catalan or any other language.

I know that it is usual for dictionaries and usage guides that are intended for native speakers to contain examples that are taken from real language use; I have not done so here. I have kept to the policy of my own teaching, which is that examples presented to people learning English should essentially be simple, and particularly that examples of vocabulary use should not be placed in sentences with complicated grammar structures while grammar examples should not be made difficult by the use of unusual vocabulary.

It is customary in linguistic works to use an asterisk to mark a reconstructed or unattested etymological form or an incorrect example. In this book I use asterisks for references, the few assumed etymologies are described as such, and incorrect examples are shown in ~~strikethrough text~~. I feel that this is more appropriate for the non-specialist reader. To avoid confusion, strikethrough has not been applied to phonetic symbols or to titles.

The phonetic symbols used here represent modern British Standard English. They are shown with descriptions and their usual pronunciations on pages 244-246 On occasion I have commented on regional varieties, and on some points connected with Welsh, but I have made no attempt to be complete. The foreign words shown here that have been adapted into English have their pronunciation shown using the symbols of standard English, which is how they are often pronounced, so as to reduce the number of symbols facing a user of this book.

Although this book contains some notes on American English, I have made no attempt to make a full comparison of the two forms of the language.

In order to clarify and demonstrate the use of capital letters throughout the text I have used lower case (small) letters in titles of articles for all words that are not normally capitalised.

As a general rule, when comparing two words I have written the title of the article so that the first in the alphabet comes first, e.g. *above & over* rather than *over & above*; but when it seemed appropriate to do so I have abandoned this policy. An ampersand (&) in the title indicates that the words are contrasted, while the word *and* indicates that they are being considered together.

Articles and the index are alphabetised letter by letter. For example, *-en adjective suffix* precedes *engage* and *-en verb suffix* follows *entrance & entry*.

Cross-references are shown in SMALL CAPITALS. Indirect cross-references are shown with an asterisk and (*ITALICS*), e.g. PRESENT PERFECT (*PERFECT ASPECT*) is a reference to the item called present perfect in the article called perfect aspect. The index contains references from keywords to articles.

For hyphenation I have generally followed the Concise Oxford Dictionary, (Tenth Edition) on CD-ROM 2001 Version 1.1, © OUP 1999, 2001, with the exception of writing *no-one, co-operate* and *co-ordinate* with hyphens. In order to show the hyphenation I have not used line-end hyphens.

The index contains an alphabetical list of words referenced to the articles in which they can be found.

This book is available in a Kindle ebook edition.

note for history articles

This book contains articles telling the history of England, Ireland, Scotland and Wales. These are intended to be informative and not controversial, though that is not always easy – especially in the case of Ireland. Nevertheless, I have tried to tell the simple accepted mainstream history of these countries; after all, I am a linguist, not a historian.

In these articles I write of the movement of peoples in the days before the Roman Empire and of the Celtic tribes that occupied the islands. Since writing them I have read of DNA evidence that suggests that those prehistoric inhabitants did not move as much as was thought and that the displacement of populations was less serious than had been believed; also that the relations between the inhabitants of those two islands and the Celts of the continent was not as strong as was supposed; in short, that the influences, such as they were, were more cultural than ethnic. I am not in a position to judge the importance or accuracy of such claims, so I have preferred to leave the articles as they were originally written with this note for information and explanation.

main changes in edition 3 (January 2011)

The previous two-column format has been abandoned. This has permitted greater flexibility in presentation, particularly with the addition of illustrations.

The table of contents now includes only main entry names.

Inconsistencies in formatting and cross-references have been corrected.

Topical articles including abbreviations have been updated to late 2010.

These articles have been added: *aid & AIDS, below & under, bleed & blood, -cester, coma & comma, conductor, death, disease & illness, Edinburgh, feed & food, -ish, judgement, lime, means, minutes, oft, so-called* and *I*. The article on *anniversaries* has been omitted as has the one on *symmetrical sentences*. So has the one on *information technology*; the increasing variety and complexity of the subject have made it impossible to describe succinctly. The list of British counties and local government authorities has been removed because the system is so confused and constantly changing that it is impossible to describe. The article *billion* has been incorporated under *numbers*.

Some Catholic authors have been added to the article on Ireland.

The tables giving the scientific names of birds, flowers and other biological items have been omitted. These dated back to the very conception of the book in 1991, when dictionaries did not always give this information despite its essential importance for interlanguage identification. Now such information is readily available on the internet. Some of the notes to these tables have been added under separate articles for *aluminium, beans, caesium, grapefruit, lime, nuts, pigeons* and *pineapple*. The scientific names of items mentioned in the text have been removed for the same reason. The list of chemical elements in alphabetical order of their symbols has been kept.

main changes in edition 4 (February 2017)

The articles *abortion & miscarriage, alliance, internet, lama & llama, miscarriage, percentages, schedule* and *their, there & they're* have been added.

An arrow ➤ has been inserted where appropriate at the foot of a right-hand page to indicate the article is continued overleaf.

Abbreviations has been updated.

Aide has been added to the article now called *aid, aide & AIDS*.

The duplicated articles *awake etc.* and *wake and awake* have been consolidated into *awake etc.*

Smog has been removed from *blend* and given its own article (like *brunch*). *Brexit* has been added to *blend*.

The figures for speakers of *Celtic languages* have been updated.

Constitution and government has been updated to include the post of Lord Speaker.

Countries and nationalities has been updated.

Dis- ➔ *dif-* has been added in *double consonants, prefixes*.

Nouns ending in *-ology* are mentioned in *-ic and –ical*.

Definitions of present and past infinitives have been added to *infinitive*.

Sperm has been added to *irregular plurals*.

Spirit has been removed from the title *ghost, phantom, spirit & spook*. It is dealt with under *ghost*.

In *modal auxiliary verbs* the sections *possibility in the present, future, or past* and *modals with the perfect aspect* have been revised. I am grateful to *Dr Brian Mott* of Barcelona University for making me aware of this need.

Musical notation has been amended to show the correct sol-fa names.

Resent/re-sent has been added to *re-* in the article *prefixes*.

The article on hyphens in *punctuation* has been amended.

A reference to intrusive *r* has been added in *r, R*.

The names *restrictive and non-restrictive* have been added to *relative clauses*.

Additional pronunciations have been added to *stationary & stationery*.

A recommendation to use *strait* (singular) has been adopted in *straight & strait*.

The article *subjunctive* has been substantially amended.

A reference to computer use has been added to *widget*.

Chav has been added to *v, V*.

The articles *chemical elements, fax, films and DVDs, football results* and *page 3 girl* have been deleted.

The article *aeroplane & airplane* has been deleted and the point included in American English.

Topical articles have been updated.

The cross-references and index have been standardised.

Formatting errors, mainly in the use of italics, have been corrected.

Many bullet points have been removed.

Some minor formatting and editing amendments have been made to facilitate the pagination of the new page size.

main changes in edition 4.1 (July 2018)

The article *hopefully* has been deleted as the controversy surrounding this word has died down since the book was first written.

The article *split infinitives* has been substantially amended to remove the advice against using them.

Some topical articles have been updated.

Some minor formatting changes and corrections have been made.

acknowledgements

My wife *Jane Harvey* transformed the handwriting in which a large part of this book was written to a computer format, she also did some of the non-linguistic research work, and she wrote the article on mathematics and much of the two articles on music.

Alison Litherland offered welcome support and encouragement in addition to reading the manuscript and making many helpful comments and suggestions.

Dr Brian Mott of Barcelona University generously gave me the benefit of his expertise in phonetics to advise me on some aspects of pronunciation and phonetic representation.

Cristian Bonucci read the third edition of this book and made a number of useful comments and suggestions.

In addition to these people I am grateful for help and support to Brian Barder, Pere Barri Soldevila, David Baxter, Alan Booth, Valerie Collins, Tony Hatfield, Natalie Herblot Flores, Hugh Jordan, Pete Kercher, Monica Masotti, Fernand Menier, Miguel Pérez Rodríguez, Colin Rosenstiel, Núria Sales, Judith Ward, and many others who answered my queries and made suggestions. In particular I am grateful to my many students who asked the questions. I have enjoyed finding the answers and writing them in this book.

A large part of this book was written during a number of working weekends spread between 1999 and 2006 at Queens' College Cambridge, where I had studied as an undergraduate. I must thank the College for its hospitality to an old member.

The main reference works that I have used are the *Oxford English Dictionary* and the *Concise Oxford Dictionary* for forms and meanings of words and for usage; *Fowler's Modern English Usage* (Oxford, second and third editions, 1965 (rev. Gowers) and 1996 (ed. Burchfield)) for usage; and the *Comprehensive Grammar of the English Language* (Quirk, R. et al., Longman, 1985) and the shorter *Student's Grammar of the English Language* (Greenbaum, S. & Quirk, R., Longman, 1990) for grammar. The *Cambridge Grammar of the English Language* (Huddleston and Pullum, 2002) was published too late to be a major reference – the main body of this book was already written in 2002 – but was consulted for certain points. *The Cambridge Guide to English Usage* (Peters, Cambridge 2004) was consulted for the fourth edition. For phonetics I have relied principally on *A Course in Phonetics and Phonology for Spanish Learners of English* (Mott, B., EUB Barcelona, 1996).

While my gratitude to the abovementioned people and reference works is wide-ranging and heartfelt, any faults that may be found in this book are my own responsibility. Any comments or suggestions will be welcome on books@lavengrobooks.com.

A

a, A /eɪ/

The first letter of the alphabet. In handwriting, and sometimes in printing, for example in the *italic* text in this book, the lower CASE letter is written ɑ.

1. It is usually pronounced /æ/ as in *bad, hat; ass, crass, lass, mass* (quantity) (see **2b**), *Mass* (Eucharist); and in *ant, can, cant, sad, that, land* etc. See BASS.

2. It is pronounced /ɑː/
   a. before *r*: *bar, hard, farm*, except when it follows /w/: *quart, war, warm, warn, water* have /ɔː/ (see **5** below).
   b. in these words with *-ass*: *brass, class, glass, grass, pass* (see **1**).
   c. before *f* followed by another consonant: *staff, draft*, except for the rather unusual words with /æ/: *gaff, faff, naff, riff-raff*.
   d. in *aunt, branch, can't, CAST, chance, command, grant, plant, stance*.
   e. in *draught, laugh*.
   f. in words with *-ath*: *bath, path*.
   g. in *calf, half, palm* and *tomato*.

3. In northern England, Wales and Ireland it is pronounced /a/ in the words in **1** and in **2 b, c, d, e** and **f**.

4. Note that *can* /kæn/ and *can't* /kɑːnt/ have different pronunciations.

5. It is pronounced /ɔː/ before *-ll* and *-lk*: *all, ball, fall, wall*; *chalk, talk, walk*; and as in **2a** above.

6. It is pronounced /ɒ/ after *w-, wh-* and *qu-*: *swan, what, wander, washed, quad, quality*, except as in **2a** and **5** above (*wall, walk*); and *wag, wax* and *quack* /æ/.

7. *ai* and *ay* are pronounced /eɪ/: *mail, laid, paid* (but *said* /e/), *day, play* but *quay* and *Torquay* (a place name) have /iː/.

8. *a* followed by a single consonant and a vowel also has this pronunciation: *male, station, potato* (except *tomato*, **2g** above) even when the *a* follows a *w*: *wade, WAGE (*SALARY), WAKE, wave*. For further comments on the pronunciations /æ/ and /eɪ/, see DOUBLE CONSONANTS.

9. *au* and *aw* are pronounced /ɔː/: *taught, taut, awful, law* except in the words *Australia, Austria, because, cauliflower, laurel*, where it is pronounced /ɒ/.

10. In unstressed syllables it is often pronounced as a SCHWA: *woman* /ˈwʊmən/, *amaze* /əˈmeɪz/, *England* /ˈɪŋglənd/.

11. The word *ANY* is pronounced /ˈeni/.

See CAN, CAN'T, CANNOT & CANT; L, L.

a- adjectives

There is a group of adjectives beginning with *a-* which are used PREDICATIVELY (*ADJECTIVES); they include *ablaze, adrift, afire, afloat, afraid, aghast, ajar, alert, alike, alive, alone, aloof, ashamed, asleep, averse, awake, aware, awash*: *The building was ablaze; The man was alive; I was asleep*. Most of them cannot be used ATTRIBUTIVELY (*ADJECTIVES): ~~the ablaze building~~; ~~the afraid child~~; ~~the awash streets~~ and an alternative way of saying this must be found: *the blazing building; the frightened child; the flooded streets*. *Alert* and *aloof* can be used attributively: *an alert guard; an aloof attitude*.

Only *afraid, alert, alike, aloof* and *ashamed* can be preceded by *very* for emphasis: *very afraid, very alert* but for example ~~very adrift~~, ~~very aghast~~ are impossible as they are NON-GRADABLE *ADJECTIVES. *Asleep* is preceded by *FAST* for emphasis: *fast asleep* (this means *deeply asleep*, not that someone has gone to sleep quickly). *Awake* is preceded by *WIDE* (*BROAD) for emphasis: *wide awake*. For *aware* see AWARE.

In all of these words, the *a* is pronounced /ə/ (SCHWA) and the stress is on the second syllable.

A

a & an

The use of the *n* depends on the pronunciation (**not** the spelling) of the following word; it is a phonetic device to prevent two vowel sounds from coming together as for example in ~~a apple~~, ~~a open door~~.

an

An is used before words that start with vowel sounds, including *heir, honour* and *hour*, which have a silent *h* /eə, ˈɒnə, aʊə/ and with their derivatives (see H, H): *He married an heiress; It will be an honour to meet you; An honest mistake; Half an hour*.

At one time *h* was silent in all words where the first syllable is unstressed; although it is now usually pronounced in words that begin with *h*, except the three mentioned above, some publishers preserve the old usage in printing: *an habitual action, an hysterical attack; an hotel; an HISTORIC document* and some people pronounce it this way with very slight or no pronunciation of the *h*.

a

A is used before all other words including those which begin with /j/ or /w/ however they are spelled: *a European country, a useful idea, a one-legged man*. This includes all words which begin with *uni-*: *a university education, a union* when it is a prefix from the Latin word *unus* meaning *one*, but not negative forms such as *an uninvited guest, an uninsured car; an unimportant event*.

This rule applies also to abbreviations and initials: *an MP* /empiː/; *a UN* /juːen/ *peace-keeping force*.

Historically several words have suffered a misplacement of the *-n* in *an*, which has been attached to the following word in a process known as metanalysis. *Newt, nickname* and *ninny* were originally *ewt, eke-name* and *inny* (slang for *innocent*) but the *-n* of the indefinite article was moved into the word itself: *an ewt* became *a newt, an eke-name* became *a nickname*, and *an inny* became *a ninny*. This process has worked both ways: *adder, apron, orange* and *umpire* were originally *nadder, napron, norange* and *non pair*.

It is usually pronounced /ə/ but when emphasised it is /eɪ/, /æ/.

See ARTICLES.

abbreviations

Abbreviations may be written with or without full stops: *AA* or *A.A.* The modern style is to omit them in groups of capital letters: *UNO, EU,* but to place them if the abbreviation ends in a lower case letter that is not the last letter of the full word: *i.e.* and *Pres.* but *Dr* and *Mr*; full stops are especially written in abbreviations such as *a.m.* to avoid confusion with words: *1 am* (time) could be confused with *1 am* (verb). They are not used in abbreviations of WEIGHTS AND MEASURES, except for *in.* (inch) to avoid confusion. However, the use of full stops in abbreviations is a matter of style; there is variation between different publishers and printers. Normally groups of initials are pronounced as separate letters: AC /eɪ siː/, but the ones printed in *italics* in the list below are pronounced as words. See ACRONYMS.

&	and	A&E	accident and emergency (*hospital department*)
@	at (EMAIL)		
$	dollar	AA	Automobile Association; Alcoholics Anonymous
€	euro		
£	pound (*money*)	AC	alternating current (*electricity*)
¥	yen	ad lib.	ad libitum (*Latin = as much as you like*)
#	number (*USA*) (the symbol's name is *hash*)		
		AD	anno domini (*Latin = in the year of our Lord, e.g. 1996 AD. *See note at end of this list*) (AD AND BC)
9/11	'nine eleven'; reference to the terrorist attacks in New York on 11 September 2001 (DATES)		
24/7	24 hours a day and 7 days a week	AGM	annual general meeting
a/c	account	AID	artificial insemination by donor

A

AIDS	acquired immune deficiency syndrome	CCTV	closed-circuit television
aka	also known as	CD	compact disc
A-level	advanced level (*exam taken at 18 years old*)	CE	CHURCH OF ENGLAND
		CEO	chief executive officer
a.m.	ante meridiem (*Latin = before midday, *See note at end of this list*) (MORNING, AFTERNOON & EVENING)	CFO	chief financial officer
		cf.	compare (Latin *confer*)
		c.f.	carried forward (*in accounts*)
		CI	Channel Islands
		CIA	Central Intelligence Agency (*USA*)
AM	[Welsh] Assembly Member		
anon.	anonymous	CID	Criminal Investigation Department (POLICE)
asap	as soon as possible		
ART	assisted reproduction techniques	cif	cost, insurance and freight
ATM	automatic teller machine	CND	Campaign for Nuclear Disarmament
Ave	avenue		
AWACS	airborne warning and control system /ˈeɪwæks/	CoE	CHURCH OF ENGLAND
		c/o	care of (*in an address*)
AWOL	absent without leave (*military*) /ˈeɪwɒl/	COD	cash on delivery
		Col.	colonel /ˈkɜːnəl/
B & B	bed and breakfast	cont.	continued
BA	Bachelor of Arts (UNIVERSITIES); British Airways	cp.	compare
		CRE	Commission for Racial Equality
BAA	British Airports Authority	cu. in.	cubic inch (WEIGHTS AND MEASURES)
Bart; Bt	baronet (HONOURS AND TITLES)		
BASIC	beginner's all-purpose symbolic instruction code (*computer programming language*)	cu. ft	cubic foot (WEIGHTS AND MEASURES)
		CV	curriculum vitae
BBC	British Broadcasting Corporation (BBC)	cwt	hundredweight (WEIGHTS AND MEASURES)
bcc	blind carbon copy (EMAIL)	d.	died
BC	before Christ (*e.g. 44 BC, *See note at end of this list*) See (AD AND BC)	DIY	do-it-yourself
		DC	direct current (*electricity*)
		DJ	disc jockey
BF	bloody fool	DNA	deoxyribonucleic acid
BMA	British Medical Association	DOA	dead on arrival (*in hospital*)
BME	black, minority and ethnic	DTT	digital terrestrial television
bn	billion	DVD	digital versatile disc
Bros	Brothers	E	east; ECSTASY (drug)
BSc	Bachelor of Science (UNIVERSITIES)	E & O E	errors and omissions excepted
		ECB	European Central Bank
BST	British summer time	ECHR	European Convention on Human Rights
BT	British Telecom		
c.	*circa* (approximately)	ECJ	European Court of Justice
C(A)T	computerized (axial tomography)	EEA	European Economic Area
C of E	CHURCH OF ENGLAND	e.g.	exempli gratia (*Latin = for example*) (E.G. & I.E.)
CAMRA	Campaign for Real ALE /ˈkæmrə/		
Cantab.	of Cambridge University (*e.g. MA Cantab.*)	EFL	English as a foreign language
		ELT	English language teaching
CBE	Commander of the Order of the British Empire (HONOURS AND TITLES)	ENE	east-north-east
		ESE	east-south-east
		ESL	English as a second language
cc	carbon copy, courtesy copy (mail and EMAIL)	ESP	extra-sensory perception; English for special purposes

3

A

Esq.	Esquire (HONOURS AND TITLES)	HE	Her/His Excellency (*title of an ambassador*)
et al.	and others (Latin *et alii, et alia* etc.)	HIV	human immunodeficiency virus
et seq.	and the following (*pages etc.*) (Latin *et sequentia*)	HK	Hong Kong
		HM	Her/His Majesty
ETA	estimated time of arrival	HMG	Her/His Majesty's Government
etc.	et cetera	HMRC	Her/His Majesty's Revenue and CUSTOMS
EU	European Union		
EZ	easy (DEVIANT SPELLING; Z, Z)	HMS	Her/His Majesty's SHIP (*official name of Royal Navy ships e.g. HMS Ark Royal*)
F	Fahrenheit (*temperature scale*)		
f.	following page etc.; loud (*music, Italian forte*) (see *ff.* below)		
		Hon.	Honourable (*title of a son of a peer or of an MP*)
FCO	Foreign and Commonwealth Office		
		HPV	human papilloma virus
FA	Football Association	HQ	headquarters
FAO	Food and Agriculture Organisation	HR	human resources
		HRH	Her/His Royal Highness
FAQ	frequently asked questions	HTML	hypertext mark-up language
FBI	Federal Bureau of Investigation (*USA*)	http	hypertext transfer protocol
		IAEA	International Atomic Energy Agency
FC	football club		
FD	Fidei Defensor (*Latin = Defender of the Faith, a title of the British monarch*) (CHURCH OF ENGLAND)	IBA	Independent Broadcasting Authority (MEDIA)
		ibid.	in the same place or reference (*book reference*) (Latin *ibidem, in the same place*)
ff.	following pages etc.; very loud (*music, Italian fortissimo*) (see *f.* above)		
		ICT	information and communications technology
FRS	Fellow of the Royal Society		
fob	free on board	i.e.	id est (*Latin = that is to say*) (E.G. & I.E.)
Fr	Father (title of CATHOLIC Priest)		
ft	foot, feet	IMF	International Monetary Fund
FT	Financial Times (*newspaper*)	in.	inches (WEIGHTS AND MEASURES)
FRS	Fellow of the Royal Society	incl.	including
G&T	gin and tonic	IOM	Isle of Man
Gb	gigabyte	IOU	I owe you (*informal*)
GB	Great Britain	IOW	Isle of Wight
GBS	George Bernard Shaw	IPCC	Independent Police Complaints Commission
GC	George Cross		
GCSE	General Certificate of Secondary Education (*school exam taken at 16 years old*)	IQ	intelligence quotient
		IRA	Irish Republican Army
		ISBN	international standard book number
GDP	gross domestic product		
GI	common soldier (*US from government issue*)	ISP	INTERNET service provider
		IT	information technology
gif	graphics interchange format	ITN	Independent Television News (MEDIA)
GMT	Greenwich mean time		
GNP	gross national product	ITV	Independent Television (MEDIA)
GP	general practitioner	IVF	in vitro fertilisation
GPS	global positioning system	JFK	John Fitzgerald Kennedy
GUI	graphic user interface	JP	Justice of the Peace
h	hour	jpeg	joint photographic experts group /ˈdʒeɪpeg/
h & c	hot and cold (*water*)		
		Jr	Junior

A

Kb	kilobyte	NE	north-east
KC	King's Counsel (*senior barrister*) (LAW)	NHS	National Health Service
		NI	Northern Ireland
LA	Los Angeles	NNE	north-north-east
lb.	pound (*weight*) (WEIGHTS AND MEASURES)	NNW	north-north-west
		No	number
l.c.	lower CASE	NSPCC	National Society for the Prevention of Cruelty to Children
LCD	liquid crystal display		
loc. cit.	in the place already mentioned (*book reference*) (Latin *loco citato*)	NW	north-west
		OAP	old-age pensioner
		OBE	Officer of the Order of the British Empire (HONOURS AND TITLES)
L s d	librae, solidi, denarii (*Latin = pounds, shillings, pence: British units of currency before 1972*) (MONEY)		
		OCR	optical character recognition
		OECD	Organisation for Economic Co-operation and Development
LSD	lysergic acid diethylamide	*OPEC*	Organisation of Petroleum Exporting Countries /ˈəʊpek/ (OIL)
LSE	London School of Economics		
m	metre; million		
MA	Master of Arts (UNIVERSITIES)	OK	satisfactory
Mb	megabyte	ono	or nearest offer
MB	Bachelor of Medicine (UNIVERSITIES)	op. cit.	in the work already mentioned (*book reference*) (Latin *opere citato*)
MBA	Master in Business Administration (UNIVERSITIES)		
		OT	Old Testament
MBE	Member of the Order of the British Empire (HONOURS AND TITLES)	OTC	officer training CORPS; over the counter (*pharmaceuticals*)
		OTT	over the top (*exaggerated*)
MC	master of ceremonies	Oxon.	of Oxford University (*e.g. BA Oxon.*)
MD	Doctor of Medicine		
MEP	Member of the European Parliament	oz	ounce (WEIGHTS AND MEASURES)
		p	penny (MONEY); QUIET (*music, Italian piano; see pp. below*); page (see *pp.* below)
Mgr	Monseigneur, Monsignor		
MI5, MI6	See MI5 AND MI6		
MP	Member of Parliament; Military Police	p & p	postage and packing
		p.a.	per annum (*Latin = yearly e.g. £40,000 p.a.*)
mp3	MPEG Audio Layer 3		
MPEG	moving picture experts group	PA	personal assistant
mpg	miles per gallon (*measure of a car's fuel consumption*) (WEIGHTS AND MEASURES)	pax	passengers (*travel industry*)
		PC	POLICE Constable; Privy Councillor (CONSTITUTION AND GOVERNMENT); Plaid Cymru (*Welsh nationalist party*) personal computer; politically correct
mph	miles per hour (WEIGHTS AND MEASURES)		
MS	MANUSCRIPT		
MSc	Master of Science (UNIVERSITIES)	PCC	Press Complaints Commission
MSP	Member of the Scottish Parliament	pdf	portable document format
		PE	physical education
N	north	PG	parental guidance (*cinema classification*)
NAFTA	North American Free Trade Agreement		
NATO	North Atlantic Treaty Organisation /ˈneɪtəʊ/	PGCE	Postgraduate Certificate in Education (*British professional teaching qualification*)
NB	nota bene (*Latin = Note! This is important!*)		

A

PhD	Doctor of Philosophy (Latin *Philosophiae doctor*) (UNIVERSITIES)	ROI	Republic of Ireland; return on investment
PIN	personal identification NUMBER	*ROM*	read only memory
plc	PUBLIC limited company	RSPB	Royal Society for the Protection of Birds
PLO	Palestine Liberation Organisation	RSPCA	Royal Society for the Prevention of Cruelty to Animals
p.m.	post meridiem (*Latin = after midday. *See note at end of this list*) (MORNING, AFTERNOON & EVENING)	RSVP	répondez s'il vous plaît (*French = please reply, used on formal invitations*)
PM	prime minister; post mortem	RTF	rich text format
PMT	premenstrual tension	Rt Hon.	Right Honourable (*title of a member of the Privy Council*) (CONSTITUTION)
PO	Post Office		
POTUS	President of the United States		
POB	Post Office box	Rt Revd	Right Reverend (*title of an Anglican bishop*)
pp	per pro (*used when one person officially signs a document in another person's name.*); very quiet (*music,* Italian *pianissimo; see p. above*); pages (see *p.* above)	S	SOUTH
		sae	stamped addressed envelope
		SDLP	Social Democratic and Labour Party (*Northern IRELAND*)
		SF	science fiction
PPS	parliamentary private secretary; post-post scriptum	SME	small and medium size ENTERPRISE
		SMS	short message service
PR	proportional representation; public relations	SNP	Scottish National Party
		sq ft	square feet
prop.	proprietor	Sq.	square
PS	post scriptum (*Latin = addition after the signature of a letter*)	SSE	south-south-east
		SSW	south-south-west
		St	saint; street
PSNI	POLICE Service of Northern Ireland	STD	sexually transmitted disease
		SW	south-west
PT	physical training	t	tonne
PTA	parent-teacher association	TB	tuberculosis
PTO	please turn over (*to the next page*)	tiff	tagged image file format
QC	Queen's Counsel (*senior barrister*) (LAW)	tn	trillion
		TT	teetotal
qv	quod vide (*cross-reference in a book*)	TUC	Trade Unions Congress
		U	universal (*cinema classification*)
R&D&I	research and development and innovation	u.c.	upper CASE
		UFO	unidentified flying object
RAF	Royal Air Force	UHF	ultra-high frequency
RAM	random access memory	UK	United Kingdom
RC	Roman CATHOLIC	*UKIP*	United Kingdom Independence Party /ˈjuːkɪp/
Rd	Road		
Revd	Reverend	*UNESCO*	United Nations Educational, Scientific and Cultural Organisation /juːˈneskəʊ/
RIP	requiescat in pace (*Latin = may he/she rest in peace*)		
RM	Royal Marines		
RN	Royal Navy		
RNA	ribonucleic acid	uni	UNIVERSITY
RNIB	Royal National Institute for the Blind	*UNICEF*	United Nations International Children's Emergency Fund /ˈjuːnɪsef/
RNLI	Royal National LifeBOAT Institute		
		UNO	United Nations Organisation

A

URL	uniform resource locator (*web page address*)	VIP	very important person
USA	United States of America	VJ day	Victory in Japan day (*15 August 1945*)
USB	universal serial bus	vs	versus
USS	United States Ship	W	west
USSR	Union of Soviet Socialist Republics	WC	water closet
		WHO	World Health Organisation
V	volt	WMD	weapons of mass destruction
v	versus	WTO	World Trade Organisation
VAT	Value Added Tax	WNW	west-north-west
VC	Victoria Cross	WSW	west-south-west
VDU	visual display unit	www	world wide web
VE day	Victory in Europe day (*8 May 1945*)	Xmas	CHRISTMAS
		yd	yard (WEIGHTS AND MEASURES)
VHF	very high frequency		

* *a.m.* and *p.m.*, and *AD* and *BC*. These abbreviations are spoken and written as the names of the letters; the full forms are not used but are given here for information.

See E.G. & I.E.

-able and -ible

These suffixes are pronounced /əbl/ and /ɪbl/ respectively. Note that *-able* is not pronounced /eɪbl/ as in the word *able*.

They usually imply a passive idea when added to verbal stems. Something that is *unmistakable* cannot be mistaken and something that is *visible* can be seen. (The verbal stem *vis-* in *visible* is Latin as the word came into English in its Latin form modified by Old French.)

There are active exceptions: *perishable* goods are goods which may perish; *changeable* weather is weather which may change; a *suitable* partner is one who suits you.

Sometimes they can be added to nouns to indicate the quality of the nouns: *comfortable, fashionable, impressionable, knowledgeable, marriageable, peaceable, objectionable, personable, pleasurable, profitable, seasonable, sizeable.*

-able is found in words with Latin *-abilis* or Old French *-able*. It is, however, a free formation and may be attached to any verb to imply the action of the verb can be done: *drinkable, washable*. In colloquial English it can be added even to MULTI-WORD VERBS: *ring-up-able, get-at-able*. Although it is assumed that the suffix is the word *able*, and that a *washable sweater* is one that is able to be washed, *able* is not in fact the origin of the suffix.

When *-able* is added to a verb of more than two syllables with *-ate*, the *-ate* is dropped: *demonstrate, demonstrable; calculate, calculable* etc. Two-syllable verbs make *creatable, debatable* etc.

When *-able* is added to a verb which ends with *-y* the *y* changes to *i*: *justify, justifiable; rectify, rectifiable.*

When *-able* is added to a verb which ends with silent *-e* the *e* is retained in *-ce* and *-ge*, where it affects the pronunciation: *pronounceable, manageable*. The suffix is dropped in other words e.g. *usable, forgivable*, but may be retained in *blameable, likeable, sizeable.*

Most words with *-ble* have *-able* because it is a free formation. As new formations cannot be made with *-ible* the number of these words is smaller. Among the commonest are *accessible, admissible, adducible, audible, collapsible, combustible, compatible, comprehensible, contemptible, convertible, corruptible, credible, defensible, destructible, digestible, dirigible, discernible, divisible, edible, eligible, exhaustible, expressible, extensible, fallible, feasible, flexible, forcible, fusible, gullible, horrible, incorrigible, indelible, intelligible, irascible, invincible, legible, negligible, ostensible, perceptible, perfectible, permissible, plausible, possible, reducible, reprehensible, repressible, reproducible, resistible, responsible, reversible, risible, sensible, susceptible, tangible, terrible, vendible, visible.*

A

abortion & miscarriage
An *abortion* is an induced termination of a pregnancy; a MISCARRIAGE is spontaneous.

above & over
Above means *higher than*: *The castle is on a hill above the town; The river Marne joins the Seine above Paris.* It is used to compare points on a scale: *Six degrees above zero; Above average; Above £50 but below £500; Inflation is expected to RISE above 4%. Above all* means ESPECIALLY.

Over means *vertically over*: *There is a light over the table; I held the umbrella over my head.* Clearly, anything that is vertically over another thing is higher than it, so in these examples it is also possible to say *There is a light above the table; I held the umbrella above my head.*

Over also means:

across the surface of something, from one side to the other
We walked over the bridge to reach the village; The plane flew over the Pyrenees while we were having lunch; An expression of happiness spread over her face.

to the place where I am or to the place where you are
Come over and see me at once; I'll send it over tomorrow morning.

on the other side of
John lives over the road from me. (colloquial)

more than
Over 18 (years old); over £50.

finished
The concert will be over by 10.30; Game over.

Over and over (again) means *repeatedly*: *I've asked him over and over (again) but he hasn't answered.*

Over all means *in general*: *It rained on a few days but over all we had a good holiday.*

All over means *covering* or *found in all parts of*: *There was water all over the floor; There are rivers all over Britain.*

See BELOW & UNDER.

abroad & foreign
Abroad is an adverb meaning *to another country* or *in another country*: *Are you going abroad for your holidays?; She lived abroad for most of her life.*

From abroad means *from a foreign country*: *They returned from abroad last month.*

FOREIGN is an adjective *related to another country*: *foreign holidays; foreign languages.*

accents and diacritic marks
English words do not have these, although they are sometimes written on foreign words used in English such as FIANCÉ. When a word is accepted as an English one the accent is gradually dropped.

Their names in English are ´ *acute*, ` *grave* /ɡrɑːv/, ^ *circumflex*, ¸ *cedilla*, ˜ *tilde*, ¨ *umlaut* (German) or *diaeresis* /daɪˈerɪsɪs/ (other languages). The names of letters with these symbols are spoken as *é e-acute, à a-grave, î i-circumflex* etc. Spanish-speakers should note that in English the word *tilde* refers only to the ˜, the mark which distinguishes *ñ* from *n*. English keyboards do not have these accents and marks. The best rule seems to be to use the accent or mark whenever possible if it makes a difference to pronunciation: *façade, cliché, Müller, Muñoz*, though some publishers ignore them almost completely or are inconsistent in their use of them in foreign names, possibly for fear of misunderstanding the complications of the large number of accents and marks in some central European languages. Publishers vary considerably in their treatment of such marks on foreign words.

accommodation
Note the spelling. This word is often misspelled by native speakers.

See DOUBLE CONSONANTS WITH PREFIXES.

A

ache, pain & sore

ache

Ache /eɪk/ (noun) refers to a continuing pain, not a sudden sharp one. It must be used in *earache, headache, stomach-ache, toothache*. It is countable: *I've got a bad toothache; Do you suffer from headaches?; I've had a lot of earaches lately.*

It can be used as a verb: *My head is aching.*

pain

Pain can be either countable or uncountable: *I've got a pain in my side; She's been suffering from pains in her arm; Are you in pain?; He has a low resistance to pain.*

Generally an *ache* is more persistent than a *pain* (countable) but *pain* (uncountable) can be very severe and persistent: *He was in great pain for the last few months of his life.*

A *pain in the neck* (*bum* (colloquial), *arse* (vulgar)) is something or someone that is a nuisance.

To take pains means *to make a great effort to do something correctly*. The adjective is *painstaking*: *After more than fifteen years of painstaking research his book was ready for publication.*

sore

Sore refers to an injury that involves ulceration, broken skin, and/or inflammation; it is noun or adjective: *His feet were covered with sores; I've got a sore throat; My eyes are sore.*

acronyms

An acronym is a word formed from the initial letters of other words such as *laser, NATO, UNESCO* and *UNICEF*. Acronyms of the names of specific organisations are treated as names and have no article: *The Secretary-General of NATO announced today...*

People often talk of the *HIV virus*, an *ATM machine*, an *ISBN number*, or a *PIN number* even though the acronyms include letters representing the words *virus, machine,* and *number*.

See ABBREVIATIONS.

actual

Actual means *real, true, not imagined*: *The actual financial results for this year differ from the budgeted prediction by 3.26%.*

Actually means *really, truly, in fact*: *He said he was a millionaire, but actually he had only rented the Rolls-Royce for the day.*

These words have no connection with time as they do in other INDO-EUROPEAN LANGUAGES. They do not mean *current, present*.

AD and BC

Although these abbreviations represent *anno domini* (Latin for *in the year of the Lord*) and *before Christ*, the full forms are very rarely used; they are spoken as abbreviations: /eɪ diː/ and /biː siː/. The forms CE (common era) and BCE (before common era) are sometimes found.

adapt & adopt

Adapt makes the noun *adaptation*. *Adopt* makes *adoption*.

adjective not adverb

Verbs of perception are followed by adjectives, not adverbs. These verbs are *feel, look, seem, smell, sound*, and *taste*: *I feel happy; She looks ill; It seemed easy.*

See SENSE VERBS.

adjectives

An adjective is a word that describes a noun or pronoun: *awake, blue* and *hot* are adjectives.

Adjectives are used in English in the expressions: *to be hot, cold, hungry, thirsty, afraid,* RIGHT, WRONG, SUCCESSFUL. We do not say ~~I have hunger~~ etc.

A

attributive and predicative

An adjective which precedes the noun is attributive: *a blue car* (see THING); an adjective is predicative when it follows a verb: *it is close; it feels hot* (subject complement, see SENSE VERBS) or when it describes the object: *I find this interesting* (object complement).

Some adjectives can only be predicative. They include adjectives related to health: ILL, *poorly, faint, well, unwell* (but not *sick*), *sore, painful*; most A-ADJECTIVES and *able, afraid, answerable, conscious* (meaning *aware*), *fond, glad, loath, subject, tantamount*.

gradable & non-gradable

Adjectives can be divided into two classes, gradable and non-gradable.

Gradable adjectives are those that have degrees in their meaning: *a bit hot, fairly old, quite difficult, rather intelligent, very wet*.

Non-gradable adjectives are those that refer to a quality that is absolute. Examples are: *fabulous, filthy, huge, incredible, priceless*; some of them are extreme synonyms of gradable adjectives: *filthy = very dirty; huge = very big*. These adjectives do not have comparative forms: ~~filthier, more incredible~~; they do not have degrees: ~~fairly filthy, quite huge~~; they cannot follow *so*: ~~so priceless that..., so huge that...~~; and they must be modified with adverbs other than *very*: *absolutely fabulous, terribly filthy, perfectly priceless*. See QUITE.

Some adjectives refer to a state that exists absolutely or does not exist at all. *Annual* and *unique* are examples; while *absolutely unique* and *almost annual* are reasonable (though the FORMER is tautological), *very annual* and *more unique* are meaningless. OPEN is non-gradable and must be qualified with *wide* not *very*. There are some anomalies: *enormous* is non-gradable and so ~~very enormous~~ is impossible, although its opposite *very tiny* is perfectly correct. Surprisingly, *extreme* is gradable: *His political views are very extreme/are more/less extreme than they were five years ago*.

Past participles used in passive constructions are non-gradable; the action defined by the verb is fulfilled so the participle in its adjectival sense is absolute: *That author was well-known in his time but is totally forgotten nowadays* (not ~~very known, very forgotten~~); *I was fully* (not ~~very~~) *persuaded by his argument*.

Some past participles have achieved the status of adjectives: *I was very interested to see that he still lived there; She was very frightened at the end of the film*; but *very* is not used with a true passive meaning: *I was extremely/deeply* (etc.) *interested by your speech; She was really/extremely* (etc.) *frightened by the monsters in the film*.

restrictive use

Adjectives can be used non-restrictively. If I talk of *my Welsh wife*, it is assumed that I have only one wife and she is Welsh. This use is similar to what is found in non-defining RELATIVE CLAUSES: *My wife, who is Welsh, is a teacher*.

adjectives, comparison

There are three degrees of comparison: higher, same and lower. For the difference between comparative and superlative forms see COMPARATIVES AND SUPERLATIVES.

higher degree comparison
one-syllable adjectives

These add *-er* for the comparative and *-est* for the superlative: *high, higher, highest; old, older, oldest; fast, faster, fastest*.

Note: *just, real, right, wrong* and the preposition LIKE can only make their comparative forms with *more, most*: *A more just decision had never been reached; I had never been more wrong in my life; She looks more like her father every time I see her*.

A final single consonant after a short vowel is doubled: *big, bigger, biggest; hot, hotter, hottest* but after a long vowel or diphthong it is unchanged: *cheaper, cooler, greater*. See DOUBLE CONSONANTS.

If they end with *-e*, they do not double it: *wide, wider, widest; free, freer, freest*.

one-syllable adjectives following *more, most*

This can be done, but it is never necessary to do so, when they are PREDICATIVE (**ADJECTIVE*) and the *than* is followed by a CLAUSE. *You are more kind/kinder than I could possibly expect.* This cannot be done with adjectives which make irregular comparative forms, or with *bad, big, black, clean, fair* (colour), *far, fast, good, great, hard, high, low, old, quick, small, thick, thin, tight, wide, young.*

This is always done when the quality of the adjective rather than the quality of a noun is being compared. The meaning is like RATHER than: *His LECTURE was more long than interesting (...was long rather than interesting).* There are no restrictions on the use of adjectives here as there are in the preceding paragraph; all adjectives can be used: *His new car is more fast than comfortable.*

Past participles used as adjectives must have *more, most*: *My right shoe is more worn than my left one.*

two-syllable adjectives

Adjectives which end with -*y* can only take -*ier*, -*iest*: *easier, happiest*; the only exception is that ADJECTIVES WITH -LY often take *more, most*: *friendlier/more friendly; leisurely/most leisurely.*

Adjectives with -*ow*, -*le*, -*er*, -*ure* and many others with the stress on the first syllable can take both forms: *narrower/more narrow; nobler/more noble; cleverer/more clever; maturer/more mature.*

Present participles and past participles used as adjectives can take only *more, most*: *The work was more tiring* (not *tiringer*) *than I had expected*; *That room is more crowded* (not *crowdeder*) *than this one.*

Other adjectives vary; some can take only *more, most* in comparative and superlative forms while others take *more, most* more commonly than -*er*. If you are in doubt, use *more, most*.

three-syllable adjectives

Negative forms of two-syllable adjectives with -*y* take -*ier*, -*iest*: *unhappier, untidiest*. All other adjectives with three or more syllables take *more, most*: *more beautiful, most intellectual.*

irregular comparative forms

Some adjectives have irregular comparative forms: *good, better, best* (for *well/better* referring to health see WELL); *bad, worse, worst; much, more, most*; some have variable comparative forms: *far, farther/further farthest/furthest; little less/lesser, least; more, much, most; old, older/elder, oldest/eldest* (for the difference in meaning see FARTHER & FURTHER; LITTLE & SMALL; ELDER). *Well-known* etc. make *better known*.

-er and -er; more...and more...

Two comparative forms of the same adjective repeated indicate an increase in the force of the adjective: *Your work is getting better and better*; *My life is becoming more and more interesting*; (*'Curiouser and curiouser!'*, a quotation from *Alice in Wonderland*, has passed into the language as an idiom despite, or perhaps because of, Alice's failure to use good English.)

most as intensifier

Most has the meaning of *very, extremely* in sentences such as *You are most kind; His speech was most interesting.*

same degree comparisons

In affirmative sentences these are made with *as...as*: *John is as old as Mary.*

In negative sentences these are made with either *as...as* or *so...as*: *The bus is not **as** fast **as** the train; The train is not **so** fast **as** the plane.*

lower degree comparisons

These are made with *less* and *least* for comparatives and superlatives respectively. All adjectives make these comparative forms in the same way. There is a difference between *This film is less boring than the other* and *This film is more interesting than the other*; between *This is your least bad result* and *This is your best result*. The first examples imply that the film is still boring and that the result is still bad, though not so much as before.

A

adjectives, order

Adjectives generally stand in the order beginning with the most general and leading to the most specific. Although the rules are complex and can change in individual circumstances the usual order, after the DETERMINER, is:
- adjectives that amplify, emphasise or de-emphasise: *certain, complete, definite, extreme, same, total.* These are NON-GRADABLE (*ADJECTIVES).
- general: *lovely, important, old* (size, age, shape).
- origin and nationality, participles, material, colour. These are non-gradable.
- any word which is closely connected with the noun to provide a single concept: *social worker; drinking water.* This can be another noun: *bus ticket.* Note that the -ING FORM used here is a GERUND used adjectivally; *drinking water* is *water for drinking,* but *running water* is *water that is running.*

So we have *An old, red maths book; A complete, beautiful, French coffee table; That horrible, red, woollen sweater.*

adjectives, use of *and* between adjectives

PREDICATIVE *ADJECTIVES have *and* before the final adjective. *His life was LONELY (*ALONE), poor, unhappy, violent and short.*

ATTRIBUTIVE *ADJECTIVES do not usually have *and* between them when the effect is to accumulate in meaning: *a hot, bright, summer's day; a dirty, old, red car.*

When attributive ADJECTIVES describe different attributes that are seen separately, *and* may be used: *a wicked and vicious tyrant; modern concrete and glass buildings. And* is always used between colours: *a red and green beetle; a blue and yellow car, a black and white film.* Note that with colours *white* is the second of two: *red and white* etc.; with three or more it can stand in any position, though *red, white and blue* are usually in that order.

adjectives with -ly

Cowardly, DEADLY, DEATHLY, *friendly, leisurely,* LIKELY, *lively, lonely, lovely, lowly, scholarly, silly, stately* and *ugly* are adjectives: *a cowardly action; a friendly gesture.*

These words cannot be used as adverbs. For an adverbial meaning the sentence must be changed: *He behaved like a coward/in a cowardly way; She gestured amiably/in a friendly way,* not ~~He behaved cowardly/She gestured friendly~~.

Gingerly, early and POORLY, and the words expressing frequency: DAILY, *weekly,* FORTNIGHTLY, *monthly, quarterly* (= every three months) and *yearly* (but not *annual/ly*), can be used as adjectives and adverbs: *a daily paper; the milk is delivered daily; an early train; the train arrived early.*

adjectives without nouns

An ATTRIBUTIVE *ADJECTIVE must be followed by a noun or pronoun; it cannot be left hanging in the air. If there is no obvious pronoun, use *one: Which do you prefer? The green one or the red one/this one or that one?* or THING: *The most difficult thing will be...; The most exciting thing about the holidays was...* See ONE REPRESENTING A NOUN.

exceptions to this rule

Certain adjectives which are used to define groups of people in society; in these cases the adjective takes a plural verb: *the rich have all the pleasure; the poor have all the problems; the healthy; the sick, the unemployed.*

Certain nationality adjectives: *the French; the Irish.* See COUNTRIES AND NATIONALITIES for the nationality adjectives that can be used in this way.

Adjectives used in abstract contexts: *A journey into the unknown; The best is the enemy of the good.*

Ordinal numbers, superlatives, *last, next, other* and *own.* These can be used without a following noun: *the second (one):* ALL *is for the best in the best of all possible worlds; the other (one); No thanks, I prefer my own.*

Some fixed expressions with prepositions: *for your own good; for good* (= forever, permanently); *in public, in private, in secret; in the nude, in the wild; in short; to the full; from bad to worse; out of the ordinary; in the extreme; above normal; in common.*

Adjectives used without nouns cannot take a POSSESSIVE: *John was the last to arrive; The last person's* (not ~~*The last's*~~) *arrival time.*

adverbs, comparison

Adverbs make their comparative forms in the same way as adjectives and, except as shown below, the article ADJECTIVES, COMPARISON can be used to refer to adverbs.

Some adverbs have irregular comparative forms: *well, better, best; badly, worse, worst; much, more, most;*

Some adverbs have variable comparative forms: *far,* FARTHER/FURTHER, *farthest/furthest; little/less/lesser, least.*

Although adjectives which end in *-y* have *-ier*, all adverbs in *-ly* (except *early, earlier, earliest*) make their comparatives with *more, most*: *more quickly* not ~~*quicklier*~~.

Often makes *oftener, oftenest* as well as *more, most often.*

The adjective is sometimes used informally instead of the adverb: *Can you write clearer, please?* (for *more clearly*). This seems to be particularly common with *quicker* (perhaps because of the analogy with *faster*): *You'll get there quicker* (faster) *on the motorway.*

adverbs, formation

Most adverbs are formed from adjectives by adding the suffix *-ly*: *quick – quickly; slow – slowly.*

If the adjective ends in *-l*, the adverb has two *l*'s: *equal(ly), beautiful(ly);* HOPEFUL(LY).

If the adjective ends in *-y*, the adverb ends in *-ily; easy - easily; happy - happily* because English orthography does not admit *y* before any suffix (but see PLURAL FORMS | NAMES).

See ADVERBS WITHOUT -LY.

adverbs, order

The usual order of end-position adverbs (see ADVERBS, POSITION) is manner, space, time:
They played happily in the garden.
They played happily yesterday.
They played in the garden yesterday.
They played happily in the garden yesterday.

This rule is not inflexible. Short adverbial expressions come before much longer ones: *They played in the garden yesterday, as happily as they had ever played in their lives. They played yesterday in the garden where I played when I was a child.*

A one-word destination adverb immediately follows verbs of movement, and ARRIVE: *They went there hopefully; We travelled home quickly.*

adverbs, position

Adverbs can go in three positions, *initial, mid* and *end*.

initial position
This is at the beginning of the sentence, before the subject: *In all probability Mary will know the answer.*

mid-position
1 In affirmative statements (except with the verb *be*) this is:
   a between subject and verb: *I always eat eggs for breakfast.*
   b between auxiliary and main verb: *I have always eaten eggs for breakfast.*

A

    c after the first auxiliary if there is more than one: *Eggs have always been served for breakfast in this hotel.*

    d In emphatic statements (except with the verb *be*) the adverb can move to a position between the subject and the first auxiliary: *I always **do** eat eggs for breakfast; I always **have** eaten eggs for breakfast; I never **would** have eaten toast for breakfast if eggs had been available.*

2 In NEGATIVE statements the adverb follows the *not*: *I do not always eat eggs for breakfast; I have not always eaten eggs for breakfast.* See ALREADY, YET & STILL.

3 With the verb *be:*

    a when there is no auxiliary the adverb goes after the verb: *I am always hungry at breakfast time.*

    b when there is an auxiliary, it follows it as in **1 b.** and **1 c.** above: *I have always been hungry at breakfast time.*

    c In emphatic statements, as above, the adverb moves to follow the subject: *I always **am** and I always **have** been hungry at breakfast time.*

    d In negative statements the adverb follows the *not*: *I am not always hungry at breakfast time; I have not always been hungry at breakfast time.*

end-position

This is after the direct and/or indirect object. For the order of adverbs of different types in this position, see ADVERBS, ORDER.

which position to choose

The position of the adverb is generally determined by three factors although there is some variability, especially in spoken language (see the table below):

    a the type of adverb.

    b whether it is a phrase or a one-word adverb. Phrases cannot stand in mid-position. The use of *very, almost, hardly* etc. before a one-word adverb does not make a phrase of it: *The repairs have (very) nearly been completed.*

    c the degree of emphasis. Initial position is usually emphatic.

It is very unusual to place an adverb between the verb and the direct object. Sometimes this is done:

- when the direct object is followed by a RELATIVE CLAUSE: *I have received from my bank the money which I need to buy the car*. This is done only in a formal style of writing or speaking. In this example the regular order (*I have received the money which I need to buy the car from my bank*) is ambiguous; it could mean that I am buying the car from the bank, not that I have received the money from the bank.

- when a MULTI-WORD VERB has an object consisting of several words:
She turned down the offer of a better job.
~~She turned the offer of a better job down.~~

    She turned the offer down.
    She turned down the offer.
    She turned it down.
    ~~She turned down it.~~

- for precise expression in legal language, especially when the object is extremely long: The Contractor shall take out and maintain <u>at its expense during the course of this present Contract and until it is completed</u> insurance that includes the following covers…

A

summary chart for adverb position

	Type of adverb	P / W	Example	I	M	E
1	certainty	phrase	in all probability, without a SHADOW of a DOUBT	✓	X	✓
2	certainty	word	probably, undoubtedly, certainly, definitely	✓	✓	X
3	degree	phrase	as a close approximation, up to a point	✓	X	✓
4	degree, approaching	word	almost, nearly	X	✓	X
5	degree, limiting	word	barely, HARDLY, scarcely	✓	✓	X
6	frequency	phrase	every month, whenever the sun shines	✓	X	✓
7	frequency, definite	word	daily, monthly	X	X	✓
8	frequency, indefinite	word	usually, often*	✓	✓	✓
9	manner	phrase	with a smile, as soon as possible	✓	X	✓
10	manner	word	happily, slowly, carefully	✓[a]	✓[a]	✓[a]
11	space	phrase	in the garden, at the airport	✓	X	✓
12	space	word	here, up, inside, northwards	✓	X	✓
13	time	phrase	on Tuesday, at that moment	✓	X	✓
14	time, definite	word	yesterday, tomorrow	✓	X	✓
15	time, indefinite	word	recently, then	✓	✓	✓

* With *very* etc. these adverbs do not lose their one-word status: *He has very often arrived late.*

examples

1. ***In all probability*** *she knows the answer. She knows the answer **without a shadow of a doubt**.*
2. ***Probably*** *it will snow. It will **undoubtedly** have started raining.*
3. ***As a close approximation*** *it will cost you $8,000. I accept what you say **up to a point**.*
4. *He **almost** broke the record. The repairs have **nearly** been completed.*
5. *It has **barely** rained all week/We have had **barely any** rain all week.*
   (Note the position of *barely any*. The adverb moves to the DETERMINER which it is modifying.)
   Hardly[b] *had she arrived at home when the phone rang.*
6. ***Every month*** *he sends his daughter a cheque for £1,000. She goes to the beach **whenever the sun shines**.*
7. *Letters are delivered **daily**.*
8. ***Usually*** *he goes home for lunch but today he's meeting a friend. It could **always**[c]/**never**[d] have been there. I don't see him **often**.*
9. ***With a smile,*** *he put the phone down. I will send you the results **as soon as possible**.*
10. ***Happily*** *he sealed the envelope and posted it. He **slowly** walked to the door. He copied her name and address **carefully**.*
11. ***In the garden*** *there was a fish pond. I'll meet you **at the airport**.*
12. ***Here*** *we find the problem. Paul drove the lorry **northwards**[e] for twenty kilometres.*
13. ***On Tuesday*** *I'm free at ten o'clock. I couldn't find the solution **at that moment**.*
14. ***Yesterday*** *it rained. I will tell you the answer **tomorrow**.*
15. ***Recently*** *she has been working very hard. I have **recently** been having a lot of problems. Have you been taking enough exercise **recently**?*

notes

a. *well* and *badly* can only go in end-position.
b. in initial position only with INVERSION.
c. *always* cannot go in initial or end-position
d. *never* cannot go in end-position and can go in initial position only with inversion.
e. *northWARDS* etc. cannot go in initial position.

See SPLIT INFINITIVE; EVEN; ONLY.

A

adverbs without -ly

Some words without *-ly* can sometimes be used adverbially. The words in question are BLOODY, CHEAP, clean, clear, close, DEAD, direct, EASY, fair, FAST, fine, flat, free, HARD, high, JUST, LATE, light, LIVE, long, loud, low, most, POSH, PRETTY (meaning *fairly*), QUICK, RIGHT, sharp, SHORT, slow, sound, STRAIGHT, tight, well, wide and WRONG. All of these words except *fast*, *long* and *well* have equivalent forms with *-ly*; a dictionary will explain the difference in meaning between the two forms.

Dead, fast, long, low, straight and *well*: Except for *well*, which can only be an adverb (except when it means in good health, see WELL), these words can be both adjectives and adverbs: *a fast train, the train travels fast*. They have no adverbial form with *-ly* (*deadly* and *lowly* are ADJECTIVES WITH -LY). As an adverb *dead* means *very, exactly*: *dead easy; dead on ten o'clock*.

Clear, close, easy, fair, free, short, tight and *wide*: The adverbial form without *-ly* is used only in certain verbal expressions. Examples are *clear (keep clear), close (come, keep, stay close), easy (go easy, take it easy), fair* (play, fight fair), free (run free), light (travel light), loud (laugh loud and long, speak loud enough), short (short-sighted), tight (hold, pack tight), wide (open wide)*. In other cases apart from these the adverb with *-ly* is used in the normal way: *clearly different; speak clearly*. *Shortly* means *soon, in a short time*. (*Fairly is the normal adverb formed from *fair*: *speak fairly of someone; treat someone fairly*. It also means QUITE, RATHER, not completely: *fairly good; fairly interesting*.)

HARD is the usual adverb: *work hard*. *Hardly* has the special meaning of ALMOST NOT.

In the other cases the forms with and without *-ly* are used in different contexts and may have very different meanings. See the article for each word.

DOUBTless is always an adverb. The adjective meaning *beyond doubt, unquestionable* is *indubitable*.

advertise

Note the variation in the pronunciation of these forms: *advertise* /'ædvətaɪz/, *advertiser* /'ædvəˌtaɪzə/, and *advertisement* /ædv'ɜːtɪsmənt/. *Advertisement* is often shortened to *ad.* or *advert*.

advice

The noun is *advice* /æd'vaɪs/; the verb is *advise* /æd'vaɪz/. The final sound of *advice* must be unvoiced because *c* before *e* is never pronounced VOICED (see C, C). Similarly LICENCE, PRACTICE and PROPHECY are nouns, while *license, practise* and *prophesy* are verbs. Although these four words all have an unvoiced last sound /s/, the spelling follows the model of *advice, advise*.

The noun *advice* is uncountable like INFORMATION and NEWS: *Let me give you some advice; He gave me three pieces of advice*.

aerial & antenna

Antenna is the technical word and is often found printed on radios, DVD players etc. However, *aerial* is the normal conversational word.

affect & effect

Affect /ə'fekt/ is a verb.

Effect /ɪ'fekt/ is a noun. If one thing *affects* another, it has an *effect* on it. *Effect* is also a verb meaning to *bring about, cause to happen*: *They effected a rapid escape; The company has plans to effect great changes*.

Although the two words are pronounced differently, the similarity leads to confusion. Perhaps for this reason, the verbal use of *effect* is not very common. Another form is *to put something into effect*.

Africa

While this word clearly relates to the whole continent, for historical reasons *Africa* is used naturally by British people to refer to sub-Saharan (black) Africa: *She was born in Africa* but *He fought in North Africa in the war. I'm going to North Africa for my holidays*.

See AMERICA.

A

ago, since & for

ago
Ago says how far in the past something happened: *She arrived ten minutes ago; Dinosaurs became extinct 65 million years ago*. Because it refers to a completed time in the past it has the PAST SIMPLE.

since
Since takes a state or action in the present and relates it to its starting point: *This town has existed since the Middle Ages*; *I have been waiting since ten o'clock*. Because it refers to the present time the PRESENT PERFECT (*PERFECT ASPECT*) is used. The PAST PERFECT (*PERFECT ASPECT*) is also possible: *I had been waiting since ten o'clock*.

for
For gives the duration of an action, continuing, or completed, or in the future:
I have lived in London for five years. (Present perfect because I live there now.)
I lived in London for five years. (Past simple because I do not live there now.) See PAST SIMPLE & PRESENT PERFECT.
I'll be there for half an hour.

aid, aide & AIDS

Aid meaning *help* is uncountable. It has no plural, but *technical aids, teaching aids* etc. have plurals. An *aide* (from French *aide-de-camp*) is an assistant to a political leader. **AIDS** is an ACRONYM of *acquired immune deficiency syndrome*.

ain't

This is a non-standard CONTRACTION representing: *am not, are not, is not, have not* and *has not*.

air-conditioned

This BACK-FORMATION is used as a transitive verb *to air-condition*:
They're going to air-condition our office. (They're going to install air-conditioning.)
Carol has bought an air-conditioned car/a car with air-conditioning.
The air-conditioning (system) has broken down again.

aisle

An *aisle* /aɪl/ is the passageway in a church between the rows of seats. By extension it is used in theatres, cinemas, trains, and planes, and also in supermarkets for the passageways between the display shelves. The ETYMOLOGY of the word is confused. It is a mixture of French *aile* (wing), *isle* and *alley*. There is no justification for the *s* but it is the standard spelling.

See COULD; FOREIGN; GHOST; ISLAND.

ale and beer

Before the introduction of hops to England the word *ale* was used to describe a drink made of fermented malt (germinated barley) or other grain. Hops were introduced into England in the fifteenth century and spread through the country during the next hundred years or so. The word *beer* was used to describe the new hopped drink. These words are synonyms nowadays. *Beer* is more common in general but *ale* is always used in *brown, light* and *pale ale*.

Lager /ˈlɑːgə/ is a kind of beer that is lighter in colour and flavour than traditional British beer; it is the kind of beer that is typical in other European countries.

Commercial *ginger ale* or *beer* is a non-alcoholic ginger-flavoured drink. Home-made ginger beer is usually alcoholic as it is a fermentation of yeast and sugar with ginger.

alive, life & live

Alive /əˈlaɪv/ is an adjective which means *having life*: *When my grandfather was alive*. It can only be used as a PREDICATIVE *ADJECTIVE. See A-ADJECTIVES. ➤

A

Living /ˈlɪvɪŋ/ is the -ING FORM of the verb *live*: *I was living in London at that time; Living in Africa helped him to understand the problems of the third world; Not a living soul knew what they had done.*

Live /laiv/ is an adjective and adverb. In broadcasting it means that something is being broadcast as it happens: *A live broadcast from the football stadium; The football match was broadcast live.* In electricity it means *carrying a current*: *Don't touch that wire – it's live; This is the live terminal of the circuit.* As an ATTRIBUTIVE *ADJECTIVE it corresponds to *alive*: *Live animals are not used in these experiments.* *Live ammunition* is designed to cause damage as opposed to *blank ammunition* which explodes but does not project a bullet or shell, or is an empty piece used for show.

Live /lɪv/ is a verb which means:
to be alive: *Shakespeare lived from 1564-1616.*
to inhabit a place: *They live in Moscow.*
to have its normal place: *That book lives on the middle shelf.*
To *live together* means *to cohabit, to live as a couple without being married.*

Life /laɪf/ is a noun: *He led a happy life* (or *He **lived** a happy, long* etc. *life.* This is the only occasion when *live* can take an object). It can also mean a biography: *Boswell's Life of Johnson.*

Lifeboat, lifeguard, life jacket, lifebelt etc. are equipment for saving life at sea.

all & everybody/everything

All is used with a DETERMINER; *everybody/thing* is used as a singular pronoun: *All the children were happy; Everybody was happy.* Not *All were happy*. *All the food was eaten. They ate everything.* Not *They ate all*.

However, in very general senses and rather dramatic language *all* can be used as a pronoun to mean *absolutely everything*: *All is not lost; If all goes according to plan; All was in vain.*

In RELATIVE CLAUSES *all* suggests a limitation or insufficiency; it is like *the only thing*: *All that you can do now is tell the police; All's well that ends well* but *Everything that was stolen was later found. Is that all you want?* expresses surprise that you don't want more while *Is that everything you want?* is a way of checking that you haven't forgotten anything. *I've done all I can* implies that I cannot do more even though this may not be sufficient for you, while *I've done everything I can* implies that I feel satisfied that I have done everything possible.

That's all and *that's everything* are equally correct meaning *there is no more*. However, *That's all* might suggest that it is unfortunate that there is no more, while *that's everything* could suggest satisfaction that everything has been dealt with. Also, *that's all* must be used when there is an uncountable reference: *Is there any more wine? No, that's all (I bought).*

all, both & most

All refers universally. **Both** refers to two things. These two words are used in the same way. The examples in this article are given with *all*, but *both* could be used in the positive examples: *All (of) the students passed the exam; All fish can swim; The students will all be examined.* In the last example *all* takes the mid-position. See ADVERBS, POSITION. The use of *all* or *both* does not AFFECT whether an ARTICLE is used.

With pronouns the usage is *All of them speak Spanish; I know all of them; They all speak Spanish; All of them speak Spanish.* Again, *both* could be used in all (of) these examples.

All can be used with an uncountable noun; obviously *both* cannot: *All the milk has been drunk.*

In the negative, *Not all birds can fly* means that some can and some cannot. *Both birds cannot fly* means that NEITHER (*EITHER AND NEITHER) of them can fly. *Not both birds can fly* is impossible. *All cats cannot fly* is possible but *No cats can fly* is more usual.

Most refers to a majority of things or of the quantity of a mass. It is used as follows: *Most (of) the students passed the exam; Most birds can fly; Most of them speak Spanish; I know most of them; Most of the milk has been drunk.*

A

alliance
This word is pronounced /əˈaɪəns/. *Ally* is pronounced: noun /ˈalaɪ/, verb /əˈlaɪ/.
See -IETY.

almost + negative
It is more usual to say *Hardly anybody could hear the speaker* than *Almost nobody could hear the speaker*. Similarly, *hardly + any-* is preferred in sentences such as *I've hardly any money; I hardly ever drink beer; She hardly said anything; I've hardly travelled anywhere this year*.

This seems to be a question of style and preference; there is no grammatical reason to prefer one or the other. However, in sentences such as *There's nothing new here, well almost nothing new*, where the *nothing* is repeated, it is usual to use the form with *almost* and a negative word.

With *not* however: *I almost didn't catch the plane* is another way of saying *I almost missed the plane; I almost failed to catch the plane*. On the other hand, *I hardly caught the plane* is not a possible construction.

alone, by oneself, on one's own & lonely
Alone is an adverb meaning
- *with no other people present, unaccompanied*, possibly intentionally and possibly not, but with no suggestion that it was a disagreeable experience: *I travelled alone; He spent the day alone. I did my work alone* means that there was no other person with me when I did it. In this case it is used in END-POSITION *(*ADVERBS, POSITION)*.
- *only, exclusively*: *George alone knew the answer.* (Only George knew the answer.) *I paid $10,000 for that picture alone.* (I paid $10,000 for that picture and for nothing else.) In this case it immediately follows the noun which it focuses attention on (*George; that picture*).

A sentence such as *I spoke to George alone* is ambiguous. It could mean *I spoke to George with no other people present* or it could mean *I spoke to nobody except George*.

By oneself and *on one's own* can also mean the same as the first meaning of *alone* above: *I travelled by myself; He spent the day on his own*. However, *I did my work by myself* can mean either that there was no other person with me when I did it or that I did it without help. These two forms should not be confused: *He spent the day by his own*.

Lone is an ATTRIBUTIVE **ADJECTIVE* meaning *solitary, separate, apart from others*: *A lone tree was visible on the horizon*.

Lonely is an adjective. When it is applied to people it means that the absence of other people was unpleasant: *I was lonely; I spent a lonely Christmas*; a *lonely hearts' club* is a club for people who want to meet other people with a view to romance but when it is applied to a place it means that the place is unpleasantly isolated: *She lived in a lonely house in the mountains*.

along, up and down the road
Unless the road in question is sloping there is really no difference between these forms.

already, all ready etc.
There is a difference in meaning between *Are they here already?; That'll be £13.65 altogether* and *Are they all ready?* (Are all of them ready?); *Did you buy them all together* (all of them together) or separately?

The compound *alright* (first recorded in 1893) is sometimes used but is less widely accepted than *already* and *altogether*. Many people reject it as incorrect and insist on *All right (?Alright), I'll give you the money; Teresa was ill last month but she's all right (?alright) now*. There is no doubt in this case: *There were ten questions in the test and I got them all right*.

already, yet & still
Already and *yet* mean *before a certain time present or past*. *Still* means that something is continuing.

➤

A

affirmative

Already is usually in the mid-position but can be placed at the end (see ADVERBS, POSITION): *I already know/knew the answer.* (I have/had found it out before then.); *They have/had arrived already.*

Still can only stand after the subject: *I still know/knew his phone number.* (I continue(d) knowing it.) not (in modern English) ~~I know/knew his phone number still~~.

negative

Yet also has two possible positions: *I don't know the answer yet* (I have not found it out by this time); *They have not yet arrived.*

Still can only stand after the subject: *I still don't/didn't know his telephone number or email address* (I continue(d) not knowing it) not (in modern English): ~~I don't/didn't know his phone number still~~.

Although *still* appears to have the mid-position (see above), unusually it keeps its position after the subject in compound verb forms: *I still haven't found out his phone number. He still won't/can't have arrived.*

The PAST SIMPLE cannot be used with *yet*: ~~I didn't know the answer yet~~. Use *I didn't know the answer at that time.*

For the type *Surely he doesn't still live with his parents; She can't still have the same car after all these years* see PREDICATION NEGATION (*NEGATION OF VERBS*).

question

Have you (already) found the answer (already)? (I am surprised that you have found the answer so quickly.)
Have you found the answer yet? (neutral)
Do you still know his phone number? (Do you continue knowing it?)

negative question

Haven't you (already) found the answer (already)? (surprise – I thought you had already found it)
Haven't you found the answer yet? (surprise that it is taking you so LONG.)
Don't you still know his phone number? (I expect that you do, and I will be surprised if you don't.)

With modal and similar auxiliary verbs *yet* and *still* are similar in affirmative sentences:
The best is still/yet to come. (The best still hasn't come/hasn't come yet.)
I have still/yet to read his latest book. (I still haven't read it./I haven't read it yet.)
We may still/yet arrive on time. (There is still a possibility./It is not impossible yet.)

other uses of *yet*

It emphasises comparatives: *The next stage was yet more difficult (even more difficult) than the previous one had been.*

It is like *but, however, nevertheless*: *She worked very hard, (and) yet she failed the examination.*

alternate & alternative

Alternate /'ɒltəneɪt/ is a verb meaning that two things follow each other in turns. It can be intransitive or transitive: *Happiness alternated with sadness; The weather alternated between sun and rain; They alternated morning and afternoon working.*

As an adjective or adverb *alternate(ly)* /ɒlt'ɜːnət/ refers to two things that happen in turns: *They work alternate weekends; They carried red and blue flags alternately.*

Alternative /ɒlt'ɜːnətɪv/ is an adjective describing other things or possibilities that are available: *an alternative method; several alternative routes. Alternative energy* is energy from sources that do not consume the earth's natural reserves of fossil fuels. It is also a noun: *Which alternative do you prefer?; We have no alternative (but to stop now).*

Although some people insist that *alternative* should be restricted to a choice between two possibilities (because of its original meaning in Latin), this is not the case. There are many examples of its use with more than two alternatives.

A

although & despite
Although is a CONJUNCTION and must be followed by a CLAUSE with a verb: *I went out although it was raining.*

Despite and its SYNONYM *in spite of* are PREPOSITIONS and must be followed by a noun: *I went out despite the rain/in spite of the rain.*

although etc.
Although /ɔːlˈðəʊ/ and *though* /ðəʊ/ are synonyms, except in cases where *though* is used to mean *however*: *I don't believe him, though. Although* cannot be used here.

Thorough /ˈθʌrə/ means *very careful, considering all details*: *a thorough examination; thorough consideration.*

Thought /θɔːt/ is the past of *think*.

Through /θruː/ is a PREPOSITION meaning passing from one side of something to the other.

Throughout /θruːˈaʊt/ means *in all parts of* either in space or time: *English is spoken throughout the world; Religion has been an issue throughout European history.*

Tough /tʌf/ means *hard, resilient, difficult*: *The meat was as tough as leather; That is a tough question.* Referring to people it can mean *resilient, liable to be violent*, an extension of the basic meaning.

Trough /trɒf/ is the open container from which a horse or other animal drinks; it is used for any long open container for liquids. It is also used for a depression in geology or on a graph, the opposite of a peak.

aluminium
This is the name used in science rather than the American *aluminum*.

See CAESIUM; SULFUR & SULPHUR.

always + continuous aspect
Always can be used with the CONTINUOUS ASPECT of the verb when the reference is to an action which is surprising or annoying: *He's always wearing that horrible old sweater; He's always talking about his work.*

amen
There are two pronunciations: /ɑːˈmen/ and /eɪˈmen/.

America
America and the adjective *American* are normally used to refer to the United States of America: *200 American dollars; the American government* even though *America* is the name of the whole continent. In very formal contexts *United States* is used: *The United States government.* North *America* comprises the USA, Canada and Mexico. *Central America* is the region between Mexico and Colombia, and SOUTH *America* is the main southern continent. *Hispano-America* is sometimes used for the Spanish-speaking countries in the continent; *Latin-America* includes Brazil as well as *Hispano-America* and possibly Quebec; *Ibero-America* is the preferred expression in Spanish diplomatic circles not only as it is more accurate but also as *Latin-America* is considered to be a French expression. *Hispanics* are people of South American origin in the USA.

AMERICAN ENGLISH is the standard name for the form of the English language that is used in the USA.

See AFRICA.

American English
Three factors have led to the strength of American influence on British English: the presence of American troops in Britain during the Second World War; American films, TV programmes and comics; and the power of the American economy. The influence is more noticeable in pronunciation

A

and vocabulary than in grammar. American words are easily assimilated into British English; a number of words which were once regarded as Americanisms are now accepted as common words in Britain. With the widespread use of the INTERNET, American English is becoming dominant and many typically American forms are appearing in British usage.

There are very few grammatical differences between the two forms of the language, and those which there are, are trivial. In American English:
- *gotten* is sometimes used as the past participle of GET.
- HAVE is used with the auxiliary *do* rather than *have got*.
- the PRESENT *SUBJUNCTIVE is used more frequently.
- SHALL *MODAL AUXILIARY VERBS) is hardly ever used except in questions.
- the PAST SIMPLE is used with *already, ever, just* etc. instead of the present PERFECT.
- some prepositions are used differently.
- American English is more innovative than British English.

The very large majority of the vocabulary is the same in the two forms of the language. There are some words for natural and social phenomena which do not exist in Britain (as there are in every country where English is spoken), and there are words which exist on both sides of the Atlantic but have different meanings.

Fall meaning *autumn, loan* as a verb, and *I guess* meaning *I suppose* were found in medieval English and crossed the Atlantic Ocean with the early settlers in America. They have now died out in Britain and are commonly regarded as Americanisms, though *I guess* is now becoming common in English worldwide.

Some words are spelled differently in American English and British English; the differences between the two forms of the language are slight, but where there is a difference, American English is usually simpler and more phonetic. This is largely due to the work of the American lexicographer Noah Webster (1785-1843) whose *Compendious Dictionary of the English Language* (1806) introduced his spelling reforms for the English language, which were eventually accepted.

GB	US	British/*American*
-ae-	-e-	gynaecology/*gynecology*
-ce	-se	defence/*defense* (but British English *defensive*)
-gue	-g	analogue/*analog*; catalogue/*catalog*
-ller, -lling, -lled	-ler, -ling, -led	traveller, travelling, travelled / *traveler, traveling, traveled*
-our	-or	colour/*color*
-re	-er	theatre/*theater*

British *American*

British	*American*		
aluminium	*aluminum*	PROGRAMME	*program*
cheque	*check*	pyjamas	*pajamas*
fulfil	*fulfill*	speciality	*specialty*
install	*instal*	syphon	*siphon*
jewellery	*jewelry*	tyre	*tire*
plough	*plow*	worshipped, worshipping,	*worshiped, worshiping,*

In American English all words have *-or*. In British English some have *-or* and some have *-our*. See -OR & -OUR.

Aluminium and *caesium* are the international scientific forms.

In computer usage British English has *PROGRAM*.

Non-standard spelling is more common in American English, notably *tonite* for *tonight* and *thru* for *through*. Though the latter is not regarded as standard it was adopted as the official style of the Chicago newspaper *The Tribune* in 1935. See DEVIANT SPELLING.

These differences exist and they cannot be ignored. Nevertheless, they are small in comparison to the language as a whole and their importance should not be exaggerated. British and American native speakers communicate efficiently and with a minimum of difficulty in understanding. People often have more difficulty in understanding strong regional accents from their own country, whether that is Britain or the USA, than in understanding each other. Except for words which pass from one form of the language to the other (mostly from American to British English) the two forms are not usually mixed and it is wise for a foreign student of English to choose one or the other and use that consistently. Here is a list of American words with their British equivalent meaning.

American	British
airplane	aeroplane
assignment	homework
attorney	lawyer
automobile	car
bathroom	toilet
bill	(bank)note
billboard	hoarding
billfold	wallet
biscuit	scone
branch water	tap water
campus	university area
candy	sweets in general
casket	coffin
check	bill (e.g. in restaurant), cheque
checkers	draughts (game)
CHIPS	(potato) crisps
closet	cupboard
COLLEGE	university
cookie	biscuit
CORN	maize
crazy	mad
derby	bowler hat
diaper	nappy
dime	10 cents
dormitory	hall of residence
downtown	in the centre of town
draft	conscription
drapes	curtains
drugstore	shop selling toiletries & cleaning items
DUMB	stupid
el	overhead (*el*evated) railway
elevator	lift
eraser	rubber
fag	homosexual (insulting)
fall	autumn
faucet	tap
first floor	ground floor
flapjack	pancake
forty-niner	gold prospector in California in 1849
fraternity	male students' social organisation
freeway	motorway
French fries	(potato) chips
G.I.	private soldier
gallon	0.83 British gallon
garbage can	rubbish bin
gas(oline)	petrol
go (food to go)	food to take away
grain	corn
hog	pig
homely	ugly
hood	bonnet (of car)
Ivy League	prestigious universities in N.E. states
Jello	jelly
jelly	jam
jumper	pinafore dress
knickers	knickerbockers, plus-fours
levee	embankment
(stand in) line	queue
liquor store	off-licence
lumber	timber
mad	angry
MAJOR	principal subject at university
mom	mum (mother)
movie	film (in a cinema)
movie theater	cinema
necktie	tie
nickel	5 cents
Old Glory	the American flag
one way ticket	single ticket
pail	bucket
pants	trousers
parking lot	car park
patrolman	policeman
penny	1 cent
pint	0.83 British pint (see WEIGHTS AND MEASURES)
POOL	game similar to snooker
pop	dad (father)
quarter	25 cents = 2 bits
railroad	railway
raincheck	a promise to do something later
real estate	property (land, houses)
realtor	estate agent

A

redwood	giant sequoia tree	subway	underground (railway)
rotary	roundabout	Thanksgiving	national holiday, fourth
round trip ticket	return ticket		Thursday in November
rubber	condom	thumb tack	drawing pin
rye	WHISKEY made from rye	traffic circle	roundabout
schedule	timetable	trunk	boot (of car)
shades	blinds, sunglasses	underpass	subway
sherbet	water ice, sorbet	undershirt	vest
sidewalk	pavement	uptown	out of the centre of town
singlet	vest	vacation	holidays
smokestack	chimney	vest	waistcoat
soda	a sweet carbonated drink	vet	ex-serviceman
sophomore	second year student	WASP	White Anglo-Saxon
sorority	female students' social organisation	windshield	Protestant windscreen
speakeasy	illegal bar during PROHIBITION	YANKEE	(a person) from New England
store	shop/store	zip code	postcode

amid(st), among(st), while (whilst) & again(st)

The first three of these, *amid(st)*, *among(st)* and *while (whilst)*, have no difference in meaning between the forms with and without *-st*. *Again* and *against* of course differ completely in meaning.

among & between

among

Among relates the position of one object to various surrounding objects as an undefined or collective group: *I was only one among many; Hungary is among the formerly communist countries of Europe; Picasso is numbered among the greatest twentieth-century painters.*

Amongst is a SYNONYM of *among*.

between

Between relates the position of an object to each of several objects considered separately: *I was sitting between John and Mary. Luxembourg lies between France, Germany and the Netherlands.*

Although *between* is COGNATE with the word TWO, there is no reason why *between* must be restricted to meaning *between two things*; indeed it is incorrect to say ~~Luxembourg lies among France, Germany and the Netherlands~~ as the other three countries are being considered separately. It is correct to say *Luxembourg is among the richest countries in Europe* as in this CASE the other countries are being considered as a group.

Between can also refer to two ALTERNATIVES: *The choice was between John and Mary. I can't see the difference between these two sweaters.*

Betwixt is an archaic SYNONYM of *between*; it is used nowadays only in the colloquial cliché *betwixt and between*.

analyser & analyst

An *analyser* is a machine or system that analyses things. An *analyst* is a person that analyses things.

ancient, antique & elderly

Ancient refers to a time before the fall of the western Roman Empire: *ancient languages, ancient civilisations*; *ancient* is sometimes used more generally to refer to something which is very old, for example an *ancient tree* or an *ancient monument*, but unless the word is used ironically or exaggeratedly, the meaning is always that the thing in question is many centuries old.

Antique is used mainly with reference to pieces of furniture or other objects of the decorative arts.

Elderly refers mainly to people and is considered more polite than *old*.

anger, surprise, insults and taboo words
This article contains words that some people may find offensive.

Like other languages, English has a number of words that are used at moments of intense emotion. Being emotional words they are not filtered through the intellect when they are spoken; for this reason the language of swearing and insulting is very strongly defined by culture and is difficult to translate from one language to another. British English differs even from other varieties of English in this respect. This article refers to British usage except where shown. Also the force of these words changes with time; when the Church was powerful, the use of religious or blasphemous expressions was considered very powerful language, so much so that the word *damn* was printed as *D—* in books published in the eighteenth and nineteenth centuries. The use of strong language is called swearing, referring to the swearing of oaths in God's name; to do so lightly was thought blasphemous. In the mid-twentieth century other non-religious words were replaced by dashes.

Words marked with * are considered offensive by some people and should be used with care. Words marked with ** are very powerful and should be used only in extreme circumstances. Many people find them deeply offensive. Many people do not swear at all, or only very mildly. In very many cases the tone of voice in which the words are spoken and the personal relations of the people involved are important in deciding the strength of the expression. However, there is now a wide degree of tolerance of these words. For example, the use of *bloody* as an intensifying adjective or adverb will give offence to some people; the word should be used with care, although it is more widely accepted now than in 1916 when the public was outraged by the use of the word on the stage in the first London performance of *Pygmalion*. These words did not really become publicly acceptable until the 1960s, when they were first included in dictionaries. Theatre critic Kenneth Tynan caused a storm of outrage when he used the word *fuck* on television in 1963. There seems to be greater tolerance of such words, especially *fuck*, on the INTERNET than in VERBAL use, where great caution should still be exercised.

A *minced* pronunciation is one which substitutes a milder or meaningless word for one that is considered offensive. As language changes people often do not know that they are using minced oaths.

Because so many strong swear words have four letters, a *four-letter word* is another way of describing a swear word.

The excessive use of such words is sometimes referred to colloquially as *effing and blinding*, referring to the constant use of the words *fuck* and *bloody*. Sometimes people speak euphemistically of *the F-word* and *the C-word*, meaning *fuck* and *cunt* respectively.

arse* (American English ass)
This is the buttocks. To fall *arse over tip* or *tit* is to fall over heavily. To *arse about* or *around* is to fool about doing nothing particular. To *lick someone's arse* means to behave in a very ingratiating way to them, to do anything to gain their favour. To call someone an *arse* means that he/she is a fool. Perhaps it comes from the use of *ass* (= *donkey* in British English) to mean a fool. The *arsehole*** (American English *asshole***) is the anus. It is a very offensive insult.

In American English *ass* is always used instead of *arse*. Americans are sometimes surprised to read of Don Quixote riding his horse Rocinante while his servant Sancho Panza follows behind on his ass.

balls*
Balls are testicles. Not surprisingly the word means manly strength or courage. *It takes balls to...* But also, and rather surprisingly, it means *rubbish or nonsense*: *Balls! A load of balls! That's balls.* To *make a balls up of something* is to do it badly, to make a mess of it; there is a verbal form *He ballsed it up*. Bollocks is an ALTERNATIVE, but it is less common in the last two examples. In 1932 Ernest Hemingway used the Spanish word *cojones* in *Death in the Afternoon*. It became popular and is sometimes used instead of *balls*.

To *ball* means to have sex; the subject is usually the man.

A

To *have a ball* is a perfectly acceptable expression meaning *to have a good time*; the reference here is to a ball as a dance.

bastard*
A *bastard* is a person whose parents were not married. In this literal sense its use is now mainly historic but it is still used as an insult.

berk**?
This means a fool. It is an abbreviation of *Berkeley* or *Berkshire Hunt*, which is RHYMING SLANG (*COCKNEY) for *cunt*. However, it is not usually considered offensive, perhaps because many people do not know its origin, though some may take offence. It is sometimes spelled *birk, burk* or *burke*.

bitch**
A bitch is a female dog. It is a powerfully insulting term for a woman though it does not refer to sexual morality. The meaning can be transferred to other things: *Life's a bitch. Son of a bitch* (sometimes written *sonofabitch* or *SOB*) is an insult to a man. It is more American than British.

As a verb *bitch* means to behave very unpleasantly to other people.

blast
This refers to a violent movement of air around a thunderbolt or an explosion. It is used as an exclamation of annoyance *Blast it/you/this machine*. It comes from *God blast you*.

bloody*
Bloody has two meanings.

Literal: *Covered with blood, bloodstained* as in *'What bloody man is that?'* (Shakespeare, *Macbeth*, I, ii, i).

An intensifier: This meaning of the word probably derives from the word *blood*; there is no evidence to support the commonly believed theory that *bloody* is a corruption of the blasphemous oath *By our lady*. It is used as an adjective: *Bloody hell! This bloody machine won't work* or as an adverb *Not bloody likely*. When it is used as an intensifying adverb, it does not have *-ly*.

Ruddy means *red*. It is used as a minced form of *bloody*.

bugger**
Buggery is anal sex; a *bugger* is a person who performs it. These are legal terms but outside legal language the words are insulting: *Buggery!; You bugger!; Bugger it/you/this machine; I couldn't/don't give a bugger.*

Bugger all means *nothing: He told me bugger all.*

Sometimes it is used jokingly among friends: *You're a silly bugger aren't you?* However, unless you are very sure of your RELATIONSHIP with the person you are talking to this usage is best avoided.

Christ
This expresses mild surprise or anger: *Christ! By Christ* is emphatic: *Yes, by Christ!; By Christ you'll regret that.* The minced form *Crumbs!* is sometimes used.

cock
A *cock* is a male bird especially of the domestic hen. The noise it makes is *cock-a-doodle-doo*. It also means a *tap*. To *cock a gun* is to raise the hammer so that it can be fired. From this if something *goes off at half cock* it fails to achieve its full intention. A *cock-up* is a mess or a badly done job. The *cock-up theory* and the *conspiracy theory* are two ways of explaining why things go wrong.

** It also means a *penis*, perhaps from the meaning *tap*. A *cocksucker* is an insult to a man, relating to the act of fellatio. A *cock teaser* is a woman who is sexually provocative but refuses to have sexual intercourse.

cunt**
This means the *vagina*. It is a very powerful word, probably the strongest four-letter word in the English language. It is used as a very offensive insult, usually addressed to a man. Until recently it was never seen in print. *Twat* means the same as *cunt* and is just as offensive.

damn /dæm/

This is a religious word. People who are *damned* are condemned to eternal punishment. As has been mentioned above, the word was once thought so powerful that it could not be printed; now, it is a fairly mild expression of annoyance or anger that does not give offence, except perhaps when used as a direct insult. Curiously, *damn* can be used adjectivally instead of the past participle.

Damn! Damn it! This expresses general anger.
Damn you! Damn this machine! This expresses specific anger against a person or thing.
Damn your eyes! This is an old-fashioned insult.
Damn me! I'll be damned! This is an expression of surprise.
This damn(ed) machine won't work. This shows annoyance or anger.
Damn all is nothing at all.
I don't/couldn't give a damn. This means *I don't/couldn't care less*.

For a number of years *damn* was the strongest swear word that could be used in Hollywood films. In *Gone With the Wind* Clark Gable famously says 'Frankly my dear, I don't give a damn' but unnaturally emphasises the word *give*. It is said that he did so because he would have preferred to say *fuck* rather than *damn*, which would have been more appropriate to Rhett Butler's character. For all of these *goddam(ned)* can be used as an alternative. *God damn it* shows the SUBJUNCTIVE of the word.

DASH (*HIT) is sometimes used as a minced form of *damn*, but also suggests violent activity.

Dash is the name of the PUNCTUATION mark used in the written form *d–*, which was used to represent *damn*.

devil

This is not now felt to be as strong as it once was. *What/Why the* DEVIL? is like *What/Why the hell?* If you are *between the devil and the deep blue sea* you have a dilemma; two alternative choices, both of which are extremely dangerous or risky. There'll be *the devil to pay* means that there will be serious trouble in consequence of an action. To *play the devil with something* is to damage something seriously (note the distinction between *pay* and *play* in these two examples). A *devil-may-care* attitude is one that gives no thought to the consequences. In *a devil of* it is an intensifier like *a hell of*: *We had a devil of a good holiday*.

fanny**

This is a complicated word. In British English it means *the vagina* but is perhaps not as strong as *cunt*. In American English it is a synonym of *ass*, which is *arse* in British English.

It is also a woman's name, short for Stephanie. The name of the book *Fanny by Gaslight* causes a certain amount of confusion and amusement.

fuck**

This means to have sex with someone, usually with the man as the subject. For many centuries it was regarded as a taboo word and was rarely found in printed work, though frequent in speech. It is used as the strongest equivalent of *damn*: *Fuck!; Fuck it!; I don't/couldn't give a fuck*. To *fuck about*, or *fuck around* is to fool about doing nothing in particular. To *fuck something up* or to *make a fuck-up* of something is to do it badly, to make a mess of something. *Fuck off!* is a very strong and insulting way of telling someone to go away. The -ING FORM *fucking* is used to intensify. It is used in the same way as *bloody* (adjective and adverb) but is even stronger. *Fucker* is a general insult. *Fuck all* means *nothing*: *He told me fuck all*.

This word is used widely on the internet, especially in the abbreviation *WTF* for *what the fuck?* This casual use should not be adopted in normal communication or conversation.

God

This expresses mild surprise or anger: *(My)* GOD! *(Good) God! By God* (an ELLIPTICAL form of *I swear by God*) is emphatic: *Yes, by God!; By God you'll regret that*. The minced forms *Gosh* and *Golly* are sometimes used instead of *God*.

A

hell
This expresses anger, which could be mild or severe.

Oh hell! Hell's bells (and buckets of blood)!

What/why/who/etc. the hell? This emphasises the question.

What the hell! Who cares? These mean *What difference does it make?*

Go to hell. This is an insult.

Not a (snowball's) chance/hope in hell means no chance or hope at all.

Come hell or high water means *Whatever obstacles or difficulties may arise*: *I won't change it come hell or high water.*

Hell for leather is very, dangerously, fast.

To beat/knock hell out of someone is to beat someone severely.

Till/when hell freezes over refers to an impossibly distant future time: *I'll wait for your answer till hell freezes over; You'll get your answer when hell freezes over.*

If you *give someone hell* or *play (merry) hell with someone*, you make their life very difficult. The affected person *gets hell*.

Get the hell out (of a place) is to leave quickly.

There'll be hell to pay means that there will be enormous problems.

To play (merry) hell with somebody/something is to cause great problems: *This weather's playing hell with my rheumatism.*

To *raise (merry) hell* (also *raise Cain*) is to cause a great disturbance.

If you do something *just for the hell of it*, you do something for fun, for no practical reason.

Like hell is an intensifier: *Run/work like hell*. It can be used as an emphatic contradiction: *'You can't do that.' 'Like hell I can't.'*

Hell's Angels are lawless leather-jacketed motor-cyclists; they originated in California, where they caused considerable civil trouble in the 1950s. They were seen in the film *The Wild One* (1954), where they were called *Black Rebels*.

prick**
As a verb this means *pierce* or PERFORATE and is perfectly acceptable at all times. If you are handling roses you might *prick your finger* on them. You can *prick a hole* in paper or material; a small hole made in that way is called a *pinprick*. When you have an injection you might feel a slight *prick*. If you have done something wrong *your conscience might prick you*. To *prick up your ears* means to start paying attention, to become alert.

**It also means a *penis*, and is used as an insulting term for a man.

pussy**
This is a term for the vagina. In Britain, though not in the USA, it is also a friendly name for a cat. See ANIMALS.

screw**
Like *fuck*, this also means to have sex. To *screw around* means to have sex with a number of partners. *Screw you/it/this machine* is an expression of anger. To *screw up* means to make a mess of something or to do it badly.

From the original meaning of the word, to *screw someone (into the ground)* means to put great pressure on them. To *screw something out of someone* is to obtain something with enormous difficulty. There is a particular association here with thumbscrews as an instrument of torture.

shit*
This means *excrement, faeces*. In this sense it is uncountable. It means *rubbish, nonsense, something very unpleasant*: *That's a load of shit; His new film's shit.* It means *cannabis resin*.

Shit! is an exclamation of annoyance or anger. If you are *in the shit* or *up shit creek (without a paddle)* you are in serious difficulty. *When the shit hits the fan* is the moment of crisis leading to something terrible. *To beat (seven shades of) shit out of someone* is to beat them severely.

To call someone *a shit* (uncountable noun) is a serious insult. In this use it is countable: *He's a (complete) shit*; *They're a bunch of shits*. *I don't/couldn't give a shit* means I don't/couldn't care less. If you have *the shits*, you have diarrhoea. It is a verb. It can be regular (*shit/shitted*) or irregular *shit, shat, shat*

Some people say *sugar* as a minced form of *shit*. This is only done as an exclamation, not in the sense of excrement.

sod*
Sodomy is anal sex. This word is used in the same way as *bugger*.

tit*
This is a slang word for a woman's BREAST. It is an insult to a man. If you *feel/look a tit* you are embarrassed. If something *gets on your tit*, you feel annoyed by it. Saying that it *gets on your wick* is acceptable.

Birds of the family *Paridae* are called *tits*. This is a different word from *tit* meaning breast and does not cause offence.

See HOMONYMS.

wank**
This means *masturbate* (of a man). A *wanker* is an insult for an unpleasant or useless person.

SUMMARY
surprise
Christ!; (My) God; (Bloody) hell; (God) damn; Shit*; Fuck** (me); Blast; Bugger** (me).*

anger		insults
(Bloody*) hell		shit*
Shit*		prick**
Damn		arsehole**
Fuck**	*you*	You (bloody*) (fucking**) bitch**
Screw**	*it*	bastard*
Bugger**	*this computer*	wanker*
		bugger

Anglican
Anglican refers to the CHURCH OF ENGLAND or any church in communion with it. As a noun it means a member of the Church of England. *Anglican* has no other meaning; it is not a SYNONYM of *English*.

Anglo-
Anglo- is a prefix meaning English that can make compounds with other words. It can stand before other nationality adjectives to indicate a relationship or connection between Britain and that country: *Anglo-American relations; Anglo-French co-operation*. Other nationality adjectives are formed in this way: *the Franco-Prussian War; Sino-Japanese relations*.

Anglo-Catholic
An *Anglo-Catholic* is a member of the CHURCH OF ENGLAND who is closer in belief to the CATHOLIC Church than to PROTESTANTISM. Contrary to what people sometimes suppose an *Anglo-Catholic* is **not** an English person who is a member of the Roman Catholic Church.

Anglo-Indian
This means a British person resident in India, or relating to the British Empire in India; it also means a person of mixed British and Indian parentage.

A

Anglo-Irish

This refers to the English establishment which colonised and administered Ireland when that country was part of the British Empire.

It is sometimes used to refer to Irish literature written in English, but this use is disliked by many Irish nationalists.

The *Anglo-Irish Agreement* (1985) was an agreement between the British and Irish governments concerning the administration of Northern IRELAND.

Anglo-Saxon

This refers to the Saxons who conquered England after the ROMAN withdrawal in the fifth century (see ENGLAND, A BRIEF HISTORY). It also refers to the language (also known as OLD ENGLISH (*ENGLISH LANGUAGE, A BRIEF HISTORY)*) which was spoken in England before 1100. In recent years it has come to be associated with countries and cultures of British origin, either in the former British Empire or in the USA as in *Anglo-Saxon capitalism, media* etc. In this sense it is used more outside those countries than in them.

Anglo-Saxon is also sometimes used to refer to basic simple words for bodily functions of sex and excretion, which are considered offensive, though some people prefer these simple English words to their Latin or Greek equivalents which they consider to be euphemisms. This is a typical example of the dual vocabulary of English, with Latin And Greek words seeming more sophisticated.

angry

You are angry *at* or *about* something, but *angry at* or *with* someone. Do not confuse *angry* and

animals

male and female names

Usually the common name of an animal is used whether the animal is male or female. However, some animals have different names for males, females and young, which are used when this distinction is necessary.

common	male	female	young
cat	tom	queen	kitten
cattle	bull	cow	calf
chicken	cock, cockerel*	hen*	chick*
deer	buck, stag	doe	fawn
dog	dog	BITCH	puppy
duck	drake	duck	duckling
elephant	bull	cow	calf
fox	dog-fox	vixen	cub
goat	billy-goat	nanny-goat	kid
goose	gander	goose	gosling
horse	stallion	mare	foal
lion	lion	lioness	cub
pig	boar	sow	piglet
rabbit	buck	doe	kitten
sheep	ram	ewe	lamb
swan	cob	pen	cygnet
tiger	tiger	tigress	cub

*Cock (but not *cockerel*), *hen*, and *chick* may be used for other edible birds: *cock pheasant; hen pheasant; pheasant chicks*. For other birds and animals use the words *male, female* and *young*: *male ostrich; female frog; young snake*.

When the sex of the animal is important, or in cases when the animal is personified, *he* and *she* can be used: *Don't be afraid of Spot* (a dog). *He won't bite you* but Spot's owner would probably refer to an unknown dog in the street as *it*.

Children have familiar names for some animals including *pussy-cat, baa-lamb* and *bunny-rabbit* (as in the cartoon character Bugs Bunny). For the plurals of animal names, see PLURAL FORMS.

animal noises

animal	verb	ONOMATOPOEIA
bull	bellow	-----
cat	miaow, purr	miaow
cockerel	crow	cock-a-doodle-doo
cow	low, moo	moo
dog	bark	woof, bow-wow
duck	quack	quack
elephant	trumpet	-----
goose	hiss	sssss
horse	neigh, whinny	neigh, whinny
lion	roar	-----
mouse	squeak	squeak
pig	grunt	oink
sheep	bleat	baa, baa
snake	hiss	sssss

animals and meat

In English the name of the meat is often different from the name of the animal: *calf/veal; cow/beef; deer/venison; pig/pork; sheep/mutton*. The probable reason for this difference is that after the Norman conquest of England in 1066 the ANGLO-Saxon farmers looked after the animals, while the French-speaking Norman aristocracy ate the meat. These names only apply to the FLESH meat; other parts of the animal have the animal name such as *ox tongue, pig's trotters* (feet). The meat of the lamb is called *lamb*. *Chicken, cock(erel), hen, boar, hog, ox* and *swine* are Anglo-Saxon in origin as is *breakFAST*, but *bacon, brawn, poultry* and *sausage* are of French origin, as are *dinner, feast* and *supper*. Rabbit, hare and other undomesticated animals have the same name for the animal and the meat.

another

This is a compound of the indefinite ARTICLE *an* and the word OTHER. It is always written as a single word. It often tends to mean *one more* rather than *a different one*: *Would you like another cup of coffee?* but *They travelled in a different train from us.*

One another means *mutually*: *They spoke to one another*.

anticipate & expect

Anticipate is frequently used informally by native speakers as a synonym of *expect* but this is regarded as incorrect by some people.

any- & some-

This article refers to *any* /ˈeni/, *anybody, anyone, anything, anywhere* and *some* /sʌm/, *somebody, someone, something, somewhere*.

Early in an English course students learn that *some-* is used in affirmative statements and *any-* is used in conditional sentences, questions and negations. This is a good basic rule, but the true situation is more complicated. *Some-* refers to a specific person, thing, or place, even though it is not identified, while *any-* refers to a non-specific member of a group. ➤

A

***some-* is used**

- in conditional sentences to imply that the condition is specific: *If someone* (i.e. one specific but unknown person) *said that you'd won $1m, would you believe them?*
- in questions which are a formality: *Would you like some coffee?; Will someone please answer that phone?*

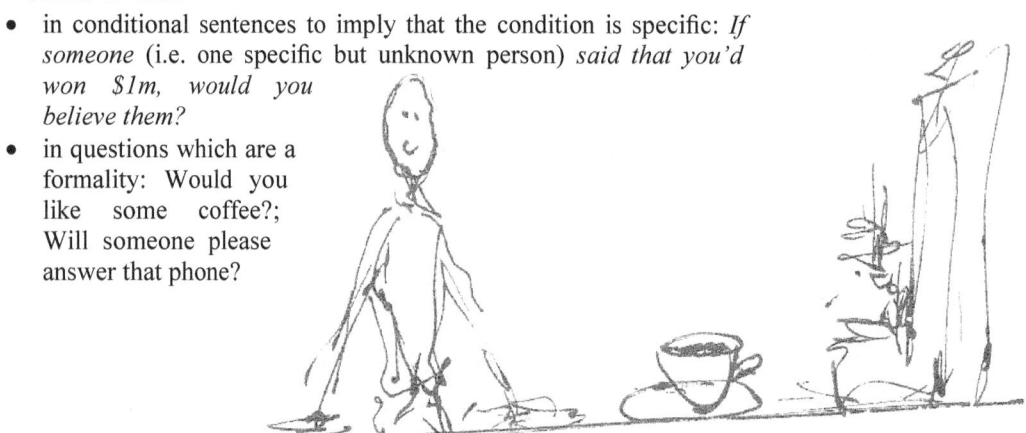

- in questions when the answer yes is expected: *'Have you got some money with you?' 'Yes, I called at the bank and got some'* (some used as a pronoun); *Is there someone there?*

Some- can be used as the subject of negative sentences: *Some people never go to the cinema; Someone who doesn't speak English is at the door.*

***any-* is used**

- as the object of negative sentences: *I had not/never seen anything so horrible; I looked for more money but I couldn't find any (any used as a pronoun.)* The negative nature of the sentence can be provided by a prefix: *I am unable to give you any more information; It is impossible for us to wait any* LONGer.
- in questions: *Have you ever seen anything so horrible?*
- in affirmative sentences when it shows that all members of a group are equally able to do something. In *Someone told me that he lived here*, *someone* refers to an unnamed but specific person; but in *Anyone in the village will tell you his address*, *anyone* shows that all the people in the village will help you, and that it does not matter which of them you ask.
- in sentences containing words which are negative or restricting in meaning, though they are not truly negative words themselves. Examples are *seldom* and *rarely; scarcely, hardly* and *barely* (note that these words also cause INVERSION): *I seldom have any time to read newspapers; I have rarely/seldom heard anything so stupid; Hardly anything had changed since my last visit*; and *the first* (and other ordinal NUMBERS) *time that: It was only the first (third) time that I had said anything to her.*

It is extremely important to understand that the *any-* forms are used in negative sentences but are not themselves negative: *Anyone will help you* is affirmative (see above). *No-one will help you* is negative. These two sentences are exactly opposite in meaning.

The compound forms are

any-	**no-**	**some-**	notes
anybody	*nobody*	*somebody*	
anyone	*no-one*	*someone*	
anywhere	*nowhere*	*somewhere*	
anything	*nothing*	*something*	
anyplace	*noplace*	*someplace*	These forms are used mainly in American English.
any time	---	*sometime(s)*	*any time* is sometimes written as one word.
anyway	*no way*	---	*no way!* is an emphatic negative response.

32

anybody and anyone
There is no difference at all between these two forms, just as there is no difference between the forms *somebody* and *someone, nobody* and *no-one*.

appointment, date & rendezvous

An ***appointment*** is a formal arrangement to meet somebody at a specified time and place: *I can't meet you on Thursday morning because I have another appointment at that time; I'd like to make an appointment with Dr Murchiston.*

A ***date*** (colloquial) is a social arrangement to meet somebody, do something with somebody, or go somewhere with somebody, usually in an amorous context: *Would you let a boy kiss you on your first date with him?* It can be used as a verb: *They've been dating for six months now.* In American English *date* can refer to the person: *Sure you can bring your date to my party.*

The word ***rendezvous*** /ˈrɒndɪvuː/ is military in origin; although, like *appointment*, it refers to a meeting at a specified time and place, the meeting may be secret and carefully planned: *We made a rendezvous under the bridge.* A *rendezvous* can also be the place: *I'll meet you at our usual rendezvous.* As a verb *rendezvous* is almost always military or paramilitary: *You will rendezvous with Capt. Miller and his men at 03.46.* The plural of the noun and the third person singular of the verb are written *rendezvous* and pronounced /ˈrɒndɪvuːz/. The PAST SIMPLE and past participle of the verb are *rendezvoused* /ˈrɒndɪvuːd/.

approve (of)

To *approve* something is to give it official confirmation and to say that action may be taken as a result: *I have approved your expenses claim.*

To *approve of something* is to have a good opinion of it: *I do not approve of your new girlfriend.* Thus, *I approve your plan* means that I give you permission to proceed with it. *I approve of your plan* means that I think that it is a good plan.

Arabic numerals

These are the numerals usually used in western writing: *1, 2, 3* etc. They are called *Arabic* because this system of writing numerals was introduced from Arab countries to replace the less efficient system of ROMAN NUMERALS. In fact the numerals are not the same as those used in writing the Arabic language.

For the difference between *Arab, Arabian* and *Arabic* see COUNTRIES AND NATIONALITIES note 1.

-arian

The words *communitarian* and *majoritarian* are used with very precise meanings in political philosophy; respectively they are a belief in communities rather than in individuals and rule by the majority. *Communitarian* is occasionally seen in an EU context as an equivalent of the French *communautaire*; this is never done officially and should be avoided to prevent ambiguity. The words ~~minoritarian~~ and ~~universitarian~~ are never used.

In general use it is best to use these nouns as adjectives: *community relations, majority opinion, minority shareholders; university finances.*

armistice poppies

The armistice that ended the First World War came into effect on 11 November 1918. This date is celebrated in the UK, the symbol of this celebration being the poppy that grew on the fields in France where much of the fighting took place. In early November many British people wear poppies that are produced for charity; these poppies are not elegant but are symbolic, and should not be mistaken for the flowers that people occasionally wear with their clothes for normal decoration.

A

arrive

This is a verb of position not of movement. It can only be used with prepositions which describe position; it cannot be used with *to*: *He arrived in the pub* BEFORE *me* but *He came to the pub by bus* and *We arrived at the airport an hour and a half before take-off* but *We travelled to the airport by taxi*. The most commonly used prepositions are *in* and *at*, though other prepositions of place, e.g. *on, over, next to*, are possible: *The plane arrived over Paris at 12.30*.

articles

Notes:
- The term *zero article* below means that neither the definite nor the indefinite article is used. The natural way of expressing this in English would be to say *no article*, but this term is reserved in grammar for the description of the lack of articles with proper nouns.
- The use of articles is a very complicated subject. The general rules below are followed by some specific cases and other cases.
- There are two articles in English: the definite article *the*, and the indefinite article *a/an*. They do not vary for GENDER, CASE or NUMBER.
- For the difference between *a* and *an* see A & AN; for the difference between the indefinite article and the number *one*, see ONE, NUMBER NOT ARTICLE.
- The correct use of articles depends partly on whether the noun is countable or uncountable. Remember that some nouns e.g. *glass* can be countable or uncountable depending on the context.

general rules
singular countable nouns

A singular countable noun must have either the indefinite article or the definite article except when there is another DETERMINER (a word such as *every, my, this, one, no*). An article is not used before a determiner ~~the my book~~. The indefinite article is used when the noun is one of many similar or identical objects and it is not clear which is being referred to.

John bought a sofa last week. There are many sofas. John bought one of them.

I ate in a Chinese restaurant There are many Chinese restaurants. I ate in one of them.

Mary is a teacher. There are many teachers. Mary is one of them. (In this use of the indefinite article with professions English differs from some other languages.)

The definite article is used with reference to something which can be identified as the only possible one under consideration when all the people involved in the communication share the knowledge required to identify the object. This identification may come from the context or from general knowledge.

John went into his living room and sat on the sofa. It is clear from the context that the reference is to the only sofa in John's sitting room.

Mary is the teacher who marked your exam. The teacher who marked your exam can be distinguished among all other teachers.

The Pope blessed us. There is only one Pope.

The sky was blue and the sun was shining. Only one sky can be seen at a time, and we assume that we are talking about the earth's sun.

If you go to Santiago de Compostela, you must see the cathedral. There is only one cathedral in Santiago de Compostela.

The Portuguese government; The Prime Minister of Greece. Portugal has only one government and Greece has only one Prime Minister.

Sometimes the definition is provided together with the noun (postmodification): *I ate in a Chinese restaurant* but *I ate in the Chinese restaurant in Castle Street*. There is only one Chinese restaurant in Castle St, so this definition is unique. In *I ate in one of the Chinese restaurants in Castle Street* the definition is restricted to the Chinese restaurants in Castle Street.

In these examples the postmodification provides a definition, not a description. In the above example, *Chinese* is a description of the restaurant, while *in Castle Street* is a definition. *I ate in the Chinese restaurant (that is) in Castle Street* is correct but *I ate in the restaurant (that is) in Castle Street ~~and (that is) Chinese~~* is not. However, in *There are Chinese restaurants in Castle Street* the phrase *in Castle Street* defines the place, not the restaurant.

In *It was the colour of dried grass* the noun *grass* is uncountable, so it has no article.

Sometimes the same noun has both articles in the same sentence: *I bought a cat and a hamster, but the cat ate the hamster.* I have already mentioned a cat and a hamster; it is clear that the only cat and the only hamster which I am referring to are the ones which I bought: *The cat (which I had bought) ate the hamster (which I had bought).*

I bought a computer last week, but the CD-ROM drive didn't work. I have not mentioned a CD-ROM drive, but because all computers have them it is clear from the context and from general knowledge that I am referring to the device in the computer which I bought.

plural countable nouns and uncountable nouns
(Uncountable nouns have no plural.) These may have zero article, definite article or ANY & SOME.
1   *Do you like roses?*
2   *Butter is made from milk.*
3   *Intelligence separates humans from animals.*

The article is not used here because the references are to roses as a class of flowers; to butter and milk as substances in general; and to intelligence as a quality in general and to humans and animals in general.

But these sentences have a definition, though it may be implicit:
1   *Do you like the roses (which we see in this garden)?*
2   *Could you pass me the butter (which is near you on the table)?*
3   *The intelligence of stone age people.*

In general the use of the definite article is the same for these nouns as for single countable nouns: *John and Mary went into the living room and sat on the new chairs; John and Mary are the teachers who marked your exam.*

Some and *any* are sometimes used in the position of articles when the focus is on the number or quantity more than on the class or general nature of the noun:
1   *John went to the garden and cut some roses.*
2   *Mary went to the market and bought some butter.*
Here the reference is not to roses and butter in general but to the number of roses which John cut and the amount of butter that Mary bought. These are unspecified, but we could reasonably ask the questions:
1   *How many roses did John cut?*
2   *How much butter did Mary buy?*

Any is used instead of *some* in questions and negative sentences: *Have you got any potatoes?; I haven't got any money.*

The difference between zero article and *some/any*: *John and Mary are teachers; Do you like dogs?*

These sentences do not have articles because the reference is to a class of people or things. The questions, ~~*How many teachers are John and Mary?; How many dogs do you like?*~~ are INVALID.

Compare **1** *Would you like some roses/tea?* and **2** *Would you prefer roses or violets/tea or coffee?* In **1** the focus is on the (unstated) number of roses/amount of tea, while in **2** the focus is on the class of flower/drink to be considered.

specific cases
the definite article
Places that are thought of generically although they have various locations. For example *cinema* and *theatre* or *seaside* used generically: ▶

A

She goes to the cinema every Monday. (There are four cinemas in her town; every Monday she goes to one of them.)
We always got to the seaside for our holidays. Last year we went to Morecambe and this year we're going to Skegness.

Certain adjectives which imply that the noun is unique such as:
- Superlative adjectives: *the biggest house; the oldest tree*
- *Next, LAST, only: the next train; the last chance; the only reason*

absence of article

No article is used with:
- Names of people and places: *Do you know John? They live in Manchester Road. The Hague* is the only city name that has an article in English; the diplomatic agreements that were signed in The Hague in 1899 and 1907 are referred to as *the Hague Convention* (not: ~~the The Hague Convention~~). In particular, *Cairo, Havana* and *Mecca/Makkah* do not have articles.
- Titles: *Where is Mr Smith?; I would like to make an appointment with Dr Jones.*
- Certain nouns which are considered as institutions rather than as places or when they are being used for the purpose for which they are intended: *in bed, on campus, at church, in college, at court, on deck, at home, in hospital, in prison/jail, at school, at sea, on stage, in town, at university* and *at work; in bed* but *stand on the bed; go to church on Sundays* but *go to the church and turn right; I have to go to school tomorrow* (to work as a pupil or teacher) but *I have to go to the school tomorrow* (as a parent to speak to a teacher). Note also *online* and *offline* for a computer connection.
- MEANS of transport with *by* e.g. *by bicycle, boat, bus, car, taxi, train, plane* as well as *on foot, horseback*. Contrast *take a/the plane, taxi* etc.
- Means of communication with *by* e.g. *by fax, mail, post, phone, radio*. Contrast *in the mail/post; on the phone; on the radio.*
- Times of day and night with *at*: *at dawn, noon, night*. See TIME | PREPOSITIONS.
- Meals considered as an institution rather than a particular event: *Will you stay for lunch? I'll ring you after dinner*. Contrast *I had lunch at Mary's; Mary gave me fish for lunch* with *The lunch Mary gave me was delicious; Mary gave me a delicious lunch.*
- Illnesses. *He suffered from pneumonia; He's got diabetes* but *I've got a cold/a TEMPERATURE; ACHE* and its compounds are usually countable: *I've got a headache; Eating unripe fruit will give you a stomach-ache.*
- Parallel structures, where the same noun is repeated: *arm in arm; day by day; from time to time* and where two contrasting nouns are used: *from father to son; from left to right.*
- Letters and numbers indicating paragraphs, sections etc. *As is mentioned in paragraph 4...; The conditions set out in section d) above; Question 3 has ten marks because it's more difficult than question 6; Look at example number 6*. The noun is not necessary in *It's mentioned in 4; The conditions set out in d) above; 3 has ten marks because it's more difficult than 6; Look at 6.*
- Nouns in three-word complex prepositions: *in accordance with; by means of*
- Some idiomatic verbal expressions: *catch sight of, give place to, give way to, keep pace with, lose sight of, lose contact/touch with, lose track of, make allowance for, make fun of, make room for, make use of, pay attention to, set fire to, take account of, take advantage of, take care of, take note of* and *take notice of.*
- The names of meat which are also the names of the ANIMALS: *Do you like chicken? I have never eaten rabbit.* The words *beef, mutton, pork, veal* and *venison* are uncountable and so can never have the indefinite article.
- *Man* (when it is used generically to mean *the human race), mankind; humankind* and *womankind. 'The proper study of mankind is man'* (Alexander Pope). For a consideration of the sexist implications of *man* used in this way with a general meaning, and of *mankind*, see INCLUSIVE LANGUAGE.

other cases

Note the contrast in *What's on the radio?/I heard it on the radio* but *The message was sent by radio; What's on television?/I saw it on television; I spoke to him on the phone* but *The message was sent by phone; The cheque is in the post* but *I'll send it by post.*

Play with musical instruments, games and sports:

The definite article is used with musical instruments: *Can you play the guitar?; The trombone is very difficult to play.*

Zero article is used with games and sports: *Have you ever played cricket?*

ABSTRACT *NOUNS* have zero article when they refer to the concept in general: *I love art.* There is still zero article when the noun is described by ATTRIBUTIVE *ADJECTIVES*: *She is studying ancient Greek philosophy.* However, when the description follows the noun (post-definition), usually with the word *of* or in a RELATIVE CLAUSE, the article must be used: *She is studying the philosophy of ANCIENT Greece; ... the philosophy that developed in ANCIENT Greece.*

The indefinite article should not be confused with the number *one*: *I bought a dog yesterday* means one of the many dogs which I could have bought. *One dog is enough in a small house* has a numerical element: *one dog, not two or three or more dogs.* See ONE, NUMBER NOT ARTICLE.

When the name of a LANGUAGE is used alone there is no article: *Do you speak Portuguese? I studied Russian at university.* In a more formal style the word *language* is used with the name as an adjective. When this is done, the definite article is used: *The Chinese language is the most widely spoken in the world.*

The INTERNET has the definite article because *net* is a countable noun.

Space, HEAVEN, and *hell* are places and do not have articles.

For the use of articles with nationality nouns see COUNTRIES AND NATIONALITIES.

artist & artiste

An *artist* is a painter or other person who produces works of art. An *artiste* is a singer or dancer or other person who performs in public.

arts and sciences

Academic subjects are divided into two fields, arts and sciences. In this sense *arts* is another name for humanities, and does not refer to painting, sculpture etc.

as

as and like

The usage differs basically accordingly according to whether the word is used as a conjunction or a preposition.

In careful usage *as* rather than *like* should be used as a conjunction meaning *in the way that*: *Do this as I do* not *Do this like I do*, though informally, and especially in American English, *like* is often used as a conjunction in such sentences as these.

When the word is followed by a noun or pronoun, *like* is correct in careful usage: *Do this like me.* For this purpose *as* may be considered as a conjunction and *like* as a preposition. See GRAMMAR.

The word *like* may be considered as a preposition in sentences such as:
1 *She looks like her mother.*
2 *Like her mother, she's a teacher.*
3 *She's a teacher like her mother.*
4 *No-one can teach like her.*

A

In **1** and **3** *like* can be modified as if it were an adjective: **1** *She looks very like her mother; She looks more like her mother than like her father; She looks more like her mother than her brother does;* **3** *She's a teacher just like her mother.*

3 and **4** can be converted into CLAUSES with *as* **3** *She's a teacher, as is her mother;* **4** *No-one can teach as she does.*

Sometimes however, *as* appears to be a preposition. There is a difference between *He wrote as a civil servant*, which means that he was a civil servant and wrote in that capacity, and *He wrote like a civil servant*, which means that he was not a civil servant but wrote in the style of one.

As is often used to state a job, role, or function: *She got a job as a sales assistant; He appeared in the play as Hamlet; I used a knife as a screwdriver* while *like* expresses a similarity: *The hotel was like a home to me; His living room was like a museum.* See LIKE.

as as a relative pronoun

As can sometimes be used as a relative pronoun referring to a clause or sentence: *His wife's French, as you know* (*His wife's French, which you know*). The RELATIVE CLAUSE (which is always non-defining and thus has commas) may be placed inside the main clause: *His wife, as you know, is French.* In this case *as* is a relative pronoun and is the subject of a clause: *As was said earlier, the results are better than was expected.* Because *as* is the subject of the clause it is not followed by any other noun or pronoun. Compare *As it was said earlier, I won't repeat it now.* Here *as* means *because* and must be followed by a subject.

as means because and when/while

As a conjunction *as* can mean *because*: *As there was no traffic in the square, I could hear the church clock striking.* It can also mean *when/while*: *As I was crossing the square, the church clock was striking.*

Sometimes this may cause ambiguity: *As I was in the square, I heard the church clock strike* could mean either *Because I was in the square...* or *When/while I was in the square...* Such ambiguity can be avoided by using other conjunctions as is shown in this paragraph.

ascend & ascent

Ascend is the verb and *ascent* is the noun.

The noun *Ascension* is practically limited to the Ascension of Christ to heaven forty days after Easter.

See EXTEND, PORTEND.

assassin

An *assassin* is a person who deliberately murders a public figure for political or religious reasons. John Kennedy, Indira Gandhi and Benazir Bhutto were all assassinated. The word is not used for private people, who are simply KILLed or murdered.

The first *assassins* were members of a medieval Muslim sect which considered it a religious duty to murder enemy leaders. *Assassin* is derived from the Arabic word meaning a hashish-smoker as the *assassins* were believed to consume hashish before killing their victims in the state of ecstasy induced by the drug; there is, however, no historical evidence to support this theory.

See KILL; THUG.

assure etc.

Assure states an insistence to remove doubt. It has a personal object: *I assure you that I knew nothing of the problem; I wish to assure you of my full support for your proposal.*

Ensure is to make sure that something happens: *I will ensure that the goods reach you this week.*

Insure is to pay money against the risk of future damage. You *insure a car, flat, boat* etc.

A

Make sure is to confirm something: *Make sure that you catch the right train; I think his phone number is 12345 but I'll just make sure.*

Reassure means to try to convince someone that their doubts or worries are baseless.

The corresponding nouns are *assurance, insurance, reassurance.*

asterisk
An asterisk (*) is used in linguistics, though not in this book (see introduction), to indicate a) that a form that is printed is incorrect, or b) that a historical form has been assumed to have existed without proof, for example the Indo-European root of *father* in the article COGNATE.

at & to
Some verbs can be followed by *at* or *to*; generally *to* is neutral, while *at* suggests aggression. You can *throw a ball to a friend* in a game, but if you *throw a stone at someone*, you want to hurt them. You can *kick a ball to another player* but *kicking sand at someone on the beach* is aggressive. You *shout to someone* when there is a loud background noise; you *shout at them* if you are angry. *Speak* and *talk* are usually followed by *to* or *with*. Using them with *at* suggests a rather aggressive style and you may find it difficult to reply because the speaker is speaking constantly.

See IN & ON (INCLUDING AT).

attach & enclose
A file that accompanies an EMAIL is *attached*. The attached file is an *attachment*. A document that is put in the same envelope as a LETTER is *enclosed*. The enclosed document is an *enclosure*.

audience, onlookers, spectators & viewers
Audience is used for the public in theatres, concert halls and cinemas, or listening to a RADIO programme: *The audience applauded loudly.* It is also used for a formal meeting with a monarch or pope.

Onlookers are people who gather to watch an event such as a cat being rescued from a tree.

Spectators are people watching a sporting event.

Viewers are people who watch television.

autarchy & autarky
Autarchy means government by a despot, an *autarch*; it is a synonym of autocracy.

Autarky means a policy of national economic self-sufficiency, without wishing to trade with other countries.

Though the two words share the prefix *auto-* (meaning self) and have the same pronunciation /ˈɔːtəki/, the former comes from the GREEK root αρχία meaning *ruling* (as *monarchy* etc.); the latter comes from the Greek root άρκεια meaning *suffice*.

auxiliary and main verbs have the same form
Sometimes a verb appears as an auxiliary and main verb together. There is nothing strange about sentences such as *I had had* /həd'hæd/ *dinner when they came. (I'd had dinner...); What do you do?* /dəjuˈduː/; *I used to use* /justəˈjuːz/ *an electric typewriter.*

In each case the auxiliary has a weak pronunciation, or is contracted. This is less clear with *used to* but note the difference in pronunciation.

See USED TO.

aware
To be aware means *to know, recognise*: *I became aware of somebody standing behind me; I wasn't aware (I was unaware) that his wife was German; Are you aware that we have to leave in ten minutes?* Generally, *aware* is a PREDICATIVE *ADJECTIVE that must be followed by *of* or a *that* CLAUSE, though the attributive constructions *aware people*, an *aware state* (for *a state of awareness*) and the predicative without *that*: *we are very environmentally aware* are found informally. ➤

A

Aware can be preceded by *very much* or *very well*: *very much/very well aware* or *perfectly aware*. *Unaware* is the negative of the adjective *aware*. *Unawares* is an adverb meaning unexpectedly: *I met him unawares. The question took/caught me unawares.*

Beware is a verb meaning *be careful, cautious, be aware of some risk or danger*. The *be* is the verbal part but it is unchangeable and thus is used only in the imperative and infinitive: *Beware of the dog. I told you to beware (of the dog).* The construction with an object (i.e. without *of*) is sometimes found in poetry or formal prose. In Shakespeare's Julius Caesar, Caesar is warned *Beware the Ides of March*.

Wary means *cautious, suspicious*. It can be attributive or predicative: *I'm wary of buying things from people in the street; I was wary, from fear of being attacked; He had a wary expression on his face; His unwary behaviour led to the attack.*

See A- ADJECTIVES.

away & out

Go away suggests a greater time and distance than *go out*. You might *go out* for dinner or *go out* to the bank, but you *go away* for the weekend or *go away* for your holidays; when you *go away* you pack your clothes and toothbrush. However, people do say *He's been out in Africa for 25 years.*

Go away is a rather rude way of saying *leave me*. *Go out* also means to have an emotional relationship with someone: *John and Mary have been going out for six months now; Who is she going out with now?*

axe, axis & axle

An **axe** (American *ax*) is a tool, usually with a wooden or metal handle, and a metal blade for chopping; the plural is *axes* /ˈæksɪz/.

An **axis** /ˈæksɪs/ is an imaginary line around which a body rotates; the earth's axis is the line joining the North and SOUTH Poles; the plural is *axes* /ˈæksiːz/. In the Second World War the *Axis* was the alliance of Germany and Italy.

An **axle** is the shaft in a vehicle on which wheels are placed and rotate.

aye and nay

These archaic words, pronounced /aɪ/ and /neɪ/, mean *yes* and *no* respectively. They are used in counting votes in Parliament, and *aye aye* is an acceptance of an order in nautical language, the equivalent of *yes*. *Aye* is commonly used now in Scotland to mean *yes*.

Aye, often spelled *ay* and pronounced /aɪ/ or /eɪ/, means *always*. It is generally archaic and poetical but is common use in Scotland.

Nay can be used to mean *on the contrary*. This is uncommon and literary.

B

b, B /biː/
The second letter of the alphabet. It is pronounced /b/.

It is silent in words which end with -*mb* such as *bomb, climb, comb, crumb,* DUMB, *honeycomb, jamb, lamb, limb, numb, plumb, succumb, thumb, tomb* and *womb*. It is silent in the derivatives of these words: *bomber, climbing, thumbs* etc. It is silent in *plumber*. It is pronounced in the nouns *timber* and *number*, which are not formed from words which end in -*mb*. It is therefore not pronounced in the adverb *numbly* formed from *numb*, or in the comparative *number*, but is pronounced in *humbly* formed from *humble* and in NUMBER in the numerical sense. It is silent in the words *debt, doubt, redoubt* and *subtle*.

back-formation
Sometimes a shorter word has been falsely assumed to be the root of a longer word; the verbs *baby-sit* and *diagnose* have been derived from the nouns *baby-sitter* and *diagnosis*. This process is known as back-formation. Other examples are *burgle, couth, edit, gestate, greed, liaise, peddle, resurrect, scavenge* and *televise*, which come from *burglar, uncouth, editor, gestation, greedy, liaison, pedlar, resurrection, scavenger* and *television* respectively.

See AIR-CONDITIONED; -SCAPE.

backside
This is a colloquial word meaning *buttocks*. Say *The back of the house, book, screen* etc.

bald & bold
Bald /bɔːld/ means without hair on the head.

Bold /bəʊld/ means *brave, daring, audacious*.

ball
To *have a ball* means to have a good time. The reference is to a *ball* as a dance.

bank
A *bank* is a financial institution where people deposit money. A *bank* is also the side of a river: *The Houses of Parliament are on the north bank of the Thames* /temz/.

A *bank of earth* is a name for a large wall of earth and a place where the seabed comes near to or above the surface of the sea is a *sandbank*.

A *bank* is not a seat.

See BENCH; HOLIDAYS.

bar
A *bar* is a long thin piece of wood or metal; a man's bicycle has a *crossbar*. Bars can be placed on windows to keep burglars out or prisoners in; someone who is *behind bars* is in prison. A door can be *barred* by fitting a bar of wood or metal to lock it. This led to the use of the word to mean any obstacle. A *colour bar* prevents people of a certain colour from employment, access to public places etc.; a *bar to promotion* is a factor, perhaps lack of qualifications, that makes it impossible to promote someone. In a more literal sense, we talk of a *bar of chocolate* or *soap*. A *bar* is the counter in a pub where drinks are served, and is also one of the rooms in the pub; people who work *behind the bar* are known as *barmen* and *bar*MAIDs, collectively *bartenders* or *bar staff*. In a court of LAW the *bar* is the rail that separates the area where the judge sits from the rest of the court. Thus *at the bar* means in court; *at the bar of public opinion* means in the considered opinion of the general public. A *BARRISTER (*LAW)* is someone who has been *called to the bar* and is allowed inside the non-public part of the court. ➤

B

Bar and *barring* mean *excepting*: *Everyone bar(ring) John agreed; Everything is ready bar(ring) accidents; He is the best doctor bar none.*

In MUSICAL NOTATION a *bar* is a vertical line (a *bar line*) dividing the composition into portions of equal duration.

bare etc.
Take care with the pronunciation and meaning of:
Bare /beə/ uncovered.
Bear /beə/ verb or animal. See HOMONYMS.
Beer /bɪə/ a drink.
Beard /bɪəd/ hair on a man's face.
Bird /bɜːd/ animal of the class Aves.

bass
In music this word is pronounced /beɪs/. The fish and the BEER *(*ALE AND BEER)* with this name are pronounced /bæs/.

bath & bathe
Bath /bɑːθ/ is a transitive verb meaning *to wash (a person or animal) in a bath*: *I was bathing the baby when you rang; It's time to bath the dog again.*

Bathe /beɪð/ (intransitive) means *to go into water for amusement*: *It is not safe to bathe in this river.* *Bathe* (transitive) means *to wash (a wound or injury) with water or other liquid*: *Bathe that cut with antiseptic and put a bandage on it.*

See INTRANSITIVE AND TRANSITIVE VERBS.

BBC
The British Broadcasting Corporation was founded in 1927 as a publicly owned corporation to replace the privately owned British Broadcasting Company Limited. Ultimately the BBC is responsible to Parliament through a BOARD of governors who are appointed by the government, but in fact it has almost complete independence in its activities. In order to preserve this independence, the BBC is not allowed to broadcast advertising or sponsored programmes on its domestic services; instead, it receives its finance from the television licence, which is a tax on television ownership (television dealers are required to report the name and address of anyone who buys a TV to the HOME OFFICE). The level of the TV licence is set by the government, and is currently (2018) £150.50 per year.

The BBC has a number of national TV and radio channels. It also broadcasts World Services for radio and TV; these services are funded from the licence fee and some advertising. The BBC is known colloquially as *Auntie*, from its traditional concern for the nation's morals in its conception of public service broadcasting, or *the Beeb*, from the pronunciation of the beginning of the name BBC. As the nature of broadcasting changes, the channels through which the BBC broadcasts on TV, radio and the INTERNET are subject to variation.

See MEDIA.

BBC English
This is another, former, name for RECEIVED PRONUNCIATION (RP), resulting from its use as the standard accent of spoken English in BBC programmes. With the rise in social respect for regional variations of English in recent decades, RP is rarely heard now on the BBC.

beach, coast & shore
Beach means a flat or sloping area of sand or small stones between the land and the sea. It is often used for recreation and comes to an end at a headland or artificial construction; a seaside town may have more than one beach. *We spent the morning on the beach and the afternoon on the cliff-top; Which beach do you prefer?*

Coast is the part of the land near the sea. *San Francisco is on the west coast of the USA; There will be fog in coastal areas; The French coast can be seen from Dover. Coast* also means to travel downhill in a car or on a bicycle without using the motor or pedals, and so figuratively, to progress without making an effort to do so.

Shore, like *beach*, means the area between the land and the sea. However unlike a *beach* it is not necessarily flat or sloping, it can be rocky for example, and is not clearly defined. *Shore* can also be used for the area at the side of a lake or large river: *The shore of Lake Kariba; The shore of the Zambezi*.

beans
There are many different varieties of beans and their English names can be confusing. Runner beans are *Phaseolus coccineus*; haricot /ˈhærɪkəʊ/ beans and French, green or kidney beans are *Phaseolus vulgaris*; butter beans are *Phaseolus lunatus*; broad beans are *Vicia faba*.

bear, bore, born(e)
This basically means *carry*. Although it is not often used with this meaning nowadays, it survives in compounds such as *waterborne* and *airborne*. A cheque, share certificate or other financial document which can be paid to the person who possesses it is called a *bearer cheque* etc. The second amendment to the Constitution of the United States of America states: *...the right of the people to keep and bear Arms, shall not be infringed*; *I will bear that in mind* means that I will include it in my considerations; a project or action that *bears fruit* is one that produces results. A woman bears a child: *Queen Anne (1665-1714) bore eighteen children; Women of childbearing age; The children borne by his second wife.* In the passive sense without *by* the past participle is *born*: *She was born in 1975*. By extension *bear* means *suffer, tolerate*: *I can't bear him; He bore his pain with dignity*.

Bear is also the name of an animal. This has no ETYMOLOGICAL connection with the verb.

been & gone
There is a difference between *She has been to Paris* and *She has gone to Paris*. The FORMER means that at some time in her life she has travelled to Paris and has the experience of having been there, whereas the latter means that she is in Paris now. These examples correspond to two different usages of the PRESENT PERFECT *(*PERFECT ASPECT)*. The first is a completed event that occurred at an unstated time in the past; the second is a state that began in the past and continues in the present.

The response to the question *Has she (ever) been to Paris?* can be either in the present perfect: *Yes, she's been there twice* or in the past: *Yes, she went with the school last year*. The question *Has she gone to Paris (yet)?* gives an answer in the past when the time is given: *Yes, she flew yesterday* but the short answer, which does not give the time, repeats the auxiliary: *Yes, she has*.

See PAST SIMPLE & PRESENT PERFECT.

before & in front of
Use **in front of** as a preposition for position: *The car in front of me was a Seat; The papers were in front of me on the table*. At one time *before* was used with a place reference meaning *in front of*, usually with personal nouns or pronouns; now *in front of* should be used. Use *before* as a preposition or conjunction with time: *Before the war, before the twentieth century, before we moved into this house*. In sentences such as *Turn off the motorway before the airport*, *before* may seem to have a place reference but in fact it really means *before you reach the airport* and is a time reference; compare *The car park is in front of the airport*. The person *before you* waiting to be served in a shop or bank is not necessarily standing *in front of you*.

Before can mean *in the presence of*: *to appear before the judge, court, notary, a committee*. Also *The* CASE *before this court; The matter before this committee*. This is rather formal.

begin & start
Both of these verbs can be intransitive or transitive and in very many cases they are SYNONYMS: *The lesson usually begins/starts at 10 o'clock, but we'll begin/start half an hour later on Tuesday*. ➤

B

However, *start* has the idea of beginning movement and must be used for machines: *I can't start the car; The car didn't start easily.* It is used for travelling *We started on Thursday morning*, although when talking of the process of travelling we can say *Our JOURNEY (*TRAVEL) began/started on Thursday morning.*

Similarly, a race, or a football match, or a film, or a church service *starts* at four o'clock. *Starting a rumour* or *a business* contains the idea of setting something into motion.

Start also means *to react in surprise*: *He started when I spoke to him.* Compare the COGNATE verb *startle = surprise*.

nouns

A *beginner* is a person who is beginning or starting a new activity, e.g. *beginners, intermediate, and advanced students.*

A *starter* is the person who indicates to athletes that they should *start* running in a race. It is also the mechanism that *starts* the action of a machine such as a car.

behave

This is a compound of *have* but it is pronounced /bɪˈheɪv/ and is not irregular. Its past tense and past participle are *behaved*.

belief

The plural of the noun is *beliefs*. The third person singular of the verb is *believes*.

belly

Belly means *abdomen*. In Victorian times the word was considered vulgar and many people still do not like it. Despite the great anatomical difference, the word *stomach* and its childish form *tummy* were adopted as euphemisms with the result that many British people talk of a *stomach-ache* to describe abdominal pain, wherever in the abdomen it may be. The *belly-button* (or *tummy-button*) is the navel; a *belly-laugh* is a loud unrestrained laugh; a *beer-belly* is the extended abdomen typical of a beer-drinker; to *bellyache* is to complain noisily or persistently.

Belly can also describe the rounded part at the bottom of a SHIP or aeroplane. Although there is now a tendency to avoid such euphemisms these words should be avoided in formal company or situations where they might give offence.

below & under

Below and *beneath* mean *lower than*; *under* and *underneath* mean *vertically below*. They correspond to ABOVE & OVER.

bench

A bench is a long seat made of wood or stone on which a number of people can sit. It is used to refer to the magistrates or judges who are trying a case: *Who is on the bench today?; He was on the bench for thirty years.*

In surveying and map-making, a *benchmark* is a mark of known position that can be used as a base for FURTHER *(*FARTHER)* measurements. Thus it is used more widely to mean a reference point or criterion.

See BANK.

beside & besides

Beside is a PREPOSITION meaning *by, next to, at the side of*: *I was sitting beside Mary; The cinema is beside the church.* If you are *beside yourself with anger* (etc.) you are extremely angry (etc.)

Besides means *moreover* (adverb) and *in addition to* (PREPOSITION): *He's the best candidate. (And) besides, he speaks the language of the country; I spoke to John besides Mary and Jim.* In questions and negatives it suggests *except, excluding*: *Who did you speak to besides John?; I didn't speak to anyone besides John.*

better
This is the irregular comparative of the adjective *good*: *A better car*; and of the adverb *well*: *You played better today.*

had better
In giving advice the expression: *you'd* (etc.) *better* is a contraction of *you* (etc.) *had better*. This is important as it affects the TAG QUESTION and SHORT ANSWER (see WOULD RATHER *(*RATHER)*): *You'd better ring him, hadn't you?*; *'Hadn't you better ring him?' 'Yes I had.'*

bi-
The prefix meaning *two* is always *bi-* (not *by-*) as in *bicentenary, bilingual* and *bicarbonate*. The spelling of BICYCLE, which often causes problems, is perfectly regular with regard to the PREFIX.

This prefix is almost always pronounced /baɪ/. Exceptions are *bigamy* and *binocular(s)* with /bɪ/. There are very many words that begin with *bi-* that are not made with this prefix. If in doubt consult a dictionary.

See BIO-.

biannual & biennial
Strictly speaking, *biannual* means *half-yearly* and *biennial* means *taking place once every two years*. However, the similarity of form, together with the similarity of pronunciation, of these rather uncommon words has led to considerable ambiguity and confusion. *Half-yearly* and *two-yearly* are perfectly good and avoid ambiguity, as do *half-monthly* and *two-monthly* for *bi-monthly*. Use *fortnightly* rather than *two-weekly*. These words are adjectives and adverbs: a *fortnightly* magazine is published *fortnightly*. A *two-monthly* gas bill is paid *two-monthly* or *every two months*.

Bible, books of
Old Testament: Genesis, Exodus, Leviticus, Numbers, Deuteronomy, Joshua, Judges, Ruth, I Samuel*, II Samuel*, I Kings, II Kings, I Chronicles, II Chronicles, Ezra, Nehemiah, Esther, Job, Psalms, Proverbs, Ecclesiastes, Song of Solomon, Isaiah, Jeremiah, Lamentations, Ezekiel, Daniel, Hosea, Joel, Amos, Obadiah, Jonah, Micah, Nahum, Habakkuk, Zephaniah, Haggai, Zechariah, Malachi.

New Testament: Matthew, Mark, Luke, John, Acts, Romans, I Corinthians, II Corinthians, Galatians, Ephesians, Philippians, Colossians, I Thessalonians, II Thessalonians, I Timothy, II Timothy, Titus, Philemon, Hebrews, James, I Peter, II Peter, I John, II John, III John, Jude, Revelation.

Apocrypha: I Esdras, II Esdras, Tobit, Judith, Rest of Esther, Wisdom of Solomon, Ecclesiasticus, Wisdom of Jesus the Son of Sirach, Baruch, Song of the Three Children, Susanna, Bel and the Dragon, Prayer of Manasses, I Maccabees, II Maccabees.

*the first/second book of Samuel, and similarly for others.

bicycle
Not ~~byciele~~, ~~bycycle~~ or ~~biciele~~.

See BI-.

big & large
With reference to physical size there is no significant difference; either word could be used to describe, SAY, a *book, table, sea, company, car, dog,* or *forest*.

Big can suggest importance: *a big mistake, a big chance* or *opportunity, the big day*. A child who moves to *the big school* has started at a secondary school and is now a *big boy* or *girl* (or at least *bigger* than before). The *big boss* is a very important person, a *big name*, a *big cheese*, a *big wheel* or a *bigwig* and may be involved in *big business*. Your *big brother* or *sister* is older than you are. *Big Brother* is the character in George Orwell's 1984 who exercises total control over people's lives. The name has been adopted for a television programme in which contestants live in a house with TV

B

cameras filming all their activities. You have two *big toes* and one *large intestine*. People have *big ideas* and *big words* (they *think big* and *talk big*); *it's big of you* means that it is generous of you to do something, though the words may be spoken ironically. If you *hit the big time* you are successful in a public career, especially entertaining, and if you do something *in a big way*, you do it *on a large scale*. If you are *too big for your boots* or are *big-headed*, your sense of self-importance is exaggerated, but if you are *big-hearted* you are generous. *Big deal!* often means ironically that something is unimportant. The *Big Apple* is New York, *Big Ben* is the bell of the clock in Westminster Tower over the Houses of Parliament in London. The *big bang* is the explosion that is believed to have started the existence of the universe. At a funfair or theme park the *big wheel* is just that, a big wheel with seats or cabins for passengers to ride on it, and the *big dipper* is the roller coaster, a kind of train in which passengers ride up and down steep slopes; the *big dipper* or *plough* is the constellation *Ursa major* (the great bear). There is no adverb *bigly*.

Someone who is *at large* is at liberty and the *people at large* are the people in general. *By and large* means generally speaking. *Largesse* /lɑːˈʒes/ is generosity. *Large*, not *big*, is used with QUANTIFIERS such as *amount, quantity, extent, proportion*. A *large number of people* is the same as *many people*. A *big number* is mathematically big. The adverb *largely* means *generally, mostly*.

bind & bound

There are four distinct but similar words.

bind, bound, bound

To *bind* is *to tie something securely in position*: *She bound a cloth around his injured arm; The prisoner was bound to the chair*.

A *bookbinder binds books*, i.e. puts the pages together in a cover.

To be bound to means that something will certainly happen: *It's bound to rain; He's bound to be late*.

A *binding agreement* is one that makes a firm obligation, and *bonds* are physical restraints or moral obligations: *bonds of friendship*. The expression *His word is his bond* means that he can be trusted absolutely. A *bond* is a certificate of debt issued by a government or a PUBLIC COMPANY, repayable on a fixed date.

To be *in a bind* is to be in a difficult or dangerous position. In compounds *-bound* suggests restriction on movement: *snowbound* (because of snow); *housebound* (unable to leave a house because of illness or injury); *deskbound* (restricted to working at a desk).

A *band* is something thin and flat (unlike CORD *(*CHORD & CORD)* or string) that is used to fasten something, for example a metal band on a wooden box. A *rubber* or *elastic band* can hold papers together. It is not clear whether *band* meaning a group of people is connected with this word. It is used for an organised group of people, especially soldiers, robbers, or murderers. A group of musicians in the army is called a *band* and the word has spread into general use for a group of musicians that is smaller than an orchestra.

bound (jump)

Bound/ed meaning JUMP is unconnected with the verb *bind, bound, bound*.

bounds (borders)

Bounds (this is a different word from the previous two examples, and is usually used in the plural) are *limits*. Something that is *beyond the bounds* of possibility is totally impossible. *Boundless enthusiasm* is unlimited. An area that is *out of bounds* is one where one cannot go. A *boundary* is a line marking the limit of land between different owners, government areas, countries etc.

bound (direction)

A fourth word *bound* indicates direction. *Bound for California* means that the destination of the journey is California. *Outward bound* and *homeward bound* refer to the two directions of a long journey. *Outward bound* courses are adventure courses for young people. *Northbound* (etc.) means travelling *northWARDS* (etc.).

bio-
The first syllable of this PREFIX is pronounced /baɪ/ not /biː/. A *biopic* is a biographical film. It is pronounced /ˈbaɪəʊpɪk/.

biscuit
This is pronounced /ˈbɪskɪt/.

See CIRCUIT.

bite & sting
Vertebrate animals *bite*; mosquitoes, gnats, midges, horse-flies, tsetse-flies, other types of fly, and bugs *bite*. Scorpions, bees, wasps and hornets *sting*; poisonous plants *sting*.

The difference is not clear-cut. *Bite* is usually with teeth, while *sting* involves sudden sharp pain and the injection of poison; the snake's teeth seem to be more important than the poison in saying that a snake *bites*, while the absence of injected poison and of sharp, immediate pain lead us to say that mosquitoes etc. *bite*. Also, a bite comes from the front of the animal and a sting from the back. The difference seems to be relatively recent.

Sting is used for the sensation felt when alcohol is put on tender skin. As a noun *sting* is the part of the animal which breaks the skin. A bee leaves its *sting* in the wound. A *sting in the tail* is an unpleasant surprise which comes at the end of something written or spoken. The reference is to a scorpion, which has its *sting* in its tail.

bleed & blood
Bleed, bled, bled is the verb. *Blood* /blʌd/ is the noun.

See FEED & FOOD.

blend
Also called a portmanteau word, a *blend* combines the parts of two words to give a combined meaning.

A *breathalyser* is a device which ANALYSES a driver's breath to measure the level of alcohol; a *motel* is a hotel designed for motorists; *paratroops* are troops who enter an area by parachute; *Oxbridge* refers to Oxford and Cambridge UNIVERSITIES. *Brexit* is the process by which Britain will leave (exit) the European Union.

See FACTION.

blink & wink

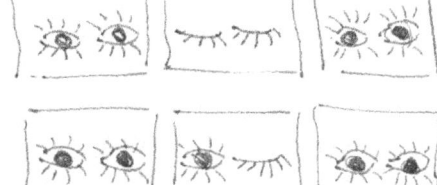

Blink is to shut both eyes involuntarily, for example when something threatening approaches them. To do something *without blinking* is to do it without showing any surprise. *Blinking* is used as a minced form of BLOODY as an intensifying adjective.

Wink is to shut one eye deliberately, to signal information.

board
A *board* is a thin, flat piece of wood, such as is sometimes used for making floors or walls of houses or SHIPS. *Board* was used for the wood which made the top of a table and so by extension means *food* in the expressions *bed and board; boarding house; boarding school*; and *a committee* which might sit round a table: *board of directors; promotion board; examination board*.

The word also has a connection with ships as can be seen in expressions such as *to board; on board; aboard* though these expressions are now also used with aeroplanes and trains. It is also found in *starboard* (the right-hand side of a ship).

See PORT.

B

boat & ship

This article compares boats and ships. For the terminology of ships see SHIP.

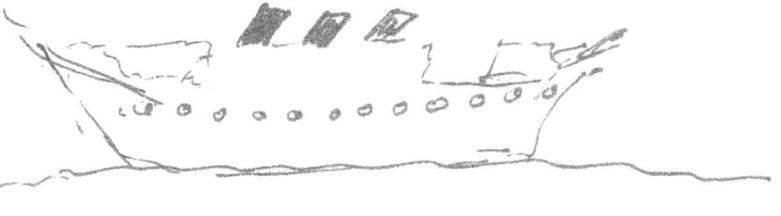

Vessel and *craft* are general words for all structures that travel on or under the water; *craft* is irregular in having no PLURAL. *Aircraft* and *spacecraft* are vehicles of any kind that travel in the air or in space.

A *boat* is smaller than a *ship*; one moved by oars is a *rowing boat*.

Any vessel that has sails is also probably a *boat* nowadays as larger *vessels* have motors, but in the days of sail and wind power larger vessels with sails were called *ships*; some sailing ships are still used for recreation and training. *Submarines* are referred to as *boats*. *Lifeboats* are boats that rescue people in difficulty near the coast.

Boats and *ships* were often personified as feminine and the pronouns *she* and *her* were used to refer to them. Now this is less common, perhaps because they have come to be seen as less romantic, or perhaps because of feminist influence.

If goods are *shipped*, they are not necessarily transported by ship. The words *shipping agent* and *shipment* also do not necessarily refer to sea transport.

See PORT; SAIL.

bookmaker

A *bookmaker* (colloquial *bookie*) is someone who accepts bets on horse races and other events. He calculates the ODDS and pays money to people who have bet on the winning horse. To *make a book* refers to the record book that is kept of who has bet how much money at what odds. This is nothing to do with printers and publishers who produce and sell books commercially.

bookshop & library

A *bookshop* is a shop which sells books.

A *library* is an institution which keeps books for borrowing or reference.

bourgeois

A *bourgeois* /ˈbʊəʒwɑː/ is a person who has *bourgeois* values and is a member of the *bourgeoisie* /bʊəʒwɑːˈziː/. The word is not used very much in English and when it is used it almost always has a derogatory implication since the *bourgeoisie* were disliked first by the aristocracy because they were below them socially, and later by the Marxists for the opposite reason. The usual modern English term is *middle class*.

bow

There are two words with the same spelling. One of these words has two pronunciations but its meanings all relate to the idea of bending.

pronounced /bəʊ/

It is the thing used to shoot an arrow. It is a knot made with two loops, typically used to tie shoelaces or worn by girls in their hair or in a *bow tie*. The *elbow* is the joint where the arm bends in the middle.

pronounced /baʊ/

There are two different words with this pronunciation.

The first is the verb related to the noun described above. It means *to bend forward from the waist as a mark of respect*. To *bow your head* is to let it fall forward as a sign of humility or shame. To be *bowed down* with CARE is to be oppressed by it. To *take a bow* is to recognise applause or congratulation, literally or metaphorically.

B

The other word is the rounded or pointed part at the front of a SHIP. Another form of this second word, *bough* (with the same pronunciation), is a poetical word for the branch of a tree. Most native speakers are not aware that these words have different origins.

bowdlerise
In 1818 the editor Dr Thomas Bowdler /ˈbaʊdlə/ (1754-1825) published his *Family SHAKSPEARE* (sic), an edition which could be 'read aloud in a family' as he had removed the parts which he judged to show 'profaneness or obscenity'. He also edited a version of Edward Gibbon's *Decline and Fall of the Roman Empire*. Thus, to *bowdlerise* is to remove words or passages which are judged to be offensive from a work of spoken or written art. A modern example is the publication of Mark Twain's *Huckleberry Finn* with the word *nigger* replaced by *slave*.

bowls & bowling
Bowls is a sport played on an area of grass called a *rink* or *green*. The object is to bowl balls (called *bowls* or *woods*) along the ground so that they are as close as possible to a small white ball called a *jack*. The bowls are about 10-15 cm in diameter and are elliptical in shape (heavier on one side than on the other) so that when they are bowled they follow a curved path instead of running in a STRAIGHT line.

Bowling or *ten-pin bowling* is an indoor sport in which large balls (approx. 20 cm diameter) are bowled along a wooden track to knock down as many as possible of the ten wooden pins at the end of it.

boyfriend and girlfriend
These are the expressions used of young people to describe a relationship which is more than social, and which has emotional and possibly (but not necessarily) sexual involvement. The words are also sometimes used of older people who are living together but are not married.

See FIANCÉ(E); PARTNER.

brand, logo & trade mark
The word **brand** refers to the particular type of a commercial good made by one manufacturer: *What brand of washing machine did you buy?*; *This washing powder is cheaper than the brand I usually use*. The word is COGNATE with the verb *burn* and originally meant the mark burnt on goods to identify them, in the same way that criminals were branded as a punishment (from which we still say figuratively that someone is *branded as a liar* etc.) or animals were branded to indicate ownership.

Brandy is made from distilled (*burnt*) wine, and was originally called *brandewine*.

A **logo** is the symbol which identifies a brand commercially.

A **trade mark**, like a *logo*, identifies a brand commercially but may be more than a printed symbol. The distinctive shape of a Coca-Cola bottle is a registered trade mark.

bread
Bread is uncountable: *Would you like some bread?*; *How much bread shall I boy?* The countable word for a complete piece of bread as it is baked is *loaf*: *Boy two loaves (of bread)*; the words *of bread* are not really necessary as *loaf* is only used for bread nowadays, though at one time it was used for sugar, as in the name of *Sugarloaf Mountain* in Rio de Janeiro, and for other things. *Loaf* is only used for the traditional type of British bread. The long type of French bread, which is becoming more popular in Britain, is known as a *French stick* or *baguette*.

Loaf (of bread) is RHYMING SLANG *(*COCKNEY)* for *head*.

Bread is a slang term for money.

Meatloaf is minced meat moulded and baked in one piece.

B

breast

Anatomically, this is the mamma in women, the organ that secretes milk; it is also used for the mamilla, the corresponding organ in a man. A woman who feeds a baby with her own milk *breast-feeds* it. More generally the word refers to the front part of the thorax. A *breast pocket* is a pocket on the front of a shirt or jacket, either a man's or woman's. The *breastbone* is the common name for the sternum. The *breast* is regarded as the part of the body where feelings and emotions are found, so *to make a clean breast of something* means to disclose or confess something fully. *Abreast* means side by side, for example *walking/cycling three abreast* because the people's *breasts* are in a line. By analogy, in animals, the breast is the front part below the head. A cat may have a white mark on its *breast*; the robin is known as robin *redbreast*. In athletics to *breast the tape* is to win a race by breaking the tape with one's breast; in swimming *breast-stroke* is a way of swimming on one's *breast*, putting the arms forwards and bringing them backwards at the same time. The word *breast* is not used for the mammary glands of other mammals except perhaps apes and monkeys.

Boob/tit: These are slang words used only for the female breast. (*Tit* as a name for several species of birds is unconnected.)

Bosom: Physically, this is a woman's two breasts considered together. It is also considered the seat of thoughts and feelings and of emotions. A *bosom friend* is a very close or intimate one. *In the bosom of one's family* expresses the intimacy and protection of a family.

Bust: This is a sculpture representing a person's head, shoulders and breast. It can also refer to a woman's *bosom* as such or be the measurement around the body at that point. It is the standard way of referring to body size.

Dug: This word can be used for the equivalent organ in animals, though *udder* is used for the baggy organs of cows or sheep.

Teat and **nipple**: These refer to the parts of female mammals where the milk is actually excreted. *Teat* is used of animals and *nipple* of humans. Both are used for a baby's bottle. *Teat* is used for condoms. *Nipple* is used for protuberances on machines, for example for lubrication, and in the names of some plants that have nipple-like features: *nipple cactus, nipplewort*.

Udder is used for cows, sheep, and goats.

bride and bridegroom

These are the words that are used on the day of the wedding, and for a time before and after it, to describe the people who are getting married. The woman is the *bride* and the man is the *bridegroom* or *groom*.

See ETYMOLOGY; FIANCÉ(E).

brief

Brief means *short in time*, usually referring to verbal communication: *a brief speech, mention, consultation, report*. A *brief* is the summary of a case that a barrister uses in court; a *briefcase* is a case for carrying documents and papers; *in brief* means *in short*; to *summarise*.

To brief someone is to provide them with the information they need for a specific action. It is especially used for legal and military actions. *Debriefing* is the process in which the people who have taken part in the action report on how it developed.

Briefs are underpants with short legs.

bring & take

Basically, *bring* means movement towards the speaker and *take* means movement away from the speaker: *Bring your work to me at the end of the lesson; Take this home and study it for tomorrow*. However, *bring* is also used to refer to a place where the speaker imagines himself to be when he is delivering the thing that he has brought: *I'll bring my report to your office tomorrow* could be said on the phone to a person who is in the speaker's office, but equally it could be said personally when neither speaker is in the office. A similar relationship exists with COME & GO.

Brit

This is a colloquial word for Briton.

See BRITAIN, BRITISH ETC.

Britain, British etc.

Britain is commonly used instead of *Great Britain*. The adjective is *British*; there is no adjective ~~*Great British*~~. For *United Kingdom* see CONSTITUTION AND GOVERNMENT.

Britannic

This is only found in the formal title *Her/His Britannic Majesty*.

British Isles, the

The geographical name given to the islands of Britain and Ireland together with the Isle of Man; sometimes the term includes the Channel Islands. The name is not popular in Ireland, but no alternative geographical name exists.

Briton

The usual formal word for a native of Great Britain. It is used in print but is not much used in speech, when people prefer to say *the British (people)* or colloquially *Brit*.

broad & wide

These two words are very similar in meaning; they both have *narrow* as their opposite and refer to a relationship that is the opposite of *long*. In some cases either of them may be used, while in other cases only one is appropriate. *Wide* refers to the distance between the edges, while *broad* refers to the expanse between the limits. *A wide road* is one which has its sides far apart; *a broad road* is one which has a great expanse of surface. Here there is no effective difference, just as someone sitting on the bank of a large river and looking at the other bank would say *This is a wide river*, as the other bank is far away. Seeing the same river from a bridge or aeroplane, this person would say *This is a broad river* as the most important aspect of its appearance is the expanse of water. *A wide door* would open to allow several people to pass aBREAST but *a broad door* shows a large and impressive piece of wood.

Broad tends to be used with the words *back* and *shoulders*, and must be used in the expression *broad-backed* and *broad-shouldered* meaning *able to bear a great load* literally or figuratively; *broad* must be used in the expressions *broad daylight,* BROAD CHURCH (*CHURCH OF ENGLAND), *broad hint, broad Lancashire* (etc.) accent or dialect, *broad facts, broad outline*; some trees have *broad leaves*. A *broadband* line is one that provides a fast connection to the INTERNET.

The jacket which covers the broad back and shoulders is *wide*, as are its sleeves and the accompanying trousers. Mouths are *wide*, and eyes may be *wide* by nature or in surprise; they may also be *wide apart* in the face. *Wide* must be used in the expressions *at wide intervals, give a wide berth to, a wide gap, a wide gulf, a wide opening, wide open* (never ~~*very open*~~), *to open wide, wide awake* (never ~~*very awake*~~) *a wide range, wide-ranging, wide distribution, the wide world.*

A *broad generalisation* is one which ignores unimportant exceptions; a *wide generalisation* includes many aspects of the subject. A *broad distinction* or *difference* is one made in very general terms; a *wide distinction* or *difference* implies that the things under consideration are very different. *Broadly speaking* means *in general terms*; *Broadly speaking you are right, but if we consider some individual cases we see that...*; *He spoke widely about European music* means that he covered many aspects of the subject. *To take a broad view of something* means to approach it tolerantly, *broad-mindedly*; a *wide view* of something is a comprehensive view. *Broadcast* originally meant *to scatter seeds over the whole surface*. See CAST.

The *Broads* are an area of wetland in eastern England. In American slang a *broad* is a promiscuous woman. This caused confusion and amusement during the Second World War among AMERICAN Air Force PERSONNEL stationed in that area who were invited to spend their free time on the local broads.

B

broke
I'm broke (not *I'm broken*) means *I have no money*. To go *broke* means *to lose all your money, to go bankrupt*.

brow & eyebrow
Brow is a synonym of *forehead*. *Eyebrows* are the lines of hair above the eyes. The *brow of a hill* is its highest point.

brunch
A BLEND of the words *breakfast* and *lunch* used to describe a meal like breakfast but which is eaten nearer to lunchtime.

business
This word is not only a SYNONYM of *commerce*. Though it is pronounced /ˈbɪznəs/, its root is *busy+ness*. It can mean a private activity: *That's my business; That's none of your business; Mind your own business*. It can mean *event, affair, state of affairs*: *This is a bad business; What a business!*

busyness
This is the state or quality of being busy: *It was a time of great busyness*. It has been formed to distinguish it from *business*, which has the same origin but which has now acquired a specific meaning that is slightly different. It is pronounced /ˈbɪzinəs/

but
In addition to its common meaning, *but* can mean *except*. *Nothing but the truth; What could I do but tell her? Everyone was there but me.*

by
This is the preposition used with works of art: *Othello by William Shakespeare; The Pastoral Symphony by Beethoven*. It is used because the name is understood as a passive agent: *Othello (written) by William Shakespeare*. It is also correct to say *Shakespeare's Othello; Beethoven's Pastoral Symphony*.

See PASSIVE VOICE.

For *by* as a time preposition, see TIME.

by-
A *by-law* or *bye-law* is one which affects only the particular town in which it is made. It comes from the Old English *b´yr* meaning a town. A *by-election* is an incidental election held in a constituency when a Member of Parliament dies or resigns from Parliament. The prefix is the PREPOSITION *by*.

See PLACE NAMES.

C

c, C /siː/

The third letter of the alphabet.

It is pronounced /k/ before *a*, *o* and *u*.

Before *e* and *i* it is pronounced /s/; exceptionally, it is pronounced /k/ in *sacerdotal* and in *sceptic* (written *skeptic* in American English), thus avoiding confusion with *septic*. See CELTS AND CELTIC.

Between vowels *cc* is pronounced /ks/: *eccentric, accent*, OCCIDENTAL *(*DICTIONARY WORDS)* except in *baccy* (tobacco), *soccer* (see FOOTBALL), and *recce* (reconnaissance), where it is pronounced /k/.

ch, CH

ch is usually pronounced /tʃ/: *child, church*.

In some words of French origin it is pronounced /ʃ/ e.g. *chalet* /ˈʃæleɪ/ *champagne* /ʃæmˈpeɪn/, *charade, Chardonnay, château, chauvinism, chic, chivalry, moustache*.

In some words it is pronounced /k/. The commonest words where this happens are *ache, anchor, archaic, archive, archipelago, architect, chaos, character* (but note the unrelated *caricature*, which has no *h*), *charisma, chasm, chem-, Christ, choir,* CHOLERA, *choral,* CHORD, *lichen* /ˈlaɪkən/, *saccharine,* SCHISM (also /sɪz(e)m/), *school, schooner, techn-*. With the exception of *ache, anchor* and *schooner* all these words are of Greek origin, and most have similar forms in other European languages, often also pronounced with /k/. In American English, and increasingly in British English, *schedule* is pronounced /ˈskedjuːl/.

Ache has this pronunciation because Samuel Johnson's influential eighteenth-century dictionary falsely derived it from αχος, the Greek word for parsley. Formerly the verb was written *ake* pronounced /eɪk/ and the noun was written *atche* pronounced /eɪtʃ/. The *h* in *anchor* and *schooner* is also not etymological. The name *Michael* is pronounced /ˈmaɪkəl/. The Hebrew word *cherub* has the usual English pronunciation /tʃ/.

In Scots English *ch* is pronounced /x/ as in the Scottish words *Ach!* (exclamation like *Oh!*), *loch* (lake), and *pibroch* (a kind of bagpipe music). It has this pronunciation in Welsh PLACE NAMES: *Machynlleth* /maxˈʌnɫeθ/.

cabs and taxi

These words are used interchangeably. There are two types of taxi. One type is usually, but not necessarily, the large vehicles commonly known as *black cabs* or *London taxis* (though they are not all black and are found throughout the country); these can carry passengers who stop them in the street. *Mini-cabs* or *private hire cars* can only pick up passengers who have made a specific booking, usually by telephone; these are specifically prohibited from responding to passengers calling them in the street. Both types must be LICENSED for public operation by the local authority.

cacaos, cocoa & coconut

Cacaos /kəˈkɑːəʊ/ is a tree that BEARS the seed pods from which cocoa and chocolate are made.

Cocoa /ˈkəʊkəʊ/ is a powder made from cacaos seeds; it is also the name of a drink made from this powder.

Coconut is the large hard brown seed of a tropical palm tree. It contains white FLESH and a white liquid.

caesium

This is the name used in science rather than the American *cesium*.

See ALUMINIUM; SULFUR & SULPHURS.

calendar

Britain adopted the Gregorian calendar in 1752. In dates written about that period the phrases *old style* and *new style* represent the Julian and Gregorian calendars respectively. When the Gregorian

C

calendar was adopted in Britain it was eleven days ahead of the Julian calendar and dates went directly from 2 to 14 September 1752. This caused great protest with the cry 'Give us back our eleven days,' partly because quarterly debts remained in force but daily wages were adjusted to the new calendar.

A rhyme to remember the number of days in a month is:
Thirty days have September,
April, June and November.
All the rest have thirty-one, excepting February clear,
Which has twenty-eight, twenty-nine each leap year.
See DAYS AND MONTHS; JUMP | LEAP.

call & call on

I'll call you tomorrow means *I'll phone you tomorrow*; *I'll call on you tomorrow* means *I'll visit you briefly tomorrow.* As *phone* and *ring* are both SYNONYMS of *call* with reference to the telephone (*I'll phone you tomorrow; I'll ring you tomorrow*), the use of *call* might be considered unnecessarily confusing, but it is well-established.

To make a call to someone means *to phone someone*; *to pay a call on someone* means *to visit someone.*

calque

A calque (or loan translation) is a word that has the same form in two or more languages. *Oversee* and *supervise* are calques because the Latin roots of *supervise* mean exactly *over/see*. Similarly, *foretell* and *predict*, *inborn* and *innate*, and *forgive & pardon* are calques.

camping

The place where you put a tent is called a *camp site*. Camping is the gerund of the verb *to camp* and its use on signs means *camping is permitted or available here*.

See PARKING.

can, can't, cannot & cant

In British English the modal verb *can* is pronounced /kæn/ and the contracted negative *can't* is pronounced /kɑːnt/. This is a useful distinguishing feature as the final *t* is not always clear, especially before another *t* or a *d*. However, in American English the two words have the same vowel sound /kan/ /kant/. The uncontracted negative is *cannot* /'kænət/. This is *can* and *not* written together. It is always written as one single word.

For the regular verb *can/ned* see the note at IRREGULAR VERBS.

The unconnected word *cant* is pronounced /kænt/. It is used to mean words that sound moral but are insincere or exaggerated. Also, it is a jargon used by a small group of people and not understood by others; it is especially used of *thieves' cant*.

capital letters

Capital letters are also called *upper CASE letters*. Printers used to keep the large letters in the upper part of the case in which they kept their type. In the seventeenth and eighteenth centuries common nouns were often written with initial capitals, although this was never a standard as it is in modern German. *Capital letters* are used for:

the first word of a sentence.

the first person pronoun *I*.

proper names of people and places: *I saw Indira in New Delhi, the Atlantic Ocean, China, Estonia, Tuscany, the West End, High Street, Windmill Avenue.* Although *heaven* and *hall* can be considered as places, they do not have capital letters.

names of days and months: *on Tuesday, in March*; also *Easter, Maundy Thursday, Good Friday, Whitsun, Christmas Day, Boxing Day, New Year's Eve* but not the names of seasons: *in autumn*.

names of planets: *Is there life on Mars?* but *the moon. Earth* has a capital letter in a list of planets: *Mercury, Mars, Earth* etc. but a small letter in *life on earth; Venus can be seen from earth*.

titles: *Do you know Mr Robertson?; This is Sir Arthur Morris; The speaker was Prof. Forster; the Duke of Wellington, Lord Derby;* however, small letters are used if the title is not specific: *He is a professor now*.

the adjectives and languages associated with countries and regions: *She's Brazilian; Do you speak Catalan? Martian* (from the planet Mars) has a capital letter but COCKNEY does not. See GYPSY.

words derived from names of people and places when the connection seems real: *Balkanisation, Christian(ity), Cyrillic (alphabet), Darwinian, Gothic architecture* and *lettering, Herculean, Machiavellian, Platonic philosophy, Leninism, Marxism, Roman alphabet,* ROMAN NUMERALS, *Thatcherite*; when the connection is less direct small letters are used: *bowdlerise, boycott, champagne, draconian, jacuzzi,* FRANKFURTER, HAMBURGER, *jersey,* MACKINTOSH (*EPONYMS), *pasteurise, platonic love, quisling, quixotic, utopian, venetian blinds*. However, there are no absolute, clear rules and a considerable amount of individual variation is found. For scientific units named after people see miscellaneous points below.

some ABBREVIATIONS even when the full name is written with small letters: *PC* (personal computer), *PTO* (please turn over), *NNE* (north-north-east).

names of political and religious organisations and of their members: *the Liberal Democrat Party, a Liberal Democrat; Protestant;* ISLAM, *Muslim; Judaism,* JEW, GENTILE, *the Roman* CATHOLIC *Church* (institution, but *the Roman Catholic church by the railway station*), *a Roman Catholic*. (Note that *conservative* and *liberal* with small letters refer to a person's character in general, not to their political opinions.)

titles of books, films etc.: the first word and important words only (generally nouns, verbs, adjectives and adverbs): *The Lord of the Rings, Gone with the Wind; the Economist*.

names of established organisations: *the British Council, Cambridge University, the Folio Society, the European Union, the Royal Air Force* and *the Royal Navy*.

trade names: *Coca-Cola, Sony, Windows*.

famous buildings and institutions: *the Houses of Parliament; St Paul's Cathedral; the House of Commons, the House of Lords*; names of SHIPS and aeroplanes: *HMS Dreadnought, Airbus, Spitfire*.

historical periods: *the Stone Age, the* MIDDLE AGES, *the Renaissance, the Reformation*, and wars: *the First (Second) World War, World War One (Two), the Crimean War*.

miscellaneous points

Names of scientists that are used as scientific units do not have capital letters, e.g. *joule, newton, watt* but when the initial letter is used alone it is written as a capital: *J, N, W*.

Compass roses on maps show either *N, S, E, W*, which are the abbreviations of the full names (see above) or *North, South, East, West*, which are the words considered in isolation, almost as one-word sentences, and therefore written with capital letters.

Points of the compass and their associated adjectives are not generally written with capital letters in mid-sentence: *Travel west for 15 km; Madras is in southern India, a northerly wind*. However, when used in geographical proper names they have capital letters: *North Korea, the West Bank, Western Samoa, East Timor, South Africa* (the country) but *southern Africa* (the region in general), *the Southern Cross*. Thus *Northern Ireland* (the constitutional name of the province) but *northern*

C

England; Manchester Road is the name of the road but *the Manchester road* is the road that goes to Manchester. See SOUTH & SOUTHERN.

The names of academic subjects other than languages do not have capital letters: *I studied physics at university; I met my history teacher on the bus.* However, these words are frequently seen with capitals on school timetables where, like points of the compass (above), they are written in isolation, and in the official names of university faculties and appointments: *the Department of Physics; the Professor of History.*

When a capitalised word has a prefix the capital letter is kept, usually with a hyphen: *un-English, pre-Christian.* The forms *unchristian, Unchristian, unChristian* and *UnChristian* are found.

Because capital letters add emphasis and importance to words, there is considerable variation in their use. Some people prefer them in expressions such as *The Pope announced today that...; The Queen will visit Zambia next year; Jesus and His disciples* (but always *Pope Francis, Queen Elizabeth II*); *The Managing Director chaired the meeting.*

A recent trend is to use capital letters in an unorthodox manner in trade names such as *easyJet, WhatsApp, WiFi.*

See INTERNET.

car

A car has a *bonnet* (American English *hood*) at the front to cover the *engine*, at the back it has a *boot* (American English *trunk*) to contain the luggage, and it has *wings* to cover the front wheels. A car has two *front wheels*, two *back* or *rear wheels*, and a *spare wheel* for use if one wheel has to be replaced; each wheel consist of a metal *hub* surrounded by a rubber *tyre*. Cars usually have four doors (two *front* and two *back* or *rear*) though many cars are *hatchbacks*, with a door at the back that lifts up. A car has a *central locking* system that allows all the doors to be locked easily at the same time from outside the car, and a *child-lock* locks the door handles from inside the car. The *headlights* are the powerful lights at the front of the car; they can be *dipped* so that they do not disturb other drivers. The *sidelights* are less powerful. Red *rear lights* make the car visible from behind, *indicator lights* show when the car is about to turn, *brake lights*

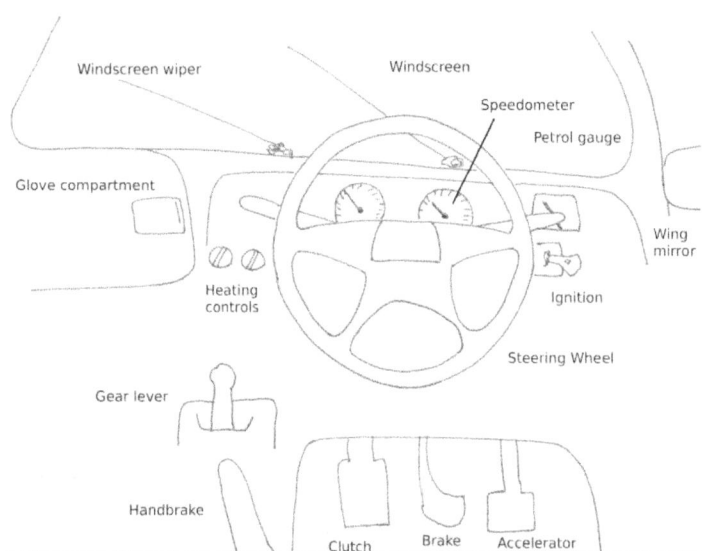

show that the brakes are being used, and *hazard warning lights* flash to show that the car is STATIONARY in a potentially dangerous position. A *petrol cape* is removed to put petrol into the *tank*. The *nearside* of the car is the side nearest to the side of the road (the LEFT-hand side in the UK) and the *off side* is the side by the centre of the road.

The picture shows the interior of a British car with the controls on the right-hand side. The panel below the windscreen is the *DASHboard (*HIT). (Gauge* is pronounced /geɪdʒ/.)

care

Basically this means *worry, anxiety.* If *you haven't a care in the world* or have *put/left your cares behind you,* you are free of all worry. From this it came to mean a concern for caution or attention:

C

Handle with care. *Careful* work is work that is done with attention to accuracy and detail; *careless* is the opposite.

Care for means *look after*: *He had to care for his sick mother* but *I don't care for horror films* means that I don't like them.

I don't care means it makes no difference to me: *I don't care who you are, you can't park there; For all I care you can go hungry*. *'But I'll be hungry.' 'Who cares?'* (implying *'I don't'*) or *I couldn't care less*.

To care about something means to be interested in or concerned about something: *He really cares about the people who work in his department*.

Another meaning has to do with responsibility for protection and preservation, looking after something. A letter can be addressed *care of* somebody (abbreviation *c/o*) and the expression *take care of* has this meaning: *Will you take care of the children while I go to the shops?* Among gangsters, *to take care of somebody* ironically means to kill that person, but also with the ambiguous meaning of taking responsibility for dealing with a piece of business. A *care label* is a label on clothes or fabric that gives advice for washing, cleaning and ironing them. A *care order* is an order for a child to be removed from his/her parents, with responsibility for his/her upbringing being taken by public authorities. A child to whom this happens is *in care*. The *caring professions* are those such as nursing and social work which involve caring for other people. A *caretaker* is a person employed to look after a building such as an unoccupied house or a public building when it is not being used. A *caretaker government* is one that is in office temporarily in an administrative capacity.

caricature
This is not connected with CHARACTER and is not written ~~charicature~~.

carnival
In Britain this is not particularly the celebration for the beginning of Lent. It means a large public celebration which may be held at any time of the year. The Notting Hill Carnival in West London is held in August.

carry & fetch
Carry has the idea of *transport*: *That is too big for me to carry; I was carrying the dinner from the kitchen when I fell*.

Fetch means to go and return with something: *Will you fetch my glasses from the garden?; The house will fetch £300,000* means that that price will be paid for it.

case
The word *case* represents two separate words that have no ETYMOLOGICAL connection.

A case is a container that is specifically designed to contain one particular item: *cigarette case, glasses case, pen/pencil case*. A *suitcase* is used for carrying clothes. A *briefcase* is a container used for carrying papers; the reference is to the use of the word BRIEF to refer to the notes that a barrister uses.

Lower case and *upper case* letters are other names for small letters and CAPITAL LETTERS respectively. Printers used to keep the small letters in the lower part of the case in which they kept their type and the capital letters in the upper part of it.

From a different origin, it means an example or occurrence of something: *An interesting case. A case of meningitis* and is used as a grammatical term (see following article).

See IN CASE.

case, grammatical
Before the Norman Conquest in 1066 English, like other INDO-EUROPEAN LANGUAGES, had case endings for nouns, pronouns and adjectives (Latin, German and Russian are examples of languages

C

where case inflections can be clearly seen). The English inflections were lost during the period when English was assimilating French influence to make modern English (see ENGLISH LANGUAGE, A BRIEF HISTORY). They have completely disappeared from adjectives, which are now invariable for case as well as for number and gender; nouns now only show variation for possessive and plural; only pronouns now have a case system. See GENDER.

A result of this is that English-speakers have largely lost the ability to recognise grammatical case. By the rules of case the subjective case should be used in *It's I; If I were he; It was she who…; Whoever did it; it wasn't I; Not I/I too; His sister's taller than he; She's as old as I; the same as I.* However, it happens so frequently in English that the subjective case is before the verb and the objective case follows it that these forms are very commonly expressed using the objective pronoun: *It's me; If I were him; It was her who…; Whoever did it, it wasn't me; Not me/Me too; His sister's taller than him; She's as old as me; The same as me.* This is especially common in informal use but is becoming more widespread. In *His sister is taller than he is* there is naturally no confusion.

The phrase *between you and I* is controversial; *between you and me* would be appropriate according to the strict laws of case following a preposition. *Between you and I* is found in SHAKESPEARE'S Merchant of Venice (act 3, scene 2) but a rule was made in about 1860 that the correct form should be *between you and me*. As a result *between you and I* is often considered incorrect and is best avoided for that reason ~~Between you and I~~; ~~The doctor saw my wife and I together~~. There are cases where *you and me* is clearly incorrect, for example ~~You and me are a good team~~, and it may be that through a phenomenon known as hypercorrection *between you and me* has been changed intentionally to *between you and I*.

See WHO AND WHOM.

cast

Basically this means *throw* but it is not used now with this meaning except in some expressions, such as *cast light, doubt on something; cast a fishing line* or *net, cast a shadow*. Less obvious collocations are *cast an eye over something, cast a vote, cast a (magic) spell. Cast* has a special meaning in the theatrical usage of deciding which actor will play which part in a play or film. *The director will cast the play on Saturday; He was cast as the villain.* From this the *cast* is the group of actors in a play or film. *Casting* is the process of deciding which actor will have which part; a *casting company* is an agency that provides suitable actors for parts in plays and films.

A *casting vote* is a deciding vote that is cast, usually by the chair of a meeting, when two sides are equal.

Molten metal or other substances can be poured into a MOULD. This process is known as *casting* and the result may be *cast iron* or for example a *plaster cast* to make an impression of something.

It is found in the compound forms:

broadcast: to transmit by radio or television (as in the British Broadcasting Corporation. See BBC.)

castaway: a person who is SHIPwrecked and has found refuge in a remote land or island.

downcast: unhappy.

forecast: to predict. See FOUR.

newscast: a news broadcast.

opencast: an opencast mine is one where the material is removed from the surface not from underground.

outcast: a person rejected by his family, society etc.

overcast: an overcast sky is one that is completely covered with cloud.

typecast: an actor is typecast when he/she always plays the same character or type of character.

caste

This is unconnected with the previous word. It means one of the social classes defined by the HINDU (*INDIA*) religion. It is pronounced /kɑːst/.

C

catholic

The basic meaning of this word (pronounced /ˈkæθlɪk/) is *general, universal*: *He has catholic tastes in music, literature* etc.; in this sense it has a lower case letter. It was used to refer to the ANCIENT Church before it divided into its western and eastern parts, and after this separation it was used by the western or Latin church to refer to itself. After the Reformation it was claimed exclusively by the part of the Western Church which remained loyal to Rome, but the Anglicans hold that the *Catholic Church* includes the CHURCH OF ENGLAND as the English continuation of the Ancient and Western Churches.

Since the REFORMATION it has generally referred to the Church of Rome; *Roman Catholic* is the term used in English law and official terminology. *Catholic* alone is used in continental countries, especially Latin ones, and is in common use in England meaning *Roman Catholic*.

cease etc.

The choice of the words listed below is determined by usage rather than by meaning.

cease

This is probably the least common of these words and means *to come to an end, to happen no more*. It is both intransitive and transitive: *The rain ceased; The noise did not cease; The rain ceased falling; Will you cease making that noise?*

There are adjectives: *ceaseless, unceasing*.

A *ceasefire* is a military command to cease firing weapons. It is also an agreement between both parties of an armed conflict to cease firing, a truce.

complete

This is transitive only. It means *to bring something to an end so that it is whole, entire, all its parts and elements are present correctly*:

I have written most of the report. I will complete it tomorrow; That completes our quota for the year.

It is a synonym of *fill in*: *Please complete this questionnaire.*

The adjective is *complete*.

finish

Intransitive and transitive. It is used of events or processes that have a planned or natural end point: *The film finishes at 8.45; She finished in second place; I'll finish the report tomorrow; Finish your dinner, and then we'll go.*

A *finishing school* is one that prepares a girl to enter high society. The *finishing touches* are the final small points that make something complete or perfect.

The *finish* or *finishing line* is the final point in a race. A *finish* is the final coating of decorative or manufactured work: a *glossy finish* for paintwork; an *oak finish* for woodwork; a *zinc finish* for metalwork.

The adjective relating to Finland is *Finnish*.

finalise

Transitive. This means *to put something into its final form, to put the finishing touches to something*: *I'm meeting the customer tomorrow to finalise the delivery arrangements.*

end

Intransitive: *The rain ended; The lesson ended early; The noise did not end; The film ends at 8.45.*

Used transitively it means that something comes to a permanent end abruptly or unintentionally: *That ended his chances of promotion; The fire alarm ended the lesson twenty minutes early.* To *end one's days* means to live the end of one's life: *He ended his days in the knowledge of his success.* To *end it all* is to commit suicide.

noun

(The) End appears at the end of a book or film.

C

To put an end to something is to prevent it from continuing: *The weather put an end to our camping holiday.*

In the end is *finally*: *In the end we decided to go to Turkey for our holidays.*

At the end refers to a position in space or time: *The park is at the end of the road; Ask me at the end of the lesson.*

End can mean *purpose*: *What end do you have in mind?; Does the end justify the means?*

No end of means a large quantity or number: *I've had no end of trouble/problems; No end of people have been asking for information.*

stop

As a verb *stop* can be used either intransitively or transitively: *The rain stopped; The noise did not stop; My watch has stopped; He stopped (his car) at the red light; The rain stopped falling; Will you stop making that noise?*

However, the stoppage is not necessarily permanent: *The rain stopped for ten minutes; The rain didn't stop once all day; The fire alarm stopped the lesson for ten minutes; He stopped smoking for six months but then he started again; After trying a number of times, he finally stopped smoking when he was in hospital.*

To *stop (up)* is to block or close an open space: *I'll stop (up) the gap between the window and the wall*. A *stop-gap* measure or solution is a temporary one. To *stop someone's mouth* is to persuade them, by bribery or otherwise, not to speak. To *stop* a stringed instrument is to press the string to the band with a finger in order to change the note that is played. An *organ stop* closes an organ pipe producing a note an octave lower. See MUSICAL NOTATION AND TERMINOLOGY.

To *put a stop to something* is to prevent it from continuing. A *bus stop* is a scheduled place for a bus to stop to pick up and set down passengers. In photography, a *stop* is the effective diameter of a lens, e.g. *f8*. A *stop* is a PUNCTUATION mark, ESPECIALLY a full stop. A *stop lamp* or *light* is a red one that shows on the back of a vehicle to indicate when it is stopping.

quit

Intransitive and transitive, meaning *stop* but unlike *stop* it must have a personal subject: *It's time for me to quit; I must quit smoking* not ~~The rain quitted~~. *Notice to quit* is an official notice from a landlord to leave a rented property.

-cede & -ceed

verb	nouns
accede	access, accession
cede	cession
concede	concession
exceed	excess
intercede	intercession
precede	precedence, PRECEDENT, precession (an astronomical term)
proceed	procedure, proceedings, procession
recede	recession
secede	secession
succeed	success, succession

These words are all derived from the same Latin root (*cedere* = *give way* or *yield*). Native speakers sometimes confuse these words and their spelling. The unconnected *supersede* is written thus.

Celts and Celtic

These words are pronounced /kelt/ etc. except for the name of the Scottish football club *Celtic* /ˈseltɪk/.

The Celts were the native inhabitants of Britain before the Roman invasion. They co-existed fairly well with the Romans but the later Germanic invasions pushed them westwards into Scotland, Wales, Ireland, the Isle of Man, and Cornwall (but see the note for history articles on page xv);

Celtic place names (e.g. *Helvelyn, Pen-y-Ghent*) are found in the SOUTH-west and north-west of England but these are not now considered Celtic areas.

Celtic languages

There are six Celtic languages. *Irish Gaelic, Scots Gaelic* and *Manx* (the old language of the Isle of Man) make up the Goidelic or Q-Celtic group, while *Welsh, Cornish* (the language of Cornwall), and *Breton* (spoken in Brittany in north-west France) make up the Brythonic or P-Celtic group. *Cornish*, which is a recognised minority language of the United Kingdom, and *Manx* were extinct but are being revived; they are known and studied today but are not used as living languages. They have about 3,500 and 100 speakers respectively.

Welsh is now spoken by 562,000 people out of a Welsh population of 3.1 million. Though it is more widely used in rural and western areas of the country than in cities, it is taught in all schools in WALES. Wales is officially bilingual, it has its own Welsh-language TV station, and the future of the Welsh language seems secure, although the strength of the traditional Welsh cultural identity side by side with the English language and English immigration into Wales is perhaps problematic. The Welsh language is also spoken by 110,000 to 150,000 people in England and a small number, perhaps 5,000, in Patagonia, Argentina.

Scots Gaelic /'gælɪk/ is spoken in the west of SCOTLAND. Its use has been encouraged officially and it is now spoken by 57,000 people out of 5.3 million. It is historically the language of the Highlands and of the Western Isles; it has never been the language of the whole of Scotland. It is spoken by 1,275 people in Nova Scotia, Canada,

Irish Gaelic /'geɪlɪk/ is spoken by some 65,000 people in Northern IRELAND, almost all from the CATHOLIC community. It is spoken by 140,000 people in the Irish Republic.

Breton is spoken by about 210,000 people out of about 4.55 million in Brittany.

Figures are taken from Wikipedia, November 2016.

censor, censure & censer

A *censor* /'sensə/ is a person who examines printed material, films etc. before publication to ensure that nothing immoral, heretical or politically offensive is published. The verb *censor* means to perform this action.

Censure /'sensjʊə/ means an unfavourable opinion, hostile criticism, disapproval or condemnation. To *censure* somebody means to express such an attitude.

A *censer* is a container in which incense is burnt during a religious ceremony.

centre & middle

We talk of the *centre* of a circle or a sphere (such as the earth) or of any other geometrical figure. From this it follows that the centre is the point round which things revolve (the sun is the centre of the solar system), the most important point. The central part of town, or town or city centre, is the most important part, though the town/city may contain a number of shopping centres which attract people from their surrounding areas. The *shopping centre* is the most important point of its own area of attraction as is shown by the fact that it may actually be outside the town itself. Similarly a *medical centre, civic centre* or *training centre* will act as a point of attraction and reference for people interested in making use of its facilities; the *centre of gravity* of a body is the point about which all the rest of the body balances; a *music centre* is an apparatus that has a RADIO and plays CDs, tapes, and/or records. The centre of an organisation is a way of referring to its headquarters; a company may have a *Central Purchasing Department*, i.e. one purchasing department for all the company's offices. *Centre* is also used to refer to the part of a sporting or military formation that is not on the flanks, and in politics for moderates who cannot be categorised as right or left.

It is possible, though unusual, to say that the sun is in the middle of the solar system; to say that it is at the mid-point is more accurate. A line or linear scale can have a mid-point but a centre always suggests a surrounding circle or sphere. Whereas the *centre* is defined as a point of revolution or attraction, the middle can be a part as well as a point and can refer to the parts of a time or process.

C

A good written composition should have a beginning, a *middle* and an end; a symphony may have a *middle movement*; if a man is called Giles Stanley Murchiston, Stanley is his *middle* NAME, and the longest FINGER can be called the *middle finger*. We have the *middle of the morning, afternoon, evening, night, week, month, year* etc. with *mid-morning* etc. These are not precisely defined except for *midday* and *midnight*, which can refer to precise times. The period between youth and old age is called *middle age*, while the MIDDLE AGES are the period from about 500 to 1500 (between the ancient world and the modern one) though in Britain this term most frequently refers to the period 1000 to 1400. Other terms with *middle* are *middle class* (between upper and lower), *Middle* EAST (between *Near* and *Far*), *middleman* (an intermediary between supplier and purchaser), *middle-of-the-road* (unadventurous between extremes) and *middle-sized* (between small and large), *middle of a crowd/battle, mid-field*. To say that someone lives *in the middle of a town, housing estate* etc., implies that they are surrounded by houses rather than being in the geometric centre, though it is improbable that they live on the very edge; if you are lost *in the middle of the forest*, you have no idea of your position in relation to the central point; similarly if your car breaks down when you are *in the middle of the mountains*. The phone can ring when you are *in the middle of washing the dishes*, though this does suggest that you had not just started or nearly finished. For *middle C* see MUSICAL NOTATION AND TERMINOLOGY.

To sum up, *centre* has a more precise, geometric sense, and is a centre of revolution, attraction or influence. *Middle* is often less precise and refers more to processes, sequences and ordered relationships and can have an idea of being among or surrounded by other things or people. The prefix *mid-* refers to the middle of a process, area, or period of time: *mid-career, mid-field* (in football), *midday, mid-Victorian*. The word *midwife* (where *wife* has its old meaning of *woman*) may refer to her *mid-position* between mother and baby, but it is more likely that *mid* derives from a preposition meaning *with*.

certain(ly) & sure(ly)

There is little difference between the adjectives in *I'm certain/sure that it will rain; Bob is certain/sure to know the answer*.

For certain/sure means *without doubt*.

There are occasions when they are not SYNONYMS. *Certain* refers to a specific example that is not identified: *A certain lady will be pleased to know that; A certain degree of skill is required; A certain John Smith* (someone called John Smith).

There are differences between the adverbs.

Certainly gives an assurance that something really is true: *He certainly* (definitely) *used to work for the BBC; Certainly he used to work for the BBC* (we may certainly say that, or it is certain that, he did). As a response, it gives a strongly affirmative impression: *'You were at the meeting then?' 'Certainly, but I didn't stay for coffee afterwards'; 'Is he reliable?' 'Certainly.'*

Surely expresses a speaker's strong belief that a statement is true, a belief that is based on experience or probability but which is not definitely proved: *Surely the weather will be good in August* (it probably will be). Compare this belief with *Certainly the summer temperatures in* SOUTHERN *Spain will be over 30° C in August* (there is no doubt that they will be). *Surely* is also used to anticipate a possible denial: *Surely you must remember where you put the tickets; Surely you haven't finished already*.

-cester

Most place names that have *-cester* are pronounces /stə/: *Gloucester* /ˈglɒstə/, *Leicester* /ˈletsə/, *Worcester* /ˈwʊstə/. *Cirencester*, however, is pronounced /ˈsaɪrənˌsestə/.

The name derives from the Latin *castra*, meaning a military camp. It is the same as *-chester* in Dorchester, Manchester etc. and Chester itself.

chap

Chap is a friendly, informal word used to refer to a man, usually a young man.

C

Bloke is a colloquial word for a man.

Fellow is also a familiar synonym for a man. See FELLOW and MATE.

Guy also is a colloquial word for a man; in American English *guys* (plural) can be men or women.

Lad is a boy or young man; it can imply a spirited, vigorous, even MACHO *(*FEMALE & FEMININE; MALE, MASCULINE & MACHO)* attitude to life as *a bit of a lad* and *laddISH*. In the plural *the lads* refers to men of any age with common working or recreational interests.

Lass is a girl or young woman. This word is not COGNATE with *lad* and is used in Scotland and the north and midlands of England. It is not used in the SOUTH of England.

character, personality & personage

Character and ***personality*** both refer to the characteristics and qualities that form a person's attitudes and behaviour. Someone with a strong, perhaps strange, character or personality is *a well-known local character*, QUITE *a character*. *Personality* cannot be used here. *Character* is also a fictional character in a book, play or film. Someone who is well-known for their television appearances for example is *a TV personality*.

Personage is not a common word but it is used to refer to important people. Sometimes it is used ironically: *A group of personages from Head Office are coming to visit our factory next week*.

cheap(ly)

Cheap and *cheaply* can both be used on most occasions: *He bought/sold it cheap(ly)*; *At that time life was held cheap(ly)*. However, in phrases such as *cheaply bought* only *cheaply* is acceptable.

See ADVERBS WITHOUT -LY.

cheer

Cheer and all its compounds suggest happiness. To be *of good cheer* is to be happy, to be in a good mood; people *cheer* when they are happy with what is happening, for example at a sports event. *Cheerful* means *happy*.

Cheers can mean *thank you* or *goodbye*; it is also a common way of making an informal toast when drinking.

chemist

The term *chemist's shop* is often used for a public commercial pharmacy where medical drugs are obtained; one large chain of commercial pharmacies in Britain uses the name *chemist* in its advertising: *I'm going to the chemist's to boy some paracetamol*. The name *pharmacy* is used in hospitals, and *pharmacology* is a different academic discipline from chemistry.

chess

The *pieces* or *men* are called *king, queen, bishop, knight, castle* or *rook*, and *pawn*. When the king is under direct attack it is in *check*. When the king is under a threat from which it cannot escape, that is *checkmate* and the game is ended. A position in which neither player can win is called *stalemate*, a word which is often used figuratively to refer to negotiations or similar situations that are not moving.

These words are not connected with the other meanings of MATE.

chest

A *chest* is a large box. By extension from that it means the upper part of the human body. This can be either internally, as in *chest pain* for example, or externally as the front surface of the body. Medals are worn on the left side of the chest.

C

child

This word and its irregular plural *children* can be used as a common term for sons and daughters: *How many children do you have?; Where do your children go to school?*

The word *child(ren)* can refer to adult(s) in the context of family relationships: *When he died he left his money equally to his three children; Her three children all live in different countries.*

childish

ChildISH refers to things related to childhood but is more frequently used to refer to an adult who behaves like a child, in a silly manner. *Childlike* is similar but sounds more positive, referring to *childlike innocence* for example.

Infantile refers to the behaviour and attitudes of an infant and is sometimes used, like *childish*, to refer to adults' behaviour.

Puerile is always pejorative, whether it refers to children's or adults' behaviour.

Juvenile is not so common; it refers to young people and was used until 1969 in the term *juvenile delinquent* to mean a person below the legal age of responsibility (but above a minimum age) who could be punished for breaking the law. In the theatre the *juvenile lead* is a young person whose character has a leading role in the PLAY, and the actor who plays that role.

Youthful means being or looking young, or having the character of youth: *a youthful appearance*; *youthful impatience.*

For other things intended for children use *children's literature, TV, sports* etc.

chip

A *chip* is a small, usually thin, piece that has been cut or broken off a larger piece. Traditionally the material was stone or wood, but the word is now used in electronics to refer to the silicon chip that is used in computer manufacture.

In British English a *potato chip* is a piece of potato, usually long and rectangular in appearance, which is deep fried and served hot with steak, eggs, hamburgers etc. The thin, approximately circular or oval, slices of potato which are eaten cold and are often sold in bags, are called *potato crisps*. In American English these are called *French fries* and *potato chips* respectively.

A *chip* is a counter or token used in gambling, in casinos for example.

Someone who is a *chip off the old block* shows typical characteristics of one of their parents or other family members. To *have a chip on ONE'S (*PRONOUNS, PERSONAL) shoulder* means to have a very deeply rooted resentment against another person or society in general. *When the chips are down* means *When a critical situation ARISES (*RISE).*

choler(a)

Choler is *anger*; the adjective *choleric* means *angry*.

Cholera is a disease caused by the bacterium *Vibrio cholerae*, with vomiting and diarrhoea.

These words are both pronounced with /kɒl/.

choral & coral

Choral /'kɔːrəl/ is the adjective from *choir* /kwaɪə/: *choral music.*

Coral /'kɒrəl/ is a hard substance created by some sea creatures and sometimes used as decoration by people.

chord & cord

Chord has two meanings:

a group of three or more musical notes played together and *a STRAIGHT line joining the ends of an arc of a circle.* See GEOMETRY *(*MATHEMATICAL TERMS).*

Cord is a thin kind of rope; as well as the literal meaning this is also used in anatomical expressions: *spinal, umbilical, vocal cord.*

Christ and Christian

These words are pronounced /kraɪst/ and /ˈkrɪstɪən/.

Christmas and New Year

Christmas Day (25 December) and *Boxing Day* (26 December) are bank (i.e. public) holidays in the UK; *Christmas Eve* (24 December) is not. The name of *Boxing Day* has nothing to do with the sport of boxing; it refers to when the collection boxes in churches were opened on Christmas Day and the contents were distributed among the poor on the following day. From that the name was given to the nineteenth-century custom of giving Christmas presents, which were called Christmas boxes, on that day.

Many of the present day customs associated with Christmas date from that time. Queen Victoria's husband Albert, who was German, introduced the idea of decorating a tree for Christmas. A *Christmas tree* is an evergreen tree (one that has needles instead of normal leaves and does not lose them in winter), usually a pine or fir. It is decorated with coloured glass balls, strings of gold and silver decoration called *tinsel*, and small lights called *fairy lights*. There is usually a fairy on the top of the tree.

People also decorate their houses with *holly* and *mistletoe*. Both are evergreen plants. Holly has hard leaves with sharp points and red berries; mistletoe is a parasitic plant with long green leaves and white berries. Although there is Christian symbolism connected with them, their use goes back to pagan (pre-Christian) times, when evergreen plants symbolised the continuity of fertility and were an important part of the celebration of the winter solstice (21 December), which marked the rebirth of the sun. Part of this fertility tradition survives today in the custom that anybody standing under the mistletoe can be kissed by anyone else.

People send *Christmas cards* to their friends and family. It is usual to send or give a card to everyone you know, even people whom you see on Christmas Day itself; some cards are religious in inspiration and many cards are sold for charity organisations. Presents are given to family members and close friends with the greeting *Happy Christmas* or *Merry Christmas*. In writing Christmas is often abbreviated to *Xmas*, where the *X* represents the GREEK letter *chi*, the first letter of Christ's name in Greek; some people pronounce *Xmas* /ˈeksməs/.

The best known symbol of Christmas is *Father Christmas*, or *Santa Claus* as he is sometimes known. He is a continuation of the tradition of Saint Nicholas, who brings presents for children on his day (6 December), but this custom is not celebrated in Britain. He lives in Lapland (northern Scandinavia) where he and his elf workers spend all year making the toys that he gives to children at Christmas. Father Christmas travels around the world on his *sleigh*, which is pulled by nine *reindeer* called Rudolf, Dasher, Dancer, Comet, Vixen, Cupid, Prancer, Donner, and Blitzen. During the night of Christmas Eve he visits each house and goes down the chimney to leave presents in the *stockings* that the children have hung by their beds. Often families leave some WHISKY and *mince pies* by the fire for him to have on his way.

Mince pies are small pies about 5-7 cm in diameter containing MINCEMEAT *(*FLESH & MEAT)*, (which is made of fruit, not meat). They are a typical delicacy of the Christmas period, but the main meal is *Christmas dinner*, which is eaten at midday on Christmas Day; it usually consists of roast turkey with a variety of vegetables, followed by a *Christmas pudding*, a very heavy, rich, boiled pudding containing nuts and dried fruits. The pudding is often served flaming with brandy. After the meal people often watch the *Queen's Speech* on television. *Christmas cake* is a rich heavy cake with dried fruit and nuts, covered with marzipan and icing (moulded sugar paste).

Although Christmas is a very important date in the Christian calendar, its religious significance in Britain is decreasing as fewer people are actively religious. Nevertheless, the traditional religious imagery is still important; many schools have *crib scenes*, representations of the scene in *Bethlehem* when *Jesus* was born. Often too they have *nativity plays* in which children play the story of *Joseph* and *Mary* going from *Nazareth* to *Bethlehem*, where they found *no room at the in* (hotel) and Jesus slept in a *manger* (container for animal feed). The *shepherds* came down from the hills to worship

C

him and the *Three Kings* or *wise men* from the east, who had followed the star, gave him presents of *gold*, *frankincense* (an aromatic gum resin used as incense) and *myrrh* (a gum resin used as a perfume). The arrival of the Kings is celebrated on *twelfth night* (6 January) but no presents are given on that day; it is the end of the Christmas period when people take down the Christmas decorations and cards that they have received.

There are special hymns called *Christmas carols* that are sung at this time celebrating the nativity. Some, such as *Once in Royal David's City* and *Away in a Manger,* are more seriously religious while others such as *God Rest Ye Merry, Gentlemen* (*May God keep you merry, gentlemen,* see SUBJUNCTIVE) and *Good King Wenceslas* (celebrating the charity of King Wenceslas of Bohemia in the tenth century) are more cheerful. One tradition is for groups of people to go from door to door singing carols to collect money for charity. On Christmas Eve churches have religious services of carols and readings from the Bible; the best known of these is in the chapel of King's College, Cambridge, which is broadcast worldwide on television and radio.

Church of England

The Church of England is the established (i.e. official) Church in England. It separated from the Roman CATHOLIC church in 1534 after Pope Clement VII refused to allow King Henry VIII to divorce Catherine of Aragon. Although there are now doctrinal differences between the Church of England and the Roman Catholic Church Henry's initial dispute was a political one with the Pope, whose predecessor Leo X had awarded him the title *Fidei Defensor* (Defender of the Faith) for a book in which he attacked Martin Luther. This title is still used by British monarchs and is seen on British coins.

The Monarch is the Supreme Governor of the Church but has no power in its running; its spiritual head is the Archbishop of Canterbury who is the Primate of All England; the other archbishop, York, has the title Primate of England. The bishops of the Church of England are appointed by the Crown, which means in practice that the prime minister appoints the person nominated by a joint committee representing elements of the Church and Government. Parliament has control over some aspects of Church affairs but Church doctrine is determined by the General Synod. The two English archbishops (Canterbury and York) and 24 bishops sit by right in the HOUSE OF LORDS *(*CONSTITUTION)*. Despite the establishment of the Church of England there is freedom of religion in England, and all positions (except that of the monarch, who must be an ANGLICAN) are open to any member of any religion.

The Church of England has 24 million nominal members and one million worshippers. It is the only established Church in the United Kingdom. The Church of Ireland, the Church in Wales and the Episcopalian Church in Scotland represent the Anglican communion in those three countries. The CHURCH OF SCOTLAND is not part of the Anglican communion.

Anglican parish priests use the title *Vicar*, both as a title and as a form of address: *The Vicar of Bray; Good morning, Vicar.* An Anglican priest is addressed and referred to formally as *The Revd John Smith* and is often referred to in speech as *Mr Smith*. Some priests, especially in the Church's ANGLO-CATHOLIC wing choose to be known by the title *Father*: *Father John, Fr Smith*.

Anglican priests are permitted to marry, though some choose to take vows of celibacy. The Church of England voted to admit women as priests, but not as bishops, in 1992; the first were ordained in April 1994. The Church is seriously divided on the issue of homosexuality among the clergy.

High and Low Church, and Broad Church

The *High Church* is a movement in the Church of England which emphasises the CATHOLIC tradition in the Church and gives a 'high' position to the authority of bishops and priests, the sacraments and other points of doctrine, discipline and ritual which distinguish the Church from Calvinist and other Protestant denominations. It is not much used in the modern Church. The Low Church is the part of the Church of England which gives a 'low' position to the authority of bishops and priests and to the sacraments. The most extreme *Low Churchman* would consider himself close to the Calvinist and other Protestant denominations. The BROAD *Church* favours a liberal interpretation of doctrine.

See CHURCH OF SCOTLAND.

Church of Scotland

In Scotland the Church of Scotland, also called the *Kirk*, is the national, but not established, Church. It is Presbyterian, i.e. it has no bishops. In Scotland the Monarch (who is also the Supreme Governor of the CHURCH OF ENGLAND) is a member of the Church of Scotland, apparently changing religious affiliation on crossing the border.

circuit

Circuit, circuitry, and *circuitous* are pronounced /ˈsɜːkɪt/, /ˈsɜːkɪtri/, and /səkˈjuːɪtəs/.

See BISCUIT.

City of London

The City of London is the ancient part of London, the part that was occupied during the Roman occupation. It has its own lord mayor, council, city government and police force, which are independent of the rest of London; its governing institutions date back to the MIDDLE AGES. It is one square mile (2½ sq. km.) in area, forming an ISLAND in the larger metropolitan area. It is the financial heart of Britain; it is the area where all BANKS and other financial institutions have their offices.

city, town & village

The difference between these is one of degree. It is not easy to be precise. In economic terms, a *city* can be said to generate its economic growth from its own local economy. A *metropolitan area* is a political name for the conurbation which has spread beyond the city's boundaries, or which has incorporated existing nearby towns.

Traditionally the definition of a city in the UK has been that it is the seat of a bishop although Birmingham was created a city before it had a bishop; because of this definition Wells and Ely, with 10,000 and 20,000 people respectively, are cities. Cities can be created by royal charter. Sunderland was created a city by Royal Charter in 1992 to mark the fortieth anniversary of the coronation of Queen Elizabeth II, and in 2002 five more cities (Preston, Newport, Stirling, Lisburn, and Newry) were created. See CITY OF LONDON.

A *town* is smaller and less economically independent than a city; historically towns were market towns for farmers from the surrounding rural area and for local administration. However, the word *town* sometimes refers to a city. If someone says *I'm going to town*, it could mean that they are going to the nearest city; similarly, *She works in town* could mean that she works in the nearest city. A *county town* is the administrative centre of a COUNTY, even if it is a city, and the *town hall* may be the meeting place for the city COUNCIL. Other languages often do not make the difference between *town* and *city* that is found in English.

A *village* is smaller than a town and a *hamlet* is very small indeed, a collection of houses without a church.

civil service

In Britain the *civil service* is the body of *civil servants* that are employed by the country's central government in London or by the regional governments in Scotland, Wales and Northern Ireland. People employed by local authorities are known as *local government officers* or *employees* or as *public servants*; they are not referred to as *civil servants*. Civil servants and local government employees collectively are public (service) employees. Very senior civil servants are sometimes referred to informally as *mandarins*.

The word *functionary* is not used formally with reference to British civil servants; it sounds pompous and is sometimes used insultingly or ironically.

C

classic & classical

Classic is used of something that is regarded as excellent or of great importance: *a classic car, example, representative, text book*. *Classics* is the study of *classical* subjects, especially Greek and Latin.

Classical refers to the art and literature of the ancient world: *classical Latin* was spoken at the height of the Roman Empire; *classical Greek* is not the language spoken in modern Greece; a *classical education* is one that concentrates on these subjects, and a *classical scholar* is an expert in them. *Classical music* is serious, traditional, conventional music, especially that of the period 1750 to 1800. *Classical science* is science based on theories developed before relativity and quantum mechanics.

clause

A clause is a group of words that contains at least a subject (S) and a verb (V). It may also contain other elements such as an object (O) or objects and one or more adverbs (A). *John (S) gave (V) Mary (O) a present (O) on her birthday (A)*.

A sentence may contain more than one clause:
1 He gave her a present and took her out for dinner.
2 He gave her a present because it was her birthday.
3a He gave her a present which she did not like.
3b He gave her a present, which she did not like.
4 He gave her a present after asking her to marry him.

In **1** the two clauses are co-ordinate (equal) and are joined by a co-ordinating CONJUNCTION.

In **2** the clause *because it was her birthday* is subordinate to the main clause *He gave her a present*. It is introduced by a subordinating conjunction.

In **3** *which she did not like* is a RELATIVE CLAUSE; a relative clause is a kind of subordinate clause. In **3a** it is a defining relative clause (she did not like the present). In **3b** it is a non-defining relative clause (she did not like his action of giving her a present).

In **4** *after asking her to marry him* is an adverbial clause.

cleave

For the differences between the forms and meanings of this word see the note at IRREGULAR VERBS.

cleft sentences

The name comes from the past participle of the verb CLEAVE, meaning *divide, split*.

Cleft sentences provide emphasis by bringing the object to near the beginning of the sentence. The normal order is *I saw John; I like his sense of humour*. The cleft sentence equivalents are *It was John that I saw; It's his sense of humour that I like*.

Usually the stress is on the complement of the verb (*John, sense of humour*) but there are other possibilities: *It was John that **I** saw; It's his sense of humour that **I** like* or *It was John that I **saw**; It's his sense of humour that I **like**.* The sentence begins with *it* even when the subject is plural: *It was the cars that were the problem*.

Note that a sentence such as *It's the book that interests me* is ambiguous in writing; it could be a cleft sentence, or it could be a sentence with a RELATIVE CLAUSE that could be written as *This is the book which interests me*. Neither of the changes introduced here (*this, which*) is possible in the cleft sentence. This ambiguity is avoided in speech by the different intonation: *It's the **book** that interests me* (cleft sentence); *It's the book that **in**terests me* (relative clause).

A cleft sentence does not have to focus on a noun:

It was $\dfrac{here, there, in the park}{then, yesterday, in 2015}$ that I met her.

C

clerk

In an office a *clerk* is person who handles paperwork but has no executive authority. This is known as *clerical work*. In a bank a *clerk* is the person who deals with the customers and counts money. An ANGLICAN priest is officially known as a *clerk in holy orders*; apart from this the word *clerk* has no religious meaning in modern English, although the adjective *clerical* also refers to the church, for example a priest wears a *clerical collar*.

See DOG COLLAR.

clever etc.

A *clever* person is one who shows a particular skill or talent in doing something and can do it easily, quickly, efficiently, and skilfully. A *clever* idea, proposal, plan or suggestion is one that shows cleverness on the part of its originator.

Astute is similar to *clever* but relates more to an analytical ability to assess situations and people.

Bright can be used to describe someone who is very cheerful, lively and animated in conversation. It is the opposite of DULL *(*DARK)*. It can also refer to someone who is very intelligent, quick-witted or clever; in this sense, it is mostly used with reference to children or people of inferior status. A *bright idea* is a clever, original one.

Brilliant means *outstandingly talented or intelligent*. A *brilliant* idea or proposal is an exceptionally good one.

Canny describes a person who shows good cautious JUDGEMENT.

Cunning refers to a way of achieving a goal that is indirect, evasive or deceitful. A *cunning plan* would be made by a *clever* person as a means of deceiving an opponent. *Cunning* can also be a noun: *There were no limits to his cunning. Cunning* is often regarded positively, even showing respect for an opponent's activities.

Intelligence is the ability to use the power of understanding, so it can be said that humans are intelligent but computers are not, although artificial intelligence is being developed. However, to say that somebody is intelligent is to say that they have a high level of understanding information, they can understand and manipulate it quickly. A certain level of knowledge is required for intelligence to be exercised, but factual knowledge by itself does not imply intelligence. *Intelligent* is the opposite of *stupid*.

Shrewd refers to a good ability to make accurate assessments of situations.

Sly is an adjective. It is similar to *cunning* in that it involves deceit or evasion, but it is always negative in connotation.

Wise describes a person who can judge the right course of action in a situation and act accordingly, one who can see and adopt the best means of reaching an end. A wise person has and uses common sense. *Wise* is the opposite of *foolISH*.

> A *word to the wise*, sometimes quoted as *verbum sap.* or *verb. sap.,* is used to imply that someone who understands a situation will easily INFER *(*IMPLY)* what is not said, or the reason why it is not said.

> The expression *none the wiser* refers to an obsolete sense of *wise* meaning *knowledge*. Similarly, the expression *as wise as before* means knowing no more than before – and usually nothing – about a matter: *I've read the instruction book but I'm none the wiser/I'm as wise as before* (I know no more than I did before).

> *To put someone wise* or *to be* or *get wise to something* refers to the gaining of information, informing someone or becoming aware of something oneself.

> A *wisdom tooth* is one of those at the back of the mouth that appear at about the age of twenty.

Witty. The word *with* derives from a Germanic root meaning *know* as in modern German *wissen*, and at one time it referred to thinking, reasoning and understanding; this meaning is obsolete, but survives in the expressions *beyond the with of...* meaning beyond someone's understanding or

C

ability, and *at one's wit's (or wits') end*, meaning that one has no idea what to think or do. Also to *bring, drive* or *put somebody to their wit's end*.

A *quick-witted* person is one who can think quickly.

Witting means *aware*, a *witting action* (one performed wittingly) is one performed intentionally. It is now usually used only in the negative *unwitting(ly)*.

To *live by your wits* means to make a living by adapting cleverly to circumstances.

To *have your wits about you* means to be mentally alert.

To wit means *that is* or *namely*: *The largest country in western Europe, to wit Germany*. It is similar to *i.e.*

Nowadays *wit* refers to an ability in speech or writing to associate thought and expression in a way that is attractive because it is unexpected, but is at the same time brilliant and amusing. A witty person is said to be a *wit*.

A *dimwit* is a person who is not very bright. See DARK.

client & customer

The traditional difference between these two is that a ***client*** pays for the services of a professional person, a lawyer, architect, accountant etc., while a ***customer*** is someone who has the CUSTOM of buying from a particular shop, though a casual visitor to a shop is also a *customer*. In the case of a private sale of a house or car, for example, the word *buyer* or *purchaser* would be used. However, in recent years banks, which used to refer to their *clients*, as was natural given the definition of a client, have begun to refer to their *customers*. Moreover, *customer* has been adopted by telecommunications companies, which USED TO have *subscribers*, and by railway companies and airlines, which used to have *passengers*. The term *customer service* seems to be gaining ground throughout the service sector of the economy.

clock & watch

Together these are known as *timepieces*.

A ***watch*** is a timepiece that is normally carried with you. At one time it was useful to make a distinction between *pocket watches* and *wristwatches*. Now that pocket watches are very rare, the word *watch* is used alone. Size is not the criterion for distinguishing watches and clocks. Even a very small timepiece that is designed to stand independently on a table, or that is part of a computer or DVD player, is a ***clock***, while a larger one designed to be carried in a pocket or worn on a wrist is a watch.

cloth(s), clothes etc.

cloth

As an uncountable noun, cloth /klɒθ/ is woven textile material. As a countable noun it refers to a piece of cloth and can be qualified as *table-cloth, dishcloth*.

clothes

This word, pronounced /kləʊðz/, has no singular; it refers to all the things made of cloth (as well as leather, plastic etc.) that one wears. It was originally the plural of *cloth* before the word *cloths* developed with its special meaning. In the days before clothing became a matter of fashion, the plural of *cloth* reasonably referred to what one wrapped around one's body for warmth and decency. When a singular is needed for *clothes*, the word *garment* is used; this has its own plural *garments*.

costume

This refers to a particular way of dressing, hairstyle, jewellery etc. of a particular nation, class or period, for example *national costume*. It is also the word used in the theatre for the clothes etc. that an actor wears on stage. A *swimming costume* is the garment worn for swimming.

dress

This uncountable noun refers to someone's clothing, especially the outer clothing considered as adornment as well as a mere covering for the body. This sense is most commonly found nowadays in the sense of a woman's dress (countable), one piece covering the body from the shoulders or BOSOM (*BREAST) to the knees or ankles and worn for elegance and adornment. *Evening dress* is the formal clothes worn on formal occasions, dinners for example, in the evenings. The *dress rehearsal* of a play is the final rehearsal, which is intended to be as close as possible to the actual running of a performance. In a theatre the *dress circle*, usually the first gallery above the floor, is a place where the audience are (or in many cases now were) expected to wear full evening dress. A *dressing gown* is a loose gown worn with nightclothes.

A *dressing* is the covering that is placed over a wound for protection and hygiene. *Salad dressing* is a sauce, usually based on oil and vinegar, used to *dress* (flavour and enrich) a salad.

club

A *club* is a long heavy stick used as a weapon; *Indian clubs* are used in athletic exercises. The stick used in golf to hit the ball is called a *club*. *Clubs* is the value of one of the suits (♣) of PLAYING CARDS.

In the seventeenth century the idea of a *club* as a solid mass led to people *clubbing together* to constitute *clubs* (the precise relation of the nouns and verb is uncertain): *sports clubs, social clubs* and so on. So a *golf club* is both the stick that is used in playing the game and the institution that manages the golf course and organises golfing and social activities. The traditional *clubs* in cities, often known as gentlemen's clubs, provide facilities for members with common interests. Some of them do not admit women members, which explains why Margaret Thatcher was the first British Conservative prime minister not to be elected a member of the Carlton Club (because she was a woman) though she was given honorary membership.

A *club foot* is a deformed foot.

People *club together* to share the expenses of buying a present or of spending time together.

To be in the (pudding) club is a slang expression meaning to be pregnant.

cockney

Cockneys are the people from the East End of London, which was the industrial and port district of the city. A true *cockney* is one born within the sound of Bow bells, the bells of St Mary-le-Bow church, the parish church of Bow, the main district in the East End.

The name *cockney* derives from *cock's egg*, which is a small strangely shaped egg laid by a young hem. It was used as a derogatory term used by country people for townspeople; it came to apply specifically to Londoners in the seventeenth century.

As well as significant vowel differences, a typical feature of cockney pronunciation is the use of /f/ and /v/ for /θ/ and /ð/ respectively at the ends of words and between vowels, giving /saʊf/ for SOUTH and /ˈbrʌvə/ for brother. Another typical feature is the use of the GLOTTAL STOP /ʔ/ (*PHONETIC SYMBOLS*) which replaces *t* between vowels and at the ends of words such as *bitten, bottom, glottal, about,* and *what*.

rhyming slang
Rhyming slang is a characteristic feature of cockney speech, where a word is replaced by a rhyming phrase: *loaf of bread* for *head*, *apples and pears* for *stairs*, *butcher's hook* for *look*, *plates of meat* for *feet*. In some cases only the first part of the phrase is used: *Use your loaf* means *Use your head - think! Have a butcher's at this* means *Have a look at this*.

cognate

Words in different languages are cognate when they share the same origin, even though the form and possibly the meaning differ. For example, the English word *stool* is cognate with the German word

C

Stuhl (which means *chair*) despite the difference in meaning. English *brother*, German *Bruder*, and Latin *frater* all derive from the assumed INDO-EUROPEAN base *bhrater*.

The relationship is sometimes surprising; the fact that the English *hundred*, Latin *centum*, and Russian *cmo* (pronounced *sto*) are related is not immediately obvious. Cognate languages are languages such as Spanish, Catalan, Italian, and Portuguese that derive from the same origin.

college

The word *college* has no precise meaning in English. Some independent secondary schools use it in their names. Some universities, Cambridge for example, are divided into *colleges* for residential and, to a certain extent, teaching purposes. The word is often used in the names of other post-school educational institutes such as *business college, college of music*. It is the name used for certain professional associations, especially scientific and artistic ones e.g. the *Royal College of* PHYSICIANS, *Royal College of Art*.

colours

The names of colours can be used as nouns: *Blue is my favourite colour. This green is too dark.*

See LANGUAGES.

coma & comma

A *coma* /'keʊmə/ is a state of deep unconsciousness, usually caused by severe injury.

A *comma* /'kɒmə/ is a PUNCTUATION mark.

come & go

The choice of which of these to use depends on the speaker's position; *come* means *move towards the speaker* and *go* means *move away from the speaker*. A standard collocation would be *come here* or *go there*. With the words *in, out* and *back* they are used as shown on the right.

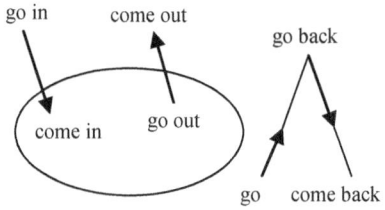

Thus, *go in* and *come in* both correspond to *enter; go out* and *come out* both correspond to *leave, depart, exit;* and *go back* and *come back* both correspond to *return*.

It is important to realise that the idea of *towards or away from the speaker* includes the idea of where the speaker imagines him/herself to be. Imagine two people who work together. They are having lunch together in a restaurant. One says *'Come to my office this afternoon and I'll show you the report.'* However, if he knows that he will be away from his office, he might say *'Go to my office this afternoon and leave your report on my desk.'*

See BRING & TAKE.

Commonwealth

The Commonwealth is a voluntary association of independent states that were once in the British Empire; Myanmar (formerly Burma but the name change is controversial), Ireland and the Arab countries that were once under British control are not members but the former Portuguese territory of Mozambique joined in 1995 as did the former German and Belgian colony of Rwanda in 2009. The monarch of the UK is the Head of the Commonwealth, but the UK has no special status in the organisation (it is not the British Commonwealth). Some countries, notably Australia, Canada, Jamaica and New Zealand, recognise the UK's monarch as their head of state, and some others choose to retain the British PRIVY COUNCIL *(*CONSTITUTION)* as their final court of appeal, but despite that all Commonwealth countries are independent; no institution in the UK has power in any Commonwealth country against the wishes of that country, and in particular the British parliament cannot legislate for any Commonwealth country or interfere in any way in its internal affairs.

C

company

A company is a commercial organisation with a legal personality which trades in goods and/or services with the intention of making a profit. It is managed for the benefit of the *shareholders* by a *board of directors* which has a *chairman*. Its internal operations are governed by its *articles of association*. A *limited liability company* is one where the *shareholders'* liability is limited to the *nominal value* of their shares. If the *shares* are sold in the stock exchange it is a *public limited company (plc)* often referred to as a PUBLIC COMPANY. If not, it is simply a *limited company (Ltd)*. The word public here refers to the fact that the shares can be owned, bought and sold by members of the public. It does not mean that the company is owned by the public in the form of the state; such a thing is a *nationalised* or *publicly owned company*. In American English, the terms are *corporation (company), president (chairman), Inc (Incorporated) (plc), stockholders (shareholders)*.

See ENTERPRISE.

comparatives and superlatives

For the making of these forms see ADJECTIVES, COMPARISON and ADVERBS, COMPARISON.

The comparative is used when two things are being compared directly: *Mary is taller than Anne; Mary is the taller daughter* clearly implies that there are only two daughters. Although this was not always so (Jane Austen could write in the early nineteenth century of *the youngest of the two daughters*), it is advisable nowadays to use the comparative RATHER than the superlative when two things are being compared.

The superlative is always used when three or more things are being compared.

The superlative is usually associated with the preposition *in*: *the tallest mountain in England; the oldest girl in the class; the highest note in the song* or with *on*: *the tallest mountain on the island; the only picture on the wall*. However, with time expressions we use *of*: *The hottest day of the year; The last week of the holidays*. See IN & ON (INCLUDING AT).

superlative with -most

The suffix *-most* is attached to certain prepositions and nouns to make a superlative adjective. It is pronounced /məʊst/, the same as the adverb *most*, but has a different origin. The words generally refer to position or direction and the commonest are *endmost, foremost, rearmost, backmost, bottommost, topmost, centremost, downmost, uppermost; easternmost, westernmost, northernmost, SOUTHernmost; inmost, innermost, outermost, leftmost, rightmost, utmost*.

compare

When things are compared to show that they are similar, use the preposition *to*: *He compared the colour of her eyes to the colour of the sky; Shall I compare the to a summer's day?* (SHAKESPEARE, sonnet 18).

When things are compared in order to analyse their similarities and differences, use *to* or *with*:
The quality's poor compared to/with what it used to be.
When I compared John's story with Jane's, I found considerable differences.
A comparison of John's story with Jane's revealed considerable differences.
With is generally used when the comparison involves a formal analysis of a number of things.

compass(ess)

A *compass* is the instrument used to find north.

A pair of *compasses* is the instrument used to draw a circle.

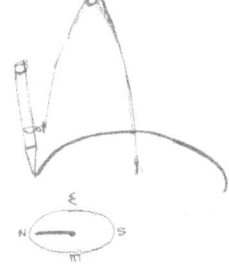

competence & competition

Competence refers to the ability or power or authority to do something. *This matter is outside my competence; I am not competent to deal with it*. The negative forms *incompetent/incompetence* are often used insultingly to refer to the inability to do something and do not refer to power or authority: *He built the wall so incompetently that it fell down*.

C

Competition refers to two or more people attempting to reach the same goal in sport, in business, in a TV show, or in other *competitive* activities. Other forms are *competitor, competitiveness*.

complacent & complaisant

These words are DOUBLETS.

Complacent /kəmˈpleɪsənt/ means *self-satisfied, relaxed, willing to let things take their course.*

Complaisant /kəmˈpleɪzənt/ means *willing to defer to or please another person or to accept what other people, do without complaining.*

complement & compliment

These words are DOUBLETS; both come from the Latin *complementum* and as nouns both are pronounced /ˈkɒmplɪmənt/, and as verbs /kɒmplɪˈment/. However, they are differentiated in meaning in English.

Complement has the idea of filling or completing: *The full complement of this section is 300 people* (the number employed when all positions are filled). *Human geography is the complement of physical geography.* (The two together complete the concept of geography.) It can be used as a verb: *Human geography complements physical geography.* The adjective is *complementary*: *Complementary angles together make a right angle; Complementary colours make white light.*

A ***compliment*** is a comment that is polite about someone, or that praises them; it can be made to or about the person. The act of doing so is *paying someone a compliment*. Saying *compliments to the chef* is a way of complimenting the person who has cooked a meal; *Compliments of the season* is a common Christmas greeting. It can be used as a verb: *She complimented him on his performance.* The adjective is *complimentary*: *She was very complimentary to him; We had complimentary tickets* (free tickets given as a compliment).

complement (grammatical)

In grammar *complement* is a term for a word or phrase that completes the meaning of the predicate. In practice this usually means that it is:

- a noun that refers back to the SUBJECT (noun complement): *Susan is my boss; Susan became the head of the department.* Here the words *Susan* and *boss* have the same reference (they are the same person) unlike *Susan saw my boss*, where the references are different and *boss* is the direct OBJECT of *saw*.
- an adjective that refers back to the subject or object (adjective complement): In *Susan was/became/got angry*, the adjective *angry* refers to the subject *Susan*. In *I left the house QUIET* the adjective *quiet* refers to the object *house (the house was quiet)* but in *I left the house quietly* the adverb *quietly* refers to manner in which I left it *(I left quietly)*. See SENSE VERBS.

Prove can be followed by a noun complement: *The operation proved a success*. However, the forms with an infinitive: *The operation proved to be a success* or with an adjective: *The operation proved successful* are more common. Although in theory SEEM can be followed by a noun complement, in practice this is extremely rare.

compound nouns

In compound nouns letter combinations such as *ph, sh, th* are not pronounced as /f/, /ʃ/ or /θ/ if they occur at the meeting point of two words that are compounded: *shepherd* /ˈʃepəd/ (*sheep + herd*), *mishap* /ˈmɪshæp/ (a compound of the PREFIX *mis-* and the root of *happen*), *dishonest* /dɪsˈɒnɪst/ and *foothill* /ˈfʊthɪl/.

comrade

This word originates from the idea of people who share a room (or chamber, a COGNATE word). It was especially used by soldiers to refer to their FELLOWS; this led to a more general use referring to close companions who shared friendship, occupation of living accommodation and the fortunes of life. Its idea of close association and equality led to its adoption by socialists and communists, who wished to avoid other social titles such as *Mr* or *Sir* that implied respect and subservience. It is rarely used in any context other than these two.

conditional sentences

Conditional sentences are usually divided into four categories numbered from zero to three.

In the examples given in this article, the *if* CLAUSE (the *protasis*) is given before the main or matrix clause (the *apodosis*). Of course, they can be reversed: *I will boy a car if I win the lottery* etc.

For punctuation of conditional sentences, see PUNCTUATION | COMMAS.

zero conditional

If water is heated to 100° C, it boils.
This has the PRESENT SIMPLE in both parts of the sentence. It refers to something that is always true. This is a normal use of the present simple: *Water boils at 100° C.*

first conditional

If I win the lottery, I will boy a car.
I am making a prediction that I will boy a car (the WILL *FUTURE is normally used for predictions) but that prediction can be fulfilled only if I win the lottery; winning the lottery is a condition for my buying a car. The opposite is also very probably true *If I don't win the lottery, I won't boy a car* and a question can be asked: *If you win the lottery, will you boy a car?*

Note that the verb tense is present in *If I win* although it refers to a time in the future. See TENSE & TIME. This is similar to the use of the present in subordinate time clauses. The use of the FUTURE to make a prediction gives a feeling that the idea is definite; there is certainly a possibility that I will win. I have bought a ticket for the lottery. If there is a definite intention, the GOING TO FUTURE can be used: *If I win the lottery, I'm going to boy a car.*

second conditional

If I won the lottery, I would boy a car.
This is far more hypothetical than the first conditional. Maybe I don't have a ticket for the lottery and am just considering the abstract possibility; maybe I do have a ticket but still think that my chance of winning is remote. The second conditional can also be used to describe hypothetical conditions that are clearly impossible to fulfil: *If the sun always shone, we would never see the stars.*

Here, the verb in the *if* clause is in the PAST SIMPLE *(If I won; If the sun...shone)* though the time must be in the future for the first example to become reality, and in the second it is a general statement with no special reference to time. The use of a past tense in such conditions is common in INDO-EUROPEAN LANGUAGES, though this is often not noticed by speakers of other languages as the use of the SUBJUNCTIVE mood obscures the nature of the tense. As the English subjunctive is almost non-existent, the use of the past tense is more apparent. Because its use, with no indication in the verb of its hypothetical nature (and that is the purpose of the subjunctive mood), seems strange, foreign speakers of English very frequently make the mistake of trying to introduce this element of uncertainty by using *would*: ~~If I would win...~~ / ~~If the sun would shine...~~ **This is wrong** (but see below*). Just as the *will* in the first conditional is not in the *if* clause (protasis), so in the second conditional the *would* is not in that clause.

*In formal letters, constructions such as this are found: *I would be very grateful if you would send me...* Here the second *would* should be understood as the past of *will* expressing willingness. See MODAL AUXILIARY VERBS.

third conditional

If I had won the lottery, I would have bought a car.
This is an impossible condition because it sets a condition for an event in the past. The lottery took place last week. I had a ticket. I did not win. The use of the PAST PERFECT *(*PERFECT ASPECT)* for a past condition is in line with the use of the PAST SIMPLE for the second conditional. In *If I had won*, the *had* is in the past (and is arguably the past subjunctive) just as *won* is in *If I won*. So, as with the second conditional, there is a tendency to say incorrectly ~~If I would have won...~~ ➤

C

other modal verbs
Other verbs than *will/would* can be used: *If I win the lottery, I may/might/will be able to boy a car; If I won the lottery, I might/could boy a car.*

Intention can be expressed in the condition with *If he's to pass the exam he'll have to work harder* or *If he's going to pass the exam he'll have to work harder*. In *If he wants to pass the exam he's going to have to work harder* the future with *he's going to* refers to present evidence. For *be to* and *going to* see FUTURE.

(Further information about this use of *may* & *might* can be found under MODAL AUXILIARY VERBS.)

Other words than *if* can be used to introduce the condition. *Unless* states a negative condition: *Unless I win the lottery, I won't be able to boy a car* (If I don't win the lottery, ...) However, *unless* has a strong idea of an exception. We say *You'd be silly if you didn't boy a car* but not ~~You'd be silly unless you bought a car~~.

Other conditional words are *as long as, so long as, assuming (that), given (that)* (formal), IN CASE, *in the event that, on condition (that), provided (that), providing (that), supposing (that)*.

The conditional sentences can be expressed in other ways:
1 *Should I win the lottery, I will boy a car.*
2 *Were I to win/If I were to win the lottery, I would boy a car.*
3 *Had I won the lottery, I would have bought a car.*

This is more formal than the usual conditional sentences, and in the case of **1** and **2** suggests a lower degree of probability.

The above conditional sentences refer to hypothetical situations. *If* is also used in sentences where it makes an assumption or confirms a fact; in these sentences verb tenses are used normally: *If you had eggs for lunch, you won't want more for dinner; If he's been here since Monday, he can't have been in Paris yesterday.*

When *will/would* means *be willing* or *insist*, it can be used in the *if* clause: *If you'll just wait a minute, I'll tell Mr Robinson that you're here; If you'd (would) stop talking, you'd (would) hear what I'm saying; If you **will** (emphatic = insist) work all night, of course you'll be tired the next day.* The second of these examples is the CASE found in formal letters: *I would be grateful if you would send payment by return of post.*

conductor
The person who drives a bus or any other vehicle is a *driver*. At one time a bus *conductor* was responsible for collecting FARES from passengers and generally managing the bus. People who sell tickets on trains are sometimes known as conductors.

An orchestral conductor manages the orchestra in a concert.

A conductor is also a substance that conducts electricity, heat etc.

conjunctions
The co-ordinating conjunctions *and, or* and *but* join two or more co-ordinate CLAUSES: *He works hard and I respect him for that; You can email me or Mary can phone me; They live next door but I never speak to them.*

When the subject of the two clauses is the same, it is not necessary to repeat the subject: *He worked hard and passed his exams; You can email me or phone me; They live next door but never speak to me.*

In fact it is not necessary to repeat any of the words of the first clause that would appear in the second.
He must have rung the doorbell and then used a key.
He must have rung the doorbell or used a key.
He must have rung the doorbell but not used a key.

In subordinate clauses the subject must be stated, even if it is the same as in the main clause: *I didn't phone because I expected to see you.* (not ~~...because expected to see you~~). Compare *I didn't phone and (I) expected to see you.*

conjuror, magician & wizard

In the modern theatrical sense of a performer who produces rabbits from hats and saws young ladies in half *conjuror* /ˈkʌndʒərə/ is more common than *magician*. The form *conjurer* is also found.

A *wizard* was (maybe still is) the male equivalent of a witch; Harry Potter went to Hogwarts to learn to be a wizard. The word is not now used of theatrical performers, though it is found with a certain ironical sense in *The Wizard of Oz*.

Conservative Party

The origins of the Conservative Party lie in the Tory party that rejected the Act of Settlement, which established the Hanoverian line of succession. The Tories were the party who supported the Stuarts and the divine right of kings against Parliament's choice of monarch. The party gained in influence during the nineteenth century, representing the land-owning and imperial interests; it became known as the Conservative Party in about 1830. Benjamin Disraeli, a baptised Christian from a Jewish family, was its best known leader in the nineteenth century. Later, with large-scale support from business, the Conservative Party came to dominate British politics in the twentieth century, though Britain's entry into the EEC caused some tensions between the business and land-owning sections of the party.

Margaret Thatcher, who was Prime Minister from 1979-1990, revolutionised British society by greatly reducing the power of trade unions, and removing state involvement from large areas of public life, from industry by the process of privatisation and also from the institutions of the welfare state such as education and health care. In the process she moved the Conservative Party, and with it the centre ground of British politics, considerably to the right and into a nationalist, anti-European stance. She was removed from the party leadership in 1990 when it became apparent to leading Conservatives that she was a liability for the forthcoming general election. Although the party won in 1992, the ensuing Conservative government under John Major was weak and unpopular and was dogged by financial and sexual scandals.

Eighteen years of Conservative rule came to an end in 1997, when the party suffered its most serious electoral defeat ever, being unrepresented in SCOTLAND and WALES and being confined in England very largely to rural areas. In the 2001 election the party fought with a nationalist anti-Europe policy but failed to regain the ground that it had lost (though it did win one seat in Scotland) and its result was seen as a further defeat. In 2005 it regained a little ground but was still in a weak strategic position. David Cameron, who was elected party leader in 2005, failed to win a parliamentary majority in the 2010 general election and the party formed a coalition government with the Liberal Democrats. In May 2015 the party won a majority in parliament. After the Brexit referendum on leaving the EU in June 2016 Cameron resigned and Theresa May took over as party leader and prime minister.

The party's colour is blue.

See LABOUR PARTY; LIBERAL DEMOCRAT PARTY.

constitution and government

The United Kingdom of Great Britain and Northern Ireland is the full official name of the country. Great Britain consists of ENGLAND, SCOTLAND and WALES. The UK is a constitutional monarchy but the constitution is not written; it consists of a number of documents, most importantly *Magna Carta* (1215), by which King John gave away some of his absolute power, and the Bill of Rights

C

(1689), which extended constitutional freedom. However, much of the basis of the British constitution is tradition and custom, changed informally as circumstances require. There is no single document, or even a single recognised collection of documents, that can be called the British Constitution, and there is no Constitutional Court to rule on its interpretation. The name Great Britain dates from the union of England and Scotland and refers to the enlargement of the country; it is not the meaning of the word *great* that is a synonym of *marvellous, fantastic* etc.

Crown and monarch

The *Crown* is a constitutional institution in Britain, equivalent to the institution known as the State in other countries. It is currently embodied by Queen Elizabeth II but it is continuous and exists irrespective of the person of the monarch. Government ministers in Britain are nominally appointed by and act in the name of the Crown. The Act of Settlement 1701 established the current line of succession to the throne by passing the throne to the German Prince George of Hanover; this established a Protestant succession after the religious problems of the Tudors and Stuarts. The Royal Marriages Act 1772 established that the monarch may not marry a Roman CATHOLIC.

The *monarch*, currently Queen Elizabeth II, who came to the throne in 1952, is the Head of State. She has a consultative role and meets the *Prime Minister* (PM) weekly. She has no direct power to decide government policy but her views can be influential. The *Crown Prince* is Prince Charles; as the ELDEST soon of the monarch he has the title *Prince of Wales*.

government

The supreme governing body is the *Privy Council*. However, this rarely meets and the country is governed by a committee of it known as the *Cabinet*. The Cabinet is chaired by the Prime Minister. The government consists of the Cabinet and a number of *junior ministers* making a total of about 60 members of the government. The prime minister and other ministers are responsible to *Parliament* for their official actions.

Parliament consists of the *House of Commons*, the *House of Lords*, and the *Monarch*. The House of Commons consists of about 655 *Members of Parliament* (MPs), one representing each *constituency* (electoral district) in the country (see ELECTIONS). The number of MPs varies every few years as constituency boundaries change. At the time of writing (November 2016) there is a proposal to reduce the number of MPs to about 600. The maximum length of a Parliament between elections is five years, but the prime minister personally can choose to hold a general election at any time before that; recent elections were held at four-yearly intervals in May 1997, 2001 and 2005, but then in May 2010. The chairman of the House of Commons is the *Speaker*, a title that originated in the responsibility of the holder of the post to speak for (represent) the House of Commons to the monarch.

The *House of Lords* is the *upper chamber* of Parliament. Originally it was the assembly of the aristocracy (peers) who held their seats by right of inheritance. In 1958 life peers were introduced; they are members for their own lifetimes but the title is not inherited. Life peers are appointed by the prime minister. Until 1999 the hereditary peers had a large majority of members, which ensured a majority for the CONSERVATIVE PARTY. In 1999 a large number of hereditary peers were removed from the House of Lords (while keeping their titles) leaving 92 hereditary peers as members, elected by themselves from among their own number. As a result the appointed life peers now have a majority. There are no constitutional limits to the number of peers of either kind. The two archbishops and 24 of the bishops of the CHURCH OF ENGLAND sit in the House of Lords, as do the country's senior judges *(Law Lords)* even though in 2009 the UK Supreme Court replaced the House of Lords as the country's highest court. House of Lords judicial decisions were made by the judges alone on legal grounds; the ordinary members did not participate in these rulings. The presiding officer of the House of Lords is the *Lord Speaker*; he or she is elected by the members. The title of Lord Speaker is used even when the post is held by a woman.

Both Houses of Parliament can originate legislation but following a reform in 1911 the House of Lords cannot delay financial legislation. It can delay other legislation from the Commons, but its powers to do so have been greatly reduced. Government ministers must be in Parliament; although it is theoretically possible for a cabinet minister to be in the House of Lords this is unusual now, especially in the case of a senior minister.

Parliament is sovereign, which means that its powers cannot be restricted in any way, not even by a constitution that exists above it. It has power to legislate as it wishes, and a simple majority (50% + 1) of members voting in both houses can approve a law, even one that in other countries would be considered a constitutional amendment. The recent changes to the composition and powers of the House of Lords and the establishment of regional assemblies in Scotland and Wales have been approved in this way. Nevertheless, European Union law takes precedence over UK law.

The Parliament meets in the *Palace of Westminster*, a royal palace. The prime minister's official residence is at *10 Downing Street*, a building that contains a large amount of office space. *Buckingham Palace* is the official residence of the monarch. *Westminster, Number Ten* or *Downing Street,* and *the Palace* represent Parliament, the PM, and the Monarch respectively. Many government offices are on a street called *Whitehall* and that name represents the official administration or CIVIL SERVICE. Downing Street is a street off Whitehall. It has only three houses. Number 11 is the official residence of the *Chancellor of the Exchequer* (finance minister) and Number 12 is the official residence of the government *Chief Whip*, who is the internal manager and disciplinarian of the governing party.

See HOME OFFICE; FOREIGN OFFICE; TREASURY.

regional and local government

In 1998 the Westminster Parliament voted to establish representative assemblies in SCOTLAND and WALES; their members are Members of the Scottish Parliament (MSP) and Assembly Members (AM) respectively. The *Scottish Parliament* has considerably more power than the *National Assembly for Wales*. Northern Ireland also has its own assembly, under a law from 1999.

The traditional system is that the *mayor* of an English town or *lord mayor* of a CITY (*provost* or *lord provost* in Scotland) is not directly elected but is elected by the councillors from among their number and serves for one year as chairman of COUNCIL meetings and as the representative of the town or city at civic functions. Traditionally the *mayoress* is the mayor's wife, who is expected to assist him on social occasions; even if the mayor is a woman she uses the title of mayor and appoints a companion to assist her though the precise terminology in this case is not clear. Because the post is not directly elected, and is held for only one year, British mayors do not have the prestige and authority of mayors in other countries. London and Manchester have elected executive mayors and other cities may ADOPT this system in the future. The local government system is rather confused and impossible to describe in detail.

Do not confuse *mayor* with the army rank of *MAJOR*.

contamination & pollution

There is a certain overlap in the meanings of these words but **pollution** is the commonly used word for environmental pollution from industry, motor vehicles, and so on. The *polluter pays principle* is well-established in debates on environmental protection. The substances that cause *pollution* are *pollutants*.

Contamination refers more to the action of chemical or infectious agents on drugs, food, or water in production or processing. Milk can be *contaminated* by unclean dairy equipment. A wound can be *contaminated* by dirt. To sum up, a river can be *polluted* by pesticides reaching it, but if the pesticides are present in the food that reaches the shops, they *contaminate* it. A river can be *polluted* by waste products from a factory, but drinking water can be *contaminated* while it is being its processed. Clothing and other equipment used in nuclear plants is *contaminated* with radiation.

Decontamination is the only negative form; the word ~~depollution~~ does not exist.

continuous & continual

A distinction can be made between *continuous* and *continual*.

C

Continuous means *never stopping at all. A continuous tape* is one which when started will never stop playing; *The wind blew continuously from the east all day.*

Continual is used to refer to something that continues during a period of time, but is not *continuous. My neighbours argue continually.*

Nevertheless, it must be said that the distinction is not always clear and *continuous* is used in senses that would require *continual* from the above definition.

continuous aspect

This is sometimes known as the progressive aspect. Only dynamic verbs have the continuous aspect. It is made up of the verb *be* and the -ING FORM of the verb. All forms of *to be*, including infinitives, can be used.

	Active	**Passive**
present	*I am working*	*It is being done*
past	*I was working*	*It was being done*
future	*I will be working*	*It will be being done*
present perfect	*I have been working*	*It has been being done*
past perfect	*I had been working*	*It had been being done*
future perfect	*I will have been working*	*It will have been being done**
conditional	*I would be working*	*It would be being done*
conditional perfect	*I would have been working*	*It would have been being done**
infinitive	*(to) be working*	*(to) be being done*
past INFINITIVE	*(to) have been working*	*(to) have been being done*

*These forms exist in theory but are rarely used.

contractions

Contracted verb forms are used naturally in speech on all occasions; indeed, spoken English that does not use contractions sounds strange and unnatural, except when the full form is used for emphasis: *I will not pay.* They are also used in informal writing such as a letter or a note to a friend, which is written as if it were a spoken communication. Newspapers usually report news without using contractions, but individual columnists may use them to suggest a more personal relationship with the reader. The use of contractions in fairly formal writing seems to be growing.

The contracted forms of *be* and *have* are as follows:

I'm, you're, he's, she's, it's, we're, you're, they're. Past *wasn't, weren't.* The forms *'tis, 'twas* and *'twill* (for *it is, it was* and *it will*) are no longer used.

I've, you've, he's, she's, it's, we've, you've, they've; Past *hadn't.*

These can be followed by *not: I'm not, you're not, we've not* etc. The ALTERNATIVE forms *you aren't, they haven't* etc. can be used, but there is no such equivalent *I ~~amn't~~* to *I'm not.* There is a negative QUESTION: *Haven't you?* etc. In the first person of *be* this is *aren't I?*, not ~~*amn't I?*~~ See TAG QUESTIONS.

There's is the contraction of THERE IS and *there has (been).* The forms *there'll (be)* and *there've (been)* are also found.

Do has the forms *don't, doesn't, didn't.* These are only used when *do* is an auxiliary verb.

MODAL AUXILIARY VERBS make *can't* /kɑːnt/, *couldn't, mayn't*, mightn't, shan't*, shouldn't, I'll* etc., *won't, I'd, she's, he'd, we'd, you'd, they'd, wouldn't, mustn't.* There are also the forms *oughtn't to, usedn't to* (see USED TO), *daren't,* and *needn't.*

*Mayn't is practically never used; *shan't* is rare. See SHALL (*MODAL AUXILIARY VERBS).

Contractions can be used in WH- QUESTIONS: *When'll we arrive?; What're you doing?; How's your mother?; What's he do at weekends? (What does he do...)* and with *do: Where d'you live; What d'you think?*

AIN'T is a common non-standard contraction of *am not, is not, are not, have not* and *has not.*

Contractions can be attached to noun phrases: *The man next door'll be able to tell you; Someone here's been causing problems.*

possible ambiguity

Note that *he's, she's,* and *it's* are common to both verbs. There is no real risk of ambiguity. It is obvious that *Mary's a doctor* and *Mary's a blue car* are *Mary is* and *Mary has* respectively (though the use of HAVE in this way is unusual), and that the context will almost certainly make it clear whether *Mary's a daughter* means that she has one or that she is one.

In the case of auxiliary verbs there is no possibility of confusion: *Mary's working* can only be the contraction of *Mary is working* (the present continuous is made with *be + -ing*), while *Mary's worked* must be the present perfect: *Mary has worked* (*have + past participle*).

However, there is genuine ambiguity in the case of irregular verbs that do not change. In *He said he'd put it on the shelf* or *They said they'd set out at 10 o'clock* the contraction could be of *had* or *would*. Because of the difference in pronunciation *She said she'd read the report* is ambiguous in writing but not in speech.

See PUNCTUATION | APOSTROPHES | MISSING LETTERS.

control

In many languages this word has the idea of checking; it does not usually have this meaning in English except for *quality control,* and *passport control*. However, even there it is only used as a noun. As a verb, passports are *checked*.

In English this word implies some measure of power, authority or direction. Someone may have a *controlling interest* in a company (i.e. more than 50% of the shares), or *be at the controls*, or *lose control,* of a car or other vehicle; some vehicles have *dual controls*. The *control tower* is the place where *air traffic controllers* direct airport movements. If you are *in control* of a car, a situation etc., you have the power to direct its course; it is *under control*; otherwise it is *out of control*. In a scientific experiment a *control group* is one that is used for comparison with the group that is the object of the experiment.

cook(er)

Although the suffix *-er* usually indicates a person who does something, a *cook* is a person who cooks and a *cooker* is the apparatus, usually consisting of an oven and gas burners or electric hotplates, which is used in cooking.

corn

In Britain *corn* is any cereal; the commonest cereals in Britain are *wheat, barley, oats* and *rye*. Malted barley is used to make BEER (**ALE AND BEER*) and WHISKY; *OATS* (**PLURAL FORMS* | *NOUNS ONLY USED IN THE PLURAL* | *PLURALIA TANTUM*) are used to make porridge, a Scottish breakfast dish. In the USA, *corn* refers to *maize*; *corn flakes* and *popcorn* are American in origin and so use the name *corn*. In Britain this plant is called *sweetcorn* or *maize* but *cornflour* is maize flour. The seeds grow on a large cylindrical *cob*; the whole thing is called a *corn cob*, and when one is served whole it is called *corn on the cob*.

A *cornflower* is a blue flower that grows in cornfields.

A *peppercorn* is the individual grain of PEPPER that is ground for use as a spice.

Corned beef is beef that has been preserved in salt.

corps & corpse

The word *corps* /kɔː/ is used for certain organised bodies of people for a special purpose. It is especially used in the army e.g. *Intelligence Corps; Royal Army Medical Corps* but also in the *diplomatic corps* and the *press corps*.

A *corpse* /kɔːps/ is a dead body.

C

could
Etymologically there should be no *l* in this word, but the attraction of *should* and *would* was so strong that *could* displaced *coude* and is now accepted as the standard.

See AISLE; FOREIGN; GHOST; ISLAND.

council & counsel
Both words are pronounced /ˈkaʊnsəl/.

A *council* is a committee of people who meet periodically. It is the usual word for the governing bodies of local government areas: *parish/town/county council*; the tax collected and spent by these councils is the *council tax*. The *Privy Council* is the monarch's body of advisors (see CONSTITUTION). Members of a *council* are *councillors*.

Counsel is a SYNONYM of *ADVICE* but is less common. *Counsel* is a word for a BARRISTER *(*LAW)* (*my counsel* means *my barrister*). In the plural it is a PLURAL WITHOUT S. In the USA lawyers are addressed as *Counsellor*. *Counselling* is the process of giving professional assistance to people who have experienced severe personal, emotional, and/or psychological difficulties.

counties
The counties are the historical administrative divisions of England; they vary considerably in size and in the power of their councils. The word *shire*, pronounced /ʃaɪə/ when it is used alone, means a county and is sometimes used to refer to the rural counties in England. It forms part of the names of some counties, and is pronounced /ʃə/: *Lancashire* /ˈlænkɪʃə/, *Yorkshire* /ˈjɔːkʃə/. Not all local government authorities in the UK are counties. The system is confused and changes frequently.

See COUNTY & COUNTRY.

countries and nationalities
The **first column** in the table below gives the name of the country or territory as usually used in English. Any recent other name is given in round brackets e.g. *Cambodia (Kampuchea)*.

The definite article is used in the names of some countries e.g. *the Bahamas*.

The **second column** gives the adjective relating to that country. Where the noun referring to a person from that country differs from the adjective, the noun is given in square brackets e.g. *Spanish [Spaniard]*. Where the name of a country's national language relates to the name of that country, the language always has the same form as the national adjective e.g. *Albanian* is the language of *Albania* (but see the notes on *Arab/Arabian/Arabic* and on *Malaysia*). No other information about languages is given. Names of languages, like nationality adjectives, are written with CAPITAL LETTERS.

The **third column** gives the capital of that country in its normal English form. Other important cities, regions or geographical features which have specific English names are given in square brackets e.g. *Brussels [Antwerp, Bruges, Ghent, Liege, Ostend]*. These forms are widely used although the modern tendency is increasingly to use the form of the name in the language of the country. This column also gives geographical names from English-speaking countries which differ in other languages.

Apart from *The Hague* no CITY has the definite article in its English name e.g. *Cairo, Mecca*.

As there is no commonly recognised system of transliteration from some languages, especially Arabic, forms used by different publishers may vary.

This table is compiled on linguistic criteria to form part of this book. It includes recent former countries, dependent territories, disputed names and certain ethnic/national groups. It implies no political or administrative significance of any kind and none should be assumed from it.

country	adjective	capital and other places
Afghanistan	Afghan [Pashtun]	Kabul
Albania	Albanian	Tiranë
Algeria	Algerian	Algiers
Andorra	Andorran	Andorra la Vella

C

country	adjective	capital and other places
Angola	Angolan	Luanda
America (see United States of America)		
Antigua and Barbuda	Antiguan, Barbudan	St John's
Arabia	Arab/Arabian/Arabic[1]	
Argentina	Argentine, Argentinian	Buenos Aires
Armenia	Armenian	Yerevan
Australia	Australian	Canberra [New South Wales]
Austria	Austrian	Vienna [the Danube]
Azerbaijan	Azerbaijani	Baku
the Bahamas	Bahamian	Nassau
Bahrain	Bahraini	Manama
Bangladesh	Bangladeshi	Dhaka
Barbados	Barbadian	Bridgetown
Belarus (White Russia)	Belarus (White Russian)	Minsk
Belgium	Belgian [Walloon, Flemish]	Brussels [Antwerp, Bruges, Ghent, Liege, Ostend]
Belize	Belizian	Belmopan
Benin	Beninese	Porto-Novo [Cotonou]
Bhutan	Bhutanese	Thimphu
Bolivia	Bolivian	La Paz
Bosnia-Herzegovina	Bosnian	Sarajevo
Botswana	Botswanan	Gaborone
Brazil	Brazilian	Brasilia [the Amazon, Rio de Janeiro]
Brunei	Bruneian	Bandar Seri Begawan
Bulgaria	Bulgarian	Sofia
Burkina Faso	Burkinese	Ouagadougou
Burma (see Myanmar)		
Burundi	Burundian	Bujumbura
Cambodia (Kampuchea)	Cambodian (Kampuchean)	Phnom Penh
Cameroon	Cameroonian	Yaoundé
Canada	Canadian	Ottawa [New Brunswick, Newfoundland, Nova Scotia, Prince Edward Island]
Cape Verde	Cape Verdean	Praia
Central African Republic		Bangui
Chad	Chadian	N'Djamena
Chile	Chilean	Santiago
China	Chinese[2]	Beijing (formerly Peking) [Guangzhou (formerly Canton), Shanghai (unchanged), Xinjiang (formerly Sinkiang)]
Colombia	Colombian	Bogota
Comoros	Comoran	Moroni
Congo, See Democratic Republic of the Congo and Republic of the Congo		
Costa Rica	Costa Rican	San José
Côte d'Ivoire	Ivorian	Abidjan
Croatia	Croatian [Croat]	Zagreb
Cuba	Cuban	Havana
Cyprus	Cypriot	Nicosia
Czech Republic	Czech	Prague

C

country	adjective	capital and other places
Democratic Republic of the Congo (formerly Zaïre)	Congolese (Zaïrean)	Kinshasa
Denmark	Danish [Dane]	Copenhagen
Djibouti	Djibouti	Djibouti
Dominica	Dominican	Roseau
Dominican Republic	Dominican	Santo Domingo
Ecuador	Ecuadorean	Quito
Egypt	Egyptian	Cairo [Alexandria, Luxor]
El Salvador	El Salvadoran	San Salvador
ENGLAND[4]	English [Englishman/woman]	London [Cornwall, the Thames]
Equatorial Guinea	Equatorial Guinean	Malabo
Eritrea	Eritrean	Asmara
Estonia	Estonian	Tallinn
Ethiopia	Ethiopian	Addis Ababa
Falkland Islands	Falkland Islands[3]	Port Stanley
Fiji	Fijian	Suva
Finland	Finnish [Finn]	Helsinki
France	French [Frenchman/woman generic plural: the French]	Paris [the Basque Country, Brittany, Dunkirk, Normandy]
Gabon	Gabonese	Libreville
The Gambia	Gambian	Banjul
Georgia	Georgian	Tbilisi
Germany	German	Berlin [Bavaria, the Black Forest, Cologne, Munich, Nuremberg, the Rhine, Rhineland Palatinate, Saxony, Silesia]
Ghana	Ghanaian	Accra
Great Britain[4]	British [Briton]	London
Greece	Greek	Athens [Corinth, Crete, Macedonia, Thessalonika, Thrace]
Grenada	Grenadan	Saint George's
Guadeloupe		
Guatemala	Guatemalan	Guatemala City
Guinea	Guinean	Conakry
Guinea-Bissau	Guinean	Bissau
Guyana	Guyanese	Georgetown
Haiti	Haitian	Port-au-Prince
Holland (see The Netherlands)		
Honduras	Honduran	Tegucigalpa
Hong Kong		
Hungary	Hungarian	Budapest
Iceland	Icelandic [Icelander]	Reykjavik
India	Indian	New Delhi [Benares, Kolkata (formerly Calcutta), Chennai (formerly Madras), the Ganges, Kashmir, Mumbai (formerly Bombay), Punjab]
Indonesia	Indonesian	Djakarta
Iran	Iranian	Teheran
Iraq	Iraqi	Baghdad [Basra]

C

country	adjective	capital and other places
IRELAND or Éire	Irish [Irishman/woman generic plural: the Irish] (also refer to Northern Ireland)	Dublin
Israel	Israeli	Jerusalem [Bethlehem, the Dead Sea, Galilee, Nazareth]
Italy	Italian	Rome [Florence, Genoa, Leghorn, Milan, Naples, Sicily, Turin, Venice]
Jamaica	Jamaican	Kingston
Japan	Japanese[2]	Tokyo
Jordan	Jordanian	Amman
Kazakhstan	Kazakhstan [Kazakh]	Astana
Kenya	Kenyan	Nairobi
Kiribati /ˈkɪriːbæs/	Kiribati	Bairiki
Korea, North	North Korean	Pyongyang
Korea, SOUTH	South Korean	Seoul
Kosovo	Kosovan [Kosovar]	Pristina
Kuwait	Kuwaiti	Kuwait City
Kyrgyzstan	Kyrgyz	Bishkek
Laos	Laotian, Lao	Vientiane
Latvia	Latvian	Riga
Lebanon	Lebanese[2]	Beirut [Sidon, Tyre]
Lesotho	Lesothan	Maseru
Liberia	Liberian	Monrovia
Libya	Libyan	Tripoli
Liechtenstein	Liechtenstein [Liechtensteiner]	Vaduz
Lithuania	Lithuanian	Vilnius
Luxembourg	Luxembourg [Luxembourger]	Luxembourg
Macedonia (previously known as the former Yugoslav Republic of Macedonia (FYROM))	Macedonian	Skopje
Madagascar	Madagascan or Malagasy	Antananarivo
Malawi	Malawian	Lilongwe, Blantyre, Zomba
Malaysia	Malaysian[6]	Kuala Lumpur
Maldives	Maldivian	Male
Mali	Malian	Bamako
Malta	Maltese	Valletta
Marshall Islands		Majuro
Martinique		
Mauritania	Mauritanian	Nouakchott
Mauritius	Mauritian	Port Louis
Mexico	Mexican	Mexico City
Micronesia, Federated States of	Micronesian	Palikir
Moldova	Moldovan	Chisinau
Mongolia	Mongolian	Ulaanbaatar
Montenegro	Montenegrin	Podgorica
Morocco	Moroccan	Rabat [the Atlas Mountains, Casablanca, Fez, Marrakech, Tangiers]
Mozambique	Mozambican	Maputo
Myanmar (Burma)	Myanmar (Burmese)	Yangon (Rangoon)

C

country	adjective	capital and other places
Namibia	Namibian	Windhoek
Nauru	Nauruan	Yaren
Nepal	Nepalese	Kathmandu
Netherlands (sometimes referred to as Holland)	Dutch [Dutchman/woman generic plural: the Dutch]	The Hague [the Hook of Holland]
New Zealand	New Zealand [New Zealander]	Wellington
Nicaragua	Nicaraguan	Managua
Niger	Nigerien	Niamey
Nigeria	Nigerian	Abuja (former capital Lagos)
Norway	Norwegian	Oslo
Oman	Omani	Muscat
Pakistan	Pakistani	Islamabad [Karachi]
Palau		Ngerulmud
Palestine	Palestinian	[Jericho, the West Bank, the Gaza Strip]
Panama	Panamanian	Panama City
Papua New Guinea	Papua New Guinean or Papuan	Port Moresby
Paraguay	Paraguayan	Asunción
Peru	Peruvian	Lima
the Philippines	Philippine/Filipino [Filipino]	Quezon City
Poland	Polish [Pole]	Warsaw [Stettin, the Vistula]
Portugal	Portuguese[2]	Lisbon
Puerto Rico	Puerto Rican	
Qatar	Qatari	Doha
Republic of the Congo	Congolese	Brazzaville
Reunión		
Romania	Romanian	Bucharest [Transylvania]
RURITANIA **(see article)**	*Ruritanian*	*Strelsau*
Russia	Russian	Moscow [Archangel, St Petersburg (formerly Leningrad), Siberia, the Urals]
Rwanda	Rwandan	Kigali
St Helena	St Helenian	
St Kitts and Nevis		Basseterre
St Lucia	St Lucian	Castries
St Vincent and the Grenadines	Vincentian	Kingstown
Samoa	Samoan	Apia
San Marino		San Marino
São Tomé and Príncipe		São Tomé
Saudi Arabia	Saudi	Riyadh [Dammam, Dhahran, the Empty Quarter, Jeddah, Mecca, Medina, Yanbu]
SCOTLAND[4]	SCOTCH, SCOTS, SCOTTISH [Scot, Scotsman/woman]	EDINBURGH [LOCH[7] Ness]
Senegal	Senegalese	Dakar
Serbia	Serbian [Serb]	Belgrade
Seychelles	Seychellois	Victoria
Sierra Leone	Sierra Leonian	Freetown
Singapore	Singaporean	
Slovakia	Slovakian [Slovak]	Bratislava
Slovenia	Slovene, Slovenian	Ljubljana
Solomon Islands		Honiara

country	adjective	capital and other places
Somalia	Somali	Mogadishu
SOUTH Africa	South African	Pretoria [Cape Town, Johannesburg]
South Sudan	South Sudanese	Juba
Spain	Spanish [Spaniard]	Madrid [Andalusia, the Balearic Islands, the Basque Country/Euskadi, the Canary Islands, Catalonia, Corunna, Majorca, Navarre, Saragossa, Seville]
Sri Lanka	Sri Lankan or Sinhalese[2]	Colombo
Sudan	Sudanese[2]	Khartoum
Surinam	Surinamese	Paramaribo
Swaziland	Swazi	Mbabane
Sweden	Swedish [Swede]	Stockholm [Gothenburg]
Switzerland	Swiss[2]	Berne [the Alps, Geneva]
Syria	Syrian	Damascus
Taiwan	Taiwanese[2]	Taipei
Tajikistan	Tajik	Dushanbe
Tanzania	Tanzanian	Dar es Salaam, Dodoma
Thailand	Thai	Bangkok
Togo	Togolese	Lomé
Tonga	Tongan	Nuku'alofa
Transnistria	Transnistrian	Tiraspol
Trinidad and Tobago	Trinidadian and Tobagan or Tobagonian	Port of Spain
Tunisia	Tunisian	Tunis
Turkey	Turkish [Turk]	Ankara [Istanbul (formerly Byzantium and Constantinople), Smyrna]
Turkmenistan	Turkmen	Ashgabat
Tuvalu	Tuvaluan	Vaiaku
Uganda	Ugandan	Kampala
Ukraine	Ukrainian	Kiev
United Arab Emirates		Abu Dhabi
United Kingdom[4]	British	London
United States of America	American, United States[7]	Washington D.C. [New York, the Rockies]
Uruguay	Uruguayan	Montevideo
Uzbekistan	Uzbek	Tashkent
Vanuatu		Vila
Vatican City State		
Venezuela	Venezuelan	Caracas
Vietnam	Vietnamese	Hanoi
WALES[4]	Welsh [Welshman/woman generic plural: the Welsh]	Cardiff
West Indies	West Indian	
Western Samoa	Samoan	Apia
Yemen	Yemeni	Sana'a
Yugoslavia (also see former constituent republics)	Yugoslavian [Yugoslav]	Belgrade
Zambia	Zambian	Lusaka
Zimbabwe	Zimbabwean	Harare

C

notes

1 *Arab* (adjective) refers to the people and culture. It is also the nationality noun. *Arabic* is used for the language and ARABIC NUMERALS; *Arabia* and *Arabian* refer to the Arabian peninsula.
2 Nationality nouns are formed without change from all adjectives ending with *-ese*. They do not change in the plural, for example *Japanese*: *two Japanese, the Japanese* (generic plural). The nouns *Seychellois* and *Swiss* are also unchangeable.
3 All island groups which use their name as the adjective make the nationality noun with *Islander* e.g. *Cayman Islander*.
4 *The United Kingdom of Great Britain and Northern Ireland* is the correct full name of the country. See CONSTITUTION. Great Britain consists of England, Scotland and Wales. *Britain* is often used colloquially as the name of the country. As there is no convenient adjective from United Kingdom the adjective *BRITISH* is often used. It is incorrect to use *England, English* etc. when referring to Great Britain or the UK. The language, however, is always called *English*.
5 There is no adjective or nationality noun for all countries. In such cases we say e.g. *the government of the Central African Republic; a person from Guinea Bissau*.
6 *Malay* is the name of the predominant language of the country and is the adjective and noun used for the predominant ethnic group.
7 *United States* is used only in formal contexts such as *United States Consulate*. In other cases AMERICAN is used to refer to people and things of the USA, even though this seems geopolitically incorrect.

county & country

County is pronounced /ˈkaʊnti/.

Country is pronounced /ˈkʌntri/.

See COUNTIES; COUNTRIES AND NATIONALITIES.

couple & pair

A *couple* can mean simply *two*: *a couple of men; a couple of rooms*, or *about two*: *a couple of hours; a couple of drinks*.

Two people who are emotionally attached, married or not, are a *couple*.

A *pair* is two things that are identical, or that are regarded as one unit: *a pair of eyes, gloves, scissors, trousers, shoes*.

See PLURAL FORMS.

cricket

Cricket is a sport that was invented in England and spread throughout the Empire. It is played professionally in England between teams representing COUNTIES. The Welsh county Glamorgan is the only non-English county in the county championship. The full members of the International Cricket Council are Afghanistan, Australia, Bangladesh, England, India, Ireland, New Zealand, Pakistan, SOUTH Africa, Sri Lanka, the West Indies and Zimbabwe. There are 92 associate members.

Cricket is played between two teams of eleven players each. The *field* can vary in size but is roughly oval in shape. In the centre is the *wicket*, a well-kept piece of grass 22 yards (20.12 metres) in length. At each end is a structure also known as a *wicket* that consists of three wooden poles (*stumps*) 28 inches (71.1 cm) in height, with two small pieces of wood (*bails*) placed across the top of them. At each wicket there is a player with a *bat* who has to defend the wicket from a ball *bowled* by a *bowler* from the opposing team (the ball must be bowled with the arm extended fully, not thrown in the usual manner).

If the batsman hits the ball, he and the man at the other end run and change places as many times as they can do so without the wicket being broken by the ball returned by one of the *fielders* from the opposing team, with at least one of the bails being removed. The number of times that the batsmen cross counts as a *run* (point scored) for the batsman who hit the ball. If the ball crosses the *boundary* line on the ground, four runs are scored; six are scored if it crosses the boundary without touching the ground. A score of a hundred runs for a batsman is called a *century*; a batsman who is out without scoring at all is said to have a *duck*.

If the batsman fails to hit the ball and it breaks his wicket, or if he obstructs it with his body, or if the ball that he has hit is caught by a member of the fielding team, he is *out* and is replaced by another member of the team. When ten batsmen are out, the team's *innings* (see NOUNS | SINGULAR WITH -S) is finished and the teams change roles. As there must always be two batsmen, one is left *not out* at the end of an innings.

The game develops in *overs*, groups of six balls (eight in Australia) bowled alternately from each end of the wicket by different bowlers. In a professional game each side has two innings; an English county game lasts a maximum of three days, while an international game (a *test match*) has a limit of five days. It can easily happen that a game ends in a DRAW, especially if the weather is bad; cricket cannot be played in rain or bad light. There is a *one-day version* in which each side bowls a limited number of overs.

A cricket ball is hard and covered with leather. It is between 22.4 and 22.9 cm in circumference and weighs between 156 and 163 grams. Bowling the ball is a highly specialised skill. Usually, the *bowler* tries to confuse the batsman as to the path of the ball, and the place and direction in which it will bounce, and sometimes he tries to hit the wicket without bouncing the ball. On rare occasions bowlers may try to intimidate batsmen by aiming the ball at the man not the wicket. A cricket ball is bowled at up to 160 kph; *batsmen* wear protective clothing on exposed and sensitive parts of their bodies.

The game is traditionally regarded as representing the spirit of fair play; to say that something is *not cricket* means that it is not fair.

Croquet /ˈkrəʊkeɪ/ is a different game from cricket. It is played on a lawn by players using wooden *mallets* (large wooden hammers) to hit wooden balls through *hoops* (metal arches).

A *cricket* is also a jumping insect of the family *Gryllidae*.

crucifixion
This is from *crucifix* and is not written ~~crucifiction~~.
See -TION & -XION.

cry
The meaning of this is similar to *call* or *shout*: *A cry for help*; *She cried out in pain*. However, crying is often accompanied by tears, especially with babies, so it also has that special meaning and is often a synonym of *weep, wept, wept*.

culinary terms
Many traditional culinary terms in English come from French, though in some ways they have been anglicised: *sauté(e)d* /ˈsəʊteɪd/ *potatoes*, *blanquette* /blɒnˈket/ *of veal*, *chicken à la* /ˈælæ/ *king*. Note the combination of English and French terms, which is common in culinary language.

current(ly) & present(ly)
Current(ly) is used for something that is happening in the present but is not permanent: *My current car; Her current boyfriend; The current week's TV schedules; He is currently working in our Liverpool office.*

Present is a synonym of *current* (*My present car* etc.) but the adverb *presently* means soon, in the near future: *I will fax you the results presently.* Not ~~He is presently working in our Liverpool office~~.
See PRESENT & PRESENTLY.

C

curriculum & syllabus

A *curriculum* (plural *curricula*) is the list of subjects that are studied in a school. If a subject is *not on the curriculum* it is not taught. *Extra-curricular activities* are school activities that are not part of the school's curriculum, for example sporting activities, interest clubs, camps etc. A *curriculum vitae* (usually CV) shows a person's educational and work experience.

A *syllabus* is the detailed list of the content of the teaching material for each subject. Its plural should be the English *syllabuses*; it is not a Latin word and there is no etymological justification for the plural ~~*syllabi*~~.

custom, customer, customs & costume

A *custom* is a habitual action; *It is my custom to eat fish on Fridays*; this is rather formal construction.

Someone who buys something from a shop is a *CUSTOMER (*CLIENT & CUSTOMER)* of that shop. A dissatisfied *customer* may withdraw his *custom* and take it elsewhere.

To *customise* a product is to adapt it to the individual requirements of the customer.

The *customs* check is the procedure by which travellers must declare items that they take into a country; they may be required to pay *DUTY (*TAX)* on these items. The people who administer this are *customs officers*. In Britain this department is known as *Her/His Majesty's Revenue and Customs*.

A *costume* is clothing worn on special occasions. It may be national costume, or the costume that an actor wears on stage, or it may be a *bathing* costume.

See CLIENT & CUSTOMER.

cut

Cut is the general term.

Carve is used for cutting decorative designs or letters in wood or stone. It is used for cutting meat to serve for eating, but a butcher *cuts* or *slices* meat in the shop.

Chop is to cut by HITTING rather than with a knife. Meat and vegetables can be chopped into small pieces. A piece of meat cut through a bone is a chop (usually pork or lamb ribs, but leg chops are cut through the leg bone). An axe is used to *chop* wood.

Hack is to cut or chop very badly, inexpertly, inelegantly, or roughly.

Slash is to cut with long movements of a knife or sword; these movements are not precisely directed. See PUNCTUATION | STROKE OR SLASH.

Slice is to cut thin flat pieces of something, bread or meat for example. A *slice* is such a piece.

Cymru

Cymru /ˈkʌmri/ is the Welsh name for WALES. *Cymraeg* /kʌmˈraɪɡ/ is the Welsh word for Welsh.

D

d, D /diː/

The fourth letter of the alphabet. It is normally pronounced /d/ but is pronounced /t/ after UNVOICED consonants at the ends of words. Thus *mist* and *missed*, *past* and *passed* are HOMOPHONES pronounced /mɪst/ and /pɑːst/ respectively. The sound is made by placing the tongue on the alveolar ridge, which is just behind the upper teeth.

See -ED AND -ES, PRONUNCIATION.

dairy, diary & daily

A *dairy* /ˈdeəri/ is a place where milk is stored, processed and distributed.

A *diary* /ˈdaɪəri/ is a book for keeping a daily record of events and thoughts or a book for noting future appointments.

Daily is an adjective or adverb meaning *every day*.

See ADJECTIVES WITH -LY.

damage & damages

Damage is usually uncountable. *Damages* is the compensation which is paid in civil LAW to someone who has suffered defamation. See PLURALIA TANTUM.

dare say

I dare say (sometimes as one word *daresay*) means *I suppose, it is probable*. It is followed by a *that...* CLAUSE. The *that* can be omitted: *I daresay he'll be late. He often is.*

For *dare* as a semi-modal verb see MODAL AUXILIARY VERBS.

dark

Dark refers to an absence of light. It is *dark* at night, or in a space with no natural or artificial light. This may be relative rather than an absolute absence of light, so a *dark room* may be one that needs light for comfort but is not totally without light. Similarly, a *dark night* could be one with little or no light from the moon or stars. With colours *dark* means that a colour reflects little light: *a dark-blue shirt; the paper is dark brown*. It is the opposite of *light*. As a noun *dark* is found in expressions such as *before/after dark* (nightfall) and *a leap in the dark*. It can mean *depressing, sad, pessimistic* as in *dark future, the dark side of things*.

Gloomy can also be used to describe *depressing, sad, pessimistic* thoughts or prospects etc. Even when it refers to physical darkness, colours, or feelings, *gloomy* (and the noun *gloom*) always suggests melancholy or depression.

Dim refers to something that produces light or is illuminated but is weak. It is the opposite of *bright*. Applied to a person it refers to somebody who is not bright intellectually, who is rather stupid and slow to understand things. See CLEVER.

In relation to people *dull* too can mean *slow to understand* or *stupid*; it also means *uninteresting, boring*, as in the saying *All work and no play makes Jack a dull boy*. A *dull pain* is not intense. *Dull colours* are not bright, and *dull sounds* are distant and unclear. *Dull*, like *dark* and *gloomy*, means there is little light. It can refer to the weather: a *dull day* or *dull weather* has no sun but is not as dark or unpleasant as *gloomy* weather.

Murky weather is like *dull* weather but is more intense, with storms threatening. Someone's *murky* past or *murky* business affairs will be dubiously honest, and something that they will want to hide.

dates

Dates can be written in three ways:

Using either the cardinal number or the ordinal number for the day: *9 February 2018* or *9ᵗʰ February 2018* (twenty eighteen or two thousand and eighteen). Both forms are spoken in Britain as

D

the ninth of February. Either the day number or the month can be put first e.g. *9 February 2018* (more common in Britain), *February 9 2018* (more common in North America).

Using the abbreviated form of the month: *9 Feb 2018, Feb 9 2018*.

Using numbers: There is a serious risk of confusion here. An American would read 9-2-18 as *September the second*. In Britain it would be understood as *the ninth of February*. Americans talk of 9-11 (spoken as *nine eleven*) to refer to the terrorist attack in New York on 11 September 2001.

Commas (*6 April, 2018*) are not necessary in the date. There is no comma in the year number: ~~2,018~~.

days and months

days

The names of the days in English were translated from their Latin equivalents in the Old English period, sometimes using the name of the equivalent Germanic GOD instead of the Roman one.

Modern English name	Old English name	Germanic god	Latin name	Roman god
Monday	Mōnandæg		lunae dies*	(moon)
Tuesday	Tīwesdæg	Tīw	dies Marti	Mars (god of war)
Wednesday	Wōdnesdæg	Odin	Mercurii dies*	Mercury (messenger of the gods)
Thursday	Thu(n)resdæg	Thor	Jovis dies*	Jupiter (king of the gods)
Friday	Frīgedæg	Frigga	Veneris dies*	planet Venus
Saturday	Sætern(es)dæg		Saturni dies	Saturn
Sunday	Sunnandæg		dies solis	(sun)

*late Latin

days with special names

Some days have special names. *Maundy Thursday, Good Friday, Holy Saturday, Easter Day* (or *Easter Sunday*) and *Easter Monday* are the days of Easter. Easter Sunday is not a fixed date; it can be as early as 22 March or as late as 25 April.

Whitsun (sometimes abbreviated to *Whit*) is another name for *Pentecost*, the Christian feast that takes place fifty days after Easter. *Whit Monday* is a HOLIDAY in some countries. *May Day* is traditionally 1 May, though in Britain the public holiday is the first Monday in May.

Christmas Eve, Christmas Day and *Boxing Day* are 24, 25 and 26 December respectively. *New Year's Eve* and *New Year's Day* are 31 December and 1 January respectively. In Ireland, 26 December is called *St Stephen's Day*.

The *Sabbath* is the day in the week for rest and religious practice. For Jews it is from Friday evening to Saturday evening (Hebrew *Shabbat* שבת) and for Christians it is Sunday. The English word comes via Greek and Latin from the Hebrew, which means *rest* as can be seen in the related *sabbatical*.

See CHRISTMAS.

months

The English names of the months all come from Latin.

January	Janus	god of doors and beginnings
February	februa	a purification feast held in this month
March	Mars	god of war
April	Aprilis	ultimately from Greek Aphrodite
May	Maia Maiestas	Roman earth goddess
June	Juno	queen of the gods
July	Julius	Julius Caesar
August	Augustus	Augustus Caesar
September	seven	*
October	eight	*
November	nine	*
December	ten	*

*These names refer to the number of the month in the Roman calendar that was used before the Julian calendar was adopted.

See CALENDAR.

death

Dead /ded/ is the adjective. *Death* /deθ/ is the noun. *DIE* (regular) is the verb.

When a person dies, a doctor issues a *death certificate* stating the medical cause of death. Before this can be determined it may be necessary to have a *post mortem (PM)*, a medical examination of the body by a pathologist. If the circumstances of death are suspicious there may be an *inquest*, a judicial investigation by a judge who holds the position of *coroner*. When the legal and medical formalities have been completed, the body is released to the family. In legal language a person who has died is known as *the deceased*. The *funeral* is organised by an UNDERTAKER and usually takes place a week or more after the death. The body is placed in a *coffin* and travels to the funeral in a vehicle called a *hearse*. Sometimes the coffin is carried on the shoulders of people who act as *pall-bearers*. The people attending a funeral are known as *mourners*, from the verb *mourn*. The sense of emotional loss caused by the death of a loved person is *grief* (verb *grieve*). Newspapers publish *obituaries* describing the lives of prominent people when they die.

In over 70% of cases in the UK there is a *cremation* in a *crematorium*; this means that the body is burnt, and the word *cremate* is not used for burning in any other sense at all. After a cremation the *ashes* are kept in an *urn*. Funerals are often conducted by religious figures, even for people who were not very religious in life, but non-religious funerals are also practised.

Pass away is a common euphemism for *die*.

See CORPS & CORPSE; EXECUTOR, EXECUTIONER & EXECUTIVE.

The noun **death** can have a countable plural when it means CASES of death: *The number of deaths from the earthquake may exceed 10,000.*

A **deathly** silence is one that suggests death. Someone who is *deathly pale* is so pale as to look dead.

Deadly refers to something that can kill: *a deadly attack; deadly poison*. Something that is *deadly boring* or *dull* is extremely boring or dull. *Deadly nightshade* is a very poisonous plant; a preparation of it called belladonna is used in medicine.

Dead can have a meaning of *precise* or *exact*: *The total is fifty-six pounds dead; He arrived dead on 10 o'clock.* To navigate by *dead reckoning* means by calculating position from the factors of time, speed and direction, with no input of information from outside the aeroplane, SHIP, or other vehicle.

debt

The *b* is silent /det/.

See B, B; DOUBT; REDOUBT; SUBTLE; RECEIPT.

deduce & deduct

Deduce means to draw a conclusion from known information by a process of reasoning; to INFER *(*IMPLY)* it. This is known as *deductive reasoning*.

Deduct means to take away or subtract: *Income tax will be deducted from your salary*.

Both words make the noun *deduction*.

defender & defendant

A **defender** is someone or something that defends in general (for *Defender of the Faith*, see CHURCH OF ENGLAND).

A **defendant** is someone who is defending a civil law suit.

demagogy

This is pronounced /ˈdeməgɒgi/. The adjective *demagogic* is pronounced /deməˈgɒgik/.

D

dependant & dependent

Dependant is the noun referring to a person who lives at the support of others.

Dependent is the usual adjective. Thus a *dependant* is someone who is *dependent* on someone else: *dependent relatives,* for example, are *dependants*.

Similarly, a **descendant** is somebody who is descended from somebody else: *He is a descendant of Charles II*. *Descendent* is the adjectival form for something that is descending; it is rare outside scientific writing. This distinction is not always observed by native speakers.

See -NCE, -NCY AND -NT.

desert & dessert

A *desert* /ˈdezət/ is an area of land with no water or trees and little or no vegetation.

Someone's *deserts* /dɪˈzɜːts/ are what they deserve: *He got his just deserts*. It is sometimes used ironically to mean that his *deserts* were an unpleasant consequence of an irresponsible action.

To *desert* (verb) /dɪˈzɜːt/ means to leave or abandon a person or place completely: *He deserted his wife and children; A deserted village*. In particular, a *deserter* is someone who *deserts* from the armed forces.

Dessert /dɪˈzɜːt/ is a name for the sweet course of a meal.

See MEALS.

despite

Despite (one word) and *in spite of* (three words) are synonyms. They are prepositions and go with nouns: *He was wearing a coat despite/in spite of the sunny weather*.

See ALTHOUGH & DESPITE.

determiners

Determiners are words such as ARTICLES (*a(n), the*), possessive PRONOUNS (*my, your* etc.), or EACH & EVERY. They determine the reference of a noun.

deviant spelling

Sometimes words are spelled phonetically; this is especially done with a small number of words to make an impact in ADVERTISING.

EZ	easy (the name of the letter z is pronounced /ziː/ in American English)
hi-fi	high fidelity (sound recording)
tho	though
thru	through
tonite	tonight
Toys R Us	Toys Are Us
while-U-wait	while you wait

Tho and *thru* are American; the spelling *thru* began as part of an American spelling reform movement but never became accepted as the standard. See AMERICAN ENGLISH.

Dunno /dʌˈnəʊ/, *kinda* /ˈkaɪndə/, *gonna* /ˈgɒnə/, and *wanna* /ˈwɒnə/ are the written representation of the colloquial pronunciation of *I don't know, kind of, going to,* and *want to*. They are sometimes seen in representation of direct speech, especially in comics, but are considered very colloquial.

A similar but more common colloquial form is *cuppa* for *cup of tea*: *Would you like a cuppa?*

dialect and foreign accents in print

Some authors make major changes to the spelling of English words to represent ways in which the words in DIRECT SPEECH are spoken by characters who use non-standard English. The result can be ungrammatical such as *It don't matter* and possibly mystifying for a foreign reader. For example, in *Harry Potter and the Philosopher's Stone* Hagrid says, *'They say there's dragons guardin' the high-security vaults. And then yeh gotta find yer way…Yeh'd die of hunger tryin' to get out, even if yeh did manage ter get yer hands on summat'* (They say there's (sic) dragons guarding the high-security vaults. And then you['ve] got to find your way…You'd die of hunger trying to get out, even if you did manage to get your hands on something.)

devil & evil

The *devil* is the spirit of *evil*. However, despite this connection in their meanings the two words have no ETYMOLOGICAL connection. *Devil* comes from Greek διάβολος and is related to the word *diabolic*, while *evil* comes from an entirely separate Germanic root.

If you are caught *between the devil and the deep blue sea*, you are in a serious dilemma, faced with two choices both of which are unattractive.

Speak (or *talk*) *of the devil* is an expression used when a person who has been mentioned in conversation suddenly and unexpectedly appears. It is not in any way offensive.

dictionaries

There is a wide range of bilingual dictionaries available for English and many other languages and the only sensible advice to someone studying English is to buy one from a reputable publisher. For reference purposes a large one is obviously better than a smaller one; it will last for many years and new vocabulary, though obviously important, is comparatively small in proportion to the total.

The INTERNET has a large number of on-line monolingual and bilingual dictionaries for English and major international languages.

There are monolingual dictionaries that are specially designed for people who are studying or using English as a foreign language. There are also monolingual dictionaries intended for native speakers. These are not likely to be of interest to most non-native speakers, though very advanced students, teachers and translators may find them interesting and useful. However, it is important to mention the Oxford English Dictionary, one of the outstanding works in intellectual history; with over 500,000 definitions it includes every word that has been used in the English language in over 1,000 years (many of which are now obsolete) with a history of how the word has been used and quotations to illustrate its usage. The dictionary is published in 23 large volumes. It is available on CD-ROM and on-line.

Dictionaries contain a large amount of highly concentrated information; a dictionary entry must be studied carefully, looking for transitive, intransitive, and reflexive verb forms, whether a word is an adverb or preposition or other part of speech, and other details of usage. With bilingual dictionaries it is sometimes necessary to check the possible translations in the dictionary against their meanings in the other part of the dictionary.

dictionary words

Some words are found in dictionaries but are hardly ever used outside them. The synonyms *architectural* and *western* are almost always used instead of *architectonic* and *occidental*.

For *folkloric* see FOLK. For *milliard* see NUMBERS | BILLION. For *petroleum* see OIL.

die

A *die* is a device used for stamping coins or for moulding material into shape.

A *die* is also a small cube with numbers from one to six, used in certain games; the irregular plural is *dice* but this word is now used as a standard singular, *one dice, two dice*, and is more common than the singular *die*.

D

die & dye
Die, died, died means to cease living; the -ING FORM is *dying*.

Dye, dyed, dyed means to colour hair or CLOTH for example by chemical means. As a noun *dye* is the substance that is used in *dyeing*.

different
Different from is the usual collocation in British English; ***different to*** is very common but is illogically considered incorrect by some people. ***Different than*** is common in American English but is unusual in Britain. It is sometimes used with a CLAUSE, probably because of the similarity to a comparative adjective as in *The city is different than (it was) fifteen years ago; The city is bigger than (it was) fifteen years ago.* It seems unnecessary to rewrite the sentence as *The city is different from what it was fifteen years ago.*

direct speech
Direct speech is the reporting of the exact words that someone has spoken: *Jane said, 'I'm hungry because I haven't eaten all day.'* The words written in direct speech are enclosed in inverted commas, also known as quote marks. For further information on the punctuation of direct speech see PUNCTUATION.

The words which present the direct speech *(Jane said)* may be inverted if they are placed in the middle or at the end of the direct speech.
'I'm hungry,' Jane said 'because I haven't eaten all day.'
'I'm hungry,' said Jane 'because I haven't eaten all day.'
'I'm hungry because I haven't eaten all day,' Jane said.
'I'm hungry because I haven't eaten all day,' said Jane.

This inversion is unusual in sentences where the subject is a personal pronoun: *'I'm hungry,' said she 'because I haven't eaten all day.'*

It is impossible if the verb has an indirect object. The only possible forms are:
'I'm hungry,' Jane told me 'because I haven't eaten all day'
'I'm hungry because I haven't eaten all day,' Jane told me.
See INDIRECT SPEECH.

discover, uncover & invent
To *discover* something is to find something unknown: *Alexander Fleming discovered penicillin.*

To *uncover* something is to remove a cover from something which you know or have good reason to believe is there, to reveal something: *He uncovered the body; The newspaper uncovered the scandal.*

To *invent* something is to create something completely new: *Galileo invented the telescope.*

discreet & discrete
Discreet means *careful, tactful, unobtrusive*: *A discreet message.* Luis Buñuel made a film called *The Discreet Charm of the Bourgeoisie.*

Discrete means *separate, distinct*: *Discrete concepts.*

disease & illness
A ***disease*** is a medical condition with recognised symptoms. There are infectious diseases and autoimmune diseases. ***Illness*** refers more to a subjective perception of bad health. We talk of *mental illness*, though some psychiatric conditions may be found to have organic causes. There is a considerable overlap between the two words.

See ILL.

dismiss, fire (out) & sack
Dismiss is the formal legal term for ceasing to employ someone; it is personal and is usually for disciplinary reasons rather than for organisational or financial reasons (this is *making someone redundant*). ***Fire*** and ***sack*** are slang terms for this.

Dissenter and Nonconformist

In Britain these names refer to members of Churches other than the Roman CATHOLIC Church which are not part of the established CHURCH OF ENGLAND or CHURCH OF SCOTLAND. They include the Congregationalists, Methodists, and Baptists among others. These groups are sometimes known as the Free Church.

do & make

do

As a main verb *do* and *does* are pronounced /duː/ and /dʌz/. As an auxiliary verb in questions they have the weak pronunciations /də/ and /dəz/: *Do they know? Does he know?* or are elided in *Do you know?* /djʊˈnəʊ/ or /dʒʊˈnəʊ/ *What does he know?* /wɒtsɪˈnəʊ/

Do is used as the auxiliary in the simple tenses: *Where do you work?; I did not know that.*

It can mean *be sufficient or suitable*: £100 *will do for the weekend; That dress won't do for a wedding. That will do* is a colloquial way of saying *That's enough.*

It is used with work and actions:
Have you done your homework?
I've got a lot of work to do.
I did the preparation yesterday.
He did languages at university.
I must do the garden this weekend.
She's having her hair done tomorrow.
I JUST did bacon and eggs.

It means *make progress*:
Pat's doing well after his operation.
'How did you do in the exam?' 'I think I did well.'
He's doing badly. He would do better if he worked harder.
He was doing 200 kph when the police stopped him.
We did 300 km today.

It is used with gerunds indicating an action: *I'll do the shopping; She used to do a lot of swimming; Have you done the ironing yet?*

What do you do? means *What is your job?*

Do is used with these expressions: *a favour, a test, an exam, business, damage, good, harm, justice, one's best, one's duty, work.*

To *do without* something means to continue without something that was desired: *We will have to do without wine because I haven't got any and the shop's closed.*

make

Followed by an object *make* tends to have the sense of create or produce: *He made a model of the Eiffel Tower out of matchsticks; I'll make you a birthday cake. Making work* means creating it: *This change has made* (i.e. created, produced) *a lot of work for my department*, while *do* is concerned with the action: *We've done a lot of work on this new project.* Compare *What are you doing?* (what activity) with *What are you making?* (possibly to a carpenter asking *Is that a chair or a table?)*

Make is used in the sense of causing or forcing somebody/thing to do something; it is followed by the bare INFINITIVE (without *to*): *He made her cry; My boss made me stay late yesterday; Money makes the world go round.* But in the passive, the infinitive with *to* is used: *I was made to stay late again today.*

It can be followed by an adjective or noun to show the result of a process: *That made me angry; They made him treasurer of the club; He will make a good teacher.* ➤

D

Make can express the result of a calculation: *Two and two make four; I make the answer 34,600;* precise time: *What time do you make it? I make it 3:24*; and financial income: *He makes £50,000 a year; I made* (a profit of) *€2,000*.

Make is used with *an appointment, arrangements, an attempt, a bed, the best of,* CERTAIN, *a charge, a choice, a complaint, a decision, a difference, a discovery, an effort, an enquiry, an exception, an excuse, fun of, a habit of -ing, a journey, a loss, love* (see MAKE LOVE), *a mistake, money, the most of, an offer, peace, a phone call, a promise, a profit, room for, a suggestion,* SURE (*CERTAIN), *a trip, use of, war*.

To *make do with something* means to accept something inferior as a substitute for what was desired. *There is no wine, so we'll have to make do with water*.

dog collar

The clerical collar that is worn by ANGLICAN clergymen is sometimes referred to informally or jokingly as a dog collar. Unlike the collar worn by Roman CATHOLIC priests, in the Anglican collar the full white ring is visible round the neck.

See CLERK.

doom, fate, destiny & destination

In ancient Greek mythology the three Fates (*Clotho, Lachesis* and *Atropos*) were the goddesses who determined the course of human life. **Fate** is thus what will certainly happen because it has already been determined; this is seen in the expression *as sure as fate*. It refers to what will finally happen (or has happened) to a person or thing: *to decide* or *seal somebody's fate*; *a fate worse than death*. **Destiny** is similar in meaning but **destination** is different, referring to the place which is the end of a journey, or to which a person or thing is being sent.

Doom refers to a fate or destiny that cannot be changed and is unpleasant, implying destruction and death. The original meaning of the word had to do with irrevocable decisions and JUDGEMENT, and this is still to be found in expressions such as *the crack of doom* as the Last Judgement in the Christian religion. Thus a *doomsday machine* or *doomsday bomb* is one that could destroy all human life. *The Domesday Book* (thus spelled) is the name of the book composed by order of the Norman King William the Conqueror in the eleventh century, in which a record was made of all land with its value and owners, an inventory of the country he had conquered.

double consonants

pronunciation

Double consonants are pronounced identically to single ones; there is no long or double consonant pronunciation except in the case of:

1 words ending with *-l* that have the suffix *-less* such as *guileless* or *soulless*,
2 words ending with *-n* that have the suffix *-ness* e.g. *meanness* or *openness*,
3 words starting with /n/ that follow the PREFIX *un-*: *unnecessary, unknown*, and also *ennoble*. This does not happen with the prefix *in-*: *innovative, innocent*. For the pronunciation of double *s* see S, S.

doubling consonants after vowels

The rules for understanding when a consonant is written single or double in English are complicated but essential. The basic rule (though inevitably there are some exceptions) is that a single consonant is found at the end of a word and after long vowels; a double consonant follows a short vowel that is followed by another vowel. For examples of pronunciation see PHONETIC SYMBOLS. Here we are dealing with two different sounds, *the short vowel sound* and *the long or diphthong sound*, which is the same as the name of the letter in the alphabet.

When *y* is pronounced as a full vowel and is not the final letter of the word, its pronunciation is identical to *i*.

D

The short vowel sound is normally found in monosyllables which end with a consonant.

	short		long
/æ/	cat, hat, man, sad	/eɪ/	cater, hate, mania, station, table, danger
/e/	bet, fed, fell	/iː/	competed, depletion, meter
/ɪ/	bit, him, hymn, lid, dribble	/aɪ/	bite, hiding, icy, oblige, BIBLE
/ɒ/	Bob, fog, hop	/əʊ/	bone, hope, hoping, notion, noble
/ʌ/	but, CUT, fun, mud, shut	/juː/	acute, computer, mutilate, tube, union
/ʊ/	bull, pudding, pull, push, put		

For irregular pronunciations of these vowels in individual words, see the appropriate article for each letter.

Words ending in -*ition* are pronounced /ɪʃən/. For -*ision* and -*ission* see s, S.

It can be seen that when a single consonant is followed by another vowel, the vowel before it is made longer; it can be said that the following vowel changes the pronunciation of an earlier one. Compare *hat* and *hate*. The final *e* in *hate* is silent, as is usually the case with a final *e* in English, but it has a function. It changes the pronunciation of the *a* from /æ/ to /eɪ/. However, when the consonant is doubled, the short pronunciation is kept.

/æ/	fattest, manner, sadder
/e/	better, stemmed, stepping
/ɪ/	bitter, hidden, richer
/ɒ/	bonnet, hollow, hopping, hotter
/ʌ/	cutting, butter, funny
/ʊ/	fuller, pulling

This explains for example why *write* and *writing* have one *t* and *written* has two; why the *g* in *big* is doubled in the comparative *bigger*; and why the adjective *bitter* /ˈbɪtə/ is different from the noun *biter* /ˈbaɪtə/ from the verb *bite*.

The verb *hit* makes the -ING FORM *hitting*, while *bite* gives *biting*. It is important to remember that the spoken language developed before the written language and the spelling is a way of representing the sounds; a double consonant protects a vowel from the effect of a vowel that follows it because the *e* or *i* can work back through the effect of one consonant to change the vowel in *bite* or *biting*, but not through two in *hitting*, *hitter* or *bitter*. It is also clear that there is no need to double the consonant in for example *heating* because the vowel in *heat* is already long.

In words that end with a consonant followed by *l* and a vowel the *l* itself acts as a vowel *table* /teɪbl/, *title* /taɪtl/, *noble* /nəʊbl/; but *rabble* /ræbl/, *little* /lɪtl/, *hobble* /hɒbl/.

In words with that have -*ange* this is regarded as a single consonant: *danger, range, strange* /ˈdeɪndʒə/ etc.

Double *r* has the same effect as any other double consonant. Although *bare, here, fire, core, cure* are pronounced with a diphthong, such words as *carry, terrible, mirror, corridor, hurry* have a short vowel.

The letter *v* is never doubled: *giving, liver, never*.

Words formed from monosyllables retain that word's original vowel pronunciation: *fur – furry* /ˈfɜːri/; *tar – tarry* /ˈtɑːri/ but *hurry, tarry* /ˈtæri/ (a verb meaning *waste time, delay*).

To summarise, the use of double consonants and the pronunciation of words that contain them are two sides of the same coin; the spelling determines the pronunciation and the pronunciation determines the spelling. A native speaker can naturally pronounce these invented words: *laggen, hetting, finner, bolly* and *nubbery* as /ˈlægən/, /ˈhetɪŋ/, /ˈfɪnə/, /ˈbɒli/ and /ˈnʌbəri/, and can also write them correctly on hearing them spoken.

Although, as always, there are exceptions to this general rule, they are very, very few. They include *dove* /dʌv/, *have* /hæv/, *give* /gɪv/, LIVE /lɪv/ (*ALIVE), *driven* /drɪvn/, *risen* /rɪzn/ *done* /dʌn/, *gone* /gɒn/ *one* /wɒn/ or /wʌn/.

This rule is a basic point of English spelling. Without it, there would truly be chaos but an understanding of it shows that the spelling of *write, wrote, writing, written, writer* or *hide, hid, hiding, hidden* obey a rule of the language and are logical in relation to that rule.

Prefixes are not affected. For example, the Greek prefix *syn*- is /sɪn/ in *synergy*. ➤

D

double consonants with prefixes

Words that have come into English from Latin, and have Latin PREFIXES, keep the spelling of the Latin original. In words such as *admit, contain, inestimable, invest, precede, profession, obliterate, subvention* it is easy enough to recognise the prefix and root. When a root begins with the same letter as a final consonant of the prefix, this is written double: *adduce, connotation, innate*. The Latin prefix and root are clearly identifiable: *ad-mit, ad-duce; con-tain, con-notation; in-estimable, in-nate* etc. In Latin, however, the final consonant of a prefix sometimes changes so that it is the same as the consonant that follows it; for example, the prefix *ex-* becomes *ef-* before the letter *f* as in the word *efficient* (*ef-ficient*, where the *ef* represents the prefix *ex-*). In these cases English follows the Latin spelling and the consonant is written double in English, once for the last letter of the prefix and again for the first letter of the root; this is the reason why *efficient* (*ef-ficient*) has a double *f* but *deficient* and *proficient* (*de-ficient, pro-ficient*) have only one. Also, when these Latin prefixes are used before a vowel, the consonant is single as in *inoffensive* and *disappear* but if the root begins with the same consonant, it is double as in *innocent* (*in-nocent*) and *dissolve* (*dis-solve*).

There is no difference in pronunciation between single and double consonants; the only difference is in the spelling (but see PRONUNCIATION above).

The following list shows the prefixes that end with consonants; compounds are shown where the prefix remains unchanged (*admit* etc.) and, where appropriate, with the prefix assimilated to the following consonant (*accuse, appear*). Because of the number of words involved, only a few examples can be given for each prefix. Some of these words, *appear* and *summon* for example, have come from Latin through French.

ad-	*admit, addition, adapt*
ad- → *ac-*	*accuse, acclimatise, accommodate, accumulate*
ad- → *ap-*	*appear*
ad- → *as-*	*assimilate, assess*
com-	*combine, compound, commemorate*
com- → *co-*	*cognate, cohabit, co-operate,*
com- → *con-*	*concentrate, connect, constant, contain*
com- → *col-*	*collateral, college*
com- → *cor-*	*correct, correspond*
dis-	*dissatisfaction, dissect, disappear*
dis- → *dif-*	*different, diffident, diffuse*
ex-	*examine, extract*
ex- → *ef-*	*effervescent, efficient, effusive*
in-	*innocent, innovate, inoffensive, inoculate.* See note below.
inter-	*interdepartmental, interfere, international*
inter- → *intel-*	*intellectual, intelligent*
ob-	*obtuse, obsolescent*
ob- → *of-*	*official, offence*
ob- → *op-*	*opposite, opportunity*
sub-	*subordinate*
sub- → *suf-*	*suffocate*
sub- → *sug-*	*suggest*
sub- → *sum-*	*summon*
sub- → *sup-*	*suppose, supplement*
syn-	*synergy, syndicate, synagogue*
syn- → *sym-*	*sympathy, symmetry*

Note for *in-*: There are two separate prefixes with the same form. The negative meaning appears in *innocent* and *inoffensive* (where the double *f* represents the prefix *ob-*). In *innovate* and *inoculate* the prefix has the same meaning as the English preposition *in*.

The word *accommodate* has two prefixes (*ad* and *cum*), which have both been assimilated.

D

Clearly not all English words with these initial letters originate as Latin or Greek prefixes, so there are words such as *acute, coral, super, open* that do not have double consonants. Suffixes can similarly produce double consonants: *mean + ness* gives *meanness, hopeful + ly* gives *hopefully*.

doublets

Doublets are pairs of words from the same origin that have developed different forms and meanings: *glamour* and *grammar, radius* and *ray, tradition* and *treason*. Some doublets are surprising: *cloak* and *clock* both derive from Latin *clocca* (bell), in the case of *cloak* because of its shape.

doubt

The *b* is silent /daʊt/. See B, B; DEBT; REDOUBT; SUBTLE; RECEIPT.

Doubt refers to uncertainty over the existence of a present or past state of affairs: *I doubt whether he had enough money in the bank when he signed the cheque; I doubt whether the population of Spain is as high as 50 million; I never doubted that you would be here on time* and uncertainty as to whether a future event will occur: *I doubt whether we will have enough money to go on holiday next year; I don't doubt that this song will be very popular.* These ideas can be expressed with the noun *doubt*: *There is an element of doubt as to whether he had enough money at the time; The question of whether (or not) he had enough money is in (open to) doubt; There is no doubt he had enough money at the time; It is beyond doubt he had enough money at the time; I have no doubt that he had enough money at the time.*

The adjective *doubtful* means unCERTAIN: *It is doubtful whether we will arrive on time.*

Doubtless is an adverb meaning *probably*: *Doubtless he had enough money at the time.*

Doubt does not imply uncertainty between two or more courses of action: ~~I doubted whether it would be faster by bus or train~~ should be *I was uncertain/I didn't know whether it would be faster by bus or train.*

down/uphill etc.

Downhill and *uphill, downstairs* and *upstairs*, and *downstream* and *upstream* are not used generally to mean upWARDS and *downwards*. However, *upstairs* can mean *to a senior position in an organisation*; and *upstairs* and *downstairs* or *below stairs* were used to refer respectively to the employing family and the servants when people had living-in servants.

Downstream and *upstream* are used to refer to relative positions in a production or organisation process in which items or ideas flow.

dozen

For non-specific numbers it is natural to speak in English of dozens rather than tens: *Dozens of people arrived late; I've told you dozens of times.* However, with numbers it is more logical to use *tens*: *tens of thousands of people*.

See SCORE.

draw

The basic meaning of this verb is *pull, take, move*. The most common use of this word is to *draw a picture*. This refers to the action of moving a pencil on the paper to create an image; it is not the basic meaning of the word.

The cowboy drew his gun (he *took* it from his holster (the case in which it is carried); it does not mean that he made a picture of his gun).

Robin Hood drew his bow (he *pulled* the string to prepare to shoot).

Draw the curtains, please (*move* them to open or close them).

He hit me so hard that he drew blood (made me bleed).

May I draw your attention to paragraph 3? (*attract* your attention). ▶

D

I went to the bank and drew £100 in cash (I *took* £100).
A hundred years ago horse-drawn vehicles were the only means of transporting goods (vehicles *pulled* by horses).
They drew lots to see who would go for help (They *took* the lots from a container).
He drew a deep breath before admitting the truth (he *took* air into his lungs).
He drew his pen across the paper and said, 'That's all' (he *pulled, moved* his pen).

Students normally first learn that *draw* means *to make a simple picture with a pencil*, and are later confused by the wide range of apparently unconnected meanings of this verb. This meaning derives from the last example above.

The compound *withdraw-withdrew-withdrawn* means *take, move away*:
I'd like to withdraw £50.00 from my current account.
Her father withdrew his consent to the marriage when his daughter's FIANCÉ *received a five-year prison sentence.*
The buyer withdrew from the contract at the last minute.

There are associated nouns. *Draught* /drɑːft/ is the usual British spelling of the word but *draft* is standard in the cases shown below; *draft* is the standard American form at all times:

We won a cake in the draw at the church fête. (The winning ticket is taken from a hat.)
He put his papers in his drawer and locked it. (A drawer is a box that can be pulled out of a table or chest.)
It is clear that the drawbacks will outweigh the advantages. (A drawback prevents you from progressing.)
Please close the window. There's a terrible draught. (The air is moving through the room.)
He usually beats me at draughts. (The pieces are moved on the board.)
I prefer draught beer to bottled beer. (The beer is taken from the barrel.)
The SHIP*'s draught is five metres.* (The depth of the ship that is below water.)
The architect asked the draughtsman for a plan of the kitchen. (A draughtsman makes a drawing.)
I enclose a bank draft for $50,000. (A draft moves money from one place to another.)
The government may abolish the draft next year. (The draft is an *American* name for compulsory military service, for which young men are taken from the population.)
The game ended in a draw/The game was drawn. (The two teams moved to the same score; they drew level.)

To *draw up* a document means *to prepare a legal document*, a will, a contract etc.: *She instructed her solicitor to draw up a new will.*

Thus a document (of any type) which is in a state of preparation is called a *draft*: *I've completed the draft of your letter/I've drafted your letter/but I haven't typed it yet.*

If you *overdraw* your bank account, you will have an *overdraft*. (The PREFIX *over* means *excessively*.)

A *drawbridge* is one that has hinges at one end so that it can be raised to prevent people from passing, for example at the entrance to a medieval castle.

A *drawing room* is a comfortable room in a house; now people usually talk of a sitting room. It was originally a *withdrawing room*, the room to which the ladies *withdrew* after dinner.

drop & fall

Drop can be transitive or intransitive. *Fall* can only be intransitive: *I dropped the egg* (voluntarily or involuntarily); *The egg dropped/fell from my hand.*

dumb

In British English *dumb* means *unable to speak* (some people are *deaf and dumb*); in American English it means *stupid* (from German *dumm* = *stupid*). American English uses *mute* for a person who cannot speak *(deaf mute)*. This usage of *dumb* is found in Britain especially in *dumbing-down*, reducing the intellectual and cultural level of, for example, an EXAMINATION or the MEDIA.

dynamic and stative

Dynamic verbs describe an action: *do, sit, walk, work, write*. They have a CONTINUOUS ASPECT, which describes a current action or state: *I was sitting on the wall* and an imperative, which orders an action: *Sit there*. *Get* as a PASSIVE AUXILIARY is dynamic.

Stative verbs are not used in the continuous and imperative forms since the state that they describe is always valid (but see FUTURE CONTINUOUS *(*FUTURE)*): ~~I'm doubting/knowing that~~ are impossible.

Some stative verbs are *be, contain, belong, depend; have, own, possess, cost, weigh, resemble; agree, believe, DOUBT, know, understand; care, hope, like, love, want, wish*, and the verbs of sense and perception HEAR, SEE, *look, feel, smell, sound, taste, seem, appear* when they describe a state rather than an action. You *hear* or *see* something involuntarily because your ears or eyes perceive it (a state), but you *listen to* or *look at* something because you actively want to (an action).

Some verbs can be either dynamic or stative. When *think* means *consider*, it is dynamic: *I'm thinking of going to France this summer; Think hard. Where did you put it?* When it means *have an opinion* it is stative: *I think he'll pass his exam*.

He's having his dinner and *Have another look* are dynamic, but *He has three cars* is stative.

I'm living in a caravan is dynamic and suggests a temporary situation, but *I live in a large flat* is stative and suggests a permanent situation.

The verb *be* can be used in the continuous and imperative forms with dynamic adjectives. These are adjectives that do not refer to a permanent and unchangeable state; they refer to a temporary state that can, and probably will, change soon and that is in the control of the person who is behaving in that way. Thus we cannot say ~~She's being thin; I'm being tall~~ but we can say *Why is he being friendly to that woman?; Don't be noisy*. Adjectives that can be used in this way include (among many others) *ambitious, brave, calm, careful/less, cheerful, childISH, COMPLACENT, conceited, cruel, efficient, enthusiastic, foolish, friendly, funny, good, greedy, helpful, impatient, jealous, kind, loyal, naughty, noisy, obstinate, patient, reasonable, rude, SENSIBLE, QUIET, shy, silly, stupid, thoughtful, tidy, vulgar, wicked, witty*.

E

E

e, E /iː/

The fifth letter of the alphabet.

It is pronounced /e/ in monosyllables that end with a consonant: *bed, hen, egg, tell, lend*.

It is pronounced /ɜː/ before single *r* in monosyllables and stressed syllables: *her, jerk, prefer, Percy*. This vowel, written *err* is also used to indicate hesitation in speech. It is pronounced /ɑː/ in *clerk, sergeant, Hertford, Derby, Berkshire*; American English has /ɜː/ in *clerk* and *Derby*.

It is pronounced /iː/ in:
- be, he, me, THE (strong), we, YE.
- words with *ee*: *feet, bee, seem*, but *-eer* is pronounced /ɪə/: *beer, deer*.
- words with *ie*: *chief, piece*, but *-ier* is pronounced /ɪə/: *fierce, pierce*.
- words with *ei*: seize, receive, protein, caffeine, weird; but *heir* /eə/, *their* /ðeə/. *-eight* is pronounced /eɪt/: *eight, freight, weight*; but *height* /haɪt/.

It has its long pronunciation in words with *e[consonant]e*: *these, even, complete* have /iː/ but *-ere* is /ɪə/: *here, mere, sincere*; or /eə/ *there*.

A silent *e* at the end of a word is lost before an inflection or suffix that begins with a vowel: *write – writing; note – notable; late – later; nine – ninISH*. *Ageing* and *mileage* are exceptions: *singeing* (from *singe*) distinguishes the word from *singing*. Also, words which end *-ce* or *-ge* keep the *e* if the first letter of the suffix is not *e* or *i*: *changeable, danceable, noticeable*.

The *e* is kept before a consonant suffix: *achieve – achievement; late – lately; white – whiteness*.

For further comments on the pronunciations /e/ and /iː/ see DOUBLE CONSONANTS.

ea

This is usually pronounced /iː/: *beat, deal, east, feast, heat, team, yeast*.

In some words it is /e/: *bread, dead*, DEATH, *head, (in)stead, threat*.

In *break, great, steak* it is /eɪ/.

Ear is /ɪə/, but *bear* and *pear* /eə/; *earth, dearth* /ɜː/; and *heart, hearth* /ɑː/.

In these verbs the infinitive has /iː/ while the PAST SIMPLE and the past participle have /e/: *deal - dealt, dream - dreamt, lean - leant, leap - leapt, mean - meant, read - read*.

each & every

These are DETERMINERS that refer to individuals in relation to their membership of a group. They are often interchangeable: *There are twelve students in each/every class*.

These words take singular verbs: *Each/every class has twelve students*.

Each focuses on the separateness and individuality while *every* focuses on the totality: *I will read a list of words and I will read each word twice; I heard every word you said*.

Each (unlike *every*) can be used as a pronoun: *There are six classes and each has twelve students; Each of the classes has twelve students; The classes (each) have twelve students (each)*.

Each other refers to a mutual relationship: *We've known each other for ten years; We read each other's letters*.

Every can be modified: *Almost every student was examined orally*.

Every can mean *to the greatest possible degree*: *There is every reason to suppose that...; There is every indication that we will succeed*.

Every is used for intervals in a series: *I phone her every day* (not *each day*); *The exams are held every six months; Every tenth unit has a revision section*.

As well as its literal meaning *every other* means ALTERNATE, *every second*: *Every other week*.

Each and every is emphatic: *Each and every room was* SEARCHed.

E

each other & themselves
Each other implies a mutual relationship, whereas *themselves* is reflexive. *John and Mary saw each other* means John saw Mary and Mary saw John. *John and Mary saw themselves* means John saw John and Mary saw Mary; or John and Mary saw John and Mary.

earth, land & soil
Earth is the name of the PLANET on which we live; when listed with other planets it usually has a CAPITAL LETTER. Meteorites, rockets and artificial satellites *fall to earth*. The *earth connection* of an electrical machine is the connection that *earths* it to prevent its becoming LIVE *(*ALIVE, LIFE & LIVE)*. It can also be used as a synonym of **soil** for the actual substance on the earth's surface in which plants grow: *rich earth/soil*. In WH- QUESTIONS, *where (etc.) on earth* it provides emphasis. The -EN ADJECTIVE *earthen* is only found commonly in the word *earthenware*, the baked clay that is used to make simple cooking and eating utensils and flower pots.

Land is the part of the earth's surface that is not sea. A journey is made *by land, or by sea, or by air*, and aeroplanes *land* at the end of their journeys. It also refers to *land* as an expanse: *to own land, agricultural* or *building land*. Someone who *works on the land* is employed in agriculture. Your *native land* is the country or region where you were born; *-land* is a suffix in the names of many countries; *Land of Hope and Glory* is a patriotic British song sung to the music of Elgar's Pomp and Circumstance March 1 (op. 39). *Land's End* is the WESTERNMOST *(*COMPARATIVES AND SUPERLATIVES | SUPERLATIVE WITH -MOST)* point of land in Cornwall, the peninsula in the south-west of ENGLAND.

ease & easy
Surprisingly, these two words have no ETYMOLOGICAL connection despite their similar meanings; the development of *easy* has been affected by *ease*. *Easy* is mostly known as the opposite of *difficult* but like *ease* it has the idea of comfort or lack of effort. An *easy chair* is a comfortable chair and a *woman of easy virtue* is one who is sexually promiscuous, but *I'm easy* means *I don't mind, I have no preference between* ALTERNATIVES; *go easy* and *easy does it* mean *be careful* or *cautious* (*easy* is an ADVERB WITHOUT -LY here).

Ease can be a noun: *To do something with ease* is to do it easily, without difficulty; if you are *taking your ease*, you are relaxing. If someone *puts you/your mind at ease*, they remove any DOUBT or fear that you had.

It can also be a verb: *Her comment eased my mind. Ease (up)* means *become less severe or stressful*: *The rain/pain will ease (up) during the night; You're working too hard. You should ease up a bit. Ease off* means *disappear gradually*: *The rain/pain will ease (off) during the night*.

Unease and *uneasy* refer to mental or emotional states rather than to physical comfort: *I tried not to show my unease about the project; I have an uneasy feeling that this will be more dangerous than we expected*.

A *disease* is a medical condition.

As military expressions, *stand at ease* means with a certain amount of relaxation as opposed to standing at attention while *stand easy* allows a more relaxed position.

East, Far East, Middle East & Near East
These terms are used in English to represent the world as seen from a European viewpoint. Although they are widely used, they are geographically inaccurate for people in many parts of the world.

Someone who has lived or worked in *the East* is referring to *the* **Far East**: India, China, Indonesia, Japan, Korea etc. *The orient* is another name for this region, and *oriental* refers to the Far East; these terms are unusual and seem dated nowadays.

Before 1918 *the Near East* was the Balkan peninsula and the Ottoman Empire, while *the* **Middle East** was the countries of Persia (now Iran), Afghanistan, the Caucasus, and what is now known as Central Asia. After the collapse of the Ottoman Empire in 1918 the term **Near East** fell out of

E

general use and the emerging Arab countries between the Mediterranean Sea and Iran, together with Egypt, became known as *the Middle East*; however, archaeologists and ancient historians retained the term *Near East* to refer to the area otherwise known as *the Middle East*. Other European languages have names for this region that translate literally into English as *Near East*.

economic(al) and economics

Economic refers to the science of economics, as in *economic problems, economic growth, economic systems*.

Economical refers to the efficient use of resources without waste. Often these are financial resources.

Economics is the name of the academic discipline. A person who studies it or is qualified in it is an *economist*.

ecstasy

Note the spelling of *ecstasy*. It is not written with *x* or *-acy*. The adjective is *ecstatic*.

The amphetamine-based drug methylenedioxymethamphetamine or MDMA is colloquially known as *ecstasy* or *E*.

See HYPOCRISY.

-ed and -es, pronunciation

In general, the *e* is not pronounced in endings such as *lived* /lɪvd/, *ruled* /ruːld/, *washed* /wɒʃt/, *jumped* /dʒʌmpt/. Note that the pronunciation of the final letter *d* depends on the preceding sound. The last sounds of *live* and *rule* are VOICED, so the *d* has its normal voiced pronunciation. This is the case when the verb ends with any of the voiced consonant sounds: *rubbed* /rʌbd/, *bagged* /bægd/, *judged* /dʒʌdʒd/ etc. However, when the last consonant sound of the verb is unvoiced, the *d* loses its voiced quality (it becomes devoiced) and is pronounced as unvoiced /t/: *knocked* /nɒkt/, *passed* /pɑːst/, *mopped* /mɒpt/. Vowels are always voiced so when a verb ends with a vowel sound, the *d* is pronounced voiced: *bored* /bɔːd/, *played* /pleɪd/. However, when the verb ends with /t/ or /d/, it is impossible to pronounce the final sound immediately joined to it, and an /ɪ/ is introduced: *decided* /dɪˈsaɪdɪd/, *ended* /ˈendɪd/, *wasted* /ˈweɪstɪd/.

This rule only applies to verb formations; certain adjectives that end with *-ed* are always pronounced /ɪd/: *crooked, dogged, jagged, naked, ragged, rugged, wicked, wretched*.

Blessed is pronounced /blest/ and /ˈblesɪd/ respectively, depending on whether it is used as a verb or an adjective. *Learned* also has the two pronunciations; as an adjective /ˈlɜːnɪd/ it means *knowledgeable, erudite*, EDUCATED.

An *aged* /ˈeɪdʒɪd/ man; a man *aged* /eɪdʒd/ fifty; a well-*aged* /eɪdʒd/ wine.

Sometimes in poetry the *-ed* is pronounced for rhythmic effect; in this case it is often marked *-èd* in writing.

There is a similar rule for the pronunciation of the endings *-s* and *-es*. If the preceding sound is voiced, it is pronounced voiced /z/: *LIVES (*ALIVE)* /lɪvz/ (verb) /laɪvz/ (noun), *rubs* /rʌbz/, *rules* /ruːlz/. If that sound is unvoiced, it is pronounced unvoiced /s/ *hats* /hæts/, and if that sound is a SIBILANT, it is pronounced /ɪz/ *kisses, judges, boxes*. This variation is purely phonetic; it applies to *s* added to third-person present verb forms, to plural nouns, and to genitive nouns.

See PRESENT SIMPLE *(*PRESENT TENSES)*.

Edinburgh

This is the capital of SCOTLAND. It is pronounced /ˈedɪnbʌrə/, /ˈedɪnbrə/ or even /ˈedɪmbrə/. *Burgh* is the Scots equivalent of the English *borough* /ˈbʌrə/.

See G, G | GH, GH.

E

educated

In English this refers to academic education as learnt in schools and universities rather than to a person's level of cultural knowledge or to his attitudes towards other people, where we say *cultured* and *polite* respectively.

The process of managing children, providing food and shelter, and teaching them social behaviour as well as more intellectual learning is *bringing up*. Someone who is *well brought up* behaves well with other people; someone who is *well educated* has been to good schools and perhaps university. There is clearly some overlap between the two.

-ee

In general the suffix *-ee* has a passive sense: an *employee* is a person who is employed, an *amputee* is a person who has had a limb amputated, an *addressee* is the person to whom a letter is addressed, a *franchisee* is someone who holds a franchise, and a *trainee* is a person who is being trained. A *payee* is a person to whom a cheque is payable (not in general a person to whom money is paid) and a *trustee* is a person who is trusted to keep or manage something, especially property or money. However, there are cases where it has an active meaning: an *attendee* (also *attender*) attends a meeting; a *refugee* wants protection; and an *escapee* escapes from prison. *Grandee*, an important, eminent or powerful person, comes from the Spanish title *grande* (a high-ranking nobleman).

See FIANCÉ(E).

e.g. & i.e.

These should not be confused.

e.g. (Latin for *exempli gratia*) means *for example*: Tropical FRUITS *e.g. mango, pawpaw and avocado*.

i.e. (Latin for *id est*) means *that is to say* and introduces an explanation: *Tropical fruits i.e. those that grow in hot countries*.

They are spoken and written as the names of the letters; the full forms are not used but are given here for reference.

See ABBREVIATIONS (a.m. and p.m.)

either and neither

These words have two different pronunciations: /ˈaɪðə/ and /ˈnaɪðə/; /iːðə/ and /ˈniːðə/. Both forms are used in British English; the latter pronunciation (with /iː/) is standard in American English.

as adverbs

According to prescriptive GRAMMAR these words can be used only with two alternatives: *Either John or Bill has written this*. However, they are easily used with three:
1 *Either John or Bill or Arthur has written this.*
2 *Neither Margaret nor Mary nor Joan was at the meeting.*

Note that **1** can be rewritten as *(One of) John or Bill...*, but that there is no equivalent for **2**. *None of Margaret...* does not seem satisfactory. An alternative, which is not universally accepted, is *Margaret was not at the meeting, (and) nor was Mary or Joan*.

A sentence such as *Mary's either out or (she) can't hear the phone* is considered by some people as INVALID because the two alternatives following *either* and *or* are not grammatically equal. To achieve this equality, the sentence should be rewritten as *Either Mary's out or she can't hear the phone*, where *Mary's out* and *she can't hear the phone* are equal CLAUSES. This is preferable in a formal style, but the former is common in colloquial use.

as a negative form of too.

'I know John.' 'I know him too.'
'I don't know John.' 'I don't know him either.'

'I know John.' 'So do I.'
'I don't know John.' 'Neither/Nor do I.' (Both are correct.)

E

Other modal verbs can be used:
'John will be there.' 'So will I.'
'I can't speak Russian.' 'Neither/Nor can John.'
See SHORT ANSWERS.

as pronouns
On either side of the gate means *on each side/on both sides*; it is the dual equivalent of *all* for three or more: *There were CORNfields on either side of the river*. The negative is *There were cornfields on neither side of the river*. However, *He was told he could stand on either side of the gate* means that it was not important which side he chose to stand on. Another example would be *There are two dictionaries on the shelf. Either (one) (of them) will give you the information you want.*

elder and eldest

These are comparative and superlative forms of *old*, used to describe family relationships; they are never used with *than*. For example *John is my elder brother; He is the eldest of six children* but *My brother is older than* (not ~~elder than~~) *I am.*

These forms are sometimes used to distinguish father and son: *William Pitt the Elder*, the Earl of Chatham, was a senior eighteenth-century British politician. His son *William Pitt the Younger* became prime minister in 1783 at the age of 24. An *elder statesman* is someone who has a lot of experience, especially in politics, and can give advice but has little direct responsibility or authority. *Elder/eldest* can only refer to people.

Officials in the Presbyterian and Mormon Churches are called *elders*.

Elder is also the name of a plant; *elderflower* and *elderberry* are used for making jelly and wine.

elections

In a British parliamentary election each party chooses a *candidate* in each *constituency* (as the electoral districts are known). Independent candidates can stand but are rarely elected. The *candidate* must appoint an *agent* as his/her legal representative and must pay a *deposit* of £500, which is refunded if he/she gains more than 5% of the votes; otherwise the deposit is lost. In the *election campaign* the candidates and their supporters *canvass* public opinion, that is they try to attract support, usually by visiting *voters* and explaining their POLICIES.

On *polling* (election) *day* the voters *go to the polls*. The *polling station* (voting place) is usually in a school and the voter marks a *ballot paper* by placing a cross against the name of his/her preferred candidate and placing the paper in a *ballot box* (a square black metal box). When *the polls close*, the ballot boxes are taken to the counting centre, which is usually the Town Hall, the *votes* that have been cast for each candidate are counted, and the candidate who has the largest number of votes is elected. If the result is close, a candidate or *agent* can ask for a *recount*. When the result is agreed, the *returning officer*, who is responsible for running the election (and is the MAYOR *(*MAJOR)*, or a member of the council, or an official), *declares the result* and the name of the elected *member of parliament* (MP).

The number of votes by which the winner leads the second-placed candidate is the *majority*. In elections for local *councils*, the system is the same but the electoral districts are called *wards* and the person who is declared elected is a *councillor*.

A typical result in a parliamentary election for a fictional Welsh constituency might look as follows.

Constituency of Llareggub	
Jones D (LD)	20,497
Evans J (Lab)	15,356
Rhys Gruffydd I (PC)	6,892
Watkin-Wynn A (C)	5,947
Majority	5,141

LD: Liberal Democrat **Lab**: Labour
PC: Plaid Cymru (Welsh Nationalist)
C: Conservative

If a member of parliament or a councillor dies or retires from politics during a parliament, a BY-*election* is called in that constituency to elect the new MP or councillor. The procedure is as described above. In elections to the Scottish Parliament, the Welsh Assembly and the European Parliament, and also in towns and cities that have directly elected MAYORS *(*CONSTITUTION | REGIONAL AND LOCAL GOVERNMENT)*, a proportional system is used for counting the votes and members are elected from a party list. In such elections there is no by-election and the next person on the party list is chosen to fill a casual vacancy.

ellipsis

This is the omission of certain words which can be clearly understood from the context. For example, *Thank you* is an elliptical form of *I/we thank you*. In *I didn't tell him yesterday but I will (tell him) tomorrow* the second *tell him* is usually ellipted (i.e. omitted).

Ellipsis is the term for the three dots (…) that indicate an omission in a quotation.

else

Else means **a)** *in addition*: *Do you want anything else?; Nobody else wanted to come* or **b)** *instead, different*: *What else could I have done?; I couldn't find John but someone else told me that…; Where else can they be?*

Else can follow *some-, any-, no-* forms (*somebody, anywhere, nothing* etc.) The genitive is made with *else's*: *Who else's car did you see?*

Somewhere else and *elsewhere* mean in some undefined place other than the one in question: *Your umbrella isn't here. It must be somewhere else/elsewhere*. But *elsewhere* also means *in* or *to all other places*: *There will be rain in the north; elsewhere it will be sunny*.

Else can follow ALL used as a pronoun, especially in *if all else fails*. As a conjunction, *else* (usually *or else*) makes a clear ALTERNATIVE. Alone, it is used as a threat: *Don't do that again, or else!*

email

In *email* addresses the *domain name* may be that of an INTERNET *service provider* (ISP) or it may be a private domain, so that an address could be

myname@isp.com spoken as *my name (one word) at I S P dot com*
or
my.name@domain.com spoken as *my dot name at domain dot com*
or
my_name@domain.com spoken as *my underSCORE name at domain dot com*

@ is a traditional English symbol to represent the preposition *at*, so its ADOPTION *(*ADAPT & ADOPT)* for use in email addresses was perfectly logical. *Email* users refer to the normal postal system as *snail-mail*.

When a reply is made to an email, an English-language system will place RE before the subject of the mail. A mail that has been received and is being sent to another person, is *forwarded* and the letters FW will be seen in the subject line. A *copy* (CC) or a *blind copy* (BCC) of a mail can be sent. These letters stand for *(blind) carbon copy* or *courtesy copy* and relate to the times when carbon paper was used for making copies of letters.

See ATTACH & ENCLOSE; SPAM.

emergence & emergency

Emergence is the process of emerging. An *emergency* is an urgent situation of risk or danger.

See -NCE, -NCY AND -NT.

employ & use

Employ is the word that is used of people who are paid for their work, especially on a regular contracted basis. Other forms are *employer, (un)employed, (un)employment*. An *employee* is a person who is employed (see -EE). In other senses *use* is now more common. If someone feels that they are being *used*, they feel manipulated or exploited unfairly.

-en adjective suffix

The suffix *-en* can be added to nouns to indicate the material that something is made of: *a woollen sweater; a wooden staircase*. Usually the *-en* form is figurative or metaphorical while the name of the material is literal.

E

a gold watch   a golden opportunity
a silk tie   silken skin
a lead weight   a leaden sky
a brass candlestick   brazen rudeness

Flaxen can describe yellow hair and *earthenware* is the name for pots made from clay. Other *-en* adjectives e.g. *leathern, oaken, silvern, wheaten* are archaic.

See -EN VERB SUFFIX.

engage

This basically means to *commit* or *promise*, and is generally used in the passive voice. Nowadays it is almost always used to mean engaged (i.e. committed) to marry somebody, although in the nineteenth century it was used more widely for social and professional commitments. The period of time when two people are engaged is their *engagement*. See MARRIAGE & WEDDING. It can also mean the action of finding people to work and starting to employ them (not the state of employing somebody): *I advise you to engage a good lawyer*.

In mechanical terms, it means to bring one part of a machine into operation with another: to *engage* first gear in a car; a phone number is *engaged* if it is in use when you dial it.

Somebody can be *engaged in a correspondence* on a certain matter, and troops can *engage the enemy* (come into battle).

England, a brief history

See the note for history articles on page xv.

In prehistoric times Britain was occupied by Celtic tribes. The Romans, led by Julius Caesar, invaded in 55 and 54 BC but were defeated; Claudius successfully invaded in AD 43 and established a permanent presence, with Britannia being incorporated as a province of the empire. When Rome was sacked by barbarians in 455 AD, the Roman legions left Britannia and Germanic tribes from the east invaded to fill the power vacuum. It is probable that the King Arthur legend is based on the activities of a leader of the resistance to this Germanic invasion. Apart from archaeological remains and the basic layout of the road system radiating from London, there are no present-day remains, physical or cultural, of the Roman occupation.

These invaders (Vikings from Scandinavia and Angles and Saxons from the mouth of the Rhine, **not** from modern Saxony) had no written records and used wood for their buildings so that very few archaeological remains are to be found. This period is known as the Dark Age. Later, England was administered centrally as a Saxon kingdom.

In 1066 William Duke of Normandy (the Conqueror) invaded from northern France. This invasion caused profound social change, in particular the introduction of the feudal system and major changes to the language as the French of the conquerors mingled with the English of the native population. The feudal system was moderated by a rebellion by the barons against King John in 1215, when they forced him to sign Magna Carta, giving them certain privileges. The Normans did not conquer Scotland, but they fortified parts of Wales, using it as a base to conquer Ireland. As they had lands on both sides of the Channel, there was considerable contact with France; the possession of the Channel Islands (Jersey, Guernsey, Alderney and Sark) by the British Crown dates from this time. However, in time the two countries separated and Calais, the last English possession on the French mainland, was lost in 1558.

After a civil war in the fifteenth century between the rival claimants of Lancaster and York, the Welsh lord Henry Tudor, who had a distant claim through the Lancastrians, won the throne. This war, really a long series of conflicts, was called The Wars of the Roses as the red rose was the symbol of the Lancastrians while the Yorkists' rose was white.

Henry's son, Henry VIII, was a popular, handsome king, with considerable artistic talent. He wrote a book on theology for which Pope Leo X gave him the title Defender of the Faith. Henry was married to a Spanish princess, Catherine of Aragon; she bore two sons and four daughters but only one daughter, who later became Queen Mary Tudor, survived infancy. Henry's desperation for a male heir led to his desire to divorce Catherine in favour of his mistress Anne Boleyn. The Pope refused an annulment, causing Henry to break with the Roman Church and establish the CHURCH OF

ENGLAND with himself as head in order to marry Anne, who bore him a daughter, later Queen Elizabeth, and a stillborn son. Henry's six marriages were all in the hope of siring a male heir to continue the dynasty; his only surviving son, who reigned as Edward VI, was caught up in the political and religious instability that followed Henry's death until the accession of Elizabeth. Her reign was characterised by great domestic concern at the political problems of a Protestant nation surrounded by CATHOLIC powers, and seaborne expansion which led to conflict with other countries, especially Spain. On her death in 1603 the throne passed to King James VI of Scotland who also became James I of England. See GUY FAWKES NIGHT.

In 1642 a civil war broke out. This was a power struggle between King Charles I (James I's son) and the forces of Parliament led by Oliver Cromwell. The Parliamentary victory was eventually to allow a greater degree of freedom and accountability than had been the case with Charles, who believed in the divine right of kings, but the immediate consequence was little more than a dictatorship by Cromwell. Charles II was restored to the throne in 1660 and was succeeded by his brother James II. James was a French puppet and foolishly tried to reintroduce Catholicism as the national religion. This proved so unpopular that Parliament sacked him in 1689 and invited the Dutch Protestant William of Orange, whose wife Mary was the Stuart claimant, to invade the country and win the crown from James, which he did. From this point the Protestant settlement was established and Catholics were not allowed to hold public office until 1830.

In 1714 the Crown passed to George, Elector of Hanover. He spoke no English, which led to an increase of power for his ministers and thus for Parliament. Parliament also solved his financial problems by taking over his land in return for an annual payment. This further strengthened Parliament's position against the Crown. The eighteenth century saw a great expansion in trade, but also the loss of the rebellious American colonies in 1776.

The French Revolution led to enormous fear in Britain both that there might be a similar revolution and that France might invade. Both fears proved groundless, and Britain's defeat of France at Trafalgar and Waterloo established the country's superpower status, with total domination of the seas and a rapidly expanding empire throughout the nineteenth century. This expansion was enhanced by Britain's leadership in the Industrial Revolution. The reign of Queen Victoria became known for strict public and private morality and for scientific, technological and philosophic advance.

In the early twentieth century war with Germany was inevitable, and the First World War destroyed not only millions of lives but a way of life that in some parts had changed little since medieval times. The rise of the LABOUR PARTY led to the eclipse of the LIBERAL PARTY as the radical opposition to the CONSERVATIVES. The Empire was weakened politically and economically but actually reached its greatest extent in the 1920s; however, there was agitation for independence in India, which was finally achieved in 1947 in the aftermath of World War II.

In World War II Britain was the only non-neutral country in Europe not to be occupied by Germany and the price of this resistance was high. After the war India was clearly untenable, and other Imperial territories became independent in the 1950s and 1960s to the extent that, except for the special case of Northern Ireland, there is no territory in the world under British political control which wishes to be independent. The newly independent countries remain in association with Britain through the COMMONWEALTH.

As a nuclear power Britain played an important role in the Cold War, but with the collapse of Communism in 1989 Britain's world role as an independent nation has declined. Closer involvement with the European Union is seen by many as the necessary future for Britain but others, still nostalgic for Britain's imperial past, are unhappy about forming closer ties with European countries. On 23 June 2016 a referendum to leave the EU was won by a margin of 52% to 48%, initiating a process known as Brexit (a BLEND of Britain and exit). At the time of writing (July 2018) the UK is close to leaving the EU.

See IRELAND, A BRIEF HISTORY; SCOTLAND, A BRIEF HISTORY; ROMAN INFLUENCE IN BRITAIN; WALES, A BRIEF HISTORY.

E

English language, a brief history

The origins of the English language lie in the invasion of England by Germanic tribes as the Roman Empire withdrew. The different linguistic origins of these peoples explain some of the differences in modern English, especially in Scotland.

As political power became centred in the south of England, the version of the language spoken there became dominant until in 1066 the French-speaking Normans conquered the country, breaking a linguistic development that would otherwise have led to a modern language rather like Dutch. As a result of the Norman invasion many of the inflections on English nouns, adjectives and verbs were lost (see CASE, GRAMMATICAL) as a simplified version of the language was developed and a large number of French words were incorporated. The use of London as the capital established the language of the south-east as the standard, and the introduction of printing in 1475 by William Caxton helped to standardise the written language. At that time spelling and pronunciation were fairly consistent, but later changes in standard spelling were insufficient to reflect changes in pronunciation. The Enlightenment in the eighteenth century saw the introduction of a number of Latin and Greek words, especially related to sophisticated intellectual activities, and the expansion of the Empire in the nineteenth and twentieth centuries brought more words into English from many other languages.

The effects of this history on modern English are clear to see. The loss of inflections led to English having great flexibility in word forms; the same word can be a noun or a verb. An *email* is a noun, but in *I'll email the report to you* it is a verb. This flexibility is possible because English, unlike other European languages, has lost the inflection that marks the infinitive of a verb and most of the inflections for tense and person.

The introduction of words of Latin and Greek origin into a language that is basically Germanic has produced a language with a very wide vocabulary and a number of examples of synonyms. *Kingly*, *royal* and *regal* (Germanic, medieval French and direct from Latin respectively) are all adjectives relating to *king*.

See AMERICAN ENGLISH.

enjoy

This verb is transitive. In the sense of *have fun* it is REFLEXIVE: *Did you enjoy yourself at the party?* Otherwise its direct object is a noun: *He enjoys life* or the GERUND of a verb: *I enjoyed talking to her.* In a weaker sense it means *to have something and use it beneficially*: *We have always enjoyed good RELATIONS with our neighbours.* Sometimes this is done ironically as in *She enjoys poor health*.

Unlike LIKE and *love*, *enjoy* is a DYNAMIC VERB: *I was enjoying myself until John arrived.*

enterprise

An enterprise is a risky or dangerous UNDERTAKING that might lead to great profit or advantage. The word is sometimes used in business and finance, especially for an unusual kind of structure, but the common word for a trading body is COMPANY. Nevertheless, the term *small and medium size enterprise (SME)* is increasingly common.

entrance & entry

Both of these mean the action of coming or going into a place. **Entrance** /ˈentrəns/ is used to refer to an actor appearing on the stage. They also mean the place where something, for example a building, a park or a harbour, is entered. An *entrance fee* is the money paid to enter a museum, exhibition, or other institution.

An **entry** is also a small passage between two houses. In accounts and other records that are kept in lists each separate item is called an *entry*. *Double-entry book-keeping* is the standard. A separate item in a diary is an *entry*.

As a verb **entrance** /enˈtrɑːns/ means to charm or enchant or delight with a feeling that can be so strong as to be overwhelming. It comes from the noun *trance* and is not COGNATE with the noun *entrance*.

E

-en verb suffix

Some monosyllabic adjectives can add the suffix *-en* to make verbs: *blacken* means *to make or become black* (transitive and intransitive). The commonest examples are *blacken, brighten, BROADen, cheapen, coarsen, dampen, darken, DEADen, deafen, deepen, FASTen, fatten, flatten, freshen, gladden, harden, lessen, lighten, liken, loosen, madden, moisten, quicken, quieten, redden, ripen, roughen, sadden, sharpen, shorten, sicken, slacken, smarten, smoothen, soften, stiffen, stouten, straighten, straiten, sweeten, tauten, thicken, tighten, toughen, weaken, whiten, widen, worsen.* Note that *deaden* refers to pain or noise; it is not a synonym of KILL. Also, *fasten* means to make firm or secure; it is not a synonym of *quicken*. This suffix cannot be added freely to words.

See -EN ADJECTIVE SUFFIX; STRAIGHT & STRAIT.

envy & jealousy

Envy /'envi/ is the feeling that someone ELSE has advantages or success that the *envious* person does not: *I envy (her) her position and salary; I am envious of her position and salary; Her position and salary are the envy of the company*. The expression *I don't envy you* is a way of saying to someone that they have problems and difficulties.

A *jealous* /'dʒeləs/ person is very strong in protecting rights or affection, sometimes to the point of obsession. A *jealous husband* is one who exercises strict control over his wife to prevent her affection from going elsewhere, whether or not this suspicion is justified. It can also be a synonym of *envious*: *I am jealous of her position and salary*.

Jealous is a DOUBLET of *zealous* /'zeləs/, which means *enthusiastic, full of zeal* /ziːl/.

epithets

In English epithets are usually preceded by *you*: *You dirty rat; You fool; You complete idiot; You wonderful woman.*

eponyms

An eponym is the use of the inventor of a thing as its name. A *sandwich* is named after the fourth Earl of Sandwich (1718-1792) who ate meat between slices of bread while he was gambling so that he would not have to leave the table; *Wellington* boots are boots in a style made famous by the Duke of Wellington (1769-1852) but now they are always waterproof rubber boots, usually black or green and known as *wellies*. The *Bodleian* Library (in Oxford), the *cardigan*, the *diesel* engine, the *mackintosh* (waterproof coat), the *Morse* code and *sadism*, are also examples of eponyms, from Sir Thomas Bodley, the Earl of Cardigan, Rudolf Diesel, Charles Macintosh, Samuel Morse, and the Marquis de Sade respectively.

In literature an eponymous hero is one whose name is also the title of the work: *Jane Eyre* is the eponymous HEROINE of the book by Charlotte Brontë.

(e)special

The difference between these two forms is not clear, but the adjective *especial* is now rare in English. Of the adverbs, *specially* means *specifically, for no other purpose*: *I cooked this specially for you; I went into town specially to buy it*, while *especially* means *above all, most of all*: *It is common in England, especially in the north.*

espresso

The Italian style of coffee is *espresso* /es'presəʊ/ meaning *expressly* i.e. freshly and immediately prepared for each customer. However, *expresso* /eks'presəʊ/ is sometimes heard from English native speakers who assimilate it with *express*.

estate

An estate is a large area of land in private ownership, usually with a house: *a country estate; a shooting estate*. An *estate agent* is someone whose business is buying, selling and managing property; the property is not necessarily a large rural estate but is usually a house or flat. A *housing*

E

estate or *industrial estate* is an area built at one time as one project with houses or industrial premises. When someone dies, their *estate* is all the property of all kinds that is left.

Estuary English

It is currently fashionable in Britain, especially among young people, to speak *Estuary English*. The reference is to the Thames estuary but the accent is heard nationwide. Its main features are the use of the GLOTTAL STOP /ʔ/ (*PHONETIC SYMBOLS*) (for /t/, *butter* /ˈbʌʔə/, *wet* /weʔ/ and the use of /w/ for /l/ *ballpoint* (pen) /ˈbɔːwpɔɪnʔ/.

See L, L.

etcetera

The pronunciation /ekˈsetrə/ instead of /etˈsetrə/ is surprisingly common, presumably because of the attraction of so many words that begin with *ex-*. It is not considered correct. The common misspelling *ect.* is also incorrect.

etymology

Etymology is the study of the origins of words and the development of their meanings; it is based on the Greek root *etumon* meaning true but it is a mistake to insist that a word used in modern English (or in any other language) should have the same meaning as it had in Old English or Latin or any other language that it may have come from. Words change in meaning, and a few examples of common words that have changed greatly from their etymologically original forms will show this clearly. (It is obvious too that these forms themselves must have their own origins, which may have different meanings again.)

Nice, from Latin *nescius* (ignorant) came into English in the late thirteenth century, meaning *foolISH, stupid, senseless*. Since then it has meant *strange, lazy, effeminate, shy, precise, subtle, unimportant, critical,* and *delicate*. Its present meaning is *pleasant*.

Snob meant a shoemaker in the eighteenth century (the actual origin of the word is unknown). It came to mean a person of the lower classes in general, then such a person who imitates the manners of people of higher classes, and in the early twentieth century it came to mean someone who looks down on his social inferiors.

Silly derives from a Germanic root meaning *luck, happiness*. In the fifteenth century it meant *pitiable*. Its meaning passed through *weak, sick, unsophisticated, humble* and *plain* before reaching its present meaning of *foolish*.

The only possible way of determining the meaning of a word is by looking at how it is generally used now. Etymology is of great interest to linguists and others, but has no authority in deciding a word's **current** meaning.

English etymology has some surprises which show the dangers of making the most obvious assumptions. *Boxing Day* is not connected with the sport of boxing (see CHRISTMAS); a *bridegroom* is unconnected with the *groom* who looks after horses; a *buttonhole* was originally a *buttonhold* (it is not the word *hole*); for *court-card* see PLAYING CARDS; a *greyhound* is not connected with the colour *grey* (its origin is unknown); *sorrow* and *sorry* are unconnected (*sorry* is the adjective from *sore*). See also FARTHER & FURTHER; EASE & EASY.

There is a tendency to invent etymologies that seem right or appropriate. Many people believe incorrectly that POSH is an acronym of PORT *out, starboard home* because these were the comfortable sides of the SHIP when people travelled to India by sea. Also, some people claim incorrectly that the word GAY acquired its meaning of homosexual as an acronym of *(as) good as you*, an attitude of self-assertion by homosexuals. These are known as FOLK etymologies.

The names of the months *September, October, November,* and *December* derive their names from the Latin numbers for seven, eight, nine, and ten. Their names were kept after a change to the calendar (the introduction of July and August) moved them from their numerical place.

See DAYS AND MONTHS.

E

even

This word has the idea of things being flat or horizontal or equal in height or smooth, free from variation, in balance (as with scales) *even-handed justice* is fair and balanced, *the balance is even*. As a verb it means *to make things level or smooth or free of fluctuations*: to *even out fluctuations in earning power* for example.

To be/get even with somebody means to have settled an account, and can also mean *to take revenge*. An *even chance* is an equal chance, *even money* means equal ODDS.

Even numbers are those that can be divided exactly by 2 (2, 4, 6, 8 and so on).

adverb

As an adverb *even* shows that a sentence contains an extreme case, strongly stating or denying it:
Even John was there.
This is believed even by people who should know better.
Even after that experience he had learnt nothing.
They don't do that, even in Scotland.
Even if we leave now, we'll arrive late.
Even though he passed the exam, he couldn't find a job.
I didn't even see him.
I won't tell you his address, not even his phone number.
It's even bigger than I thought.
It's even more difficult than last year's exam.

Like ONLY, *even* usually takes the mid-position but can move next to the word that it focuses.

ever

In WH- QUESTIONS *ever* adds emphasis; it is written as a separate word:
Why ever did you do that?
What ever happened next?
Where ever did you buy that hat?
How ever did you escape? (compare *However, did you escape?*)
When will they ever learn?

As pronouns and adverbs, these are written as one word:
You can have whatever you want.
Whoever you meet, don't say what has happened.
Get here however you can.
Whenever I fly, I feel nervous.

ever & always

At one time *ever* meant *always*; it is not used in that way generally now but that meaning has survived in certain expressions. *For ever* means *permanently, always*: *I'll love you for ever; He's forever complaining* (see CONTINUOUS ASPECT); *I came here in 1984 and I've lived here ever since (then)*.

Ever is used in comparisons: *His books are as interesting as ever; Her work is better than ever*. This could be considered as *... as they ever were; ... than it ever was*.

Ever since (not ~~always since~~) emphasises the complete nature of the time: *We've lived in this house ever since our wedding; Ever since they arrived they've been complaining.*

An *evergreen* tree or plant is one that does not lose its leaves in winter, one that is always green.

Everlasting means *eternal* or *perpetual*: *He told her of his everlasting love for her*.

Ever after refers to the cliché ending of a romantic story or fairy tale, when the hero and HEROINE marry: *And they lived happily ever after*.

E

everyday & every day

Everyday is written as one word when it is an adjective meaning *common, regular, not special*: *This is our everyday cheese*. Note that the ADJECTIVE cannot be predicative: ~~*This cheese is everyday*~~.

As an adverb it is written as two words: *I eat this cheese every day*.

examination & test

Examination is the usual word for the process of assessing someone's knowledge or ability at school or university, or in an application process for a job. A ***test*** is simpler and less formal. For example in a school children might have a test every few weeks but an exam every term. *Test* is used in combination with other words to imply test of status or achievement: *blood, breath, intelligence, performance, pregnancy* etc. *test*.

In the UK a *driving test* determines whether a person should be given a driving licence.

A *test match* is an international cricket or rugby match; a *test ban* is a ban on the testing of nuclear weapons.

excuse

The verb is pronounced /eksˈkjuːz/; the noun is /eksˈkjuːs/. When an *excuse* is made for an action, it is often the CASE that the *excuse* is false.

executor, executioner & executive

An ***executor*** /egˈzekjʊtə/ is a person appointed to ensure that the provisions of a will are carried out (executed). The female form is *executrix*.

An ***executioner*** /eksɪˈkjuːʃənə/ is a person who carries out a death sentence. Although *execute* /ˈeksɪkjuːt/ and *execution* have a general sense of performing or carrying out a task, when necessary they refer specifically to a death sentence. The prisoner is *executed*.

An ***executive*** /egˈzekjʊtɪv/ is a person in a company or other organisation who has the authority to execute agreed POLICY, to take *executive* action.

expect, hope & wait for

Expect means to look at an event as certain or nearly certain. It can be followed by an INFINITIVE, a CLAUSE or an object and infinitive:
I expect to have the result on Thursday.
I expect that I will have the result on Thursday.
He expects me to support him.

or by an object alone:
I expect the result on Thursday.
You can't expect any help from him.
I expect payment at 30 days.
You are expected to be here 30 minutes before we leave.

A pregnant woman is said to be *expecting* a baby: *She's expecting her baby in October; She is an expectant mother*.

In colloquial speech it is used as a synonym of *suppose*: *I expect he's already there; I expect she was very unhappy*.

Hope is less strong than *expect*, and expresses a desire that something will happen or be the case, or a belief with no solid evidence to support it. *I hope to have the result on Thursday* is less certain than *I expect...*

In Britain, if you are planning a barbecue in the summer, you say *I hope the weather will be good*, but in Spain you say *I expect the weather will be good*.

It is intransitive, so we have *I hope to have the result on Thursday* and *I hope that I will have the result on Thursday* but not ~~*I hope the result on Thursday*~~; and *He hopes that I will support him* but not ~~*He hopes me to support him*~~.

Wait for refers to something that will certainly happen in the future but not immediately. You *wait for a bus*; in the doctor's SURGERY you sit in the *waiting room.*

experience

As an uncountable noun this word refers to the knowledge which someone has acquired by doing something, or the length of time during which they have been doing it: *You can rely on his great experience; She has twenty years' experience as a nurse.*

As a countable noun it is something memorable which has happened to a person: *I had a strange experience yesterday.*

When used as a verb it has both meanings: *He is a very experienced pilot; We have never experienced such weather in July.*

extend & extent

Extend is the verb and *extent* is the noun; the noun *extension* also exists.

Extent is the area, range or scope of something; *to a great extent* is *to a great degree.*

Extension refers to the act or result of extending something: an *extension* to a building; a telephone *extension.*

See ASCEND; PORTEND.

F

f, F /ef/

The sixth letter of the alphabet. It is pronounced /f/ except in the word *of* /ɒv/, but note that *off* is pronounced /ɒf/. See OF & OFF.

For the plurals of words that end in *-f*, many of which change to *-ves*, see PLURAL FORMS.

faction

In addition to its usual meaning of a group within a larger organisation, especially a political one, that disagrees with the position of the organisation as a whole, faction is a BLEND of fact and fiction, referring to a book or film that is fictional though based on fact. The film *Titanic* is an example of this.

false friends

Quite often an English word is similar in form to a word in another language but differs in meaning; this makes correct and careful use of a DICTIONARY essential. False friends obviously vary from language to language but it is worth mentioning that ACTUAL in English means *real, effective* and does not mean *current* as the equivalent does in other European languages. It also happens that an English word is used in other languages with a different meaning; for example, some languages use the English word *smoking* to describe what in English is called a *dinner jacket*. A smoking jacket was a nineteenth-century term for a brightly coloured jacket in which men relaxed while smoking after dinner.

familiar

This word is not used with relation to *family*. We talk of *family finances, family relations* etc. In sociological texts the word *familial* is found.

Familiar is used to mean that something is well-known: *to be familiar with something* or *something is familiar to somebody*; *a familiar face*. To be *familiar with somebody* suggests a very close relationship.

A witch's *familiar* is the creature which accompanies her as her attendant and servant.

family relationships

Your *father* and *mother* are your *parents*. Their parents, your two *grandfathers* and *grandmothers*, are your *grandparents*. If it is necessary to distinguish them you talk of your *maternal* or *paternal grandmother* etc. Your grandparents' parents are your *great-grandparents*, and a *great* is added for each generation before that.

Your *sons* and *daughters* are your *children*, and their children are your *grandsons* and *granddaughters*, collectively your *grandchildren*. Your grandchildren's children are your *great-grandchildren*, and a *great* is added for each generation after that.

Your parents' brothers and sisters are your *uncles* and *aunts*. Their wives and husbands are also called *aunts* and *uncles*. If it is necessary to be precise, you can talk of your *uncle/aunt by marriage*. The children of your uncle and aunt are your *cousins*; there is no distinction in English between male and female cousins but usually the context establishes this quickly: *My cousin Sarah/My cousin and his wife/I'll ask my cousin what she thinks about it*. The precise term for people who share common grandparents is *first cousin* or *cousin GERMAN; second cousins* share a great grandparent. In fact, *cousin* is often used for all such relationships.

You may have *brothers* and *sisters* (for the common term see SIBLING). Their sons and daughters are your *nephews* and *nieces*, and their children are your *great-nephews* and *great-nieces*, as you are their *great-uncle* or *great-aunt*.

A married man or woman has a *wife* or *husband*; the common term is *spouse*. Your spouse's RELATIONS are your *father-in-law, mother-in-law, sister-in-law* and *brother-in-law*. Together, your spouse's family are your *in-laws*. Your son's wife and your daughter's husband are your *daughter-in-law* and *son-in-law*. *In-law* RELATIONSHIP does not extend beyond these degrees: *My wife's cousin, Tom's aunt and uncle*. Also, the spouses of your brother and sister are your *sister-in-law* and *brother-in-law*. There is no English term to describe the relationship between a husband's parents and his wife's parents.

A *step-* relationship, *stepfather, stepmother, stepsister, stepson* etc., is one that has come about as a result of a second marriage where there is no blood relationship. Your *half-brother* or *half-sister* is one who has one parent in common with you. Usually, it is not necessary to define these relationships so precisely.

fare

Originally this was a verb meaning *travel*. It no longer has that meaning by itself, but it survives as a noun meaning *the money that has to be paid to travel*: *bus-, plane-, train-, taxi-fare* etc. *I've got my fare, economy-class fare*. By metonymy a taxi-driver uses the word to refer to his passengers: *I was looking for a fare*.

In certain expressions it also refers to food, especially with regard to its quality or quantity: *simple, good, coarse, usual, Christmas fare*. *A bill of fare* is a menu. In this sense the word is old-fashioned, but it is sometimes used to give a traditional impression.

Warfare is a state of war or the act of conducting a war. The word is used with an adjective: *chemical, biological, psychological, trench, land, sea, air, legal warfare*.

Welfare is a state of well-being and prosperity. A *welfare state* is one that intends to ensure the welfare of its citizens through government action.

A WAYfarer is a traveller, especially one who is walking. The word suggests a long journey. A *seafarer* is a sailor.

Farewell means *goodbye*, but is used when the people are separating for a long time, or for ever. Sometimes the more poetical form *fare you well* or *fare THEE well* is used.

A *thoroughfare* is a public road.

A *fieldfare* is a bird (Turdus pilaris); its name is perhaps connected with *fare*.

A *fanfare* is an impressive, ceremonious sound made with trumpets, often as a welcome on official occasions. It is an imitation of the sound and has no connection with *fare*.

As a verb, *fare* is used but it means progress rather than travel: *How did you fare?* (How did things go?); *I fared well/badly*. (Things went well/badly for me.)

farther & further

These are the irregular comparative forms of *far*, adjective and adverb. Both adverbs can mean *greater in distance*: *John swam to the farther/further shore*; *further* is more common than *farther*; *further* is used to mean *more, extended*: *further information on page 94; further education*.

Farther is a variant of *further*, which in Middle English was the comparative of FORTH not of *far*. The comparative of *far* was *farrer*. However, *farrer* fell out of use and *farther* and *further* became the comparative forms of *far*.

fast

This word has three meanings; the first two are from the same root.

1 *Firmly fixed, not easily moved*. If a door is *fast shut* or a drawer is *stuck fast* it cannot be moved. Someone who is *fast asleep* is deeply asleep and cannot be awoken easily (it does not mean that he/she has fallen asleep quickly). A *fast colour* is one that does not fade or wash out. The verb *fasten* comes from this sense.

2 *Quick(ly), rapid(ly)* (*fast* is an ADVERB WITHOUT -LY). *A fast train is one that travels fast*. A clock or watch that is *fast* is one that is ahead of the true time (the opposite is *slow*). A *fast person* is one who lives extravagantly (*fast*) and is devoted to pleasure and often immorality. On a motorway the *fast lane*, correctly the overtaking lane, is for vehicles that are overtaking others. It is often used by vehicles that are travelling faster than others. ▶

F

3 Unconnected with the previous meanings is *fast* meaning *a period of time when food is not eaten*, often for religious reasons. The word *breakfast* comes from this meaning. It is also a verb: *A fast day* is a day when people *fast*.

feed & food
Feed, fed, fed is the verb. *Food* is the noun.
See BLEED & BLOOD.

fellow
As well as the meaning shown under CHAP, *fellow* is also used to refer to the senior members of OXBRIDGE *(*BLEND)* colleges, and to some or all members of prestigious academic bodies such as the *Royal Society* and the *Royal College of Surgeons*.

Used before a noun *fellow* refers to people who are in the same category as the speaker: *My fellow students; Fellow Scots! A fellow teacher*. It is usually pronounced with the stress on the first syllable /ˈfeləʊ/ but when it is used with another noun, the stress is on the second noun, with the *fe* having the secondary stress /ˌfeləʊˈstjuːdənts/.

See MATE.

female & feminine; male, masculine & macho
Female and *male* are the biological words used of people, animals and plants. Despite the similarity of forms, they are ETYMOLOGICALLY unrelated, deriving from Latin *femella*, (the diminutive of *femina*, a woman) and *masculus* (male) respectively, though the word *male* influenced the development of *female*. They are also used of machinery, electric plugs etc. for projecting parts that fit into sockets. *A male chauvinist* is a man who believes that men are superior to women; sometimes the fixed expression *male chauvinist pig* is used. *Male* and *female* can be used as nouns. The poet Kipling (1865-1936) wrote *The female of the species is more deadly than the male*.

Masculine and *feminine* refer more to men and women socially or in terms of behaviour than biologically, especially in relation to the commonly observed attributes of the sexes. These terms are GRADABLE *(*ADJECTIVE)*, whereas *male* and *female* are non-gradable. *Masculine* and *feminine* are the grammatical terms used to describe the gender of nouns.

Macho /ˈmætʃəʊ/ and *machismo* /məˈtʃɪzməʊ/ (/məˈkɪzməʊ/ is occasionally heard but does not correspond to the Spanish origin of the word) refer to exaggerated virility, as shown by film characters such as Rambo, James Bond, and Indiana Jones. They come from Spanish, where *macho* is the normal word for *male*.

few
Few(er) is used with countable nouns and *little/less* is used with uncountable nouns. However, native speakers often use *less* with countable nouns: *less books, people, years*. When this refers to a quantity rather than to a number, it is perfectly acceptable in forms such as *(No) less than fifteen minutes, 200 miles, £3000*.

fiancé(e)
Fiancé is masculine; the feminine form is *fiancée*; both are pronounced /fiˈɒnseɪ/. These words are used to describe two people who have become ENGAGED. They are sometimes written with accents as they are French words.

See BRIDE.

find, found, founder & foundry
There are four different unconnected words here.

find, found, found
Things can be found by chance: *I found a £5 note in the street*, or after searching: *I found my glasses in the bathroom*.

Find is used in the expression: *I find it difficult/impossible/easy/ridiculous etc. to...*

F

It can mean *to conclude from the evidence*: *As a result of my investigation I find that his action was incorrect.* A court *finds* a DEFENDANT guilty or not guilty.

Find out is to obtain information: *I'd like to find out about Spanish classes* or to learn a fact, the truth etc. *I found out his nationality by chance; I found out that he had German nationality.*

A *finder* is a person who finds something. A *foundling* is a baby whose parents are not known, one that is found.

found(ed)

To *found* an institution means *to establish* it: *The college was founded in 1446; He founded his business empire in the 1930s.*

If one thing is founded on another, it is based on it: *This book is founded on fact; It's my belief, founded on experience, that...; 'We look forward to a world founded on four essential human FREEDOMS'* (US President Franklin D. Roosevelt).

Foundation is the act of founding: *The foundation of the CHURCH OF ENGLAND by Henry VIII*; or the basis on which something is founded: *This book has a solid foundation in fact.*

The *foundations* (usually plural) of a building are the part BELOW the ground that support the rest of the structure. The *foundation stone* is a stone laid ceremonially to mark the start of work on a building.

A *foundation course* is a preliminary, usually general, course of study at a university. A *foundation cream* is the basic cream used in make-up.

A *founder* is a person who founds something.

The *Founding Fathers* were the American statesmen who founded the USA.

founder

As a verb *founder* means *sink* of a ship: *The Titanic foundered on her MAIDEN voyage.* See GENDER.

foundry

A *foundry* is a *place* where metal or glass is melted and moulded into shape.

fingers & toes

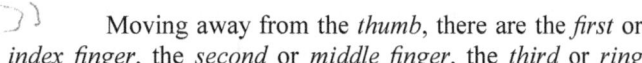

Moving away from the *thumb*, there are the *first* or *index finger*, the *second* or *middle finger*, the *third* or *ring finger*, and the *fourth* or *little finger* (*pinky* in American English). The word *finger* is only used in relation to the hands; the parts of the feet that correspond to fingers are called *toes*. BIG and LITTLE *toes* have special names; the other toes do not.

fisher & fisherman

A man who catches fish for a living or for sport is a *fisherman*. *Fisher* is an English surname. An *angler* is someone who catches fish with a rod and line. *Angling* is also known as *fishing*.

flags

The official flag of the United Kingdom is the *Union Flag*, often referred to as the *Union Jack*. It was first used in 1606 to represent the Union of ENGLAND and SCOTLAND. It is a combination of the crosses of St George (square red on white) for England and St Andrew (diagonal white on blue) for Scotland. In 1801, following union with IRELAND, St Patrick's cross (diagonal red on white) was added. WALES is not represented on the flag. The flag is not perfectly symmetrical; the broader white

F

stripe must be UPPERMOST *(*COMPARATIVES AND SUPERLATIVES | SUPERLATIVE WITH -MOST)* at the side by the flag pole. It forms part of the flags of Australia, New Zealand and some other COMMONWEALTH countries, and of the US state of Hawaii.

The flag of the *European Union* has a blue background with a circle of twelve gold stars. The number of stars does not change.

The flag of the United States of America is known as the *Stars and Stripes,* or *Old Glory,* or the *Star-Spangled Banner.* The thirteen horizontal stripes represent the thirteen original states and there are fifty stars representing the current states. While the number of stripes remains constant, more stars are added as more states join the Union.

flammable

The traditional word for something that burns easily is *inflammable*, where the PREFIX *in-* is the Latin word meaning *in* or *into* and is not a negative prefix; the word is related to *inflame*. However, because of the possible risk of misunderstanding, *flammable* is now used for substances that burn and *non-flammable* is the word for those that do not.

Fleet Street

Fleet St is a street in central London which was for many years the centre of the newspaper industry. The term *Fleet St* came to be SYNONYMOUS with the national press. In the 1980s the introduction of new printing technology led the newspaper proprietors to move to new premises away from the Fleet Street area. Nevertheless, the term is still sometimes used with its original meaning.

flesh & meat

Flesh is the muscular part of an animal or person between the skin and the bones. It is also the soft part of a fruit. Meeting or knowing someone *in the flesh* means *in reality* as opposed to by reputation.

Meat is the flesh of animals used as food. It does not normally include fish and poultry. At one time it meant food in general and still has this meaning in the obsolete *sweetmeat* and in *mincemeat*, which is a mixture of dried fruit and spices and is used in mince pies (see CHRISTMAS); mincemeat does not contain meat as such, but does traditionally contain suet (an animal fat from around the kidneys). Vegetarian mincemeat is available.

folk

This is pronounced /fəʊk/ and has the plural *folks*. *Folk* is now uncommon as a separate word meaning *people* but it is still commonly found in compound words such as *country folk* (people who live in the country not a town); *townsfolk*; *kinfolk*; *north-country folk* (people from the north of England, or any other country); *menfolk* and *womenfolk* (men and women in general or particularly in a family). These words do not change in the plural, but in *my folks, the folks back home* (meaning family) the plural is used as separate individuals are being considered.

Folklore is the traditional wisdom and stories of a people (*lore* means traditions and knowledge). The adjective *folkloric* exists but is rarely used; instead it is more common to talk of *folk music, customs, dance, memory, wisdom* etc. If a general adjective is needed, *traditional* or *quaint* would be

football

Football is the usual name in English for the sport that is played worldwide. It is governed in the UK by the Football Association, from which it has taken its other name of *soccer* /'sɒkə/ (note the unusual spelling).

Rugby, which is also sometimes called football by its players and supporters, is a game in which an oval ball can be kicked or carried by the players with the aim of placing it on the ground behind the opponents' goal line. The goal is shaped like the letter H and points are scored for kicking the ball through the top of it. *Rugby Union*, with teams of fifteen men, is the main version of the sport in Britain; in England it is a middle and upper class sport, being played in PUBLIC SCHOOLS, but in Wales, Scotland and Ireland it is popular throughout society. It is also played in France and a number of COMMONWEALTH countries and is increasing in popularity elsewhere. *Rugby League* is a version of the game that is played in the north of England and in some other countries; it has teams of thirteen men.

American football is superficially similar to rugby in that it has H-shaped goals and is played with an oval ball that can be carried, but is in fact a completely different game. *Australian football* is another different form of the game.

fore-

This is a PREFIX to many nouns and verbs with the meaning *in front of, ahead, in the future*: *forearm, forego, forehead, forename, foresee, foreskin.*

forego & forgo

Forego means *preCEDE*: *the foregoing paragraph*. It is a compound with the prefix *fore-* meaning to go ahead.

Forgo means *to abstain from, to choose not to have, use or do something*.

foreign

Note the pronunciation /ˈfɒrɪn/ and spelling of this word. It does **not** end with *-ing*; it is **not** ~~foreing~~. The gradual inclusion of the *g* in the sixteenth to eighteenth centuries was a mistake, perhaps from confusion with the word *reign* /reɪn/.

Foreign is an adjective; the noun is *foreigner*, a person from a *foreign* country. For the adverb see ABROAD & FOREIGN.

See AISLE; COULD; GHOST; ISLAND.

Foreign Office

The Foreign Office, correctly the Foreign and Commonwealth Office since 1968, is the Department of State responsible for the UK's external relations. It is headed by the Foreign Secretary.

foreign words and names

The question of whether or not to translate the names of places and institutions in non-English speaking countries is nothing to do with language; it depends very much on two factors: how easy it is for an English speaker to recognise the original and how easy it is to translate the name itself. It is easy, for example, to translate the Spanish *Guardia Civil* into *Civil Guard* in English; it is less easy to translate the German *Bundestag* (the lower house of the German Federal Parliament) into English. In practice, solutions to this problem are found for each case individually and may vary from one person or situation to another. There can be no general rule.

It is unwise to translate parts of addresses corresponding to street, square, avenue etc. into English. These exist as proper names in their own language, and certainly a post office wants to receive mail from other countries with addresses written on them in its own language, not in English.

When a foreign word is used in English it is usual to give the word a pronunciation similar to the original, but how close this in fact is depends on the speaker. With time, words become naturalised and acquire pronunciation using English sounds but sometimes not obeying normal rules of pronunciation, for example *Beethoven* (/ˈbeɪthəʊvən/ not /ˈbiːθəʊvən/). The German *z* retains its /ts/ pronunciation in *Mozart* /ˈməʊtsɑːt/ and *Nazi* /ˈnætsi/ or /ˈnɑːtsi/.

The following places have English forms of their names. The forms in italics are historical; they are not in current use: Archangel, Athens, Azores, Balearic Islands, *Brunswick* (Braunschweig), Bucharest, Cairo, Canary Islands, Cologne, Copenhagen, Corsica, *Corunna* (A Coruña, Spain), Crete, *Danzig* (Gdańsk, Poland), Florence, *Hanover**, *Leghorn* (Livorno, Italy), Lisbon, Milan, Moscow, Naples, Rome, *Saragossa*, Sardinia, Seville /səˈvɪl/, Shanghai, Sicily, St Petersburg, Stockholm, Turin, Venice, Vienna, Warsaw.

*This name is always used in referring to the Hanoverian monarchs of the UK (George I to Victoria (1714-1901). ➤

F

Beijing, Guangzhou and *Xinjiang* are now used for *Peking, Canton* and *Sinkiang*; *Mumbai, Chennai* and *Kolkata* are used for *Bombay, Madras* and *Calcutta*. *Yangon* and *Myanmar* are used for *Rangoon* and *Burma*. See COMMONWEALTH; COUNTRIES AND NATIONALITIES.

Names of foreign people are not translated except in the case of historical (not modern) royalty: *Henry IV* of France, *Philip II* of Spain, *Emperor Charles V*, but *King Juan Carlos* of Spain; also *Charlemagne* /ˈʃɑːləmeɪn/ rather than *Charles the Great*. Names of Russians tsars are translated up to and including *Nicholas II* (*Peter the Great, Catherine the Great*) but Иван, which is the Russian for *John*, is kept as *Ivan* /ˈaɪvən/ (*Ivan the Terrible*). All Popes' names are translated into English: *Benedict XVI; Francis*.

Classical personal names are used in the nominative CASE: *Socrates, Herodotus, Augustus, Tacitus, Claudius*, but *Homer, Pliny, Livy*.

forget

Forget is a compound of GET, though the prefix *for-* has no meaning nowadays. The past participle *forgotten* represents an unusual past participle of *get*, which is still sometimes found in *gotten*.

See IRREGULAR VERBS; AMERICAN ENGLISH.

forgive & pardon

These words are synonyms but *pardon* is more formal. It is the legal term; a criminal can be *pardoned* or receive a *pardon*. *I beg your pardon* is a common way of apologising; it is more formal than *I'm sorry*. *Pardon* is also used more in theology. *Forgive* and *pardon* are also CALQUES.

former and latter

These are used to make reference to each of two previously mentioned concepts. An example of this use can be found in the article AUTARCHY & AUTARKY. The reference must be very clear. If there is any doubt, as for example when the items are expressed lengthily, it is better to restate them briefly than to expect a reader to study one or more paragraphs to identify the references.

forth & fourth

Forth is an adverb meaning *forwards, onwards* in space or time; it is only used now in certain fixed expressions: *back and forth* means *backwards and forwards*; HENCE*forth* means *from now* and *thenceforth* means *from then*; *and so forth* is the same as *and so on*; a *forthcoming* event is the next one in the future: *the forthcoming Eighth World Congress on...*; a *forthright* person or comment is one that is direct and outspoken; *forthwith* means *immediately*.

The *Forth* is the name of a river in Scotland.

Fourth is the ordinal number corresponding to *four*.

fortnight

A *fortnight* is a period of two weeks; the origin of the word is *fourteen nights*. It has the adjective/adverb FORTNIGHTLY (*ADJECTIVES WITH -LY). *A fortnightly magazine; it is published fortnightly*.

four-letter words

A large number of swear words in English have four letters, so the term *four-letter word* is used to mean *swear word*.

See ANGER, SURPRISE, INSULTS AND TABOO WORDS.

frankfurter

A *frankfurter* is a smoked sausage of the type made in Frankfurt (*-er* is the German suffix added to towns and cities to indicate origin there). This is also the origin of HAMBURGER and *wiener* (*Wien* is the German name for *Vienna*). These names are not written with CAPITAL LETTERS.

freedom & liberty

These are synonyms but have different collocations.

F

freedom

The four freedoms proclaimed by American President Franklin D. Roosevelt in 1944 are *freedom of speech, freedom of religion, freedom from want, freedom from fear;* other expressions with *freedom* are *freedom fighter; freedom of action; freedom of assembly; freedom of conscience; freedom of expression; freedom of speech.*

liberty

If you are *at liberty to do something*, you are free to do it without restriction.

To *take the liberty of doing* something is to do something that you have no right to do: *As you were not here I took the liberty of opening this letter.*

To *take liberties with somebody/something* means to act with a degree of freedom or familiarity that is unjustified.

The *Statue of Liberty* is in New York harbour.

friend

This word is pronounced /frend/ not /frjend/.

fronting

Fronting means placing something at the beginning of a sentence, out of its normal position. This is done to repeat a word and continue the theme of the idea:

'John made a suggestion.' 'Huh! A suggestion you call it. It was more like an order.'
'We climbed the hill.' 'Hill you say! It was a real mountain.'
'He said he was married.' 'Well, that I knew already.'

Sometimes a speaker's thoughts are not very clearly defined and an idea appears before its grammatical framework:

'We stayed in a lovely hotel. The Crown it was called. And very good beer they serve there too.'
'And John, where did he stay?'
She's very beautiful, your sister I mean.

Fronting is not always colloquial but it always relies on a context for the fronted item to be understood:

Arthur said he didn't like Lizzy. That much I knew already.
That Arthur didn't like Lizzy I knew already, but that he had been married to her came as a complete shock to me. (In this case the position of the object in the first CLAUSE balances that of the subject of the second clause.)
He says that he once climbed Mount Everest but whether that's true I don't know.
I know some people at work but others I never speak to.
Whether I can finish this tomorrow I can't say just now.
See INVERSION.

fruit(s)

Fruit is usually uncountable: *Fruit is healthy; I must buy fruit.* Its plural is sometimes used with reference to different kinds of fruit (*fruits of the forest*), though often it is expressed as *kinds of fruit.* As the result of an action it can be plural: *fruits of his labours* but an action BEARS *fruit.* Fruit trees are known by the name of their fruit: *apple tree, cherry tree, pear tree* etc.

-ful and -less

The suffix *-ful* is the adjective *full* but as a suffix to nouns it always has only one *l*. The corresponding adverb ends with *-fully*. It is used to make adjectives meaning *having* or *characterised by* the quality of the noun: *beautiful, hopeful, graceful, useful.* It is also added to nouns to make a noun that describes the quantity contained by the noun. A *spoonful of medicine* is the quantity that can be contained in a spoon: *Take one spoonful of medicine after meals.* The PLURAL is *-fuls* (*two spoonfuls of medicine*). Note that this refers to the quantity; *two spoons full of medicine* refers to two real spoons, each of which is full of medicine. ➤

F

The suffix *-less* also makes adjectives from nouns; it is the opposite of *-ful*, making adjectives that mean *without the quality of the noun*. Note that these suffixes do not always correspond: *hopeless, graceless, useless* but not ~~*beautiless*~~; *hairless, jobless* and WORTHLESS but not ~~*hairful, jobful, worthful*~~.

Topless refers to a person, especially a woman, who is naked from the waist upwards.

fumes, smoke, steam & vapour

These words are used metaphorically with overlapping meanings but basically they can be defined as follows:

Smoke is the result of burning. It can refer specifically to smoking tobacco: *No smoking; The room was full of smoke.* *The big smoke* is a city, often specifically London.

Fumes (the word is usually used in the plural) refers generally to a gas or smoke or vapour especially when it is harmful or unpleasant. Some chemical substances give off unpleasant or dangerous *fumes*. *Fume cupboards* are used in chemistry laboratories to handle such substances. *To fume* means to be angry.

Vapour has a scientific meaning of a fluid that fills a space like a gas.

Steam is the vapour formed by boiling water.

fun and funny

Fun is a noun describing an enjoyable state. It can be used informally in positions where it appears to be an adjective. *The party was (good) fun; We had a fun time* and even sometimes *we had a very fun time*. If you *do something for fun* you do it for enjoyment and no other reason; something said *in fun* is said jokingly, not seriously; a *fun-run* is a long-distance race that is run more for fun than for competition; to *make fun of somebody* is to mock or ridicule them; a *funfair* is a place of entertainment with attractions, rides and so on but not so big as a theme park; *fun and games* is amusing or exciting activity: *There'll be fun and games when he sees what you've done here.*

The derived adjective *funny* has two meanings, neither of which corresponds to the meaning of the noun:
- Amusing: *Charles told me a very funny joke.*
- Strange or unusual or suspicious: *There's a funny smell here.*

These two meanings are sometimes referred to as *funny ha-ha* and *funny peculiar* respectively. There is room for ambiguity: *Something funny happened yesterday; He's a very funny man.*

future (verb forms)

There are several ways of expressing the future in English; the differences between them are not always clear.

will/shall + infinitive

This is the nearest to a neutral future in English to describe known, certain, future events (for the use of *shall* see MODAL VERBS, SHALL/SHOULD): *Christmas Day will be a Sunday in 2022; Our flying time will be two hours and twenty minutes; Will you be at the meeting?; I might be able to lend you £10,000 but when will you pay it back?* (discussing the predictable mechanics of repayment. See *going to* below.)

It is often used after *hope, think, expect* etc. *I think you'll pass; I hope you'll be there.*

It is used in first CONDITIONAL sentences.

It is used for spontaneous offers, promises, and threats: *I'll collect you at ten o'clock; You'll live to regret it. I'll get it* (i.e. answer the phone).

going to + infinitive

This is used to refer to the fulfilment in the future of something that is intended or evident in the present:

present intention

I'm going to buy a new car next week. When are you going to repay me the £100 you owe me? (implying that a present intention has been expressed but not fulfilled; i.e. this is a reminder. See *will/shall* + *infinitive* above.)

The intention can be a strong determination: *I'm going to finish this before I go home, howEVER long it takes.*

present evidence

He's going to break the record. (His time is very good at present.)
It's going to rain. (The sky looks very dark.)

present continuous

This refers to a future event arising from a present plan or arrangement. The plan has been made before the moment of speaking: *I'm flying to Spain next weekend; She's having a party on Saturday; I'm seeing the doctor about it on Thursday.*

Clearly, the difference between an intention and a plan or arrangement is small; in many cases the *going to* and *present continuous* futures are effectively interchangeable: *I'm buying a new car next week. She's going to have a party on Saturday. I'm going to see the doctor about it on Thursday* but not ~~When are you repaying me the £100 you owe me?~~ as the intention (rather than a plan or an arrangement) is an essential part of the idea behind the question.

The present continuous with future meaning is used with DYNAMIC verbs: *Where are you HAVING lunch?; I'm playing squash tomorrow; Mary's taking her daughter to the hospital this afternoon; We're meeting the employees' representatives at 10.00 a.m. on 14 March.*

The present continuous cannot be used for events that are outside human control as they are not planned: ~~It's raining this afternoon; A hurricane's hitting the coast on Tuesday.~~

Though there is no rule, it is in the nature of plans and arrangements rather than intentions that they are in the fairly near future.

plans arrangements and predictions

The similarity between the present continuous and going to futures is clear with the verbs *go* and *come*, which are not usually used with *going to*: *Are you going to go to your mother's?* is repetitive and *When are you going to come back?* seems contradictory.

The *will* future (above) *Will you be at the meeting?* could also be expressed as *Are you going to be at the meeting?*

As these events can be repeated, there is a similarity to the use of the present simple for habitual actions: *The train has been delayed. It will/is going to leave at 10.40* with a slight change in meaning from prediction to intention.

~~Are you being at the meeting?~~ is impossible because *be* has no stative continuous form (but see PASSIVE VOICE). However, *Are you attending the meeting? Are you going to attend the meeting?* and *Will you attend the meeting?* are all possible.

I'll come after dinner is a spontaneous offer.
John's coming after dinner is an arrangement that has been made.
John'll come after dinner says when he's willing and able to come.

present simple

The present simple with future meaning (see TENSE & TIME) is common in subordinate CLAUSES.
CONDITIONAL: *What will you do if you win the lottery?*
Time clauses: *Will we arrive before the film starts?*

It is used in main clauses to refer to things that are very definitely based on a calendar or timetable: *Next term starts on 10 January; The next train leaves at 10.20; What time does the film start?*

It is used in cases where the present continuous could also be used: **1** *I fly to New York on Tuesday;* **2** *I'm flying to New York on Tuesday.* **1** emphasises the timetable aspect; **2** emphasises the plan. ▶

F

future continuous
Like other CONTINUOUS TENSES (*CONTINUOUS ASPECT*) this is used to refer to an interruption; when one instantaneous action occurs while a continuous action is occurring: *When you come back, I'll be cooking dinner.*

It is used for the future as a matter of course: *We'll be flying at 35,000 feet.* It is also used to express a future event that will happen in the normal course of things with no direct involvement of will, spontaneous decision, or intention. It is reassuring to hear the captain of a plane say *Today we'll be flying at 12,000 metres and we'll be landing at Rome at 12.35. We expect that the weather will be sunny when we land.*

So, the question *When will you be repaying the £100 you owe me?* is more tactful than *When are you going to repay the £100 you owe me?*

It is also used in *He'll be wishing he'd taken his umbrella* (STATIVE VERBS (*DYNAMIC AND STATIVE VERBS*) can be used with a continuous form in this construction) and in *I'll be closing early on Thursday*, although *close* is instantaneous and is not usually used in the continuous form.

be to + infinitive
This is used to refer to a future arrangement or plan: *They are to hold an official investigation.*

It is used especially to imply a requirement: *Everyone is to be here at six o'clock* (this is effectively the same as *Everyone must be here* but sounds less commanding in tone).

An intention expressed in a condition: *If he's to pass that exam, he'll have to work harder than he is doing.* This is similar to *If he's going to...* See CONDITIONAL SENTENCES.

be (just) about to + infinitive
This is used to express something in the very near, even immediate, future; using *just* emphasises the immediacy: *I am about to phone him. Do you want me to ask him?; We're just about to leave.*

which to choose?
The differences between these ways of expressing the future are not clear cut; often the same idea can be expressed in different ways with slight differences in meaning. To take an example from *be to + infinitive* above: *They are to hold an official investigation* could be rewritten as:

They will hold an official investigation. (Inevitably)
They are going to hold an official investigation. (Intention)
They are holding an official investigation. (With future reference clear from context.) (Plan)
They'll be holding an official investigation. (Natural course of events)
They are to hold an official investigation. (Intention, possibly requirement)
They are about to hold an official investigation. (Starting very soon)
~~They hold an official investigation~~ is impossible for this example because there is no regular timetable or schedule element. But the present simple is found in expressing the timetable: *They are holding an official investigation. It **opens** at 10.00 a.m. on Monday 14 March.*

future in the past
Reference can be made to a past time when something was seen as being in the future:

will becomes would
She would live to regret what she had done (note that *would* here is the past of *will*; see TENSE & TIME) (This is a rare literary use.)

was going to
I was (just) going to ring the bell when the door opened. (Intention, often unfulfilled.)

past continuous
I was going to Spain the following weekend. (The plan had been made before the time referred to.)

past simple
Would we arrive before the film started? is not a conditional idea. It is the past equivalent of the example at present simple (above) *Will we arrive before the film starts?*, where a present tense in a subordinate time CLAUSE refers to future time. See TENSE & TIME.

future continuous
This cannot be used in the past as it clearly refers to the future as seen from the present.

be (was/were) + infinitive
This refers to
an arrangement in the past: *He was to be married the following week.*
a requirement: *Everybody was to be here at six o'clock (but some people still haven't arrived).*
destiny: *She was to live to regret what she had done.*

be (just) about to
This refers to something, perhaps an unfulfilled intention, that was very close in the future: *I was just about to leave when the phone rang.*

future perfect
This is a rather unusual verb form. It refers to an action that will be completed before a defined time in the future: *I'll have finished the report by five o'clock.* Note that *by* sets a final TIME limit: *The flowers will have come and gone by your next visit.*

G

G

g, G /dʒiː/

The seventh letter of the alphabet. In handwriting the lower CASE letter is written g.

It is normally pronounced /g/ before *a, o* and *u*. It is usually pronounced /dʒ/ with *ge-* and *gi-*: *gentle, giant, gerontology*, but /g/ in *get, give, gynaecology*.

Exceptions are *gaol* /dʒeɪl/ (the traditional spelling of *jail*), *margarine* /ˌmɑːdʒəˈriːn/ (commonly *marge* /mɑːdʒ/), and *mortgagor* /ˈmɔːgɪdʒə/ (the borrower in a mortgage contract). See T, T.

It is not pronounced in words that end *-ng*: *sing* /sɪŋ/, *ring* /rɪŋ/, and their inflected forms: *singer* /sɪŋə/, *ringing* /rɪŋɪŋ/ etc. but it is pronounced in *finger, hunger, linger,* MONGER /fɪŋgə/ etc., where it is not an inflection; *danger* and *messenger* are /deɪndʒə/ and /ˈmesɪndʒə/.

It is silent before *n* at the beginning or end of a word as in *gnash, gnat, gnaw, gneiss, gnome, gnostic, gnu; align, benign, campaign, champagne, design,* FOREIGN, *malign, reign, sign, sovereign*.

When *gn* is between two vowels the *g* is pronounced: *agnostic, benignant, ignorant, malignant, magnet, signature* etc. except in inflected forms of verbs: *signing, aligned*.

In words of French origin it is pronounced /ʒ/: *regime* /reɪˈʒiːm/, *bourgeois* /ˈbʊəʒwɑː/. The Italian word *gnocchi* is pronounced /ˈnjɒki/.

See GARAGE.

gh, GH

Ghana, ghastly, gherkin, ghetto, ghost, and *yoghurt* are pronounced with /g/. See GANDHI.

When *-gh* is written at the end of a word or in *-ght* (see below) it represents a letter called *yogh* (ʒ, Ʒ) that was used in English until the fifteenth century to represent a palatal fricative sound. In modern English its pronunciation is very variable. After *-igh* it is pronounced /aɪ/: *high, thigh* etc.

Words ending with *-ough* have no regular pronunciation in modern English.

/aʊ/ *bough, (snow)plough, slough* (a swamp), *Slough* (a town), *Hough* (surname).
/ʌf/ *Clough* (surname), *enough, rough, slough* (shed skin), *tough*.
/ɒf/ *Bough* (surname), *cough, trough*.
/əʊ/ *dough, (al)though*.
/uː/ *through*.
/ə/ *thorough, borough*, both with /ˈʌrə/; Scots *burgh* /ˈbʌrə/ as in EDINBURGH /ˈedɪnbʌrə/.

In Irish personal and place names that have *gh* it is pronounced as /h/ between vowels and is not pronounced at the end of a word: *Callaghan* /ˈkæləhən/, *Fermanagh* /fəˈmænə/.

The combination *gh* is used in the transliteration of words from other languages. Outside specialist circles it is pronounced /g/.

-ght, -GHT

When *-ght* is inside or at the end of a word, the *gh* is not usually pronounced.

-aught and *-ought* are both pronounced /ɔːt/ except where indicated: *bought, brought, drought* /draʊt/, *fought, nought, ought, sought, thought, wrought; caught, daughter, draught* /drɑːft/, *fraught, naught, naughty, slaughter, taught;* but *laughter* /lɑːftə/.

-ight is pronounced /aɪt/: *blight, fight, fright, light, right, might, night, sight, slight, wright*.

For *-eight* /eɪt/ see E, E.

gain, earn & win

Gain means *to acquire something,* usually something advantageous: *gain an advantage, gain employment, gain recognition;* or *to increase, to gain weight, gain importance: I have gained £5,000 because my investments have increased in value; gainful employment* is paid employment. A CLOCK or watch that is running fast *gains* time: *My watch gains five minutes a week.* See LOSE.

G

Earn is related to work. *He earns £50,000 a year; At last he is earning again after being unemployed for so long.* What is earned is not necessarily money: *I have earned a break, a holiday* (after working so hard); *He has a well-earned reputation for honesty.* Earned income is money received in return for work; *unearned income* is money received from interest, rent etc.

Win refers to some kind of struggle, fight or competition: *The Roundheads won the English Civil War; I won £50,000 in the lottery; He won the gold medal.*

games and sports
You *play* games and sports: CHESS, *football, tennis, squash* etc.

You *go swimming,* SAILING, *fishing* etc. (activities that end in *-ing*, including *go shopping*). See GO + -ING.

You DO other activities: *exercises, athletics, aerobics, karate, yoga.*

You *go sailing* (etc.) *a lot* but you *do a lot of sailing* (etc.)

Gandhi
The name of the Indian Nationalist leader is often written incorrectly as ~~Ghandi~~.

garage
This is usually pronounced /ˈgærɑːdʒ/ or /ˈgærɑːʒ/ though /ˈgærɪdʒ/ is sometimes heard. It is the building in which motor vehicles are stored (private houses and bus operators have *garages*) and also the place that sells petrol, oil etc. (also called a *petrol station*) and which also possibly repairs and services vehicles.

Garage music takes its name from the *Paradise Garage*, a dance club in Manhattan.

-gate
Following the American political scandal that originated in the Watergate Hotel in 1972, the suffix *-gate* has been attached to other sources of political scandal.

gay
Traditionally *gay* meant *cheerful, brightly coloured.* In the late 1960s homosexuals began to use it as a public word to describe themselves, and now the word has almost entirely lost its original meaning.

See QUEER.

gender
Nouns in English do not have inherent gender; they cannot be classified as masculine and feminine according to their inflections (as in Russian or Latin) or according to the article that they take (as in Spanish or German). Pairs of nouns representing male and female people (*man/woman; uncle/aunt; monk/nun*) and animals (*stallion/mare; dog/bitch*) can be found, but with the exception of the few nouns that have a feminine suffix (*actress* etc.) the gender of a noun (differently from the sex of the person or animal it represents) can be defined only in terms of the PRONOUNS that can represent it; it is the pronouns, not the nouns, in English that truly have gender. The pronouns in question are *he, she, it, who* and *which*.

Clearly, words such as *man, boy, king, uncle* have *he*, and *woman, girl, queen, aunt* have *she*, while *doctor, artist, officer, child, parent, cousin* have *he* or *she* depending on the sex of the person in question; *who* is used as the interrogative pronoun: *Who saw you?* and the relative pronoun: *The doctor who saw me is Spanish.*

Equally clearly, words such as *book, table, music, sky, computer, water, honour* have *it* and *which* as their pronouns.

The remaining classification is not clear. GROUP NOUNS have *who* or *which* as seems appropriate in the context. ▶

G

It is perfectly acceptable and normal to use *it* (but *who* rather than *which*) for a baby or a young child, especially when its sex is unknown or is not clearly seen (e.g. under BREAST: *A woman who feeds a baby with her own milk breast-feeds it*).

Animals that are personalised, or that have obvious sexual characteristics such as *bull* and *cow*, can have *he* and *she* as appropriate but almost always have *which* rather than *who* as the relative pronoun. In practice this personalisation is usually limited to mammals and some birds, especially those kept as pets.

The word SHIP used to be regarded as feminine and was referred to by *she*: *The Titanic sank on her* MAIDEN *voyage*. However, this seems to be uncommon in modern usage.

gender & sex

Gender is the term used in grammar to distinguish the different classes of nouns: masculine, feminine and neuter.

Gender is used instead of *sex* sometimes euphemistically and sometimes to refer to social rather than biological differences; this use is particularly common in feminist writing and is used before the noun: *gender issues, studies* etc.

Sex is the biological difference between male and female animals and plants as found in their reproductive systems.

gentle, genteel & Gentile

Gentle means *soft, tender, mild*: *gentle words*; *a gentle breeze* was blowing; *treat me gently*. In the days of greater social class distinction than we now have a *gentleman* was a man of good social position who was expected to behave according to an honourable code of behaviour. This sense has practically disappeared although it is commonly used in addressing a group of PEOPLE (**PERSON AND PEOPLE*): *Ladies and gentlemen* and it is sometimes used instead of *man* as a polite way of referring to a stranger. The female equivalent of *gentleman* is *lady*; although *gentlewoman* exists, it is very rarely used nowadays.

Genteel refers to the behaviour and attitudes of gentleFOLK, but is now often used sarcastically or ironically of people who try to imitate refined sophisticated attitudes and fail in the attempt. *Genteel poverty* refers to the living conditions of people who try to maintain the values of gentlefolk but do not have the necessary money to support that way of life.

Gentile (with CAPITAL LETTER) refers to a person who is not JEWISH: *She married a Gentile*.

geographical location

Scotland is (to the) north of England; Wales is (to the) west of England; France is (to the) SOUTH of England.

London is in	*the south-east of England.*
	south-eastern England.
Glasgow is in	*the south of Scotland.*
	southern Scotland

North, south, east and *west* make adjectives with *-ern*: *northern* /ˈnɔːðən/, *southern* /ˈsʌðən/ etc.

Wales divides into two parts, *North Wales* and *South Wales*. Wrexham is in North Wales and Cardiff is in South Wales.

German & german

Both words are pronounced /ˈdʒɜːmən/.

German is the adjective relating to Germany.

The unrelated word **german** with a small *g* means having two parents or grandparents the same as in *brother german* or *cousin german*. The variant *germane* /dʒɜˈmeɪn/ means *relevant*: *That is not germane to the discussion*.

G

gerund

The gerund is the part of the verb that behaves as a noun. It can be the subject or object of a verb: *Smoking can damage your health; I like swimming.*

It can follow a preposition: *Don't swim after eating a large meal.* In this example the gerund *eating* is both a noun in that it follows a preposition and a verb in that it has its own object: *a large meal.*

Because the gerund is a noun it is sometimes felt that it must be preceded by a genitive:
1. *His/John's forgetting the appointment was unfortunate.*
2. *I can't ignore his forgetting the appointment.*
3. *I don't like his/Robert's being out so late.*

In **1** and **2** the genitive is usual, and it is quite common in *I can't ignore our Deputy Production Manager's forgetting the appointment.* But when two or more genitives are involved, it becomes difficult: ~~I can't ignore both the Deputy Production Manager's and his secretary's forgetting the appointment~~ is unacceptable. It must be either written as *I can't ignore both the Deputy Production Manager and his secretary forgetting the appointment* or totally re-formed as *I can't ignore the fact that both the Deputy Production Manager and his secretary forgot the appointment.*

In sentences like **3** *I don't like him/Robert being out so late* the form without the genitive is preferred in informal style when the subject is not a person: *I was delayed by the train leaving twenty minutes late.* In *I don't like him being out so late,* the words *him being out so late* are the object of *like.* This is different from *I saw him crossing the road,* where only *him* is the object of *saw.* It can be written as *I saw him as he was crossing the road.* ~~I saw his crossing the road~~ is impossible.

See -ING FORM; PARTICIPLE CLAUSES.

get

(*Get, got, got* in British English; in American English the past participle *gotten* is common. It is found in British English in the compounds *beget* and *forget, -got, -gotten.*)

This word has a large number of meanings, many of which are phrasal verbs, but they can generally be placed in three groups. Because of the number and range of words that it can replace it is common in informal and colloquial use, but it is usually avoided by careful writers because its use suggests a lack of care and thought in choice of language.

obtain
Get (buy) *a new car.*
Get (obtain) *a good job.*
You'll get (achieve) *nothing by flattery.*
Get (gain*) the better of somebody.*
He got (acquired) *a reputation for honesty.*
He got (scored) *two goals in the first half.*
I get (calculate as the result) *452.36.*
She had got (received) *a letter from Mary.*
She gets (receives/earns) *£30,000 p.a.*
They got permission to leave early.
I got no answer.
Did you get (find) *the information?*
I must get (have) *some sleep.*
Get a sight of (manage to see) *something.*
He got (caught) *flu when he was on holiday.*
We arrived too late to get lunch.
He got (hit/shot) *me in the arm.*
I can get (receive) *40 TV channels.*
I've been trying to get you (reach you by phone) *all morning.*
I'll get it (answer the door/phone etc.)

For *have got* referring to possession see HAVE.

➤

G

reach and arrive
We'll get there tomorrow.
When will we get to the mountains?
We'll get as far as the river and then have a rest.
We're getting somewhere/nowhere. (We're (not) making progress.)
We'll get as far as Unit 6 before the holiday.

It is followed by prepositions of movement in PHRASAL VERBS *(*MULTI-WORD VERBS)*: *get into* (enter), *get out of* (leave), *get over, get through, get round* etc. In these senses there is often an implication of difficulty in reaching the goal or destination.

This can also be used transitively: *I can't get that song out of my head; It was impossible to get the car into second gear.*

become
Get better, worse, rich, hot, rid of something etc. With a present participle it means to start doing something: *get going, get talking to somebody.* This sense is found in the use of the verb as an auxiliary for the passive voice e.g. *get dressed, get married* when the verb refers to a single action rather than a continuing action or a state.

ghost

Etymologically there should be no *h* in this word, which was spelled *gost* until the late fifteenth century. However, William Caxton (c. 1422 - c. 1491), the first English printer, had spent a large part of his life in the Low Countries and was influenced by the Dutch spelling of the word when he printed it. The etymologically false spelling thus became established and is now the only acceptable form.

Nowadays *ghost* only refers to the spirit of a dead person who returns to haunt a place or a person, but the older meaning of *spirit* is still found in the religious name *the Holy Ghost* for *the Holy Spirit*.

See AISLE; COULD; FOREIGN; ISLAND.

ghost, phantom & spook

These words are synonyms but are used differently.

Ghost /gəʊst/ is the common word for the spirit of a dead person: *Have you ever seen a ghost?; The ghost of Ann Boleyn can be seen in the Tower of London.* A place with ghosts is *haunted*. *Phantom* and *spook* are not commonly used for these ghosts, though a film and later a musical were made from Gaston Leroux's book translated into English as *The Phantom of the Opera*.

Phantom refers to something that is totally illusory, an invention of the mind. It is often used ATTRIBUTIVELY: a *phantom limb* (which produces *phantom pain*) is one that is imagined to be present by a person who has lost a limb; a *phantom pregnancy* is one which shows the normal symptoms but does not exist in fact.

A ***spook*** is a colloquial word for a spy. *Spooky* means *sinister* or *ghostly*.

-ght and -gth

A number of English words end with *-ght*: *light, might, right*; *bought, caught* etc. In these words the *gh* represents the Middle English letter *yogh* (ȝ, Ȝ, see GH, GH *(*G, G)*). It is not pronounced in modern English.

The abstract nouns *length* and *strength* (from *long* and *strong*) are completely different in formation; the vowel of the adjective has changed with the addition of the suffix *-th*. This suffix is pronounced /θ/, the regular pronunciation of *th*, so these words are pronounced /leŋθ/ and /streŋθ/. Learners of English sometimes confuse them and write ~~lenght, strenght; ligth, nigth~~.

girl

This word has been used to apply to adult women as well as children in expressions such as *girlfriend, his new girl, girl-talk, all girls together* but in recent decades feminists have claimed that

G

the word is insulting, perhaps because of its association with *serving girls*, ESPECIALLY black ones in the USA.

Girlie (not *girly*) magazines, shows etc. show fully or nearly naked women.

glass & glasses

Glass (uncountable) is the substance that windows etc. are made of. A large piece of *glass* is called a sheet; a small piece in a composite window is a PANE: *The top pane is broken. Crystal* is used to refer to high-quality glass.

A *glass* (countable) is a drinking vessel made of *glass*. It can be any shape or size and can be described as a *water glass, wine glass, beer glass* etc. Nowadays such drinking vessels are sometimes made of plastic. It is not easy to know how to describe them. A *plastic glass* seems to be the best solution.

Glasses (always plural) are the things that many people use to correct defective eyesight. Each individual piece of glass in them is called a *lens*. See PLURALIA TANTUM *(*PLURAL FORMS)*.

A *spyglass* is a small telescope.

A *magnifying glass* is a lens that produces a magnified image.

See SPECTACLE(S).

God & god

The name *God* has a CAPITAL LETTER when it refers to the monotheistic religions Christianity, ISLAM and JUDAISM. *Allah* and *Jehovah/Yahweh* also have capital letters in English. It has a small letter when used for the gods of other religions, although the god's own name has a capital letter: *The Roman goddess Venus was the equivalent of the Greek Aphrodite, the goddess of love and beauty.*

golf club

It is interesting to note that, though there is no ambiguity in meaning, a *golf* CLUB is both the implement that is used to hit the ball and the social institution to which golfers belong and which organises their games and competitions.

go + -ing

With verbs describing a sporting or physical activity we use *go ...ing*. *I went swimming every day; He goes fishing on Saturdays*. Some other verbs used with this construction are *angling, cycling, fishing, hunting, jogging, riding, shooting, shopping, SKIing*.

See GAMES AND SPORTS.

grammar

Early attempts to analyse English grammar started by using Latin and Greek as models. The parts of speech used in Latin were applied to English with the result that some categories, which are still used in describing English at a fairly simple level, are not satisfactory; in particular, the class of adverbs has a wide variety of words allocated to it. Also, the distinction between conjunction and preposition is not easy to make in the case of AS & LIKE.

Prescriptive grammar is the application of rules that must be followed; again, these rules were initially derived from Latin and proved to be inappropriate. Examples are the ban on SPLIT INFINITIVES and the placing of a PREPOSITION AT THE END of a sentence; an insistence on the use of WHOM could also be considered prescriptive. Modern grammars, like dictionaries, prefer to describe what happens rather than prescribe what should happen. In general *descriptive grammar* is more tolerant of the change that inevitably takes place in a language. However, in this book, because learners of a language have a very reasonable desire to know what is right and what is wrong, or at least what is and is not acceptable, a degree of prescriptiveness will be found.

The tradition of prescriptive grammar is stronger in the USA than in Britain. This is probably because of the desire of millions of non-English-speaking immigrants to find a clearly defined standard.

G

grammar school
The first grammar schools in England were founded in the sixteenth century, or even earlier in some cases. The name comes from the teaching of Latin grammar in schools of that time. In the twentieth century grammar schools were secondary schools that specialised in more academic subjects. Following the introduction of compulsory education (1870) and the increase in mass culture they provided a way for the growing middle class to obtain an education similar to that provided previously only in PUBLIC SCHOOLS.

grapefruit
A *grapefruit* is a large, yellow or pink citrus fruit (*Citrus paradisi*). It has its name because it grows in bunches like grapes.

grass & lawn
Grass is a plant of the family *Gramineae*. It is used in gardens and parks to provide a pleasant green surface. An area planted with grass and treated carefully is a *lawn*.

In Britain, *grass* is a slang word for marihuana (cannabis).

gray & grey
Gray is no longer used for the colour in British English, though it remains standard in American English. Both forms are used for the surname.

Greek alphabet
The letters of the classical Greek alphabet are transliterated into English as follows:

Name	UPPER CASE	lower case	English equivalent
alpha	Α	α	a
beta	Β	β	b
gamma	Γ	γ	g
delta	Δ	δ	d
epsilon	Ε	ε	e
zeta	Ζ	ζ	z
eta	Η	η	e
theta	Θ	θ	th
iota	Ι	ι	i
kappa	Κ	κ	k
lambda	Λ	λ	l
mu	Μ	μ	m
nu	Ν	ν	n
xi	Ξ	ξ	x
omicron	Ο	ο	o
pi	Π	π	p
rho	Ρ	ρ	r
sigma	Σ	σ*	s
tau	Τ	τ	t
upsilon	Υ	υ	u
phi	Φ	φ	ph
chi	Χ	χ	kh**
psi	Ψ	ψ	ps
omega	Ω	ω	o

* ς at end of word

** This letter was transliterated as *ch* in Latin. This spelling has been preserved in English words such as *character*. See CH, CH *(*C, C)*.

Modern Greek (ELOT) transliteration is similar but has v for beta and f for phi.

greetings

Strictly, *Good morning* is used as a greeting until twelve o'clock midday but many people use it until lunchtime, which may be a little later. See MEALS. *Good afternoon* is used until about five or six o'clock and *good evening* is used after that for the rest of the evening. *Good night* is the equivalent of *goodbye* and can be used in the evening. It is perfectly possible to say *good night* to someone at eight o'clock in the evening and then to say *good evening* to someone else an hour later. *Good day* is rather rude in modern British English and should not be used; it is common in Australia.

How do you do? is used only as a formal greeting between two people who are meeting for the first time. Both people say *How do you do?* and there is no response; the question is a mere formality. Normally, when friends and acquaintances meet, they ask *How are you?* or *How are you keeping?* or more informally *How's life?*, *How are things?*, or *How's things?* (sic, singular verb with plural subject).

On leaving each other people say *Goodbye*, less formally *Bye-bye* or *Bye* or CHEERS. This can be followed by (*I'll*) *see you later/tomorrow/on Tuesday/at the meeting*/etc. or simply *See you*. (*I'll*) *see you anon* means at some unspecified time in the future.

British people shake hands on first meeting, as they say *How do you do?* but not usually on other occasions. Kissing is not usually part of social greeting outside the family and close friends; men never kiss each other in social greetings.

group nouns

Group nouns (e.g. *army, committee, team*) may take either a singular or a plural verb depending on whether the speaker thinks of them as a single unit or as a collection of individuals:
Newtown United is the best football team in the country.
Newtown United are playing Oldville Town on Saturday.

A group of soldiers was approaching.
A group of soldiers were approaching.

In many cases there is little effective difference between the two forms.

Any following pronouns must agree with the number given to the subject: *The government has announced its plans to abolish income tax; The government have never been as popular as they are at the moment.*

The word *number* behaves similarly to group nouns. In sentences such as *A large number of BICYCLES were in the road* the verb is plural because the effective subject is *bicycles*. The sentence could be rewritten as *Many bicycles were in the road*. However, in the sentences *The number of bicycles in the road was very high* and *The number of students was divided by two* the verb is singular because the subject really is the singular word *number*.

See POLICE; SINGULAR AND PLURAL.

grow

grow into/out of

If a child has a piece of clothing which is too big, a parent might say *You'll grow into that sweater soon*, meaning that the child will grow to be the same size as the sweater so that the sweater will fit. *She's grown out of those jeans* means that the girl has grown so much that her jeans no longer fit her.

grow up

This means to become an adult either physically or emotionally. It does not mean simply to become taller. *Grown-up* means *adult*: *grown-up clothes*; *grown-ups here, children there*.

guerrilla

In English this refers to the person, not the organisation: *A group of guerrillas attacked the bus*; it can be used as an adjective: *guerrilla warfare, guerrilla bands*. It is pronounced /gəˈrɪlə/, the same as the ape *gorilla*.

G

gulf
The *Gulf* (with a capital *G*) is the sea between Iran and the Arabian peninsula. It was formerly known as the *Persian Gulf* but the name was changed out of respect for Arab opinion.

gun
A *gun* is a firearm of any size or type. *He's got a gun* could refer to a small pistol or a shotgun or rifle, but the largest artillery piece is also a *gun*. If a precise definition is necessary, there are specific names that can be used, *pistol, revolver, rifle, shotgun, machine gun* etc.

guts
This word (also in the singular) literally means *intestine*. It is used (always in the plural) as a strong word meaning courage or determination. *To hate someone's guts* means to hate them very deeply.

Catgut is the name for the dried intestines of several animals (but not the cat) used to make strings for musical instruments.

Guy Fawkes night
On 5 November people light bonfires and set off fireworks to celebrate the failure of an attempt on 5 November 1605 to blow up the Houses of Parliament while King James I was opening the Parliament. This was a desperate action by a Roman CATHOLIC group to prevent the consolidation of the Protestant monarchy with James I, who had succeeded Queen Elizabeth in 1603 (see ENGLAND, A BRIEF HISTORY). Guy Fawkes /fɔːks/ was found in the Parliament building as he was preparing to set off the explosion and his name is associated with this action, though he was not one of the leaders of it. The evening of 5 November is known as Guy Fawkes night or bonfire night; a model of a man, known as a guy, is burned on the fire. These guys are often made by children, who show them in the streets in the days and weeks before bonfire night and collect money for them. This is perfectly acceptable and is **not** regarded as a form of begging. Fawkes was executed for treason but not by burning.

Guy is a common friendly word for a man.

See CHAP.

gypsy
The spelling *gypsy* is now more common than *gipsy*, reflecting the former belief that these people came from Egypt. The word should have a CAPITAL LETTER *(Gypsy)* when it refers to Romani people but is used with a lower case *g* in other contexts.

See ROMAN.

H

h, H /eɪtʃ/

The eighth letter of the alphabet.

Some people pronounce the name of this letter /heɪtʃ/.

It is pronounced /h/ and in RECEIVED PRONUNCIATION is always pronounced at the beginning of a word except in *heir, honour* and *hour* and their derivative forms: *heiress, honourable, hourglass* etc. It is not pronounced in *annihilate,* /əˈnaɪleɪt/ *annihilation, vehement* /ˈviːmənt/, and *vehicle* but it is pronounced in *vehicular*. It is not pronounced in words that end with *vowel-h*: *cheetah* /ˈtʃiːtə/, *pharaoh* /ˈfeərəʊ/.

Although it is pronounced in other words, it is quite common to see such forms in print as *an hypothesis, an historic day*, i.e. *an* is used before a word beginning with *h* and an unstressed syllable. See A & AN.

It is usually silent in place names ending in *-ham*. *Clapham* /ˈklæpəm/, *Durham* /ˈdʌrəm/ but *Caversham* and *Haversham* have /ʃəm/. It is pronounced in *West Ham* /west hæm/ and *East Ham* /iːst hæm/. The surname *Bentham* is pronounced /ˈbenθəm/.

See PLACE NAMES.

hamburger

This name refers to the city of Hamburg in Germany (see FRANKFURTER) but is not written with a CAPITAL LETTER. It has no connection with the meat *ham*, which has never been an ingredient of hamburgers. However, perhaps because of this potential misunderstanding, *hamburgers* are sometimes called *beefburgers*, or increasingly JUST *burgers*. A *cheeseburger* is a hamburger with cheese.

Handel

The composer *George Frideric Handel* (1685-1759) was born in Germany as *Georg Friedrich Händel*. He lived in London for many years and became a British subject in 1727. In English his name is always written as *Handel* /hændl/.

happen

Happen can have a personal subject; this indicates that something has occurred by chance. It is followed by an infinitive: *I happened to read about you in the paper yesterday; If you happen to see Bill, ask him to ring me.*

hard & hardly

Hard is an adjective, but it is also used as an adverb meaning *with a great effort*: *work, run, look, study, push hard.*

Hardly is a synonym of *scarcely*: *The film had hardly begun when the fire alarm sounded.*

Sometimes this implies difficulty: *I could hardly speak*. But this is not always the case: *I opened the door with difficulty* (I opened the door but it was difficult to do so) is different from *I hardly opened the door* (I barely, scarcely opened it; I opened it just a little).

See INVERSION.

have

When referring STATIVELY (*DYNAMIC AND STATIVE) to possession, *have* can be used in three different ways:
1 *I have some money; I haven't any money; Have you any money?*
2 *I have got some money; I haven't got any money; Have you got any money?*
3 *I have some money; I don't have any money; Do you have any money?*

1 is mostly British and is formal. It is not very common though it is found in certain fixed expressions: *I haven't a clue; What have we here?* ➤

H

2 is also mostly British and is informal.

3 is standard American English, but is becoming more common in British English.

In **1** and **3** *have* is a main verb itself meaning *possess*, whereas in **2** it is an auxiliary verb making the present perfect of *get*. There is no difference at all in meaning but ADVERBS IN MID-POSITION respect this fact: *I always have money; I have always got money.*

Note that *have got*, like plain *have*, expresses stative possession and contrasts with *have* in other tenses: *He has a moustache. He has had it for five years; He has got a moustache. He has had it for five years*. When *have* is used DYNAMICALLY to refer to an action, **3** must be used: *What did you have for breakfast? I didn't have a shower yesterday.* As this sense, unlike possession, refers to an action, a CONTINUOUS ASPECT verb is possible: *He's having a rest at the moment.* Thus there is a difference between the questions *Have you got bacon for breakfast?* (possession, stative) and *Do you have bacon for breakfast?* (action, dynamic).

When *have* is used as an auxiliary to make the present perfect it behaves like any other auxiliary verb with inversion for questions: *Has he eaten his dinner?* and no other auxiliary in negatives: *He has not eaten his dinner.*

have and causation

Have + past participle means *to cause something to be done*:
I have my hair cut by my neighbour. (With *by* to introduce the passive agent.)
We're having an extension built to the house. (As above, a dynamic action can use the continuous of *have*.)
I have my neighbour cut my hair.
I'll have him repair it next week.

Informally, GET can be used in these examples:
I got my hair cut last week.
We're getting an extension built...
I'll get him to repair it next week.
See INFINITIVE for BARE INFINITIVE and INFINITIVE WITH *TO*.

other uses of *have*

He had his car stolen last week has the same structure as the causative *have* above. However, this (presumably) refers to his experience rather than his causing it to happen.

You have two more patients waiting to see you, doctor. This is similar to *There are two...* but is more personal.

I have a friend working in Zambia. (A friend of mine is working/I have a friend who is working in Zambia.)

pronunciation

Have and *has* are pronounced regularly: /hæv/ and /hæz/. However, in *have to* (see *must* in MODAL AUXILIARY VERBS) the pronunciation is /'hæftuː/ and /'hæstuː/. Thus, *I have* /hæv/ *two cars. She has* /hæs/ *to go now.*

haven & heaven

A ***haven*** /'heɪvən/ is a harbour. Nowadays the word is used generally for a refuge, a place of SAFETY, more than for a real harbour but the word is found in place names such as *Newhaven* and *Whitehaven*.

Heaven /'hevən/ is the religious concept of eternal paradise. See HEAVEN & SKY.

The words are unconnected. A *tax haven* is a place where money can be invested outside the control of national tax authorities. It is a refuge not a paradise.

healthy, sane, & sanitary

Healthy refers to general physical, medical health. It is also used figuratively: a *healthy respect* for somebody; *healthy development*; *a healthy imagination*.

Sane and *insane* refer only to mental health.

Sanitary refers to things that affect hygiene and health. A *sanitary engineer* deals with *public health* systems, especially drains. *Sanitary towels* are the absorbent pads worn by menstruating women.

The words *health(y)* and *wealth(y)* should not be confused.

hear & listen

Hear is involuntary. You *hear* something because the sound comes to your ears.

Listen is voluntary. It implies some attention from the person listening. When it is used transitively it is used with the preposition *to*: *Listen to me; I was listening to the radio.*

Compare *see* and *look* under SEE.

heaven & sky

Heaven /ˈhevən/ is the religious concept of paradise. See HAVEN & HEAVEN. *Sky* is the name of what is seen above the earth.

hello

This is the usual spelling. *Hallo* and *hullo* are sometimes found. All three forms are pronounced /həˈləʊ/.

help

Can't help means that something is unavoidable: *I can't help thinking that; I couldn't help overhearing what you said.*

hence

There are adverbs in English that refer to movement to or from a place.

	here	there	where
to	hither	thither	whither
from	hence	thence	whence

Although these words are not all in colloquial use now, they are still sufficiently common to be WORTH mentioning here.

Typical usage is *They live ten miles hence; We walked thither; Whither are you going?; Whence have you come?* *From* is sometimes used unnecessarily with the *-ence* forms: *from thence* etc.

The following forms and usage are common nowadays.

Hence means *from now*: *Ten days hence I will be on holiday;* HenceFORTH means *from now on: Henceforth this information must be presented on form ABC123.*

Thence means *from then* and *thenceforth* means *from that time on.*

Hence means *for this reason*: *Expenses have been exceptionally heavy, hence profits are lower than was expected.*

Whence means *from which, for which reason: Resources are low, whence it follows that the project must be cancelled.*

Hitherto means *up to this time: Hitherto this information has been presented on form XYZ789. Hitherto* is also used to mean *up to that time.*

The remaining forms *whenceforth, thitherto* etc. can be constructed but are never found in modern English.

here-, there- and where- with prepositions

Here-, there-, and *where-* can combine with prepositions to make words relating to *this* (*here*), *that* (*there*), and *which* (relative pronoun) (*where*). For example, *hereafter* means *after this, thereafter* means *after that;* and *whereafter* means *after which*. Often these words are used in formal language. The combinations that can be made (excepting some that are archaic) are with *-abouts, -after, -by, -fore, -in, -inafter, -of, -to, -tofore, -under, -upon,* and *-with*.

notes

They live somewhere here/thereabouts (near here/there).

H

It'll cost €10,000 or thereabouts (about that price).
Whereabouts do they live? (approximately where?)
His whereabouts is/are unknown. (location)

Hereafter, like HENCE*forth*, means *from now on, in the future*. *The (life) hereafter* is *life after death*.

Therefore is a common adverb meaning *for that reason*.

Wherefore means *why, for what reason?* It is now only used in the colloquial phrase *the whys and wherefores* meaning *the reasons*. However, in SHAKESPEARE'S Romeo and Juliet, Juliet says 'O Romeo, Romeo! wherefore art THOU [are you] Romeo?' As the true meaning of *wherefore (why)* is not widely known, people who are not FAMILIAR with the PLAY sometimes assume that this simply means *Oh Romeo, where on EARTH are you?* and quote it when they have lost someone or something.

Hereinafter is used in legal documents to mean *from this point on*: *Megacomputers plc (hereinafter the employer)...* *Thereinafter* is similar but refers to a different document. ~~Whereinafter~~ is not used.

Hereto means *to this matter*: *That is not relevant hereto.*
Thereto is similar to *hereto*; it also means *additionally*: *...a salary of £50,000 p.a., with a bonus thereto in respect of...*
Whereto: *...a salary of £50,000 p.a., whereto a bonus will be paid in respect of...*

Heretofore is *before this time*; *theretofore* is *before that time*.

Hereunder and *thereunder* use *under* to mean *later in a docume*nt. ~~Whereunder~~ is not used.

Herewith is common in letters: *I enclose herewith a copy of the contract*. *Therewith* and *wherewith* are not used.

Wherewithal is a noun meaning *the money needed for something*: *We do not have the wherewithal to take on this project.*

Whereas is a conjunction making a contrast. In formal legal language, in contracts for example, it has the special meaning of *taking into consideration the fact that*.

heroin & heroine

Heroin is the name of a drug derived from morphine. The drug was unfortunately so named because it made its users feel like heroes, before its addictive properties were understood. *Heroine* is the feminine of *hero*. Both are pronounced /ˈherəʊɪn/.

highbrow

*High*BROW is an informal term for *intellectual*. Below that, in decreasing order of intellectualism, there are *middlebrow* and *lowbrow*. Note that brow is a synonym of forehead; it is not the same as *eyebrow*. A *highbrow* can also be called an *egghead*.

high(ly)

High is the adverb (ADVERB WITHOUT -LY) for the usual meaning of *high*: *The plane was flying higher than usual; You are singing too high*.

Highly means *very, greatly*: *highly probable, highly selective.*

I think highly of him means that I have a high opinion of him.

high street

The *high street* is the main street of a town, usually the main shopping street. This is a general name; it is not necessarily the actual name of the street. *High street banks* are banks that offer accounts to ordinary members of the public rather than specialist investment banks.

H

hijack
A vehicle, typically an aeroplane, can be *hijacked*, and the passengers would say *We were hijacked*. Individual people can be *kidnapped* and are then normally held for ransom.

hire, rent & let
These words are largely similar in meaning but there are differences in usage.

Hire can be used of people, meaning *to begin to employ people*, especially in the phrase *hire and fire*. It means both to give and to obtain the temporary use of something in return for payment: *If we hire a car, it will be cheaper than going by train; There's a place on the lake where they hire (out) rowing BOATS; Boats for hire; DVD hire*.

Rent is the usual word with relation to property. Like *hire* it can be used for receiving or acquiring the use of something: *I rented this flat before I bought it; They rented their house (out) while they were abroad; House for rent*. *Rent* is the money paid for this: *I pay £100 per week in rent*. It is sometimes used for other things. Cars can be rented as well as hired. In Britain some people *rent TVs and DVD machines* suggesting that rent is considered more long-term than hire. *Car rental* is more common than *car hire*. *Rent-a-mob, rent-a-crowd* are terms suggesting that people are easily found for any purposes. A *rent boy* is a young homosexual prostitute.

Let. This verb refers to property. When property is let, rent is paid on it. The unrelated noun *lease* can refer to the contract, and to the period of time for which it is valid: *a long lease; the lease expires next year*. Commercially, *leasing* is a financial process by which a company acquires assets by paying a sum to the owner; the property in the goods is transferred after a certain number of payments have been made over a certain period of time.

historic & historical
Historic refers to something that is of great importance in history, or which makes it: *a historic victory, discovery, day, event*.

Historical refers to history as a whole: *historical evidence, analysis, research*; something that is *historical* happened in a *historical* period not in *prehistoric* (curiously, not *prehistorical*) times; something that is of purely *historical* interest has no current relevance or application.

As the American commentator William Safire pointed out in 1992, 'Any past event is *historical*, but only the most memorable ones are *historic*'.

See -IC & -ICAL.

hit etc.
This article contains sub-articles on the two main words *hit* and *strike* followed by these words in alphabetical order: *bang, bash, batter, beat, belt, bump, butt, dash, flog, kick, knock, pound, punch, slap, smack, thrash, thump*.

hit, hit, hit
Hit is the most general of these words. It is transitive except when compounded with certain adverbs such as *hit back* and *hit out*. You can hit somebody or something with a part of your body (hand, head), with a hand-held instrument (hammer, stick) or with something that is thrown or projected (ball, bullet). One thing can hit another: *The apple hit the roof as it fell from the tree; I hit my head on a low door frame*. You can be hit by something that comes forcefully to your mind: *The importance/seriousness/ difficulty/danger etc. of the situation only hit me later*. *Hit* can mean affect badly: *He was hit hard by the financial recession; The country was hit by an earthquake*.

The usual noun for the act of hitting something is *blow*. The usual verbs are *deal* and *strike*: *That dealt a blow to my hopes; Strike a blow for freedom*. It can mean a sudden problem: *His resignation is a serious blow for the company*. *Hit* can be used as a noun but is usually limited to these three meanings:

A success: *That pudding was a hit with the children*.

H

The number of people visiting a website: *Our site had 10,000 hits last month*, or something found by an INTERNET search engine: *The search gave me 13,974 hits.*

A killing or robbery: *We'll make the hit on Saturday* means that the robbery or the killing will be committed on Saturday; the context will make the meaning clear. A *hit man* is a hired killer. A *hit list* can be either a list of people to be killed or a list of hits in an internet search engine.

strike, struck, struck & stricken; stroke

Strike is a general word like *hit* but is not always synonymous:

John struck Bill (on the head) (with a bottle).
The arrow struck him in the arm.
He struck and struck again.
The sound of the CRICKET bat striking the ball.
The horses' hoofs struck sparks from the road.
As the sun rose the light struck the house.
The snake struck suddenly.
The storm/earthquake struck the town at night.
The attacker struck terror into his victim.

It is commonly used with the noun *blow*:

John struck Bill such a blow that he fell unconscious.
He struck him a blow on the head.
They struck a blow for freedom.

It is used in non-literal senses:

It strikes me that he's not telling the truth. (It occurs to me…)
It strikes me as a ridiculous idea. (It seems to me…)
I was struck by his suggestion. (…interested, impressed…)
She wore a striking dress. (…impressive, dramatic…)

It is used with adverbs, prepositions and adjectives:

He was struck down by a heart attack.
Her hopes were struck down.
He struck at her with a whip.
This strikes at the foundation of civilisation.
She struck out in anger. (…attacked…)
He will strike back if he is struck.
I will strike out all references to you.
The doctor/lawyer was struck off for professional misbehaviour. (…removed from the list of qualified professional people…)
The band struck up a march (…started playing…)
I was struck dumb by his rudeness (…extremely surprised; *dumbstruck* and *thunderstruck* can both be used as adjectives with this meaning.)
The blow struck him dead.
The lightning struck him blind.

You *strike a match* to make it burn; before matches were invented, people talked of *striking a light* with flint and steel. LIGHTNING *strikes*: *The church was struck by lightning.* The saying *lightning never strikes twice in the same place* means that an unexpected event is unlikely to be repeated. In the THEATRE *the scenery is struck* (taken down and removed) at the end of the show; *to strike camp* means to take down the tents. On a sailing SHIP, *the sails are struck* (taken down from the masts). This is the meaning that is used when employees of a company *strike* by refusing to work in order to force the company's management to increase their pay or to improve other working conditions. *Striking the sails of a ship* or *striking one's tools* was an expression of a refusal to work. See STRIKE (NOUN) below. Now it is used with no object: *They struck for a 5% wage rise.* A *clock strikes* when it makes a noise to indicate that an hour, half hour or quarter hour has passed. This does not refer to alarm clocks, which *go off* at the time for which they are set: *The clock struck one; The clock was striking half past three as I entered the church; I heard six o'clock strike*. In mining *to strike oil, gold* etc. means to find a deposit underground. See STRIKE (NOUN) below. To *strike a bargain/deal* means to agree one. To *strike a balance* means to choose a moderate course between two extreme alternatives or to achieve a balance between two different forces: *We must strike the right balance between work and pleasure*. To *strike up an acquaintance/friendship with someone* means to start and establish it. To *strike out* means to begin moving in a direction: *They jumped into the water and struck out for the shore; He struck out eastwards*. If something *strikes a* CHORD, it creates an emotional response or a has a strong effect.

Type that has a horizontal line through it (~~like this~~) is called *strikethrough*. It is used in this book to indicate examples of incorrect usage.

Stricken is an alternative past participle of *strike*. It means *severely affected by some difficulty or emotion*. It is especially found in compounds such as *panic-stricken, poverty-stricken, guilt-stricken, grief-stricken*.

stroke (noun)

This is the commonest noun connected with the verb *strike*. It is a synonym of *blow* to refer to the act of hitting and in particular we say *strike a blow* not ~~strike a stroke~~; it has a wider range of meanings. A number of *strokes of the cane* or *lash* was given as a punishment. A *stroke* is a common name for ictus (cerebral thrombosis, embolus, or haemorrhage). If something is done *at one stroke*, it is done with one blow, all at once: *At one stroke he lost his family, his friends and his fortune*. As a clock *strikes the hour*, the noun *stroke* can refer to that: *The shop opened on the stroke of nine* (at nine o'clock exactly).

The expression *a stroke of work* is found in negative sentences: *You haven't done a stroke of work all day*. In swimming, different *strokes* are different styles of movement: *breaststroke, backstroke, crawl, butterfly stroke*. In rowing, one movement of the oars is a *stroke*. In a BOAT with more than one person rowing, the stroke is the one sitting at the back of the boat, who sets the pace for the others. In golf, tennis etc. a *stroke* is not only the act of hitting the ball but also the style with which it is hit: *I must improve my golf stroke*. So *to put someone off his stroke* means to disturb or distract someone who is concentrating. A *piston-stroke* is the whole movement of a piston. A *stroke of luck* is an unexpected piece of good luck. A *stroke of the pen* refers to the act of authorising something: *With one stroke of the pen I could destroy his happiness*. A *stroke* is a name for the symbol / (also called a slash).

stroke (verb)

Whereas *strike* means to hit something violently, *stroke* means to touch it softly, to caress the body, hair etc. of a person or animal.

strike (noun)

Strike is also a noun. While *stroke* as a noun refers to the act of hitting, *strike* is an attack. The snake *made a strike* at my boots. In military language, a *strike* is an attack; *first-strike capability* is the capability to deal a massive blow at an enemy before he has time to act. In *mining* a *strike* is the act of striking oil, gold etc. See *strike* verb, above. A *lucky strike* is one that is made by chance. This is the origin of the name of the cigarette brand *Lucky Strike*; it is not to be confused with a *stroke of luck*. See *stroke* noun, above.

A *strike* is when EMPLOYEES refuse to work because of a complaint against the employers. See *strike* verb, above. Note that this is not from the meaning of *strike* as an attack. Initially people *go on strike* then they *are on strike*. A *hunger strike* is when someone refuses to eat so as to put moral pressure on somebody else. A *rent strike* is a refusal to pay rent. In ten-pin bowling a *strike* is when all the pins are KNOCKED down with the first BOWL.

bang

This is an ONOMATOPOEIC word referring to the noise made when one thing hits another: *Don't bang the door*, but it is used also to mean *hit*: *I banged my head on the door frame*. ▶

H

It can be intransitive: *The door was banging all night; I banged on the wall because my neighbours were making too much noise.* To *go bang* or *go off with a bang* means to explode: *The gun went bang/went off with a bang.* It can be a noun: *I heard a bang/I got a bang on my head. Bang goes...* means that something disappears suddenly as in an explosion: *Bang goes any possibility of leaving early; Bang went £1000.* The *big bang* theory proposes that the universe began at one moment with an enormous explosion. As both verb and noun *bang* means to have sexual relations with someone (transitive and intransitive).

bash

This means *to hit very heavily, damaging the object that is hit*. If one car *bashes* another the damage is more severe than if it *bumps into* it or *knocks it*, but is probably short of severe damage or destruction (this would be *smashing* rather than *bashing*). *To have a bash at something* means to attempt it: *I once had a bash at playing the violin*. A *bash* is a slang word for a party or a social event.

batter

This means *to hit with repeated blows* to the EXTENT that the recipient of the blows is damaged or broken: *They battered down the door*. It is used to describe domestic violence, *battered wives* or *babies*. Something that has been used hard over time such as books, a BOAT or SHIP, a car, a suitcase could be *battered*. *Batter* is similar to POUND but suggests a more irregular attack: the waves *pound* on the shore regularly, but they *batter* a ship in a storm.

beat, beat, beaten

This means *to hit repeatedly*; beating a person or animal suggests an intention to harm or punish. In schools where corporal punishment was used, a *beating* was usually administered with a cane. To *beat someone up* means to beat a person severely by *punching* and *kicking*. A carpet is beaten to clean it. A drum is beaten. Eggs and cream can be beaten in the kitchen. A bird beats its wings. It can be intransitive: *A bird's wings beat; The sun was beating down; The waves were beating on the shore; A drum beats; A heart beats.* In war, sport or other competition *you beat your opponent*. To *beat time* means to indicate the pace of a piece of music, either to follow it or to lead the musicians. Music that has a strong rhythm can be said to have a *beat*; this is the origin of the name of the musical group *The Beatles*, who became famous in the early 1960s with songs that had a powerful beat. The name of the group is a HOMOPHONE of *beetles* (insects). The noun *beat* is also used for a *drumbeat* and *heartbeat*. A police officer's *beat* is the route that he/she patrols. *I'm dead beat* (not *beaten*) means I am very tired, exhausted, but *He's a deadbeat* means that he is a WORTHless person. In music, the *offbeat* is the unaccented beat: *The clarinet comes in on the offbeat*. In other contexts the word is an adjective meaning *unusual, eccentric*: *an offbeat idea, suggestion*. In music a *downbeat* is a strong beat and an *upbeat* is a weak one. In other senses the words are used as adjectives; *downbeat* means *pessimistic, unhappy* and *upbeat* means *optimistic, cheerful*. To BROWbeat someone means to exert strong moral force on a person with looks and words but without physical violence. *Weather-beaten* means affected by long exposure to wind and rain: *a weather-beaten face, weather-beaten luggage.*

belt

This means *to hit someone with a belt*, but is used generally for a violent physical attack on a person, or physical punishment. *I'll belt you* is a general threat of violence. *Belt up* is a slang expression for *be quiet*.

bump

This is an ONOMATOPOEIC word suggesting *a heavy collision of two objects*: *My car bumped into his as I was parking it; I bumped the car while I was parking it*. The protective bars at the front and back of a car are called *bumpers*. *I bumped my head on the low door frame. He fell with a bump* means he fell heavily. A *bump* is an irregularity on the surface of something: if you hit your head on a door frame, you will probably have a *bump* on your head later. A *bumpy* road is one with a broken, uneven surface; a *bumpy* journey is one on such a road; and a *bumpy* flight is one in turbulent air. To *bump someone off* is a slang expression meaning to kill them.

butt
This means *to hit with the head*, as rams (male sheep) do. To *butt into* a conversation or into someone's private business means to force oneself into it.

dash
This suggests hitting with force: *The rain was dashing against the windows; The SHIP was dashed to pieces on the rocks; He dashed the cup from her hands; That dashed our hopes of arriving early*. It can be a deliberate act of throwing a thing: *He dashed the cup to the ground*. In horse-drawn carriages a *dashboard* was a board that protected passengers from mud and stones that were dashed up by the horses' hoofs. In motor vehicles this has been adapted to refer to the panel under the windscreen containing the instruments. See CAR.

Dash also means to move quickly, to rush: *I must dash; He dashed into the room*.

Dash is used as a minced form of *damn*: *Dash it! Dashed if I know*, but as *damn* has lost its strength as a swear word, the use of *dash* is decreasing.

Dash is also a PUNCTUATION mark (–).

flog
This means *to beat with a stick or whip as a punishment*. *Flogging* was a common punishment in the army and navy, and in PUBLIC SCHOOLS. *To flog a dead horse* is to make a great effort that can produce no result. *That subject has been flogged to death* means that it has been discussed in such detail and at such length that nothing new can be said about it. *Flog* is a slang word meaning *sell*.

kick
This means to *hit with the foot*: *kick a ball*. It can be a noun: *the horse's kick broke his arm*. If a drink *has a kick in it*, it is surprisingly strong. *You get a kick out of* something that is exciting, and if you *do something for kicks* you do it only for FUN and excitement, not for profit or advantage. *To kick the bucket* is a slang expression meaning *to die*.

knock
This is an ONOMATOPOEIC word, referring to *one hard thing hitting another*. You can knock at a door with your knuckles or with a metal *knocker* to announce your presence. You can *knock on a wall* to indicate that your neighbours are making too much noise (see BANG); you can *knock a nail into a piece of wood* with a hammer, and you can *knock some sense into someone's head*; you can *knock a hole in a wall*. To *knock something off* is a slang expression meaning to steal it; to *knock someone off* is a slang expression meaning to kill them.

In Britain to *knock someone up* means to knock at their bedroom door to AWAKEN them: *I'll knock you up at 7.30 tomorrow morning*. But in American English it only means to make a woman pregnant; the possibility for surprised misunderstanding is great. It is also a noun. A nasty *knock* could be a physical blow or an emotional shock. I heard a *knock* at the door means that I heard the sound of someone knocking. If a blow to the head makes you unconscious, you are *knocked out*.

pound
This means to hit with repeated heavy blows: *Pound the garlic in a mortar; Someone was pounding at the door*. A policeman *pounds the BEAT*, referring to the heavy rhythmic fall of his steps. See BATTER.

H

punch
This means *to hit with a closed fist*; it can be used as a noun (*throw a punch*). It also means to make a hole in paper, metal, leather etc. and is the name of the tool used for doing so. You can *punch a piece of metal* or *punch a hole in a piece of metal*.

slap
This means *to hit with an open hand*. To *slap someone's face* expresses anger, but to *slap someone on the back* is an expression of congratulations. Children are sometimes punished by being *slapped* on the legs or hands. A *slap on the wrist* is often used figuratively for a punishment or criticism. *Slap and tickle* is light-hearted amorous play, kissing and cuddling, snogging (slang).

smack
Like *slap* this means *to hit with an open hand*. It is more common than *slap* in the sense of physical punishment (except for *a slap in the face*).

A HOMONYM *smack* means to have a flavour or taste of: *This sauce smacks of garlic*. It is used figuratively: *This smacks of corruption*.

thrash
This is a form of *thresh*, which means *to beat CORN* to separate the usable grain from the unusable chaff. It is used to describe great personal violence, suggesting repeated heavy blows, possibly with a weapon such as a stick or whip: *I'll give you a thrashing; I'll thrash you within an inch of your life*. By extension it means to beat an opponent completely: *The team thrashed their opponents 5-0*. To *thrash about/around* means to make uncontrolled violent movements: *He panicked and started thrashing around*. A reference to the original meaning of threshing corn is found in the expression to *thrash a subject* (etc.) *out*, meaning to discuss a subject in great detail, making all points very clearly. As a noun, a *thrash* is a lavish party like a BASH.

thump
This represents the noise of something hitting hard and heavily, with a fist or other hard, heavy instrument. A heavy bag (but not a solid box) makes a thumping noise as it hits the ground. If you are nervous or excited, your heart might be *thumping*. To *thump out a tune* is to play it very heavily.

holidays
Public holidays in the UK are officially known as BANK holidays, being days when the banks must close, so no financial activity can take place. Apart from *Christmas, New Year* and *Easter* all bank holidays fall on Mondays. The bank holidays are: *1 January* (New Year's Day), *Good Friday, Easter Monday, the first Monday in May, the last Monday in May* (Spring Bank Holiday), *the last Monday in August* (Late Summer Bank Holiday), *25 December* (Christmas Day), *and 26 December* (Boxing Day). If CHRISTMAS Day, Boxing Day or NEW YEAR'S Day falls on a Saturday or Sunday, the following Monday and, if necessary, the Tuesday, are also holidays to maintain the overall number in the year. In Northern Ireland *12 July* (the anniversary of the Battle of the Boyne in 1690, where William of Orange defeated James II, see IRELAND, A BRIEF HISTORY) is a bank holiday.

See DAYS WITH SPECIAL NAMES.

H

Home Office
The *Home Office* is the Department of State responsible for the UK's internal affairs. It is headed by the *Home Secretary*.

homonym
There are two types of *homonym*.

homographs
Homographs are words that are written identically but are different in meaning: CASE is an example, meaning a container or, for example, a legal case. ROW is an example of a homograph with different pronunciations: /rəʊ/ is a linear arrangement and /raʊ/ is an unpleasant noise.

homophones
Homophones are words that are written differently but have the same pronunciation: *meat/meet, cent/sent/scent, waist/waste, plane/plain* are examples of homophones. English has a large number of homonyms and they are the basis of a lot of English humour: *'How do you keep cool at a football match?' 'Sit next to a fan.'* The word *fan* has two meanings; it is a supporter of a football team and a cooling device. Such jokes are known as *puns*.

honours and titles

honours
The Prime Minister can create both hereditary and life *peers* (the *peerage*, members of the House of Lords see CONSTITUTION) and can confer other honours. He also creates about twenty *knights* a year. A *knighthood* allows the holder to put the title *Sir*, always spelled with a capital *S*, before his name; the equivalent title for a woman is *Dame*. This gives the holder considerable social prestige but no direct power; a knight is **not** a member of the House of Lords. *Knighthoods* are given to public figures, actors, sports personalities, business people for example, and to senior civil servants, politicians, and military officers. A knight is never referred to as *Mr*; he is, for example, *Sir Paul McCartney*, and is addressed formally as *Sir Paul* (not ~~Sir McCartney~~). The surname is not used alone with the title.

Although they can be given at any time, knighthoods are usually announced twice a year, on New Year's Day and on the Queen's official birthday (a Saturday in June). These lists also include honours to other public figure. As well as the various orders of knighthood there are the awards of *Commander, Officer* and *Member of the Order of the British Empire*, recipients of which put the letters *CBE, OBE* and *MBE* respectively after their names, as well as various other honours to public figures of all kinds. Each complete list contains several hundred names. An attempt is being made to spread honours more widely among the public.

titles
The forms of aristocratic titles in English are

emperor	*empress*
king	*queen*
duke	*duchess*
marquis/marquess /ˈmɑːkwɪs/	*marchioness* /mɑːʃəˈnes/
earl	*countess*
viscount /ˈvaɪkaʊnt/	*viscountess*
baron	*baroness*

notes
1. *Marquis* and *marquess* are different forms of the male title. The female is *marchioness*.
2. *Earl* is used for British titles such as the *Earl of Chester*, and *Count* for European titles, the *Count of Barcelona*, the *Count of Monte Cristo* for example. *Countess* is used for a woman who holds a British earldom in her own right, and for the wife of an *earl* or *count*.
3. Life peers all have the rank of *baron*.
4. The title of *baronet* is an inherited knighthood. A baronet is not a member of the peerage. It is written as *Sir Arthur Williams Bt* or *Bart*. ➤

H

Peers, especially *barons*, are usually known by the title *Lord*: *Lord Palmerston, Lord Smith*. *Judges* are addressed as *Your Honour* or *My Lord*, which is often written informally as *m'lud* /məˈlʌd/.

Sir and *madam* are the usual words used in speech to show respect to a stranger or to a superior in the police or armed forces, though in these organisations the equivalent of *sir* is *ma'am* /mɑːm/: *Yes, ma'am*. *Gentlemen* and *ladies* are the plural forms: *Good morning, sir; Can I help you, madam?; Excuse me, gentlemen/ladies*. This usage is quite different from *Sir* as the title of a knight. The equivalent nouns are *gentleman* and *lady*: *There's a gentleman to see you; A lady asked me to give you this*. However, a woman who runs a brothel is known as *a madam*.

hot

As well as referring to temperature, *hot* means *spicy* with relation to food; a dish that is strongly flavoured with PEPPER or curry for example is *hot*. This is a standard term used on restaurant menus and in labelling curry sauces. The opposite to *hot* in this case is *mild*.

hour

Hour is not normally used for exact time but is used in *at a late hour, at an early hour, at that hour*, where *hour* means time. An *hour* is a period of sixty minutes. A teaching session is called a *class* or a *lesson*; the word *hour* is not used for this purpose even if the lesson is exactly sixty minutes long. The *small hours* are the hours after midnight which have small numbers: *We stayed talking into the small hours*. The *eleventh hour* is the last possible moment for doing something. *Office hours* and *shop hours* are the times when the office or shop is open.

See TIME.

house & home

A ***house*** is a building designed for people to live in. It is a separate building, not a flat, though a house can be divided into a number of flats: *They've bought a new house; Our house has been painted*. It is used for royal houses, i.e. dynasties: *The House of Windsor*, and for the *Houses of Parliament* (*House of Commons* and *House of Lords*).

Home is more personal and emotional. *My home* is not only the physical building but includes all its associated characteristics; someone who is from a *good/bad home* has a good or bad family background; your *homeland* is the land that you come from; a *nursing home* or CARE *home* is a residential institution that provides care for sick or old people; a *homeless* person has no permanent address; a sports team plays *at home* (on its *home ground*) or away; a *home page* is the entry page to a website; you invite your guests to *make themselves at home* or *feel at home*; the *home counties* are the counties surrounding London, and the HOME OFFICE is the government department that deals with internal affairs.

Note that there is no DETERMINER in the expressions: *be at home* and *go/come home*.

human etc.

Human is the biological word for the genus *Homo* to which *human beings* belong, unlike animals, Martians, and fairies. To say that someone is *only human* is to say that they show the typical failings and weaknesses of mankind. *Human rights* are the rights common to all of MANKIND *(*INCLUSIVE LANGUAGE)*.

Humane treatment of other people or animals is treatment that shows compassion or tries to avoid suffering.

Humanism is the culture of individualism that developed from the Renaissance. In English it also refers to an ethical philosophy based on human behaviour and considered as a rational alternative to religious faith.

Humanity means both people collectively, and the humane feelings typical of mankind.

hybrid compounds

This is the name for words such as *humankind, speedometer, television, homosexual*, which have a mixture of etymological roots in their formation. Some people dislike them but a large number of them are well established in the language and are often unnoticed. *Homophobia* (hatred of homosexuals) seems to have been formed in the mistaken belief that *homo* in *homosexual* is the Latin *homo* (man). In fact it is the Greek *homo* (same) as in *homogeneous*.

hyper- & hypo-

These two prefixes are opposite in meaning: *hyper-* /ˈhaɪpə/ means an excess while *hypo-* /ˈhaɪpəʊ/ means an insufficiency. Care must be taken with them as there is a tendency for both to be pronounced /ˈhaɪpə/. A clear pronunciation will distinguish between them. This is particularly important with *hyperglycaemia* /ˌhaɪpəglaɪˈsiːmɪə/ and *hypoglycaemia* /ˌhaɪpəʊglaɪˈsiːmɪə/.

hypocrisy

The influence of words ending with *-cracy*, e.g. *aristocracy* and *democracy*, leads some native speakers to write *hypocracy*. This is incorrect. *Hypocrisy* has the same basic form as *hypocrite*.

See ECSTASY.

I

i, I /aɪ/

The ninth letter of the alphabet.

It is pronounced /ɪ/ in *hit, SHIP, thin* etc. This vowel is difficult for speakers of some languages but it is important to distinguish it from the different vowel /iː/, which is normally written *ee* or *ea*. It is true that /iː/ is longer in English than /ɪ/, but the difference is of quality as well as quantity. They are different sounds.

It is pronounced /aɪ/

- in its long pronunciation when followed by a single consonant and a vowel: *line, mile, size, write* etc. However, in *give* and *live*, and before *-ve[consonant]* e.g. *given, river, liver, rivet*, it is /ɪ/. *Driver* and *diver*, made from verbs, are /draɪvə/ and /daɪvə/. (For further comments on /ɪ/ and /aɪ/ see DOUBLE CONSONANTS.)
- in the combination *-ight*: *bright, fight, sight*.
- in monosyllables ending *-ild* and *-ind*: *child, mild, wild; bind, blind, find, grind, hind, kind, mind, rind, wind* (as a verb, but *wind* as a noun is /wɪnd/).

i and *y*

When a word that ends with *-[consonant]y* has an inflection, the *y* changes to *ie*.

- plural nouns: *lady, ladies*.
- comparative and superlative adjectives: *happy, happier, happiest*.
- verb inflections: *carry, carries, carried, carrier; cry, cries, cried, crier*; the -ING FORM is *carrying* etc.

Verbs that end with *ie* follow the pattern *die, dies, died* but *dying*.

With suffixes the *y* changes to *i*: *beauty, beautiful; study, studious; forty, fortieth*.

The *y* does not change in words such as *plays, playing, studying* (but *studies, studious*).

See SKI.

i before *e*

The combinations *ie* and *ei* can both be pronounced /iː/. A common spelling rule in English is *i before e except after c*. It is true that the usual spelling is *ie*: *believe, chief, niece, priest*, and that *cei* is found in *ceiling* and words with *-ceive* and *-ceipt*: *conceive, conceit; deceive, deceit; perceive, receive, receipt*; but it also has this pronunciation in *seize, weird*, and the name *Keith*. The combination *cie* is found in words such as *science, society, conscience; species* /ˈspiːʃiːz/ is the only word where *cie* is pronounced /iː/. *Eiderdown, height, kaleidoscope*, and EITHER AND NEITHER are the only common words with *ei* pronounced as /aɪ/. In a number of words it is pronounced /eɪ/ *eight, freight, neighbour, weigh(t), beige, veil, vein* but in other cases the pronunciation of *ei* varies from word to word.

-ic and -ical

There are a large number of adjectives that end in *-ic* and/or *-ical*. About 55% always have only *-ic*, 25% always have only *-ical*, and 20% can have either. Examples are:

-ic only: *alcoholic, basic, dramatic, plastic*.
-ical only: *chemical, practical, radical*.
both forms: *geographic(al), ironic(al), problematic(al), symmetric(al)*.

There seems to be a preference in American English for *-ic* (the AMERICAN *National Geographic* magazine and the British *Royal Geographical Society*) but this difference is far from clear.

Whether these words have *-ic* or *-ical*, they have their stress on the syllable that precedes the suffix: *alcohólic, práctical*.

Adjectives relating to geographical or cultural ideas always have *ic*: *Arabic, Baltic, Icelandic, Teutonic* as do names of chemical compounds: *chloric, oxalic*, SULFURic.

Nouns ending in *-ology* make adjectives in *-ical*: *biological, ideological, zoological.*

When the root is a noun ending in *-ic*, the adjective is always *-ical*: *logical, musical, topical.* Apparent exceptions are *alcoholic, comic, plastic.* However, these nouns have been made from the adjectives, not vice versa.

The adverb is always *-ically* except for *publicly* though ~~*publically*~~ is sometimes seen, as are the incorrect forms ~~*incidently*~~ and ~~*accidently*~~ (thus spelled from the pronunciation).

Sometimes the two forms have different meanings.

See CLASSIC; ECONOMIC; HISTORIC; POLICY & POLITICS ETC.

-ics

Words ending with *-ics* refer to matters of study or activity: *acoustics, athletics, aerodynamics, economics, ethics, linguistics, mathematics, politics, tactics* etc. As the name of the study or activity the words are singular: *Athletics is part of the Olympic Games; Linguistics is the study of language; Politics is the art of managing power in a society.*

However, when different aspects of the matter are considered these words are regarded as plural: *His politics* (i.e. his political opinions) *are disgusting; The economics of the situation make it difficult to find a solution; Such acoustics are unusual in a concert hall of this age.* Note that when these words are plural they usually have a DETERMINER.

idioms and metaphors

These are examples of language use where words do not have their usual meanings. Some metaphors (but few idioms) are common to different cultures. They should not be translated from one language to another without certainty that the translation will be comprehensible; otherwise they can be misleading or even ridiculous.

-iety

Words ending in a consonant followed by *-iety* are pronounced with /'aɪəti/: *anxiety, piety, (in)sobriety, notoriety, (im)propriety, variety, impiety, society.*

See ALLIANCE.

if & whether

In some cases *if* and *whether* are interchangeable. *If* tends to be more common in informal usage of sentences of this type:
Do you know if/whether you're staying for dinner?
I don't know if/whether she has arrived yet.

Can you tell me if/whether you're staying for dinner or if/whether you're leaving this afternoon?
I don't know if/whether she has arrived or if/whether she has been delayed by the weather.

These examples have two balanced parts and can be rewritten as:
Can you tell me if/whether you're staying for dinner or leaving this afternoon?
I don't know if/whether she has arrived or been delayed by the weather.

However, *if* cannot be used in sentences of the following types:
Whether you stay for dinner makes no difference. (subject CLAUSE)
The problem is whether we'll have enough food. (COMPLEMENT clause)
It's a question of whether we'll have enough food. (preposition complement)
You haven't answered my question, whether we have enough food. (apposition)
She doesn't know whether to stay for dinner. (*to*-infinitive following)

In all of the above examples *whether or not* can be used but ~~*if or not*~~ is incorrect: *Do you know whether or not you're staying for dinner?* but *Do you know if/whether you're staying for dinner or not?* is correct with EITHER *if* or *whether.*

In some CASES there is ambiguity: *I'll tell you if I can do it* could mean *If I can do it I will tell you so (and if I can't do it, I won't tell you)* or *I'll tell you whether I can do it (or whether I can't do it).*

I

ill

words connected with health.

Ill is the usual word meaning *in poor health*: *I was taken ill on Tuesday; If you feel ill, go to the doctor; She's been ill for six months*. It usually follows the noun but can go before it, especially when it is preceded by an adverb: *He was a very ill man when I met him; Terminally/mentally ill patients*.

POORLY (an ADJECTIVE WITH -LY) can be used instead of *ill* in the first set of examples: *I was taken poorly on Tuesday* but not in the others: ~~He was a poorly man when I met him~~.

Usually, **sick** is used before the noun: *The sick man stood up and walked to the door*; but *sick* does not describe a chronic or permanent state so *He was a sick man when I met him* is improbable and ~~Terminally/mentally sick patients~~ is impossible. An employed person who is *ill* or *poorly* will probably *go sick* (present a *sick note* to report that he is unable to go to work) and will be *off sick* for a period of time, during which he will receive *sick pay*. Someone who is *ill in bed* might *rise from her sick bed* to answer a KNOCK *(*HIT)* at the door.

Used PREDICATIVELY, *sick* has the idea of nausea or vomiting: *I feel sick; I'm going to be sick*. In British (but not American) English *to be sick* specifically means *to vomit*: *He was sick three times last night* and as a noun *sick* is the substance that is vomited: *I had to clean the sick off the floor*. *Being ill in bed* is clearly different from *being sick in bed*. *Morning sickness* is a nausea that commonly accompanies pregnancy. Some people are *seasick* or *carsick* (etc.); *travel sickness* is the general word for this. People who go away from home may feel *homesick*, not physically but emotionally affected by the lack of familiar elements of home life, while a *lovesick* young person separated from his or her lover can be difficult to manage. A *sick mind* is one that is mentally disturbed, and a *sick joke* is one that makes fun of illness, death and the LIKE. If you are *sick* of people telling you what to do, you have had enough of it, you are fed up with it. If it is very serious, you are *sick and tired* or *sick to death* of it. A *sickie* is a slang word for time taken off work when one is not really ill.

If someone's health deteriorates or improves they become *worse* or *better* respectively. *Better* is ambiguous. It can obviously mean that a patient has improved: *I feel better than I did last week*, but it can also mean *fully recovered*: *You'll be better next week; Don't come back to work until you're (feeling) better*. *Ill*, *poorly* and *sick* do not have comparative forms.

other uses of *ill*

As well as its connection with poor health *ill* has a general meaning that something is poor, bad, or wrong; indeed, *ill health* is another way of saying *bad* or *poor health*.

Ill will is animosity or bad feeling. It is a CALQUE of *malevolence*. An *ill wind* refers to the arrival of unpleasant circumstances, problems, or difficulties. It is a reference to the proverb *It's an ill wind that blows nobody any good* meaning that however bad things are, someone will always benefit from the situation. *Ill* is common as an adverb before a past participle: *ill-advised, ill-built, ill-informed, ill-judged, ill-matched, ill-prepared, ill-presented, ill-suited*. To *think* or *speak ill* of someone is to have or express a low opinion of that person, and if you *take something ill* you accept it unhappily or unwillingly or are offended by it.

See DISEASE & ILLNESS.

illegible & unreadable

Illegible is used to refer to something that is physically impossible to read because of the nature of the text; it may be badly handwritten or physically damaged.

Unreadable is a personal JUDGEMENT on an author's style: *I have tried on several occasions to read X but I find his books unreadable*.

imply & infer

To **imply** something is to suggest it indirectly.

To **infer** something is to deduce or conclude it from evidence. Native speakers sometimes use *infer* to mean *imply*.

The corresponding nouns are *implication* and *inference*. The adjective *implicit* describes something that is implied but is not stated openly; it is the opposite of *explicit*.

in & on (including at)

For the use of these with time expressions see TIME | TIME PREPOSITIONS.

in

In means *inside a three-dimensional space*: *in the room, in the car, in a box, in the water* (a diver or a fish). A photograph, picture or mirror is regarded as such a space: *Who can you see in this photo?; I caught a GLIMPSE (*SEE) of her in the mirror. In* with two-dimensional space means *within the boundaries of*: *in the field, in Liverpool, in Catalonia.*

on

On means on the surface of something: *on the floor, on the wall, on the ceiling, on the side of the box, on the table, on the line, on the water* (a BOAT or a bird).

On is used with fairly small islands that can be considered as one place: *We spent our holiday on the Isle of Man; Nelson Mandela was imprisoned on Robben Island* but *in Britain, in Cuba*. No precise distinction can be made with regard to size.

A town or farm for example may be *on a river, on a border,* or *on the coast.*

notes for in & on

This distinction between *in* and *on* also applies to books and newspapers: *It's in the dictionary, it's in today's newspaper, it's on page 94* (inside the physical book or newspaper but printed on the surface of page 94).

A table can be *in the corner of the room* (surrounded by the walls in the corner) and a building can be *on the corner of the street* (on the surface of the part of the street that makes the corner).

In is also used in relation to concepts that are metaphorically spatial: *in the circumstances, in this situation, in danger, in my opinion, in the nature of such animals*; each of these can be considered as an enveloping cloud analogous to a three-dimensional box or room.

In or *on* is used in almost all cases with COMPARATIVE AND SUPERLATIVE adjectives: *the longest river in Europe; the oldest girl in the class; the biggest house on the ISLAND.*

If you are *on the road* you are travelling. A house or petrol station for example may be *on the road to Manchester*. A cinema or shop for example is *in a certain street* in Britain but in American English it is *on the street.*

You speak to someone *on the phone*, you hear something *on the radio*, but you see a PROGRAMME *on TV.*

You travel *on a bus, plane, train* etc. but *in a car or taxi.*

in & into

Into combines the ideas of entering and arriving: *She came into the room; Put it into the box. In* is often used colloquially here.

on to & onto

As the equivalent of *into*, when it combines the ideas of moving to and arriving on something, both forms are acceptable, though in Britain some people regard one-word *onto* as non-standard; in American English it is standard: *The cat jumped onto the table*. But it must always be written as two words when this idea of movement is not present, for example when it is part of a MULTI-WORD VERB: *I will now move on to the next part of my speech; He passed his cold on to me.* In each of these examples, the *on* could stand as an adverb as the last word of a sentence: *I will now move on; He passed his cold on.* ▶

I

We drove on to the beach means that we continued driving until we reached the beach; *We drove onto the beach* means that we drove our car off the road so that it was on the beach. These two sentences are differentiated in speech by intonation.

Clearly, when the *to* is part of an infinitive it cannot be combined with *on*: *When the others went home, he worked on to finish the report on time.*

See ON AND UPON.

at

At is more difficult to define precisely; it refers to a spatial relationship that is not covered by *in* or *on*. For example, if you are waiting for a bus you are *at the bus stop*, though you may be a few metres away from the actual stop because you are sheltering from the rain. Someone the same distance from the bus stop but who is waiting for a taxi would probably say they caught a taxi *near* or *next to* the bus stop or *a few metres from* it. The difference is whether you think that there is a connection between you and the bus stop.

Similarly, a person is *at work* but *in her office* (she spends part of her time at work in the canteen drinking coffee and chatting with other people), *at home, at school (at the local comprehensive, at Eton), at university (at Cambridge)*. Someone standing *on the end of a bridge* is on the bridge; someone *at the end of the bridge* is not necessarily on it. Meeting someone *at the corner* of the street is not as precise as standing *on the corner*. Countries can be *at war* (but *in a state of war*) or *at peace*. *At* is the preposition used with *sea* to refer to people in SHIPS: *He's at sea now; He spent most of his life at sea.* If you are *all at sea*, you are totally confused. *You'll have to change trains at Birmingham* or *She's at Birmingham* (understood to mean Birmingham University) but *She's in Birmingham* (perhaps living there or just there for the day).

In the end means *finally*: *We had a lot of problems but in the end it all went well. At the end* refers to the end of a process, time period, or physical object: *See me at the end of the lesson; I'll pay you at the end of the month; My house is at the end of the street.*

At is used with points on a scale: *Water boils at 100° C.; At his best he is excellent.*

You can be *good, excellent, bad, terrible at* something: *good at swimming; terrible at maths.*

There is a difference between sitting *on a table* and sitting *at a table*.

At one time *at* was used in places where *in* is now used with names of places: *I bought the cheese at Liverpool.*

With MULTI-WORD VERBS there is often no apparent logic in the choice of preposition: *depend on* but *trust in. Look at, look in* and *look on* all mean different things.

in case

Followed by a CLAUSE, this is used to describe a precautionary measure against something that might happen: *Take an umbrella in case it rains; I washed your blue sweater in case you needed it.* Also *I don't think it will rain but take an umbrella (JUST) in case.*

Lest is a very formal equivalent of *in case*: *Take an umbrella lest it rain.* Note that the high degree of formality requires the use of the SUBJUNCTIVE mood.

In case as used above is different from *In case of rain* (if it rains) *the party will be held indoors*.

See CASE.

inclusive language

The increased awareness of feminism in recent decades has led to changes in many languages as people try to find language that does not discriminate between men and women. Languages are affected differently according to their nature; in English the problem is found in two main areas, agent nouns (those that name jobs or positions) and pronouns.

agent nouns

There are two ways in English of making feminine forms, with *-ess* and by changing *-man* to *-woman*.

-ess

This suffix has been used since the MIDDLE AGES as a means of indicating a female agent. Some are solidly fixed in the language: *abbess* (female of abbot), *ambassadress* (female ambassador or wife of an ambassador), *duchess* (and other titles), *goddess, governess* (obsolete name for a private teacher*), heiress, hostess, lioness, mayoress* (usually the wife of a MAYOR *(*MAJOR)*), *mistress, peeress,* PRIESTESS (not Christian religion), *shepherdess, stewardess* (usually now *flight attendant* or *cabin crew*) on a plane. HEROINE and *landlady* are also well established as is the distinction between *widow* (woman) and *widower* (man).

Actress, authoress and *waitress* are commonly used, though people are beginning to question the need for separate female forms of these words. *Poetess, directress* and *manageress* are rarely seen nowadays. Forms in *-rix* (corresponding to Latin *-or*) such as *directrix, aviatrix* are no longer used except for the legal term EXECUTRIX. It is interesting to note that these names were used proudly by women in the early twentieth century precisely to show that women were doing those jobs, but now that it is not surprising that this is the case the trend is away from such specific indication. As nurses are traditionally thought of as female, *male nurse* is a common term for a man working in that profession. MASTER, meaning an expert in a trade or art is perhaps less common now than it used to be but it is difficult to find a suitable female equivalent; *mistress* is not appropriate.

A number of jobs were traditionally done by men; for example *businessman, chairman, fireman, policeman, seaman*. As this work is now often done by women, these are often changed to *businesswoman* or *business person* (plural *business people*), *chairperson* or *chair, firefighter, police officer, seaFAREr*.

It can be used for babies, where GENDER seems irrelevant: *The baby fell off the bed and landed on its head.*

mankind

Mankind means people in general. In Old English *man* meant a person of either sex as well as a male person; it is still sometimes used in this sense, but less frequently now. Despite this, some people prefer the word *humankind* as being non-discriminatory while others object to it as a HYBRID COMPOUND. Here *kind* is a noun meaning *race* or *family*; it is connected to KIN *(*KITH AND KIN)* and has nothing do with *kind* as an adjective.

pronouns

A problem arises in the third person pronoun, where the gender of the pronoun is related to the sex of the person to whom it refers. The pairs of words involved are: *he/she; him/her; his/her* and *himself/herself*, and when a general singular reference is made to a teacher, doctor or driver for example, there is no satisfactory solution: *When a teacher speaks to a child, he or she must...; A doctor must respect his/her patients*. Such forms are inelegant in print and almost impossible in speech. Some people choose to use the masculine pronouns, or rather the more probable one: *In 2030, whoever is the President of Iran will find that his country...; A primary school teacher may have up to thirty children in her class.*

In colloquial language and journalism this may be acceptable, but in professional work publishers sometimes try to overcome the problem by alternating masculine and feminine forms in the text. This can be difficult for the reader: *A primary school teacher may have up to thirty children in her class but he has more resources available than her grandparent* (to avoid *grandfather* or *grandmother*) *did*. Some publishers alternate these forms in successive chapters of a longer book. In a short text such as a job advertisement, or a text that is for reference more than continual reading such as a contract, the alternative forms *s/he, he or she, him/her* etc. are often used. These too can be alternated *she or he, her/him*. One convenient solution that is sometimes appropriate is to use a plural: *Primary school teachers may have up to thirty children in their classes* or a definite article: *A primary school teacher may have up to thirty children in the class.* One increasingly popular solution is to use *they* forms with singular reference: *When a teacher speaks to a child, they must...; A doctor must respect their patients*. This seems unusual but is becoming more widespread. It is especially useful when a pronoun has to refer to an impersonal word such as *anyone* or *somebody*. The easiest and most elegant solution is to use the appropriate part of *they, them* etc.: *Anyone who needs a ticket must bring their money tomorrow; Nobody could do it, even if they wanted to*. Although this use is criticised as illogical, it has been found in English since the sixteenth century and seems to be becoming the modern standard. However, it causes problems in extended sentences; the following is adapted from the second paragraph of the article on MULTI-WORD VERBS: *to put someone through is to make a telephone connection for them, to put them through the telephone system that is between them and the person they want to speak to*. The repeated use of the plural pronoun is inappropriate to the obviously singular nature of the person in question. Similarly, *Anyone who has found themselves alone in a forest at night...* sounds unusual; the combination of singular and plural is strange.

It would seem logical for a neutral pronoun to be used instead of both *he* and *she*; several such words have been proposed, but none has made any significant progress. Oddly perhaps, there has been no proposal that *it* should replace the two pronouns that refer to the sex of the person in question.

See ONE | PRONOUNS PERSONAL.

India & Hindu

India and *Indian* refer to the country. *Hindu* (adjective and noun) refers to the religion of *Hinduism* and its followers but there are many Indians who are not Hindus. *Hindi* is the official language of India. *Hindustani* is still sometimes used for the lingua franca of North-west India. Because of Christopher Columbus's mistake in thinking that he had ARRIVED in Asia when in fact he landed in America, the NATIVE peoples of the American continent are also *Indians*, though *native-American* is increasingly the preferred term.

indirect (reported) speech

Usually in indirect speech when the reporting verb moves into the past, a process known as backshifting takes place; this means that the verb that is reported moves into the past. The principle is clearest in the transformation of a sentence such as *He has worked/he worked in Paris* into *He said that he had worked in Paris* (past or present perfect → past perfect). Here the normal use of the past perfect refers to one action preceding another (He had already worked in Paris before he spoke). The *that* is optional: *He said he had worked in Paris*. Backshifting is a general change but see the notes below for precise information about how it is applied in different tenses.

direct	indirect	backshift
He works part-time.	He worked part-time.	present → past
He's working.	He was working.	present → past
He worked there last year.	He (had) worked there last year.	past → past or past perfect
He's never worked in Paris.	He had never worked in Paris.	pres. perf. → past. perfect
He'd never worked in Paris.	He had never worked in Paris.	past perfect → past perfect

modal auxiliary verbs

He will never work again.	He would never work again.
He may never work again.	He might never work again.
He cannot work.	He could not work.
He must work. (obligation)	He must work/he had to work.
He must work in York. (logical deduction)	He must work in York.
He should work harder.	He should work harder.
He would rather work in Spain.	He would RATHER work in Spain.
He might never work again.	He might never work again.
He couldn't work for six weeks.	He could not/had not been able to work for six weeks.
He had better work harder.	He had better work harder.
He ought to work harder.	He ought to work harder.

For further information on the past and present of modal verbs see the articles on MODAL AUXILIARY VERBS and TENSE & TIME.

He	said explained stated whispered told me suggested denied	that...	

A number of verbs can be used to introduce the indirect speech.

When what is reported in the indirect speech is still valid at the time of reporting, backshifting is not obligatory: *He told me that his sister is a doctor.*

There is no backshifting if the reporting verb is in the present simple: *I think he's stupid; She says that she's lost her purse* or in the present perfect: *I have often suggested that he is not really the best man for the job.*

The present simple is used to report words from famous authors or works that have current validity: *Shakespeare writes in 'As You Like It' that all the world's a stage; The Bible tells us that adultery is sinful.*

Changes are sometimes necessary to time and place expressions in indirect speech with respect to the direct speech original. For example *today → that day, now → then, tomorrow → the following day, here → there, this → that, myself → him/herself*. These changes are obvious from the context.

The above examples relate to statements. Other types of utterance can be converted to indirect speech, making the same changes.

questions
yes-no
Are you working? I asked if/whether she was working.

alternative
Are you working or not? I asked if/whether (or not) she was working (or not).

wh-
When will he start working? I asked when he would start working.

Note the word order in the WH- QUESTION; it is not *I asked him when would he start working*. It is *I asked her where her husband was* not *I asked her where was her husband* and *Do you know where the station is?* not *Do you know where is the station?*

exclamation
What a good worker you are! I told him what a good worker he was.

imperative
Work harder. I told him to work harder.

Indo-European languages
Like almost all languages spoken in Europe, English is a member of the Indo-European family. Indo-European languages are also spoken in Iran, Pakistan and India. In origin English is a Germanic language; although the typical Germanic inflections have been lost (see ENGLISH LANGUAGE, A BRIEF HISTORY), a comparison of English irregular verb forms and use of MODAL AUXILIARY VERBS with their equivalents in modern German makes this relationship perfectly clear. Other Germanic languages are German, Dutch, and the Scandinavian languages. Russian and related Slavic languages are spoken in eastern and central Europe. The CELTIC languages, which were once spoken across much of Europe, survive in Wales, Scotland, Ireland, Cornwall, the Isle of Man and Brittany in north-west France.

Proto-Indo-European, the parent of all the modern languages, probably developed in the Danube area of Europe some time before 3000 BC. Between 2000 and 1000 BC the modern groups began to appear. There are no records of Proto-Indo-European, but it has been possible to reconstruct it from the evidence of modern languages.

Other modern languages spoken in Europe are Finnish and Estonian, and the more distantly related Hungarian, all of which are Uralic languages; Turkish is distantly related to these. Basque is spoken

I

in northern Spain and south-western France. Although there is no evidence, it seems reasonable to suppose that it is the descendant of one of the languages spoken in Europe in the Stone Age before Indo-European languages became dominant. There are suggestions that it may be related to modern Caucasian or North African languages, or to ancient Iberian, but nothing has been proved.

inferior and superior

These words are not normal comparative forms. One thing is *inferior* or *superior to* another (not *than*).

They refer to quality; they are not synonyms of *lower* and *higher*. They do not necessarily have to be used in comparisons. An *inferior wine* is one of low quality in absolute terms.

infinitive

There are two forms of the infinitive, the BARE (or plain) *infinitive* (without *to*) and the infinitive with *to*. The present infinitive is the normal infinitive of the verb with or without *to*; the past infinitive is *(to) have+past participle*.

the bare infinitive

This is used:

- following modal and semi-modal verbs: *I must, can, will* etc. *go*.
- following *let*: *They let him go* (but *They allowed/permitted him to go*). Passive: *He was allowed/permitted to go* but not ~~He was let go~~.
- with *make*: In the expression *make somebody do something/make something happen*: *He made her cry; We will make him pay for the* DAMAGE. But note the passive with *to*: *He will be made to pay for the damage.*
- in expressions where it is represented by *do/does/did* in the other CLAUSE: *What my proposal will do is make things fairer; Ask him his address was all I did.*
- following causative HAVE: *I'll have him repair it tomorrow.*
- following sense verbs: *I saw him cross the road*. But note the passive: *He was seen to cross the road*. For the difference between this and *I saw him crossing the road* see SENSE VERBS under INFINITIVE OR -ING?
- following *know*: *I have never known him* TELL *(*SAY ETC.) a lie*. But note the passive: *He has never been known to tell a lie.*
- following prepositions of exception: *I did everything but/except tell him the answer.*
- following *why*: *Why stop now?; Why spend more than you have to?; Why not go on Sunday?; Why not phone her now?*

See RATHER | WOULD RATHER; BETTER | HAD BETTER.

the infinitive with *to* (full infinitive)

This form of the infinitive is used after certain verbs (see INFINITIVE OR –ING?) and in some other constructions.

As the subject or complement of a verb:
To live there must be expensive.
For you to live there must be expensive.
It must be expensive to live there.
It must be expensive for you to live there.
I'm pleased for him to have won.
His response was to call me a liar.
His response, to call me a liar, was unfair.
It's good/bad/(un)natural for him to sleep so much (or *...that he should sleep so much*). See COMPLEMENT (GRAMMATICAL)

As the direct object of a verb:
I require/expect/need/want/would like everyone to be here at eleven o'clock. (Note that ~~I require etc. that everyone should be here~~ is not possible.)

I like to smoke a cigar after dinner. See INFINITIVE OR -ING?
I told them when to arrive; I showed him how to do it. (with a WH- QUESTION word)
I expect to arrive at ten o'clock.

As the complement of an adjective: *I'm very pleased to meet you; I'm happy to TELL (*SAY ETC.) you that you have won first prize.*

In the infinitive of purpose. In *I used a computer to calculate the result* and *I went to the shop to buy a pair of shoes* the infinitive is used to express the purpose for which the main action was taken.

postmodification

Postmodification (cases where the descriptive information about a noun follows it) with the *infinitive with to* is found in

infinitive clauses

The first guest to arrive was Mary could be rewritten as *The first guest who arrived was Mary* because the subject of the infinitive CLAUSE *(the first guest)* is the same as the subject of the main verb *(Mary)*. This is not always the case. In the sentence *The man for you to ask is John* the subject of the infinitive clause *(you)* is different from the subject of the main verb *(John)*. This clause can be rewritten as *The man you should ask is John.*

The man to ask is John is ambiguous; it could be personal or impersonal depending on the context and can be rewritten as either *The man you should ask is John* or *The man everyone should ask is John.*

Similarly, in these examples
1 *The time for you to leave is 10.00.*
2 *The time at which you should leave is 10.00.*
3 *The time at which to leave is 10.00.*

1 *The place for them to stay is the King's Arms.*
2 *The place at which they should stay is the King's Arms.*
3 *The place at which to stay is the King's Arms.*

sentence 3 could be personal or impersonal depending on the context. This construction can be used in the passive voice: *The matter to be discussed today is of great importance.*

apposition

1 *His request for people to arrive early was ignored.*
2 *His request to arrive early was ignored.*
3 *His attempt to break the record succeeded.*

These can be rewritten:
1 *His request that people should arrive early was ignored.*
2a *His request that people should arrive early was ignored.* (different subject)
2b *His request that he should arrive early was ignored.* (same subject)
3 This cannot be rewritten with a *that* CLAUSE.

See NEGATIVE INFINITIVE *(*NEGATION OF VERBS)*.

Verbs with *object + infinitive* are described in INFINITIVE OR -ING?

infinitive or -ing?

For the infinitive without *to*, see MODAL AUXILIARY VERBS and BARE INFINITIVE under infinitive.

verb + infinitive with *to*
absolute infinitive only

Some verbs are followed by an absolute infinitive with *to*: *I want to be alone; We expect to arrive at ten o'clock.* Among these verbs are *afford, agree, arrange, attempt, beg, choose, claim, dare, decide, expect, fail,* HAPPEN, *help, hope, long, manage, mean* (= intend), *need, offer, prepare, pretend, promise,* REFUSE, *seem, want, yearn.*

For *dare, help, need,* see MODAL AUXILIARY VERBS | SEMI-MODAL VERBS. ➤

I

absolute infinitive or object + infinitive

Ask, beg, expect, help, intend, need, want and WISH can be used with an absolute infinitive: *She asked to go* (She asked, she went) or with an object before the infinitive when the subject changes: *She asked John to go* (She asked, John went.)

For ADVISE, *intend* and *recommend*, see VERB + -ING below.

object + infinitive only

Some verbs cannot have an absolute infinitive; they must be followed by an object and infinitive. Among these are AID, *allow, appoint, assist, cause, challenge, command, compel, dare*, enable, encourage, entitle, entreat, forbid, force, implore, incite, induce, inspire, instruct, intend, invite, lead, oblige,* ORDER, *permit, persuade, prompt, provoke, remind, request, stimulate, teach,* TELL *(*SAY ETC.), tempt, trust, urge, warn.*

*In this sense *to dare someone to do something* means *to challenge someone to do something.*

See VERBS OF MENTAL PERCEPTION below.

With sentences such as *I allowed him to go home* and *Bill encouraged Ben to speak* it is very important to note that verbs that have an object and infinitive cannot be used with a *that* clause. The forms ~~She asked that John go~~ and ~~Bill encouraged Ben that he speak~~ are absolutely impossible in English. It should be emphasised that *want* is in this category: You *want somebody to do something.* For example *I want you to be here at ten o'clock* not ~~I want that you are here at ten o'clock~~.

Passive forms can be made of these verbs with the exception of *want* and *need*: *John was asked to go; Ben was encouraged to speak.*

verbs of mental perception

The verbs *believe, consider, expect, feel, find, know,* PROVE, *show,* SUPPOSE and THINK fall into the category of verbs that can only be followed by an object and infinitive with *to*: *She believes him to be a millionaire; We considered her to be the best candidate; I expected her to have arrived by now* (the past INFINITIVE is used with the PAST SIMPLE). These sentences can always be rewritten as *She believed that he was a millionaire* etc. and in fact the form with *that* is more common, but the infinitive provides the passive with the personal subject: *He is believed to be a millionaire; She was considered to be the best candidate; She was expected to have arrived by then.* See HE IS SAID TO BE ETC. *(*PASSIVE VOICE).*

verb + -ing

Some verbs are followed by -ing. Among these are *admit,* ADVISE, *anticipate, appreciate, avoid, begrudge, can't help, can't stand, carry on* (continue), *consider, contemplate, delay, detest, deny, dislike, don't mind, endure* (tolerate), *enjoy, entail, envisage, escape* (avoid), *excuse* (FORGIVE), *fancy, finish, foresee, forgive, give up, grudge, have difficulty (in), imagine, include, intend, involve, it is (not) worth, it is no good, it is no/little* etc. *use, justify, keep* (continue), *mention, mind, miss, necessitate, pardon, postpone, practise, prevent, propose, put off, recall, recollect, recommend, report, require, resent, resist, risk, stand, stop, suggest, tolerate, suggest.*

Examples:
I admitted stealing the book.
I appreciate you(r) (see GERUND) *coming so quickly.*
Can you imagine owning a villa in Spain?
I can't stand being cold.
Mary suggested going for a walk in the park.

Advise, intend and *recommend* can have an object and infinitive: *I advise/recommend you to leave early; They intend her to marry him.*

deserve, need, require, want

With these verbs the -ING FORM has a passive meaning:
He deserves thanking most sincerely (to be thanked).
This chapter needs revising (to be revised).

This requires thinking about (to be thought about).
My hair WANTS washing (needs to be washed).

both infinitive and *-ing* possible with different meaning
afraid
I am afraid to go out in the dark means that it is dark now and I do not want to go out. *I am afraid of going out in the dark* means that as a general rule I do not want to go out when it is dark.

go on
With an infinitive it means to proceed from one action to another: *I've spoken about the past. Now I'll go on to talk about the present and the future.* With the -ING FORM *go on* means *continue*: *He went on talking about the past without mentioning the present or the future.*

like
LIKE, *love, dread, hate, loathe* and *prefer* can be used with either the infinitive or the gerund; the -ING FORM is much more common.

	adore		
	like		
	love		Other tenses can be used: *I loved/will prefer/had hated watching TV.*
I	prefer	watching TV.	The infinitive is used with the conditional (see LIKE): *I would like* (etc.)
	hate		to watch TV.
	loathe		
	dread		

It is also used in *I like to watch the TV news before I go out to work*. Here, the emphasis is on liking the potential ability to do so, rather than on the enjoyment obtained from the action (*I like watching…*) It refers to the habit: *I have the habit, which I like, of watching the TV news…*

regret
I regret to say/TELL (*SAY ETC.) you/inform you that I have damaged your car is a rather formal way of expressing regret at the moment of speaking, whereas *I regret not working/having worked harder earlier* and *I'll never regret telling/having told him the truth* refer to an action that comes earlier in time than the regretting.

remember & forget
With the infinitive these refer to the future with respect to the time of remembering/forgetting:

Remember to lock the door when you go out.
Of course I'll remember to lock the door.
Did you remember to lock the door?
In each case the act of remembering is earlier in time than the locking of the door.

With *-ing*: in *Do you remember locking the door?* and *Of course I remember locking the door* the act of locking is recovered from the memory; it takes place earlier in time than the remembering.

Forget is similar:
Don't forget to lock the door.
Of course I won't forget to lock the door.
I forgot to lock the door.
but can only have *-ing* with a negative verb: *I haven't forgotten/I can't forget locking the door for the last time when I left the house for ever.*

These words can have an object and *-ing*: *I remember him telling me about his childhood; I'll never forget him telling me about his childhood.*

sense verbs
SENSE VERBS can be followed by either an infinitive or an -ING FORM with different meanings.

The infinitive is used for a completed action: *I saw him come out of the shop; I heard him lock the door.* ➤

I

The -ING FORM is used for an action that has not been completed: *I saw him walking along the road; I can feel something moving.* Note the correspondence with the continuous aspect of the verb: *He was walking along the road when I saw him.*

stop
With an infinitive it means stopping movement or action in order to do something else: *I stopped to buy a newspaper at a kiosk; The bus stopped to let the passengers get on.*

With a gerund *stop* means to stop an action that is in progress: *I stopped writing and looked at her; I stopped buying newspapers last year* (because they were too expensive).

The two forms can be combined: *I stopped writing to look at her; She stopped working to make herself a cup of coffee.* The infinitive following *stop* is the infinitive of purpose.

try
To try to do something is to make an attempt in the hope of succeeding:
I tried to open the door but it was impossible.
He's trying to break the world record.
Try to wear a blue hat. (If you can wear one, it will help me recognise you.)

Try with a noun object means *to experiment with something*: *Try more ice; Try John*. The object can be a gerund/-ING FORM of a verb:
Try putting more ice in it. (Perhaps that will make it cold enough.)
Try asking John. (He might know the answer.)
Try wearing a blue hat. (It would probably look better than that red one.)

both infinitive and *-ing* possible with the same meaning
Some verbs can be followed by an infinitive or *-ing* with no difference in meaning.
I intend to go/going to Scotland next year.
She began to cry/crying.
It's started to snow/snowing.
It continued to snow/snowing all night.
I can't bear to see/seeing him in pain.

Note that the continuous form *I'm intending going to Scotland next year* is possible but ~~She's beginning crying; It's starting snowing; It's continuing snowing~~ are not. In these three cases the infinitive must be used: *She's beginning to cry; It's starting to snow; It's continuing to snow.*

~~I can't be bearing~~... is impossible as BEAR is a stative verb.

With an object we can say *I'm intending him to go to university; That started her crying.* (Note that to start somebody doing something is an instantaneous action and so it has no continuous form: ~~He was starting her crying~~.)

The prepositional verbs *depend on* and *rely on* can be used as follows with no difference in meaning: *You can depend/rely on him to arrive on time* and *You can depend/rely on him/his arriving on time.*

which to use
Overall, the question of whether to use a gerund or an infinitive is one that causes problems for students, who are faced with an apparently arbitrary division of verbs into categories.

In fact a distinction can be made. The infinitive is used in the case of a potential or hypothetical action which takes place after the time of the main verb:
I want to go.
He agreed to pay me.
I'll need to go to the bank.
We arranged to meet.

The -ING FORM refers to the performance or continuing nature of the action (it is the form used in the CONTINUOUS ASPECT of verbs). In these examples, it is possible to consider the verb as relating to a real, possibly continuing, action or state:
I admitted (the action of) *stealing the book.*

I appreciate your (your action of) *coming so quickly.*
Can you imagine (the state of) *owning a villa in Spain?*
I can't stand (the state of) *being cold.*
Mary suggested (the action of) *going for a walk in the park.*

In this light we see that verbs that can take both forms with different meanings are reflecting this difference.

future potential	performance
I am afraid to go out in the dark.	*I am afraid of going out in the dark.*
Remember to lock the door.	*I remember locking the door.*
I tried to open the door.	*Try asking John.*
I stopped to buy a paper.	*I stopped writing.*
I like to watch the TV news...	*I like watching TV.*
I'd like to watch TV.	
I regret to tell you...	*I regret not working.*
I won't forget to lock the door.	*I haven't forgotten locking the door.*
I'll go on to talk about the present.	*He went on talking about the past.*

The future potential refers to the future as at the time of the action described by the verb, which can be the past or future at the time of speaking; see REMEMBER & FORGET above.

See USED TO.

information

This word is uncountable like ADVICE and NEWS: *some information* or *a piece/some pieces of information* but not ~~an information~~.

-ing form

For most purposes the terms GERUND and present participle are perfectly adequate. The gerund is the part of the verb that is used as a noun: *Smoking damages your health; I'm looking forward to meeting you* and the *present participle* is the part used in the continuous tenses: *He's watching television; They were playing football.*

However, there are a small number of borderline cases where it is not easy to make this distinction, so the term -ING FORM is commonly used in grammar books.

See PARTICIPLE CLAUSES.

inner, interior & internal

These words differ in the way they are used RATHER than in meaning.

Your **inner** thoughts, feelings and emotions are your most private ones. The *inner* compartment, space etc. is the opposite of the *outer* one that surrounds it. An *inner circle* is an exclusive group of people and the *inner city* is the area near the centre. The opposite is *outer*.

The **interior** of a country is the part away from the coast. *Interior decorators* specialise in decorating the insides of buildings. In many countries the *Ministry of the Interior* deals with the countries *internal* affairs. An *interior angle* is an angle inside a geometrical figure. The opposite is *exterior*.

Internal is an adjective referring to what is inside something: *internal trade, internal injuries*; *internal arguments, correspondence, relations* (inside an organisation); the *internal-combustion engine* is what powers motor vehicles. The opposite is *external*.

in order to

This describes a purpose: *(In order) to turn the machine on, press the red button.* In the above example, the *in order* is unnecessary; sometimes however, it avoids ambiguity:
1 *This is an important step and it is necessary to increase production.*
2 *This is an important step and it is necessary in order to increase production.*

Sentence **1** is ambiguous. The *it* could refer to *step*: *This is an important step, which is necessary to increase production.*   ➤

I

In this case the sentence would mean the same as **2**. On the other hand, the *it* could be impersonal and the second CLAUSE would then be grammatically unrelated to the first: *This is an important step and production must be increased.* In **2** it is totally clear that the step is necessary for production to be increased.

instead of

This means *in place of* (*stead* is the Old English *stede* meaning *place*). Although *stead* does not now have this literal meaning, it is possible to say *in my* (etc.) *stead* for *instead of me* (etc.) This is rather literary.

A *homestead* or *farmstead* is a name for a farmhouse and its associated buildings.

A *bedstead* is the framework of a bed (originally it was the place where a bed was placed).

insulate & isolate

Insulate means to prevent electricity, heat or sound being conducted. Electric cables have to be insulated. *Thermal insulation* reduces the heat loss from a building.

Isolate means to separate from other things. An *isolated village* is a remote one; people suffering from infectious diseases are *isolated* from others. A problem can be *isolated* (i.e. separated and identified) before it is dealt with. In chemistry *isolation* is the preparation of a substance in pure form. *Isolationism* is a national policy of isolation or separation from other countries, avoiding involvement in international affairs, particularly applied to the USA the 1930s, when it did not join the League of Nations.

interest

This word has several meanings:

Interest is something that arouses your curiosity, that makes you wish to learn more. It can be both uncountable: *I have little interest in sport* and countable: *His interests include fishing and stamp-collecting.* It can be a verb: *The cinema has always interested me; I have always been interested in the cinema.*

If you have an *interest* in something, it can affect you directly; a *financial interest* could be an investment in a company or a bet on a horse race. An *interested* PARTY is someone who has a financial or other interest in something.

Interest is money paid by a debtor for a loan; in this sense it is uncountable.

negative forms

The verb *interest* has two negative participle forms: *uninteresting/uninterested* and *disinterested*. These correspond to **1** and **2** above respectively:

I find his work uninteresting; I am completely uninterested in your problems.

A disinterested observer would say that...; Your opinion is not exactly disinterested; here *disinterested* is a synonym of IMPARTIAL (**PARTIAL*).

The use of *disinterested* to mean *uninterested* seems to be increasing but it is advisable to maintain the difference in meaning.

The noun *disinterest* corresponds to *disinterested* but in the absence of a noun ~~uninterest~~ it is also used to mean a lack of interest. *My disinterest in football is well known* is common but controversial. *Lack of interest* is unambiguous and safe.

internet

This word has the definite ARTICLE because *net* is a countable noun: *I read it on the internet; The internet has changed communications.* When it was new it had a capital letter but now it is written with a small *i*.

intoxication & poisoning

Intoxication (etc.) means *poisoning* and is used with this sense in medicine. However, in general use *intoxicated* only means *drunk*.

intransitive and transitive verbs

An *intransitive verb* is one that does not have an object. The verbs in these sentences are intransitive: *The dog is barking; Rain was falling; I walk to work.*

A *transitive verb* is followed by a direct and/or indirect object: *John saw Mary* (DO); *Tell me** (IO); *Tell me the time.* (IO + DO); *He gave his money to charity.* (DO + IO).

*In the example with IO only, the DO is understood (see ELLIPSIS): *Tell me (the time); Tell me (that you love me).*

Many verbs can be transitive or intransitive: *I'm reading (War and Peace); I'm leaving (the office) now.* Some verbs are always intransitive. Examples are *go, come, fall, sit*. Some verbs are always transitive. Examples are *bring, have, receive.*

invalid

An *invalid* /ˈɪnvəlɪd/ is a person who is weak from illness or is disabled. *Invalid* /ɪnˈvælɪd/ is the opposite of *valid*.

inversion

after adverbs

When a sentence begins with an adverbial phrase or CLAUSE that is negative or restricting in meaning, the verb is inverted, i.e. it has the order which it would have in a question, auxiliary – subject – main verb, although the sentence is not a question. This is done in a formal style of English and is usually found in writing more than in speech as the adverbial expression is placed at the beginning of the sentence for emphasis:
Never did I think of stopping.
We looked for the address everywhere but nowhere could we find it.
Nowhere else is the problem so serious.
In no circumstances will he come here again.
Only by working hard will he succeed.
Rarely have I seen such good work.

These sentences can be rewritten using the normal order as:
I never thought of stopping.
We looked for the address everywhere but we couldn't find it anywhere.
The problem is not so serious anywhere else.
He will not come here again in any circumstances.
He will only succeed by working hard.
I have rarely seen such good work.

In speech the emphasis could be provided by word stress: *I **never** thought of stopping; We looked for the address everywhere but we couldn't find it **anywhere**.*

When a sentence starts with a subordinate adverbial clause, the verb in the main clause, not the adverbial clause, is inverted: *Not until I had arrived in the restaurant **did I find** that I had left my credit card at home.* It is not: ~~Not until had I arrived...~~

Sometimes, in rather formal language, the clauses can make a very long introduction. For example: *Only after Hofmannsthal had made it clear to him that this was only intended as a small opus and an intermediate work in thanks to Max Reinhardt, with whose assistance he had succeeded in bringing off the Dresden première of the 'Rosenkavalier' as an unparalleled success, **did Strauss warm** to the project* and *Only after the motor car had become an essential piece of personal equipment, both because it allowed a greater degree of personal mobility than ever before and because it played an increasing role as a status symbol for the average citizen, **did it become** apparent that it would cause pollution problems in cities.*

Hardly, scarcely and *no sooner* are similar in meaning; they cause *inversion* in a following verb. However, there is a difference in the case of *no sooner* which is a comparative adverb and must be followed by *than*.

I

Hardly/scarcely had I got home when the phone rang.
No sooner had I got home than the phone rang.

after *so*
So followed by an *adjective* or *adverb* also causes inversion:
So great was the problem that a solution could never be found.
So slowly did they react that the cost doubled.

Some examples of adverbial expressions which cause inversion are:

never/at no (other) time	*seldom/rarely*
nowhere/in no (other) city/country etc.	*only by...* with GERUND
not only (inversion in main clause)	*only after...* (inversion in main clause)
in no circumstances	*only if...* (inversion in main clause)
on no account	*only in this way*
no sooner...than	*only then*
hardly/scarcely...when	*only when*
hardly/scarcely ever	*so* with adjective or adverb

investigation and research

Research (noun and verb) and *researcher* are the normal words in academic life, with *research assistants, grants* etc. though *investigate, investigation, investigator* are often found, especially with *principal investigator*. Companies invest money in *R&D&I* (research and development and innovation). *Investigate* and its derivatives are the usual words for police and similar investigation.

Ireland, a brief history

See the note for history articles on page xv.

In discussing Ireland it is important to distinguish between the words *Ireland* /ˈaɪələnd/ (the name of the country) and *island* /ˈaɪlənd/ (the geographical nature of Ireland).

The first inhabitants of Ireland date back into prehistory but the arrival of the Celtic Gaels in about 350 BC was a decisive event as they took control of the island for themselves. The Roman occupation of Britain never extended to Ireland, though there were contacts through trade. In the fifth century AD St Patrick, the patron saint of Ireland, introduced Christianity and Roman culture to Ireland, where it remained alive during the Dark Ages. The Anglo-Saxon tribes that occupied England never crossed to Ireland, although some Vikings settled there independently founding the city of Dublin. The tribes of medieval Ireland developed a system of local kings under a high king who had some overall control but there was no real central government of the island as one unit.

In 1166 the Norman English entered Ireland and, with the authority of the Pope, claimed sovereignty, taking large areas of land and establishing the Norman feudal system of land ownership instead of the traditional system. The northern kingdom of Ulster resisted the occupation, while other Gaelic chiefs submitted. Unrest and rebellion continued, and as direct English authority weakened the strength of the native Irish together with the oldest settled Norman families grew until, in the fifteenth century, Ireland achieved a degree of independence under a mixture of Gaelic and Norman feudal landowners. The arrival of the Tudors in England stopped this development as they attempted to re-impose English rule, but the Reformation and Henry VIII's break with the Roman CATHOLIC Church was not acceptable in Ireland and to the long-established Norman-English settlers. Irish resistance to English rule continued among both the ancient Irish people and the old-established Norman-English landowners. This led to a complex situation of varying systems of government, with England only having full control over the area around Dublin known as the Pale (the expression *beyond the pale* meaning *unacceptable* comes from this).

The resistance of Catholic Ireland was strengthened by hopes of help from Spain, but this never materialised. Towards the end of the sixteenth century England under Queen Elizabeth I was still trying to establish complete control by planting colonies of English settlers in the rebellious provinces; and the most rebellious of all was Ulster in the north. However, Irish resistance there came to an end, leaving the way open for Protestant settlers from England and Scotland, the Scots being radical Presbyterians, Protestants but not from the CHURCH OF ENGLAND. English rule was now firmly established in Ireland, with Catholics excluded from public office, and during the English civil war Cromwell's Protestant troops occupied Ireland with great force and violence, taking land for themselves and imposing military rule on the Irish and ANGLO-IRISH population.

After the restoration of the monarchy in England with Charles II, the accession of the Catholic James II in England raised optimism in Ireland; when James was replaced by William III, he looked to Ireland for support but was defeated there by William at the Battle of the Boyne in 1690. This finally established the Protestant succession in England, and thus Protestant control of Ireland, but it was also a matter of great importance in Europe as it marked the end of the power of Louis XIV of France and was welcomed in some Catholic courts.

Laws were passed in England and Ireland to establish the Church of England as the only officially established church; members of other denominations were excluded from the professions and public life. During the more relaxed eighteenth century many aristocratic families converted to Anglicanism, thus losing their association with the mass of the people while acquiring political power and influence. The American and French revolutions found an echo in Ireland; while the Catholics had many reasons for opposing English rule, the Protestants, who were treated only slightly better, were developing radical theories of equality and democracy. Eventually, this discontent of Catholics and Presbyterians led to a rebellion in 1798 under the leadership of a Protestant called Wolfe Tone. The rebels hoped for support from France, but this did not materialise and the rebellion was suppressed by the British authorities. Following this, in 1800 the Act of Union formally and completely incorporated Ireland in the United Kingdom; the Parliament in Dublin, which had been dominated by English interests, was closed and Ireland was represented in the British Parliament in London. Ireland had no degree of independence at all. This situation continued during the nineteenth century with the Irish people, Catholic and Protestant, feeling oppressed and exploited by a foreign government and by landlords, many of whom who had little or no interest in the well-being of the people who worked their land. Gradually, voting rights and access to education were given to Catholics, as they were in Great Britain, and an Irish party led by Daniel O'Connell began to achieve representation and influence in the London Parliament with Catholics and Protestants working to win some kind of local power based in Ireland.

Then, in the 1840s, disaster struck. Ireland was an agricultural country with very little industry or trade, these being based in England and Scotland. But three-quarters of the land was used for growing wheat (the price of which was kept artificially high by the landowners) and other crops, while half of the people in Ireland were desperately poor and living entirely off potatoes. So, when disease destroyed the potato crop in 1845, a famine occurred that continued until 1848 when, despite some rather late public and private relief measures, death and emigration had reduced the population of Ireland from eight million to 6½ million (massive emigration continued for many decades; the population of all of the island of Ireland even now is about five million). This famine led to further unrest and rebellion against the Union. Political pressure continued in Ireland and in London, where the LIBERAL prime minister William Gladstone was sympathetic to Irish claims; the CONSERVATIVE PARTY supported the Protestants, who were generally richer than the Catholics and who were opposed to breaking the Union as were some middle-class Catholics. Protestantism was particularly strong in Ulster, where Scottish Presbyterians had settled the land in the early seventeenth century, and in 1886, when Gladstone proposed Home Rule (as self-government was known) their absolute rejection of it, with the support of the Conservative opposition in Parliament, defeated Gladstone when, despite the support of the Irish party led by Parnell, some of his own party voted against him. In 1892 Gladstone succeeded in passing Home Rule through the House of Commons but was defeated in the House of Lords by powerful Conservative opposition. In 1912, after the power of the Lords had been reduced, a third attempt was made to pass Home Rule. Ireland would have achieved a great degree of self-government but there was still powerful opposition from the Conservatives and the Ulster Protestants, who by then had a power base in the growing manufacturing city of Belfast. Identifying themselves strongly with the Protestant succession in England following the victory of William III (of Orange) over James II (Stuart), they prepared for armed resistance to the British government in the event of Home Rule being passed and the Union being dissolved. The outbreak of the First World War in 1914 made it impossible for the Home Rule Act, which had already been approved by the King, to become law.

Although many Irishmen fought in the British army in the war, England's weakness was Ireland's opportunity and at Easter weekend 1916 a rebellion in Dublin proclaimed an Irish Republic. This uprising was suppressed by the British and most of the leaders were executed. Although directly it was a failure in itself, it set the tone for Anglo-Irish relations when the war ended. It was claimed that Britain, which had fought a war for the rights and freedom of small nations, could no longer deny Home Rule to Ireland; but still the Protestant Unionists with English Conservative support opposed this, maintaining their threat to use armed force if necessary to protect the Union from the British Crown, however paradoxical that position might seem. Meanwhile, the Irish nationalist party Sinn Féin was growing in strength and calling for a completely independent Irish republic. A compromise was proposed by which most of Ireland (26 counties) would have Home Rule but the six of the nine counties of Ulster in which the Protestants had a majority of the population would remain in the Union with their own Parliament. This was accepted by the Ulster Protestants but the Catholic Nationalists were divided between those who were willing to accept it and those who insisted on a republic of the whole island. Thus in 1921 the Irish Free State came into existence with internal opposition from Republicans, which led to a civil war. Northern Ireland came into existence in the north of the country; it and the Free State were entirely separate political units.

The Free State was heavily dominated by the Roman Catholic Church and followed a strongly Nationalist political policy and an AUTARKIC economic policy. In 1937 the remaining slight connections with the UK were broken and in 1948 the country became a republic, maintaining a constitutional claim to sovereignty over the six counties of Northern Ireland. Northern Ireland itself, with a large Protestant majority, continued to have an Irish identity while expressing strong emotional and patriotic loyalty to the British Crown and the Protestant religion, mostly in its extreme Presbyterian form. In the 1960s it became clear that the Catholic population of Northern Ireland was suffering from discrimination at the hands of the Protestant government, in which they had not been able to participate during almost fifty years of its existence, and that they were denied the normal rights of other UK citizens. Catholic protests against this situation in 1969 were met with extreme Protestant violence in Belfast on a scale that required the intervention of the British army, the Protestant police of Northern Ireland not being appropriate to control the situation. Further continued Protestant opposition to Catholic involvement in the government led the British government to abolish the Northern Ireland Parliament and govern the province directly from London. Meanwhile, the IRA (Irish Republican Army, with reference to the republic declared in Dublin in 1916), which had been mostly quiet for some decades, returned to activity with a terrorist campaign aimed at removing Britain finally and completely from Ireland and establishing a single republic in Ireland, while Protestant paramilitary organisations appeared fighting a terrorist campaign against any concession to Catholic Nationalist interests. Sinn Féin gave tacit support to the IRA, but in the 1990s the Republican Movement began to look for a political rather than a military solution and agreed to work in a government in Northern Ireland that shared power between Catholics and Protestants, looking for closer relations with the Republic, which in turn had adopted a more tolerant social and economic policy and removed from its constitution the claim to sovereignty over the whole island of Ireland. The Good Friday Agreement of 1998 helped the peace process and in 2005 the IRA disarmed, but in Northern Ireland the two communities are still divided. However, some normalisation was achieved in the early summer of 2007 with the re-establishment of the Northern Ireland Assembly. In recent years the Republic has enjoyed spectacular economic growth but this proved to be unsustainable and Ireland was very badly affected by the 2010 world financial crisis.

At the time of writing (November 2016) the future of the peace process is uncertain as the UK's planned departure from the European Union (Brexit) would close the border between Northern Ireland and the Republic.

In Ireland as a whole the Gaelic Celtic tradition has remained strong as a focus of national identity although the social upheaval of the Famine and other social changes in the later nineteenth century led to a great decline in the use of the Irish language. Cultural and intellectual activity has always been powerful in Ireland, with writers such as Swift, Wilde, Synge, Joyce, Shaw, Heaney and O'Nolan, and Ireland has a very rich fund of musical and visual art. Because of the history of emigration, large Irish communities are found all over the world, especially in the USA, Canada, Australia, and naturally Britain.

See ENGLAND, A BRIEF HISTORY; SCOTLAND, A BRIEF HISTORY; WALES, A BRIEF HISTORY.

irregular verbs

This is a complete list of basic English irregular verb forms. However, compound verbs which follow the pattern of the root e.g. *arise, become, behold* are not normally given here.

This list shows the common forms used in modern British English though occasional variations are found. The notes include comments (which are not intended to be exhaustive) on forms used in American English. A complete list of compounds and possible variations can be found in a dictionary.

With very few exceptions (*cost* and *quit*), the verbs listed below are Germanic in origin; verbs that are of Latin origin are almost always regular. Thus, if a verb is a monosyllable or a compound of a monosyllabic Germanic root, there is good reason to suppose that it might be irregular.

An asterisk (*) indicates that the verb is described in the notes that follow this list. Where alternative forms are given but there is no Note, the first form is more common in modern British English.

abide*	abode/abided	abode/abided	cost	cost	cost
be	was/were	been	creep	crept	crept
BEAR*	bore	born/borne	cut	cut	cut
BEAT (*HIT)	beat	beaten	deal	dealt	dealt
beGET	begot	begotten	dig	dug	dug
begin	began	begun	DO	did	done
bend	bent	bent	DRAW	drew	drawn
bereave*	bereft/bereaved	bereft/bereaved	dream*	dreamt/dreamed	dreamt/dreamed
beseech*	besought	besought	drink*	drank	drunk/drunken
	beseeched	beseeched	drive	drove	driven
bet	bet	bet	dwell*	dwelt/dwelled	dwelt/dwelled
bid*	bade	bidden	eat	ate	eaten
bid*	bid	bid	fall	fell	fallen
bind	bound	bound	feed	fed	fed
bite	bit	bitten	feel	felt	felt
bleed	bled	bled	fight	fought	fought
blow	blew	blown	find	found	found
break	broke	broken	flee	fled	fled
breed	bred	bred	fling	flung	flung
bring	brought	brought	fly	flew	flown
build	built	built	forbid	forbade	forbidden
burn*	burnt/burned	burnt/burned	forGET	forgot	forgotten
burst	burst	burst	forsake	forsook	forsaken
buy	bought	bought	freeze	froze	frozen
can*	could	(been able)	GET*	got	got/gotten
CAST	cast	cast	gild*	gilded/gilt	gilded/gilt
catch	caught	caught	gird*	girded/girt	girded/girt
chide	chid	chidden	give	gave	given
choose	chose	chosen	go	went	gone
cleave*	see note	see note	grind	ground	ground
cling	clung	clung	grow	grew	grown
clothe*	clothed/clad	clothed/clad	hang*	hung/hanged	hung/hanged
come	came	come	have	had	had

hear	heard	heard	show	showed	shown
heave*	heaved/hove	heaved/hove	shrink*	shrank	shrunk/shrunken
hew	hewed	hewn	shrive	shrove	shriven
hide	hid	hidden	shut	shut	shut
HIT	hit	hit	SING	sang	sung
hold	held	held	sink*	sank	sunk/sunken
hurt	hurt	hurt	sit	sat	sat
keep	kept	kept	slay	slew	slain
kneel	knelt/kneeled	knelt/kneeled	sleep	slept	slept
know	knew	known	slide	slid	slid
lay	laid	laid	sling	slung	slung
lead	led	led	slink	slunk	slunk
lean*	leaned/leant	leaned/leant	slit	slit	slit
leap*	leapt/leaped	leapt/leaped	smell*	smelled/smelt	smelled/smelt
learn*	learnt/learned	learnt/learned	smite	smote	smitten
leave	left	left	sow	sowed	sown/sowed
lend	lent	lent	speak*	spoke	spoken
let	let	let	speed*	speeded/sped	speeded/sped
LIE	lay	lain	spell*	spelt/spelled	spelt/spelled
light*	lit/lighted	lit/lighted	spend	spent	spent
lose	lost	lost	spill*	spilt/spilled	spilt/spilled
make	made	made	spin	spun	spun
mean	meant	meant	spit	spat	spat
melt*	melted	melted/molten	split	split	split
meet	met	met	spoil*	spoilt/spoiled	spoilt/spoiled
mow*	mowed	mowed/mown	spread	spread	spread
pay	paid	paid	spring	sprang	sprung
PROVE*	proved	proved/proven	stand	stood	stood
put	put	put	stave*	staved/stove	staved/stove
quit	quit/quitted	quit/quitted	steal	stole	stolen
read/riːd/	read /red/	read /red/	stick	stuck	stuck
rend	rent	rent	sting	stung	stung
rid	rid	rid	stink	stank	stunk
ride	rode	ridden	strew	strewed	strewn
ring*	rang	rung	stride	strode	stridden
rise	rose	risen	STRIKE*	struck	struck/stricken
run	ran	run	string	strung	strung
saw	sawed	sawn	strive	strove	striven
SAY	said	said	swear	swore	sworn
SEE	saw	seen	sweep	swept	swept
seek	sought	sought	swell	swelled	swollen
sell	sold	sold	swim	swam	swum
send	sent	sent	swing	swung	swung
set	set	set	take	took	taken
sew	sewed	sewn	teach	taught	taught
shake	shook	shaken	tear	tore	torn
shave*	shaved	shaved/shaven	tell	told	told
shear*	sheared	shorn/sheared	THINK	thought	thought
shed	shed	shed	thrive*	throve/thrived	thriven/thrived
SHINE*	shined/shone	shined/shone	throw	threw	thrown
shit*	shitted/shit/shat	shitted/shit/shat	thrust	thrust	thrust
shoe	shod	shod	tread	trod	trodden
shoot	shot	shot	WAKE*	woke	woken

WEAR	wore	worn	win	won	won	
weave*	wove/weaved	woven/weaved	wind	wound	wound	
wed	wed/wedded	wed/wedded	wring	wrung	wrung	
weep	wept	wept	WRITE	wrote	written	
wet	wet/wetted	wet/wetted				

notes

Some verbs have both regular and irregular forms, e.g. *burned* and *burnt*. As verbs (rather than as the adjectival use of a past participle) both forms are acceptable, the difference being of little importance. As a general rule, American English prefers the regular form.

abide: *Abode* is the past of the archaic use of this word meaning *to live* (to be resident in a certain place, not to be alive); it is also a noun meaning *place of residence*. The regular form (with *by*) means to *conform to, obey* rules etc.

BEAR: *Born* is the past participle when it means *be born* of a baby; *borne* is used for *carry, tolerate*.

bereave: *Bereft* means *lacking in, without*: *bereft of ideas, bereft of taste*; *bereaved* means *deprived by death*: *bereaved at an early age*.

beseech: Both forms are used.

bid: *Bid-bade-bidden* is an old form meaning *order, command*. *Bid-bid-bid* means offer a price for something, for example at an auction.

burn: *Burned* (often pronounced /bɜːnt/) and *burnt* are both used. *Burnt* is found as an attributive adjective: *burnt sugar, burnt cork*. As there is no effective difference, the regular *burned* is preferable.

can: The verb can meaning *to put food in a can to preserve it* is unconnected with *can, could* and is regular: *We canned most of our peas; canned meat*.

cleave: These are two separate verbs that coincidentally have the same infinitive: *cleave*.
One is transitive and means *split, divide*; it is unusual except in literary and certain technical use. It is irregular with variable past forms *cleaved, clove,* and *cleft*, and past participle forms *cloven* and *cleaved*. Its past participle adjective form is also variable, *cloven-footed, cloven hoof* but *cleft lip, cleft palate*, CLEFT SENTENCE, *in a cleft stick* (in a dilemma).
The other verb is intransitive and regular: *cleave/d* means *to stick* or *adhere*. It is rather uncommon.

clothe: *Clothed* is the usual form. *Clad* can be used in collocations with adverbs: *insufficiently clad, richly clad*; in forms such as *a leather-clad motor-cyclist, tree-clad hills, snow-clad mountains*; and in certain technical terms: *a building clad* (covered, faced) *with marble*. The verb *clad* (*We will clad the building with marble*) is a BACK-FORMATION from this.

dream: Both forms are used. They are pronounced *dreamed* /driːmd/, *dreamt* /dremt/. *Dreamed* is more common. As there is no effective difference, the regular *dreamed* is preferable.

drink: *Drunk* is the usual form and is the predicative ADJECTIVE: *He was drunk when he arrived*, but *drunken* is used as the attributive ADJECTIVE: *A drunken driver, drunken behaviour*.

dwell: *Dwelt* is preferred.

GET: *Gotten* is used in American English in the sense of *obtained*: *Have you gotten your plane tickets yet?* In British English it is found only in *ill-gotten* (obtained immorally or illegally) and in the compounds *begotten* and *forgotten*.

gild: *Gilded* is the usual form. *Gilt* is sometimes used as the adjective, especially in *gilt-edged securities* (reliable investments in stocks and shares).

gird: *Girded* is the usual form. *Girt* is sometimes used but it is unusual. The word *gird* itself is a literary word.

hang: *Hung* is the usual past participle. *Hanged* is the usual past participle for killing a person by hanging, and was used by judges passing death sentences; however, *hung* is often found in this sense.

heave: *Heaved* is used when the word means *pull*. *Hove* is used in the nautical senses: *The SHIP hove into view* (*came into sight*), which is used commonly in non-nautical speech, and *the ship hove to* (stopped moving).

kneel: *Knelt* is much more common.

lean: *Leaned* is the common form and is preferred; it is regular and avoids confusion with *lent* (past of *lend*). *Leant* /lent/ is also found in British English.

leap: *Leaped* (predominant in American English) and *leapt* /lept/ (predominant in Britain) are both used.

learn: Both forms are used. *Learned* is pronounced /lɜːnd/ or /lɜːnt/. *Learnt* /lɜːnt/ is more common in British English than in American. As there is no effective difference, the regular *learned* is preferable. When it means *knowledgeable*, *learned* is pronounced /ˈlɜːnɪd/.

light: *Lit* is the past and past participle of the verb: *He lit the fire*, and the predicative ADJECTIVE: *The lamps were lit*; the attributive form is *lighted*: *A lighted cigarette* except when it is with an adverb: *A well-lit road*. *Lighted* is more common in American English.

melt: *Melted* is the usual adjective: *melted cheese*. *Molten* is used when a high temperature is involved: *molten iron, lava* etc.

mow: Both forms are used as the past participle of the verb. *Mown* is used as the adjective: *Newly mown grass*.

PROVE: *Proven* is unusual in Standard English except as an attributive ADJECTIVE in expressions such as *proven ability, strength* etc. It is standard in American English and in Scotland, where *not proven* is a verdict in LAW cases.

ring: *Ring* is irregular meaning the sound a bell makes, and thus meaning to make a phone call. It is regular when it means *to make a ring round*: *The city was ringed by mountains*.

shave: *Shaved* is the verb but *shaven* is used adjectivally.

shear: *Shorn* is used for cutting wool from sheep. *Sheared* is used for cutting metal.

SHINE: *Shone* /ʃɒn/ is used for light: *The sun shone; He shone a light*. *Shined* is used meaning polished: *He shined his shoes*.

shit: All forms are used.

shrink: *Shrunken* is the attributive ADJECTIVE: *a shrunken population*

sink: *Sunk* is used for the verb. Both forms are used as the attributive ADJECTIVE in different collocations.

smell: *Smelled* and *smelt* Are both used in British English. *Smelled* is standard in American English. As there is no effective difference, the regular *smelled* is preferable.

speak: See SPAKE.

speed: *Sped* is used for moving quickly: *He sped away*. *Speeded* (sometimes with *up*) is used with the idea of acceleration: *He speeded up when he left the town* and of travelling at a dangerous or illegal speed: *He speeded through the town*.

spell: Both forms are used. *Spelled* is especially common in American English.

spill: Both forms are used. *Spilt* is fixed in: *It's no use crying over spilt milk*.

spoil: Both forms are used. *Spoiled* is especially common in American English.

stave: Both forms are used in the sense of breaking. In *stave off* meaning to avert danger *staved* is usually used.

STRIKE *(*HIT)*: *Stricken* is only found in certain expressions: *panic-stricken* etc.

thrive: The regular *thrived* is more common than the irregular form.

wake: This is the usual form. For the full usage of *wake, waken,* and *awaken* see WAKE ETC.

weave: The irregular form is used for the manufacture of CLOTH. The regular form means to move from side to side avoiding obstacles: *She weaved (her way) through the crowd*.

See PASSED & PAST.

-ise and -ize

Both forms are used in verbs such as *standardise/standardize, recognise/recognize*. The origin of this difference goes back to Ancient Greek; the Greek suffix -ιζειν was represented in Latin by -*izare*. In French this was changed to -*iser* and a number of French words with this ending, which had been newly formed in French and did not come from Greek, passed into English. Some British writers and publishers prefer one, some the other, and some publishers accept both in their house style. In American English the -*ize* suffix is standard. However, there are some words that do not have this origin. For this reason it seems more convenient to use -*ise* consistently.

The words that must always be spelled with *-ise* are ADVERTISE, ADVISE, *arise, chastise, circumcise, comprise, compromise, demise, despise, devise, dis(en)franchise, disguise, enfranchise,* ENTERPRISE, *excise, exercise, expertise, franchise, improvise, incise, merchandise,* PREMISE, *prise* (force open), *promise, reprise, revise, supervise, surmise, surprise, televise.*

-ish
This is a suffix that means *about, approximately*. It can be added to both nouns and adjectives: *foolish* means *silly* or *unwise, like a fool*; *babyish* means CHILDISH or *immature*; a *reddish* brown is a brown COLOUR that has a lot of red in it; and *sixish* means *at about six O'CLOCK*.

Islam
Islam is the name of the religion. The adjective is *Islamic*. Islam has two main forms, *Sunni* and *Shia*; their followers are known as *Sunnis* and *Shiites*. *Islamism* is the political belief held by *Islamists* that society should live according to the *Sharia law*. **Muslim** is a noun referring to a follower of Islam; *Moslem* is sometimes found. The **Koran**, also *Quran* or *Qur'an*, is the *Islamic* holy book. **Muhammad** or *Mohammed* is the prophet of Islam. **Allah** is the Islamic name for GOD. *Arabic* is the language of *Islam*, although many Muslims are not Arabs. As Arabic words have to be transliterated, there are several ways of spelling the names of the holy book and of the prophet. Note the use of CAPITAL LETTERS in these terms.

The older English form *Mahomet* should be avoided as it is considered insulting, as is the use of the word *Mohammedan* to refer to a *Muslim*. *Mussulman* is an archaic word.

island
The *s* is silent; the word is pronounced /ˈaɪlənd/. Etymologically there should be no *s* in this word as it derives from the Middle English *yland*, which meant *island*. However, in the sixteenth century the borrowed French word *île* was associated with the English word *iland*, Latin scholars knew that the French spelling *île* represented an earlier form *isle*, so the English spelling was adapted to a false etymology from Latin *insula* through French.

Island is the usual word. *Isle* is used in poetry and in proper names: *the* BRITISH ISLES *(*BRITAIN, BRITISH), the Isle of Man, the Isle of Wight.*

See AISLE; COULD; FOREIGN; GHOST.

it to postpone a subject
Sometimes *it* is placed at the beginning of a sentence to allow the subject to be postponed. The technical term for this is extraposition. It must be understood very clearly that this is done only when the subject is a CLAUSE (i.e. it contains a finite verb) or is an INFINITIVE. It is not done when the subject is a noun (but see FRONTING):
~~She is very beautiful your sister.~~
Your sister is very beautiful.

~~It was very good that dinner.~~
That dinner was very good.

It is done in cases such as these:
It will be impossible (for us) <u>to finish on time</u>.
It's a disaster <u>to lose this election</u>.
It doesn't matter <u>what he says</u>.
It has been announced <u>that the exam will be next week</u>.
It is thought <u>that he is in Paris</u>.

Some of these sentences can be rewritten with the underlined part as the subject: *(For us) <u>to finish on time</u> will be impossible*; *<u>To lose this election</u> is a disaster*; *<u>What he says</u> doesn't matter* but ~~*That the exam will be next week has been announced*~~ and ~~*That he is in Paris is thought*~~ are not possible.

These sentences can be written using the -ING FORM of the verb (GERUND) as a subject: *<u>Finishing on time</u> will be impossible (for us)*; *<u>Losing this election</u> is a disaster*. ▶

I

In the sentences *It will be impossible (for us), <u>finishing on time</u>* and *It's a disaster, <u>losing this election</u>* the extrapositional clause is separated by a slight pause in speech, which can be shown in writing as a comma, as if this part is an afterthought that has been added to make perfectly clear what the *it* subject refers to. See FRONTING. As the -ING FORM is used as a gerund (a noun) in such sentences it will be seen that there is a parallel with *She is very beautiful, your sister* and *It was very good, that dinner*, where *your sister* and *that dinner* amplify and explain the subject. This is clear in the sentences with *it*, which is clearly not impersonal in reference as it can be replaced by *that*, which has a specific reference: *That's a disaster, losing this election; That was very good, that dinner*. The point is made with full clarity by expanding these sentences further: *That's a disaster – losing this election, I mean; That was very good, that dinner was*. It is also done in sentences with *It doesn't* MATTER: *It doesn't matter what you do*.

Extraposition can also apply to objects: *I found it difficult to learn Russian* but not ~~*I found to learn Russian difficult*~~. *Can you get it into your head that we are not French?* is correct (the use of *it* as an object maintains the English rule that an adverb (*into your head*) cannot stand between verb (*get*) and object (*that we are not French*)). ~~*Can you get into your head that we are not French?*~~ is incorrect. ~~*Can you get that we are not French into your head?*~~ is unacceptable because the object is too long to balance the adverb. See ADVERBS, POSITION. These sentences can be rewritten using nouns (a gerund in the first example): *I found learning Russian difficult; Can you get the idea/fact that we are not French into your head?*

its & it's

This is simply a reminder that *its* is the POSSESSIVE of it and *it's* is the CONTRACTION of *it is* and *it has*. Many native speakers confuse them. Other pronouns (*hers, ours, yours, theirs*) do not have apostrophes in the possessive but contractions do have them.

J

j, J /dʒeɪ/
The tenth letter of the alphabet. It is pronounced /dʒ/.

When this sound appears at the end of a word, it is written -*ge* as in *age, judge*. The words *haj* /hædʒ/ (Muslim pilgrimage), *raj* /rɑːdʒ/ (British Empire in INDIA), and the monument the *Taj* /tɑːdʒ/ *Mahal* are the only words used in English that end with the letter *j*.

Jacobean etc.
These adjectives and nouns are derived from the Latin *Jacobus* (James).

Jacobean refers to the time of King James I of England (1603-25); it is particularly used of the architecture, furniture, and literature of that period.

The *Jacobins* were leaders of the French Revolution. The name had earlier been used for Dominican friars. They took it as they met in a Dominican friary.

Jacobite refers to the followers of King James II of England after he was removed from the throne, and to those of his son.

See ENGLAND, A BRIEF HISTORY; SCOTLAND, A BRIEF HISTORY.

jam & marmalade
Jam is conserved FRUIT with sugar. While many kinds of fruit are used to make jam, this kind of food is called *marmalade* when it is made of citrus fruit. While the large majority of marmalade is made of oranges, it can be made of lemons or limes. Marmalade contains pieces of the skin of the fruit. Ginger marmalade is also sometimes found, containing pieces of ginger.

jeans
The name *jeans* comes from the city of Genoa in Italy. Although *jean* was originally the name of the material, this is not commonly used now. The material is usually known as *denim*: a *denim shirt*, a *denim bag*. This name derives from the town of Nîmes in the south of France. However, *jeans* seems to be coming into use for *jeans shirt, bag* etc.

Jew, Judaism, Hebrew, Israel and Israeli
Each of the three words *Jewish*, *Hebrew* and *Israeli* has a specific meaning. They are not interchangeable.

Jew is a noun referring to a person of the *Jewish* faith; the feminine is *Jewess*. *Judaism* is the name of the religion. *Jewry* refers to *Jews* as a whole, as a religious community. The *Torah* is the *Jewish* holy book. *Hebrew* is the name of the ANCIENT language which is now used in its modern form as the official language of the State of *Israel*. *Israeli* is the adjective relating to that state.

Note the use of CAPITAL LETTERS in these terms.

John Bull
John Bull is a character representing the typical Englishman. He is shown in pictures and cartoons as an eighteenth-century English gentleman, not an intellectual but strong and determined. He is often seen with the Union FLAG on his waistcoat and with a bulldog, a symbol of determination and persistence.

See UNCLE SAM.

judgement
In British English *judgment* is the term used for a formal decision made by a judge or court and *judgement* is used in other contexts, for example the ability to make a correct or wise decision. In American English *judgment* is usual in all contexts.

J

jump

This article also includes *bound, hop, leap, skip, spring*.

jump

The basic word is *jump*. Athletics recognises the *long jump*, the *high jump*, and the *triple jump* (formerly *hop, skip/step and jump*). It can be transitive or intransitive with a preposition: *He jumped (over) the stream; The horse jumped (over) the fence.*

If you are suddenly happy you *jump for joy* and if you are suddenly surprised or frightened you *jump out of your skin*, or simply *jump*: *You made me jump*. To *jump at an offer* means to accept an opportunity very willingly, as a wild animal *jumps at its* PREY, while to *jump on someone* means to attack them either physically or verbally; again it is a metaphor of an animal attacking. To *jump down someone's throat* means to attack verbally, to criticise fiercely and suddenly. To *jump to it* (the *it* is never specified) means to act quickly when it is necessary to do so. A sailor who *jumps (his)* SHIP deserts it. To *jump the gun* means to start acting before the signal is given (from athletics. Sometimes a runner starts running before the starting gun sounds), to *jump the queue* means to take ones turn before it is due, and to *jump the lights* is to drive away from traffic lights before the green light shows.

Jump leads are cables that transfer electricity from the battery of one vehicle to another to *jump start* it. A *jump seat* is a folding seat, as is found in typical British black TAXIS *(*CAB)*. A *jumper* is a sweater (as well as a person or animal that jumps) and someone who is *jumpy* is nervous.

bound

Bound is similar to *leap* in general meaning (to jump upwards or forwards) but apart from that is only used in the expression to advance by *leaps and bounds*. This word is not connected with any other meaning of BIND.

hop

Hop means to jump on only one leg or to move by a series of one-leg jumps. Originally, however, its meaning was similar to *jump* as is seen in the name of the insect the *grasshopper* and in the colloquial *hop in/on* a vehicle. Small birds and frogs *hop*.

The noun *hop* is the act of hopping, but if a journey is made in *three hops* that means three stages. If you are *caught on the hop* you are unprepared.

The forms of *hop, hopping, hopped* /hɒp hɒpɪŋ hɒpt/ should not be confused with *hope, hoping, hoped* /həʊp həʊpɪŋ həʊpt/.

The unconnected word *hop* is the plant used in making beer.

See ALE AND BEER.

leap

Leap means to jump forcefully. *He leapt up from his chair* suggests a more energetic action than *jumped* or *sprang*. It can also suggest jumping as far forwards as possible. Salmon *leap* out of the water as they swim up rivers from the sea to their breeding grounds. It can mean a great step in advancement of knowledge or experience; Neil Armstrong stepping onto the moon in 1969 said 'That's one small step for a man, one giant leap for MANKIND' *(*INCLUSIVE LANGUAGE)*. A *leap in the dark* is a major step into the unknown. A *leap forward* is a major advance; to advance by *leaps and bounds* is to advance quickly. Your *heart leaps* with sudden excitement. Something that *leaps to the eye* is obvious. A *leap year* has 366 days, with 29 days in February (see CALENDAR).

skip

Skip means to jump lightly and gracefully, and to move by skipping, but now it is mostly used for the game of *skipping* over a rope or to mean omitting or passing over something: *You can skip chapter ten; Let's skip classes today.*

spring

Spring, sprang, sprung as a verb has the idea of sudden movement; nowadays it is rarely used as a synonym of *jump* in the basic sense but is found in expressions such as *spring into action* and *Where did you spring from?* when someone appears suddenly.

If something *springs apart* it breaks or separates into pieces that fly away from each other.

If a SHIP, pipe or other container *springs a leak* water starts flowing in or out when it should not do so.

As a noun *spring* seems to have a strange variety of meanings but they all relate to the idea of sudden origin or movement.

A *spring* is a place where water comes (springs) from the ground.

Spring (formerly the *spring of the year*) is the first season, the season when the year begins. *Spring cleaning* is a thorough cleaning of a house or room; the name refers to the custom of cleaning a house when it was opened in spring after having been closed all winter. The effective use of this is seen in the expression *spring and fall*, though now fall meaning autumn is only found in American English.

A *spring tide* occurs before and after the new and full moon it has the greatest difference between high and low tides.

A *spring* is a piece of metal that springs back to its original position if it is pressed out of shape. Springs are used in the suspension of motor vehicles and in mechanical watches. A metal wire turned into a spiral shape is a spring; small springs are used to hold batteries in position, in TV remote control units for example.

summary

bound/leap: great movement upwards or forwards; leaps and bounds.
jump: basic term, athletics.
hop: jumping on one leg; grasshopper and birds.
spring: sudden movement or start of activity.
skip: light, graceful movement; skipping with rope.

just

As an adjective, *just* means *fair*: *a just decision, a just reward*. The corresponding adverb is *justly*: *he was treated unjustly, He was justly given compensation.*

Just can also be an ADVERB WITHOUT -LY with a range of meanings.

exactly, precisely

That is just what I was thinking; You are just the man I want to speak to; Just when did they arrive?

a moment ago

They have (only) just arrived.

simply, merely, only (colloquial)

We are just good friends (i.e. not lovers); I'll just have a sandwich; I just can't understand it.

barely, hardly

I just finished it in time; Just a moment.

positively (emphatic, colloquial)

It is just wonderful/marvellous/brilliant etc.

It's just as well (that)... means *It's a good thing (that)...*: *It's just as well (that) you told me they're divorced now.* ▶

J

Just about is *almost exactly* or *almost completely: just about here; just about finished.*

In *just IN CASE* the *just* is emphatic: *Take an umbrella just in case.*

Just now means *at this moment: It isn't raining just now* and *a little time ago: He was here just now.*

Just so is like *exactly*; it expresses agreement.

K

k, K /keɪ/

The eleventh letter of the alphabet. It is pronounced /k/. It is written -*ck* after a short vowel except in TREK and *yak*.

It is not pronounced in the combination *kn-* at the beginning of a word: *knack, knackered, knapsack, knave, knead, knee(cap), kneel, knickers, knife, knight, knit, knob, knock, knot, know, knowledge, knuckle*; it is pronounced in *acknowledge* /akˈnɒlɪdʒ/.

kh, KH

This combination is not naturally English. It is used in the transliteration of words from other languages, especially Russian, *Khrushchev* for example, and Asian languages: *Bokhara, Khomeini, Khan, Sikh*. It represents the sound /x/ but is usually pronounced /k/ in English.

Keats and Yeats

The surname of the English Romantic poet **John Keats** (1795-1821) is pronounced /kiːts/. The surname of the Irish Nationalist poet **William Butler Yeats** (1865-1939) is pronounced /jeɪts/.

Keynes

The surname of the economist **John Maynard Keynes** (1883-1946) is pronounced /keɪnz/. The name of the city of **Milton Keynes** is pronounced /kiːnz/.

kill

Killing is not necessarily an act of deliberate violence. People can be killed accidentally in natural disasters or accidents, and smoking, drink or overwork can kill people.

See ASSASSIN.

kith and kin

The term *kith and kin* means *friends and relatives*. However it is strongly emotional and is used especially with reference to groups of British people experiencing extreme difficulty in remote parts of the world. *Kin* and *kinfolk* are sometimes found meaning one's own family. One's *next of kin* are one's closest relatives, especially in the context of people to be informed in the event of accident, illness, or death.

know

Know, knew, known is a STATIVE VERB *(*DYNAMIC AND STATIVE)*; it refers to the state of having knowledge, not the process of acquiring it: *I (already) knew that he was Russian* but *That was the moment when I found out/learnt/ discovered/got to know that he was Russian*. For this reason, knowing a person is the state of knowing his/her character well; it is not the act of meeting or getting to know a person.

knowledge

This word (pronounced /ˈnɒlɪdʒ/) is uncountable in that it has no plural form (~~knowledges~~). However, it is used with the indefinite ARTICLE when it refers to a particular branch of knowledge: *A knowledge of German will be useful for this job*.

known

A *known criminal* or a *known expert* in a subject is someone known to be a criminal or an expert; a *well-known* (not ~~very known~~) *criminal, writer, expert, musician* is one who is famous, or at least whose name is known to many people, while a *little-known* one is the opposite. The COMPARATIVE *(*ADJECTIVES, COMPARISON)* forms are *better known* (not ~~more known~~) and *less known*. See ADJECTIVES | GRADABLE & NON-GRADABLE.

L

l, L /el/

The twelfth letter of the alphabet. It is pronounced /l/.

It is usually silent in *almond* /'ɑːmənd/, though the spelling influences some people to pronounce it. It is silent in words that end with *-al[consonant]*: (pronounced with /ɑː/) *calf, calm, (be)half, balm, palm, qualm;* (pronounced with /ɔː/), *chalk, talk, walk;* also FOLK /fəʊk/. It is silent in COULD, *should,* and *would.*

There are two different pronunciations (allophones) of *l* in English. Clear *l* is used before vowels: *laugh, lip, lot* and between vowels: *follow, Helen*. After vowels, especially back vowels (see PHONETIC SYMBOLS) at the end of a word or before a consonant, the allophone dark *l* /ɫ/ is used; here the back of the tongue is raised, and sometimes even a vowel sound is produced instead of the consonant. This explains what has happened in the words listed above (*calf* etc.): the *l* has become so dark that it has become assimilated into the preceding vowel. In ESTUARY ENGLISH it is pronounced /w/ *ballpoint pen* /'bɔːwpɔɪnʔ/.

In Welsh *ll* is pronounced /ɬ/. This sound, which is not found in English, is a voiceless alveolar lateral fricative; it is pronounced with the tongue in the same position as for /l/ but the sound is not voiced in the larynx; this produces a kind of blowing sound. It is difficult for English speakers, who often replace it with /l/, /kl/, or /θl/. This sound is found in many Welsh PLACE NAMES.

A similar sound, an unvoiced *l*, is found in English after unvoiced consonants e.g. play /pl̥eɪ/, clean /kl̥iːn/ etc., though the difference is not usually noticed by native speakers.

Labour Party

The Labour Party was founded in 1900 as the Labour Representative Committee, a pressure group to promote the interests of labour against those of capital. Initially it worked with the LIBERAL government to achieve its aims, though its own parliamentary strength was growing. After the First World War, the Labour Party increased in strength as the Liberal Party declined in popularity. In 1924 the Labour Party formed its first government with Liberal support. Some social legislation was passed but the government fell a few months later. In 1929 another minority Labour government was formed; in 1931 unemployment caused a major government crisis and the Prime Minister Ramsay Macdonald formed a national government of all parties. This was unacceptable to the party, which expelled him.

In 1945 an election was held at the end of the Second World War; the Labour Party won a large majority with Clement Attlee as prime minister. This government wanted to build a new Britain; it nationalised essential industries such as the railways, coal and steel, and founded the National Health Service. In the 1950 election its majority fell to five and in 1951 it lost the election to the Conservative Party. Labour was returned in 1964 and governed until 1970, and was returned again in 1974, but in 1979 there was severe industrial difficulty, especially with workers in the public sector, and the Labour Party again lost power in that year's election.

A deep internal debate began in the Party and in 1981 four leading members left to found a Social Democratic Party. See LIBERAL DEMOCRAT PARTY. In 1983, under Neil Kinnock's leadership, the party began to unify around a centre-left position and restore its popularity, and in 1993 internal changes gave party members the power to determine policy, which had previously been held by trade unions.

In 1994 Tony Blair became leader and in 1997 Labour was returned to power with a large majority after eighteen years of Conservative government. Blair continued to move the party away from its socialist past and in the 2001 election his party maintained its dominant position in British politics, although the government's support for the American invasion of Iraq led to a very great amount of internal dissent. In 2005 Labour again won a general election, but with a smaller majority than it had enjoyed. In July 2007 Blair resigned as leader and was succeeded by Gordon Brown, who proved unable to raise the party's popularity. Labour lost the general election in May 2010, and Ed Miliband was elected as leader in October 2010. He resigned after the party's defeat in May 2015 and was replaced by Jeremy Corbyn, who is on the left of the party.

The party's colour is red.

See CONSERVATIVE PARTY; LIBERAL DEMOCRAT PARTY.

lama & llama

A *lama* is a Buddhist priest.

A *llama* is a South American animal ((*Lama glama*).

Both words are pronounced /ˈlɑːmə/.

languages

The names of languages can be used as nouns:
1 *His Russian is poor.*
2 *Mary speaks excellent German.*
3 *Mary speaks German excellently.*

Note that in **2** *excellent* is an adjective describing the noun object *German*, and in **3** *excellently* is an adverb modifying the verb (S V O Adv).

The names of languages are always written with CAPITAL LETTERS.

See COLOURS.

language skills

There are four language skills. *Listening* and *reading* are the passive skills, and *speaking* and *writing* are the active ones. It is normal for a person using a foreign language to have better passive than active skills; that is to say, it is possible to recognise more words and expressions than they can use. This is the natural case in a speaker's native language.

late, latest & last

late

The common meaning of *late* is after the usual or expected time: *The meeting started late; I'm sorry I'm late; The train was ten minutes late.*

It can also mean *dead* in forms such as *The late Princess Diana; My late husband.*

Sometimes this is used to mean *former*: *The late president; Our late mayor* but this is not advisable as it can lead to confusion. It is better to say *the former president; Our ex-mayor*.

Lately is a synonym of *recently*; a *Johnny-come-lately* is a newcomer, someone who has recently arrived.

The COMPARATIVE of *late* is *later* /ˈleɪtə/. *Latter* /ˈlætə/ is used with *former* to refer to two previously mentioned concepts.

See FORMER AND LATTER.

latest

Latest means *most recent*: *the latest news, fashion, gossip, information, report. Have you heard the latest?* means *the latest news.*

last

Last is used in time expressions: *last year, my last birthday, last Christmas* and in series: the *last station* is the most recent one that the train stopped at, not necessarily the end of the line. There is, however, a difference with artistic or academic composition *Schubert's last symphony was unfinished.*

lavatory

This was once the common word for both the container and the room (it is sometimes in a different room from the bath in British houses) but *loo* and *toilet* are now more common; *bog* and *khazi*

L

/kɑːzi/ are slang names. Public lavatories are often called *public conveniences*; picture symbols have usually replaced the labels *Gentlemen* and *Ladies*.

law

A *lawyer* is someone who is qualified in the law, though the word is also used for people studying law at universities. Not all lawyers practise but those who do are divided into *solicitors* and *barristers*. A *solicitor* handles legal paperwork, preparing wills, dealing with property transfer, and writing contracts. Some, but not all, solicitors are notaries, which means that they can certify the authenticity of documents. Many people have a permanent RELATIONSHIP with a solicitor, as with other professional advisers. In the event of any difficulty with the police a solicitor is the legal advisor who represents and initially defends a suspect. If a case goes to court, the solicitor prepares the details of the case and passes them on to a *barrister*. A barrister is a professional *advocate* who argues a case in *court*, though solicitors increasingly are allowed to represent their CLIENTS in court. Some senior barristers are appointed as *Queen's Counsel* (*QC*); a barrister who becomes a QC is said to *take silk* on accepting the title. See COUNCIL & COUNSEL.

A *magistrate* or *justice of the peace* is usually a lay person (i.e. is not a professional lawyer) appointed to manage the first hearing of criminal cases; some magistrates, mostly in London, are paid professional lawyers, and are called *district judges*. When the police have sufficient *evidence* they pass it to the *Crown Prosecution Service* who present the case in the name of the Crown. A magistrate can decide cases and impose a penalty up to a limit of £5,000 and/or six months' imprisonment, or up to twelve months for certain more serious *offences*; in fact magistrates deal with 95% of all prosecuted crime. Above that limit, and when a case is of a type that cannot be heard by a magistrate, cases are sent to a Crown Court, where they are heard by a *Judge* and in some cases a *jury* consisting of twelve members of the public chosen at random. The jury decides the *verdict* (whether the *prisoner* (the *accused*) is *guilty* or *not guilty*) and in the event of a guilty verdict the judge decides the *sentence* (punishment).

In a *civil* case one PARTY (the *complainant*, formerly the *plaintiff*) *sues* the other (the *defendant*) by issuing a *claim form* (formerly a *summons,* plural *summonses*), which is an order from a court to appear at a certain time. Civil courts do not have juries except usually in *libel* (defamation) cases, where the jury not only decides in favour of one party but also decides the level of DAMAGES, and in cases of serious claims against the police.

If one party is unsatisfied with the result, they can, in certain circumstances, *appeal* against the ruling of a criminal or civil court by taking the case to the *Court of Appeal*, or *Appeal Court*. The final court in the UK was the House of Lords until 2009, when this role was transferred to the SUPREME COURT (*CONSTITUTION AND GOVERNMENT | GOVERNMENT). Being a judge is not a separate legal profession; judges are appointed from among the barristers (and now occasionally the solicitors) by the Lord Chancellor, who is a senior judge himself. *Barristers* are so called because they are allowed inside the BAR *of the court*, which separates the public part of the court from the part used by lawyers and other people involved in the process. Being *called to the bar* is the process of being appointed as a *barrister* and the *Bar Association* is the body that represents barristers. The name *solicitor* comes from the solicitor's role in finding work for a barrister. The *Law Society* is the solicitors' professional association.

In the United States there is not the difference between solicitors and barristers that there is in Britain. The name *attorney* is used to describe a practising lawyer. A *District Attorney* is employed by the State to prosecute cases.

Scotland has its own legal system, which is independent of that in England and Wales. The equivalents of *solicitor* and *barrister* are *writers to the signet* and *advocate* respectively. Crown prosecutions are brought by the *procurator fiscal*.

British laws are known as acts (a law is an act of Parliament) and are referred to as for example *the Finance Act 2010; the Immigration and Asylum Act 1999.*

L

lead
Lead /led/ is the metal with symbol Pb and atomic number 82.

Lead /liːd/ can be a noun or verb relating to showing people the way or being at the head of a group of people who are following. As a verb it is irregular: *lead, led, led.*

lecture(r)
A *lecture* is a speech given to an audience for the purpose of education or instruction. It is particularly used in universities. Despite the word's ETYMOLOGY, it has no association in modern English with the idea of reading. University teachers are known as *lecturers* although lecturing is only a small part of their work.

left and right
Apart from their meanings describing position, these words have other meanings: *left* is the past and past participle of *leave*, and *right* is the opposite of *wrong*. For this reason it is best to use *left-hand* and *right-hand* as adjectives when describing position; *the left-hand seat, the right-hand door* (*the right door* could mean *the correct one*), and *left-wing* and *right-wing* in political terms: *left-wing policies, a right-wing party*. In adverbial expressions this is not so important: *turn left; the second door on the right; he is on the left of his party; the party has moved to the right.*

See RIGHT(LY); WRONG(LY).

legal, legitimate, lawful & licit
All of these mean *in accordance with the law*; *licit* is not commonly used. *Legal* also means *connected with the law*: *legal studies* (i.e. the study of the law) lead to a *legal career* (as a lawyer). *Legitimate* is also used for a child born to married parents (though this is no longer used in English law), or for an argument or opinion that is rationally based. The opposite forms are *illegal, illegitimate, lawless,* and *illicit*. *Illicit* has moral implications: *an illicit romance.*

lemming
A lemming is a small Arctic rodent. Its population fluctuates greatly and at periods of high population large numbers of lemmings migrate to find new habitat; inevitably some die in the process. In 1958 Disney produced the film *White Wilderness*, which showed dead lemmings that had been placed by film-makers at the foot of a cliff to illustrate the film and claimed that the animals had committed suicide by deliberately running in large numbers over the edge of the cliff. The film was so influential that this falsehood was believed in the English-speaking countries and the lemming has passed into the language as a metaphor of a mass rush into a dangerous or suicidal situation.

-let
The standard English diminutive ending is *-let*, as in *booklet, cutlet* (though not from *cut*), *eyelet, hamlet* (a small village, see PLACE NAMES), *leaflet, piglet, platelet* (a blood cell fragment (thrombocyte), not a small plate for food); a *starlet* is a minor film star. This suffix is not widely applied in modern English though joking forms are sometimes made. It is only used with monosyllables. *Bracelet* is a diminutive, though the original form *bracel* is obsolete. *Pamphlet, couplet, sterlet* (a young sturgeon), and DOUBLET, *triplet* etc., are not diminutives but have other etymologies.

letters
If the name of the person who will receive the letter is unknown, a formal letter should start *Dear Sir*, or *Dear Madam*, or *Dear Sir/Madam*, (note the comma following the salutation); a letter to a company or other organisation as a whole is addressed *Dear Sirs,*; letters to newspapers begin with *Sir* alone. A letter such as a personal reference that has no specific addressee is headed *To whom it may concern.* The conventional ending for such formal letters is *Yours faithfully,* before the signature. When the addressee's name is known it should be used: *Dear Mr/Mrs/Dr/Prof.* etc. *Hill,*;

L

these letters conventionally end with *Yours sincerely,*. Other, less formal, endings such as *Yours truly, Sincerely yours,* are also found. The abbreviation *ref.* (reference) is used in *Our ref.: Your ref.:*

The following sentences are commonly found in formal letters:

Thank you for your letter of [DATE].
I am writing in response to your advertisement in today's/yesterday's [newspaper] or *in the [newspaper] of [date].*
I must (regretfully) inform you that ... /I regret to inform you that...
I am pleased to be able to tell you that...
I would like to take this opportunity to mention...
Please reply at your earliest convenience. (This means *as soon as possible* and is an abrupt comment.)
I look forward to receiving your reply/payment as soon as possible. (This is more polite because *look forward to* is associated with pleasant events.)
I would be grateful if you would/could send... at your earliest convenience/as soon as is convenient/as soon as possible. See CONDITIONAL SENTENCES.
Please do not hesitate to write/phone/contact me/us if you have any further queries/require further information.
Looking forward to hearing from you/meeting you, (written immediately before *Yours faithfully/sincerely*).

The letters *p.p.* (*per pro*) are placed before the signature when a letter or other document is signed by someone else, a secretary for example. The words *Dictated by X and signed in his/her absence* are sometimes used. The letters *c.c.* introduce the list of people to whom copies are sent. CONTRACTIONS should not be used in formal letters.

Personal letters can obviously vary immensely depending on the relations between the correspondents. They might begin (*My) dear, (My) dearest,* or *(My) darling X,*; typical endings in approximately increasing degrees of intimacy are *Yours, Kind regards, Best wishes, Love, All my love, Love and kisses*. The letter *X* is used to represent a kiss. Contractions should be used in personal letters; they represent the words as they would be spoken personally.

See ATTACH & ENCLOSE.

Liberal Democrat Party

The word *liberal* was first used in its political sense in British politics in the early years of the nineteenth century when it was used to describe the advanced (progressive) members of the Whig party who wanted to reform Britain's constitutional system to provide greater freedom and democracy; the word was taken into English from other European languages, especially Spanish and French. After the great parliamentary reform of 1832 the advanced Whigs and the radicals became known as Liberals. The first Liberal prime minister was William Ewart Gladstone, who held office three times in the second half of the nineteenth century. His governments passed a number of socially progressive measures including secret ballots in ELECTIONS and compulsory education; he reformed the army, abolishing the system of purchasing commissions, and he tried unsuccessfully to introduce Home Rule (autonomy) for IRELAND. ABROAD, he pursued what would now be called an interventionist foreign policy in defence of human rights.

Herbert Asquith's Liberal government came to power in 1908 and in 1912 it reformed Parliament, significantly reducing the power of the House of Lords. In 1916 he was replaced as prime minister by David Lloyd /lɔɪd/ George (commonly known as Lloyd George), who followed a more aggressive war policy. Lloyd George lost office in 1922, when the Labour Party replaced the Liberal Party as the main progressive force in British politics. The party went into a deep decline, with only six MPs in the 1960s. Then the party's fortune improved and in 1981 it formed an alliance with the Social Democratic PARTY, which had broken away from the Labour Party; the two parties merged in 1988 to form the Liberal Democrat Party. Under the leadership of Paddy Ashdown the party increased greatly in strength. Philosophically it is in the European social-liberal tradition, calling for individual freedom within a welfare state. It is the only British political party that is, and always has been, in favour of closer British involvement with the European Union. After short periods of leadership by Charles Kennedy and Sir Menzies /ˈmɪŋɪs/ Campbell (see Z, Z), Nick Clegg became leader in December 2007. In the 2010 election the party increased its vote share but won fewer seats and entered a coalition government with the Conservative Party. It was defeated badly in the May 2015 election. Clegg resigned and was replaced by Tim Farron. In 2017 Farron was succeeded by Vince Cable.

The party's colour is orange.

(In the USA, the word *Liberal* has a different meaning. Liberals are people who prefer to increase the power of the central government rather than having power exercised by States and individuals. This is more like European social democracy.)

See CONSERVATIVE PARTY; LABOUR PARTY.

licence & license

In British English *licence* is the noun and *license* is the verb; James Bond is *licensed to* KILL. This difference can be remembered with reference to ADVICE AND ADVISE, where the spelling reflects the pronunciation. However, this is often ignored, especially with *licence* being used for the verb. A person or company that *licenses* another person or company to do something is the *licensor* and the one that receives the *licence* is the *licensee*. See -EE.

An OFF-*licence* is a shop that sells alcoholic drinks to be drunk off the PREMISES, i.e. they must be taken away from the shop.

In American English *license* is standard for both noun and verb.

See ADVICE; PRACTICE; PROPHECY.

lie & lay

lie, lay, lain

This is intransitive and means *to be in a horizontal position*: *His land lies close to the Welsh border; I lay on the beach all morning; I could happily have lain in the sun all afternoon, if I hadn't had*

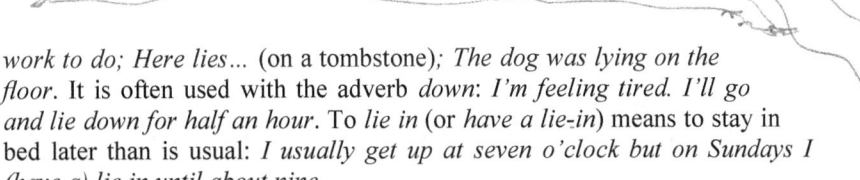

work to do; Here lies... (on a tombstone); *The dog was lying on the floor*. It is often used with the adverb *down*: *I'm feeling tired. I'll go and lie down for half an hour*. To *lie in* (or *have a lie-in*) means to stay in bed later than is usual: *I usually get up at seven o'clock but on Sundays I (have a) lie in until about nine*.

lay, laid, laid

This is transitive form of *lie, lay, lain* and means *to place something in a horizontal position*: *Lay the books on the table; They laid the injured woman on the stretcher and carried her to the ambulance; They're laying electric cables in the main road*. To *lay the table* is to place on a table the things that will be used for serving and eating the meal. Birds and some other animals *lay eggs*.

Native speakers sometimes confuse these verbs: *I ~~laid~~ on the beach all morning; The cat was ~~laying~~ on the bed; ~~Lie~~ him on the bed*, and write ~~layed~~ for *laid*. This is incorrect.

lie, lied, lied

This is intransitive and means *deliberately to say something that is untrue*: *Don't lie to me. I know who you were with last night; He was lying through his teeth; He's never lied in his life*. It a powerful word that excludes any possibility of a mistake or misunderstanding. Often it is better to say *That is not true; I'm sure that's not the case* or some other similar expression. ▶

L

Lie is often used as a noun: *He's never told a lie in his life; There are lies, damned lies, and statistics* (attributed to British Prime Minister Benjamin Disraeli). A *white lie* is a tactful statement which is not true but which is used for social purposes: *I'm afraid he's not in at the moment. Can you call back later?* (He's having his lunch.)

A *liar* is a person who tells lies.

This word has no connection with *lie, lay, lain.* The similarity is coincidental.

lay (adj.)

A *lay* person is someone who is actively involved in a church but is not in holy orders; *a lay preacher* preaches a sermon in church but is not ordained; together the *lay* people in a church are the *laity.* It also means someone who is interested in or involved with a profession, but is not professionally qualified, especially law and medicine: *To put something in terms that a lay person can understand.* Some committees on professional standards or ethics include *lay members.* This word is unconnected with the above verbs.

A *lay figure* is an artificial model or dummy with joints used by artists to show the shapes of the human body and to hang clothes on. This also is not related to any of the other meanings.

lighting, lightning & lightening

Lighting is a system for providing light to a building, street etc.

Lightning is the flash caused by an electrical discharge between a cloud and the ground.

Lightening is the -ING FORM of the verb *lighten*, which means **1** to become lighter in brightness (*the sky lightened*) or intensity (*the rain lightened*) and **2** to make lighter in weight (*to lighten someone's load*).

like

verb

Be careful to distinguish between these three forms:

I like playing tennis. (Playing tennis always gives me pleasure.)

I'd (I would) like to play tennis. (Just now, playing tennis would give me pleasure; this could be a suggestion.)

I like to play tennis on Saturday afternoons. (This is a habit which gives me pleasure.) See INFINITIVE OR -ING?

preposition

Like is also a preposition meaning *similar to*: *He looks like his father; These mountains are like the Alps* and *in the same way as*: *Do it like this/like me.*

... and the like means *and similar people and things.*

The like(s) of you means *People like you.* It is nothing to do with *your likes* or *dislikes* (the things that you like or dislike). See AS.

filler

There is a modern slang tendency to use *like* as a filler in speech: *I was like waiting for the bus like, when this man like came up to me and asked me like...* This should be avoided in any but the most informal context.

likely

Likely is an ADJECTIVE WITH -LY connected with the idea of probability. Sometimes it is a synonym of *probable*: *It is likely/probable that he will come.* It can be used with a personal subject: *He is likely to come.*

It can be used in British English as an adverb with *more, most,* or *very*: *He'll most likely/probably come tomorrow.* In American English it can be used freely as an adverb synonym of *probably*: *He'll likely come tomorrow.*

lime

This botanical name refers to two completely different things: the citrus FRUIT *Citrus aurantifolia* and the trees of the *Tilia* genus, which are also called *linden* trees.

liquor & liqueur

Liquor /ˈlɪkə/ is used generally to mean alcoholic drinks, especially spirits. It is also sometimes used in cooking to mean *water* or *liquid*.

A ***liqueur*** /lɪˈkɜː/ is a sweet distilled alcoholic drink, sometimes flavoured with herbs, which is usually drunk after a meal.

little & small

Little (as an adjective) and *small* can both refer to size or importance. However, *little* can have emotional overtones. A *small difficulty* is a relatively unimportant one but *I can't think about every little difficulty* emphasises their unimportant nature; *a small boy* is one who is not big but *a little boy* implies a friendly, affectionate view of him; *little ones* can mean *children*. Similarly, *a lovely little house; a happy little man* are more affectionate than the same phrases with *small* but *little* can also suggest disapproval: *a silly little girl; you little fool.*

Both words are used in fixed collocations:

little

Little is used with animal names to indicate the smaller or smallest one with that name. The *little owl* is the smallest British owl. The *Little Bear* is a star constellation distinct from the Great Bear; the word is used similarly in place names such as *Little Crosby* and *Great Crosby*; and in *little* FINGER and *toe*. *Little green men* are imaginary invaders from space.

small

Small is used in these expressions:

The *small intestine* or *gut*.

E. F. Schumacher's phrase *small is beautiful,* meaning that small-scale systems and institutions are preferable to large-scale ones.

The saying *(it's a) small world, isn't it?* expressing surprise at meeting someone in an unexpected place, or other similar coincidence.

The *small print* of a contract is the detailed conditions, which are often printed in small type; it is often used metaphorically: *You should have read the small print* simply means *You should have read it more carefully*.

Small change is money in coins rather than notes.

Small letters are not CAPITAL LETTERS.

A *small businessman* is the owner of a small business.

Small ads (ADVERTISEMENTS) are newspaper advertisements that occupy a few lines of print in a column, perhaps with a small picture.

Small capitals are capital letters printed at the same size as small letters. They are used for cross-references in this book.

The *small hours* are the early hours of the morning after midnight.

The *smallest room* is a euphemism for the LAVATORY.

Smalls or *small clothes* are underwear.

comparative forms

Only *small* makes a comparative form: *smaller, smallest*. The comparative forms of *little* (*less, least*) are used when *little* is a QUANTIFIER, not an adjective.

loathe, loath

Loath /ləʊθ/ is an adjective meaning *very unwilling: He was loath to admit his mistake.* ▶

L

Loathe /ləʊð/ is a verb meaning *hate, detest*: *I loathed working for that company.*

Loathsome is the adjective: a *loathsome person* or *animal* is one that inspires *loathing* or disgust.

loch

Loch /lɒx/ (see PHONETIC SYMBOLS) is the Scottish form of the English word *lake*: *Loch Lomond, Loch Ness*. There is said to be a famous monster living in Loch Ness.

A *sea loch* is one that is connected directly with the sea like a Norwegian fjord. The Irish word *lough* has the same pronunciation. English people often pronounce these words as /lɒk/.

lollipop lady/man

A *lollipop* is a sweet on a stick; lollipops are often round and flat. People who control traffic outside schools use large round signs on sticks to warn drivers to stop so that children can cross the road. Because these signs look like lollipops, these people are informally called *lollipop ladies/men/women*.

long

As an adverb *long* refers specifically to time, meaning for a long time.
1. *I have long thought/believed that...*
2. *How long did you live in Africa? Not long.*
3. *I hadn't been waiting long when the bus came.*

Short cannot be used adverbially.

See TIME.

1 is the only form in which *long* is used to mean *for a long time* in affirmative statements. We do not say *I waited long* but *I waited (for) a long time.*

The comparative and superlative forms are used: *I lived in Africa longer than John, but Bill lived there (the) longest.*

Long can be used with *too* and *enough*: *I had waited too long; I had waited long enough.*

The usage *He won't have that painting as long as I live* has led to the use of *as/so long as* in conditional sentences: *I feel safe as long as you're here* (= provided that...)

So long is an informal way of saying *goodbye*.

Someone who is *not long for this world* is expected to die soon.

Long ago means in the distant past: *I knew him long ago.*

Before long means *soon*: *We'll know before long.*

No longer means that something that was once the case is not so now: *They no longer live here.*

All day/week/etc. long emphasises the continuing nature of something: *All year long the situation became worse.*

A *lifelong* friend is one you have known all your life.

With a hyphen *long* can precede a participle: *A long-lost friend; a long-felt desire* or an -ING FORM: *His long-suffering wife; long-wearing material.*

longitude

The pronunciation is /ˈlɒndʒɪtjuːd/ or /ˈlɒŋgɪtjuːd/. The incorrect pronunciation as if it were written *longtitude* is sometimes heard.

lose, loose & loss

Lose /luːz/, *lost, lost* is the verb. *I have lost my watch.* A clock or watch that is running too slow *loses time*: *My watch loses five minutes a week.* See GAIN, EARN & WIN.

Loss /lɒs/ is the noun associated with *lose. His death was a sad loss; The company made a loss of £22,000,000 last year.*

Loose /luːs/ is an adjective meaning *unrestrained*: *loose hair, a loose dog* or the opposite of *tight*: *a loose shirt.* The word is not etymologically connected with *lose/loss*.

lot

A lot is a group of things, especially items for sale at an auction.

*A **lot of*** meaning *much* or *many* is used in all kinds of sentences: *I've got a lot of time; Have you got a lot of books?; I haven't got a lot of time.* Lots of is a colloquial alternative: *I've got lots of time; Have you got lots of books?; I haven't got lots of time*

Much and **many** are usually only used in negative sentences and questions: *I haven't got much time; Have you got many books? Much* is uncountable and *many* is countable. They can be used in negative sentences and questions instead of *a lot of*: *I haven't got much time; Have you got many books?* In affirmative sentences they are rather formal: *I have given much thought to it; Many people believe it.*

They are used with adverbs: *Too much, so much, very many.*

M

m, M /em/
The thirteenth letter of the alphabet. It is pronounced /m/.

It is silent initially in *mnemonic* /nɪˈmɒnɪk/.

Magdalen(e)
Magdalen and *Magdalene* are colleges in Oxford and Cambridge universities respectively; both are pronounced /ˈmɔːdlɪn/.

Mary Magdalene /ˈmægdəlɪn/ is a biblical character.

maid and maiden
These two words share the same origin meaning a girl or young unmarried woman but are used differently.

A *maid* is a female domestic servant. Sometimes the word is used jokingly to refer to a young woman.

A *barmaid* is a woman who works behind a BAR in a pub or hotel.

A *bridesmaid* is a girl who accompanies a BRIDE at her wedding.

A *chambermaid* is a woman who cleans rooms and makes beds in a hotel; this used to be the name for a woman who did this work in a private house.

A *dairymaid* or *milkmaid* is a woman who works in a DAIRY.

A *housemaid* is a female servant in a house. *Housemaid's knee* is an inflammation (bursitis) affecting the kneecap (patella).

A *mermaid* is an imaginary animal that lives in the sea, with the head and body of a woman and the tail of a fish.

A *nursemaid* is a woman who is employed to look after small children, a nanny.

An *old maid* is a rather rude name for an elderly woman who has not married.

Maiden is not used nowadays to refer to a young woman literally.

A *maiden aunt* is one who has never married.

Maidenhead is the state of virginity; physically, it is the hymen. It is also the name of a town in Berkshire.

Maidenhood is virginity, the state of being a *maiden*.

A woman's *maiden NAME* (see PERSONAL NAMES) is her surname before she marries.

In CRICKET a *maiden over* is one in which no runs are scored.

A SHIP's *maiden voyage* is the first that it makes.

The first speech that a new Member of Parliament makes in the House of Commons after being elected is his/her *maiden speech*.

major
An army rank immediately above captain; it should not be confused with MAYOR (*CONSTITUTION | REGIONAL AND LOCAL GOVERNMENT).

See MILITARY RANKS.

make love
At one time *make love* meant to approach someone with the intention of establishing a loving relationship or to flirt. In the twentieth century it came to mean precisely to have sexual relations with someone. It is important to bear this in mind when reading books written before the middle of that century.

M

manuscript
Despite the origin of the word (Latin *manuscriptus* = written by hand), this can be used of the original of a work presented for publication, even if it is typed or prepared in electronic format by computer. It is abbreviated MS.

marriage & wedding
Marriage is the state of being married and the continuing relationship: *a long/happy/second marriage*. The *marriage bed* is used as a metaphor for the sexual relations of a married couple; a *marriage bureau* is an agency that arranges marriages; a *marriage certificate* (or *lines*) is the certificate that confirms that a marriage has taken place; a *marriage licence* is the licence to marry if there are no *banns* (formal announcement in church of an intention to marry); a *marriage settlement* is the agreement on the division and use of property between the spouses; a *marriage of convenience* is one that is made for practical purposes such as guaranteeing financial arrangements or acquiring citizenship of a country. *Marriage* is sometimes used to mean the ceremony itself and the accompanying celebrations; some newspapers have announcements of *Births, marriages, and deaths*. Some people are involved in *arranged* or *forced* marriage.

However, *wedding* is more common for the ceremony; it is found in *wedding anniversary, cake, day, dress, guest, night, photo, present, ring, video*. A *wedding breakfast* is the meal served to guests after the *wedding ceremony* (at any time of day) and the *wedding march* is a march played when the bride enters the church.

If John and Mary become ENGAGED, that is their commitment to *marry* or, as is more commonly said, to *get married*. In Britain when a man PROPOSES to a woman he usually gives her a diamond ring, which she wears on the third finger of her left hand. After the wedding they will *be married*. (Note the difference between the DYNAMIC AND STATIVE forms of the passive voice in *get married* and *be married*). *John marries Mary* and *Mary marries John*; and *the priest marries them (to each other)*. Then *John is married to Mary*.

On the day of the wedding, and perhaps for a few days beforehand and afterwards, *bride* and *bridegroom* or *groom* are used to refer to the woman and man respectively.

See ETYMOLOGY.

master and mistress
Both these words refer to someone who has power over others; the *master and/or mistress* are the heads of a household, and the phrase *master and servant* shows the nature of the relationship. In the merchant marine the *master* is the officer in command of a vessel and *captain* is a rank: Captain Smith was the master of the Titanic. A *schoolmaster* or *schoolmistress* is a teacher; this is used mostly in independent schools, and in the school the simple terms *master* and *mistress* are used: *my history master, your gym mistress*. The *headmaster/mistress* is the person in charge of the school. A *master*, for example a *master carpenter*, is a person with great skill in a trade who can teach others known as apprentices or pupils. A *master's degree* is a higher degree at a UNIVERSITY. An *old master* is a painter from a time in the past, especially in the great period of European painting from the thirteenth to the seventeenth century, and a *grand master* is a top international CHESS player. A *master document* or record is an original one from which copies are made. The *master bedroom* in a house is the biggest one. In general rather than specific terms we can say that a woman is a *mistress* of her subject, meaning that she is an expert at it. However, a man's *mistress* is a woman other than a wife with whom he has a prolonged sexual affair.

As a verb to *master* something is to control a situation or to bring people or land under one's control. To *master* a subject or art is to acquire a good command of it. The noun is *mastery*: *His/her mastery of French cooking was impressive*. There is no female form of the verb or of *mastery* that can be used in relation to women.

See MR ETC.

M

mate

The commonest meaning is as a colloquial equivalent of FRIEND. However, with animals it applies to the animal's sexual partner, which is definitely not the case with human beings; the *mating season* is the period for selection of partners and for reproduction.

With certain trades it can mean an assistant: *a carpenter's mate*. A *mate* is an officer on a merchant SHIP; the *first mate* is second in command under the MASTER.

It can also be used of a person who is in the same situation: *classmate, flatmate, room-mate, workmate*. In these expressions there is no implication that the people are necessarily personal friends. This meaning is similar to that of FELLOW but it relates to the location rather than to the category of people (cf *fellow students*).

An *inmate* is a permanent resident in an institution such as a prison or a hospital.

This word is unconnected with the terms used in CHESS.

material

In addition to its general meaning, this has the specific meaning of CLOTH, textile: *I must buy some material to make a dress.*

mathematical terms

arithmetic

The names of the four basic arithmetical operations are *addition* (+), *subtraction* (-), *multiplication* (x) and *division* (÷). These operations are spoken as follows:

$4 + 2 = 6$

Four and two	is / are / make / makes / equals	six.
Four plus two / Four added to two	is / makes / equals	

$4 - 2 = 2$

Four minus two	is / makes / equals	two.

Four take-away two is a form that children sometimes use.

$4 \times 2 = 8$

Four twos	are	eight.
Four times two	is / makes / equals	

Four by two is sometimes used, especially in referring to rectangular dimension.
See X, X.

$4 \div 2 = 2$

Four divided by two / Four over two	is / makes / equals	two.

4^2 is *four squared*; 4^3 is *four cubed*; 4^4 is *four to the fourth, four to the power four* and so on with ordinal numbers. 4^n is *four to the nth* /enθ/, *four to the power n*.

$\sqrt{4}$ is *the square root of four; root four*; $\sqrt[3]{4}$ is *the cube root of four*.

For fractions see NUMBERS.

algebra

In algebra letters are pronounced with their normal alphabet names and do not have plural forms:

$(2x + 3y)^2 = 42$

two x /tuːeks/ *plus three y* /θriːwaɪ/ *all squared equals forty-two.*

$$\frac{2x + 3y}{\sqrt{2}} = 42$$

two x plus three y all over root two equals forty-two.

$4(2x + 3y) = 42$

four times two x plus three y equals forty-two.

$9 \times 6 = 42_{(13)}$

nine times six is forty-two to base thirteen.

An *equation* containing terms involving no higher power than squares is a *quadratic* equation. If the highest power is three it is *cubic*, with four it is *quartic*, and with five it is *quintic*. The roots of a quadratic equation are given by the formula:

$$x = \frac{-b \pm \sqrt{b^2 - 4ac}}{2a}$$

x equals minus b plus or minus the square root of b squared minus four a c all over 2 a.

geometry

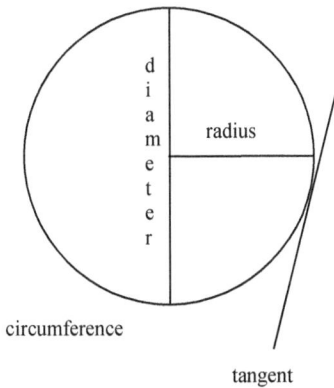

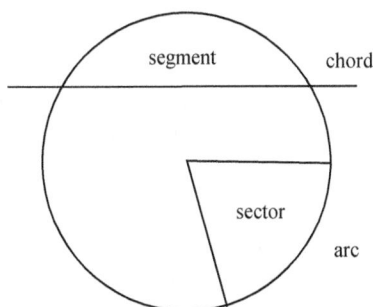

CHORD /kɔːd/; *circumference* /səˈkʌmfərəns/; *diameter* /daɪˈæmɪtə/; *tangent*/ˈtændʒənt/ See CHORD & CORD; RADIO, RADIUM & RADIUS. π is the GREEK letter *pi* /paɪ/.▶

M

Angles are measured in *degrees* or *radians*: there are 360° or 2π radians in a circle. An angle of 90° is a *right angle*, one of less than 90° is *acute*, between 90° and 180° it is *obtuse*, and greater than 180° it is *reflex*.

Plane figures with different numbers of STRAIGHT sides are:
3   triangle
4   quadrilateral
5   pentagon
6   hexagon
7   heptagon
8   octagon
9   nonagon
10 decagon

Triangles can be *right-angled*, with one angle being 90°. The side OPPOSITE the right angle is the *hypotenuse* /haɪˈpɒtənjuːz/. Triangles can also be *equilateral* (all three sides equal), *isosceles* /aɪˈsɒsəliːz/ (two sides equal), or *scalene* (no sides equal).

trigonometry

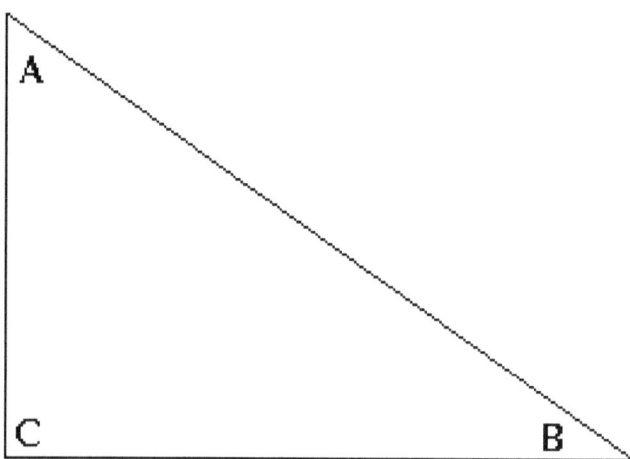

In a right-angled triangle where C is the right angle and the side A – B is the hypotenuse the *sine* of angle A is $\frac{BC}{AB}$, its *cosine* is $\frac{AC}{AB}$, and its *tangent* is $\frac{BC}{AC}$

Different types of quadrilateral are:
parallelogram: both pairs of opposite sides equal and parallel.
rectangle: parallelogram with adjacent sides meeting at right angles.
square: rectangle with adjacent sides equal in length.
trapezium: one pair of opposite sides parallel.

The regular Platonic solids are *tetrahedron* (4 faces), *cube* (6 faces), *octahedron* (8 faces), *dodecahedron* (12 faces) and *icosahedron* (20 faces). These words make PLURAL FORMS with *-hedra* or *-hedrons*.

matter & mind

It doesn't matter means that it is not important, it has no significance. It can be used alone as a response to a comment or situation: *'I finished your bottle of water.' 'It doesn't matter. I've got another one'* or with a following comment describing what it is that doesn't matter: *It doesn't matter what you do; It doesn't matter who you are. You can't come in*. It can be made personal: *It doesn't matter (to me* etc.*) what you do*. It is similar to *I don't care what you do; It makes no difference to me what you do*.

I don't mind is obviously personal. It is similar in meaning to *It doesn't matter*: *I don't mind what you do* but it has more an implication of objecting to something. It is a form of *Do you mind?* as in *Do you mind if I smoke?*

maybe

This is one word when it means *perhaps*: *Maybe I'll be late tomorrow*. It is two words when it is a modal verb: *I may be late tomorrow*.

meals

Breakfast is the first meal of the day. The traditional English breakfast of cereal with bacon, eggs, sausage etc. followed by toast and marmalade is served in hotels but is rarely eaten in full in private homes. Cheese and cold meat are not normally eaten for breakfast. A FAST is a period when people do not eat, sometimes for religious reasons; thus the name *breakfast* refers to the meal that breaks the overnight fast, the first food taken for some time. Where we now say *I had breakfast* people used to say *I broke my fast* but this is unusual nowadays.

Elevenses is a name given by some people to a mid-morning coffee break with biscuits; of course the name comes from the time of eleven o'clock.

Lunch is usually a light meal, maybe a sandwich or a meal on one plate. It is usually eaten at some time between 12.00 and 14.00. Office workers normally have between thirty minutes and an hour for lunch.

Brunch is a BLEND of breakfast and lunch. It is often served as a late breakfast or early lunch on Sundays as a buffet.

Tea is a snack or light meal in mid-afternoon consisting of tea with cake, biscuits and perhaps sandwiches. In this regard *tea* is a meal, not only a drink. If you are invited to tea in an English home you will be expected to eat. Young children normally have a cooked tea as they go to bed before dinner.

Dinner is the main meal of the day and is usually eaten between 18.00 and 20.00. Some people, especially on Sundays, eat dinner at midday and have a more substantial *tea* (sometimes called *high tea*) at about 17.00 or 18.00.

Supper is a snack or light meal of biscuits, fruit, and/or sandwiches eaten during the evening at about 21.00 or 22.00.

Clearly this can only be a guideline; there is considerable variety in individual eating habits.

Restaurants in Britain may stop taking orders for lunch at about 14.00 and dinner at 21.00, or even earlier. Pubs that sell cooked meals do not usually have an open kitchen all the time that they are selling drinks.

means

Means has the *s* in the singular and does not change: *One means of transport; two means of transport*.

media

For the BBC see SEPARATE ARTICLE.

As well as the BBC there are private commercial television channels in Britain, which receive money from advertising; they are Independent Television (known as Channel Four), Channel Four and Channel Five. Broadcasting, including the BBC, is supervised and regulated by the Office of Communications, known as Ofcom. Also, there are many satellite channels showing a wide variety of programmes.

The main written media are the newspapers. The daily newspapers in fact appear only on six days of the week; the Sunday newspapers are separate, although in some cases they are associated with daily

M

papers. British newspapers are divided into two categories, the serious papers, which are called broadsheets from the name of the large pages on which they are printed (though most have now adopted a smaller page format), and the more popular and sensational tabloids, also so named from the page size, which is much smaller than that of the broadsheets. It is usual in Britain for newspapers to adopt strong political positions, and at election times they usually express an open opinion and recommendation for one party or another.

The **Times** is the oldest and probably the best known of the serious daily newspapers; it is conservative in outlook, as is the **Sunday Times**. The **Daily Telegraph** and **Sunday Telegraph** are also conservative. The **Guardian** and the (Sunday) **Observer** are closer to the Labour Party. The **Financial Times** (FT) is respected, but naturally its news focuses on economic and financial affairs.

Among the tabloids, the **Daily Mail** and **Mail on Sunday** represent the voice of the right-wing conservative middle class, as do the **Daily** and **Sunday Express**. The **Daily** and **Sunday Mirror** generally support the Labour Party, and the **Sun** changes as the views of its readers change; having supported the Conservative Party in the 1980s, it changed its support to Labour in the 1990s but supported the Conservatives again in the 2010 and 2015 general elections. All the tabloids give a lot of space to items that are not strictly news, show business gossip and human interest stories for example. The **Sun** and **Mirror**, which together sell about 5 million copies a day, also carry a lot of scandal and sensationalised information.

There are also weekly newspapers and magazines. The **Economist** carries general British and international news (not only economics and business) with science and art reviews, and comments from a conservative point of view. The **New Statesman** carries left-wing comment, while the **Spectator** is more right-wing. The **Times Literary Supplement** has serious literary reviews. **Private Eye** is a magazine published every two weeks which carries very strong satirical articles and has a reputation for its good cartoons.

There is also a very wide range of specialist newspapers and magazines in the UK dealing with a wide range of different matters.

meter & metre

A *meter* is a device for measuring a flow: *electricity meter, taxi meter*.

A *metre* is a standard unit of length (100 cm).

Both are pronounced /miːtə/. In American English both forms are spelled *meter*.

MI5 and MI6

MI5, officially known as the Security Service, is the UK's domestic agency to counter foreign espionage and domestic political unrest. It is responsible to the HOME SECRETARY (*HOME OFFICE).

MI6, officially known as the Secret Intelligence Service, is the UK's intelligence-gathering (i.e. espionage) agency. It is responsible to the FOREIGN SECRETARY (*FOREIGN OFFICE).

Until the 1980s these agencies were so secret that no official government statement would even recognise their existence. Now they are officially recognised and the names of their Directors are publicly announced. Since the collapse of Communism they have concentrated on countering international terrorism and organised crime in the UK as well as on security problems in Northern Ireland.

middle age & Middle Ages

Middle age is the period in a person's life between being young and being old. The adjective is *middle-aged*. See -ED & -ES, PRONUNCIATION.

The *Middle Ages* (with CAPITAL LETTERS) are conventionally the period between the fall of the western Roman Empire in the fifth century and the fall of Constantinople (1453) with the fifteenth-century Renaissance in Europe; sometimes the period is taken as starting in 1000. The adjective is *medieval*.

military ranks

British military ranks for officers and other ranks are as follows:

Royal Navy	Army & Royal Marines	Royal Air Force
Admiral of the Fleet	Field-Marshal	Marshal of the Royal Air Force
Admiral	General	Air Chief Marshal
Vice-Admiral	Lieutenant-General	Air Marshal
Rear-Admiral	Major-General	Air Vice Marshal
Commodore	Brigadier	Air Commodore
Captain	Colonel	Group Captain
Commander	Lieutenant-Colonel	Wing Commander
Lieutenant-Commander	Major	Squadron Leader
Lieutenant	Captain	Flight Lieutenant
Sub-Lieutenant	Lieutenant	Flying Officer
Midshipman	Second Lieutenant	Pilot Officer
Warrant Officer	Warrant Officer 1st Class	Warrant Officer
Chief Petty Officer	Warrant Officer 2nd Class	Flight Sergeant
Petty Officer	Staff Sergeant	Chief Technician
Leading rate	Sergeant	Sergeant
Able Rate	Corporal	Corporal
Ordinary Rate	Lance Corporal	Junior Technician/Senior Aircraftsman/Leading Aircraftsman
	Private	Aircraftsman

Note:
- The pronunciation of *colonel* /ˈkɜːnəl/, *lieutenant* /lefˈtenənt/, and *sergeant* /ˈsɑːdʒənt/.
- The difference between an army captain and a naval captain.
- The Royal Marines equivalents of *Staff Sergeant* and *Private* are *Colour Sergeant* and *Marine* respectively.

minister & ministry

In government a *minister* (person) is responsible for a *ministry* (institution). In Presbyterian churches the clergyman is known as the *minister*.

minute

The period of sixty seconds is pronounced /ˈmɪnɪt/.

A small steak served in a sandwich is a *minute* /ˈmɪnɪt/ *steak*.

The *MINUTES* /ˈmɪnɪts/ are an official report of a meeting.

The adjective meaning *very small* is pronounced /maɪˈnjuːt/.

minutes

The minutes of a meeting are the official record of what was said and agreed. They are written in the PAST SIMPLE because they describe what happened in the past. Naturally, they make great use of INDIRECT SPEECH with backshifting of verb tenses.

miscarriage

Mis- is a PREFIX meaning that something is done wrongly.

A *miscarriage* is a spontaneous ABORTION. A *miscarriage of justice* is a judicial mistake. There is a verb *miscarry*: *She miscarried after two months; Sadly, our plans miscarried.*

modal auxiliary verbs

This article has an introduction followed by sections dealing with ability, permission, and possibility; these together cover the verbs *can, be able, may,* and *might*. There are sections dealing separately with the verbs *must, ought to & should, shall & should,* and *will & would* followed by

M

sections covering the use of modal verbs with the PERFECT ASPECT (*She might have come*) and with the CONTINUOUS ASPECT (*He may be coming*). The final section deals with semi-modal verbs (*dare* and *need*).

introduction

Like other Germanic languages English has modal verbs that modify other verbs with relation to willingness, possibility, obligation, and other moods. They are also used to indicate some future and conditional forms.

present	past*
can	could**
may	might
must	–
shall	should
will	would

*It is very important indeed to understand that with the exception of *could*, which is the past of *can*, the use of the word *past* with respect to modal verbs has no connection at all with chronological time. Those words are used when a past form of the verb is required for reasons of syntax. See INDIRECT SPEECH; TENSE & TIME.

** *Could* is also the conditional of *can*.

Modal verbs have four things in common that distinguish them from other verbs:
- They have no *s* in the third person singular: *he can, it must*.
- They are followed by a bare infinitive (without *to*): *You may go, It will rain*.
- They make question and negative forms without *do/does/did* as auxiliary verbs: *May I go? She must not go.*
- They are defective, i.e. they do not have all tense forms, and they have no infinitive forms. When necessary, this deficiency is made up by using other verb forms.

Modal verbs are used to indicate such ideas as possibility, ability etc.:

ability	can/could	obligation, compulsion	must; have got to
possibility	can/could; may/might	tentative inference	should, ought to
permission	can/could; may/might	obligation (suggestion)	should, ought to
logical necessity	must; have got to	prediction	will, would, shall
logical impossibility	cannot	volition, willingness	will, would

The dividing lines between these categories are not always clear.

ability and permission

Ability and permission, though different, are connected; a lack of permission often effectively leads to a lack of ability. If a child is not allowed to leave a classroom, or an employee is not allowed to leave the office early, in practice they recognise a lack of ability; and if permission to overDRAW a bank account is not given, no way except robbery will offer the ability to obtain the money.

ability (physical or mental) in the present, past, future or conditional

Ability is expressed with *can/be able;* these examples refer to the ability to do something:
Can you lift this box? Can you speak Russian?
I could run 100m in twelve seconds when I was young.
He could lift that box if he wanted to.
He won't be able to lift that box.
If I had more money, I could buy a bigger car. (This is ambiguous between the abstract possibility of buying a car and the more realistic ability to do so.) *Can* is usually used with SENSE VERBS: *I can see you.* For the difference between *can* and *be able to* see below.

permission

You may overdraw your account by £200.
You can overdraw your account by £200.

With reference to permission *may* is rather more formal and is less common than *can*. **May** is only used in the present tense; in the past and conditional *could* must be used: *When I worked in a library I could borrow as many books as I wanted; If I worked in a library I could borrow as many books as I wanted.* These sentences can be rewritten using: *... I was allowed to borrow as many books ...* and *... I would be allowed to borrow as many books ...*

Might (see below) is not an alternative to *may* used for permission.

M

ability and possibility

In some cases ability can be considered as a kind of possibility, where the possibility depends on the existence of the ability.

possibility in the present, future or past

Anyone can make a mistake.
We will be able to have the barbecue outside if the sun shines.
We could expect no other result.

These sentences can be rewritten as:
It is possible for anyone to make a mistake.
It will be possible for us to have the barbecue outside if the sun shines.
No other result was possible.

However, there are cases of possibility that do not include an element of ability. *May* refers to the possibility that a specified proposition is or will become true. Thus it can be replaced by *perhaps* (and, of course, MAYBE is interchangeable with *perhaps*).
She may be here now = Perhaps (maybe) she's here now.
It may rain this afternoon = Perhaps (maybe) it will rain this afternoon.

In sentences of this kind *might* can be used instead of *may*: *She might be here now.* *Might* is sometimes said to show a lower degree of possibility than *may*, but this difference is not universally recognised and to a large degree the two words are interchangeable.

The above examples refer to possibility in the present or future; possibilities of this kind in the past are expressed with the past INFINITIVE: *She may have arrived.* See below (MODALS WITH THE PERFECT ASPECT).

For future possibility *could* can be used: *I could/may/might finish it tomorrow.* But the negative form must be with *may/might*: *I may/might not finish it tomorrow.* *I could not finish it tomorrow* is not used because it means *It would be impossible for me to finish it tomorrow...* and can be understood as an ELLIPTICAL form of a second conditional sentence *...even if I worked as hard as possible.*

It could/may/might rain this afternoon are three correct and more or less equal forms.
It may/might not rain this afternoon are also both correct and possible.
It could not rain this afternoon is impossible because it refers to an ability to rain rather than to the possibility of rain falling.

Might is not always an alternative to *may*. Both are possible in *If I work very hard, I may/might finish it tomorrow* but only *might* is possible in *If I worked very hard, I might finish it tomorrow* because the second conditional requires a past tense of the auxiliary verb. See the introduction to this article and TENSE & TIME.

In all of these sentences, adding *well* after the modal verb increases the degree of certainty: *I could/may/might well finish it tomorrow.*

ambiguous *may*

The sentence *A married woman may keep her maiden name instead of taking her husband's surname* is ambiguous. If the *may* expresses permission, the sentence says that she is allowed to keep her maiden name; on the other hand, if it expresses possibility, it says that it is possible but not certain that she will do so. See MR ETC. This ambiguity can be avoided by using *can* for permission and *might* for possibility:

A married woman can keep her maiden name instead of taking her husband's surname.
A married woman might keep her maiden name instead of taking her husband's surname.

Does the sentence *We may pay your travelling expenses* refer to permission or possibility? Does it mean that we are allowed to pay your expenses, or that perhaps we will pay them but this is not certain?

The British Board of Film Classification is the body that determines the suitability and availability of films and DVDs in the UK. It says that DVDs classified as 18R may not be supplied by mail order. It is clear from the context that this is a prohibition (i.e. a denial of permission) rather than a possibility, but it is expressed formally. See AMBIGUOUS MUST below.

can and be able

The infinitive of *can* is *be able to*, which supplies the other parts of the verb.

I expect to be able to give you an answer tomorrow. (Ability)
I hope to be able to drive next week. (Permission)

I'll be able to pay you next week. (Ability)
You'll be able to borrow more money when you've repaid the present loan. (Permission)

I've never been able to ride a bicycle. (Ability)
I've never been able to go home early. (Permission)

In the present and conditional (except for the category of possibility) both *can* and *be able* are possible for ability:
I can/I am able to walk 6 km in an hour.
Can you/are you able to lift this box?
Can you/are you able to speak Russian?
If I had more money, I could/would be able to buy a bigger car.

and for permission:
You can/are able to overdraw your account by £200.
If I worked in a library, I could/would be able to borrow as many books as I wanted.

but not in the sense of possibility:
Anyone could make a mistake at some time.
Anyone was/would be able to make a mistake at some time.

In the past there is a difference between *could* and *was/were able to*. *Was able* implies that the action was completed and thus that it took place on one specific occasion rather than being a general ability in the past.

My TV was repaired yesterday so I was able to see the football match. (I did watch it.)
Were you able to buy a ticket at the door? (If so, I assume that you did.)

Could refers to the general past of *can*:
I could run 100 METRES *in twelve seconds when I was young.* (Ability)
When I worked in a library, I could borrow as many books as I wanted. (Permission)

This difference does not apply in negative sentences:
I couldn't/wasn't able to see the football match.
Couldn't you/weren't you able to buy a ticket?
I couldn't/wasn't able to run 100 metres in 12 seconds when I was young.
Even though I worked in a library, I couldn't/wasn't able to borrow as many books as I wanted.

Only *was/were able* is possible when the action refers to one particular occasion in the past, rather than to a general ability: *After negotiating for three hours I was able to get the price reduced by 10%* but *He could always persuade people to give him a discount.*

In the negative there is no difference: *After negotiating for three hours I couldn't/wasn't able to get the price reduced at all* and in passive verb forms *be able to* is not used: *On that day alone tickets could be bought at a 10% discount; On that day alone tickets were able to be bought at a 10% discount.*

In conditional sentences *He could lift that box if he wanted to* suggests that he has the strength to do so but is unwilling to lift it whereas *He would be able to lift that box if you took the books out of it* shows that on this occasion his strength is insufficient to lift it.

Cannot (written as one word) in the present means that something is impossible. It is the negative of *must* used for **logical necessity** (see below). *You cannot be tired.* (I know you have not been working very hard.) See **impossibility** under MODALS WITH THE PERFECT ASPECT below.

Could is used in polite requests: *Could you tell me the time please?; Could you help me with this?*

M

must
This verb is used in cases of:

logical necessity
Logical necessity refers to a statement that is a clear inference from observed facts:
You must be tired. (I know how hard you've been working.)
He must be very rich. (He has a big house and an expensive car.)
You must be joking. (I find that hard to believe.)
This must be the one I lost. (I recognise it.)

Question and negative forms are made with *can*: *Can this be the one you lost?*; *You can't be serious.*

obligation/compulsion
You must be at the exam centre at nine o'clock on Saturday morning; We must all try to find a solution; I must stop smoking.

Must has no form except the present; in other tenses *have to* is used: *We'll have to be at the airport at three o'clock; He had to get up very early; I've always had to work at night.*

Have to can be used in the present (note the pronunciation *have to* /ˈhæftuː/ and *has to* /ˈhæstuː/).

There is a difference between *have to* and *must*. *Must* implies that the requirement or obligation has been determined by the speaker.

You must be at the exam centre at nine o'clock on Saturday. (This is very close to being an order.)
We must all try to find a solution. (I am telling everyone, including myself, to do so.)
I must stop smoking. (I know that it is necessary and I am telling myself so.)

Have to is less personal; it implies that the requirement or obligation comes from outside the speaker.

You have to be at the exam centre at nine o'clock on Saturday. (That is when the exam starts.)
We all have to try and find a solution. (That is what we have been told to do.)
The doctor says that I have to stop smoking.

This example contrasts *must* and *have to*:
The goods must be delivered this week (because that is when the customer needs them and I have accepted the obligation to meet his needs) *although the contract only says that they have to be delivered before the end of this month/don't have to be delivered before the end of this month.*

The difference between *must* and *have to* is not always clear and is sometimes ignored by native speakers. When an obligation has been imposed externally, it is often accepted internally; this leaves a grey area where both forms are acceptable with little if any difference in meaning:
I have to go now because my train leaves in half an hour. (I accept the obligation that comes from outside.)
I must go now. My train leaves in half an hour. (I am imposing this obligation on myself because of the external circumstances.)

There is no significant difference between *must* and *have to* in passive verb forms: *This work must/has to be finished by Thursday.*

ambiguous *must*
The sentence *You must give him money* is ambiguous. It could be an obligation or it could be logical necessity. He has no other source of income; no-one else is likely to give him money; therefore he receives his money from you. In fact, the context makes the meaning clear, as does the intonation in speech. See *ambiguous may* above.

must not & don't have to
Must not expresses a prohibition, which is a negative obligation: *He must not go; We mustn't be late.*

Don't have to expresses a lack of obligation, which leaves a free choice open: *You don't have to go (but you can/may if you want).* ~~We don't have to be late (but we can/may if we want)~~ is meaningless in normal contexts.

M

ought to and should

These verbs are used interchangeably to indicate

tentative inference

All the examples below could be rewritten with *ought to*.

Tentative inference means that the speaker does not know for sure that something is true but supposes that it is: *We should arrive before lunch; Inflation should remain below 3%.*

The meaning of a tentative inference is close to an expectation: *I expect we will arrive before lunch; Inflation is expected to remain below 3%.*

obligation/recommendation

This is not as strong as the obligation/compulsion of *must*. The speaker has less authority to impose his/her will or is less confident that the action described will happen. *You must stop smoking* is an order. *You should stop smoking* is a piece of ADVICE, a recommendation, as is *You should water those plants less often.*

You must water those plants less often suggests a degree of authority in the speaker that sounds strange in the context of the sentence.

This lack of certainty in *should* as compared with *must* is clear in these two examples, which refer to certainty (logical necessity); *should* is impossible:
He must be very rich. (He has an expensive car.)
~~He should be very rich.~~ (He has an expensive car.)

These two examples refer to an unfulfilled expectation; *must* is impossible:
The train should be here now (but it isn't).
~~The train must be here now~~ (but it isn't).

shall & should

Should is the past of *shall* (see TENSE & TIME); see OUGHT TO AND SHOULD above.

The traditional rules of prescriptive GRAMMAR say that *shall* is the correct modal verb for use in the first person singular and plural of the future. This was regarded as being standard in SOUTHern England, but in other parts of the English-speaking world the system was not observed. The subtleties of the difference between *I shall work* and *I will work* are so great that one respected authority has stated, 'if anyone has

singular	plural
1 *I shall go*	*we shall go*
2 *you will go*	*you will go*
3 *he/she/it will go*	*they will go*

been brought up among those who use the right idiom [i.e. in southern England], he has no need of instruction; if he has not, he is incapable of being instructed because any guidance that is short and clear will mislead him and any that is full and accurate will be incomprehensible to him.' (H. W. Fowler and F. G. Fowler, The King's English, Oxford, 1906.)

Examples such as *I will always love you* (that is my will) and *We shall arrive before lunch* (neutral prediction) will be read in older books and occasionally heard even in current speech, but it is now considered correct to use *will* in the first person future in affirmative and negative sentences. The widespread use of *I'll* and *we'll* makes it impossible to determine which is being used.

Shall is still current in question forms, where it is used for making offers and suggestions: *Shall I open the window for you?; Shall we finish now?* It is also used with WH- WORDS in questions about offers and suggestions. *What shall we do now?; Where shall we go?; How shall I do it?*

With *when* and *how* a difference can be made between
When shall we arrive? (*When would you like us to arrive*, asking for a suggestion or information) and *When will we arrive?* (Question for information to a car driver, train CONDUCTOR etc.)

This difference is also found in TAG QUESTIONS.
We'll arrive after lunch, shall we? (Rising intonation asking for information.)
We'll arrive after the film starts, will we? (Falling intonation in response to being told estimated arrival time.)

Shall I/we is also the tag question following *Let's*: *Let's go out for dinner, shall we?* (rising intonation asking for confirmation of a suggestion.)

will & would

These verbs are best known as auxiliary verbs for the FUTURE and CONDITIONAL forms. However, they are basically connected with volition or willingness; as a noun, your *will* is what you wish to happen, and the word has a precise meaning in that a person's will is their statement of what is to happen to their property on death. For that reason an emphatic *will* in the future can express a strong desire rather than a simple prediction (this was the basis of the shall/will distinction described above in SHALL & SHOULD); similarly *would* can express a strong desire or intention in the past: *He would go there even though I asked him not to. Would* is the past of *will*, as is seen in the backshifting that takes place in INDIRECT SPEECH. This is commonly seen in negative senses: *I've asked him and he won't tell me* is a refusal, not a simple prediction, and *I asked him but he wouldn't tell me* is a refusal in the past. This is grammatically complete; it is not a part of a conditional sentence. Surprisingly perhaps, these can be used with an inanimate object as the subject: *My car won't start. I'll be late; I'm sorry I'm late. My car wouldn't start.* For *would* with repeated actions in the past see USED TO.

modals with the perfect aspect

In addition to the direct past of modal verbs (*could, had to* etc.) described above, they can combine with the PAST INFINITIVE (*have* + past participle) to give a present, future, or past modal relevance. This usage is found in the third CONDITIONAL. It cannot be done with modal verbs expressing ability, permission and volition; it is used in cases of:

(im)possibility

1 *He could/may/might have arrived.* (It is possible that he has arrived but we do not know.)
2 *He may/might not have arrived.* (It is possible that he has not arrived but we do not know.)
3 *He could/might have arrived earlier if his car hadn't broken down.* (It was possible for him to arrive earlier but his car broke down.) *May* is not possible here because the third CONDITIONAL requires a past tense in the protasis (*if* clause).
4 *He cannot have arrived.* (It is impossible that he has arrived.) Only *cannot* is possible.

In examples **1** and **2** above *may* and *might* refer to the present possibility (PRESENT PERFECT *(*PERFECT ASPECT)*) that he has arrived and is here now.

In these examples
1a *He could/may/might have attended the meeting last week.*
1b *He might have attended the meeting last week.*
2a *He may/might not have attended the meeting last week.*
2b *He might not have attended the meeting last week.*
3 *He could/might have attended the meeting last week if his car hadn't broken down.*

1a and **2a** correspond to *It is possible that he attended/did not attend* (PAST SIMPLE) *the meeting but we do not know*, but *might* (**1b** and **2b**) can mean *It was possible that he would not) attend the meeting but he did not do so.* Thus *might have* is ambiguous. See POSSIBILITY IN THE PRESENT, FUTURE OR PAST above. This distinction is not always observed; a British TV personality who had been involved in a car crash said 'I may have died,' suggesting that he did not know whether he was dead or alive.

logical necessity (see must above)

You must have been tired. (I know how hard you had been working.)
He must have been very rich. (He had a big house and an expensive car.)
You must have been joking. (I found that hard to believe.)
That must have been the one I lost.

At one time *must have* was the equivalent of *would have had to* in conditional sentences. This is not so now, but is still found occasionally.

Question and negative forms are made with *can*: *Can/could that have been the one you lost?*; *You can't/couldn't have been serious.*

M

prediction

See FUTURE PERFECT (*PERFECT ASPECT).

obligation/recommendation

You should/ought to have stopped smoking.
You should have exercised more often.

inference

The train should have arrived by now.

modals with the continuous aspect

Modal verbs are found with the CONTINUOUS ASPECT (*be* + *-ing*):

(im)possibility

He may/might be coming; He can't be coming.

logical necessity

He must be working; You must be joking.

prediction

See FUTURE PERFECT (*PERFECT ASPECT).

obligation

You should not be/ought not to be working now.

The perfect and continuous aspects can be combined: *He can't have been coming; She must have been joking.*

semi-modal verbs

Dare and *need* are semi-modal or marginal modal verbs. In affirmative sentences they have a third-person *s* and an infinitive with *to*: *He dares to refuse the offer; He needs to accept the offer*. In question and negative forms they can be used as modal verbs: *Dare he refuse the offer?; Need he accept the offer?; He daren't refuse the offer; He needn't accept the offer*. However, this is not necessary; the non-modal verb (*Does he dare to refuse...*) is always possible and is more common. See NEEDN'T HAVE & DIDN'T NEED TO.

money

Britain adopted the decimal system in February 1971. The *pound* is divided into *100 pence* (singular *penny*, plurals *pence* for a sum of money and *pennies* for individual coins; see PENCE AND PENNIES). Prices are written and spoken as *13p = thirteen p* /piː/ or *thirteen pence*; *£26.80 = twenty-six pounds eighty* or *twenty-six eighty*; *£4.50 = four pounds fifty* or *four fifty*, never ~~four and a half pounds~~. The current pound coins have different versions for England, Scotland and Wales, but all circulate in all parts of the country. Scottish and Northern Irish banks have the right to issue their own banknotes. These are backed by the Bank of England and have the same value as Bank of England notes. Hotels and shops in England and Wales will normally accept Scottish and Northern Irish notes, but are not obliged to do so; banks will always change them for Bank of England notes.

Under the pre-decimal system the pound was divided into twenty shillings (abbreviation *s* from Latin *solidus*) and each shilling was divided into twelve *pennies* or *pence* (abbreviation *d* from Latin *denarius*), giving 240 pence in a pound; the pound symbol itself (£) itself derives from the Latin *libra*.

Books written before 1971 include names of old coins. A ***bob*** was a shilling (5p), written as 1s. or 1/- and a ***florin*** was two shillings (10p); a **half crown** was one eighth of a pound, two shillings and six pence, written 2s 6d or 2/6 and spoken as *two and six*; a ***halfpenny*** existed as a coin, 4s. 2½d. or 4/2½, spoken as *four and twopence ha'penny* /ˈtʌpəns ˈheɪpni/; and a ***farthing*** was a quarter of a penny, £3 19s 11¾d or £3 19/11¾ spoken as *three pounds nineteen and eleven, three*. ***Crowns*** worth five shillings were produced only on ceremonial occasions and never circulated generally. A *sovereign* was a pound coin made of gold which circulated until 1917. A ***guinea*** was £1 1s. (= £1.05) and was used by doctors, lawyers and other professional people as a sum for giving their fees, and also in art auctions.

M

-monger
A monger /ˈmʌŋgə/ is a trader or dealer, but the word is only used in certain compound forms: *costermonger* (a person who sells fruit, vegetables etc. in the street from a barrow), *cheesemonger*, *ironmonger*, and *fishmonger* are the only ones in common use; it has a derogative transferred meaning in *gossipmonger*, *rumourmonger*, *scandalmonger*, *scaremonger*, *warmonger*, *whoremonger*. The verb ~~mong~~ is never used nowadays.

Mongol
A *Mongol* is a person from Mongolia. The word *mongol* (with a small *m*) used to be used to refer to people suffering from Down's syndrome, but this is not done now.

moral & morale
As an adjective ***moral*** /ˈmɒrəl/ is concerned with what is right and wrong in human behaviour; as a noun it is the moral lesson that can be DRAWN from a story.

Morale /məˈrɑːl/ is a noun referring to the psychological attitude or behaviour of a person or group of people, especially with regard to their confidence and discipline; if *morale* is high, people are happy in their work but if it is low, *morale-raising* or *morale-boosting* activities should be UNDERTAKEN.

morning, afternoon & evening
The *morning* lasts until 12 O'CLOCK midday, which is known as *noon; afternoon* is the time after this although often lunchtime is regarded as the divider between the two. The *evening* is less precise. It begins at about 6 p.m. or perhaps when people arrive HOME *(*HOUSE & HOME)* from work and lasts until the time when people go to bed for the night. However, times such as 02.00, 03.30 can be *two o'clock at night, half past three in the morning*.

motion verbs
Usually, verbs describing motion are not used without an adverb such as *back* (*to an original position*), *in, out, down, up* (also meaning *towards the speaker*), *on* (*continuing*), *over, round*: *Come here* or *Come in* and *Go away* or *Go back* rather than simply *Go* and *Come*.
Come back here.
They swam back to our side of the river.
I'll pay that money back next week.
The dog ran in through the door.
Sit down. (*Sit* without an adverb is used for dogs; it is considered rather abrupt for people.)
Put your bags down.
They cut the tree down. (They cut it and it came down.)
They knocked the old station down. (The knocking it made it fall down.)
The plane flew up to 30,000 feet.
A lady walked up and asked the time. (*Up* = approaching the speaker.)
They cycled on for another ten miles.
I'll drive over/round after dinner. (To your house.)
John's coming over/round after dinner. (To our house.)
She took the candle away and came back with a new one.

mould
Three different words share this spelling and pronunciation /məʊld/. They mean:
1 A shape into which something is placed in liquid or paste form so that when it becomes solid it takes the shape of the mould.
2 A fungus that grows on cheese, damp walls etc.
3 A kind of earth that crumbles and breaks easily.

These are different words with different origins. They are not connected.

M

moustache, sideboards and whiskers

A *moustache* is hair growing on a man's upper lip; it can be used of a woman who has an unusually hairy upper lip.

Sideboards (also known as *sideburns*, after General Burnside who wore them) are hair grown down the side of a man's face in front of his ears.

Whiskers are hairs growing on a man's face, especially on his cheeks. They are also the long hairs by a cat's mouth.

A *beard* (*BARE*) is hair growing on the chin and perhaps lower cheeks. Some animals, goats for example, have beards.

mow

This means to *cut grass or cereals*. Now it is mostly used for cutting grass in a garden with a lawnmower.

See GRASS & LAWN.

Mr etc.

The title that is used before a man's name is *Mr* /ˈmɪstə/.

Miss is used for an unmarried woman of any age and *Mrs* /ˈmɪsɪz/ (a contraction of MISTRESS (*MASTER*)) is used for a married woman. *Mrs* must be followed by the woman's husband's name. A woman who chooses not to use her husband's surname traditionally uses *Miss* and her maiden name, though nowadays *Ms* /mɪz/ or /mʌz/ is more common. *Ms* is a title which, like *Mr*, does not indicate if the person is married or single. It has been promoted in the USA by feminist groups and is widely used in Britain. It is a convenient way of addressing a woman, personally or in a letter, when you know her name but do not know (and possibly are not at all interested in knowing) whether or not she is married.

MASTER is the title for a boy.

Mr, *Mrs*, *Miss*, and *Ms* are not written in full. However, the written forms *mister* and *missus* or *missis* exist; they are written, often in DIRECT SPEECH, to represent a vulgar form of address instead of *sir* and *madam*: *Hey, missus! Excuse me, mister.* Some men talk of *my/his* or *the missus* to mean *my/his wife*: *As I said to the missus yesterday...*; *He was there with his missus.* *Miss* and *Master* are never abbreviated.

Traditionally, a woman takes her husband's full name for formal purposes: Jane Robinson, wife of Paul Robinson, would be *Mrs P. Robinson*, though if she were divorced or widowed, she would be *Mrs J. Robin*son. This custom is no longer observed. She is always *Mrs J. Robinson* but the couple are *Mr and Mrs P. Robinson*. Another custom that is no longer observed is to be found in Jane Austen's books; in *Emma* for example *Mr Knightley* is the ELDER brother of *Mr John Knightley*, and *Miss Elizabeth Bennet* is the younger sister of *Miss Bennet*.

These titles are not used with forenames alone except in the special case of a polite, respectful reference to distinguish one of a group of brothers, perhaps business partners, who of course all have the same surname. *Mr John asked me to give you this paper, sir.*

Esquire (abbreviated *Esq.*) is an old title for a gentleman, which followed the name: *Fitzwilliam Darcy, Esq.* It was never combined with any other title such as *Mr* or *Sir*.

Academic titles are not doubled to show that the holder has more than one: ~~Dr Dr~~ *Mary Jones*, ~~Prof. Dr~~ *Chris Evans*, but *Prof. Chris Evans PhD*, *Prof. Sir Chris Evans* are used.

See PERSONAL NAMES.

M

multi-word verbs

The name *phrasal verb* is sometimes used as a general term for verbs that fall into three distinct categories: *prepositional verbs*, *phrasal verbs*, and *phrasal-prepositional verbs*. Together, these are also known as *multi-word verbs*. The preposition or adverb that is associated with the verb is known as the particle.

In general these verbs are metaphors, and in some cases this can be seen easily. To GET *over* (recover from) *an illness* is comparable to *getting over* a physical obstacle and returning to normal progress and to *get round a problem* is to avoid it, to pass round the side of it, as one could with a physical obstacle. To *put something across* is to transfer information (the idea of putting it across a space between two people is easy to understand) and to *put someone through* is to make a telephone connection for him, to *put him through* the telephone system that is between him and the person he wants to speak to. However, there are many cases where the metaphorical meaning has been lost and the real meaning is very difficult or impossible to DEDUCE from the verb and particle.

There are thousands of these verb combinations in English; it is impossible to give even a partial list of common examples here without being so selective as to make the list practically useless. What follows is an analysis of the different kinds of multi-word verb and a description of how they are used. Prepositional and phrasal verbs are an important part of the English language, especially in colloquial use; anyone learning English must have an understanding of how they work and what they mean. Fluency in using them actively is desirable but in most cases there is a one-word synonym that can be used, although this will often seem less colloquial.

prepositional verbs

These are verbs which are followed by a preposition and a noun. The verb can be intransitive or transitive.

intransitive prepositional verbs

Here, the verb is intransitive; the preposition, however, has its own object: **Look at** page 94; It **depends on** the weather; I **thought about** you then; She was **listening to** the radio.

In these cases the preposition is very clearly associated with the verb; in fact, they can be seen together as single verb units in which the object of the preposition is the object of the verb/preposition unit as a whole (even though the intransitive verb itself obviously has no object):

S	V	O	A
	Look at	page 94.	
I	thought about	you	yesterday.

This is especially clear in cases where a single-word synonym of the prepositional verb can be found (in this case, the verb itself is transitive, and the prepositional object of the intransitive prepositional verb becomes the direct object of the one-word transitive verb):

S	V	O	A
	Study	page 94.	
I	considered	you	yesterday.

This transitive nature of the prepositional verb unit can be seen in its ability to make passive forms:

Subject	Aux. Verb	Main Verb	Agent	Adverb
That page	was	looked at studied	by everybody	yesterday.
You	were	thought about considered		
The weather	can't be	depended on		at that time of year.

Note the position of the preposition in these sentences. See PREPOSITIONS AT THE END (DEFERRED PREPOSITIONS).

An adverb is not normally placed between a verb and its direct object. See ADVERBS, POSITION. ~~Study carefully page 94; I considered deeply you yesterday~~. This is also true of prepositional verbs: ~~Look at carefully page 94; I thought about deeply you yesterday~~. But the adverb can be placed in the

209

prepositional verb between the verb and the preposition: *Look carefully at page 94; I thought deeply about you yesterday.*

The preposition can be separated from the verb in other ways:
'Which page do we look at?' '(At) page 94.'
'Where do we look?' 'At page 94.'
Look at page 94 and (at) page 134.
I looked at page 94 more than (at) any other page.

The preposition in a prepositional verb is only used with its object: *I looked but I couldn't see anything* (not ~~I looked at but I couldn't see anything.~~); *Think harder; It depends.*

prepositional verbs and free combinations

Passive forms can be made from prepositional verbs: *I'll look after your mother; Your mother will be looked after; I'll write to you; You will be written to; It depends on the weather; The weather cannot be depended on.*

However, *I'll write after lunch* and *I'll phone from the hotel* are free combinations: *after lunch; from the hotel* are adverbial phrases; the prepositions *after* and *from* are associated with the nouns *lunch* and *the hotel* more than with the verb *write*. The passive forms ~~Lunch will be written after~~; ~~The hotel will be phoned from~~ seem ridiculous.

A further distinction between prepositional verbs and free combinations is found in the WH-QUESTION. With prepositional verbs this is related to the object and is a pronoun, WHO(M), *what* or *which*: *Which page shall we look at?; Who(m) will you look after?; What does it depend on?* In free combinations the *wh-* word in the question is an adverb: *When will you write?; Where will you phone from?*

There is no clear difference between the forms of prepositional verbs and free combinations. Take the example *I'll look for your book*. As has been noted above, if the object is not stated, the preposition is not used: *You needn't do anything. I'll look (for your book)*. This can be changed to a sentence with an adverb of manner or place: *I'll look very carefully/in the living room* or of time: *I'll look later; I'll look after lunch*. It is clear, however, that *I'll look after your mother* and *I'll look after lunch* are different; the FORMER is a prepositional verb and the latter is a free formation. Compare *Your mother will be looked after* and ~~Lunch will be looked after~~. But, while the free combination in *I'll look after lunch* (with the understanding that I mean that I will look for your book when lunch is finished) cannot make a passive sentence, the prepositional verb *look after* meaning *take responsibility for* can do, so *I'll look after lunch* (I will make sure that it is cooked and served) makes the normal passive: *Lunch will be looked after (by me)*. Sentences such as *I'll look after lunch* are clearly ambiguous, and only the context can make the meaning clear in writing and, usually, in speech.

transitive prepositional verbs

These verbs have two objects, one following the verb and one following the preposition.

Subject	Verb	Direct object	Preposition	Prepositional complement
I	thanked	him	for	the present.
That company	provided	the city	with	electricity.
	Confine	your comments	to	the facts.
This vaccine	will protect	you	from	polio.

Passive sentences can be made from these verbs.

Subject	Verb	Preposition	Noun	Agent
He	was thanked	for	the present	(by me).
The city	was provided	with	electricity	(by that company).
Your comments	must be confined	to	the facts	(by you).
You	will be protected	from	polio	(by this vaccine).

As with the intransitive prepositional verbs above there is a difference between these forms and free combinations. This can be seen in the *wh-* questions: *I thanked him for the present; I thanked him after dinner; What did you thank him for?; When did you thank him?*

phrasal verbs

While a prepositional verb consists of a verb combined with a preposition, in a phrasal verb the particle is an adverb. Phrasal verbs come from the Germanic roots of English vocabulary; in many cases there is a single-word verb of Latin origin that has more or less equivalent meaning: *get out = escape*; *get by = survive*; *put up with = tolerate*. However, the use of phrasal verbs is natural, and the excessive use of Latin synonyms, especially in informal language, leads to a rather strange style.

Phrasal verbs can be intransitive or transitive. In origin they are idioms that have become fixed; in many cases they have lost any connection with the actual meaning of the words.

intransitive

Some intransitive phrasal verbs are *The lift has broken down; The plane took off on time.*

transitive

Examples of transitive phrasal verbs are (see below for the position of the adverb) *They're doing (up) the church (up)* (...restoring, improving...); *Have you put (away) your toys (away)?* (...put them in their normal storage place?)

Free formations in phrasal verbs are found when the verb and adverb have their normal meanings: *He walked past without saying a word; Go away!; The sun came out.*

Phrasal verbs often describe movement; the verb defines the movement, and the adverb the direction.

phrasal verbs and prepositional verbs

	DO + particle	Particle + DO
phrasal	I'll look his address up.	~~I'll look up it.~~
	I'll look it up.	I'll look up his address.
prepositional	~~I'll look it at.~~	I'll look at it.
	~~I'll look page 94 at.~~	I'll look at page 94.

When a phrasal verb has a direct object, the adverbial particle can precede or follow it: *I'll look up his address* and *I'll look his address up* are both valid. Contrast this usage with the prepositional verb: *Look at page 94* is valid, but ~~*Look page 94 at*~~ is not because the preposition *at* must precede its object but when the object of a phrasal verb is a pronoun, the adverb particle must follow it.

An adverb cannot be placed between the verb and particle in a phrasal verb.

	DO + adverb	Adverb + DO
phrasal	I'll look up his address now.	~~I'll look now up his address.~~
prepositional	I'll look at page 94 now.	I'll look now at page 94.

In a RELATIVE CLAUSE the particle cannot precede the relative pronoun.

	RC + particle	particle + RC
phrasal	The address which I looked up.	~~The address up which I looked.~~
prepositional	The page which I looked at.	The page at which I looked.

A prepositional verb can have an adverb between the verb and the preposition: *Look carefully at page 94*. But a phrasal verb cannot have an adverb in this position: ~~*I'll look later up his address.*~~

The prepositional particle can precede a relative pronoun or *wh-* word:
That's the page I looked at. / That's the page at which I looked.
Which page did you look at? / At which page did you look?

This cannot be done with the adverbs of phrasal verbs:
That's the address I looked up. / ~~*That's the address up which I looked.*~~
Which address did you look up? / ~~*Up which address did you look?*~~

In a phrasal verb the particle is normally stressed while in a prepositional one it is not: *Which address did you look **up**?; Which page did you **look** at?*

M

phrasal-prepositional verbs
These are verbs that are followed by both an adverb and a preposition; the verb can be intransitive or transitive.

intransitive
I will not put up with such behaviour.
We're looking forward to our holiday.
You'll never get away with that.

Passive forms are sometimes possible: *Such behaviour will not be put up with* but even when they are formed, the structure seems complicated and a synonym is usually preferred: *Such behaviour will not be tolerated.*

transitive
Some phrasal-prepositional verbs have two objects, one following a transitive verb and one following the preposition:
They put his failure down to his illness. (= *They attribute his failure to his illness.*)
You will have to take the matter up with the manager. (= *You will have to consult the manager about the matter.*)

The only passive that is possible from this is *His failure was put down to his illness; The matter will have to be taken up with the manager.*

general comments
Several difficulties surround the study of multi-word verbs for non-English speaking students of English. Apart from the number of these verbs, any combination can be made freely. *The refugees will be helicoptered out to safety tomorrow* is perfectly comprehensible and correct, but no dictionary will give *helicopter out* as a phrasal verb.

Some particles can be prepositions only, some can be adverbs only, and some can be either, so *I looked up his address* is a phrasal verb, and can be rewritten as *I looked his address up* but *I looked up the hill* is a freely combined prepositional verb, and cannot be rewritten or made passive as the phrasal verb: *His address was looked up.*

A further difficulty is that a multi-word verb can have a number of different meanings.
1   *I looked up the hill.* (Prepositional verb: literal meaning.)
2   *Things are looking up.* (Intransitive phrasal verb: improving.)
3   *I looked up his address.* (Transitive phrasal verb: find information in a list or directory.)
4   *He looks up to his father.* (Phrasal prepositional verb: respects.)

In **1** the literal meaning is clear. In **4** the metaphorical meaning is easy to understand. **2** can be seen as a metaphor if *up* is considered to represent improvement. Although *look* is a reasonable verb to use in **3**, it is impossible to see why *up* is used as the particle; its use seems to be totally random.

Will the explosive go off? could mean, according to the context: *Will it explode?* or *Will it deteriorate?*

Make up is a phrasal verb with a number of completely different meanings:
She made up her face. (used cosmetics)
He made up a story. (invented)
I owe you an hour's work. I'll make it up next week. (compensate)
They made up their quarrel. (settled, resolved)

In fact, *up* as a particle in phrasal verbs often has a meaning of *completely* and, with a little imagination, it is possible to see each of these sentences as referring to the completion of an action to its full extent. This meaning is clearer in examples such as *Eat up your dinner; We closed the house up when we went on holiday; Fill it up.* (Fill it (e.g. the petrol tank of a car) *up to the top.*)

The particles in multi-word verbs are prepositions and adverbs. Some can only be one or the other, while others can be preposition or adverb depending on the sentence:

prepositions only: *against, among, as, at, beside, for, from, into, like, of, onto, upon, with* etc.

M

prepositions or adverbs: *about, ABOVE, across, after, along, around, by, down, IN, OFF, on, over, past, round, through, under, up* etc.

adverbs only: *aback, ahead, apart, aside, astray, away, back, forWARD(S), home, in front, on top, out, together* etc.

It fell off. (Phrasal verb, *off* is an adverb.)
It fell off the table. (Prepositional verb, *off* is a preposition.)

summary of types
prepositional verbs
intransitive
Look at page 94; It depends on the weather; He climbed down the mountain. (*down* is a preposition.); *He climbed down from the lorry.* (*down* is an adverb indicating direction; *from* is the preposition defining the starting place.) It is incorrect to say ~~He climbed down the lorry~~.
Compare *She came in* (adverb) and *She came into the room.* (Preposition)

transitive
I thanked him for the present; He was thanked for the present; That company provided the city with electricity; The city was provided with electricity.

phrasal verbs
intransitive
Come in; The plane took off on time.

transitive
They're doing the church up; The church is being done up; Have you put (away) your toys (away)?; Have your toys been put away?

phrasal-prepositional verbs
intransitive
I will not put up with such behaviour; We're looking forward to our holiday.

transitive
They put his failure down to his illness; His failure was put down to his illness; You will have to take the matter up with the manager; The matter will have to be taken up with the manager.

noun forms
Phrasal verbs make GERUNDS: *We like dressing up; Taking it up with the manager is no guarantee of success; After making up their quarrel the two men became good friends.*

They also make nouns. For example *I get together with my friends once a month; My friends and I get together once a month; My friends and I have a get-together once a month.* This noun is different from the gerund, which refers to the action: *Getting together with my friends once a month is very pleasant.* There are very many other such nouns; they may be connected with a hyphen or written as a single word (the rules for deciding which to use are very complex): *make-up, set-up, take-away, runaway.*

mummy
Mummy is a familiar word for *mother*. It is most commonly used by children.

A *mummy* is a dried and preserved dead body, for example those of ancient Egyptian kings and queens.

Tutankhamun loves his mummy is a very silly joke. See HOMONYMS.

musical instruments
The usual instruments of a symphony orchestra are:
Strings: violin, viola, cello /ˈtʃeləʊ/, double BASS /beɪs/.
Woodwind: clarinet, oboe, cor anglais /kɔːrˈɒŋgleɪ/ (also English horn), bassoon, flute, piccolo
Brass: trumpet, cornet, trombone, tuba, French horn.
Percussion: drums, kettle drums (timpani), cymbals, triangle.

M

An orchestra is *conducted* by a CONDUCTOR (not ~~director~~), who uses a *baton*. The *leader* of the orchestra is the principal violinist. See MUSICAL NOTATION AND TERMINOLOGY.

musical notation and terminology

In musical notation in Britain the letters are the constant, absolute names of the notes while the *sol-fa* /ˈsɒlfɑː/ names are relative. Below are three scales showing this system.

scale of C major

letter name	C	D	E	F	G	A	B	C
sol-fa name	do	re	mi	fa	sol	la	ti	do

In this scale of C major, the lower C is on a *ledger* /ˈledʒə/ *line*. This is MIDDLE C.

scale of F major

letter name	F	G	A	B♭	C	D	E	F
sol-fa name	do	re	mi	fa	sol	la	ti	do

scale of E minor

letter name	E	F♯	G	A	B	C	D	E
sol-fa name	do	re	mi	fa	sol	la	ti	do

Here the notes are followed by *dots*. They are *dotted crotchets*.

The sol-fa names of these notes are pronounced: do /dəʊ/, re /reɪ/, mi /miː/, fa /fɑː/, sol/sɒl/, la /lɑː/, ti /tiː/. Sol is also called so /səʊ/.

F♯ is F sharp; B♭ is B flat; C♮ is C natural.

𝄞 treble clef /klef/; 𝄢 BASS /beɪs/ clef.

When no note is to be played, a symbol indicates a *rest* (*semibreve rest* etc.)

The *key signature* shows the *sharps* and *flats* associated with the key in which the music is played.

The *time signature* shows the speed and rhythm of the music. The lines on which the notes are written are the *stave*.

The music is divided into *bars* by vertical lines called *bar lines*.

M

The names of these notes are (American names in brackets):
    1 semibreve /ˈsemɪbriːv/ (whole note)
    2 minim (half note)
    3 crotchet (quarter note)
    4 quaver (eighth note)
    5 semiquaver (sixteenth note)
    6 demisemiquaver (thirty-second note)
    7 hemidemisemiquaver (sixty-fourth note).

A *symphony* is a piece of music for a full orchestra, normally consisting of four movements. A *concerto* /kənˈtʃɜːtəʊ/ is a piece for one or two solo instruments, accompanied by an orchestra. A *concert* /ˈkɒnsət/ is a public or private occasion where music is performed.

Musical works are described as for example *Beethoven's third (Eroica) symphony, in E flat major; Schubert's eighth (Unfinished) symphony, in B minor; Mozart's piano concerto number 10 (Moonlight Sonata), in C sharp minor.*

See MUSICAL INSTRUMENTS.

N

n, N /en/

The fourteenth letter of the alphabet. It is pronounced /n/.

It is not pronounced in words that end *-mn*: *column, damn, hymn*.

It is pronounced longer than normal in words in which *n* follows a PREFIX that ends with *n*: *ennoble, unnecessary*, with the exception of the prefix *in-*: *innate, innocent, innovate*.

naive

This is pronounced /naɪˈiːv/. It is the feminine of the French *naïf* and is the form almost always used in English (the French masculine *naïf* is sometimes found as an artistic or philosophical term). It is usually written *naive* but sometimes as *naïve*. The noun is *naivety, naïvety,* or *naïveté*.

native

This word naturally implies a connection with a place by birth. To describe someone as *a native of EDINBURGH* or *a native Scot* is common and acceptable, as are *native CITY, town, country, land* and *language*. Someone who has spoken a language since starting to speak is a *native speaker* of that language, and a person who has lived in a country so long as to adopt the habits and customs of that country has *gone native*. However, the use of the word *native* with offensive racial implications during the age of the Empire has led to a certain sensitivity in its use with regard to black or brown people. *Native American* is now the preferred term for the indigenous people of the USA but not Canada, where *Canadian INDIAN* is preferred.

-nce, -ncy and -nt

In general the words with *-nce* are derived from verbs and refer to actions and processes: *assistance, furtherance, penance, reference, reminiscence*; or to a quality or state: *arrogance, relevance, patience*; or to something possessing that quality: *protuberance, resemblance, difference*. The words with *-ncy* refer to the quality: *efficiency, fluency*, or state: *expectancy, infancy, pregnancy, presidency*. However, this distinction is not always clear in practice: *During the Spanish Presidency of the EU; consistence* and *consistency* are interchangeable.

These words derive ultimately from Latin but they changed in their progress through French into English and they do not necessarily correspond to the original Latin forms in the use of *a* or *e*; in particular, many English words with *a* come from Latin words with *e*. Moreover, there are inconsistencies as in *ascendant* and *descendent*, and in *assistance, consistence, existence, resistance*, and *subsistence*, which all come from the same Latin root *-sistentia*.

For all of these reasons, in the choice of *-nce* or *-ncy*, and in the choice between *a* and *e*, a DICTIONARY should be consulted in cases of uncertainty. There are so many of these words that it is not possible to list them here.

See DEPENDANT & DEPENDENT; EMERGENCE & EMERGENCY.

needn't have & didn't need to

I needn't have phoned to tell him the news because he knew already means that I phoned him. I did not know that it was not necessary for me to do so.

I didn't need to phone to tell him the news because Mary had already told him means that I did not phone him because I knew that it was not necessary for me to do so.

negation of verbs

The negative words *not* and *never* are placed in the same position as mid-position ADVERBS (after the first auxiliary verb): *They will not come; He has never seen her; I should not have believed him*. As with mid-position adverbs they follow parts of the verb *be*: *He is not Spanish; We were not there*. For more specific information see ADVERBS, POSITION; CONTRACTIONS; HAVE; INVERSION; TAG QUESTIONS.

ANY is used in negative sentences: *I didn't see any SHIPS; There isn't any reason to go; She doesn't know anybody; Don't touch anything* but forms with *no* can be used ALTERNATIVELY: *I saw no ships; There is no reason to go; She knows nobody; Touch nothing.*

In the sentence *John didn't give Mary the money yesterday* the whole idea of John giving money to Mary is negated; none of this happened at all. Stress can be used to indicate that some of the elements in this sentence are negated while others remain valid:

John *didn't give Mary the money yesterday.* (Peter gave it to her.)
*John **didn't** give Mary the money yesterday.* (You're wrong to say that he did.)
*John didn't **give** Mary the money yesterday.* (He lent it to her.)
*John didn't give **Mary** the money yesterday.* (He gave it to Jane.)
*John didn't give Mary the **money** yesterday.* (He gave her the diamonds.)
*John didn't give Mary the money **yesterday**.* (He gave it to her last week.)

Contractions with *let's* make the negative forms *Don't let's go; Let's not go.*

Contractions with USED TO make the negative forms *He didn't use(d) to smoke; He used not (usedn't) to smoke. Didn't used to* is illogical in grammatical terms but is used. See USED TO.

negative questions

Negative questions are mostly found in speech, where the CONTRACTIONS are used: *Didn't you know that?; Can't you help me?; Why haven't you ever said anything?*

If the uncontracted form is used, the negative word stands between the subject and the infinitive: *Did you not know that?; Can you not help me?; Why have you never said anything?* The reason for this is that the negative *You did not know that* is contracted to *You didn't know that* and then the negative contraction *-n't* moves together with the auxiliary verb *did* as one word. In the uncontracted form, it stands in its normal position immediately before the main verb.

negative infinitive

The negative INFINITIVE is made with *not to + infinitive*: *I hope to arrive on time. I hope not to be late; You have a right not to be disturbed; It was a mistake not to have made better plans.* The auxiliary *do/does/did* is not used in negative infinitive forms; a common mistake for non-native speakers is to say things such as ~~I hope don't be late~~ (*I hope not to be late*).

transferred negation

Verbs expressing opinions (e.g. *believe, expect, imagine, suppose,* and *think,* but not *hope*) or perception (e.g. *appear, seem, feel as if, look as if, sound as if, smell as if, taste as if*) usually take the negation that would seem logically to apply to the other verb. *I don't think I've read that* is more natural than *I think I haven't read that* though the second is perfectly correct grammatically. Other examples of transferred negation are:

She doesn't expect to pass the exam.
She doesn't believe she'll pass the exam.

It doesn't appear to be raining.
It doesn't look as if it's raining.

They do not seem to understand.
It doesn't look as if it is going to rain.

The transferred negation is more common and the sentence has a generally negative tone. In the untransferred form, the verb has a strong positive meaning: *She expects not to pass the exam* clearly states that she has analysed her chances and her expectation is that she will not pass. See PREDICATION NEGATION below.

I don't remember reading that means that I have no memory of reading it, but *I remember not reading that* means that I have distinct memory of deciding not to read it.

I didn't tell him to do it means that someone else told him to do it or that he decided to do it himself, but *I told him not to do it* means that I prohibited him from doing it. ▶

N

I don't know that he is here means that I have no certain knowledge about his presence, but *I know that he is not here* means that I have certain knowledge that he is not here.

A sentence such as *I didn't say that* includes transferred negation as the negative applies to the object: *I didn't say that. I said something different.*

However, with appropriate emphasis the meaning changes: *I didn't **say** that – but I thought it.*

See ONLY and predication negation below for similar use of stress to change the focus of a sentence.

predication negation

Usually a negative word negates the auxiliary verb: *I can't go to her wedding* means that it is impossible for me to go. However, *I can not go to her wedding* means that it is possible for me to decide not to go.

In *This treatment can not only reduce damage but (can) also raise life expectancy* the negation of the predicate is clearly shown by the possibility of omitting the modal verb *can*: *This treatment can not only reduce damage but also raise life expectancy.* Both infinitives, *reduce* and *raise*, follow *can* but only the first is negated.

This use of *can not*, written as two words, is pronounced with a clear stress on the *not* as part of the adverb phrase *not only*, and the contraction (*can't*) is never used.

I know not one teacher who would agree with that is an emphatic way of saying *I don't know one teacher who would agree with that.*

double negatives

Sentences such as *I don't know nothing* and *I never saw nobody* are considered completely unacceptable in modern standard English. However, they have existed throughout the history of the language (examples can be found in Shakespeare). They are very common as a way of strengthening a negative idea, but are never found in any writing or speech that is considered standard or correct.

Although the above sentences are unambiguous in meaning, the rule is usually explained by the statement that two negatives cancel each other and make a positive idea, and it is true that such examples, though unusual, can be found:
'Why did you say nothing?' 'I didn't say nothing. I asked two questions.'
Nobody had nothing (i.e. everybody had something) *to eat, though some people didn't have much.*
I can't not go (i.e. I can't decide not to go, refuse to go) *to her wedding.* (Predication negation, see above.) Sentences such as *Your behaviour has not been unnoticed; I am not unhappy with the decision* are common and correct.

negative-only words

Some words are only used in the negative. Examples are:

disconcerting	*impromptu*	*inept*	*nonplussed*	*unrequited*
disconsolate	*inadvertent*	*inevitable*	*uncalled for*	*unruly*
disgruntled	*inchoate*	*insipid*	*uncouth*	*unwieldy*
dishevelled	*incognito*	*misgivings*	*ungodly*	*unwittingly*
dismay	*incommunicado*	*misnomer*	*unkempt*	
immaculate	*incorrigible*	*nonchalant*	*unheard of*	
impeccable	*indefatigable*	*non-committal*	*ungainly*	
impetuous	*indomitable*	*nondescript*	*unmitigated*	

These have no positive forms, though the BACK-FORMATION *couth* is sometimes seen.

news

This word is uncountable like ADVICE and INFORMATION: *Have you heard the news?*; *He told me some interesting news*; *There isn't much news*; *The news is very bad.*

Although this word has a final *s* (and was originally plural) it has no singular. It is wrong to say *I read an interesting new in this morning's paper.* The correct form would be *I read an interesting piece of news/article in this morning's paper* or simply *I read something interesting in this morning's paper.*

It is also used for the news PROGRAMME on TV or radio: *When is the news on?; The news is on at six o'clock.*

niggardly
This means *mean* (the opposite of generous). It has no connection with the offensive word *nigger* and there is no reason to avoid using it.

nightmare
A *mare* is a female horse but in this word it is an obsolete name for a female monster that sat on people's chests while they were sleeping and gave them bad dreams.

-(n)naire
Note the variation in the spelling of these words:
billionaire, concessionaire, doctrinaire, millionaire but *legionnaire, questionnaire.*

no, none, not one & no-one

no
No can be placed before a noun:
I know no teachers. (Plural countable noun.)
There is no reason to believe that. (Singular countable noun.)
I have drunk no alcohol for three months. (Singular uncountable noun, object.)
No money is available for entertainment. (Singular uncountable noun, subject.)

The first three of these can be rewritten as:
I don't know any teachers.
There isn't any reason to believe that.
I haven't drunk any alcohol for three months.
with no significant difference in meaning. The last cannot be rewritten in this way as it is the subject of the verb: *Not any money is available for entertainment.*

The construction *be + no + countable noun* can mean more than a simple negation, suggesting that something is unsatisfactory or imitation:
He is no actor. (He may appear on stage but cannot be considered as an actor.)
That was no accident. (Even though it appears to be one.)
Thus we have expressions such as *It is no coincidence that*...

No can be placed before a comparative:
I have no more money; This year's EXAMINATION is no more difficult than last year's; This car is no faster than that one; They no LONGer live here.

none
None /nʌn/ originated as a compound of *not one* but now also corresponds to *not any.*
I know none. (I don't know any.)
There is none. (There isn't any.)
I have drunk none. (I haven't drunk any.)
None is available (but *Not any is available* is not possible, see above.)

Despite its etymology *none* can be singular or plural depending on the context; it is like a GROUP NOUN, though the group has zero members.

I have six pens and none is the right colour. (Singular, only one is required. It can be rewritten as *There is not one that is the right colour.*)

There are six people here and none of them want to go. (Plural, it can be expected that more than one will want to go. It can be rewritten as *All of them do not want to go.*)

The idiomatic phrase *No problem* means that something can be done without difficulty.

N

not
Not is the word that makes other words and ideas negative: *Not now; Not here; Not Mary; Not in my house*.

not one
Not one can be used with countable nouns to give emphasis: *There is not one reason to believe that*.

no-one
No-one is the same as *nobody*. It can be written as *no one* or hyphenated as *no-one*, which distinguishes it from the construction *No one person is strong enough to lift it* (no single person, no person alone) while avoiding the confusing appearance of *noone*.

See LONG (for *no longer*).

Nobel & noble
Nobel is pronounced /nəʊˈbel/ in the name of the *Nobel prizes*.

The adjective *noble* is pronounced /ˈnəʊbl/.

non-British English
English is a world language and naturally there are different varieties of it around the world. The main version other than British English is AMERICAN ENGLISH. Other important varieties are to be found in Australia and New Zealand, where it is not always possible to identify a New Zealander as not being Australian and vice versa; nor can a Canadian always be distinguished from an American. There are distinct varieties in SOUTH Africa and in the rest of Africa, in INDIA, and in Jamaica. The standard forms of these variations show very little grammatical difference from British English, though there are considerable differences in vocabulary. Within Britain SCOTLAND has *Lallans*, an English dialect with its own spelling and pronunciation, but it is only to be found in a restricted literary field; it is not used generally.

nouns

countable and uncountable
Nouns can be divided into the two categories: *countable* and *uncountable*. Uncountable nouns are also known as mass nouns.

As the name IMPLIES, countable nouns can be counted numerically and have plural forms: *three cats, six books, ten million dollars*. They can also be subdivided: *half an hour, 0.563 of a kilometre*.

Uncountable nouns cannot make plural forms or be subdivided. Examples are *music, air*. It is impossible to speak of ~~two musics~~ or ~~half an air~~.

Some nouns can be countable or uncountable depending on the context. *A cake, a cheese* (countable) refer to the whole piece as made, while *some cake, some cheese* (uncountable) refer to a piece of unspecified size that is cut from it.

Plural forms of normally uncountable nouns can be used to refer to different kinds: *Three different wines were served with the meal*.

Note that *money* is uncountable, though *euros, dollars, pounds* etc. are countable.

Some words which may be countable in other languages are uncountable in English. Examples are ADVICE, *behaviour, equipment, evidence, knowledge, information, news*. The need to specify a number is met by using the word *piece* or *item*: *a piece of advice, three pieces of information, two new items of* NEWS.

For the use of articles with countable and uncountable nouns see ARTICLES.

See also QUANTIFIERS.

gender, case, and plural forms
English nouns do not have GENDER as such although the PRONOUNS *he, him, his, she, her, it* and *its* vary with the sex of the referent. With the exception of the possessive they have no indications of CASE, and with very few exceptions English nouns make their PLURAL FORMS with *(e)s*.

N

proper and common nouns
Nouns are divided into two main groups, proper nouns and common nouns.

Proper nouns are written with initial CAPITAL LETTERS. See PLURAL FORMS; ARTICLES. Common nouns can be countable or uncountable, and concrete or ABSTRACT.

abstract nouns
Common abstract noun endings are *-ness, -(i)ty, -ence/y, -ance/y, -hood*. Note *safety* but *unsafeness*.

singular with -s
Some nouns that end with *-s* are singular. These are the DISEASES *AIDS* (an ACRONYM of acquired immune deficiency syndrome), *measles, mumps, shingles,* and *rabies;* and also *gallows*.

The word *barracks* (the building(s) where soldiers live) usually has a final *s* but is often used with a singular verb or article: *The barracks is...; They live in a barracks*.

The CRICKET term *innings* has the same form in singular and plural.

MEANS and series /'sɪəriːz/ are countable but invariable between singular and plural: *one means/series, two means/series*.

See -ICS; NEWS; STRAIGHT AND STRAIT.

summary

	concrete	abstract
countable	shoe, SHIP, cabbage, king	problem, thought
uncountable	wax, water, ALUMINIUM	happiness, music

nouns as adjectives
It is a curious feature of English that when a noun is used adjectivally its form is in many cases (but not always) singular though it is logically plural. A *toothbrush* cleans teeth and *footwear* is worn on the feet; a *corkscrew* removes corks and a *bottle bank* is for recycling bottles; a *car manufacturer* makes cars and a *bookseller* sells books.

nowadays
Nowadays makes a contrast between the present and the past: *Nowadays not many people use typewriters; People use computers nowadays*.

numbers
English uses ARABIC NUMERALS (which are not the symbols used in the Arabic language).

Care must be taken to distinguish between numbers with *-teen* and those with *-ty*. The FORMER have the stress on EITHER syllable /'θɜːtiːn/, /θɜːˈtiːn/; the latter have a clear difference between a stressed first syllable and a weak second one /'θɜːti/. However, in speech this difference is not always easy to identify, and it is not unusual for people to check what is meant by pronouncing the words very clearly, or even by saying for example '*Did you say fifty, five zero?*'

Ordinal numbers are formed by adding *-th* to the cardinal number; *first* (1st), *second* (2nd) and *third* (3rd) are irregular, and numbers with *-ty* make *twentieth* (20th) etc. Only the last element makes an ordinal number: *fifty-second* not ~~fiftieth-second~~. They are used whenever it is appropriate to do so, in DATES and in examples such as *I live on the seventeenth (17th) floor; It's his fifty-second (52nd) birthday next year*.

Fractions are made with *half, third, quarter* and then the remaining ordinal numbers: ⅔ is *two thirds,* ¾ is *three quarters,* ⅚ is *five sixths* /sɪksθs/ and so on.

2,500 is *two and a half thousand* not ~~two thousand and a half~~, which is 2,000½.

See PERCENTAGES; MONEY.

numbers in writing
When numbers are written by hand in English, *one* /wʌn/ is a single vertical stroke (l), though it is often printed (1 or 1); *seven* has no cross (7). This can be confusing for people from countries where these numbers are written by hand as 1 and 7. ➤

N

Note the variant spelling of some forms: *four, fourteen, **forty**, fourth; five, **fifteen**, **fifty**, **fifth**; eight, **eighteen**, **eighty**, **eighth** /eɪtθ/; nine, nineteen, ninety, **ninth**.*

Commas separate thousands, millions etc. A point indicates a decimal fraction.

When numbers are written as words a HYPHEN *(*PUNCTUATION)* is placed between the tens and units but not in any other position. €327,934.69 is *three hundred and twenty-seven thousand nine hundred and thirty-four euros and sixty-nine cents.* For the use of *x* to separate numbers see x, X.

billion etc.

Traditionally in Britain this was one million million, 1,000,000,000,000 or 10^{12}, while in the USA it is one thousand million, 1,000,000,000 or 10^9. However, the American usage is now standard in Britain. The word *milliard* is not used in English. To avoid any possible confusion it might be wise to say *three thousand million pounds.* The number 10^{12} is called a *trillion.* Increasingly large numbers by a power of 10^3 are *quadrillion, quintillion* etc.

abbreviations

Million, billion and trillion can be abbreviated as *m, bn* and *tn*: *£3.6m, €42bn $2tn.*

Roman numerals

Roman numerals are used in English for some purposes. They are used for kings, *Henry VIII* (Henry the Eighth), and sometimes for chapters in books, articles in contracts, numbered points in a document, and page numbers in the introduction to a book.

1	*I*	12	*XII*	40	*XL*	200	*CC*
2	*II*	13	*XIII*	49	*XLIX*	400	*CD* (or *CCCC*)
3	*III*	14	*XIV*	50	*L*	500	*D*
4	*IV**	15	*XV*	60	*LX*	900	*CM* (or *DCCCC*)
5	*V*	16	*XVI*	70	*LXX*	1000	*M*
6	*VI*	17	*XVII*	80	*LXXX*	1900	*MCM* (or *MDCCCC*)
7	*VII*	18	*XVIII*	90	*XC*	1995	*MCMXCV*
8	*VIII*	19	*XIX*	99	*XCIX*	1999	*MCMXCIX*
9	*IX*	20	*XX*	100	*C*	2000	*MM*
10	*X*	21	*XXI*	101	*CI*	2001	*MMI*
11	*XI*	30	*XXX*	144	*CXLIV*	2002	*MMII*

*4 is usually shown as IIII on CLOCK faces.

various points

A and *one* are both used with *hundred, thousand* etc. Unless it is necessary to distinguish between the article and the number there is no significant difference between *a hundred* and *one hundred*. See ONE, NUMBER NOT ARTICLE.

Sentences such as *Eight (out) of the twenty students passed the exam* can be written with *of* or *out of;* it makes no difference. But *Eight out of twenty was the highest mark* must have *out of* in giving a mark, SCORE etc.

Zero is predominantly American but is widely used in Britain. In situations where a group of numerals do not represent a total number they are read separately, *8042* (a telephone number, reference number, postcode, room number etc.) is read *eight-oh-four-two,* where *oh* is the letter *O,* although the letter and numeral are different *(O, 0).*

Once /wʌns/ and *twice* mean *one time* and *two times. Thrice* (three times) is archaic. The form is *twenty-one times,* not ~~twenty-once~~. The number *0* is *nought* or *zero: five minus five is nought/zero.* A decimal number *0.5* is spoken as *nought/zero point five.*

In FOOTBALL and rugby *nil* is used for a zero score; *2-0* is *two-nil.* In tennis the word *love* is used; *15-0* is *fifteen love.* See CRICKET.

A point is used to indicate decimal numbers. In handwriting it is usually at the mid-height of the numerals *4·36,* while in print the full stop symbol is used on the base line *4.36.*

Thousands, millions etc. are separated by commas when written as numerals, but commas are not used in year numbers: *2018* etc. *Hundred, thousand* etc. are not used in plural forms: *£300 (three hundred) pounds, 5,000 (five thousand) people* but *hundreds of pounds, thousands of people.*

The suffix *-fold* means *times*. If something increases *tenfold*, it increases ten times, by a factor of ten.

See GROUP NOUNS.

number with *be*

When the subject and complement of *be* are different in number, the verb takes the number of the subject: *The problem was the cars parked on the pavement; The cars parked on the pavement were the problem.*

nut

A nut is any hard seed or fruit in a hard shell, e.g. *almond, hazelnut, pistachio*, or *walnut*.

O

o, O /əʊ/

The fifteenth letter of the alphabet.

It is normally pronounced /ɒ/: *hot, from,* GOD. It has this pronunciation in *bomb* /ɒ/ (with silent final *b*) but note *comb* /əʊ/, and *tomb* and *womb* with /uːm/.

It is pronounced /əʊ/ in words that end with *-ld*: *bold, cold, fold, hold, old*; in words ending in *-oe*: *foe, hoe, roe, oboe* but *shoe* /ʃuː/; and in *go, ho, so,* and *no*. For pronunciation of DO and TO see the individual articles.

One is pronounced /wʌn/. *Move* and *love* are pronounced /muːv/ and /lʌv/. *Some* and *done* are pronounced with /ʌ/. *Gone* is pronounced /gɒn/.

For further comments on the pronunciations /ɒ/ and /əʊ/, see DOUBLE CONSONANTS.

oa is pronounced /əʊ/: *coal, goat, road* but BROAD /ɔː/; *oar* is /ɔə/: *board,* OAR, *roar, soar*.

oi and *oy* are /ɔɪ/ *boil, boy, doyen* /ˈdɔɪən/, *foyer* /ˈfɔɪeɪ/. *Porpoise* and *tortoise* have two pronunciations /pˈɔːpəs/ and /pˈɔːpɔɪs/.

ou is pronounced /aʊ/: *mouse, round, south* except in some words of French origin: *cagoule, croup, douche* and *route,* and also *uncouth,* where it is /uː/. *Our* is /aʊə/ in *flour,* HOUR, *our, scour, sour* but is /ɔə/ in *court, dour, four, gourd, mourn, pour, tour, your*. In words of two or more syllables that end with *-our* (e.g. *colour*) it is /ə/. *Scourge* is pronounced /skɜːdʒ/. MOULD is pronounced /məʊld/.

ow has two pronunciations:

/aʊ/ *allow,* BROW, BOW, *bowel, brown, browse, clown, cow, coward, crowd, crown, down, drowsy, flower, fowl, frown, gown, how, howl, kowtow, now, owl, powder, power, prowl,* ROW (noise), *shower, sow* (female pig), *towel, tower, town, vow, vowel, wow*.

/əʊ/ *arrow, barrow, below, blow, borrow,* BOW, *bowl, bungalow, crow,* FELLOW, *flow, follow, glow, grow,* KNOW (but *knowledge* /ˈnɒlɪdʒ/), *low, marrow, meadow, mellow, (to)morrow, mow, narrow, own, pillow,* ROW (line), ROW (propel a BOAT with an OAR), SHADOW, *show, slow, snow, sorrow, sow* (seeds), *sparrow, swallow, tallow, throw, tow, widow, willow, window, yellow*.

oar & row

An *oar* is the thing (sometimes called a blade) that is used to ROW /rəʊ/ a BOAT.

objects, direct and indirect

Consider these sentences:
1 *John gave Mary a book.*
2 *John gave a book to Mary.*
3 *John paid Mary £1,000.*
4 *John paid £1,000 to Mary.*
5 *John told Mary a story.*
6 *John told a story to Mary.*
7 *John told Mary that she was beautiful.*
8 *John said to Mary that she was beautiful.*
9 *John persuaded Mary to go home.*
10 *John persuaded Mary that she should go home.*

In all of these sentences *John* is the subject (S) and *Mary* is the indirect object (IO); the other element in the first six sentences (*a book, £1,000, a story*) is the direct object (DO). Sentences **2**, **4**, and **6** are unusual but correct.

When both objects are nouns or pronouns the normal order is S V IO DO: *John gave Mary a book; John gave her it*.

When the objects are one noun and one pronoun the only correct possibilities are *John gave her a book; John gave it to Mary*. This is because the preference is to place a shorter object before a longer one. For this reason the normal order with two noun objects is changed and sentences like **2** are used when the indirect object is considerably longer than the direct object: *John gave a book to his elderly Spanish aunt Mary* not ~~John gave his elderly Spanish aunt Mary a book~~, and *John gave a book to Mary, whom he had known since he was a child* not ~~John gave Mary, whom he had known since he was a child, a book~~.

o'clock

This is a CONTRACTION of *of the clock* but it is never written or spoken in full.

odd

This word has a wide range of meanings as adjective and noun.

adjective

As an adjective it means *strange, unusual*: *That's odd, There's something odd about her; There's an odd smell here.* With people it means *eccentric*: *I found him rather odd.*

Odd numbers are *1, 3, 5, 7, 9, 11* etc. (The others, *2, 4, 6* etc., are EVEN numbers.)

Odd can mean a surplus: *£47 odd* (*forty-seven pounds odd*) means some pence more than £47 but less than £48. *Forty-odd people* means a number from 41 to 49 inclusive. The HYPHEN (*PUNCTUATION*) is particularly important in this case; *forty odd people* means forty strange people. In speech the stress is different: ↗*Forty-odd* ↘*people,* ↗*forty* ↗*odd* ↘*people.*

If someone is wearing *odd socks*, they are wearing socks that do not match. *Odd socks* are also the socks in the drawer that have no partners.

Two *odd volumes* of an encyclopaedia are two volumes separate from the rest of the set.

Odd jobs are pieces of work that are unconnected: *I spent the morning doing some odd jobs in the house.* An *odd-job man* is someone who takes casual work of different kinds.

The *odd man out*, or *odd one out* is one that is different from the others in a group, not necessarily of people. In *apple, pear, banana, cat, cat* is the *odd man/one out* because it is an animal and not a fruit.

noun

As a noun the word is used in the plural:

It makes no odds (it isn't important)	whether you tell him now or tomorrow.
	which school she went to.

To be at odds with somebody or something means *to be in disagreement or dispute*: *He's been at odds with his neighbours for twenty years; That opinion is at odds with the facts.*

Over the odds means above an accepted limit: *You'll have to pay over the odds to get a ticket so late.*

Odds and ends refers to unconnected things or pieces of work (compare *odd jobs*): *We still have to buy a few odds and ends; I've just got a few odds and ends to finish.*

Odds and sods is a variant of this but is usually applied to people.

odds for proportion and chance

Odds is the term used to describe proportional chances, especially in betting: *I'll give you odds of 5-1* (spoken as *five to one*) *against that horse winning the race.* This means that if the horse loses, you will give me a certain sum of money (e.g. £100), and if it wins I will give you five times that sum (£500).

Long odds represent a small chance (100-1, 1000-1); *short odds* represent a good chance (2-1); EVENS (1-1) is when the chances are equal; an *odds-on chance* (1-2) is a possibility of more than 50% (see OFF for *off-chance*), I will give you £50 if the horse wins and you will give me £100 if it does not. Odds can *lengthen* and *shorten* (become *longer* and *shorter*) as the situation changes and the balance of probability changes. If the *odds are in your favour*, your chances of success are high. If you *win against (all) the odds* you have had great difficulty or opposition.

In statistics the term *odds ratio* is used.

O

of & off

of

The pronunciation of *of* can be given as /ɒv/ but as the word is almost always weak, its pronunciation is /əv/ or /v/.

In fact these two words were originally different forms of the same Old English word which meant *away, away from*; this meaning survives partly in the word *off* but has been lost in *of*, which is used mostly to indicate a relationship of possession or connection: *The front of the house, the King of Spain*. It seems strange to use a word suggesting separation to indicate possession or connection; the reason is that *of* was used in the Middle Ages to translate the French word *de*, which was used for possession. The history of the meaning of the word is very complex.

As a preposition, *of* follows a number of verbs (see MULTI-WORD VERBS) and nouns and adjectives. See PREPOSITIONS.

off

Off has the strong form /ɒf/. The old RECEIVED PRONUNCIATION /ɔːf/ is still heard.

Off expresses the idea of motion or direction from a place. It can be used with verbs: *run off, drive off, fall off, send off*. It is used in a large number of MULTI-WORD VERBS, sometimes with its literal meaning, but often in a combination in which its meaning has been lost, for example *show off* (behave arrogantly), *come off* (succeed).

Off can mean *not at work*: *I'll be off next week; Mary's off sick; He takes too much time off*. It can also mean *bad* referring to food: *This milk, meat, cheese etc. is off*; *socially bad-mannered*: *It was off of him not to tell you that he was coming*; or *slightly ill*: *I'm feeling a bit off*.

As a preposition *off* means that one thing is no longer on or in contact with something else. *The book fell off the shelf; The farmers were forced off their land.*

The *offside* of a vehicle is the side nearer to the centre of the road (i.e. the right-hand side in Britain). A car has an *off front wheel* for example. (The other side is the *near* side.)

An *off chance* is an improbable one: *I'm sure he's not at home but I'll ring on the off-chance (that he is at home)*.

An *off-licence* is a licence to sell alcoholic drinks that will not be drunk in the shop where they are bought, in other words they will be drunk *off the* PREMISES. It is also the name of the type of shop: *Go to the off-licence and buy a bottle of wine*.

Electrical apparatus such as a TV or light is *off* when it is not operating; a tap is *off* when it is closed and water is not coming out of it.

In football, hockey and other sports a player is *offside* if he/she is in a position that is not allowed between the ball and the opponents' goal.

official & officious

Official attitudes, duties etc. are those that relate to an *office* (position of responsibility) that someone holds in an organisation. An *official* statement is one that is made with the authorisation and responsibility of that person or organisation. A *semi-official* statement is one that is made on the understanding that its source cannot be quoted, and thus its accuracy cannot be checked or guaranteed. *Unofficial* activities etc. are those that LIE outside the limits of official ones. The British monarch celebrates her/his *official birthday* on a day in June, when the weather may be pleasant, whenever the birthday really falls.

In the language of diplomacy, ***officious*** formerly had a meaning similar to *semi-official* as described above. Though similar words with that meaning are in common use in other languages (French *officieux*, Spanish *oficioso*, Italian *ufficioso*), in English *officious* has the sense of interfering in other people's affairs by insisting on helping when such help may not be desired. No doubt this more common meaning has led to the disuse of the diplomatic meaning.

O

of for have
MODAL AUXILIARY VERBS are sometimes followed by *have*: *can't have, must have, shouldn't have* etc. and in such cases the *have* is pronounced /əv/. This is also the usual pronunciation of *of*, which leads a number of native speakers who do not think of the words that they are using to write the incorrect forms ~~can't of, must of, shouldn't of~~ etc.

offshore
Offshore means *at a distance from the* SHORE *(*BEACH)*: an *offshore oil platform*; an *offshore wind* is one that is blowing from the coast to the sea; *offshore companies, funds* etc. are registered or located abroad, in a tax HAVEN. An ISLAND, SHIP, reef etc. can be *off the coast of Australia* for example.

offspring
This refers to children and adults in the sense that they are produced by their parents; it is a synonym of *descendant* and is the term used in genetics. It does not mean *child* in any other sense; it is incorrect to say ~~How many offspring do you have?~~ or ~~Stop behaving like an offspring~~. It does not change in the plural ~~offsprings~~.

oft
This form of OFTEN is not used alone but is found in compound forms: *oft-quoted, oft-repeated* etc.

often
Two pronunciations, /'ɒfən/ and /'ɒftən/, are commonly used. Originally the *t* was silent (see T, T) but in the early twentieth century, with the spread of literacy following universal education, the pronunciation that reflected the spelling came into use. Now both are heard, with no special regional or class distinction. /'ɒfən/ is the more common pronunciation. The former RECEIVED PRONUNCIATION /'ɔːfən/ is still heard sometimes.

oil
As *oil* emerges from the ground it is *crude oil* or simply *crude*; its scientific name is *petroleum*, but this is now only commonly used in geology and the name of the Organisation of Petroleum Exporting Countries (OPEC). The oil company BP was originally British Petroleum. In commerce it is generally known simply as *oil*: *the price of oil, oil company* etc. The refined product is also *oil* when used for lubrication. The fuel for most cars and some other road vehicles is called *petrol* in Britain and *gas* in the United States. This is from the name (*gasoline*) of the refined product and must not be confused with *gas* in its normal meaning, which is also sometimes used for powering vehicles. Most heavy vehicles and some cars use *diesel* instead of *petrol*. *Mineral oil* is sometimes described as such to distinguish it from *vegetable oil*, which is used in cooking.

OK
This means *all right, accepted*, and is very widespread. Despite considerable argument about its origin it seems clear that it began in 1839 in the USA as a joke representing the pronunciation of *all correct* (*orl korrect*). *To OK* something is to APPROVE it, and *That's OK by me* means that *I am in favour, I approve*. It is sometimes written *okay*.

on and upon
There is no difference in meaning at all between these two prepositions; the modern preference is for *on*: *The book is on/upon the table; You can rely on/upon him; On/Upon leaving the cinema, turn right*.

There are certain fixed expressions in which *upon* is always used:
Once upon a time. (The traditional beginning of a fairy tale.)
Upon my word/soul. (A rather old-fashioned expression of surprise.)
Thousands upon thousands. (Many thousands.)

Some place names use one form or the other to indicate the river that town is on: *Newcastle-upon-Tyne; Henley-on-Thames*.

O

one, number not article

It is important to distinguish between the number *one* and the article *a(n)*.

Three children were walking down the street. One boy came into my garden and stole some apples from my tree while the other two stayed outside.
A boy came into my garden yesterday and stole some apples from my tree.

Here English sees a clear difference between the number in the first example, one boy not two or three boys (which would have been possible), and the article in the second example. It was a boy, not a girl, or a man, or a woman, or a Scot, or a well-known local apple-thief who stole my apple. The use of the indefinite article identifies the noun as singular but the nature of the noun rather than the number of them is the important matter.

A spoonful of sugar makes lemon juice pleasant to drink.
One spoonful of sugar won't be enough for that amount of lemon juice.

In the first example the important point is that lemon juice may be sweetened with sugar to make it drinkable; although the words *a spoonful of sugar* are clearly singular, the tone of the sentence is to give advice rather than precise instructions. The second sentence on the other hand states a precise quantity of sugar, not two or three spoonfuls.

This difference of focus on what is the important part of the idea is reflected in the pronunciation. The article is unstressed but the number is stressed.

A /ə/ bóy; A spóonful of sugar
Óne /wʌn/ boy; Óne spòonful of sugar

Sometimes it must be made clear that the article is meant to be a singular; in this case it is stressed like the number *one* and is pronounced /eɪ/. *I said á spoonful, not thrée.* The words *a spoonful* are repeated as direct speech, and the article *a* is stressed heavily.

one representing a noun

One can be used to avoid repeating a noun: *I need a pen. Have you got one?* (= *a pen?*)

It can be used with DETERMINERS; in fact it must be used with them because an attributive ADJECTIVE must be followed by a noun.	*I need a pen. Give me*	*that one.* *that one on the table.* *the blue one.*
If the required determiner is possessive, the appropriate possessive is used.	*I need a pen. Give me*	*yours.* *Jane's.*
The plurals are	*I need some pens. Give me*	*those (ones).* *the ones on the table.* *the blue ones.* *yours.* *Jane's.*

See ADJECTIVES WITHOUT NOUNS; THING.

only (positions)

Only usually goes in the MID-POSITION FOR ADVERBS: *I **only** saw John* means that I saw John and nobody else. However by moving the word and changing the stress the meaning can be changed:
*Only **I** saw John.* (nobody else saw him.)
*I only **saw** John.* (I didn't speak to him.)
*I saw only **John**.* (I saw nobody else.)

EVEN operates in the same way.

O

onomatopoeia

This is the use of invented words to represent sounds. Sometimes they represent real objects: *cuckoo, puff-puff, bow-wow* (children's words for *train* and *dog* respectively) but usually the words intend to reproduce the sound: *bang, buzz, crash, creak, hum, thump, whirr*. English is rich in such words and often they are very close in meaning: *whizz* and *whoosh, creak, croak* and *squeak*. It is impossible to attempt to describe them here.

See ANIMAL NOISES.

open

Open is NON-GRADABLE *(*ADJECTIVE | GRADABLE & NON-GRADABLE)*, so it cannot be modified with *very*. The word which is used is *wide*: *The door was wide open when I arrived; 'Open wide,' said the dentist.*

opposite & in front of

If one thing is *opposite* another it is on the other side of something from it. The *opposite sides* of a square do not join; the adjacent ones do join.

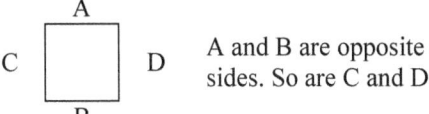 A and B are opposite sides. So are C and D.

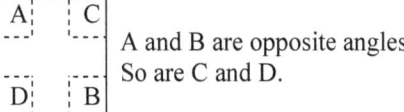 A and B are opposite angles. So are C and D.

Arthur and Helen are sitting *opposite* EACH OTHER at this table. However, Arthur's papers are on the table *in front of* him because their position is described in relation to the front part of his body.

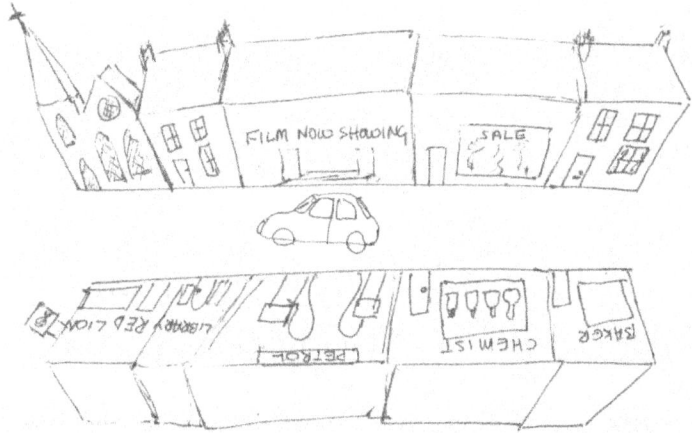

A street can have *opposite* sides. The church is opposite the pub, the cinema is opposite the GARAGE, but the car is parked *in front of* the cinema. ▶

O

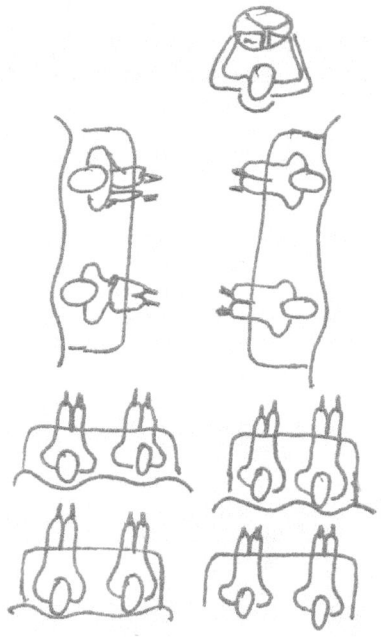

In this British bus (with the driver on the right) the passengers behind the driver are sitting opposite each other and some of the passengers at the back of the bus are sitting in front of other passengers.

The *front* or *front line* is the most advanced part of an army as it faces the enemy. *Front* does not mean *forehead*.

-or & -our

A well-known difference between British and AMERICAN ENGLISH is the spelling of words such as *colour/color* and *harbour/harbor*. However, there are a number of words that have *-or* in British English; many of them are agent words (the person or thing that performs an action) such as *inventor* or *reactor*. A dictionary should be used to distinguish between those words that have *-or* and those with *-er*. There are too many to list here.

Below is a list of words that end with *-or* in British English; it includes some words that are in fact, but do not seem obviously to be, agent words, e.g. *cursor, vector*.

adjectives
Anterior, ulterior; interior, exterior, inferior, superior; junior, senior.

nouns
CENSOR, *cursor, décor, error,* LIQUOR, *manor, meteor, motor, pallor, razor, rotor, stupor, tailor, torpor, tremor, vector, warrior.*

Rigor is written without *u* in the medical sense but is written *rigour* when it means *thoroughness* or *strictness*. The adjective is *rigorous*. The French expression *de rigueur* /ˌdərɪˈɡɜː/ means that something is required by social convention or fashion. The following Spanish words used in English have *-or*: *condor, matador, picador*.

See -OUR WORDS WITH SUFFIXES.

order

In organisations such as the army or police *orders* are commands that must be obeyed, but *order* is the perfectly normal word in commerce for the process of asking for something that is not immediately available: *We haven't got that model in stock but we can order it for you; I must cancel my newspaper order while I'm on holiday.* A waiter asks *Can I take your order?* or *Are you ready to order?* In this sense it has no authoritarian tone.

A *standing order* is a permanent instruction, especially to a bank, to pay the same amount or perform the same action at regular intervals.

O

other

Other is unusual as an adjective because it can be used as a pronoun, in which case it has a plural: *That's my opinion but others may disagree; I've found two shirts but I don't know where the others are.*

Every other has its literal meaning: *February is unusually short with only 28 or 29 days. Every other month has at least thirty.* It also means EACH second one in a series: *We receive a gas bill every other month* i.e. January, March, May, July, September and November.

See ANOTHER; EACH OTHER & THEMSELVES.

-our words with suffixes

Words that end in *-our* (in British English) lose the *u* when they make suffixes with *-ous*: *humour/humorous, rigour/rigorous*, with *-ant*: *deodorant*, with *-ation*: *elaboration*, or with *-ise*: *glamorise, vaporise*. With the suffixes *-ed, -ist, -ite*, and *-able* the *u* is retained: *behaviourist, coloured, favourable, honourable*.

See -OR & -OUR.

out of & outside

Out of is a compound preposition implying movement; it is the opposite of *into*. *Outside* is a preposition of position; it is the opposite of *inside*. However, *out of* can also describe position, especially when it can be considered as the result of movement: *The rubbish is out of the house now; Is the car out of the garage?* This has led to expressions such as *out of date; out of order; out of place; out of reach*. Where permanent position or absence of movement is implied *outside* must be used: *The hill was outside the city wall; The tree stood outside the house; He was waiting for me outside the cinema.*

overlook, overview, oversee & oversight

Overlook has two meanings:

To look at something from a higher position: *The hotel overlooks the sea.*

To ignore something, either deliberately or accidentally: *I will overlook your lateness on this occasion, but you must arrive on time in future; I overlooked the need to tell John personally.*

An *overview* is a general view, a summary: *An overview of the latest situation.*

Oversee means *supervise. The project will be overseen by Arthur Black.* An *overseer* is a *supervisor*. (*Oversee* is a CALQUE of the Latin *supervise*.)

Oversight is a noun; it corresponds to the meaning of *overlook* as an accidental failure to notice something. *As the result of an oversight this work has not been done.* It also means supervision, corresponding to *oversee*.

overseas

This is a logical SYNONYM for *ABROAD* given that Britain is an island, but it suggests a considerable distance. European countries would probably not be described as being overseas from a British point of view.

P

p, P /piː/

The sixteenth letter of the alphabet. It is pronounced /p/.

It is not pronounced in *cupboard* /ˈkʌbəd/ and *raspberry* /ˈrɑːzbərɪ/, or in words which begin with *p* followed by *n*, *s* or *t*: *pneum-; psalm, pseudo-, psych-; ptarmigan, ptero-, Ptolemy, ptomaine*.

ph

This is pronounced /f/ in words such as *graph, photo-, phono-*. The origin of this pronunciation is that the Romans used these letters to transliterate the GREEK letter *phi* and these words have passed from Latin into English with this spelling. The word *phoney* appears to be an exception to this as its origin is unknown.

The combination *ph* is not pronounced /f/ when it occurs at the join point in compound words such as *haphazard* /hæpˈhæzəd/ and *shepherd* /ˈʃepəd/.

See COMPOUND NOUNS.

Pacific & peaceful

These are synonyms but in practice modern usage has *Pacific* for the name of the ocean and *peaceful* for all other senses.

palace

In Britain a *palace* is an official residence of the royal family or of a bishop; the *Palace of Westminster*, the building in which Parliament meets, is a royal palace. The word is not usually used for a private residence, however grand it is; the exceptions are *Blenheim Palace*, the residence of the Duke of Marlborough, and *Dalkeith Palace* near EDINBURGH, which is now used by the University of Wisconsin. The very ornate pubs of Victorian times were ironically called *gin palaces*.

palindromes

A *palindrome* is a word or phrase that reads the same forwards and backwards. Examples are *radar, noon, dad, peep, poop, gig, madam, deified, Malayalam* (a language). There are palindromic sentences, for example *Madam, I'm Adam* (perhaps the first words spoken in the world); *Sex at noon taxes; A man, a plan, a canal – Panama!* (reference to Ferdinand de Lesseps, who built the Panama canal).

pane of glass

Each separate piece of glass in a window is called a *pane*: *The kitchen window has four panes. The top right-hand pane is broken.*

pantomime

Unlike a *mime*, a *pantomime* is not silent. It is a traditional Christmas show, which can trace its origins to the Commedia dell'Arte, though it has changed very much since then.

A pantomime is based on a fairy story and involves a love story. Two young people meet and fall in love, they have problems (such as lack of money or parental disapproval) which they overcome, and at the end of the show they marry. One strange feature is that the young man (the *principal boy*) is always played by a woman, while the course of the show is directed by the *dame*, a humble woman with a heart of gold, a part that is always played by a man. It must be made very clear indeed that this cross-dressing is perfectly open, there is no attempt to hide the sex of the person playing the part, and a pantomime is most definitely **not** a TRANSVESTITE show. In addition to these characters there is always a *devil* character and a good *fairy* who fight against each other to control the development of the story. In this fight between good and evil, good always wins.

A pantomime is a show for families and especially for children, who enjoy the singing and dancing and bright costumes; in fact children from the audience are often invited on to the stage at the end to sing a song with the dame.

parallel
Note the spelling. This adjective has no adverb form *parallelly*. Use *in parallel*.

parking
The place where cars may be parked is a *car park*. The sign *parking*, which has been taken into many other languages to mean *car park*, is the gerund of the verb *to park* and indicates that *parking is available*.

See CAMPING.

parson
A *parson* is a PROTESTANT (usually ANGLICAN) clergyman. The word should not be confused with *person*. The words are DOUBLETS.

partial
This has three meanings:

Wrongly favouring one side in a JUDGEMENT *or decision*; a judge, football referee etc. must be *impartial*. This is the same meaning as DISINTERESTED *(*INTEREST)*.

If you are *partial to* something, you like it: *I am partial to toasted cheese.*

Referring to a part, incomplete: *a partial success, a partial defeat*.

participle clauses
A participle CLAUSE is one in which the present participle (-ING FORM) or past participle is used alone; it can be considered as a reduction of a CONTINUOUS ASPECT verb when it contains a present participle. The sentence *While/When/As I was cycling along the street, I saw a dog* can be rewritten as *While/When cycling along the street, I saw a dog* (NB not *As cycling along the street, I saw a dog.*) or simply *Cycling along the street, I saw a dog.*

It is wrong to say *Cycling along the street, the dog ran away from me* because this suggests (grammatically, though illogically) that the dog was cycling. This construct is known as an unattached or dangling participle. The first part must have a finite verb to make the change of subject clear: *As I was cycling along the street, the dog ran away from me*.

With a past tense *Having seen the dog I cycled away from it* is the same as *When I saw/had seen the dog I cycled away from it*.

A past participle is used to express a passive meaning: *Annoyed by the dog, I looked for its owner*.

It is essential for the subject of both clauses to be the same: *On turning the corner I saw that I was going in the wrong direction* means *When I turned the corner I saw that I was going in the wrong direction*.

By walking to work I saved money and became fitter means *As a result of walking to work I saved money and became fitter*.

See GERUND.

partner
A *partner* is someone with whom an activity is shared; a *business partner* is someone who shares the expenses, profits and losses of a business. A *partner* can also refer to a spouse and is a popular term for a member of an unmarried couple or of a GAY couple.

party
The ROMANCE-language origin of this word implies a division; this has led to a number of meanings that seem to have little connection. ▶

P

A group of people responsible for taking decisions frequently divides into opposing groups; these are called *parties*. *Political parties* have their formal existence but they began as such divisions and the word *party* is still applied to such divisions in any body of people or society in general: *the anti-war party*.

A group of people who are given a particular task could be an *advance party, search party, working party* and so on. This led to the idea of a group of people meeting for pleasure: *a hunting party, a fishing party, a house party* (of people staying in the same house for a few days), or a *party of friends* to go on holiday together. This in turn developed into a *party* as a purely social event: *a dinner party, birthday party* etc.

From the same origin, a *party* is a separate person or group of people, or a company or other organisation, that is a participant in a legal action or a contract. A *third party* is one that is not directly involved in the action or contract.

passed & past

Passed is the PAST SIMPLE of the verb *pass*: *He passed me without speaking; She passed her exam*.

Past is a noun, *the past*; an adjective, *past events*; a preposition, *walk past the cinema*; and an adverb, *He walked past without speaking to me*.

Both are pronounced /pɑːst/.

passive voice

English verbs have two voices: *active* and *passive*.

In the passive voice the subject corresponds to the object of the equivalent *active* sentence. For this reason the passive can only be used with transitive verbs. The preposition *by* is used to introduce the agent.

Othello was written by Shakespeare corresponds to *Shakespeare wrote Othello*. *Othello* is the subject of the passive verb *was written* and the direct object of the active verb *wrote*. *Shakespeare* is the subject of the active verb *wrote* and is the agent of the passive verb *was written*.

The passive is used when the focus of attention is on the subject rather than the agent: *Othello was written by Shakespeare; Faust was written by Marlowe* or when it is not possible, or not desirable, or not necessary to name the agent: *This wine is made in Italy; Unfortunately, your DVD recorder was damaged while it was being repaired; Nowadays more food can be grown on a hectare of land than was possible 100 years ago.*

The passive is a useful way of avoiding a long subject: *The new hospital will be built by Ferguson and McDonald, a Scottish construction company which has a good record of building health centres but has not yet built anything on this scale* is preferable to *Ferguson and McDonald, a Scottish construction company which has a good record of building health centres but has not yet built anything on this scale, will build the new hospital.*

The passive voice is widely used in scientific writing because it provides anonymity, focusing on the action rather than the actor.

formation

The passive is formed by the appropriate form of *be* or *get* (see below) and the past participle of the verb.

	simple	continuous
present	It is done	It is being done
past	It was done	It was being done
future	It will be done	It will be being done
present perfect	It has been done	It has been being done
past perfect	It had been done	It had been being done
future perfect	It will have been done	It will have been being done*
conditional	It would be done	It would be being done

	simple	**continuous**
conditional perfect	*It would have been done*	*It would have been being done**
infinitive	*(to) be done*	*(to) be being done*
past INFINITIVE	*(to) have been done*	*(to) have been being done*

*These exist in theory but are very rarely used.

It has infinitive forms: *This letter must be sent this week; This letter cannot be sent this week; I expect this letter to be sent on Tuesday; I expected this letter to have been sent before I returned.*

The same sentence, *Her arm was broken,* can refer to an action: *Her arm was broken in the accident* and to a pre-existing state: *Her arm was broken when I saw her.* See DYNAMIC AND STATIVE.

get as auxiliary

Sometimes GET is used as the auxiliary in passive sentences; this is only done in colloquial language. It is used with its meaning of *become*: *They're getting married next year; I got dressed and went downstairs; We're getting confused now; I don't want to get involved with another woman; The story got told again and again.*

The idea of becoming or reaching a new state is clear in *I got up, got washed, and got dressed.* The sentence *I was up, was washed, and was dressed* would refer to the state of being, not the dynamic process of becoming, *up, washed,* and *dressed.* (*Get* is dynamic and *be* is stative. See DYNAMIC AND STATIVE; MARRIAGE & WEDDING.) *Get lost* is a rude way of saying *Go away.* For adverb position see HAVE.

passive from indirect object

Unusually, English has a passive construction in which the subject corresponds to the indirect object of the equivalent active sentence. *Mary was given a book (by John)* corresponds to *John gave Mary a book.*

This is used as a way of associating the indirect object and the verb in a passive construction and placing the object of the active sentence at the beginning of the passive sentence to give it prominence while avoiding the need to state who performed the action.

He was given a gold watch when he retired.
He was told to go home. (ordered, instructed. See TELL *(*SAY)*).
He was told that his wife had passed her driving test. (informed. See TELL *(*SAY)*).
He was sent details of his new job.

Compare *He was sent to the company's New York office,* where *he* would be the direct object of the active sentence: *The company | sent | him | to its New York office* (S | V | DO | Adv) with *He was sent details of his new job* corresponding to *The company | sent | him | details of his new job* (S | V | IO | DO).

See OBJECTS, DIRECT AND INDIRECT.

he is said to be etc.

Sentences with verbs of mental perception have two passive forms:

| People | think
believe
suppose
expect
know | that
he | is in Paris.
has gone to Paris. |

correspond to

| It is | thought
believed
supposed
expected
known | that
he | is in Paris.
has gone to Paris. |

and to

P

| He is | thought
believed
supposed*
expected
known | to | be in Paris.
have gone to Paris. |

*SUPPOSED TO here has the meaning *should*.

Of these passive forms the second is more widely used.

See *verbs of mental perception* under INFINITIVE OR -ING?

works of art

The association of the author, composer etc. with a work of art is considered as a passive construction, though the verb (*written, composed, painted* etc.) is not stated: *Don Quixote by Miguel de Cervantes; The Pastoral Symphony by Beethoven; The Adoration of the Magi by Rubens*.

past participle

The past participle of regular verbs is used with the auxiliary verb *have* in the verb forms of the PERFECT ASPECT and with the auxiliary verb *be* to make the verb forms of the passive voice. It is made by adding *-(e)d* to the infinitive. In IRREGULAR VERBS the form of the past participle is variable; it is the third of the three essential parts for learning an irregular verb.

past simple

The past simple tense of regular verbs is made by adding *-(e)d* to the infinitive. In IRREGULAR VERBS the past tense varies; it is the second essential part of an irregular verb.

past simple & past continuous

past simple

The past simple refers to events or states which are completed, and which occurred in a period of time which is completed; it does not matter whether the event is in the distant or recent past.

Single events:

The Normans invaded England in 1066. (The invasion and the year are completed.)
I spoke to Jenny yesterday. (My conversation with Jenny and yesterday are completed.)

STATIVE *(*DYNAMIC AND STATIVE)* or habitual events:

In Roman times people owned slaves. (Roman times are completed and people no longer own slaves.)
I played football when I was at school. (I don't play football now and my schooldays are completed.)

However, the reference is to the completed nature of the action of playing football at school; whether or not I play it now is irrelevant. In *I played football when I was at school and I still play football* the reference to the present (*and I still play football*) is a separate present statement.

The time reference does not have to be clearly stated. In *I played football at school* the words *at school* identify the time as being completed in the past because it is known that the speaker is not at school now.

The past simple is used in narratives, in novels, MINUTES of meetings, and reports for example; the time is not usually stated on each occasion because it is clear from the context.

past continuous

The past continuous refers to an action that continued for a period of time and perhaps was still not complete at the end of that time. In *I was watching TV while she was cleaning the car* it is understood that both actions are now completed though it is not clear which finished first. If the past simple is used *I watched TV while she cleaned the car* the meaning is very similar, but the focus is more on the completion of the two actions than on their continuing nature.

The past continuous is commonly used with the past simple to refer to an instantaneous action that interrupts a continuing one: *I was watching TV when the phone rang; Julius Caesar was talking to* his generals when a messenger arrived* or that takes place during it *I turned the TV off when the phone was ringing.*

However, two past simple verbs with *when* express consecutive instantaneous actions: *I turned the TV off when the phone rang* (The phone rang then I turned the TV off.)

Like the present continuous, the past continuous can mean that the state of affairs was temporary: *I had recently arrived in the town and was living with friends until I found a place of my own.*

See CONDITIONAL SENTENCES; INDIRECT SPEECH; PAST SIMPLE & PRESENT PERFECT; PERFECT ASPECT.

past simple & present perfect

For a general discussion of the perfect tenses, see PERFECT ASPECT.

Learners of English often have great difficulty in deciding which of these two tenses to use. The important thing to remember is that the past simple refers to a past time period that is completed while the present perfect refers to a time period that extends into the present and presumably into the future. It is essential to understand that **the difference is whether or not the time period is completed; the distinction does not depend on whether the action itself is completed**. Nor is it important whether the action was in the recent or distant past. In the past simple the action must be completed because the time period in which it took place is completed, but in the present perfect the action may be complete or it may be continuing in the present.

1a *I played football when I was at school.*
Past simple because the time period is completed.

1b *I have played football all my life/since I was a boy.*
Present perfect because the time period *extends into the present.*

1c *I have played football a few times but I didn't enjoy it.*
Present perfect because the understood time period (in my life) in which I have played football extends into the present.

Similar examples are:

2a *I lived in Africa from 1980 to 1982/for two years.*
Past simple because the time period is completed.

2b *I have lived in Africa all my life/since I was a boy/for two years.*
I live there now; the action extends into the present.

2a and **2b** both contain the adverbial phrase *for two years.* The verb itself makes it clear that in the FORMER I no longer live there but in the latter I do.

2c *I have lived in Africa.*
This states that I have the experience of living in Africa but I do not live there now. It gives no information about when this experience was or how long it lasted.

Because the time period to which the present perfect refers continues in the future there is a theoretical possibility in examples *1c* and *2c* that the action can be repeated. I could theoretically play football again or I could return to Africa to live at some point in my life if I wanted to.

Thus we say:
I wrote six EMAILS yesterday.
I have written four emails today. (I am at work and I can write more emails today.) but
I wrote six emails at work today. (It is now the evening, I have finished work, and the time period described by *at work* is completed.)

I have written six emails this morning. (It is still the morning now; the morning is not completed. It is theoretically possible that I will decide to write some more emails this morning, whether or not I actually do so.) but
I wrote six emails this morning. (It is now the afternoon; the morning is completed. It is obviously impossible for me to write more emails this morning.) ▶

P

The question of whether or not the time period is complete or not is clearly related to whether the subject is alive or dead.

SHAKESPEARE wrote 37 plays. (Shakespeare is dead; he can write no more plays.)
J. K. ROWLING has written about 20 books. (She is still alive; she can write more books.)
Thus, if someone says *John has always been interested in the theatre* it is definite that John is alive, but after John's death this changes to *John was always interested in the theatre*.

Since relates a time in the past to the present, so it is used with the present perfect. *For* can relate past and present in this way (see above): *John has worked for Megacomputers plc since 2005/since he moved to Wales/for over ten years.*

IMPORTANT. The use of the present simple (**PRESENT TENSES*) (*John works for Megacomputers plc since 2015*), which is standard in many languages, is incorrect and impossible in English. The present perfect **must** be used in such constructions.

John worked for Minicomputers plc/from 2008 to 2015/until he moved to Wales/for seven years. We know that John works for Megacomputers plc now. This tells us that he worked for Minicomputers plc in the past. Here *for* refers to a completed time in the past.

Conversations often change from the present perfect to the past simple as they become more precise:
- *Ask George. He's lived in Africa.*
  Has he? When was he there? (Change of tense here as the conversation moves from general to specific.)
  I think he lived in Nigeria some time in the 1990s.
- *Have you ever eaten snails?*
  Yes, I ate them during my first visit to Paris. That was when we went there with a school trip.
- *I've been very busy recently. Two weeks ago I spoke at a congress in Berlin and then I flew directly to Moscow. When I got back here I had a big report to write and...*

See PERFECT ASPECT; PAST SIMPLE & PAST CONTINUOUS.

pay
This is used as follows: *You pay a bill; You pay €2.00; You pay a waiter; You pay €2.00 for a cup of coffee; You pay a waiter €2.00 for a cup of coffee; You pay €2.00 to the waiter for a cup of coffee; You say to the waiter 'I would like to pay (for my coffee).'*

Work can be *paid* or *unpaid*.

pedagogy
This is pronounced /ˈpedəɡɒɡi/ or /ˈpedəɡɒdʒi/ with *pedagogics* /pedəˈɡɒdʒɪks/.

pence & pennies
Pence is the plural for a sum of money: *It costs 75p* (seventy-five pence).
Pennies is the plural for the individual coins: *A bag full of pennies; Two pounds' worth of pennies.*
See MONEY.

pepper
The word *pepper* in English has two separate meanings. The small dried berries (*peppercorns*) of *Piper nigrum* can be *black* or *white pepper*.

The fruit of the genus *Capsicum* is also called *pepper*. The large ones, sometimes known as *sweet peppers*, are often called *green* or *red peppers* depending on their colours, or *bell peppers*. *Chilli* or *cayenne peppers* have a very strong flavour.
See HOT.

percentages
In English percentages are used like NUMBERS; they do not have articles. We say *Inflation has risen by 2.3%; Support for the government has fallen by 6% this year.*

P

perfect aspect

For comparison and contrast of past simple and present perfect see PAST SIMPLE & PRESENT PERFECT. For further details about the future perfect see FUTURE.

There are three perfect forms: *present, past,* and *future*. They are formed with the appropriate tense of the verb *have* and the past participle.

present perfect

This is used:

- for states (stative verbs) that began in the past, continue in the present, and will probably continue in the future: *I have lived here for over 20 years; He's always supported that team; She's never owned a car.*
- for events that occurred (DYNAMIC verbs) at some time in the past; the time is not stated and the event could have happened at any time up to the present: *England has been invaded successfully only once in the last thousand years; John has spoken to the Prime Minister.* Perhaps John sees the Prime Minister every day and this is routine; perhaps he is a person who would not normally expect to speak to the Prime Minister and it is a great honour. This sentence alone does not provide this information.
  Note that in the first example the event happened nearly 1,000 years ago and in the second it was perhaps only a few seconds ago. The distance in the past is not important. The important point is that they are occurrences in the past that can theoretically be repeated in the future.
  The action can be repeated: *I have seen that film six times; It has rained on six days this month* but we do not know when any of those six times was, or for how long, or the date of any of those six days.
  There is room for ambiguity here between state and event. *He has been sent to prison* could mean that he is in prison now, or that at some time he was sent to prison but has since been released.
- in questions about a person's experiences: *Has John spoken to the Prime Minister?; Have you (ever) eaten octopus? Ever* is often used in questions referring to a person's lifetime experience rather than to a recently expected event, but it is not necessary in such questions.
- for completed actions that began in the past and lead to a current or future state:
  I've washed the car. (I am telling you that it is clean.)
  I've got the car out of the garage. (Now you can put the suitCASES into it.)
  I've bought a new camera. (We will be able to take photos on our holiday.)
- for reporting news (this is similar to the previous use): *The president has resigned; There's been an accident; John's bought a new car.* Adding *just* shows that the event is very recent: *I've just cut my finger; The lights have just gone out; I've just heard that Simon's in town.*
- with SINCE. The time reference can be with a noun or a verb (*since* as PREPOSITION or CONJUNCTION): *I haven't seen him since Christmas; I haven't seen him since he broke his arm.*
- in future sentences such as *It will be the first time that I have travelled outside Europe.*

For *Once I've spoken to him I'll let you know what he thinks* see TENSE & TIME.

present perfect continuous

This is made with the present perfect of *be* (*I have been* etc.) and the -ING FORM of the verb: *I have been running; It has been raining.*

As is usual with the CONTINUOUS ASPECT the present perfect continuous refers to an event or action that is in progress for a period of time and is used with DYNAMIC verbs. It may continue in the present when a time period is stated: *I've been waiting for half an hour; It's been raining all morning.*

Like the simple aspect it can imply that an action is temporary: *I've been going to bed late too often recently; I've been working for Mr Lewis since my boss went on holiday.*

When no time period is stated, this suggests that an action has recently finished; this is analogous to the news-reporting use of the present perfect simple: ➤

P

It's been raining. (I can see that the ground is wet.)
Have you been running? (You look hot.)
'Why are your hands dirty?' 'I've been repairing the car engine.'

In these cases it is not clear that the action is completed. At this moment it is not raining and I am not repairing the car but these actions will possibly, though not necessarily, be restarted. *I've repaired the car engine* is a statement that the work is complete. *I've been repairing the car engine* is an explanation for my dirty hands; it does not say whether the work is complete.

Compare these questions and answers:
'Have you repaired the car engine?' 'No, not yet, I've still got another hour's work.'
'Have you been repairing the car engine?' 'Yes, all morning but I haven't finished yet. I've still got another hour's work.'

past perfect

This is also known as the *pluperfect*. It is made with *had* + the past participle. It refers to two events or states in the past and places one before the other: *I had known her for five years when I married her; They had moved into their new house when Stephen was born; I had phoned him five times by six o'clock; We'd been waiting for two hours before they told us that the flight was cancelled.*

This is made clearer by adding *already*: *I had already known her for five years when I married her.*

If *before* is used, the past simple can be used instead of the past perfect: *I knew her/had known her for five years before I married her.*

It can be used with *since*: *She had lived in Spain since she left university*. This means that at a certain time in the past she had lived in Spain. It does not necessarily mean that she lives there now.

The past perfect continuous is used similarly to the present perfect continuous with appropriate changes.

See INDIRECT SPEECH; CONDITIONAL SENTENCES.

future perfect

This is used for an action that will be completed before a certain time: *I'll have written the report by Thursday*. The future perfect continuous is similar to the present perfect continuous with appropriate changes; it is not used much.

See PAST SIMPLE & PAST CONTINUOUS; PAST SIMPLE & PRESENT PERFECT.

perforate, pierce, prick & punch

These are all similar in meaning.

Perforate is the word used for making a row of holes in paper so that a part can be torn off.

Prick is the word used for breaking the skin with a needle, thorn etc.; a *pricked* balloon will burst. If you prick yourself, the needle ***pierces*** the skin; some people, especially women, have *pierced ears*; *body piercing* has become popular in recent years.

Punch implies force, hitting with a fist or making a hole in wood, leather, paper, and other substances. *Punch*, from a different origin, is the name of a mixed alcoholic drink.

personal & personnel

Personal /ˈpɜːsənəl/ is an adjective relating to one's private intimate affairs.

Personnel /pɜːsəˈnel/ is a noun meaning the people that work in an organisation. The *personnel department* is responsible for ENSURING *(*ASSURE)* that its personal relations run well. Increasingly now this is known as *human RESOURCES*.

personal names

how names work

The custom of passing a *surname* down through the generations began in the thirteenth century in England. Commonly these names were taken from the father's forename with the addition of *son*: *Jackson, Johnson, Robertson, Wilson*; from the place of origin, *Crosby, Oldham, York*; and from trades, *Baker, Cook, Thatcher*. Other common surnames are of geographical origin, *Dale, Heath, Hill, Moor*; *North, South, East* and *West*; or colours, *Black, Brown, Green, White*.

If a man is called Alan James Crosby, his *surname* is Crosby; Alan and James are his *forenames* or *Christian names*, or Alan is his *first name* and James is his *second* or *middle name*. British people commonly have two forenames and usually use the first of them; this man would probably be known as Alan Crosby. However, it is not strange to find a person who has only one forename, or more than two, or who does not use his/her first forename. Alan James Crosby is his *full name*.

When a woman marries, she usually takes her husband's surname and uses it instead of the one she has previously used (which is her MAIDEN *name*); there is no legal obligation to do so, but the custom is so widespread as to be normal. Thus if Alan Crosby married Alison Jean Hill, she would become Alison Crosby; their children would be Christopher John Crosby and Catherine Mary Crosby, probably known as Christopher and Catherine. In some cases the parents might use the mother's maiden name as one of the children's forenames: Christopher Hill Crosby.

In a case where a woman chooses to keep her own name instead of taking her husband's surname, as women who are public figures often do, the children usually have their father's surname as described above. Children of unmarried mothers take their father's surname if he recognises the children as his own. A married woman who uses her husband's surname can continue to use it and any associated title after he dies or if they divorce; Princess Diana remained Princess of Wales after her divorce from Prince Charles. The author Agatha Christie was born Agatha Miller; she became famous for her detective stories while married to Archie Christie and continued to use that surname for her books after her divorce and even after her remarriage. Her second husband was the archaeologist Sir Max Mallowan; socially she was known as Lady Mallowan but her books were published under the name of Agatha Christie, her first husband's surname.

Some people have a *double-barrelled surname*, i.e. one that consists of two surnames joined by a hyphen. These two names together make one surname, so the children of George and Mary Brown-Windsor will have the surname Brown-Windsor. Often a double-barrelled surname is the sign of an upper class family, but other couples sometimes join their surnames with a hyphen in order to pass both names on to their children. There is a process called *deed* POLL that allows people to change their surnames; a deed is a formal legal document.

Since the word *name* can refer to forename, surname or full name, the answer to the question *'What is your name?'* varies according to the circumstances. In an informal setting it would be normal to reply *'James'*, while a more formal response would be to use the surname *'Bond'*. The formula *'Bond, James Bond'* (surname then forename and surname) is quite common for giving one's name.

common forenames
Many names have friendly or diminutive forms. The list shows names that have variant forms. For example, it is particularly common to add *-y* or *-ie* to monosyllabic names: *Johnny, Frankie, Katy*. These diminutive forms and other variations are not always shown here.

male names

Abraham	Abe
Alan, Allan, Alun, Allen	Al
Alastair, Alasdair	Al
Albert	Al, Bert
Alexander	Alex, Alec, Sandy
Alfred	Al, Fred
Andrew	Andy
Anthony /ˈæntəni/	Tony
Arthur	Art, Arth
Barry	Baz
Benjamin	Benjy, Benny
Bernard	Bernie

P

male names

Bertram	Bert
Cecil	Cec /ses/
Charles	Charlie
Christopher	Chris
David	Dave
Donald	Don
Edward, Edwin	Ed, Ted, Ned
Francis	Frank
Frederick	Fred
Gareth	Gary
Geoffrey /ˈdʒefri/	Geoff, Jeff
Harold	Harry, Hal
Henry	Hal
Ian, Iain /ˈiːən/	
Jacob	Jake
James	Jim
Jeffrey	Jeff
John	Jack
Jonathan	Jon
Joseph	Joe
Leslie	Les
Malcolm /ˈmælkəm/	Mal
Matthew	Matt
Michael /ˈmaɪkəl/	Mike, Mick
Patrick	Pat, Patsy, Paddy
Peter	Pete
Richard	Dick, Rick
Robert	Bob, Rob
Stephen, Steven	Steve
Theodore	Ted
Thomas /ˈtɒməs/	Tom
Timothy	Tim
Vivian, Vivien	Viv
Walter, Wallace	Wally
Warwick	Rick
William	Bill, Will

female names

Ann, Anne, Anna	
Bernadette	Bernie
Charlotte	Charley, Lottie
Christine, Christina	Chris, Tina
Diana	Di /daɪ/
Dorothy	Dot
Elizabeth	Liz, Beth, Bess, Bet, Libby. Lizzy
Frances	Fran
Jacqueline	Jackie, Jacqui
Joanne, Joanna	Jo
Josephine	Jo, Josie
Lesley	Les, Lee
Margaret	Maggie, Meg

P

female names

Mary, Marie	Moll(y), POLL(y)
Nicola	Nickie
Patricia	Pat, Patsy, Patty, Tricia
Rebecca	Becky
Stephanie	Fanny
Susan, /ˈsuːzən/ Susanna, Suzanne /suːˈzæn/	Sue, Suzie
Victoria	Vicky
Vivienne	Viv

notes for personal names

Anthony, almost always pronounced /ˈæntəni/, was originally spelled *Antony*. SHAKESPEARE uses this spelling. *Thomas* and *Theresa* are pronounced with /t/.

There are a number of personal variations on the spelling and familiar forms of names.

Jane, Jayne, Joan, Joanne, Jean(ne) are all feminine forms of *John*.

Noël/Noelle, Leslie/Lesley, Francis/Frances and *Vivian(en)/Vivienne* have the same spoken form for men and women. *Hilary* and *Evelyn* are the only names that are common to both sexes (the writer Evelyn Waugh married a woman called Evelyn). Some short forms (e.g. *Pat, Chris*) are common to both sexes.

Mary is not used as a man's name as it is in countries with a CATHOLIC tradition. *Jesus* and *Angel* are never used as men's names.

A name with *Mac* at the beginning is Scottish in origin (*Mac* is the SCOTS GAELIC *(*CELTS AND CELTIC)* for *son* but, like *Johnson* etc., these are normal surnames, not patronymics). These names may be written as *MacDonald, Macdonald, McDonald, Mcdonald*. Alphabetical lists vary in their treatment of forms written like McDonald; some list them all under Mac and others follow strict alphabetical order.

Many Irish names have *O'* at the beginning, for example *O'Connell, O'Daly*.

Some surnames have great differences between spelling and pronunciation: *Beauchamp* /ˈbiːtʃəm/, *Cholmondeley* /tʃʌmli/, *Featherstonehaugh* /ˈfænʃɔː/, *Frazier* /ˈfreɪzə/, *Lloyd* /lɔɪd/, *Mainwaring* /ˈmænərɪŋ/, *Ruthven* /ˈrɪvən/, *Sandys* /sɑːndz/, *St John* /ˈsɪndʒən/, *Strachan* /strɔːn/, *Waugh* /wɔː/, *Yeo* /jəʊ/; for *Dalyell, Dalziel* and *Menzies* see Z, Z. In such cases it is perfectly acceptable to ask how someone's name is spelled or pronounced; this is especially true in the USA because large-scale immigration from all over the world has produced a wide variety of names.

Some people have an unpronounced *e* on the end of their name. Examples are *Browne, Clarke, Greene* /braʊn/ etc. People who have such names may say *My name is Greene with an e (on the end)*.

Welsh speakers use a patronymic with *ap* (son of): *Dewi ap Huw* is David son of Hugh. A normal surname may be used together with this. Some of these forms have come to be used as normal surnames, with the *p* incorporated into the surname: *Pugh, Pritchard, Probert, Price/Preece* (son of Hugh, Richard, Robert, Rhys) for example. Wales is unusual in having a small number of surnames. It has been estimated that 39 surnames include 95% of Welsh people. Some common Welsh surnames are *Davies, Davis, Evans, Jones, Griffiths, Owens, Morgan, Lloyd* and *Williams*. In Wales *Dai* /daɪ/, *Dafydd* /ˈdavɪð/ and *Dewi* /ˈdewi/ are all forms of David, the patron saint of Wales. *Siôn* /ʃɔːn/, *Ieuan* /ˈjajan/, *Ioan* /ˈjɒan/ are Welsh forms of John; *Ian* and *Iain* /ˈiːən/ are Scottish forms. In Ireland *Sean* /ʃɔːn/ and *Seamus* /ˈʃeɪməs/ are forms of John and James respectively. The Welsh, Scottish and Irish forms are often used in English. *Dafydd Wigley* is a Welsh nationalist politician and *Sean Connery* is a Scottish actor. These forms are used in English. The Welsh and Scottish forms are not translated.

Note the spelling of *John*. It is sometimes spelled incorrectly as ~~Jhon~~ by non-native speakers.

Nicknames in general are outside the scope of this book, but some surnames have typical nicknames that are commonly associated with them: *Nobby Clarke, Dusty Miller*, and *Chalky White*. ▶

P

Tommy, in full *Tommy Atkins*, is a common colloquial name for a British private soldier. See MILITARY RANKS.

Bloggs is used as a non-specific common name: *Joe* or *Fred Bloggs* is the man in the street. Public records show a very small number of people (about fifteen) called *Bloggs*; possibly they are not genuine.

For plural forms of names see PLURAL FORMS.

person and people

For almost all purposes *people* is the effective plural of *person*. It can follow a number and takes a plural verb: *1,500 people have bought tickets*; *the people who were* (not *was*) *present*. However, *people* is not plural in origin. It comes from Latin *populus*, and has its own singular and plural forms corresponding to community, tribe, race, nation or ethnic group. So it is perfectly correct to speak of *a warlike people*; *a peace-loving people*; *the peoples of Europe*; Winston Churchill wrote *A History of the English-Speaking Peoples*.

Person too has its own plural *persons* which is found sometimes, although *people* is usually more natural. It is used especially in more formal contexts, when the people are thought of as individuals: *Maximum capacity 8 persons* (in a lift), and in legal and constitutional language: *The crime was committed by a person or persons unknown* (always written this way); *The committee shall consist of seven persons*. The use of *persons* to mean individual people is more common in American English than in British English.

For *chairperson* etc. see INCLUSIVE LANGUAGE.

phonetic symbols

The phonetic symbols used in this book are shown below with examples of the commonest correspondences between spelling and sound. There are many exceptions in English spelling.

The symbol /ː/ after a vowel indicates that it is long. With one exception, English vowels are either long or short; some vowels are always long and others are always short. The exception is words that end with a consonant and *-y*. In these words the *y* is pronounced /i/, a short version of vowel number 1: *very easily*: /ˈveriˈiːzɪli/. However, this is not of critical importance because there are no pairs of words that are differentiated in pronunciation by this difference. See THE.

The symbols ˈ and ˌ indicate that the following syllable has the primary or secondary stress respectively, e.g. *recollect* /ˌrekəˈlekt/.

monophthongs /ˈmɒnəfθɒŋz/

The standard numbering system for English vowels and their phonetic descriptions are as follows:

No.	Phonetic symbol	Example word(s)	Description (position and lip posture)
1	/iː/	see, sea, piece, seize, these	Front, unrounded, almost fully close
2	/ɪ/	sit, hymn	Front, slightly retracted, almost half-close
3	/e/	bed	Front, unrounded, half-close/half open
4	/æ/	cat	Front, unrounded, half-open/open
5	/ɑː/	arm, calm, pass (see A, A), heart	Almost fully back, unrounded, fully open
6	/ɒ/	hot, what	Back, rounded, half-open/open
7	/ɔː/	born, board, broad, court, bought, saw, Paul, walk, fall	Back, rounded, half-open/ half-close
8	/ʊ/	put, book	Back/central, rounded, close/half-close
9	/uː/	moon, do, move, group, cute, rude, lunar, due, fruit, new	Almost fully back, rounded, almost fully close
10	/ʌ/	run, love	Front/central, unrounded, open/half-open
11	/ɜː/	her, fur, sir	Central, unrounded, half-open/half-close
12	/ə/	Many. See SCHWA.	Central, unrounded, half-open/half-close

P

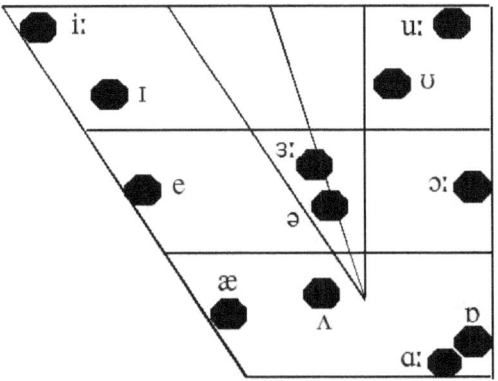

The quadrilateral on the left shows the approximate place of articulation of the English vowels. It represents the effective area of the mouth in which vowel sounds are produced by the different positions of the tongue. The dots represent the highest point of the tongue during the articulation of each of the vowels.

diphthongs /ˈdɪfθɒŋz/

1 /eɪ/ day, lain, made
2 /əʊ/ no, know*, rode, road
3 /aɪ/ my, die, high, ride
4 /aʊ/ how*, house
5 /ɔɪ/ boy, boil
6 /ɪə/ near*, beer, tea, here*
7 /eə/ hair, there*, tear*
8 /ʊə/ poor, sure, curious

*Note the two pronunciations of these groups of letters: -ow, -ere, -ear.

It is interesting to note that almost all the English vowels can be found in words of the pattern b*d: bad, bard (a poet, especially SHAKESPEARE), bed, bird, bid, bead, bod (slang for body, person), board, bud /bʌd/, (bud is pronounced /bʊd/ in the north of England), bead, booed, Bude (place name), Diphthongs: bide, bowed, bade, bode, bared, beard, Boyd (a surname).

See DOUBLE CONSONANTS.

consonants

	Example word(s)	Type	Position	VOICED/unvoiced
/p/	pen	plosive	bilabial	unvoiced
/b/	but	plosive	bilabial	voiced
/t/	top, missed	plosive	alveolar	unvoiced
/d/	dog	plosive	alveolar	voiced
/k/	cat, kid, quit, chemist	plosive	velar	unvoiced
/g/	get	plosive	velar	voiced
/f/	few, photo	fricative	labio-dental	unvoiced
/v/	voice	fricative	labio-dental	voiced
/θ/	thin	fricative	dental	unvoiced
/ð/	this	fricative	dental	voiced
/s/	sit, city, psychology	fricative	alveolar	unvoiced
/z/	zoo, plays, lives	fricative	alveolar	voiced
/ʃ/	she, station, mission	fricative	post-alveolar	unvoiced
/ʒ/	decision, measure	fricative	post-alveolar	voiced
/h/	he	fricative	glottal	unvoiced
/x/*	loch	fricative	velar	unvoiced
/tʃ/	chip, church	affricate	post-alveolar	unvoiced
/dʒ/	jar, judge	affricate	post-alveolar	voiced
/m/	man, bomb	nasal	bilabial	voiced
/n/	no, know, gnome, pneumatic	nasal	alveolar	voiced
/ŋ/	ring, ink	nasal	velar	voiced
/l/**	leg, bull	approximant	alveolar	voiced
/r/**	red, write	approximant	post-alveolar	voiced
/j/	yes	approximant	palatal	voiced
/w/	we, wheel	approximant	labio-velar	voiced

➤

P

*For /x/ see LOCH

**The letter *l*, shown here as /l/, has two variations (allophones), *clear l* and *dark l*. The pronunciation of *r* varies considerably throughout the countries of the English-speaking world.

See L, L and R, R.

glottal stop

The glottal stop /ʔ/ is not normally a recommended feature of standard English, though it is commonly found in words such as *button* /'bʌʔn/. It is used in a number of regional pronunciations, particularly in London, and is spreading throughout Britain. It is especially common in the speech of younger people.

See ESTUARY ENGLISH; PRONUNCIATION.

physician & physicist

A ***physician*** is a medical practitioner, commonly known as a doctor: *I'll ask the doctor; His sister's a doctor*. In the UK they are members of the Royal College of Physicians.

A ***physicist*** is someone who is qualified in physics.

pigeons

These are generally the grey and white birds found in cities; the *wood pigeon* is found in rural areas. The *dove* is the symbol of peace. In politics, *hawks* are people who favour an aggressive policy and *doves* are those who prefer peaceful means.

pineapple

A pineapple is a tropical FRUIT (*Ananas comosus*). It is unrelated to the pine tree or the apple.

place names

The meaning of many English place names is unknown or not immediately clear, though many have a suffix which is an old word meaning a farm or place where people lived; such suffixes are *-by*, *-ton*, *-don*, *-thorp(e)* and *-wick*. The Scandinavian influence on the north and east of England is clear in the large number of place names there that have *-by* (farm, town), *-thorp* (village), or *-thwaite* (clearing). Very few place names in England have CELTIC origins: *Thames*, *Avon* (from a Welsh word for river), *Wye*, and *Ouse* are among them. Names of Roman origin are those with *-port* (meaning *port*) or *-chester* or *-CESTER* (from Latin *castra*, a military camp). Names with *-cester* are pronounced /stə/: e.g. *Leicester* /'lestə/, *Worcester* /'wʊstə/. The suffix *-mouth* refers to the mouth of a river, *-ford* and *-bridge* show places where a river could be crossed, *-kirk* refers to a church, and *-HAVEN* is a harbour. In all such names, the stress is on the first part of the word. As they are COMPOUND NOUNS, *Clapham* and *Eastham* are pronounced /'klæpəm/ and /'iːstəm/; the *ph* and *th* do not make one sound as they usually do in English.

As with PERSONAL NAMES, place names can be pronounced in surprisingly strange ways: *Kirkby* /'kɜːbi/, *Maghull* /məˈgʌl/, *Scarisbrick* /'skeəzbrɪk/, *Belvoir* /'biːvə/, *Derby* /'dɑːbi/.

See KEYNES; MAGDALEN(E).

In Wales, Scotland, Ireland and Cornwall many place names are in the CELTIC LANGUAGES of those areas. Thus, in Wales many coastal towns begin with *Aber-* (river mouth) and the name of the river: *Aberystwyth*. Many Welsh places have Welsh and English names that are not always similar: *Caerdydd/Cardiff*, *Abertawe/Swansea*. Very many Welsh place names begin with *Llan-*, which means church and village (rather than the church building, which is *eglwys*) and is associated with the name of the village saint. Because of the nature of the Welsh language, in which initial consonants change in certain circumstances, it is not immediately clear that *Llanfair*, *Landdewi*, and *Llanbedr* refer to St Mary, St David, and St Peter respectively. Many such names (e.g. *Llangollen, Llandudno, Llanmadoc*) refer to Welsh saints in ANCIENT times, who were local hermits and are not recognised by the modern Church. For the pronunciation of Welsh *ll* see L, L.

Many Scottish mountains have *Ben* in their names from the Gaelic *beann*, a mountain. *Ben Nevis* (1,343 metres) is the highest mountain in the UK.

P

For English forms of place names in other countries see COUNTRIES AND NATIONALITY and FOREIGN WORDS AND NAMES.

See CELTS AND CELTIC; G, G | GH, GH.

planets
The names of the planets in order away from the sun are *Mercury, Venus, Earth, Mars, Jupiter, Saturn, Uranus* and *Neptune. Pluto* is no longer recognised as a planet.

playing cards
A normal *pack* (US *deck*) of 52 playing cards consists of four *suits*: ♣ *clubs*, ♦ *diamonds*, ♥ *hearts*, ♠ *spades*. Each suit has thirteen cards: *ace*, two to ten, *jack* or *knave, queen, king. Jack/knave, queen* and *king* are known as *face cards* or *court cards*, though the natural idea of the royal court is a corruption of the original name of *coat cards*, which refers to the decorative clothes of the people shown on these cards. Some games use a *joker*, which is a card that can represent any other card in the pack.

See ETYMOLOGY.

play (noun)
In the theatrical sense the word means *a dramatic representation* and does not need to be specified: *His new play;* SHAKESPEARE *wrote 37 plays; A play within a play.*

playwright
A *playwright* is a person who writes plays. The word is based on *wright*, a person who makes or builds things; it is not *playwrite*. *Wright* is found as a surname, but it is not used alone in its original meaning to describe an occupation; compounds such as *cartwright, shipwright, wheelwright* are found.

plenty
Usually found in the construction *plenty of*, it is in fact a pronoun meaning an excessive quantity of something. Note that it does not mean a large quantity in absolute terms. *I've got plenty of money* could mean *I have more money in my pocket than I can reasonably expect to spend this evening*. It does not necessarily mean *I am very rich*.

There is an adjective *plentiful*: *Oranges are plentiful at this time of year*.

plural consistency
Plural nouns are usually followed by consistent plurals: *They took their coats off; They left in their cars.*

plural forms
Almost all plurals in English end with *s*. After a sibilant sound an *e* is written if there is not already one there: *box/boxes; judge/judges*. In this case the *e* is pronounced.

See -ED AND -ES, PRONUNCIATION. Nouns ending with *-ful*: *cupful, handful* etc. make *cupfuls, handfuls* not *cupsful*. See -FUL & -LESS.

Gas and *bus* make the plurals *gases* and *buses*, not *gasses* and *busses*. See DOUBLE CONSONANTS.

compound nouns
Compound nouns normally add the *s* at the end: *assistant managers, grown-ups, gin-and tonics, handfuls*; but note *passers-by, Secretaries-General* (of the UNO), *brothers-in-law* (etc.) and *women doctors*. ➤

P

names
Personal names and place names make normal plurals: *three Johns; the Smiths and the Joneses; both Newcastles*. Proper names are considered to be unchangeable so exceptionally a final *y* is not changed: *two Marys; the Parrys*.

words ending with -*f*
Words ending with -*f* (single *f*) usually make plurals with -*ves*: *thief, thieves; wife, wives*, though *hoofs* and *roofs* are found and *proof* always makes the plural *proofs*. The usual plural of *dwarf* is *dwarfs* but J. R. R. Tolkien deliberately used the plural *dwarves* in The Lord of the Rings.

words ending with -*o*
Words ending with -*o* present a problem. Words that are felt to be fully English have -*oes*. Examples are *buffaloes, cargoes, dominoes, echoes, heroes, mosquitoes, potatoes, tomatoes, torpedoes, volcanoes*. Others such as *banjo, flamingo, fresco, grotto, mango* are variable between -*oes* and -*os*, while more unusual words (*aficionado, crescendo* /krɪˈʃendəʊ/, and *inferno*, for example) have -*os*, as does *logo*. There is variation among publishers' styles.

Where the *o* follows a vowel, the plural is -*os*: *cameos, embryos, kangaroos, studios, videos*.

Abbreviated words have -*os*: *demos* (demonstration), *euros, hippos* (hippopotamus), *kilos, photos, pianos* (pianoforte), *rhinos* (rhinoceros), *typos* (typographical error).

words ending with *y*
Words ending with a consonant followed by *y* make their plurals with -*ies*: *ladies, ferries* etc. See *i* and *y* under I, I. Words ending with -*ey* make their plurals with -*eys*: *abbeys, donkeys, journeys, monkeys* etc.

tomato's etc.
For plural forms that are often written incorrectly as ~~tomato's~~ etc. see *apostrophe* under PUNCTUATION.

plurals without *s*
irregular plurals
Common examples are *brother, brethren* (for fellow members of a religious organisation, not for FAMILY RELATIONSHIPS); *child, children; foot, feet; goose, geese; louse, lice; man, men; mouse, mice; ox, oxen;* PENNY, *pence;* PERSON, *people; sheep, sheep; tooth, teeth; woman* /ˈwʊmən/, *women* /ˈwɪmɪn/.

Hunters and zoologists often treat the names of wild animals as uncountable when thinking of the general idea of the animal: *We saw lion, giraffe and elephant*, but as countable when thinking of individuals: *a herd of fourteen elephants; One male and three female lions. Sheep, deer* and *cod* never make plural forms.

Mongoose is not a compound of *goose* and makes the plural *mongooses*.

Cannon and *fish* do not usually change in the plural; OFFSPRING and *sperm* never change. *Craft* does not change when it refers to BOATS AND SHIPS but it has the regular plural *crafts* when referring to practical artistic activities.

Latin, Greek, and Hebrew words
As knowledge of Latin and Greek decreases in English-speaking countries, the natural ability to make and use plurals of words from these languages is disappearing. However, some of these forms are still used. Latin words make their plurals as in Latin when used scientifically: *formula, formulae; larva, larvae;* RADIUS, *radii; stimulus, stimuli; bacterium, bacteria; consortium, consortia; genus, genera* but with -*s* as they become more accepted as EVERYDAY English words: *albums, areas, circuses, museums*. For *consortium, maximum*, and *minimum* both forms (-*a* and -*ums* are used). For ETYMOLOGICAL reasons *referendums* should be used (it is a Latin gerund, not a second declension noun), though *referenda* is quite common. *Octopus* is not a Latin word and must have the English plural *octopuses*. *Syllabus* is not a Latin word and must have *syllabuses*. *Virus* has the plural *viruses* for both medical and computer viruses. *Series* and *species* /ˈspiːʃiːz/ do not change as the final *s* is

from the Latin original: *one series/species*; *two series/species*. *Alumnus* and *alumna* are respectively former male and female members of a university; they make the plurals *alumni* and *alumnae* respectively. Books have *indexes* but statistical indicators are *indices*; books have *appendices* but people have *appendixes*.

Greek words normally have Greek plurals: *analysis, analyses; crisis, crises; thesis, theses* but *metropolis* makes *metropolises; criterion, criteria; tetrahedron* etc., *tetrahedra* or *tetrahedrons; phenomenon, phenomena*; but *electron, proton, neutron*, and *pentagon* etc. make regular plurals.

When plurals are required (see the comment on wild animals above), *hippopotamus* and *rhinoceros* make *hippopotamuses* and *rhinoceroses*.

The Hebrew words *cherub* /'tʃerʌb/ and *kibbutz* make *cherubim* and *kibbutzim*.

agenda, stamina, bacteria, data and media

Agenda and *stamina* are singular nouns in English although they are plural in Latin.

Bacteria is the plural of *bacterium*. Although the plural is more common, the singular must be used where appropriate: *the E. coli bacterium*.

In Latin *data* and *media* are plural and are usually used in the plural in English. *Data* has the singular *datum* in English but *item of data* or even *number* is commonly used as a singular. Often, especially in computing, *data* is regarded as an uncountable noun on the analogy of INFORMATION: *This data is new*. However, in academia it is generally plural.

MEDIA is the Latin plural of *medium* but the word is sometimes used in the singular when it refers to the communication media: press, radio, TV. This usage is not generally accepted.

nouns only used in the plural

pairs

Some things consist of two equal parts which are always used together. Examples are some tools and instruments such as *binoculars*, GLASSES, *pliers, scales*, scissors*, SPECTACLES, *tweezers*, parts of the body such as *ears, eyes* and *feet*, and CLOTHES such as *braces, gloves*, JEANS, *knickers, (under)pants, pyjamas, shorts, tights, trousers, (swimming) trunks*.

*Scales are a balance consisting of two balanced pans for weighing things. However, the name is also used for other machines that weigh, e.g. *bathroom scales*.

These words only exist in the plural: *Those scissors are mine; 'Where are your new trousers?' 'They're on the bed'; She's got (some) new glasses*.

When a number is required, we use *pair of*: *She's got a new pair of glasses; I've bought three pairs of jeans*.

Singular and plural can be mixed: *'I bought this pair last week.'*
'How much was it/were they?

See COMPASS(ES).

pluralia tantum

Some words are only used in the plural, or have a different meaning in singular and plural. They include:

make *amends*	*brains* (intellectual ability)
arms (weapons)	*clothes*
in *arrears*	*clubs, diamonds, hearts, spades* (suits of
arts/humanities (academic discipline)	PLAYING CARDS, but *play a club*)
under the *auspices* of	*congratulations*
bowels, intestines (but the large/small *intestine*)	*contents* (of a book etc.)
	credentials ▶

P

CUSTOMS (examination on entering a country)
damages
earnings, funds (money)
fumes
GUTS (intestines, courage)
heads and tails (in tossing a coin)
heavens (in the exclamation *Good heavens*)
honours (UNIVERSITY course)
mains (supply of water, gas, electricity)
manners (social behaviour)
MINUTES (the record of a meeting)
oats
ODDS (chances)
outskirts
pains (to take pains)
particulars (details)
premises
regards (friendly wishes)
remains (the part that remains of a building, meal etc.)
savings (money that has been saved)
stairs
surroundings
thanks
troops
tropics (the area in general but the *Tropic* of Cancer/Capricorn)
valuables (valuable items)
wages
wakes (holiday)
WITS (*CLEVER) (intelligence, ability: *live by your wits*)
writings (literary WORK).

For nationality words (*the Spanish* etc.) see COUNTRIES AND NATIONALITIES. See NEWS; NOUNS | SINGULAR WITH –S.

police

There are 43 independent police /pliːs/ forces in England and Wales and one for all of Scotland. In England and Wales they are under the control of COUNTY or CITY councils or, in some areas, groups of such councils. They are also subject to control by elected Police and Crime Commissioners who serve for four years; in London and Manchester this role is assumed by the elected mayors. Each police force has its own specialist units in traffic, anti-terrorism, serious crime, and other aspects of police work. The *Criminal Investigation Department* (CID) are the detectives in each police force; they work in *plain clothes* i.e. not in uniform. The *Special Branch* of each police force deals with criminal threats of a political nature. Although each police force is independent, and there is considerable rivalry between forces, there is formal co-operation among the Chief Police Officers of the different forces and within the HOME OFFICE (Interior Ministry) and Scottish Government. There is no nationally controlled police force operating generally in the UK, although MI5 AND MI6 exist to combat national and international serious and organised crime. There are also some forces with national responsibility for specific issues. Two examples are the *British Transport Police*, which operates solely on the railway network and related property and the *UK Atomic Energy Authority Police* which is responsible for the security of nuclear installations and transport.

British police routinely wear body armour and carry various types of baton (sticks), tear gas or pepper sprays, and handcuffs; they are not usually armed with firearms (except in Northern Ireland) but a range of firearms, including tasers, is available for use in certain situations and some police, especially those working as bodyguards or protecting government or diplomatic buildings, are always armed. Increasingly, police officers on normal patrol duties are armed.

Scotland Yard is the name of a building in the Whitehall area of London that was used by the followers of the Scottish King James VI when he went to London in 1603 to take the English throne as James I (see ENGLAND, A BRIEF HISTORY) and was the official residence of Scottish kings in London; that is the origin of the name. In 1842 it was used as the headquarters of the Metropolitan (London) Police, who moved to New Scotland Yard in Parliament Street in 1890 and to their present office in New Scotland Yard in 1967. The police of the CITY OF LONDON are independent of the Metropolitan Police.

Scotland Yard is the name of the headquarters of the Metropolitan Police; it does not have, and never has had, any national authority. However, before the police reorganisation in the mid to late sixties many smaller local forces did not have the resources for major investigations and needed to call in the specialists from the large London force; this is how it has gained its international reputation through detective stories and films.

Some police forces in older counties are known officially as the *Constabulary* (*Lancashire Constabulary*, *Hampshire Constabulary* etc.) Those in London and in more recently formed counties where a number of smaller forces were combined are known simply as police forces (*Metropolitan Police*, *Merseyside Police*, *West Midlands Police*). In Northern Ireland the *Royal Ulster Constabulary* changed its name to the *Police Service of Northern Ireland* in 2001.

The rank structure of a police force outside London is as follows:
Chief Constable
Deputy Chief Constable
Assistant Chief Constable
Chief Superintendent
Superintendent
Chief Inspector
Inspector
Sergeant
Constable

The Metropolitan Police is headed by a *Commissioner* with *Deputy* and *Assistant Commissioners*, as is the CITY OF LONDON Police. These forces also have the rank of *Commander* between Chief Superintendent and Commissioner. CID officers have the ranks *Detective Constable*, *Detective Sergeant* etc. up to *Detective Chief Superintendent*.

The building in which police officers work and where members of the public can find them is called a *police station*. It is usually indicated by a blue lamp above the main door.

Although police is a GROUP NOUN it is treated as plural when it refers to the officers as a group: *Three hundred police were on duty at the football match; The police are coming; Have the police arrested anyone? It was the police who were in difficulties.* See CLEFT SENTENCES. It is singular only on the occasions that it is used alone to mean police force or system of policing: *The Metropolitan Police is headed by a Commissioner (above); Merseyside Police has announced that ...;* RURITANIA *has a powerful secret police.*

Note:
The police officer who arrested the murderer was congratulated.
The police (officers) who arrested the murderer were congratulated.
The police force which arrested the murderer was congratulated.

The term *police officer* is now used instead of *policeman*. See INCLUSIVE LANGUAGE.

Traffic wardens are civilians employed by local authorities to control parking and place tickets on illegally parked cars. They are not police officers and have no police powers.

Many police forces employ uniformed civilian staff to assist with routine patrol duties and in dealing with minor offences. Depending upon the force, they are known as *Community Support Officers*, *Community Safety Officers*, *Community Patrol Assistants* or similar titles. They have no police powers and are unable to arrest or search suspects. They wear uniforms that are in many cases similar to those of regular police officers, but they do not wear the police officers' distinctive chequered bands on their headgear.

policy & politics etc.

Policy /ˈpɒlɪsi/ is the course of action or strategy adopted by a government, company, other organisation, or an individual. A document stating the terms and conditions of an insurance contract is also called a *policy*.

Politics /ˈpɒlɪtɪks/ is the science and art of government at any level from international affairs to the most local decisions. It can also refer to the power and status relationships involved in *office politics*, *committee politics* etc. Aristotle wrote a book called *Politics*. A *politician* /pɒlɪˈtɪʃən/ is a person who is involved in *politics*. A *polity* /ˈpɒlɪti/ is a particular form of civil organisation, administration

P

or government of a state or of an organised society that does not have the full mechanism of a state. The usual adjective is *political*: *political activity, political parties*; the other adjective *politic* /ˈpɒlɪtɪk/ means wise, tactful, diplomatic: *A politic decision*.

Polite means courteous and well-behaved in dealing with other people.

These words have three different origins:

The words connected with politics and state organisation, including this meaning of *policy*, come ultimately from the Greek *polis* meaning a city; the word POLICE /pliːs/ also has this origin.

The word *policy* as used in insurance terms is from French, and probably ultimately from Greek *apodeixis* meaning *evidence, proof*.

The adjective *polite* comes originally from the Latin word *politus*, which means *polished*.

poll

This is an old word meaning a *head*; it is pronounced /pəʊl/. It is not used in this sense now but is found in some expressions. It is used to mean an ELECTION because the easiest way to count people is to count heads; this was done before elections in Britain became secret in 1872. The word is now commonly used in *opinion polls*, where a number of people are *polled* to provide a representative sample of public opinion. A *poll tax* is a tax charged equally on every person. The introduction of such a tax in Britain (1 April 1989 in Scotland, 1 April 1990 in England; withdrawn in 1993) was extremely unpopular. It was not, as was reported in several newspapers around the world, a POOL *tax*.

There is a legal process called *deed poll*, which can be used to change one's surname legally. This word is indirectly connected with *poll* meaning *head*.

A *redpoll* is a bird which has a red head.

Poll /pɒl/ (short for *Polly*) is a familiar form of the name Mary. It is also used as a general name for a parrot.

pool

A *pool* is a small body of water occurring naturally. Pools suitable for swimming in are called swimming pools, but now swimming pools are usually artificial.

A *pool* is also the result of people contributing money or other resources to a common fund. Businesses may *pool* their capital; friends on holiday together may pay money into a *pool* for food and other common expenses. *The pools* (usually plural) is a system of betting on football matches where the money paid is *pooled* and distributed to the winner or winners; this idea also lies behind the name of the game *pool*, which is similar to billiards and snooker.

Some companies and other large organisations have a *car pool* where cars are provided in common for employees, a group of friends or neighbours might organise a car pool to take each other's children to school, and journalists in difficult conditions might form a *pool* to exchange information that they have gathered.

Although these two words (pool of water and common RESOURCES) have different origins, they are associated in the minds of many people.

poorly

This is:

- the adverb from the adjective poor: He sang poorly; This house is poorly built.
- an ADJECTIVE WITH -LY meaning ILL: I feel poorly; She has been poorly for some time.

popular

This refers to the people in general as in *a popular movement, a popular uprising, the popular press*; it also means *well liked*: *a popular teacher, a popular singer*. POLITICIANS *(*POLICY & POLITICS* ETC.*)* are concerned with *popularity*. *Pop music* is popular music.

252

P

port

ships

On a SHIP, the left-hand side facing forward is *port* and the right-hand side is *starboard*. These words are sometimes used for aeroplanes as well.

Like a harbour, a *port* is the place where ships make contact with the land for shelter or to load and unload, but unlike a harbour the name can be used to refer to the town or city as a whole, and can be part of the town's name: *Port Erin, Bridport*. A *free port* is an area near the harbour or docks or near an airport where goods are exempt from customs duty and other taxes.

A *port* was an opening in the side of a ship used for loading or for the guns. Initially the left-hand side of a ship was called *larboard*, but this was so similar in sound to starboard that it was more convenient to use the word *port* for the left-hand side of the ship because it was the side facing the port when the ship was in harbour. The ship was steered with a long pole on the right-hand side so it was convenient to have the port (the opening) on the left-hand side, and to place this side against the port (i.e. the land) to keep the steering pole free. Either of these reasons may be why the left-hand side of the ship is called *port*. A *porthole* is the round window in the side of a ship.

wine

Port is a strong wine from Portugal which was shipped from Oporto (which means *the port* in Portuguese). It is usually red, though white port is made; it is traditionally drunk in Britain after a meal. The Roman name for Oporto was Portascale, which gives the name of the country.

porter

All of the above definitions derive ultimately from the Latin *porta* meaning a gate. This is also the origin of the word *porter* as the person responsible for guarding the gate of a town or building. However, a different origin (Latin *portare*) gives the word *porter* as someone who carries things, especially luggage at railway stations and airports. *Porter* is also the name of a kind of dark beer that is not common nowadays. It is believed that its name comes from the fact that it was drunk by the porters who carried goods in towns and cities.

portal

A *portal* is a large impressive door or gate.

portend & portent

Portend is the verb and *portent* is the noun.

See ASCEND; EXTEND.

posh

This means *very good, stylISH, fashionable*: *a posh car, restaurant* etc. It can also mean associated with the upper class: *a posh accent, a posh school*. As well as being an adjective it is also an ADVERB WITHOUT -LY. In parts of Britain where there is a strong regional accent *talking posh* means speaking in RECEIVED PRONUNCIATION, which is associated with the upper classes; this distinction is becoming less strong as regional accents become more acceptable.

The origin of the word is uncertain but despite popular belief it is not derived from the initials of PORT *out starboard home*, the more expensive (because less sunny) side of the SHIP on a VOYAGE *(*TRAVEL)* between Britain and India in the days of the Empire.

See ETYMOLOGY.

possessive

The word *genitive* is also used, especially with reference to GRAMMATICAL CASE.

English has two ways of showing possession with nouns. One corresponds to the Old English genitive case, while the other (periphrastic) form uses the preposition *of*. The genitive (sometimes, but not in Britain, known as the Saxon genitive), is made with *-'s* or *-s'* (for the use and position of the apostrophe see APOSTROPHE, POSSESSION under PUNCTUATION). This is used with human beings

P

and animals: *John's car; the teachers' cars; the dog's bed; the fish's tail.* It can be doubled: *My neighbour's uncle's car.* It can be predicative: *This book is Mary's; That car is the doctor's.*

This genitive can be used with royal numerals: *Henry VIII's wives* (spoken as Henry the Eighth's wives); *Pope John XXIII's reforms*; and it can be attached to noun phrases: *The man next door's car; The King of Spain's daughter.*

An adjective qualifies the noun which immediately follows it, even if that noun is a genitive. Compare:
1 *John's new car* (John, as a proper noun, has no article and is the DETERMINER for car.)
2 *The teacher's new car* (the teacher has a new car).
3 *The new teacher's car* (the new teacher has a car).

In **2** and **3** the article *the* refers to *teacher*; *teacher's* is the determiner for *car*.

it is used
- with time expressions: the day's journey, a week's holiday, two years' work, today's newspaper, September's phone bill.
- with sake: for heaven's, pity's, goodness', old times' sake (as well as personal forms: for my father's etc. sake).
- in certain expressions:
  The church is a stone's throw away (very close).
  Keep him at arm's length (at a distance).
  He was at death's door (close to death, perhaps a personification of death).
  I'll keep her out of harm's WAY (safe).
  I want my money's worth/ten dollars' WORTH (with *worth*).
  I can see it in my mind's eye (in my imagination).

Although the passive BY is used with artistic works, the possessive can also be used: *Othello by William Shakespeare; Shakespeare's Othello; Van Gogh's Sunflowers; Beethoven's Pastoral Symphony; Branagh's Hamlet.* (Kenneth Branagh both played the part of Hamlet and directed the film.)

It seems that the use of the genitive is increasing slowly in modern English: *Africa's main problem, the car's windscreen wipers.* However, when the RELATIONSHIP is a connection rather than possession the periphrastic *(of)* form must be used: *the top/bottom of the hill; the front/back of the bus; the city of London.*

Partitive genitives clearly cannot have the *-'s*: *a bottle of wine, a dose of medicine.*

It can clarify postmodification:
The doctor's son who lives near me. (The son lives near me.)
The son of the doctor who lives near me. (The doctor lives near me.)

double possessive
Mary's brother lives in Italy suggests that she has only one brother. If it is necessary to make it clear that she has several brothers, one of whom lives in Italy, there are two possibilities: *One of Mary's (three) brothers lives in Italy* and *A brother of Mary's lives in Italy.*

The second is known as the *double possessive* or the *post-genitive*. If a pronoun is used instead of the proper name, it is the independent form of the possessive pronoun: *A brother of mine, yours, his, hers* etc. This construction is limited to personal possessors: *A wheel of my car's* is not possible. This construction makes it possible to distinguish between *A picture of Picasso* (one showing him) and *A picture of Picasso's* (one belonging to him). *A picture by Picasso* is one painted by him.

possessive with two people
Note the difference between:
John and Mary's house is in Mill St. (John and Mary live in the same house.)
and
John's and Mary's houses are in Mill St. (They live in different houses.)

pound

This is both a unit of currency and a unit of weight. The two are connected; originally the money value of the pound was that of one pound weight of silver. Throughout history the pound has varied in weight. Now it is 454 grams. The abbreviation for pound weight is *lb (8lb)* and for money *£ (£8)*. Both these abbreviations refer to the Latin word *libra*. See STERLING; WEIGHTS AND MEASURES.

A *pound* (a separate word) is a place for keeping stray animals. Now it is also used for the place to which the POLICE take badly parked cars.

As a verb *to POUND (*HIT)* (a separate word from the preceding two) means to *hit* or beat something heavily and repeatedly.

practice & practise

In British English *practice* is the noun and *practise* is the verb. The noun *practice* gives the adjective *practical*. This difference can be remembered with reference to ADVICE and *advise*, where the spelling reflects the pronunciation. In many cases, however, this distinction is not observed.

In American English *practice* is used for noun and verb.

See ADVICE; LICENCE; PROPHECY.

pray, praise & prey

pray /preɪ/

This is the act of communicating a wish to GOD, a saint, or other object of worship. A *prayer* is the way in which the wish is expressed; it is not the person who is praying.

praise /preɪz/

To *praise* somebody or something is to say how wonderful or excellent that person or thing is. It has a religious use *praise God and the saints* but the word is unrelated to *pray*. The noun also is *praise*.

prey /preɪ/

Animals that kill and eat others *prey* on them: *Lions prey on antelopes*. As a noun, the antelope is the lion's natural *prey*. Animals that *prey* on others are *predators*; birds that do so are known as *birds of prey*.

precedent & president

These are pronounced *precedent* /ˈprɛsɪdənt/ and *president* /ˈprɛzɪdənt/.

prefer

The basic construction is *prefer X to Y*: *I prefer tea to coffee*.

The comparison does not have to be stated directly: *Most people had coffee but some preferred (to drink) tea; I prefer to stand even if there are PLENTY of seats*.

Usually, when *prefer* is followed by a verb, the verb is the infinitive with *to* as in these examples, but when the continuing nature of the action is strong the gerund can be used: *Most people were having coffee but some preferred (drinking) tea; I prefer standing even if there are plenty of seats*.

It is possible to say *I prefer standing to sitting even if there are plenty of seats* but it is clear that a sentence like ~~I prefer to stand to to sit even if there are plenty of seats~~ is ridiculous. The solution is *I prefer to stand RATHER than sit even if there are plenty of seats* or *I would rather stand than sit even if there are plenty of seats* but not ~~I prefer to stand than sit even if there are plenty of seats~~ or ~~I prefer to stand to sitting even if there are plenty of seats~~.

prefixes

For doubling of consonants in prefixes (*sufficient, oppose* etc.) see DOUBLE CONSONANTS WITH PREFIXES. Negative prefixes (*un-* and *in-*) are described separately below. For the use of hyphens with prefixes see PUNCTUATION | HYPHENS.

ante- means *before*: *antecedent, antenatal*. It is less common than *pre-*. (Be careful not to confuse *ante-* and *anti-*.)

P

anti- and *contra-* mean *against*: *anti-abortion, anti-European, contraceptive*. Of the two, *anti-* is more common.

BI- /baɪ/, *tri-* /traɪ/ and *quadri-* /'kwɒdri/ mean *two, three,* and *four* respectively: *bilingual, tripartite, quadrilateral*. See BI-; BIANNUAL & BIENNIAL.

co- means *with, joint*: *co-author, co-driver*, a *co-educational school* is for boys and girls together.

counter- also means *against* or *in competition with* something: *counter-attack, counterbalance, counter-espionage*; *counterpart* is an equivalent in a different situation: *The Prime Minister and his Spanish counterpart*.

dis- is a prefix expressing negation. A *disobedient* person is one who does not obey. More commonly, however, it expresses not a direct negative but the idea that is no longer valid. An *unused* toy has never been used but a *disused* railway line (one that has fallen into disuse (for pronunciation see USE)) is no longer used; a *dislocated* shoulder is one that has left its normal location; *displaced* PERSONS were people who had to leave their homes after World War II (such people are now called refugees); a *disinfectant* removes existing infection. Sometimes it is not clear whether an absolute negation or a removal of a quality is meant. Have a *disloyal servant* and a *disordered mind* always been so or have they changed their status? See DISINTERESTED (*INTERESTED*). *De-* is similar to *dis-*: *decentralise, destabilise*.

ex- means *out of* in Latin: *exclude, exempt, expatriate* but often this is not obvious in the meaning in English (*exercise, experience*). It also means *former*: *ex-president, ex-boyfriend, ex-Yugoslavia*. In this meaning it is always hyphenated. *My ex is my former PARTNER*.

extra- means *outside*. *Extra-curricular activities* are those that are offered in addition to a school's normal CURRICULUM. *Extraterrestrial beings* come from outside the earth; and something *extraordinary* is outside ordinary experience.

FORE- means *in front*: *forearm, forehead* or *preceding*: *forefather, forego*, or *future*: *foresee, foretell, forecast*. It is found in *before*.

in- has two meanings as a prefix. In addition to being a negative prefix it can be *in* (the preposition): *innate* is a synonym (and a CALQUE) of *inborn*.

inter- means *between*: *interchange, international*. Do not to confuse *intra-* and *inter-*. *Intradepartmental* communication takes place within one department but *interdepartmental* communication takes place between different departments.

intra- means *inside*. *Intravenous* medicine is given directly inside the vein.

mal- means that something is done badly: *a malnourished child* is not properly fed. *Malware* is software that is intended to damage computers, viruses for example.

mis- means that something is done wrongly: *misunderstand, mishear* /mɪsˈhɪə/, *mislead, mistake*. See MISCARRIAGE.

multi- and *poly-* mean *many*: they are Latin and Greek respectively: *multilingual, multiplication, multi-access*; *poly-* is used widely in philosophy and chemistry: *polyglot, polytheism, polygamy, polyester, polypropylene*.

non- has a negating effect. It can be added to nouns: *non-availability, non-recognition, non-driver, non-scientist* and to adjectives: *non-German, non-military, non-fattening, non-English-speaking*. It is usually followed by a hyphen but *nonconformist, nonentity* and *nonsense* are written unhyphenated.

over- means *excessive(ly)*: *overpay, overcook*. *Overtime* is time worked by an employee in addition to the normal contracted hours.

post- means *after*: *post-war, postmodern*.

pre- means *before*: *pre-war, precondition*.

re- means *again*: *reappear, recheck, rewrite*. It is a free formation and is very common. In some words it has a meaning of mutual or opposed action: *react, repel, resist*. It is hyphenated before an *e*: *re-elect*, and to show that it has the literal meaning of doing something again; in this case it is clearly pronounced /riː/. To *reform* /rɪˈfɔːm/ something is to improve it, and to *re-form* /riːfɔːm/ (equal stress) it is to form it again. To *recover* something is to get it back after a time, and to *re-cover* something is to cover it again. *Relaying* information is different from *re-laying* a carpet. To *resent* is to feel bitter or indignant and *re-sent* refers to something that has been sent again

sub- means *below*: *subordinate, subcommittee, submarine, subatomic.*

under- can mean *insufficiently*: *underpay, undercook*; it sometimes has its literal meaning: *undercut, underlie, undermine.*

Obviously, there are words that begin with these letters in which they are not prefixes.

negative prefixes

For *non-* see above.

The two negative prefixes in English are *un-* and *in-* (with *il-*, *im-* and *ir-*: see below). *Un-* is native to the English language and *in-* comes from Latin. However, this is of no use in deciding which prefix to use, since very many words of Latin origin have negative forms with *un-*: *unexciting, undecided, unstable.* There are, however, certain points that can be mentioned:

Prefixes are not used with short adjectives or ADVERBS WITHOUT -LY that have specific opposite forms: ~~unslow(ly)~~, ~~unfast~~; ~~unthick~~, ~~unthin~~.

-un:

un- is used with past participles: *undecided, uninterested, uncompleted*, and present participles: *unceasing, uncomprehending.* Sometimes these forms can include prepositions: *an uncalled-for comment, unheard-of behaviour.*

un- is now the usual form for making new negative forms.

-in:

in- etc. (see *inflammable* below) is used with most words ending with *-ant/-ent* and *-ance/y*, *-ence/y*: *incessant, infrequent, irrelevance, inconsistency*. But *unadjacent, unambivalent, unapparent, unbalance, unconfident, unimportance, unobservant, unpleasant, unrepentant.*

Inflammable is not a negative. See FLAMMABLE.

in- is not used with words that already have *in-*: *unintelligent, uninformed* are the only possibilities.

Words beginning with *l*, *m* and *r* that would make negatives with *in-* make it with *il-*, *im-* and *ir-*: *illegal, immodest, irresponsible.* The consonant is doubled in these cases as it is assimilated by the following consonant. See DOUBLE CONSONANTS (PREFIXES).

in- is also a Latin prefix meaning *in*, therefore not all words beginning with *in-* are negative: *innate, inoculate.*

Prefixes can vary in different forms of the same word: *unable, inability; uncivil, incivility; unequal, inequality; unjust, injustice; unquiet, inquietude; imbalance, unbalanced; unstable, instability, destabilise.*

There are these cases where nouns with *un-* are not used:
Disconnected, unconnected, disconnection; ~~unconnection.~~
Disinterested, uninterested, disinterest; ~~uninterest.~~
Dissatisfied, unsatisfied, dissatisfaction; ~~unsatisfaction.~~

premiss & premises

These two words are variants of each other (see DOUBLETS); normally they are used as follows but the second is sometimes used with the former meaning.

A ***premiss*** (or *premise*) is a statement that logically leads to another. If the *premiss* of an argument is false, the argument will be INVALID or untrue. Its plural is *premisses*. *Premise* is also used with this meaning.

Premises (plural) is a formal term for a house or any other building with its land, outbuildings etc. It is a rather formal, legal word.

P

prepositions
Some words listed below as adjectives are past participles; they can of course be followed by the word *by* to introduce an agent in the passive voice (st. = something; sb. = somebody).

with adjectives

absent from
accustomed to
afraid of
ahead of
allergic to
amazed at
amused at
angry about st.
angry with/at sb.
annoyed about st.
annoyed with/at sb.
answerable for
anxious about
ashamed of
astonished at
averse to
aware of
bad (etc.) at
bad for
blind to
bored with
brilliant at
capable of
certain about
certain of
clever at
close to
concerned about
concerned with
confident of
conscious of
contented with
contrary to
convenient for
crazy about
critical of
curious about
delighted with
dependent on
different from
disappointed with
disgusted with
doubtful about
due to
eager for
excited about
experienced in
faithful to

familiar with
famous for
fed up with
fit for
fond of
for free
frightened of
full of
glad about
good (etc.) at
good for
for good
grateful for
guilty of
happy about
hesitant about
honest about
hopeless at
independent of
inferior to
intent on
interested in
jealous of
keen on
late for
mad about
married to
mistaken about
new to
patient with
peculiar to
pleased with
positive about
prepared for
proud of
qualified for
ready for
responsible for
sad about
safe from
satisfied with
scared of
selfish about
sensible about
sensitive about
sensitive to
separate from
serious about

shocked at
sick of
sick with
similar to
sincere about
in short
sorry about st.
sorry for sb.
suitable for
superior to
sure about
sure of
surprised at
suspicious about
terrified of
thankful for st.
thankful to sb.
thrilled about
tired of
uneasy about
used to
useful for
weak at
worried about
wrong about

before nouns
by accident
in advance
on account of
in addition to
in advance
by agreement with
in answer to
by appointment
on approval
by arrangement
on arrival
by association
under attack
in attendance
on average
on balance
on behalf of
at the beginning of
in the beginning
in brief
in business
on business

out of business
in cash
out of character
in charge of
by cheque
by credit card
in the circumstances
under the
  circumstances
in common with
in company with
in comparison with
in competition with
on condition that
in connection with
under consideration
out of control
under control
under cover
in credit
by chance
by choice
in danger
out of danger
out of date
up to date
by day
in debt
without delay
on demand
in demand
in difficulties
in duplicate
on duty
off duty
at ease
at the end
in the end
for example
in exchange for
in fact
in fashion
out of fashion
in favour of
on file
on fire
under fire
on foot

P

in future	at the moment	on purpose	in theory
in gear	in motion	on the radio	on time
in general	by name	in (out of) reach	in time
under guarantee	by nature	in receipt of	at times
on guard	in need of	on receipt of	in town
for good	need for	with reference to	out of town
in half	by night	with regard to	on trial
by hand	at night	in relation to	on top of
in hand	for nothing	for rent	in touch with
on hand	at short notice	in reply to	on tour
by heart	on occasion	in respect of	on trust
on heat	on offer	in response to	in turn(s)
for hire	in operation	at rest	in use
on holiday	in my opinion	in return for	out of use
at home	by order	at risk	on vacation
in honour of	in order (to)	for sale	in vain
in ink	out of order	on sale	in view of
for instance	in pain	from scratch	by virtue of
by invitation	in particular	at sea	at war
on a journey	on paper	in search of	in the way
on land	at peace	in season	on the way
at last	in pencil	out of season	on the whole
by law	in person	in sight	at work
at least	by phone	on sight	in work
at length	in place	at speed	out of work
at liberty	out of place	in spite of	in writing
for life	from my point of view	on stage	after nouns
in line with	in possession of	in/out of step	affection for
on loan	in practice	in/out of stock	admiration for
in the long run	out of practice	in store	demand for
in love	at present	on strike	interest in
in luck	in private	in style	lack of
by mail	in principle	supply of	love of
on the market	on principle	by surprise	market for
by means of	in progress	in tears	
in/out of mind	in public	on the telephone	
by mistake		on television	

double prepositions

Sentences such as these, where the adverb particle of a MULTI-WORD VERB is followed by a preposition that is the same word, are perfectly correct: *I didn't know I was being looked at at the time; You must hand your work in in the morning break.* The adverb has a full (strong) pronunciation but the preposition is weak (unstressed). For prepositions with time expressions see TIME.

prepositions at the end (deferred prepositions)

There is a tradition in English prescriptive GRAMMAR that a sentence should never end with a preposition. As with SPLIT INFINITIVES this rule is based on Latin grammar, where a preposition must stand before the noun (the name *preposition* derives from this requirement). However, this is inappropriate to the nature of English as a Germanic language, and it is very common in English to find a preposition as the last word in a sentence.

This occurs:
1 in passive sentences:
   No-one has looked at this letter.
   This letter has not been looked at.

➤

P

2. in sentences such as:
   It is interesting to talk to him.
   He is interesting to talk to.
   It is not worth worrying about that possibility.
   That possibility is not worth worrying about.

3. in WH- QUESTIONS with prepositional verbs:
   What are you talking about?
   Who are you looking at?
   Who did you sell your house to?
   Whose car are you standing next to?

4. in RELATIVE CLAUSES:
   This is the book (that) I was talking about.
   That's the girl (whom/that) I was looking at.
   He's the man (that/whom) I sold my house to.
   It's my car (that) you're standing next to.

Because of the tradition of prescriptive grammar, some people prefer a different form for the examples in **3** and **4** above, especially in a formal style:

3a. in WH- QUESTIONS with prepositional verbs:
   About what are you talking?
   At whom are you looking?
   To whom did you sell your house?
   Next to whose car are you standing?

4a. in relative clauses:
   This is the book about which I was talking.
   That's the girl at whom I was looking.
   He's the man to whom I sold my house.
   The car next to which you are standing is mine.

However, the sentences in **3a** and **4a** are pedantic and pompous and should not be used.

Not all prepositions can be deferred: *The door we came in through* is acceptable (*through* has its spatial meaning) but ~~*The person whose carelessness the money was lost through cannot now be found*~~ is not acceptable (*through* means *because of*). This must be *The person through whose carelessness the money was lost cannot now be found.*

Complex prepositions are not usually deferred: ~~*The person whose carelessness the money was lost because of cannot now be found*~~.

present & presently

Present refers to current events or time; *at present* means *now*.

Presently means *soon, shortly*. It is not the adverb corresponding to *present* (use *currently*). However, its American meaning of *now, at present* seems to be becoming more common in Britain.

present tenses

present simple

The *present simple* is identical to the infinitive except in the third person singular which usually adds *s*: *reads, works, says*.

If the last sound is a SIBILANT it adds *es*: *kisses, buzzes, washes, judges*. (Note that this is a phonetic rule that applies equally to noun plurals. See -ED & -ES, PRONUNCIATION.)

-es is also added if the last letter is a pronounced vowel (*go, goes; fly, flies*). See I AND Y *(*I)*.

It is used to describe:

- states that existed in the past, exist in the present, and are expected to exist in the future: *Trees have green leaves; We live in Barcelona; Zebras live in Africa*; and habitual or repeated actions:

How often do you go to the cinema?; He drinks black coffee; He works in the library. These actions are not necessarily taking place at the time of speaking: *He drinks black coffee* means that this is his habit; it says nothing about whether he is drinking black coffee at present. Frequency adverbs (e.g. *often, never, usually, twice a week, every year*) can be added to the habitual present: *I go to the cinema twice a month; He drinks black coffee for breakfast every morning; He usually works in the library.*

- phenomena that are always true: Water boils at 100° C; Falling objects accelerate at 9.8 m/sec^2.
- instantaneous actions such as commentaries: *Smith passes to Jones, and Jones scores* (a football commentary); *I enclose a cheque for £360* (a commentary on one's own action).
- acts that are performed by the utterance of the words: I apologise for what I said; I ask you to welcome our speaker; John and Mary Smith invite you to the wedding of their daughter. Thank you is an ELLIPTICAL form of I/we thank you.

For *I'll ask him when he arrives* see TENSE & TIME.

Jokes and anecdotes are often told in the present as the speaker vividly imagines the situation that he/she is describing. However, it is extremely unusual to use the present tense (*historic present*) in a written narrative.

See PAST SIMPLE.

present continuous

The present continuous is used to describe situations that are taking place at the moment of speaking: *He is reading a book; I am sitting on a chair; John is standing by the window*. Verbs that describe states are not used in the CONTINUOUS ASPECT: ~~I am knowing that~~; ~~He is liking Indian food~~. See DYNAMIC AND STATIVE.

The present continuous is used to describe a situation that is temporary:
She's living with friends (until she finds a place of her own).
I'm working in a museum (during the university vacation).
I'm working for Mr Lewis at the moment (because my own boss is on holiday).

The sentence *She usually drives to work but she's going by train this week because her car's being repaired* shows the difference between the present simple used for habitual action and the present continuous for a temporary state of affairs.

We can say *She usually drives to work but she sometimes goes by train* but not ~~She usually drives to work but she is sometimes going by train~~ because the temporary nature of *she's going by train this week* is incompatible with the repetition implied by *she sometimes goes by train.*

For the present simple and present continuous with future meaning see these under FUTURE.

with always etc.

When used with *always, constantly, continually* etc. it expresses annoyance or disapproval: *My neighbours are always ROWING; He's always asking me to go and feed his dog.*

For *He's being silly* see DYNAMIC AND STATIVE verbs.

pressure & -pression

The noun is *pressure* and not ~~pression~~, but with prefixes the forms are *compression, depression, expression, impression, oppression, repression, suppression.*

pretend

In modern use this refers to a claim that is untrue, whether to trick someone: *He pretended to be a millionaire* or as a game or joke: *Let's pretend to be animals in the zoo.*

A *pretender* is someone who claims a throne or title. In British history the *Old Pretender* and the *Young Pretender* were Stuarts (the son and grandson of James II) who claimed the throne of England in the eighteenth century. See SCOTLAND, A BRIEF HISTORY.

The noun for the act of pretending is *pretence*; a *pretension* is a claim to a quality.

P

pretty

This is pronounced /ˈprɪti/. It refers to a thing or person that is attractive and delicate, beautiful but not overwhelmingly so. With people it is used of young women and children more than of men. It has an adverb: *The room was decorated very prettily; She arranges her hair prettily.*

A *pretty mess* is, ironically, an unpleasant situation. A *pretty penny* is a considerable amount of money.

If you are *sitting pretty* (sic, not *sitting prettily*) you are lucky enough to be in a comfortable or advantageous position.

As an adverb *pretty* can be an equivalent of RATHER or *fairly*: *pretty good/big* etc. Here it does not change.

See ADVERBS WITHOUT -LY.

priceless

Priceless and *invaluable* mean that it is impossible to fix a price or value for something: *a priceless painting; your invaluable assistance.*

Valueless and WORTHless both refer to things which have no value.

priestess

Women who are priests in the CHURCH OF ENGLAND are known as (*women*) *priests*. The word *priestess* is used only to refer to non-Christian religions.

primate

A *primate* is a mammal of the highest order, including apes, monkeys, and man.

A *primate* is also an ANGLICAN archbishop. The Archbishop of Canterbury is the *Primate of All England*; The Archbishop of York is the *Primate of England*.

prize

A *prize* is won in a competition, lottery, game etc.: *first prize, the NOBEL prizes*. (Do not confuse *prize* /praɪz/, *price* /praɪs/, and *prise* /praɪz/ (force open)).

An *award* is given for outstanding achievement by a group of people who decide who is to receive it. The Oscars are called the *Academy Awards* because they are awarded by the American Academy of Motion Picture Arts and Sciences.

A *reward* is given in return for good behaviour, for example finding and returning something that has been lost.

produce

The verb *produce* is pronounced with the stress on the second syllable. The usual noun to describe something that is produced is *product* stressed on the first syllable. The noun *produce* with first syllable stress is used only for agricultural produce, for example DAIRY *produce*.

See STRESS DIFFERENCES.

programme

Programme is the British spelling; *program* is American.

However, *program* is standard in Britain in connection with computers. It is pronounced /ˈprəʊɡræm/ in noun and verb forms. There is no STRESS DIFFERENCE between the two forms.

P

progressive
This is used by some people as an alternative name for the verb forms of the CONTINUOUS ASPECT: *present progressive* etc.

Prohibition
When this word is written with a capital letter it refers to the legal prohibition on the manufacturing and selling of alcohol that was in force in the USA between 1920 and 1933.

pronounce and pronunciation
The second syllable of these two words is spelled and pronounced differently: *pronounce* /prəˈnaʊns/, *pronunciation* /prəˈnʌnsɪeɪʃən/. Some native speakers make the mistake of saying and writing ~~*pronounciation*~~ /prəˈnaʊnsɪeɪʃən/ from the verb *pronounce* instead of *pronunciation*.

pronouns, personal
The CASE system in English is very limited in comparison with other INDO-EUROPEAN LANGUAGES. See ENGLISH LANGUAGE, A BRIEF HISTORY. Adjectives and nouns lost their inflections in the MIDDLE AGES. With the exceptions of the possessive of nouns, personal pronouns are the only words in English that show variation according to grammatical CASE.

	Singular			Plural		
Case	1	2	3	1	2	3
Subject (nominative)	I	you	he, she, it	we	you	they
Object (accusative)	me	you	him, her, it	us	you	them
Possessive pronoun (DETERMINER)	my	your	his, hers, its	our	your	their
Possessive (absolute)	mine	yours	his, hers*	ours	yours	theirs
Reflexive	myself	yourself	himself, herself, itself	ourselves	yourselves	themselves

*The absolute (independent) form of *it* is never used.

See GROUP NOUNS; THOU; WHO AND WHOM.

one
One can be used as an impersonal pronoun: *One doesn't talk about that kind of thing.* This is found in formal use. The other forms are *one's* and *oneself*: *If one buys oneself a car, one's way of life will change.* This can seem repetitive; it can be rewritten as *Buying a car will change one's way of life.*

However, in colloquial speech, *you* is used impersonally: *If you buy yourself a car, your way of life will change.* Dictionaries often use *one* in definitions as an impersonal pronoun; this must usually be changed before the phrase in question can be used as desired. See PASSIVE VOICE for impersonal use.

we
We in English can be exclusive or inclusive.

Exclusive (another person and I, but not you): *May we go now please, Mr Jones?; When we've finished the report I'll put it on your desk.*

Inclusive (you and I and possibly another person): *Mr Jones says we may go now; We must be sure to leave on time.*

The inclusive use of *we* is extended to use by:
- **authors:** As we have seen in chapter 6…; … so we can assume that…
- **doctors and nurses:** *How are we today?* (How are you?); *We'll feel better after a week in bed* (The reference could be second person: *You'll feel better...* or third person: *He/she'll feel better...*). Some people dislike this, feeling that it is condescending to the patients. ▶

P

- **newspaper editors:** We have the original documents in our possession; We believe that the government has made a mistake.

The *royal we* is an extreme example of this inclusive use; it is only used in formal royal language when the monarch refers to him/herself personally as *we* instead of *I*. When prime minister Margaret Thatcher's first grandchild was born in 1989, she declared *We have become a grandmother*.

possessive pronouns

	determiners			independent items
	my			mine
	our			ours
	your			yours
These are	your	books	These books are	yours
	his			his
	her			hers
	its			---
	their			theirs

Possessive pronouns vary depending on whether they are used as DETERMINERS or as independent items. Note that the neuter pronoun *it* does not have an independent POSSESSIVE pronoun: *These are the dog's things* can be followed by *That's its bowl* but not ~~That bowl is its~~.

pronouns with nouns in apposition

Pronouns can be associated with nouns to include or exclude the speaker: *We students will not accept these changes; You Germans drink a lot of beer*. The pronoun *we* or *you* is not essential here and is usually omitted when it is clearly known that the speaker or the person spoken to is a member of the group in question. A third person form ~~they Germans~~ is not necessary because the absence of a pronoun implies the third person form.

See REFLEXIVE VERBS.

pronunciation

It is not possible here to provide a complete guide to English pronunciation; information will be found in the articles PHONETIC SYMBOLS, -ED & -ES, PRONUNCIATION, and in the articles referring to individual letters.

It is clear that English pronunciation does not correspond to the spelling; part of the difficulty is that English has more vowel sounds than available symbols to represent them, so it is necessary to play tricks with the five vowel letters (*a, e, i, o, u*) to represent the vowel sounds (DOUBLE CONSONANTS). However, it is worth mentioning that this lack of correspondence is because the spelling was largely fixed in the fifteenth century with the introduction of printing, when it represented a close approximation to the sound of the spoken words. Since then the pronunciation has changed, especially as a number of letters that were once pronounced have become silent (*brought, palm*), but the spelling has not been updated. Also, a large number of Latin and Greek words have been introduced into the language. These words do not always conform to traditional norms of English spelling and pronunciation.

Naturally, the problems that learners of English experience will depend on the sound structure of their own language. However, some common problems are worth mentioning:

Unlike many languages, English has a stress-timed rhythm. That is to say, the frequency at which strong stresses occur in a sentence is approximately equal. So, if a sentence has a number of unstressed syllables together, they have to be pronounced more quickly. The numbers below the words show the number of syllables in the stress unit; the final *e* in the words *unstressed* and *syllables* is not pronounced at all:

Só, if a	séntence has a	númber of	únstressed	sýllables to	géther
3	4	3	2	3	2

The divisions of this sentence all take the same time to say, the stressed syllables come at regular intervals, and some of the unstressed syllables (the underlined ones) are pronounced as SCHWA. This

P

rhythm is typical of English and explains why it sounds strange to speakers of some other languages. It also explains why some words have different pronunciations (strong and weak) depending on their position in the sentence.

Frequently the last consonant sound of an English word is voiced: *joined* /dʒɔɪnd/, *played* /pleɪd/, LIVES, /lɪvz/ and /laɪvz/, *runs* /rʌnz/, *dogs* /dɒgz/, *good* /gʊd/, *rob* /rɒb/. These consonants must be pronounced voiced; they must not be *devoiced* (i.e. pronounced as unvoiced consonants); e.g. /lɪfs/, /rʌns/ are incorrect.

Final consonants of words must be pronounced in almost all cases; this is especially true of words ending in *-(e)d* and *-(e)s*: *tables* /teɪblz/ not /teɪbl/ *said* /sed/ not /se/.

There are some well-known instances of silent letters: *iron* /'aɪən/, *hour* /'aʊə/, *honour* /'ɒnə/, *fasten* /'fæsn/, *castle* /kɑːsl/, *island* /'aɪlənd/, *half* /hɑːf/, *walk* /wɔːk/, but it is not so widely known, even by native speakers, that other written letters are not pronounced (silent letters in bold): CA**T**HOLIC /'kæθlɪk/, *choco**l**ate* /'tʃɒklət/, *han**d**kerchief* /'hæŋkətʃiːf/, *inte**re**sting* /'ɪntrəstɪŋ/, P**O**LICE /pliːs/.

The sounds /l/ (clear *l*, see L, L) and /r/ are not identical. /l/ is pronounced with the tip of the tongue firmly touching the alveolar ridge behind the upper front teeth. The pronunciation of *r* is variable (see R, R) but in standard English it is pronounced with the tongue in almost the same position as for clear *l* but not quite touching the alveolar ridge, behind the front teeth.

Letters are not always used to represent their expected sounds. For example, many native speakers say for *Mary and I* /'meərɪənaɪ/, *goodbye* /gʊ'baɪ/, *half past* /hʌ'pɑːst/, *football* /'fʊpbɔːl/ and *in Manchester* /ɪ'mæntʃestə/, even without being aware of what they are doing. /'kʌbəd/ is the standard pronunciation of *cupboard*.

The GLOTTAL STOP /ʔ/ *(*PHONETIC SYMBOLS)*, which is not usually taught to students of English as it is not recommended in RECEIVED PRONUNCIATION (except before *n* as in *button* /bʌʔn/), is common throughout the UK.

Foreign words that have not been accepted as fully English are pronounced in imitation of the original pronunciation, varying with the degree to which the speaker is familiar with that language.

Double consonants are not pronounced any differently from single ones; they are no longer in *rubber, funny* than in *cubic, money* (but see N, N).

When speaking, and especially when reading aloud in English, many learners tend to separate words by the spaces between them on the page. This is incorrect; in any spoken language the words are connected. Connecting them can make pronunciation much easier, especially for speakers of languages that present problems with final consonants in English. For example the sentence *I found another egg* is naturally pronounced in the units as shown divided here without any pauses: *Ifoun|danothe|regg* /aɪ'faʊndə‚nʌðə'reg/ and not (with pauses): *I | found | another | egg*.

For linking and intrusive *r* see R, R.

See ESTUARY ENGLISH; SPELLING; VOICED AND UNVOICED CONSONANTS.

propaganda

In English *propaganda* almost always refers to dishonest, misleading, political or religious propaganda RATHER than to natural spreading of information.

proper terms

There are many of these in English, but many were invented for FUN and seem never to have been used. The following list is of words in common use:

flock	birds, sheep	*pride*	lions
gang	crooks, thieves	*school**	whales
herd	cattle, elephants, giraffes, zebras	*shoal*	fish
litter	kittens, puppies (new-born)	*string*	racehorses
pack	hounds, other hunting dogs, wolves	*swarm*	bees

*This is not the educational establishment; it is a DOUBLET of *shoal*.

P

prophecy & prophesy
Prophecy /ˈprɒfɪsi/ is the noun; *prophesy* /ˈprɒfɪsaɪ/ is the verb. This difference can be remembered with reference to *advice* and *advise*, where the spelling reflects the pronunciation.

See ADVICE; LICENCE; PRACTICE.

propose
Apart from its normal meaning *propose* has a special meaning: *if a man proposes to a woman*, that means that he is proposing MARRIAGE, that he is asking her to marry him. The nouns *proposal* and *proposition* are generally synonyms, although *proposition* has a particular meaning in logic and mathematics. However, if a man *propositions* a woman, he is making a crude offer to have sex with her.

See INFINITIVE OR -ING?

Protestant
Protestant (with capital letter) is now only used in the religious sense. People who protest in other situations are *protesters*.

prove
This is pronounced /pruːv/ and means *to show or demonstrate that something is true*. The noun is *proof*. It does not mean to *test* except in the PROVERB *the proof of the pudding is in the eating* (that something should be judged by its final outcome).

It can have a noun complement: *He proved (to be) a good friend*.

When a will is left by a person who has died, it must be *proved*, i.e. the EXECUTOR must show that it is valid, before the ESTATE can be passed to the heirs.

The past participle is usually the regular *proved* but the irregular *proven* is occasionally seen and is common in American English. It is also common in Britain as the attributive ADJECTIVE: *proven validity, proven experience*.

In Scottish law *not proven* is a verdict between guilty and not guilty, that the evidence is insufficient to justify either of these.

proverbs
Some typical English proverbs are

A bird in the hand is worth two in the bush.	A present possession is better than possible gain, even if the gain would be greater.
A fool and his money are soon parted.	Foolish people spend their money unwisely.
A stitch in time saves nine.	A problem that is not solved immediately will become worse.
Absence makes the heart grow fonder.	People are liked better when they are not present all the time.
ALL's well that ends well.	Even if things go badly, a satisfactory conclusion is pleasant.
All that GLITTERS (*SHINE) is not gold.	Things are not always attractive, even if they SEEM to be.
Don't count your chickens before they are hatched.	Don't ANTICIPATE success.
Don't cross your bridges until you come to them.	Don't anticipate difficulties.
Don't look a gift horse in the mouth.	It is rude to examine a gift for possible faults. (A horse's teeth show its age.)
Don't put all your eggs in one basket.	Don't risk everything at the same time.
Every cloud has a silver lining./It's an ill wind that blows nobody any good.	There is some good aspect to every difficulty.

Half a loaf is better than no BREAD.	Something that is unsatisfactory is better than nothing.
He who laughs last laughs loudest/longest.	The final winner might not be the one who expected to win.
If you don't like the heat then get out of the kitchen.	If you can't stand stress and pressure, avoid situations where they are found.
It never rains but it pours.	When one thing goes wrong, other problems will ARISE *(*RISE & ARISE)*.
Let sleeping dogs LIE.	Don't interfere when things are satisfactory.
Look before you LEAP (*JUMP).	Consider carefully before committing yourself.
Make hay while the sun SHINES./STRIKE while the iron is hot.	Take advantage of a situation that may not last long.
Many hands make light work.	Work is done more quickly with a lot of help. (Compare *Too many cooks spoil the broth.*)
Marry in haste, repent at leisure.	A spontaneous action may be regretted later.
People who live in glass houses shouldn't throw stones.	Don't attack other people on a point where you are vulnerable yourself.
The early bird catches the worm.	The first person in position gets the best advantage.
The last straw that broke the camel's back.	(Often quoted as *It was the last straw*.) Something that is small in itself but combines with others to provoke a crisis.
The PROOF (*PROVE) of the pudding is in the eating.	Something should be judged by its final outcome.
There's many a slip 'twixt cup and lip. (*'twixt*, for *betwixt*, is an archaic word meaning *between*. See TWO.)	Many things can go wrong between planning and performance.
There's no smoke without fire.	Suspicions are usually justified.
To kill two birds with one stone.	To achieve two objectives with one action.
Too many COOKS spoil the broth.	If too many people are doing a job, they will interfere with each other's work.
Waste not, WANT not.	Do not waste resources and you will not want (in the sense of need) anything.
When the cat's away, the mice will play.	People will take advantage of freedom from control.
You can lead a horse to water but you can't make it drink.	You can give someone an opportunity, but you cannot make them use it.
You can't judge a book by its cover.	First or superficial impressions can be mistaken.

publicly

The form ~~publically~~ is occasionally used by English-speakers. It is not standard.

See -IC & -ICAL.

public schools and public companies

public schools

In Britain *public schools* are private schools which charge fees and *public companies* are private companies; the explanation for this apparent contradiction lies in the nature of the word *public*.

The term *public school* dates from the MIDDLE AGES, when it described schools that were what would now be called non-profit-making foundations or endowments providing education for members of the public. It had a rather variable meaning, contrasted with private schools, which were financed and operated by their owners, and with teaching at home by private tutors. In the mid-nineteenth century public schools began to accept pupils from the country in general, rather than from their local area, which gave another aspect to the name, *public school* being understood as a boarding school. At that time they provided an education with a strong emphasis on classical languages and culture, history, and sport, which served to train young men for the administration of

P

the Empire; a *public-school* education was regarded as typical of the upper classes, giving them an elite attitude and a certain social style: the typical English gentleman in fact. Men and women who had been to public schools (the first girls' school opened in 1634) formed strong bonds of identity with their schools (probably because they were boarding schools; the children lived there during term time) and wearing the *old school tie* was a symbol of this identity and a signal to others that the wearer had been to a public school. It is interesting to note that *tie* also means *link, bond, connection*, so the *old school tie* is not only the garment but is an expression of the identity and cohesion of those who wear it. Men and women from public schools also developed a distinctive accent (see RECEIVED PRONUNCIATION) which encouraged group identification and a sense of elitism.

These schools still exist, though as British society changes, their role is changing. The best known are Winchester (1382), Eton (1440), and Harrow (1571) for boys and Cheltenham Ladies' College (1841), Roedean (1885), and Benenden (1923) for girls. They now refer to themselves as *independent schools* but the name *public schools* is still in common use. The schools that are paid for out of public funds, which in other countries are called *public schools*, are referred to in Britain as *state schools*, even though they are administered by local education authorities not by the central government of the state.

public companies

Similarly, *public companies* are those which sell their shares to members of the public on the Stock Exchange; they have the letters *plc (public limited company),* always small letters, after their names. Companies *in public ownership* are *nationalised, publicly owned* or *state owned companies*, though almost all of these have now been privatised.

punctuation

In English, punctuation is the marks placed in a written text to make it easier to understand. It is not the allocation of points in a competition. See SCORE.

Punctuation marks are used to divide the text into meaningful sections and to give information about the structure of the sentence. There is a certain degree of individual variation in the use of punctuation, especially commas.

The punctuation of direct speech is described under the section QUOTATION MARKS below.

The most commonly used punctuation marks are:

full stop (American English *period*) .

The full stop marks the end of a sentence.

A sequence of three full stops marks an omission in a quotation (see ELLIPSIS). It also marks a pause or hesitation in direct speech.

It is used in EMAIL and website addresses. In this case it is called a *dot*.

It is sometimes used in ABBREVIATIONS though usage varies among publishers and writers.

It is commonly omitted in abbreviations where the last letter of the abbreviation is also the last letter of the full word: *Dr Foster, Mr Cameron, Mrs Thatcher* but *Capt. Kirk, Pres. Obama, Prof. Edwards, Wed., cont., fut. perf.*

It is not used in British English to mark a group of initials expressed entirely as capital letters: *AD, BC, BA, MA, BBC, EU, MP, NATO, NB, UNO.*

It can be sometimes used to mark a group of initials expressed as small letters: *a.m., p.m., i.e., e.g.* As these letters represent separate words *(ante meridiem, post meridiem, id est, exempli gratia)* they must never be joined in handwriting. If a sentence ends with such an abbreviation, only one stop is required: *She arrived at 6.30 p.m.*

It is not used with question marks and exclamation marks.

It is used to mark decimal numbers: *2.500* is exactly *2½*. In this case it is called a decimal point. See NUMBERS | NUMBERS IN WRITING.

The full stop can be used to separate hours and minutes in TIME: *She arrived at 6.30.*

semicolon ;
The semicolon provides a less heavy break than a full stop; it is easier to read texts that have CLAUSES separated by semicolons. There are many examples of semicolons in this book.

colon :
The colon is used mainly to introduce lists and examples: *The following teachers will be accompany the party: Mr Robertson and Ms Sparrow.*

It is not usually found between CLAUSES but is used formally in sentences in which one clause introduces the contents of another: *He told me the truth: he had been applying for other jobs.*

It is used to separate hours and minutes in TIME written as numbers: *She arrived at 6:30.*

comma ,
Look at these sentences:

Two main CLAUSES should not be separated by a comma; a semi-colon or full stop should be used.
Two main clauses should not be separated by a comma. A semi-colon or full stop should be used.
~~Two main clauses should not be separated by a comma, a semi-colon or full stop should be used.~~

The last sentence is an example of a comma splice: two main clauses separated by a comma. This is considered incorrect and should be avoided. The other sentences are acceptable. Clauses can of course be joined by conjunctions: *The orchestra finished playing and the audience applauded.*

When the sentence contains more than two such clauses, the earlier ones may be separated by commas with a conjunction before the last as in a list:
The orchestra finished playing, the conductor turned to face the audience, and everyone applauded.
The orchestra finished playing, the conductor turned to face the audience, but no-one applauded.

This is the most problematic stop to use; it provides the detailed management of sentence structure. There are definite rules to cover some cases, especially non-defining RELATIVE CLAUSES, but in others it is more a question of style and common sense; to a certain extent, a comma in print represents a slight pause in speech.

commas are used
- to separate items in lists: *I bought bread, water, sausages, bacon and eggs.* Usage varies concerning a comma before the word *and*. Some people write *I bought bread, water, sausages, bacon, and eggs.* Putting a serial comma in this position clarifies lists where an item itself includes the word *and*: *I went to Harrods, Selfridges, and Marks and Spencer.* An example is found in the introduction to the article SEE: *This article includes see, look, watch, gaze and stare, and glance and glimpse.* The serial comma is also known as the Oxford comma because it is the house style of Oxford University Press.
- between adjectives: *A battered, old, black car.*
- after the salutation in a LETTER:
Dear Mr Robertson, We were pleased to receive your letter of 24 August 2018.
- to represent a full stop in DIRECT SPEECH: *'I'm hungry,' Jane said.*
- to mark a parenthesis:
There is no reason, in my opinion, to abandon the project.
President Kennedy, who was elected in 1960, did not live to complete his first term of office. (The non-defining RELATIVE CLAUSE is, in fact, a parenthesis.)
He seems, however, to have been a loving father.
He arrived late and, because the box office was closed, was unable to buy a ticket.
A common mistake is to mark the parenthesis wrongly as in ~~He arrived late, and because the box office was closed, was unable to buy a ticket~~. Commas used to mark parentheses must, like brackets, be opened and closed in pairs.
- after a subordinate CLAUSE which stands before the main clause, especially in conditional sentences: *Although he has never been to an English-speaking country, he has a good idiomatic knowledge of the language; If I win the lottery, I will buy a car*

after words such as *however, nevertheless, therefore.* ▶

commas are not used
between subject and verb: *The old man who had bought me a drink turned out to be your uncle* (not *... bought me a drink, turned out ...*) except in sentences such as *Those [differences] which there are, are trivial* in the article on American English, where the verb is repeated and there is a pause in speech.

quotation marks and punctuation of direct speech '...' "..."
These are also known as *quote marks* or *inverted commas*. Except for works by a very small number of idiosyncratic authors such as James Joyce, William Golding and Alan Paton, who have persuaded their publishers to use other punctuation, DIRECT SPEECH is always punctuated with quotation marks. Single '...' or double "..." marks can be used. Double marks are usually used in handwriting for clarity, but printers and publishers choose their own styles.

In *'I am coming,' he said* the comma after *coming* represents the full stop in the original sentence (*I am coming.*).

In *He said, 'I am coming.'* only one full stop is used. It is not *'I am coming.'.*

Note the positions of the question marks in *He said, 'Are you coming?'* and *Did he say, 'I'm coming'?* No full stop is placed in addition to the question mark (see below). Note the comma after *said/say*, which unusually appears between the verb and its object.

Whether single or double quotation marks are used in a narrative, the other kind is used for quotation within a quotation: *He continued his story, 'I said to him, "What are you doing here?" and he replied, "The same as you, I suppose."'* and *He continued his story, "I said to him, 'What are you doing here?' and he replied, 'The same as you, I suppose.'"* Notice the single and double quotation marks together at the ends of these examples.

dashes and brackets – (...) [...]
These can be used to mark a parenthesis :

dash –
Three members – Tom, Dick and Harry – offered to organise a concert.
Three members–Tom, Dick and Harry–offered to organise a concert.

round brackets (...)
Three members (Tom, Dick and Harry) offered to organise a concert.

A dash has either a space before it and a space after it or no space before it and no space after it. Note the difference between *The concert was organised by three members (Tom, Dick, and Harry)* and *The concert was organised by three members – Tom, Dick, and Harry*. The bracket marking the parenthesis is closed but the dash is not.

square brackets [...]
These are used to distinguish additional material or comment from original material: *He said that the horse belonged to Tom [Pierce]; It was reported in the Southport Visiter [sic].* (The newspaper really does spell its name that way.)

apostrophe '
The apostrophe was introduced into English from the sixteenth to the eighteenth century; present conventions for its use date from the middle of the nineteenth century and are given in these rules. Many native speakers are inconsistent in the use of apostrophes and much informal written English suffers from an epidemic of apostrophe misuse. In particular, many people use a non-standard apostrophe to make a plural of a word ending with a vowel: *fly's, opera's, potato's, tomato's, banana's, apple's*. This is known informally as the greengrocer's apostrophe. George Bernard Shaw never used apostrophes in his work, writing CONTRACTIONS as *didnt, wont, cant* etc.

The apostrophe has two functions: firstly, to indicate POSSESSION (where it represents the Old and Middle English inflection *-es*); and secondly, to indicate a letter or letters that are not pronounced.

P

possession

The apostrophe with *s* indicates POSSESSION: *John's car*. When the noun has a regular plural the apostrophe follows it: *the teachers' books* but when the plural is irregular the apostrophe precedes it: *the men's clothes*. The possessive of *parents-in-law* (and similar forms) presents an insoluble problem. I recommend *My parents-in-laws' house*, which seems to be the most natural spoken form with a plural apostrophe.

Usually, when a name ends with *s*, write -*'s*: *Thomas's room; Charles's car; Mrs Jones's office, St James's St*. These are pronounced /'tɒməsɪz/ etc. but if the last syllable is pronounced /ɪz/, write *Mrs Bridges' kitchen, Moses' leadership of his people*.

It is usual to write -*s'* in classical names (pronounced /ə'kɪliːz/ etc.): *Achilles' heel* or *friend* but *Achilles tendon; Pythagoras' theorem*; and *Xerxes' fleet*; also *Jesus' disciples*.

With *sake* it is *For heaven's sake; For GOD's sake; For Charles's sake* but *For goodness' sake*.

The time expressions *A week's holiday; A month's rest* must have the apostrophe, and it is generally written in the plural forms: *Two weeks' holiday; Three months' rest*. However, this plural use sometimes seems adjectival, so *Two weeks holiday; Three months rest* are acceptable.

Many commercial names that are originally possessive forms of the name of the founder or founders are written without apostrophes: *Barclays Bank; Harrods; Diners Card; Lloyds Bank* (but *Lloyd's Insurance*). This absence of the apostrophe is often a matter of design in corporate logos; it also seems to be especially popular when the name is written entirely in CAPITAL LETTERS, e.g. *BARCLAYS BANK*, and is also seen in street-name and other signs: *QUEENS LANE, KINGS PARADE, PORTERS LODGE*.

missing letters

In CONTRACTIONS an apostrophe represents a missing letter or letters: *I'm (I am), you've (you have)*. *He's, she's, it's* are the contracted forms of both *he is, she is, it is* and of *he has, she has, it has*. *It's* is the contraction of *it is* and *it has*; *its* is the possessive form of *it*. See WHO'S & WHOSE. *He'd, she'd, it'd* are the contracted forms of both *he had, she had, it had* and of *he would, she would, it would*. *I'd better* is the contraction of *I HAD BETTER (*BETTER)*; *I'd rather* is the contraction of *I WOULD RATHER (*RATHER)*. This difference is important in making TAG QUESTIONS and SHORT ANSWERS.

Apostrophes are sometimes used to indicate the pronunciation, with some letters omitted, of *fish 'n' chips, rock 'n' roll* and *fo'c'sle (forecastle*, the front part of a SHIP); *o'er* and *ne'er (over* and *never)* are poetical forms. Sometimes, though rarely nowadays, an apostrophe is used at the beginning of a word or number to indicate that the first letters or digits are missing: *'cello (violoncello), 'flu (influenza), 'phone (telephone), 'plane (aeroplane), Andy was born in '65; I'd like a bottle of the '91*. This is not recommended. In written direct speech the apostrophe is sometimes used to indicate non-standard pronunciation, especially a missing *h*: *'I 'eard 'im go'; Huntin', shootin' and fishin'* are the traditional country activities in the pronunciation of upper class country people who drop their *g*'s. See DEVIANT SPELLING.

It is not necessary to write an apostrophe in the plural of abbreviations or numbers: *25 MPs, the 1990s*; this was done (*25 MP's, the 1990's*) to indicate that some letters were missing. There is of course an apostrophe in the possessive: *an MP's secretary*.

It is not necessary to use an apostrophe in the plural of a word which is not a noun: *His comments were full of ifs and buts*. For reasons of clarity an apostrophe is written in the plural of the name of a letter: *There are 2 t's in 'written'* but *there are four 3s in my phone number*.

See O'CLOCK.

hyphen -

There is very wide variation in the use of hyphens to make compound words; a progression can be seen from the nineteenth-century forms: *to morrow, any one, some body* through *to-morrow, any-one, some-body* in the early twentieth century, to the modern standard forms *tomorrow, anyone, somebody*.

P

The following rules apply to British English; American English may vary. Even in Britain, the situation with regard to hyphens varies constantly and different publishers have different styles. The Oxford University Press style manual says 'If you take hyphens seriously, you will surely go mad'.

hyphens are used in
- compounds of a noun with an adverb, especially those made from MULTI-WORD VERBS: *let-down, break-in.*
- compound adjectives such as *icy-cold, home-made, red-hot.*
- compound adjectives made of *well + past participle* when they are used attributively: *a well-known architect, a well-loved author* but not in predicative use, where the adverb has its usual grammatical status: *that architect is well known for his use of floral patterns.*
- based on present or past participles, for example *a well-prepared speech*, but *the speech was well prepared* and *the clothes are newly washed*; also those that are formed from nouns in the same way as participles: *one-legged, short-sleeved.*
- other descriptive phrases that consist of more than one word: *a Spanish-English dictionary, a bus-rail interchange, a management-union meeting, a house-to-house enquiry, a face-to-face interview* but *the enquiry was carried out house to house the interview was conducted face to face.*
- numbers between tens and units **only**: *two thousand five hundred and forty-two.*
- compounds with a single capital letter: *H-bomb, X-ray.*
- family relationships with *-in-law*: *mother-in-law,* and with *great*: *great-uncle, great-grandson.*
- words with these PREFIXES: *ex-, half-, non-, quasi-, self-*: *ex-husband, half-dozen, non-payment, quasi-independent, self-service*; and sometimes with *pre-* and *post-*. *Co-author, co-editor,* and *co-worker* have hyphens to avoid possible confusion in reading unhyphenated forms. The hyphen is sometimes used in *co-ordinate* and *co-operate* though these are frequently seen unhyphenated. For *recover* and *re-cover* etc. see PREFIXES.

hyphens are not used in
- compound adjectives made of an adverb ending with *-ly* and a past participle: *newly washed clothes, a badly presented speech.*
- Compound adjectives that are seen as a single concept: *equal opportunity employer, secondary school teacher.*
- scientific names, even in long names or in names that contain a repeated vowel: *ethylenediaminetetraacetic acid, diisopropylfluorophosphate.*

The rules for breaking words with hyphens at the end of a line of printed text are very complex and differ between American and British usage; they should be considered as an aspect of typography rather than language. In handwriting it is best as far as possible to avoid breaking words at line-ends. See SYLLABLES.

question mark ?
This is used at the end of a direct question: *Have they arrived?; Where are my glasses?* It is not used in an indirect question: *I don't know if they have arrived; I am not sure where your glasses are* but *Do you know if they have arrived?; Can you tell me where my glasses are?* are direct questions: *Do you know...?; Can you tell me...?*

The question mark contains its own full stop; an extra one is not written: ~~Have they arrived?.~~

A question mark is not written before the end of a sentence: *Can we finish this on time is the question we must ask ourselves* not ~~Can we finish this on time? is the question we must ask ourselves.~~

exclamation mark !
This is used at the end of an exclamation: *Good heavens! What a surprise!* and in other sentences that are not technically exclamations but which contain an element of urgency or surprise: *Come here!; He couldn't tell me!; Isn't he stupid!* Note that the last example is structurally a question but

the exclamatory sense seems to dominate. As with the question mark, the exclamation mark is not followed by a full stop.

stroke or slash /

This is used to mark alternatives: *and/or; this/next week*. The symbol \ that is found in website addresses is called a *backslash*. If it is necessary to distinguish them, / can be called a *forward slash*.

See CUT | SLASH.

pundit

Pundit is a word of Indian origin meaning a learned person. In English it means an expert in a subject. When used as a title with an Indian name, for example *Pandit* Nehru (the first prime minister of India), it is written thus.

Q

q, Q /kjuː/

The seventeenth letter of the alphabet. In English words it is found in the combination *qu*, which is pronounced /kw/: *quick, equal.*

In words of French origin that end with *-que* it has the French pronunciation /k/: *Basque, bisque, boutique, brusque,* CALQUE, *cheque, grotesque, mosque, mystique, oblique, picturesque, unique* among others, and also in *chequer* /ˈtʃekə/, *marquee* /mɑːˈkiː/, *quay* /kiː/, and *queue* /kjuː/.

In some words transliterated from Arabic it is written without the *u* that always follows it in English: *Iraq(i), Qatar, al Qaeda.* In such cases it is usually pronounced /k/ in English, though the sound that the Arabic letter represents is not found in English and is pronounced rather differently.

The name of the Australian airline Qantas is pronounced /kwɒntas/. It is an ACRONYM of Queensland and Northern Territory Aerial Services.

quantifiers

These vary as the noun in question is countable or uncountable.

countable	uncountable
all	all
both	—
each/every	—
most	most
many	much
number	deal, amount, quantity
a lot of/lots of	a lot of/lots of
some, several, various, diverse	some
(a) FEW, fewer, fewest	(a) LITTLE, less, least
not … any	not … any
no, none	no, none

quarter, term & trimester

A *quarter* is each of the three-month periods into which the year is divided for financial and other purposes (January to March; April to June; July to September; October to December).

A *term* is one of three periods into which the academic year is divided.

A *trimester* is a period of three months but is used only to refer to the periods of human pregnancy.

See SEMESTER.

queer

This means *strange, odd, eccentric.* However, since the 1920s, and especially since the early 1970s, it has been used to refer derogatively to a male homosexual as an adjective or noun. This meaning has become almost universal in modern usage. At one time comments such as *he's a bit queer* or *he's a queer fellow* were a reasonable way of describing a man who was rather eccentric or unusual, but the word cannot be used now to refer to a man without the idea of homosexuality being inevitable. Homosexuals sometimes use the word themselves but this is a self-referential use for members of a group. Used otherwise it is regarded as an insult.

See GAY.

questions

As a general rule questions in English have the word order *auxiliary verb – subject – main verb.*

Aux	S	V	O	Adv
Do	you	know	Jane?	
Can	you	pay		now?

Q

	Aux	S	V	O	Adv
Please	may	I	go		early?
When	will	she	arrive?		
	Have	you	seen	this film	before?

When a sentence contains more than one auxiliary verb, the subject follows the first one:

Wh- word	Aux₁	S	Aux₂	V	O	Adv
	Should	I	have	known	that?	
	Would	the teacher	have	believed	it?	
What	had	you	been	thinking of?		
	Will	she	have been	waiting		long?
How/where	will	you	be	cooking	it?	

Exceptions to this are questions with *who* or *what* as the subject; they have the normal SVO order (the same as non-question statements): *Who did it?; Who would have expected it?; What was broken?; What would have been the best solution?* but this does not apply when *WHO(M)* or *what* is the object: *Who(m) had you been thinking of?; What did you do?*

The verb *be* makes questions with simple inversion: *Are you here?; Is he Japanese?*

See HAVE; WH- QUESTIONS.

quick

The common modern meaning of this is FAST, *rapid*. Its sense of *living* is archaic but is still found in expressions such as *the quick and the dead* in the Apostles' Creed, and in *quicksand*, moving sand, which is extremely dangerous. *Quicklime* is calcium oxide (CaO) and *quicksilver* is mercury (Hg). *Cut to the quick* means cut into the living flesh; it can also mean *deeply insulted*. A *quick-tempered* person becomes angry quickly or fast because their temper is *quick*, i.e. alive.

Colloquially, *quick* rather than *quickly* is sometimes used as an adverb: *Come quick; A 'get rich quick' scheme*, but it is considered incorrect to do so generally. It is standard in compounds e.g. *quick-acting, quick-drying, quick-talking*. *Quick* can be used alone to tell someone to move or do something quickly. *'Quick, get out and close the door.'*

quiet & quite

These are completely different words with different pronunciations: *quiet* /ˈkwaɪət/ and *QUITE* /kwaɪt/. They must not be confused.

quite

This is a confusing word as it means:
1 *completely, totally, absolutely* and
2 *fairly,* RATHER, *to a degree.*

The second meaning is fairly new, being first recorded in 1854. Examples of usage are:
1 *It is quite impossible; That is quite a different proposal; I was quite alone; You are quite right; I quite agree.*
2 *I quite often go to the cinema; It was quite hot yesterday; He lives quite near the station; It is quite a difficult book; I quite like his books.*

The examples under **1** are non-GRADABLE *(*ADJECTIVES)*, while those under **2** are gradable.

Similarly with verbs: *I quite agree* means that I completely agree but *I quite enjoyed the party* means that it was enjoyable but I have been to better ones.

Note the position of *a* with *quite*: *quite a different proposal; quite a difficult book*. In the non-gradable examples shown under **1** above *quite* can stand in the normal position for adjectives. ▶

Q

When it does so, it strengthens the meaning: *a quite different proposal* means the same as *quite a different proposal* but is more emphatic.

Negative forms used with verbs always have the meaning *not completely*: *I don't quite agree; I don't quite like his literary style.*

Not quite with adjectives means *not completely*: *not quite full*; or *not exactly*: *not quite right*.

When it is used directly with a noun, it has the meaning *very good* and is COMPLIMENTary: *He is quite a cook; That was quite a party*.

Quite (so) is a very positive response: *'I think he's an excellent cook.' 'Quite (so).'*

R

r, R /ɑː/

The eighteenth letter of the alphabet. It is represented phonetically by /r/.

The pronunciation of this letter in modern RECEIVED PRONUNCIATION is different from many other languages. The tongue is almost in the same place as for /t/ and /d/ but does not touch the roof of the mouth. In RP it is pronounced only **before** a vowel, i.e. at the beginning of, or in the middle of, a word: *rat, red, bring, pronounce, bury, hurry*.

It is not pronounced when it is before a consonant: *hard* /hɑːd/, *fort* /fɔːt/, *Bert* /bɜːt/. It is not normally pronounced when it is the last letter of a word: *other* /'ʌðə/, *far* /fɑː/, *near* /nɪə/, but it is pronounced when such words are followed by another vowel: *other items* /ˌʌðər'aɪtəmz/, *far away* /ˌfɑːrə'weɪ/, *near enough* /ˌnɪərɪ'nʌf/.

Many speakers use a linking *r* in cases like *brother and sister* /ˌbrʌðərən'sɪstə/, where the first word ends with a written *r*. When the letter is not written it is called an intrusive *r* as in *Sheila and I* /'ʃiːlərənˌaɪ/, *law and order* /ˌlɔːrən'ɔːdə/ (the *d* in *and* is often omitted), or even *drawing* /'drɔːrɪŋ/ as a way of connecting the vowel sounds.

In other forms of English it is pronounced differently. In Scotland it is rolled, i.e. pronounced more strongly than in England. In some parts of south-east England it is pronounced /w/: *rat, red, bring, pronounce, bury, hurry* /wæt/ etc. In American English there is a retroflex *r* with the tip of the tongue curled back a little.

rh, RH

This combination of letters represents the GREEK letter ρ (rho) and is pronounced exactly like normal *r*; the *h* makes no difference at all to the pronunciation. It is found in words of Greek origin: *rhesus, rhododendron, rhombus*.

radio, radium & radius

Radio is the method of sending messages by electromagnetic waves. It is also the apparatus that sends or receives such messages: *Send it by radio; Buy a radio*.

Radium is a radioactive chemical element (Ra).

Radius (plural *radii*) is the distance from the centre of a circle to the perimeter; it is also the name of a bone in the FOREarm.

rather

This is the comparative of the archaic adverb *rathe* meaning *quickly, soon, early*. Although *rathe* itself is never found nowadays, its meanings have survived in *rather*, which often implies a preference. Like QUITE and PRETTY it is used to modify adjectives and adverbs, meaning *to a certain degree but not completely*: *This story is rather interesting; He did it rather quickly*. There is no difference between *a rather interesting story* and *rather an interesting story*.

Unlike *quite* and *pretty* it can be used:
- with comparative forms: *This is rather easier/more difficult than I expected; He did it rather earlier/more quickly than I expected; That was a rather easier question than I had expected*.
- with *too*: *This is rather too difficult for me; He did it rather too quickly; That is rather too difficult/rather too difficult a question*.
- with prepositional phrases: *He was rather in the way; I felt rather under stress*.

Rather can be used to change the meaning of what has been said: *He told me a story; (or) rather he told me a lie; I'm not complaining about his clothes but rather about his hygiene*.

When the subject changes: *I'd rather you told me the truth; I'd rather you didn't mention this conversation to her* the second verb is in the past although the time reference is in the future; this expresses the hypothetical nature of the idea. See SUBJUNCTIVE.

R

The idea of preference is clear in such sentences as *He's lazy rather than stupid; He should be criticised rather than praised; Rather than complain, I'll forget all about it; I'll forget all about it rather than complain.*

Confusion between sentences such as *He was complaining rather than criticising* and *I'll forget it rather than complain* leads to illogical forms such as ~~I'll forget about it rather than complaining~~.

The phrase *rather you than me/I* means that I would rather you did something than do it myself: *'This could be very difficult.' 'Yes. Rather you than me.'*

Rather can be an emphatically affirmative response to a question: *'Did you have a good holiday?' 'Rather.'* In this case the stress is on the second syllable /rɑː'ðɜː/. This usage is British and is rather old-fashioned nowadays.

would rather

Would rather describes a preference: *Where would you rather be?; I would rather be sitting on a beach (than in my office).* Note the position of *not* in the negative (predication negation): *I would rather not be sitting here.* The contraction is often used: *I'd rather be sitting on a beach.*

It is important for TAG QUESTIONS and SHORT ANSWERS to remember that the auxiliary verb is *would* (see HAD BETTER (*BETTER*)): *'You'd rather be sitting on a beach, wouldn't you?' 'Yes, I would.'*

In all of these examples *sooner* can be used instead of *rather*: *Where would you sooner be?* etc.

receipt

The *p* is silent: /rɪ'siːt/.

See B, B; DEBT; DOUBT; REDOUBT; SUBTLE.

received pronunciation

Standard English pronunciation, also known as received pronunciation (RP), developed as the pronunciation of the south-east of England. Of course there have always been regional variations in pronunciation but that accent was dominant among educated upper class people throughout the country in the late nineteenth century (see PUBLIC SCHOOLS). It became known as Oxford English, and later as BBC ENGLISH when the BBC adopted it in the 1920s as its standard pronunciation style for announcers and newsreaders. This was intended as a way of introducing a national standard but in some parts of the country and among some social classes it was seen as the elitist accent of the upper or educated classes of the south-east of England and was unpopular for that reason. In the 1970s social attitudes changed and regional accents became acceptable though still with variations; Scottish accents have always seemed acceptable, Irish and Welsh less so, and sometimes rural accents are thought to be more acceptable than urban ones. However the situation is still changing, and fashion in this, as in so many things, can change. Many BBC newsreaders now have regional accents.

As with so much of British life, social class plays an important part in the degree of acceptability of accent and the differing images of people who speak with different accents are of social importance. The use of received pronunciation by educated people and the upper classes was considered by others as a means of establishing, recognising, and reinforcing a social and political elite that excluded from its membership and influence those who did not speak in that way. For this reason, many people who wished to advance socially deliberately rejected their natural regional and class accents and (with varying degrees of success) imitated the accents of the people they wished to associate with. At the same time, some of the more unusual features of received pronunciation disappeared as pronunciation was in some cases adapted to spelling (e.g. OFF is no longer pronounced /ɔːf/, and OFTEN and *orphan* are no longer HOMOPHONES pronounced /ɔːfən/); a new standard pronunciation, which is basically RP but which has noticeable regional variations has come into being. Thus, while it is still true that in some parts of the UK (especially Scotland, Northern Ireland, parts of northern England, Wales, and parts of south-west England) strong regional accents are still found, in almost all the country a large number of people speak a form of English that is close to the standard pronunciation that is usually taught to foreign students and that is represented by the PHONETIC SYMBOLS used in this book.

See PRONUNCIATION; U & NON-U.

recessive accent

Although English pronunciation is far from regular, one phenomenon is that French words that entered the language after the Norman Conquest became adapted to the Germanic custom of stressing the first syllable: *nature, courage, village*. This pattern is to be found with French words that have entered the language more recently such as *menu, garage*, and is also found in the modern tendency to stress the first syllable (rather than the second) of *innovative*. In some longer words the stress is unpredictable or even variable (*centrífugal/centrifúgal, cóntroversy/contróversy, vóluntarily/voluntárily*). In cases of doubt, a DICTIONARY should be consulted.

redoubt

The *b* is silent: /rɪˈdaʊt/.

See B, B; DEBT; DOUBT; SUBTLE; RECEIPT.

reduplicated words

These are words that repeat the first part, usually changing the vowel or initial consonant, for effect.

argy-bargy	dispute, quarrel.
arty-farty	exaggeratedly or pretentiously artistic.
bow-wow	the noise a dog makes; a child's name for a dog. See ANIMAL NOISES.
bye-bye	goodbye.
dilly-dally	waste time.
ding-dong	the noise of a bell; a fight.
easy-peasy	very easy.
hanky-panky	trickery; immoral behaviour, especially sexual.
harum-scarum	wild, uncontrollable (of a person).
higgledy-piggledy	confused, disordered.
hocus-pocus	trickery, especially with complicated and confusing language.
mumbo-jumbo	meaningless ritual; confusing language.
puff-puff	a child's name for a steam engine or train.
shilly-shally	hesitate.
teeny-weeny	very small.
willy-nilly	whether or not I (etc.) want to do it or like it.

reflect & reflex

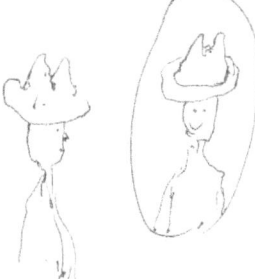

Reflect and ***reflection*** (rarely written *reflexion*, see -TION & -XION) refer to light or other things (air or water for example) being reflected from a surface; a *reflecting telescope* is one that uses a mirror to produce its image. Your behaviour can *reflect* your character. They can refer to deep thought or consideration: *I was reflecting on the effect the French Revolution on the development of the modern world; On reflection, I don't think that he is the right man for the job.*

➤

R

A *reflex* camera is one in which the picture is formed by a combination of mirror and lens. The word is also used for physiological *reflex(ive) actions* such as sneezing or BLINKING. A *reflex* angle is one of more than 180°.

For REFLEXIVE VERBS see the following article.

reflexive verbs

In English these are used only when the object is the same person or thing as the subject: *I fell but I didn't hurt myself; He caught a GLIMPSE (*SEE) of himself in the mirror.*

The reflexive pronouns are *myself, yourself, himself, herself, itself, oneself, ourselves, yourselves, themselves. Yourselves* is the only form of *you* that has an identifiable plural. The non-standard *theirselves* (cf *ourselves*) is sometimes heard.

A reflexive pronoun cannot be used as the subject of passive sentences: *I didn't hurt myself; ~~Myself wasn't hurt by me~~.*

The same pronouns are used to give emphasis: *She paid for herself* (reflexive); *She paid for it herself* (emphatic); *I myself have often said that. It was written by (me) myself* is the emphatic passive equivalent of *I myself wrote it.*

Reformation

In modern use this word (with a CAPITAL LETTER) only refers to the sixteenth-century movement in the Roman CATHOLIC Church that led to the establishment of PROTESTANT Churches. *Reform* is the usual word for change and improvement.

refuse

The verb meaning to indicate unwillingness is pronounced /rɪˈfjuːz/. The noun meaning *rubbish* is pronounced /ˈrefjuːs/.

regional names

Birmingham is sometimes called *Brum* and the people from that city are *Brummies*. Glasgow and Manchester have the adjectives *Glaswegian* and *Mancunian*, which are also used as nouns for the people: *She's a typical Mancunian.* Similarly, Liverpool has *Liverpudlian* (from *puddle* for *pool*) but the people from the city are known as *Scousers* and *Scouse* is another adjective and the name of the local dialect of English. Originally, *scouse* is the name of a stew, *lobscouse*, which was popular with sailors. Someone from the area of Newcastle-upon-Tyne in the north-east of England is a *Geordie* /ˈdʒɔːdi/ (from the name *George*). This is also the name of the local dialect. These adjectives are used for personal and cultural characteristics. We do not say ~~a Mancunian car~~, or ~~the Liverpudlian city council~~. In the case of an institution associated with a town or CITY we use its name as an adjective: *Liverpool city council; Stansted airport; Manchester cathedral.*

See COCKNEY.

register

A *register* is a list of people or other items; a person who keeps a register is a ***registrar*** and the place where a register is kept is a ***registry***. In Britain a *register office* is the government office where births, marriages, and deaths are recorded; a *register office wedding* is one performed in a register office instead of a church. The name *registry office* is quite commonly used colloquially. All British cars must be *registered* and carry a *registration plate*. These words are used for *registering* in a hotel, *registration* as a voter, and similar procedures. A *registered letter* is one that receives special security treatment in handling.

relation, relationship & relative

The difference between *relation* and *relationship* is not always clear. Basically, a ***relation*** is the way in which people or things are related and a relationship is the state of being related. However, this is not always reflected in practice: *Your view bears no relation to the facts* (it is totally unconnected with reality); *We lived next door to them for ten years and always had good relations with them.*

R

Countries have *diplomatic relations*. *In relation to* is the same as *as regards, with respect to* or is the same as *relative to* (below).

A ***relationship*** is the state of having relations with other people: *We always had a good relationship with our neighbours; His relationship (or relations) with his boss was (or were) never very happy.* *Relationship* now has the specific meaning of an emotional and sexual personal relationship: *I'm not in a relationship just now.* So, while a teacher should have a good relationship with his pupils in general, he should not have a relationship with any of them in particular.

One thing can be ***relative*** to another; a *relative increase* is different from an *absolute increase*; *relatively wealthy* means wealthy in relation to another group of people. A RELATIVE CLAUSE is one that relates two nouns. *Relative* (noun) is synonymous with *relation* meaning a family member.

Relativity is the state of being *relative*. Einstein wrote two theories of *relativity*.

A ***relational*** database is one that is structured to recognise the *relation* or *relationship* of stored items of information.

relative clauses

There are two types of relative CLAUSE, *defining* (also known as *restrictive*) and *non-defining* (also known as *non-restrictive*).

defining (restrictive) relative clauses

In *The man who sold me this painting said it was by Picasso* the relative clause *who sold me this painting* defines the man in question; without it we do not know which man said that the painting was by Picasso. This relative clause is an essential part of the sentence. The relative pronoun *who* is the subject of the relative clause. An ALTERNATIVE way of saying this, without changing the meaning in any way, is *The man that sold me this painting said it was by Picasso*. Some writers always prefer *who* to *that* for a human reference.

When the subject of the main clause is neuter, we have *The painting which/that is hanging on my wall is by Picasso*. Again there are two possible relative pronouns (*which* and *that*). There is no difference between them.

The relative pronoun can be the object of the relative clause: *The man WHO(M)/that I saw said it was by Picasso*. Here the relative pronoun *who(m)* or *that* is the object of the relative clause *who(m)/that I saw*. (For the use of *who(m)* see WHO AND WHOM). When it is the object it can be omitted: *The man I saw said it was by Picasso*. With neuter nouns we have: *The taxi which/that I took was red; The taxi I took was red*.

For defining relative clauses the possible relative pronouns are:

	personal	**neuter**
subject	who, that	which, that
object	who(m), that, (none)	which, that, (none)

In some cases the choice of relative pronoun is limited. These are discussed below.

non-defining (non-restrictive) relative clauses

In *The salesman, who knows a lot about art, says it is by Picasso* the relative clause *who knows a lot about art* does not define the salesman; it gives extra information about him. It is not an essential part of the sentence: *The salesman says it is by Picasso* is perfectly valid. This relative clause is expressed in speech by a short pause before and after it. In writing this pause is represented by commas. It would be possible, though unusual, to place the non-defining relative clause in brackets: *The salesman (who knows a lot about art) says it is by Picasso.* ➤

R

When the subject of the main clause is neuter, we have *That large painting, which was very expensive, is by Picasso.*

When the relative pronoun is the object of the relative clause we have *The salesman, who(m) I respect greatly, says it is by Picasso; That painting, which I bought yesterday, is by Picasso.*

For non-defining relative clauses the possible relative pronouns are

	personal	neuter
subject	*who*	*which*
object	*who(m)*	*which*

Compare these two sentences:
defining: *The painting which is hanging on my wall is by Picasso.*
non-defining: *That painting, which is hanging on my wall, is by Picasso.*

The sentence with a defining relative clause has *The painting...* with the definite article; the painting is defined in the relative clause. The sentence with the non-defining relative clause has *That painting...*; the more precise DETERMINER *that* defines the painting; we know which painting is under consideration before the relative clause begins because it is indicated at the time of speaking or it has been mentioned earlier. The relative clause is used to provide extra information about the painting that has already been defined.

The different types of relative clause can be combined in one sentence: *The painting that is hanging on my wall* **1***, which is by Picasso* **2***, is the one I bought yesterday* **3***.*
1 Defining – subject
2 Non-defining – subject
3 Defining – object

When the relative clause includes a prepositional verb the possibilities are:
defining personal: *The man (that) I bought it from says it is by Picasso; The man from whom I bought it says it is by Picasso.*

non-defining personal: *My next-door neighbour, whom I bought it from, says it is by Picasso; My next-door neighbour, from whom I bought it, says it is by Picasso.*

defining non-personal: *The painting (that) I told you about is by Picasso; The painting about which I told you is by Picasso.*

non-defining non-personal: *That painting, which I told you about yesterday, is by Picasso; That painting, about which I told you yesterday, is by Picasso.*

See WHO AND WHOM.

Sometimes a non-defining relative clause refers to another clause, not only to a noun; in these cases the relative pronoun *which* is always used: *He didn't know the answer, which surprised me; We've got no potatoes, which means we can't have chips.* Sometimes these sentences can be written as:
I don't think we've got any potatoes, in which case we can't have CHIPS. (I don't think we've got any potatoes. If it is true that we haven't, we can't have chips.)
There are no potatoes, for which reason we can't have chips. (There are no potatoes. For that reason we can't have chips.)

Sentences with *where* can be defining or non-defining and use commas in the same way as relative clauses do: *The house where I was born has been knocked down; My former house, where we held our anniversary party, has been knocked down.*

What is sometimes used as a relative pronoun but this is considered non-standard or vulgar: ~~*The painting what I bought yesterday.*~~

The relative pronoun is the subject or object of the verb. No other pronoun is needed: ~~*The man who he sold me this painting...*~~; ~~*The man I saw him said...*~~

summary
That is possible only in defining relative clauses; *who* and *which* can be used in all types.

religion

The CHURCH OF ENGLAND and CHURCH OF SCOTLAND have official status in those countries but except for the restrictions on the monarch (see CONSTITUTION) there is total freedom of religion in all walks of public life, though certain individuals may be prejudiced against members of certain religions.

rely & trust

Trust relates to faith or confidence:
You can trust her to repay the money.
Would you trust him with your car?
I wouldn't trust him an inch.
Trust me. I'm a doctor.
If our information can be trusted, the river is three miles away.
I couldn't trust myself to answer politely.
In God we trust. (The motto of the United States.)
You shouldn't have been so trusting.

It can be a noun:
Put/place your trust in his abilities.
You can have it on trust. (I trust you to pay for it or return it in the future.)
I must ask you to take this on trust. (i.e. to believe me although I give you no justification or reason to do so.)
Thank you for your trust.

When money is *in trust*, its management is in the hands of *trustees* instead of the person who owns the money. A *unit trust* is a common fund in which people invest their money, which is invested and managed professionally. Dividends are paid in proportion to a person's participation. In North America this is called a *mutual fund*. A *trust* is an arrangement by a group of companies or traders to work together to keep prices high and reduce competition. It is another name for a *cartel*. Laws against this practice are called *anti-trust* laws. A person who can be trusted is *trustworthy*. See -WORTHY.

Rely is closer to *depend* in meaning; it suggests confidence rather than faith: *Now that he is an INVALID he relies on his wife for everything; You can rely on his JUDGEMENT.*

In some cases the words can be interchanged with little difference in meaning. *You can trust his judgement* and *You can rely on his judgement* are close in meaning.

However, in:
1 *You can trust him with your car.*
and
2 *You can rely on him to treat your car well.*
it is necessary in **2** to state clearly what is implicit in the trust or faith shown in **1**.

In the above example *Now that he is an invalid he relies on his wife for everything* the meaning of dependence is clear. We can assume that he *trusted* his wife before he became an invalid, but because he was independent in movement he did not have to *rely on* her then.

The adjectives are *reliant* and *reliable*: *He is reliant on his wife; He is very reliable.*

remember & remind

Remember is the general word. *Recollect* /ˌrekəˈlekt/ and *recall* mean *remember* but suggest that the information is not immediately available in the memory and that an effort is necessary to find it. The differently pronounced word *re-collect* /ˌriːkəˈlekt/ means *to collect again*. See PREFIXES.

As with SENSE VERBS, *can* is often used as an auxiliary verb with *remember*: *I can remember the first space flight; Can you remember*

R

where you put the key?; She can never remember her own phone number.

To **remind** is to ensure that somebody does not forget information that is already known: *He reminded me to pay the gas bill.*

See INFINITIVE OR -ING?

repetition of subject

Sometimes in casual conversation native English speakers might say *My brother, he lives in Germany now; Liverpool, it's in the north-west of England.* This is clearly not standard usage, but it is quite common. It is found especially when the idea has not been fully thought out at the moment of speaking; there is an analogy here with one aspect of FRONTING.

replace & substitute

To *replace X with Y* means that Y is used instead of X. To *substitute X for Y* means that X is used instead of Y. The standard usage is as follows:
Computers have replaced typewriters in offices.
Typewriters have been replaced by computers in offices.
Companies have replaced their old typewriters with computers.
Companies have substituted computers for their old typewriters.
It depends on whether you are dealing with the thing that is going in or the one that is coming out. However, a non-standard use is sometimes found: *Typewriters have been substituted by computers.*

Football commentators often say *X has been substituted by Y; Y has substituted (for) X* perhaps because the new player is officially called the *substitute*.

resources, recourse & resort

resources

Resources (the word is usually found in the plural) are MEANS, stocks, reserves, supplies, or assets that are available for use when required. A country's *natural resources* are its natural wealth, usually referring to minerals and energy. *Human resources* are the employees of a company, managed by the human resources (HR) department. This term is now generally used instead of PERSONNEL. A *resourceful* person is one who is good at finding solutions to problems and difficulties.

recourse

To *have recourse to* something means to *have something available* or to *make use of it*. It is not frequently used: *Because we couldn't START (*BEGIN & START) the car we had recourse to the bicycles.*

resort

As a noun it is similar to *recourse*:

Without a car | we had no other resort but the bicycle.
a bicycle was our best resort.
we resorted/had to resort to the bicycle.

In the last resort means *as the last possibility*: *The police will try to solve the problem peacefully, but in the last resort armed action may be necessary.*

When it is used as a verb its meaning is similar to this: *The police tried to arrest the kidnapper without resorting to violence.*

A *resort* is also a place that people go to for holiday or relaxation: *a holiday/ TOURIST/seaside/mountain/SKIING/health resort.*

rest

The word *rest* is usually connected with relaxation: *to rest* or *to have a rest*. However, it also means a lack of movement. So a *restful day* is a relaxing one with little or no activity, but a *restless night* is not one with no relaxation, for example a night spent working, but is one with disturbed movements while trying to sleep; compare for example the *restless wind* or *sea*, which never stops moving. If a car or other moving object *comes to rest* it stops moving and if it is *at rest* it is STATIONARY.

A *rest* is also something on which a gun or other thing can be placed for support. *Unrest* is opposition, perhaps physical, to authority.

The unrelated noun *rest* means *remainder*: *I'll take this and you can have the rest*.

right and wrong

People learning English or using it as a foreign language naturally want to know what is right and what is wrong; this is not always an easy question to answer. As a look at the list of IRREGULAR VERBS or the article -ISE & -IZE will show, there are areas where English is rather imprecise.

Many native speakers say *He don't live here no more* (see NEGATION OF VERBS); *He AIN'T me father*. Here it is easy enough to compare these forms with a standard and say that they differ from it.

Another problem is word order. Rules are given above for ADJECTIVE ORDER, but it is possible to invent unusual contexts for sentences which would break some of those rules. Despite the basic rules that students learn, the subject does not always stand before the verb in affirmative sentences with the object following it (see FRONTING). A basic rule of English is that an adverb cannot stand between verb and object but sometimes, for example when the object is very long, this may be the only sensible way of making the sentence.

Language – any language – is not a branch of engineering, where things are absolutely possible or impossible. It is a means of human expression and thus is, and can be, no more logical, consistent, and obedient to pre-existing rules than the creative mental process that produces the desire for expression in the first place can be. It is more like art, another form of human expression, and as in art the only sensible advice is: First learn the rules, and **then** decide how and when to break them.

There is no English Academy as there is in other languages to provide universally accepted rulings on what is right or wrong in spelling or grammar, although there is very widespread agreement among linguists and publishers as to what is acceptable in formal language. The style of Oxford University Press and its DICTIONARY are highly regarded, though there is room for disagreement; see the INTRODUCTORY NOTES for my own variations from it. However, the grey areas, where variation is possible, represent a very small part of the language as a whole.

right(ly)

There are two adverb forms: *right* and *rightly*.

right

This means *to the right-hand side* as in *move/turn/keep right*.

It also has a generally positive meaning that something is or should be done *immediately*, *exactly* or *correctly*:
Go right on (STRAIGHT ahead).
Right now/away (immediately).
Come right back (directly, immediately).
Right here, right on the target (exactly).
Behave right; do it right; if I understand you right (correctly).
Right to the top, right round the hill, right into the house (all the way, completely).

It is found as an adverb in certain TITLES (*HONOURS AND TITLES*): *Right Honourable, Right Reverend, Right Worshipful*.

Right, left and centre means everywhere in all directions, indiscriminately: *People were running around right, left and centre; He's been asking questions right, left and centre*.

R

rightly

This means justifiably or in the right way: *Rightly, he decided to go home; He acted rightly; He was found guilty, and rightly so; I thought, rightly or wrongly, that he was mad.*

It is often used with a past participle: *He was rightly described, condemned, promoted* etc.

See LEFT AND RIGHT; WRONG(LY).

rise & arise

Rise, rose, risen is intransitive and means *go, move or come up.* It is used in cases of literal, physical movement: *The sun rises in the east; He rose from his seat when Mary entered the room; Arthur had not risen when his visitor arrived.* (He had not got up, he was still in bed.) Prices, percentages, rates, indices etc. also *rise.*

Arise, arose, arisen is intransitive and means *appear, become noticeable.* It does not have the literal meaning of *rise* but is used to refer to problems, questions, difficulties doubts, and other abstract ideas: *A doubt has arisen regarding his ability; If any questions arise, please refer them to me.* The RELATIONSHIP between these two words, *rise* and *arise,* is very similar to that between ROUSE & AROUSE.

Raise-raised-raised is transitive and means to *lift* or *move something upwards.* It can be either literal or figurative in use: *The divers raised the SHIP from the seabed; They have raised their prices; That joke always raises a laugh; It's a good idea, but how will you raise the money?*

It also means to *grow vegetables or breed animals*: *They raise their own carrots; These animals were raised in Lancashire* and thus *to bring up people*: *He was born in Liverpool and raised (brought up) in Birmingham.*

To *raise a point/subject/question* etc. at a meeting is to start a discussion about it.

To *raise your voice* means to speak more loudly, perhaps in anger: *You'll have to raise your voice. I can't hear you; Don't raise your voice to me.*

To *raise your eyebrows* is to show surprise or disbelief.

Give rise to means *cause, produce, result in*: *His behaviour gave rise to considerable disTRUST; The bad weather has given rise to many problems.*

road

English has a large number of words to name roads. In an urban area **road** and **street** are interchangeable (*Oxford Road, Oxford Street*). However, a street must be in an urban area and have buildings on its sides whereas a *road* can be the road through a rural area that links two urban areas; if it passes between fields or through woods from one town to another it is a road. Thus the road leading out of a town often has the name of the town which it leads to: *Liverpool Road, Manchester Road, Oxford Road* etc.; this is always *road.*

A **lane** was once a narrow road in a town or a small country road linking two villages; perhaps it still is but if those villages have grown and the lane between them has been built up and been adapted for heavy traffic, it may still be called a *lane* but have no evidence of its narrow rural origins.

A **motorway** is a main road designed for vehicles; it is not open to pedestrians or animals. It is divided into two *carriageways* for traffic travelling in different directions and each carriageway is divided into *lanes.*

Despite its ETYMOLOGY a British **avenue** is not necessarily wide with trees along the sides. It is a name that may be chosen for no obvious reason to be given to a road that is about 100 metres long and barely wide enough for two cars to pass, and which is a dead end.

There are certain fixed expressions: *No through road* but *crossroads* and *one way street.*

A *dead end* (a road with no exit) is also called a *cul-de-sac.* This French term means *the bottom of the bag.* Common abbreviations are *Rd (Road); St (Street); Ave (Avenue).*

See WAY.

rob & steal
People and institutions can be **robbed**: *Three masked men robbed the bank in Dale Street; She was robbed of her life's savings.*

Steal, stole, stolen is used for the things which are stolen: *Thieves stole her jewellery; All her jewellery was stolen.*

rogue
A *rogue* is a dishonest person. Sometimes it is used jokingly: *Let's see what the young rogue's done.* Used adjectivally it refers to something that is not normal in a way that cannot be explained easily: *a rogue value, a rogue result, a rogue state.*

Roman
Roman is the adjective referring to the city of Rome; it is used to refer to ancient and medieval Rome, for example the *Roman Empire*. The word is not used to refer to modern Rome, though the *Roman CATHOLIC Church* is centred there.

Romanesque is a style of architecture with round arches that was common in mediaeval Europe.

Romance ultimately relates to Rome, coming from the Latin *romanicus*. Now it commonly refers to an atmosphere or sense of unreality or wonder, or to romantic love. *Romance languages* are those that are derived from Latin: *Spanish, Portuguese, French* etc.

Romansh is a Romance language spoken in the Swiss canton of Grisons.

Romania (also *Rumania*) is a European country.

Romani: This word refers to GYPSIES; it is the name of their language and of the people in that language; the name is unconnected with Rome or Romania. The language is a corrupted form of Hindi that has absorbed words from many European languages. A *Rom* is a male gypsy in the Romany language but the word is sometimes used in English to refer to the people.

Roman influence in Britain
Most of what is now Britain was part of the Roman Empire. A number of archaeological remains from those days have survived and have been recovered, but the only part of the Roman administration of *Britannia* that has survived into the present is the layout of the main roads (not the modern motorways) radiating from London. In parts these still follow the routes of the Roman roads. All other Roman physical and cultural influences disappeared from England after the country came under the control of the Germanic tribes; in particular, no influence of the Latin language remained from the days of Roman rule. Apart from a few Latin words that entered English via Germanic languages in the early MIDDLE AGES, the influence of Latin on modern English dates only from the Norman conquest in 1066.

Roman influence, especially the Roman Christian Church, did survive in Wales, Ireland, parts of Scotland and the north-east of England during the period of English history that is known as the *Dark Ages*. The Angles, Saxons and other Germanic tribes that invaded Britain were not Christian.

See CHURCH OF ENGLAND; ENGLAND, A BRIEF HISTORY; IRELAND, A BRIEF HISTORY; SCOTLAND, A BRIEF HISTORY; WALES, A BRIEF HISTORY.

rouse & arouse
Both of these words are transitive.

Rouse means *to WAKE someone up*. It is used in cases of literal, physical awakening: *Will you rouse me at half past seven, please?; I was roused by the sound of the birds singing.*

Arouse means *to cause or increase an intellectual or emotional state*. It does not have the literal meaning of *rouse* but is used to refer to anger, enthusiasm, and other abstract ideas: *His suggestion aroused my interest; My curiosity was aroused to such an extent that I investigated the matter further.* It also used for *sexual arousal*, being *sexually aroused*. The RELATIONSHIP between these two words is very similar to that between RISE & ARISE.

R

row
There are three separate words with two pronunciations.

A *row* /rəʊ/ is a STRAIGHT line of people or things: *a row of seats in a cinema; a horizontal row of cells in a computer spreadsheet; a row of plants in a garden.*

To *row* /rəʊ/ a BOAT is to make it move by using OARS.

A *row* /raʊ/ is a loud, unpleasant noise. Thus it means *a loud argument*: *I had a row with my wife/boss this morning.* It can be a verb: *My neighbours are always rowing.*

See ALWAYS WITH PRESENT CONTINUOUS *(*PRESENT TENSES | PRESENT CONTINUOUS | WITH ALWAYS ETC.)*

Rowling
The name of the author J. K. Rowling is pronounced /ˈrəʊlɪŋ/.

rule
A *rule* is a principle that governs something: *The rules of the game.* *As a rule* means *generally*. A *ruler* is a person who rules or governs, or a piece of wood or metal with measurements marked on it used for ruling STRAIGHT lines. To *rule something in* is to accept it as reasonable or include it; to *rule it out* is the opposite, to reject it as unacceptable.

Ruritania
The fictional Kingdom of Ruritania, particularly its capital Strelsau, was the setting for the novel *The Prisoner of Zenda* (1894) and others by Anthony Hope. Hope's Ruritania is an autocratic, German-speaking, CATHOLIC country between Saxony and Bohemia; however, the films made from the novel and references to the country in the media present it as a picturesque, romantic, fairy-tale kingdom with a much less precise location.

Russian
Russian words written in the Cyrillic script are transliterated into English as follows:

UPPER CASE	lower case	*l. c. italic*	English equivalent	UPPER CASE	lower case	*l. c. italic*	English equivalent
А	а	*а*	a	Р	р	*р*	r
Б	б	*б*	b	С	с	*с*	s
В	в	*в*	v	Т	т	*m*	t
Г	г	*г*	g	У	у	*у*	u
Д	д	*д*	d	Ф	ф	*ф*	f
Е	е	*е*	e	Х	х	*х*	kh /x/
Ё	ё	*ё*	ë, e	Ц	ц	*ц*	ts
Ж	ж	*ж*	zh	Ч	ч	*ч*	ch
З	з	*з*	z	Ш	ш	*ш*	sh
И	и	*и*	i	Щ	щ	*щ*	shch
Й	й	*й*	i, y*	Ъ	ъ	*ъ*	" (*hard sign*)
К	к	*к*	k	Ы	ы	*ы*	y
Л	л	*л*	l	Ь	ь	*ь*	' (*soft sign*)
М	м	*м*	m	Э	э	*э*	é, e
Н	н	*н*	n	Ю	ю	*ю*	yu
О	о	*о*	o	Я	я	*я*	ya
П	п	*п*	p				

*only used after vowels

S

s, S /es/

The nineteenth letter of the alphabet. It is pronounced /s/, /z/, /ʃ/ or /ʒ/.

it is pronounced /s/

At the beginning of a word, before both VOICED and unvoiced consonants: *smell*, SPOT.

In the PREFIX *mis*. However, it is pronounced /z/ in *misanthrope* and *misery*, which do not have this prefix.

In the prefix *dis-* but it is pronounced /z/ in *disaster*, *disEASE* and *dissolve* and also in *dismal*, which does not have this prefix.

Before an unvoiced consonant: *asking, hospital, instance, obscure, western*.

After an unvoiced consonant: *asks, cakes, coughs, hats, mops*.

In the suffixes *-sive* and *-sity*: *evasive, university*.

Usually when written *ss* but it is pronounced /z/ in DESSERT, *dissolve, hussar, possess* /pəz'es/, *scissors*. See /ʃ/ below.

In words that end *-lse, -nse, -pse, -rse*: ELSE, *dense*, CORPSE, *course* but it is pronounced /z/ in *cleanse* /klenz/ and *parse*.

In some other words with *-se*. Among them are *base, case, cease, chase, crease, dose, goose, grease, horse,* LOOSE, *louse, mouse, purchase, release*.

In these words that end with *-ise* (with /aɪs/): *concise, paradise, precise*; (with /ɪs/): PREMISE, *promise, treatise*; also in *porpoise, tortoise*. See O, O.

In *house, excuse*, REFUSE, USE as nouns.

Usually at the end of a word after *a, i, o,* and *u* (*gas, this, chaos, bus*); in all words with *-us* and *-ous*; but it is pronounced /z/ in *as, does, has, his, is, was*.

In CENSURE and *tonsure*.

it is pronounced /z/

Between a vowel and a voiced consonant: *husband, raspberry* /'razbərɪ/, *cosmos, charisma;* in these words with *res-*: *reserve, reside, residue resilient, resist, resolve, resonant, resource, result, resume, resurrect*.

When *s* is added to a noun or verb that ends with a voiced consonant or a vowel: *jobs, phones, seas, ways; gives, sends, frees, plays*.

Between vowels: *easy, reason*.

In words that end in *-ISE* /aɪz/ except for those listed above.

In some words that end *-se*. Among them are *cheese, hose, lose, phase, rise, rose, these*.

In *house, excuse, refuse, use*, when they are used as verbs.

it is pronounced /ʃ/

In the combination *sh*: *short, fish*.

In the suffix *-ssion*: *mission, suppression*.

In *issue, fissure, pressure, sure* (also ASSURE, *ensure, insure*), and *tissue*.

it is pronounced /ʒ/

In words that end with [vowel]*sure* e.g. *leisure, measure, pleasure*.

In words that end with *-sion*: e.g. *decision, inclusion, vision* except following *er*, when it is /ʃ/: *diversion, immersion, version*.

silent *s*

It is silent in AISLE /'aɪl/ and ISLAND /'aɪlənd/.

S

sh, SH
See above.

It is not pronounced /ʃ/ when it occurs at the join point in compound words such as *dishonour* and *mishap*.

See COMPOUND NOUNS.

safe & save
Safe /seɪf/ is the adjective. It is also a noun referring to a strong container in which money and other valuable items are kept.

Save /seɪv/ is the verb.

Save can also mean *except*, but this meaning is not found in current English except sometimes in legal documents.

safety & security
Both of these are to do with protection from danger.

Safety is protection from natural risks: *The flooded river threatened the village's safety*; or unintentional man-made dangers: *safety at work; the safety of drugs*. Note the endings of the abstract nouns: *safety* but *unsafeness*.

Security is protection against deliberate human activity: *The company's security department is investigating the theft; A security guard is on duty at the factory all night*.

Safety regulations ensure that an aeroplane can fly with the minimum risk of mechanical or human failure. *Security staff* ensure that terrorists do not board the plane. *Safety at work* refers to physical safety in the workplace; *job security* is the certainty that you will not lose your job.

A *security* is a name for a financial instrument such as a share certificate. *Security* for a loan is the valuable object that is offered as a guarantee of repayment.

sail

A *sail* is the piece of cloth used on a *sailing* SHIP or BOAT to catch the wind and move it; if a ship is *sailing* it is moving. However, the word has survived the change from *wind* to other power, and a ship in motion is still *sailing*, and a *sailor* is a person who *sails a ship/boat* or *sails on one* (transitive or intransitive). When a ship leaves PORT it *sails* or *sets sail* (from the positioning of sails to allow a ship to move). The arms of a windmill are also called *sails*.

salary & wage
A *salary* is paid, usually monthly, to people in professional or administrative employment. It is quoted annually: *I earn £50,000 a year*.

A *wage* is (or *wages are*, both forms are used) paid daily or weekly to a manual worker. It is quoted weekly: *I earn £300 a week*.

same, very & -self (reflexive pronouns)
Same means *identical*; it is the opposite of *different*.
Apples are the same price as pears.
Apples cost the same as pears.
John lives in the same street as Mary.
John and Mary live in the same street.
The same system is used in all departments.
The TV news showed the same pictures again and again.
TV channel 1 showed the same pictures as channel 2.

I saw channel 1 and then changed to channel 2, but the pictures they were showing were (JUST) the same.
The TV news was showing the same pictures as before.
He went to the same school as me/I did.

In the above examples, *as* is used to make the comparison; there are occasions when *the same* introduces a RELATIVE CLAUSE and is followed by *that*.
1 *You stayed in the same hotel as me/I did.* See CASE, GRAMMATICAL.
2 *That's the same hotel (that) we stayed in.*

Sentence **1** can be converted into *You and I stayed in the same hotel* but no such conversion is possible with sentence **2**. However, **2** can be converted into *That's the very hotel (that) we stayed in* or, as above: *That's precisely/exactly/just the hotel (that) we stayed in.*

In this case *very* is used as an adjective (usually it is an adverb): *You are the very man I wanted to speak to; That is the very hotel we stayed in.* These sentences could be rewritten using adverbs: *...precisely/exactly/JUST the man/hotel...*

Because of the precise definition, THE is almost always the DETERMINER used, though possessive forms are possible with personal characteristics or physical features and in a rather dramatic context: *Those were her very words; His very silence was frightening; My very blood ran cold.* However, if there is an attributive ADJECTIVE before the noun, *very* reverts to its usual role of intensifying the adjective: *Those were her very last words; His very unusual silence was frightening; My very own blood ran cold.*

REFLEXIVE pronouns can be used to add intensity. They are used in apposition: *I **myself** wasn't able to lift it; I wasn't able to lift it myself; The hotel (itself) wasn't damaged (itself) but some cars parked nearby were.*

sanction

This confusing word means to *authorise* or *approve*, and also to *attach a penalty* to something. It is also used as a noun. This confusion arises from its origin in Latin *sanctio(n-)*, from a root meaning *to make sacred or inviolable*. Sometimes *diplomatic* or *trade sanctions* (meaning an embargo) are applied to a country, but apart from this it is best to avoid the word.

sans

Pronounced /sænz/ this means *without*, as it does in French. It is not used in modern English but SHAKESPEARE'S line from *As You Like It* (act 2, sc. 7) that man's life ends *Sans teeth, sans eyes, sans taste, sans everything* is so well known that modern writers sometimes adapt the phrase.

SAS

The *Special Air Service* is the elite regiment of the British Army, not of the Royal Air Force. The equivalent in the RAF is the Parachute Regiment and in the Royal Marines it is the *Special BOAT Service* (SBS).

saw & see-saw

Saw is the past of *see*.

A *saw* is a tool used for cutting wood.

A *see-saw* is a thing that children play on, a long BEAM *(*SHINE)* of wood or metal with a seat at each end. It is supported in the middle and as the children move in their seats, the beam pivots on its MID *(*CENTRE & MIDDLE)* point and the ends move up and down.

say etc.

say, said, said /sed/

This is the usual word for linguistic expression. It is used to present DIRECT and INDIRECT SPEECH.
He said, 'I'll see you tomorrow.'
He said (that) he would see me the following day.
Will you say why you did that? ➤

S

What can you say/can be said in favour of this proposal?
Say what time you'll arrive.
Say which you prefer.
'Which do you prefer?' 'Oh, I can't really say.'
Shall we say (agree on) *the red ONE?*
We must have a meeting soon, say (for example) *the end of this month.*
If you pay a deposit of, say, 10% of the price, I'll reserve it for you.

Say is used with defined words in a text: *You say your prayers; A priest says Mass.*
You can say that again expresses strong agreement.
I'll start when you say the word (give me an order or permission).
Say when (indicate when I have given you enough food or drink).

tell, told, told

Tell is similar to *say* but (with the exceptions noted below) it is concerned with passing information and it must have a personal indirect object. It is not used with DIRECT SPEECH.
He told me (that) he would see me the following day.
Will you tell me why you did that?
Tell me what time you'll arrive.
Tell me which you prefer.
Please tell me your name.
That's what she said, I tell you. (I ASSURE you.)
He told me how he cooks/how to cook rice.

Will you tell us what happened?
I told (warned) you not to trust him.

He told us the story of when they went to Moscow.
He told me a joke.
I'll tell you a secret.
To *tell somebody to do something* is to say what they should do and can effectively be like giving an order:

She told us to be here at 10.00.
We were told to be here at 10.00. See PASSIVE VOICE.
Do as/what I tell you.
Do as/what you're told.

tell without an indirect object

He told the story of when they went to Moscow.
He told a joke.
'Is he telling the truth?' 'I don't think he has ever told a LIE.'
Has he learned to tell the time yet? (to read the time from a clock.)
Now you know our plan but you must promise not to tell (not to reveal it).
I'll tell (on you). (I'll reveal your secret in public or to the authorities, for example to a teacher in a school. It is a rather CHILDISH expression.)
I couldn't tell (determine) *which road to take.*
Can you tell the twins apart? (Distinguish between them.)
As far as I can tell, he's Irish. (From the available evidence.)
The strain was telling (on me). (Having a noticeable effect.)

other expressions

To tell tales is to reveal embarrassing information about someone.
You're telling me expresses strong agreement.
That would be telling. (That would mean revealing too much information).
A telling comment or *blow* is a strong, effective one.
There's no telling what he'll do. (It's impossible to know.)
Tell me another; Tell that to the marines. (I don't believe you.)

S

The word *tell* originally meant *count*. A *teller* is a bank employee who counts money; an *automatic teller machine* (ATM) is a bank machine that issues money. The word *teller* is only used in banks and for people who count votes in ELECTIONS; in supermarkets money is taken by a *cashier* /kəˈʃɪə/.

speak

Speak, spoke, spoken is usually intransitive: *I spoke to him yesterday; We spoke about his proposal; Speaking for myself* (giving my own opinion); *I can't speak for John* (on his behalf).

Transitively it is used with languages: *Can he speak Swedish?*

To speak your mind is to give an honest opinion.

To speak out is to speak freely and openly.

His honesty speaks for itself (is very obvious, needs no further support).

His silence speaks volumes (is very significant).

Is there any more NEWS? *Not/nothing/none to speak of.* (Not/nothing/none WORTH mentioning.)

If you are *on speaking terms* with someone you have a reasonable but not intimate RELATIONSHIP.

A *speaker* is someone who speaks, at a meeting or congress for example. *The Speaker* is the Chairman of the House of Commons; the origin of this title is that he/she speaks for (i.e. represents) the House to the Monarch. The person who speaks officially on behalf of a group of people or an organisation is a *spokesman, spokeswoman* or *spokesperson*. See INCLUSIVE LANGUAGE.

A *loudspeaker* is an electric device for reproducing sound.

A *speakeasy* was a place where illegal alcohol was sold during PROHIBITION in the USA.

Doublespeak is language that is ambiguous or confusing, often deliberately so.

Newspeak is a word invented by George Orwell in his book 1984 to describe the corrupted language used in political PROPAGANDA.

talk

Talk is usually intransitive and means *to communicate verbally*. In some cases it is interchangeable with *speak*: *I talked/spoke to him yesterday; We talked/spoke about his proposal*.

To talk someone into or *out of something* is to persuade or dissuade them. *Someone has talked* means that someone has revealed a secret; *people will talk* means that they will start gossiping. When *money talks*, it exercises its power.

Talk of introduces an emphatic statement: *Talk of delays! It took me an hour to* GET *here; Talk of incompetence! I waited half an hour and still didn't* GET *served*.

A *talk* is a speech or LECTURE; *talks* are negotiations; *talk* is rumour or gossip. *Now you're talking* expresses strong agreement. If you *talk* BIG you are boasting or exaggerating; if you are *talking shop* you are talking about your business or profession, and if you are *talking nineteen to the dozen*, you are talking without stopping and are the sort of person who could *talk the hind leg off a donkey*. But if you are *talking through your hat* you are talking nonsense unlike someone who *knows what he's talking about*, who is talking with authority on a subject.

-scape

The word *landscape* has given RISE to a number of formations such as *seascape, cityscape, roofscape, moonscape*.

schedule

Two pronunciations /ˈskedjuːl/ and /ˈʃedjuːl/ are used.

schism

This was traditionally pronounced /ˈsɪz(ə)m/ but the pronunciation /ˈskɪz(ə)m/ is now frequent.

schwa

This is the name for the sound represented in the International Phonetic Alphabet by the symbol /ə/. It can be represented by all vowel letters in English. It is always unstressed in pronunciation and is

S

often very short, being the minimum vowel sound that is needed to move from one consonant to another. *Schwa* is the name of the letter representing this sound in the Hebrew alphabet, and the name has been adopted in linguistics.

See PHONETIC SYMBOLS | MONOPHTHONGS.

score

Originally this was a cut or mark made on a piece of wood, metal, stone etc. This use survives in some expressions. The skin of meat can be *scored* before it is cooked, a *goal* or *point* is *scored* (i.e. marked in the record) in sports and games, and *to score a game* means to keep the *score*; the *score* is the situation at any time in the game, for example the *half-time score*. '*What's the score?*' is the question asked about a game in progress; the *final score* is the result. A mistake in writing can be *scored out* (crossed out) and a word can be emphasised by *underscoring* (underlining) it; the symbol _ is called an *underscore*.

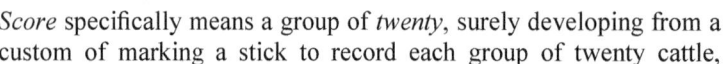

Score specifically means a group of *twenty*, surely developing from a custom of marking a stick to record each group of twenty cattle, sheep etc. as a means of recording the total number. Now it is not used to mean precisely twenty but is found in expressions such as *scores of people, people by the score* (in considerable numbers). *Threescore years and ten* (seventy) is considered the natural life of MANKIND (*INCLUSIVE LANGUAGE)* according to the Bible (Psalm 90:10), and in the Gettysburg address Abraham Lincoln spoke of what had happened *fourscore and seven years ago*. However, such usage seems unusual to modern ears.

To *settle a score* means to pay off an account or meet an obligation; it can also mean to take revenge.

From its meaning of scoring goals or points in a game, *score* has developed a slang meaning of being successful in buying drugs or for a man succeeding in having sex with a partner.

In music, the *score* is the written representation of the music. A piece of music can be *scored* for a full orchestra, for a piano etc.

To *know the score* means to be up to date with events, to have full knowledge of the background to a situation.

See MUSICAL NOTATION AND TERMINOLOGY.

Scotch, Scots & Scottish

Scot and *Scotsman/woman* are the usual nouns for the people of Scotland. *Scottish* is the usual adjective though *Scots* is sometimes used adjectivally. *Scotch* is used in certain fixed expressions: *Scotch broth, egg, mist, pancakes, terriers* (dogs), *whisky*. A *Scotch egg* is a hard-boiled egg wrapped in sausage-meat and fried. *Scotch* by itself can mean Scotch whisky: *I'll have a Scotch; a bottle of Scotch*.

To *scotch a rumour* is to counter it, to make it ineffective. To get off *scot-free* is to escape without punishment. *Scotch tape* is the trade name of a kind of transparent adhesive tape. None of these three meanings is connected with Scotland.

Scotland, a brief history

See the note for history articles on page xv.

The Roman invasion of Britain extended to Scotland, but the Highland area was never conquered and in 122 AD a wall was built to separate Scotland from the rest of the island. This is known as Hadrian's Wall and is now wholly in England; parts of it can still be seen. Following the Roman withdrawal the occupation of England by Germanic tribes spread into south-east Scotland while Celtic tribes, some native to Scotland and some from Ireland, occupied much of the rest of the country. The Vikings from Scandinavia occupied coastal areas and islands in the north of Scotland. The Celtic tribes gradually united and a border with England was established close to where it is now. *Macbeth* was King of Scotland from 1040 to 1057, but SHAKESPEARE's play has little basis in historical reality; a number of elements in it were written to please King James VI, who had become James I of England a few years earlier.

The Norman invasion of England also spread to Scotland. Although Scotland remained separate, many Norman knights received land in Scotland and regarded the King of England as their feudal chief. This state of affairs led to constant dispute and misunderstanding as to the precise relationship between the two countries, the Scots claiming a greater degree of independence than the English were willing to recognise.

In 1297 William Wallace began to act against English power in Scotland. He may have had personal reasons for hatred of the English but his guerrilla campaign proved popular. After initial success he was defeated and captured by the English in the following year; he was tortured and killed. In 1306 Robert Bruce became king, leading the party that wanted independence from England. Despite great differences among Scottish political and military leaders (medieval Scotland's constant problem) Bruce defeated his domestic enemies and in 1314 defeated the English army at the Battle of Bannockburn; in 1320 Scotland declared that it was independent of England, independence that was recognised by the pope. For many generations though, Scotland was to suffer internal problems of government and royal succession, some accidental and some arising from political conflict; constant fighting on the border with England further weakened the country.

In the sixteenth century Reformation religious ideas started to grow in Scotland. James V's opposition to Reformation led to a dispute with Henry VIII of England (his uncle), who revived the English claim to Scotland. James died in 1542 and his daughter Mary Stuart (Mary Queen of Scots) became Queen. She was six days old.

Scotland's relations with England were poor; it was a CATHOLIC country at a time when Protestant England felt insecure as a result of being surrounded by Catholic neighbours. War continued between Scotland and England, and the young queen was taken to France for her safety and married to the son of the King of France, who saw her as a means of acquiring Scotland, and perhaps England, for himself. Meanwhile, the Reformation in Scotland was taking a more extreme Protestant course than in England and in 1561, after her husband's death, Mary returned to a Scotland divided on religious grounds. Her second husband was killed, possibly by the man she later married, and then she was taken prisoner by her opponents. She escaped and tried to return to power (her baby son had been crowned King James VI) but her attempt failed. Instead of seeking exile in France, she appealed to her cousin, Elizabeth I of England, for help in 1568. Mary was an embarrassment to Elizabeth. Scotland fell into civil war, Mary was imprisoned in England, and was seen as a focus of Catholic conspiracy. In 1582 she was executed.

When Queen Elizabeth I of England died in 1603, James VI of Scotland was the legitimate heir to the English throne. James moved to London (see Scotland Yard in POLICE) and governed Scotland through a Privy Council. He returned to Scotland only once. The crowns of Scotland and England were united though the countries remained separate and independent.

Religious dispute continued in Scotland in the seventeenth century with the National Covenant as an expression of Protestant identity. Though divided, Scotland was strong and tried to influence the English Civil War by supporting the Parliamentary side, in the hope of introducing Scottish Presbyterianism to England, but this religion was not sufficiently popular there. Scotland continued to try to influence the situation in England, and for many years Scotland suffered internal religious and political dispute. The departure of James VII (James II of England), and the failure of a rebellion in his support, led to further political trouble and war, with King William III of England (William of Orange) wanting to establish his authority in Scotland. Scotland was weakened politically and economically by a disastrous attempt in the 1690s to establish a colony in Darien (Central America), and in 1714 under Queen Anne (the last Stuart monarch) Scotland and England were united as the United Kingdom. Attempts by rebellion in 1715 and 1745 to restore the Catholic Stuart line in

S

Scotland failed, and Scotland remained part of the United Kingdom, participating fully in its affairs though it kept its different legal and educational systems. The failure of the 1745 rebellion led by Prince Charles Edward Stuart (Bonny Prince Charlie [*bonny* is a Scottish word meaning good-looking, attractive]) led to a major reorganisation of Scottish society that coincided with the Industrial Revolution. This involved the destruction of the traditional power of the Highland clans (tribes), who had supported the 1745 rebellion, and in the following hundred years they were largely removed from their land (the Highland Clearances) to make way for sheep farming; many emigrated to Canada (Nova Scotia), Australia or New Zealand. In the eighteenth century Scotland participated actively in the intellectual development of the European Enlightenment.

In the nineteenth century nationalism developed as a political force in Scotland, promoted by the writer Sir Walter Scott, though he personally supported the Union with England. Tartan, the typical Scottish clothing pattern of coloured lines and squares, became extremely fashionable at this time and has remained an essential part of Scottish culture to the present day. The wearing of the kilt was also part of this process; the garment that a Scottish man wears is most definitely not called a skirt. The kilt and associated Highland dress is acceptable at any level of social formality and in any formal situation.

During the twentieth century political support for independence, or at least a measure of separate government, grew in Scotland; in 1999 the Scottish Parliament, with wide-ranging powers to govern Scotland internally, was opened. Scotland rejected independence in a referendum held in 2014 but voted to remain in the European Union in the 2016 UK referendum. Its future is uncertain at the time of writing (July 2018).

The population of Scotland is a little more than five million.

The Scots have a distinctive way of speaking English; the letter *r* is rolled (pronounced strongly) in all positions and the glottal stop is widely used. A form of English known as Lallans is used to represent the way English is spoken in parts of Scotland, but this is a minority literary use; in general, English is written in Scotland exactly as in England, though in some words *ch* represents /x/ e.g. *loch* /lɒx/ (= lake). For Scots Gaelic see CELTS AND CELTIC.

See ENGLAND, A BRIEF HISTORY; IRELAND, A BRIEF HISTORY; WALES, A BRIEF HISTORY.

search (for)

To *search for* something means to look for something thoroughly; it is stronger in meaning than *look for*.

To *search* a place or person means to conduct a thorough examination; the police can *search* a house or a person, or luggage in an airport. A *strip search* is when the person's body is examined directly. In computing a text file or a data base can be *searched*, and a *search engine* is a PROGRAM that is designed to do this. *Search me* in response to a question means *I have no idea*.

see

This article includes *see, look, watch, gaze & stare,* and *glance & glimpse.*

see

See implies involuntary action because one's eyes happen to be pointing in the direction of something: *I saw Mary in the cinema; How many birds can you see in this picture?* In the second example the seeing is the natural inevitable consequence of the deliberate action of *looking*: *How many birds can you see in this picture? You'll have to look (at it) very carefully to see them all* can be compared with *I didn't see Mary in the cinema – but I wasn't looking for her.*

The cross-references in this book are introduced by the word *see.*

look

Look at implies a deliberate intention to direct one's eyes at something and pay a lot of attention to it: *Look carefully; You're not looking.*

It has *at* when it is transitive.

'Have you looked at his web page recently?' 'Yes, I had/took a look at it last week.'

Look at page 94 (spoken, e.g. a teacher to a class).

In combination with other particles (see MULTI-WORD VERBS): *Look for, up, out* there is a sense of deliberate action. *Look out!* is a warning of danger.

Compare *see* and *look* with HEAR & LISTEN.

watch

Watch is used in relation to paying attention to things that are moving: *I watched him climbing the stairs; I watched the fish swimming in the river*. It also means to *look at* or *observe* something with considerable care or attention:
I will watch your progress with interest.
The detective watched the house.
Will you watch my bags while I go for a cup of coffee?
We must watch the company's financial development.
He's watching his weight. (*Weight-watchers* is a self-help group for people who want to lose weight.)
Watch your step is a warning to take care, perhaps literal if the ground is unsafe, or perhaps metaphorical in more general situations.
Watch it is a general warning or threat.
Watch out is a warning of danger.

A *watchman* is an old name for a security guard; a *watchdog* is a dog kept to guard property and is also used colloquially to refer to supervisory bodies. To be *on watch* means to be vigilant, referring to the police, military etc. On board a SHIP a *watch* is a period of duty.

See CLOCK & WATCH.

gaze & stare

These both mean *to look at something without moving the eyes*, but **gaze** can have the idea of looking for a fairly long time, admiringly or without really concentrating: *He gazed into her eyes; She sat gazing out of the window*.

Stare also means to look for a long time without really seeing: *She sat staring out of the window* but it can also imply an emotional intensity or concentration, even aggressiveness, that is lacking from *gaze*: *She sat staring at the door, not believing that he had left her life for ever; Do you have to sit staring at your computer all day?* (To a child) *Stop staring at that man. It's rude to stare at people.*

glance & glimpse

A **glance** is deliberate: *I glanced at the map; Take a glance at this; We exchanged glances.*

A **glimpse** is unintentional, involuntary: *I glimpsed him entering the shop; I caught a glimpse of him in the cinema.*

seem

Seem is not usually followed by a noun alone (noun COMPLEMENT): ~~It seemed a prison~~. But *It seemed like a prison; It seemed to be a prison; It seemed as if it were a prison* or *It resembled a prison*. *Seem* often has an adjective complement: *He seems interesting; It seemed longer than it really was.*

See SENSE VERBS.

semantic change

Words do not have meanings that are fixed throughout history; like all other aspects of language they change with time. While this is not usually a problem for most people in the course of a lifetime (but see GAY; QUEER), it is important to remember this when reading older texts. A good example of the wide range of possible changes is the word *nice*: it comes from Latin *nescius* (ignorant) but at different times it has meant *stupid, elegant, strange, lazy, effeminate, luxurious, shy, fastidious,*

S

precise, careful, cultured, difficult to understand, subtle, thin, unimportant, critical, delicate, detailed, discriminating, very accurate, and *appetising,* as well as the current meaning of general approval. Another example is the word *quaint* (see FOLK), which originally meant *wise* and now means *strange* or *unusual*; at one time *meat* meant food in general (see FLESH & MEAT) and *man* meant a person, not necessarily a male one. See INCLUSIVE LANGUAGE.

It is obvious that language written several centuries ago may contain words that have changed their meaning completely since then, and even in the course of a few decades problems and misunderstanding can arise (see MAKE LOVE). It follows that a word can have no real, intrinsic meaning; the only meaning that a word can have is the meaning that is generally attached to it and this, like all fashions, can change over time.

See ETYMOLOGY; RIGHT AND WRONG.

semester

A *semester* is a university course or term lasting six months. See QUARTER, TERM & TRIMESTER. In business and accountancy this is a *half year*.

seminar & seminary

A *seminar* is a teaching or training session in which a group of students interact with the teacher and each other.

A *seminary* is a place where Christian priests or Jewish rabbis are trained.

sense verbs

SEEM is used for general impressions, when the information is received through a variety of means:
It seems that the party is about to start; He seems to be an intelligent man.

When the information is received through one sense the appropriate sense verb is used.
It sounds as if the party is about to start; He sounds intelligent.
It looks like coffee; He looks like his father; It looks as if it is going to rain.
It tastes like tea; It tastes of pepper.
It smells like cocoa; It smells as if something has gone rotten.
It smells of paint.
I feel hot; These shoes feel uncomfortable.

Note the four possible structures:
verb + as if + CLAUSE
verb + like + noun
verb + of + noun
verb + adjective

correct	incorrect
That soup looks good.	~~That soup looks well.~~
You sound tired.	~~You sound tiredly.~~
I feel hot.	~~I feel hotly.~~
That soup smells spicy.	~~That soup smells spicily.~~
That soup tastes horrible.	~~That soup tastes horribly.~~

As is the CASE with *seem* the five verbs that describe sensory perception (*look, sound, feel, smell, taste*) are followed by adjectives not by adverbs. See COMPLEMENT (GRAMMATICAL).

Well is used adjectivally to mean *in good health*, so *I feel well* is not an exception. *I feel good* is different meaning *I feel happy, satisfied*.

The auxiliary verb used with sense verbs is almost always *can* RATHER than *do*; it is used in affirmative sentences as well as questions and negatives: *What can you see? I can see a house; I can't hear anything; Can you taste the garlic?; I can feel something moving.*

For the use of the *infinitive* or *-ing* to follow sense verbs, see SENSE VERBS in that article.

sensible & sensitive

Sensible generally means *showing wisdom or common sense*, the opposite of *foolISH*.

Sensitive means *acutely affected by external stimuli or mental impressions*.

There is little difference between *sensibility* and *sensitivity* in relation to human feelings whether physical or mental, though *sensibility* can also suggest awareness of something rather than sensitivity to it. *Sensitivity* is more common.

sentence

Apart from its linguistic meaning, a *sentence* is a punishment imposed on a criminal by a court; it is the punishment itself rather than the decision or JUDGMENT in general. The sentence is decided by the judge: *He received a life sentence; He was sentenced to pay a fine of £1,000.*

See LAW.

sever & several

Sever means *cut, separate, divide*; *several* means a small number, more than two.

He has severed links with his former company means that he has cut them, that they no longer exist. *He has several links with his former company* means that he kept some of his links after he left the company and still has them.

shade & shadow

Shade is an absence of direct light.

A *shadow* is an image projected by a body under a light. A body between two or more lights will have a number of shadows. If you walk on the sunny side of the street, your *shadow* will follow; on the other side, you will be *in the shade.* There are a number of uses of these two words, which are not always clearly distinguished.

shadow

If there is *not the shadow of a doubt*, or something is PROVED *beyond a shadow of a doubt*, it is absolutely certain.

If someone is *a shadow of his former self* he has lost a lot of his former strength.

Eyeshadow is make-up applied around the eyes.

Five o'clock shadow is the growth of hair that can sometimes be seen on a man's face in the afternoon or evening.

In Britain the official spokespersons of the parliamentary opposition are known as *shadow ministers* (the *shadow Foreign Secretary* etc.)

To *shadow* someone is to follow and observe them secretly.

To *overshadow* is to place in a shadow, protect from the sun; it is often used metaphorically to indicate that one person or thing is more important than another.

shade

In colour, a *shade* is a precise colour; *an attractive shade of blue*, thus *all shades of opinion* represent the complete range of opinion.

With comparative adjectives *a shade* means a little: *a shade better; a shade colder.*

An *eye-shade* is a device that fits above the eyes to protect them from damage caused by strong lights.

A *lampshade* covers a lamp to reduce the GLARE *(*SHINE)* from the bulb and sometimes to direct the light.

A *sunshade* is something that gives protection from the sun, a parasol (like a large umbrella) or a cloth cover for a terrace.

A *shady* place is one that is in or has a lot of shade. A *shady* person or business is one that is probably dishonest.

To *shade* is to screen something from the light, or to make a part of a picture darker.

S

Shakespeare

William Shakespeare (1564-1616) is generally regarded as the greatest English writer; he is sometimes known as the *Bard* (a CELTIC word for a poet). He was born in Stratford-upon-Avon in the Midlands, but little is known of his early life. He moved to London and became a member of a theatrical group known as the Lord Chamberlain's Men, which became London's leading theatrical company. They used the Globe Theatre (which has now been rebuilt near its original site), and changed their name to the King's Men in 1603, when James I came to the throne. See ENGLAND, A BRIEF HISTORY.

Shortly after his death a collection (folio) of his work was made; until then the plays had had no definitive form, being passed informally and by memory from one actor to another. His 37 dramatic works are generally divided into *Comedies*, *Tragedies* and *Histories*. The Histories describe the civil wars that led to the Tudors winning the throne of England and are now seen as justifying the dubious Lancastrian claim. He also wrote 154 sonnets and some longer poems. Because of the small amount of information surrounding his life that is available, and because there is no record that he ever went to university, a theory developed that the plays were not written by Shakespeare but by someone else. Several candidates have been proposed as the possible author but there is no convincing evidence to support this theory and professional scholars dismiss it.

Shakespeare was writing at a time when the English language was developing rapidly and he contributed a large number of new words and expressions to it. Though his language is clearly modern English and can generally be read and understood by a modern reader, it shows considerable differences from contemporary language; editions published for British schools and general readers require glossaries. The folio text is never changed or 'translated' into contemporary language, even when the plays are performed as being set in the present or future.

Shakespeare is the standard way of spelling his surname. However, this standardisation only came about in the twentieth century; before that a large number of variations in the spelling were found including two different forms of the name in his will. The adjective used to refer to Shakespeare's works is *Shakespearean* or less frequently *Shakespearian*.

See BOWDLERISE.

His plays are:
Two Gentlemen of Verona, 1590-1
Henry VI Part 1, 1592
Henry VI Part 2, 1592
Henry VI Part 3, 1592
Titus Andronicus, 1592
Richard III, 1592-3
The Taming of the Shrew, 1593
A Comedy of Errors, 1594
Love's Labour's Lost, 1594-5
Richard II, 1595
Romeo and Juliet, 1595
A Midsummer Night's Dream, 1595
King John, 1596
The Merchant of Venice, 1596-7
Henry IV Part 1, 1596-7
The Merry Wives of Windsor, 1597-8
Henry IV Part 2, 1597-8
Much Ado About Nothing, 1598
Henry V, 1598-9

Julius Caesar, 1599
As You Like It, 1599-1600
Hamlet, 1600-1
Twelfth Night (or What You Will), 1601
Troilus and Cressida, 1602
Measure for Measure, 1603
Othello, 1603-4
All's Well That End's Well, 1604-5
Timon of Athens, 1605
King Lear, 1605-6
Macbeth, 1606
Antony and Cleopatra, 1606
Pericles, Prince of Tyre, 1607
Coriolanus, 1608
The Winter's Tale, 1609
Cymbeline, 1610
The Tempest, 1611
Henry VIII, 1613

shew

This is an obsolete form of *show*.

shine etc.
This article includes descriptions of the following words: *beam, glare, gleam, glimmer, glisten, glitter and sparkle, gloaming, glow,* and *twinkle.*

shine - shone - shone
This is the base verb for giving out light. *The sun shines, the moon shines, a light or torch shines; you shine a light or torch on something.* Polished wood, metal or leather *shines*. Something that shines is *shiny*: *a shiny coin* or *a shiny nose*. When the verb is transitive, meaning *polish*, it is regular: *well-shined shoes*.

beam
A *beam* is a strong piece of wood or metal used in building. It was used originally in English to mean a pillar or column of light as seen in religious paintings and now means any similar projection of light; *sunbeams* and *moonbeams* come from behind clouds; theatre spotlights and cinema projectors throw *beams* of light in a dusty atmosphere, as does sunlight entering a dusty room. As a verb it is mostly used to describe someone who is smiling happily.

A *beemer* or *beamer* is a colloquial name for a BMW motorcycle or car.

glare
This means to shine so strongly that the light is too brilliant to be comfortable. The sun *glares* in the tropics and also when it is low at sunrise and sunset. Spotlights *glare* at actors and other people who are in their light. It is a noun; public figures have to work in the *glare of publicity*.

A *glaring light* is unpleasant, so to *glare at somebody* means to show a very strong expression of anger on your face (without speaking) so that the person who sees it feels uncomfortable.

A *glaring contradiction* or a *glaring error* is one that is very obvious.

gleam
This is like *shine* but is much less strong. It cannot be used for the sun or moon, but a torch in the distance could be gleaming, as could one that is seen through a hedge or fence, for example. The lights of a house or town gleam in the distance. It is used to describe a bright look in someone's eye.

Gleam is often used as a noun: *a gleam of sunlight, a gleam of hope, of humour, of interest. There was a wicked gleam in his eye.*

glimmer
This is rather like *gleam* but is not used very much as a verb. A *glimmer of hope, knowledge* etc. is a very slight indication.

glisten
This is to shine like something that is wet. Fresh snow *glistens* in the sun.

glitter and sparkle
These both mean *to shine with a number of small points of reflected light*. The sea can *glitter* and *sparkle* when the sunlight is reflected from a surface broken by wind. Diamonds *glitter* and *sparkle*. The *glitterati* are the famous stars of society and show business. The name is made from the word *literati*, literary intellectuals.

gloaming
This word is used to describe evening twilight. It is a noun; there is no verb ~~gloam~~.

glow
Something *glows* when it is so hot that it gives out light but is not burning; it has no flame. A fire that is dying down *glows;* red-hot metal *glows*. Someone's cheeks or nose *glow* if they seem very red. As a noun *glow* refers to this light; it can also refer to a strong feeling, *a religious glow, a hospitable glow* as if a person were giving out such heat and light.

A *glow-worm* is a beetle, the female of which gives out light.

S

twinkle
This is used to describe a faint light at a distance that is not firm; it varies in strength. Stars *twinkle* in the night sky, and distant lights *twinkle*. Someone has a *twinkle in their eye* when they are amused, but do not show any great facial expression.

ship
As a verb this can mean to send goods for commercial purposes by any means, not necessarily by sea.

The BOW /baʊ/ of a ship is the front point and the *stern* is the back; the *fore* is the front part and *aft* means towards the stern. *Forward*, sometimes pronounced /ˈfɒrəd/, means towards the front. A ship's *beam* is its width at its widest point and its *draught* is the depth of it that is underwater. On a merchant ship the *hold* is the space for storing *cargo*. The direction of a ship's movement is controlled by a blade at the stern called the *rudder*. A ship's speed is measured in *knots*; one knot is one *nautical mile* per hour. A nautical mile is different from the land mile (*WEIGHTS AND MEASURES*); it is exactly 1,852 metres, which is close to its original definition as one minute of latitude on a line of longitude, or one minute of any great circle.

Apart from *galleys*, which were used in ANCIENT and medieval times and were propelled by OARS and sometimes manned by slaves, until the nineteenth century ships were moved by the action of the wind on SAILS. European *square-rigged* ships, with the *sails* at right angles to the length of the ship, typically had three *masts, foremast, mainmast* and *mizzen mast* in order from bow to stern, a *bowsprit* projected from the bow and a *figurehead*, usually in the form of a female figure, decorated the bow. The *quarterdeck* was the raised part at the stern where officers commanded the ship. On these ships the officers had *cabins* but the crew slept in *hammocks*, which hung in the pace between the *decks*. The *helmsman* controlled the rudder, and thus the ship's direction, by turning the ship's *wheel*. *Clippers* were fast nineteenth-century sailing ships. The traditional Arab sailing ship is called a *dhow* /daʊ/ and the typical Chinese sailing ship is a *junk*.

In the nineteenth century steamships were developed. These used coal as fuel for their engines and the smoke from the engines came out of large conical structures called *funnels*; now gas, diesel or nuclear fuel are used. *Liners* carried passengers around the world. NOWADAYS most merchant ships are *tankers*, which carry OIL or gas, or *container ships*. The officers command these ships from the *bridge*.

A *submarine* travels underwater. A *cruise ship* carries passengers for pleasure; a *cruiser* is a naval, military ship. A *ferry* is a ship that sails backwards and forwards between two places.

Although steamships do not use sails, the word is still used for a ship's departure: *The ship sails at 22.00*. A *sailor* is a member of the crew of a ship.

See BOAT & SHIP; GENDER; PORT.

short
Short has two adverb forms:

Short means *suddenly* or *earlier than expected*: *We had to cut the meeting short; He just stopped short of insulting me*.

Shortly means *soon*: *I'll know the answer shortly; They arrived shortly before 10 O'CLOCK*.

See ADVERBS WITHOUT -LY.

short answers
In English it seems rather abrupt to answer a question with a simple *yes* or *no*. We usually extend the answer:
Do you know Mary? Yes, I do./No, I don't.
Has Fred arrived? Yes, he has./No, he hasn't.
Can they swim? Yes, they can./No, they can't.
Have there been any phone calls? Yes, there have./No, there haven't.

S

As with TAG QUESTIONS the short answer repeats the subject as a pronoun and the auxiliary verb. Contractions cannot be used in affirmative short answers: ~~Yes, he's.~~ Sometimes the *yes* or *no* is omitted:
Will Tim be here tomorrow? He will/He won't.
Might it rain this afternoon? It might/It might not.

With two or more auxiliary verbs, the first is used and the others are optional:
Couldn't she have arrived earlier? Yes, she could (have)/No, she couldn't (have).
Will you have been working? Yes, I will (have) (have been)/No, I won't (have) (have been).

The use of the correct auxiliary verb comes naturally to native speakers, even in long sentences: *'Could that man she was with last night be the new boyfriend she's been talking about so much lately?' 'Yes, he could.'*

short questions

WH- QUESTIONS that have a PREPOSITION AT THE END can be shortened in informal usage.

I went out last night.
Where did you go (to)? – Where to?
Who did you go with? – Who with?
What did you go for? – What for?

sibilant sounds

The name comes from the Latin *sibilare* (to hiss, whistle). The sibilant sounds typically are the letters *s* and *z*; phonetically they are /s/, /z/, /ʃ/ and /ʒ/ though they can be represented by a number of letters: *box* /bɒks/, *price* /praɪs/, *judge* /dʒʌdʒ/ and *catch* /kætʃ/ all end with sibilant sounds. For the importance of sibilant sounds in the pronunciation of certain words see -ED & -ES, PRONUNCIATION.

sibling

Siblings are the children of a common parent or parents, but the word is only used in anthropology, biology, sociology, education, and so on. *Sibling rivalry* is the term for the jealousy that can arise among siblings. In normal language use the only common expression is *brothers and sisters*: *How many brothers and sisters do you have?*

similes

A *simile* /ˈsɪmɪli/ is a metaphorical comparison: *His feet were (as) cold as ice; She stood out like a goddess; He answered me as bold as brass*. As with IDIOMS AND METAPHORS, the cultural element does not always translate from one language to another. Note the spelling of the singular *simile*, and the plural *similes* (not ~~similies~~).

since

This is pronounced /sɪns/, not /saɪns/ or /siːns/.

sing & song

Sing-sang-sung is the verb. *Song* is the noun.

single etc.

Single, sole, and *only* refer to only one example when there could be more than one. *Sole* and *only* are very largely synonyms as attributive ADJECTIVEs though *only* is more common: *The only/sole Scot in the room; My only/sole complaint was about the food.*

Single could be used in the above examples but tends to be used with the indefinite article *a* or *one* as an emphatic way of saying *only one*: *I do not have a single free moment; One single opponent stood in her way.*

Single is often contrasted with *double*: *singles tennis* has one player on each side but *doubles* has two; *single cream* has less fat than *double cream*. It has the idea of one at a time: a gun can fire *single shots* instead of repeating. A *single person* is unmarried, a *single bed* or *room* is designed for one person (unlike a *double bed* or *room*), and a *single ticket* will take you to your destination but a *return ticket* will take you there and bring you back again. ➤

S

Sole used in this sense is unrelated to the noun (*sole*) meaning the bottom part of a shoe. The name of the edible fish (*sole*) comes from the same Latin word as the *sole* of a shoe or foot, because of its shape.

Only is defining by nature and naturally goes with the definite article. However, it is used with *an* is in the expression an *only child, son, daughter.*

Unique refers to something of which only one example exists: *This stamp is believed to be unique*, or which is different from everything else in its class: *The elephant is unique among animals in having a trunk*. Because its meaning is *absolute* (it is a non-gradable ADJECTIVE) it should not be given a comparative or superlative form (~~more/most unique~~) and should not be modified with adverbs such as *totally, absolutely, quite,* though it is perfectly reasonable to say that something is *nearly unique*. However, the word is used in this way by native speakers when it tends to mean *unusual* or *outstanding*: *a most unique house* or *a very unique opportunity* will be found, though careful users of the language consider them to be unacceptable.

See ADJECTIVE | GRADABLE & NON-GRADABLE.

singular and plural
lot, number and variety
Nouns such as *lot, number, variety* often have a plural verb in sentences such as *A lot of towns have museums; A large number of people were at the concert; A variety of artistic styles are on display*. This is because the subject is considered to be *towns, people, styles*. Compare *Many towns have museums* etc. The verb is singular in sentences such as *The number of people at the concert was greater than expected; The variety of artistic styles on display was poor*. See GROUP NOUNS.

together with
A singular verb is used in sentences such as *Together with the garden the house measures 150 m^2; The house together with the garden measures 150 m^2* even though the totality of the subject is plural.

singular verb with quantities
A singular verb is used in sentences such as these, where the plural noun represents a quantity rather than a countable number: *€100 was more than I had expected to pay; A thousand kilometres is too far to drive in one day; A few months isn't long enough to form an accurate opinion.*

ski
This word is of Norwegian origin but is regarded as an English word. It is a noun and a verb. Its forms are *ski* /skiː/ *skis* /skiːz/ *skiing* /ˈskiːɪŋ/ *skied* /skiːd/ *skier* /ˈskiːə/. Do not confuse it with *sky* /skaɪ/, which makes the plural *skies* /skaɪz/.

skirt
A *skirt* surrounds a woman's body and thus the word has developed the idea of surrounding. The *outskirts* (always plural) of a city are its suburbs and surrounding rural area; a *skirting board* is the continuous board that covers the bottom few centimetres of a wall, joining it to the floor.

Skirt is used as a verb: *The city is skirted by mountains; The ring road skirts the town; The river skirts the castle grounds; The* SHIP *skirted the coast.*

Skirt and *shirt* are DOUBLETS, but their meanings are clearly different.

For *kilt* see SCOTLAND, A BRIEF HISTORY.

slang
Slang is extremely informal language. It is innovative, variable and subtle, changing in form quickly especially among young people. Many slang words fall out of fashion and disappear from the language while others become accepted as normal words over time. Speakers who are not totally familiar with how to use slang expressions should be very careful in using it as it is easy to use terms that are strange, out of date, or otherwise inappropriate or even offensive.

See RHYMING SLANG *(*COCKNEY).*

S

smog
Smog is a BLEND of the words smoke and fog used to describe air pollution which is similar to fog but which is due to smoke in the atmosphere.

so & such
Note the different word order in *The film was so good that I saw it twice* and *It was such a good film that I saw it twice.*

so-called
In English *so-called* is not a neutral way of giving the name of something. It has a pejorative connotation, suggesting that the name is used inappropriately: *Her so-called friends told the newspapers what she had been doing.*

solder & weld
Solder is an alloy that is melted and used to join pieces of metal or wire. They are then *soldered*.

Welding is the process of heating pieces of metal and forcing them together so that they join and become one; the *weld* is the joint that is made in this way. Very high temperatures are required for welding.

solidarity
This word came into English from French in the mid-nineteenth century; it still seems a little foreign. It is used in trade union and socialist politics but is unusual in general social, colloquial use.

The corresponding adjective ~~solidary~~ is never used.

south & southern
South is pronounced /saʊθ/. *Southern* is pronounced /'sʌðən/.

spake
Spake is an obsolete form of the past of *speak* (now *spoke*); *Thus Spake Zarathustra* is a common translation of Nietzsche's *Also Sprach Zarathustra*. *Spake* is sometimes used deliberately, and perhaps sometimes ironically, in modern English to indicate that a serious statement has been made.

spam
Unwanted EMAIL is called *spam*. This name comes from a brand of canned pork called *Spam* made by the Hormel Corporation, but the connection is indirect and does not suggest any criticism of the quality of the meat. The unwanted mail is written with a small *s*, whereas the meat has a capital letter.

The use of the name for junk email comes from a sketch performed in 1970 by the Monty Python comedy group. It is set in a café in which, ridiculously, everything on the menu contains Spam, often in wildly exaggerated quantities such as *Spam, egg, Spam, Spam, bacon and Spam* (though the canned meat can be eaten directly, it is often grilled or fried). A group of Vikings appears in the café, singing a song in which every word is *Spam* and which drowns the rest of the scene. It is this complete predominance of Spam in the sketch that has caused the name to be used for email that also drowns out all normal communication. The sketch can be found on YouTube.

spectacle(s)
A *spectacle* is a show, but *spectacles* are GLASSES for improving eyesight: *a pair of spectacles, a spectacle case.*

spelling
English spelling is notoriously complicated and unphonetic. Although a national standard was coming into existence in the late Middle Ages, there was considerable variation in individual spelling, which lasted until mass printing in the nineteenth century led to standardisation. Even so, there are differences in style between individual publishers in, for example, preferring one or other form of -ISE OR -IZE or in the use of CAPITAL LETTERS or HYPHENS *(*PUNCTUATION)*. ▶

S

Part of the problem is that medieval pronunciation is still reflected in the spelling of words (with *gh* for example) even though that pronunciation has changed; a further point is that the five vowel letters (*y* as a vowel is always pronounced as *i* would be) are insufficient for the twenty vowel sounds (twelve monophthongs and eight diphthongs) found in English (see PHONETIC SYMBOLS), so they have to be used in combination. Some words entered English from French in the MIDDLE AGES and have acquired English pronunciations: *royal* /ˈrɔɪəl/ and *bullet* /ˈbʊlɪt/ for example, but modern French words have French pronunciations: *ballet* /ˈbæleɪ/, *quiche* /kiːʃ/. Words that entered English directly from Latin retain the Latin spelling (see PREFIXES); and when they are Latin forms of Greek words, or when Greek words are taken directly, they have the letter combinations *ch, ph, rh, th* and the letter *y* pronounced as a vowel. The result is that although a large majority, perhaps 80%, of English words are spelled in accordance with some phonetic or etymological rule, these rules are so complicated that it is often easier to learn the pronunciation or spelling of the individual words themselves in each case. The fact that the really irregular spellings are common words makes the situation seem worse than it really is.

Several suggestions have been made for spelling reform in English. Reformed spelling would make it easier for native speakers as well as foreign learners (teaching spelling and reading is complicated but is an essential part of language teaching in primary schools in English-speaking countries); it might also save paper if the number of letters in words could be reduced. However, it has always proved impossible to agree on a standard reformed spelling system or revised alphabet. A further point is that the variety of spoken English is so great that a reform based on RECEIVED PRONUNCIATION would represent little improvement for English speakers in Scotland or India, while different reforms for different varieties of spoken English would destroy the unity of the written language. Spelling reform would also remove much of the enormous amount of etymological evidence of the growth and development of the language that is reflected (and, some would say, fossilised) in standard spelling. Nevertheless, a limited degree of reform could easily be applied which would abolish the social and educational distinction shown by the ability to spell and use, for example, DEPENDANT & DEPENDENT and LICENCE & LICENSE.

See AMERICAN ENGLISH; PRONUNCIATION.

split infinitive

Earlier editions of this book had a discussion of the problems arising from splitting or not splitting infinitives, ending with the conclusion:

> However, despite all this it must be said that there is still, RIGHTLY or WRONGLY, a considerable feeling among English speakers that a split infinitive is wrong. Sometimes it seems natural to do so but a decision to split an infinitive deliberately should never be taken lightly.

That advice was mentioned approvingly in the review in Modern English Teacher in 2009. However, in 2018 even the Economist newspaper, which is conservative in matters of style, has given up the ban and it seems clear that no purpose is served by repeating it here. For reference, I give description of what a split infinitive is.

Splitting an infinitive, which means placing an adverb between *to* and the infinitive of the verb, is one of the great taboos of prescriptive GRAMMAR.

Examples are:
I expect to happily settle into my new home.
I expect to fully support your attempt.
Are you sure you want to completely remove this PROGRAM and all its components?
and the famous mission statement of the USSS Enterprise in the TV series *Star Trek*:
To boldly go where no man has gone before.

The reason why the split infinitive is so strongly criticised is that prescriptive grammar is based on Latin, and in Latin it is impossible to do this. However, it does seem natural to English speakers to do this occasionally, presumably because the adverb precedes the infinitive as it does in the MID-POSITION *(*ADVERBS, POSITION)* with auxiliary verbs.

S

sport
Sports, not ~~sportive~~, is used as the adjective: *sports clothes, equipment, ground, writer*. As well as typical *sports* such as football and tennis, the word refers to the *country sports* of *hunting, shooting* and *fishing*; a *sports coat* or *jacket* is an informal jacket, usually made of tweed, that would be worn for such activities. *Sports* that involve killing animals are known as *blood sports*.

spot
Spot has the idea of a mark or a place. A blue tie with yellow *spots* has round yellow decorative marks on it. If it has a small stain of oil or paint, that too is a *spot*, so a *spot* can be a stain. If someone's character is *spotless*, it is totally free of any bad points. A *spot* is also a pimple, acne, the skin inflammation that TEENAGERS in particular suffer from. In football the *penalty spot* is the mark from which a penalty kick is taken. It can also be a precisely identified place: *This is a good spot for a picnic; This is the very spot where he fell down.*

As a verb it is *identify, notice*: *I spotted him as the winner before the race; I spotted him in the crowd.*

Some people observe trains or planes as a hobby. This activity is known as *train/plane spotting*.

stairs & steps
Stairs are found inside a building and are used to move from one floor to another. A set of stairs is a *flight (of stairs)* and the structure including its supports is the *staircase*. The open space occupied by stairs in a building is the *stairwell* (but a lift moves in a *lift shaft*).

Steps are generally external or in the entrance of a building, connecting two areas at different levels. Some buildings have a *flight of steps* outside the door. A *doorstep* is a single *step* up to the door of a house, and inside a building there may be a set of a few *steps*, but not enough to be a flight of stairs. A *stepladder* is a small ladder with flat steps and a folding support behind it.

stationary & stationery
Stationary means not moving: A *stationary* car.

A *stationer* is a person who sells paper, pens, and other items for writing and use in offices. These things collectively are **stationery**.

Stationary and *stationery* are both pronounced /ˈsteɪʃənəri/ /ˈsteɪʃənri/ or /ˈsteɪʃnəri/.

sterling
Sterling was the name of a medieval English silver penny, so the POUND *sterling* (originally a pound's weight of sterlings) came to mean English currency, separately from that of any other country, and is also used (*sterling silver*) to define the quality of standard silver.

The name is not connected with the Scottish town of Stirling. It is still used as the name of the currency: the *sterling exchange rate, a sterling crisis*, but as Britain is now the only significant country to use the pound as a unit of currency, the need to define the POUND *sterling* as being different from, for example, the *Egyptian* or *Cypriot pound* has become less important.

stile, style & stylus
A *stile* is a step for crossing a fence, wall, or hedge.

A *style* is a way or fashion of doing things.

A *stylus* was the writing tool used with wax tablets, and was also the needle device for reading records on record players that used vinyl discs.

story & storey
A *story* (plural *stories*) is a tale, a narrative, often but not necessarily fictional.

A *storey* (plural *storeys*, American English *story, stories*) is a floor in a building. If a building has six storeys it has (in Britain) a ground floor, first floor etc. so the top storey is the fifth floor. In the USA the first floor is at ground level, so the top floor of an American six-storey building is the sixth floor.

S

straight & strait

A *straight* line, road etc. is one that has no bends or curves. A straight line is the shortest distance between two points. *Straight* means *honest*; a criminal who *goes straight* abandons a life of crime. The *straight and narrow* is an honest and morally acceptable way of living. A *straight answer* is a clear, honest one. *Straight* also means *heterosexual*, as opposed to GAY. A *straight WHISKY* is one that is not diluted by water or any other liquid. *Straight away* means *immediately*.

Strait means *narrow* or *tight* but is archaic as an adjective except in *straitjacket*, which is a garment with long sleeves used to restrain a violent prisoner or mental patient. A *strait-laced* person has very strict puritan moral values. As a noun it is used to mean a narrow passage of water connecting two seas, e.g. the *Strait of Dover* between England and France or the *Strait of Gibraltar* between Spain and Morocco. The plural *Straits of Dover* etc. was once common but the singular form is commonly used now. There is no difference in meaning. If you are in *dire straits* (always plural) you are in a very serious or dangerous situation. Someone in *straitened circumstances* is restricted by poverty.

See ADVERBS WITHOUT -LY; -EN VERB SUFFIX.

stress differences

noun and verb

The following words (among others) have the stress on the first syllable when they are used as nouns and on the last syllable when they are used as verbs:

accent	*incense**
addict	*incline*
attribute (verb /əˈtrɪbjuːt/)	*increase*
combine	*insult*
compound	*object**
conduct	*offset***
conflict	*overflow***
conscript	*permit*
*console**	*present*
contest	PRODUCE
*contract**	*progress*
contrast	*prospect*
*converse**	*protest*
convert	*rebel*
convict	*record*
decrease	*refund*
*defect**	REFUSE*
DESERT*	*reject*
dictate	SUBJECT*
discount	*survey*
escort	*suspect*
*exploit**	*torment*
export	*transfer*
extract	*transport*
finance	*upset***
import	

*These words differ significantly in meaning between noun and verb.

**Offset, overflow* and *upset* are of the only words here of Germanic origin. The others are of Latin origin with a Latin PREFIX.

In the case of *advocate* the pronunciation changes but the main stress remains on the first syllable: noun /ˈædvəkət/, verb /ˈædvəkˌeɪt/.

S

With some prefixes there is a change of pronunciation. Nouns starting in *re-* have variable pronunciation but the verbs have /rɪ/; prefixes that contain an *o* (*pro-, com-, con-*) have variable pronunciation in nouns and /ə/ in verbs. See PROGRAMME.

This difference is not a standard feature; for example, the following have the same stress (on the second syllable) in noun and verb: *concern, consent, dislike, display, dispute*.

noun and adjective

A similar difference is found between *content* and *INVALID* as nouns, stressed on the first syllable, and *content* and *invalid* as adjectives, stressed on the second syllable. As an adjective *compact* usually has the stress on the second syllable but in *compact disc* it is on the first. *Suspect* has the stress on the first syllable as both noun and adjective.

verb and adjective

Perfect has the stress on the second syllable as a verb and on the first as an adjective.

strip

To *strip* something is to remove the cover from it; *strip paper off a wall, strip the bark off a tree*. Intransitively, *to strip (off)* means to undress; a *striptease* is an entertainment in which someone undresses.

A *strip* (noun) is a long narrow piece: *a strip of paper, a strip of land*. This is related to the word *stripe* and is unconnected with the verb *strip*.

To *tear someone off a strip* is to rebuke them angrily.

strong verbs

In the grammar of Germanic languages, strong verbs are ones that change an internal vowel, e.g. *swim, swam, swum*. In modern English grammar we talk of IRREGULAR VERBS.

studio & study

A *studio* is a room where an artist, architect, sculptor, painter, photographer etc. works. It is the place where a cinema film is shot or a TV programme is recorded and/or processed.

A *study* is a room, perhaps in a house, which has books and is used for reading, writing, and other intellectual activities.

subject

subject before verb

Except in QUESTIONS the grammatical rule is that the subject of a verb must be before the verb, even if the subject is long: *An old man I had never seen before, with a long beard and wearing a dark suit, asked a question.* This is not elegant, and sometimes a way can be found to change the order by using a passive construction: *A question was asked by an old man that I had never seen before, with a long beard and wearing a dark suit.* Or by more radical rewriting: *An old man asked a question. He had a long beard and wearing a dark suit. I had never seen him before.* It is QUITE impossible in English to construct a sentence such as ~~Asked a question an old man I had never seen before, with a long beard and wearing a dark suit~~.

In formal legal language a very long subject is acceptable: *In all the insurance policies subscribed in accordance with sections 5.1.1, and 5.1.2,* **the Purchaser, the Contractor and all the sub-contractors, suppliers, financiers (if there are any) and other agents and companies involved in the project that is the object of this present Contract, whatever interest and/or liability they may have or may be attributable to them therein**, *shall have the status of insured parties*.

subject must be stated

In English each verb must have its subject clearly stated (with one exception described below). The almost complete lack of inflections in English verbs makes this necessary; languages with highly inflected verb forms (Spanish and Russian for example) do not need to state the subject each time that a verb is used. ➤

S

The exception is in co-ordinate CLAUSES that have the same subject: *I came in, took my coat off, and sat down; John has written a book but not directed a film; Did he walk or come by bike?* Note that it is not normally necessary to repeat the auxiliary verb. However, *Mary can sing and dance* could mean that she can do both at the same time, while *Mary can sing and she can dance* makes it clear that these two abilities are considered separately.

subjunctive

The subjunctive mood is a standard feature of INDO-EUROPEAN LANGUAGES. It indicates doubt, uncertainty, or the hypothetical nature of a verb. Its use in English is so limited that students, especially beginners, are sometimes told that it does not exist or that they can ignore it. However, it is impossible to progress far in English without meeting it in one way or another. As a verb mood, the subjunctive contrasts with the indicative (the usual verb form) and the imperative moods. It is independent of tense and voice. Some languages have a number of subjunctive tenses but English has only two, present and past.

past subjunctive

This is identical to the past simple (affirmative and negative) and thus cannot be identified by its form, except in the case of the singular of the verb *to be*: *I were, you were, he/she/it were, we were, they were.*

it is used

- in second CONDITIONAL sentences (but is only identifiable in the singular of *to be*):
  If I were rich I would buy a new car.
  She would agree with me if she were here.
  If it weren't raining we could eat outside.
  He would never have said that unless he were sure of his facts.
  If I were you I'd catch the earlier train. (I advise you to catch the earlier train.)
- with WISH or *if only* to give a present meaning (see TENSE & TIME): *I wish he weren't so rude; I wish I were richer; If only she were as clever as her brother.*
- with *as though/as if*: *He spoke to me as though I were one of his servants; It looked as if it were going to snow heavily.*

In all these cases *was* is used colloquially instead of *were*, but is not considered correct in formal use.

As in other Indo-European languages, a past tense is used to indicate a hypothetical, conjectural situation; because of the nature of English, the subjunctive mood of the past tense can be seen only in the verb *be*. However, *I wish I had more money* and *If only she knew as much as her brother* can be considered to have unmarked subjunctive verb forms.

present subjunctive

This is identical to the infinitive in all persons and numbers and is thus only identified in affirmative sentences, in the third person singular, by the lack of the *s*: *I work, you work, **he/she/it work**, we work, they work* except in the case of the verb *to be*: *I be, you be, he/she/it be, we be, they be.*

The negative is formed without any auxiliary, and is therefore identifiable in all persons: *I not work, you not be* etc.

The present subjunctive is found only in a very formal style of English and is mostly used after certain verbs when the meaning of the verb concerns something which is not in the present; such as *ask, command, demand, insist, order, propose, recommend, request, suggest*. It is effectively obsolete in British English but is found in American English.

In earlier editions of this book I wrote at length about examples such as:
*All I ask is that he **reply** to my letter within a reasonable period of time.*
and
*I suggest that they **not proceed** with the building work until the situation on the ground is clearer.*

In 2018 the only reasonable advice is not to use such forms at all. They will not be found in contemporary language and seem very strange. These sentences would now be constructed as:

*All I ask is that he **replies** to my letter within a reasonable period of time.*

and

*I suggest that they **do not proceed** with the building work until the situation on the ground is clearer.*

Rather more formally, they could be:

*All I ask is that he **should reply** to my letter within a reasonable period of time* or *All I ask is **for him to reply** to my letter within a reasonable period of time.*

and

I suggest that they should not proceed with the building work until the situation on the ground is clearer.

I said in earlier editions of this book:
> In some cases it is possible to use either the present subjunctive or the present indicative, though the meaning will be different. This is the case with words such as *essential, important/importance, vital*, which can refer either to a future possibility or to a present state of affairs. Consider these sentences: *It is important that he speaks RURITANIAN* and *It is important that he (should) speak Ruritanian*. The first of these sentences refers to a definite person whose ability to speak Ruritanian is known; it might be said in the context of considering whether he is or is not a Ruritanian spy. The second sentence refers to a necessary requirement of a hypothetical person needed to fill a particular job. However, in practice the form with -*s* is very widely used in all cases.

That is even more the case now. The ambiguity is there but it seems that the context makes the meaning clear and the sentences could easily be worded differently. Moreover, this problem only occurs in the third person singular. If a politician says that it is 'fundamentally important that we listen to the British people', it is impossible to know if *listen* is indicative or subjunctive. Does she mean that they **do** listen or that they **should** listen? Presumably that they should do so, with the subjunctive meaning.

The present subjunctive is used in certain fixed expressions such as:

Be that as it may, ...
Far be it from me to criticise but ...
(God) bless/damn you (etc.)
God rest ye merry, gentlemen. See CHRISTMAS.
God save the Queen.
Heaven forbid (that...)
If need be, ...
Long live the Queen.
Serve you (etc.) right.
She'll (etc.) be 87 come Tuesday.
So be it.
Suffice it to say that ...

At one time it was used after *if: If music be the food of love, play on,/Give me excess of it* (William Shakespeare, Twelfth Night I. i. 1601) but this is never done in modern English.

The present subjunctive is never used after *when* as this is considered to be a definite prediction or statement: *I'll ask him when he arrives in the office* (predictive future); *He always has a cup of coffee when he arrives in the office* (regular event). For *lest* see IN CASE.

May can be used to express ideas that would require a subjunctive in other languages: *May you have a long and healthy life; May you never lack anything.*

Let too can express a subjunctive idea, though in *Let him do what he wants* it is not entirely clear, apart from the context, whether it has a subjunctive meaning or means *allow*.

subtle
The *b* is silent: /sʌtl/.
See B, B; DEBT; DOUBT; REDOUBT; RECEIPT.

success
The noun *success* is used in *His success in the exam was unexpected; Let's drink to our future success.* ▶

S

Other forms use the verb: *If we succeed with this project, the company will expand*; or the adjective *If we are successful with this project, the company will expand*. The form ~~have success~~ is never used.

suit & suite

Suit /suːt/ or /sjuːt/ is used in a *suit of clothes* (for a man or a woman) or *armour*, a *lawsuit* and any of the four suits of PLAYING CARDS. *To follow suit* is to do the same as somebody else (a metaphor from card games): *Our host sat down and everyone ELSE followed suit*.

Suite /swiːt/ is used in a *suite (of rooms)* in a hotel, a *suite of furniture* (matching sofa and armchairs, or table and chairs) and a *musical suite*.

sulfur and sulphur

In 1990 the International Union of Pure and Applied Chemistry recommended the use of *sulfur* for scientific use rather than *sulphur*. Though the form with *-ph* is traditional in British English, it is unusual in that the word does not derive from a Greek origin. It comes indirectly from Arabic.

summons

The plural of the legal term *summons* is *summonses*.

See LAW.

supposed to

I suppose that he's in Madrid is similar in meaning to *I believe, imagine, think that he's in Madrid*. The past is *I supposed* /sʌˈpəʊzd/ *that he was in Madrid*. However, the passive form of this sentence: *He is supposed* /sʌˈpəʊst/ *to be in Madrid* has a different meaning: *He ought to be in Madrid* with the implication that he is possibly not there. Note the different pronunciation, influenced by the following *t*. The negative uses TRANSFERRED NEGATION *(*NEGATION OF VERBS)*: *He is not supposed to be in Madrid*.

surgery

The room, house, or office where a *general practitioner* or *family doctor* receives and examines patients is called his/her *surgery*; the times when he/she does so are his/her *surgery hours*, even if the doctor does not in fact practise surgery on those PREMISES. British doctors do not usually wear white coats and they receive patients in their *surgeries* in normal clothes. *Surgeons* in Britain do not use the title *doctor* whatever their academic qualifications may be: *Ms Martin will examine you tomorrow before the operation*. As dentists are officially called *dental surgeons*, the same applies to them: *I'd like to make an appointment with Mr Foster*.

By extension, MPs and local councillors talk of their *surgeries* to mean the times when they are available for consultation by members of the public.

swine & pig

A *swine* is a pig but in British English it is not often used in that meaning. In general use it is used as a personal insult, especially for a man, or for something that is very difficult or unpleasant: *I've had a swine of a day*. It is used with DISEASES; *swine flu, swine fever*.

syllables

Because of the varied nature of the vocabulary of the English language, division of words into syllables is a very complicated matter and conventions vary between British and American English. For practical purposes, a word should not be broken at a line end in print at a place that is too close to the start or end of the word, or at a place that can give rise to momentary confusion such as breaking *therapist* as *the-rapist*. In handwriting people prefer as far as possible not to break a word at the end of a line.

See PUNCTUATION | HYPHENS.

sympathetic

In many European languages there is a word similar to this: Spanish *simpático*, French *sympathique*, German *sympatisch*, Russian *симпатичный* for example. These words describe a person's character and are best translated into English as *pleasant, good-natured* or *kind*. English *sympathetic* means showing interest and concern for another person's difficulties or sadness and corresponds more to Spanish *compasivo*, German *mitleidend*: *The POLICE officer was very sympathetic when I reported the burglary, but said that there was little possibility of recovering the stolen goods.*

See FALSE FRIENDS.

synonyms

Synonyms are words that have the same meaning; it is convenient to say that, for example, *intelligent, bright, brilliant, clever, gifted, talented* are synonyms (see CLEVER) though there are shades of meaning that distinguish them. In some cases synonyms cannot be used in all constructions: *It is likely/probable that he will win* and *He is the likely/probable winner* but *He is likely/~~probable~~ to win*.

A *thesaurus* is a dictionary of synonyms.

Words with opposite meanings are *antonyms*.

syringe

Syringe is usually pronounced /sɪrˈɪndʒ/.

T

t, T /tiː/

The twentieth letter of the alphabet. It is pronounced /t/. The sound is made with the tongue on the alveolar ridge, just behind the upper teeth.

It is silent:

- when the combination *st* is followed by a consonant in pronunciation though not necessarily in spelling: *castle, Christmas, fasten* /fæsn/, *listen* /lɪsn/, *whistle* /wɪsl/; similarly, OFTEN /ˈɒfən/ (some speakers), *soften* /sɒfən/.
- in some French words that end with *-et* pronounced /eɪ/: *ballet, beret, bidet, bouquet, buffet, Cabernet, chalet, crochet,* CROQUET (*CRICKET), *duvet, gourmet, parquet*. However, others, notably *banquet* /ˈbæŋkwɪt/ and *bullet*, have an English pronunciation.
- It is silent in *mortgage* /ˈmɔːɡɪdʒ/.

In words that end with *-ture* it is pronounced /tʃə/: *creature, nature, temperature* /ˈtemprɪtʃə/.

In words that end in *-tion* it is pronounced /ʃən/.

th, TH

This combination is pronounced /θ/ or /ð/.

It is pronounced /ð/ between vowels: *either, other, weather* but *nothing* /θ/ (it is a compound word: *no + thing*).

It is pronounced /ð/ in form words, i.e. words that help to build the sentence rather than contribute to its meaning: *that, this, then, there, with* etc.

It is generally pronounced /θ/ in words that have meaning: *bath, both, thing*. It is pronounced /θ/ before *r*: *three, threat*.

It is not pronounced /θ/ when it occurs at the join point in compound words such as *hothouse*, and in *Thames* /temz/ (the river) and the herb *thyme* /taɪm/. The PERSONAL NAMES *Theresa, Thomas* and *Anthony* are pronounced with /t/.

tag questions

form

Like other languages, English has a way of adding words to a statement to make a question and invite the hearer to respond. The way in which this is done is more complex in English than in other languages, involving both verb structure and intonation.

The structure of tag questions is simple enough to describe and understand, but their use requires a fluency in language management that learners find considerable difficulty in acquiring. A tag question takes the auxiliary verb from the main CLAUSE and turns it into a question using the auxiliary verb and a pronoun. An affirmative sentence has a negative tag question and vice versa.

John has lived in Paris, hasn't he?
Mary hasn't lived in Moscow, has she?
Your brother will be there, won't he?
She can swim, can't she?
The school is open now, isn't it?
The hospital isn't far away, is it?
He likes ice cream, doesn't he?
She doesn't eat liver, does she?
I'm right, aren't I?
I'm not right, am I?

With more than one auxiliary, only the first is used: *You could have arrived earlier, couldn't you?; He can't have been working all night, can he?*

In a negative tag question, the verb has the form of the CONTRACTION (but see below).

In the present simple and past simple tenses the auxiliary verb *do, does, did*, is used in the question although there is no auxiliary verb in the main clause.

The verb *be* has no auxiliary verb in its questions. The first person negative is *aren't I?* not ~~*amn't I?*~~

The contraction *mayn't* is not used, so the negative tag question presents a problem. The following are sometimes heard but are dubious:
permission: *I may start now, mightn't/can't I?*
possibility: *It may rain this afternoon, mightn't/won't it?*

The forms *I can start now, can't I?* and *It might rain this afternoon, mightn't it?* are both preferable and more probable.

use and intonation

Tag questions have two different purposes in conversation. One is to indicate to the other speaker: *I have said something that I know is true. I will ask you a question so that you can agree with it and take a turn in the conversation.* The main clause and the tag question both have a falling tone:
You live in ↘ Paris, ↘ don't you? (a positive answer is expected; a negative answer would be a surprise.)
Yes, I do. I moved there a year ago.
But you don't speak ↘ French, ↘ do you? (a negative answer is expected; a positive answer would be a surprise.)
No, not really but I am trying to learn it.

In these cases the tag question does not represent a real question; the answer is known and it is merely an invitation to the other speaker to continue the conversation in a particular direction. A negative question expects a positive answer and vice versa.

The other purpose of tag questions is to ask for confirmation of a statement. In this case, the tag question is a real question genuinely asking for information, or at least of confirmation of what has been said; it does not necessarily expect the answer to be positive or negative. Here the tag has a rising tone:
1 *You live in ↘ Paris, ↗ don't you?*
1a *Yes, I moved there a year ago.*
1b *No, I don't. I left Paris last year and now I live in Rome.*
2 *You don't speak ↘ French, ↗ do you?*
2a *Yes, I do. I've lived in Paris for five years.*
2b *No, I'm sorry I can't help you there.*

There is another type of tag question, which is positive and positive. With a falling intonation this is used to show that the speaker has inferred a fact from information:
My phone number is 00 33 1 23 45 67 89.
Oh, you live in ↘ Paris, ↘ do you?

But with a rising tone it can be used to express sarcasm, suspicion, and criticism.
And you can speak French like a ↘ native, ↗ can you?
So he wants to play it ↘ that way, ↗ does he?
You've been walking in the ↘ rain again, ↗ have you?

The inference expressed by this tag question can be seen in the use of *Oh, and,* or *so,* at the start of the sentence.

There is no negative equivalent: ~~*You don't live in Paris, don't you?*~~

After imperative forms the tag question is:
Phone me ↘ tomorrow, ↗ won't you?
Phone me ↘ tomorrow, ↘ won't you?
Phone me ↘ tomorrow, ↗ will you?

They are in increasing order of strength. The last is rather rude and is effectively a command. Other forms are possible with the above variations in intonation and positive/negative verb forms: *Put the*

T

TV on, can't you?; *Put the TV on, will somebody?* The only negative imperative is *Don't phone me* ↘*tomorrow,* ↘*will you?* This is quite a strong request or plea (***Please*** *don't phone me tomorrow*); the tag softens the force of the imperative verb.

No intonation is marked in the examples in this paragraph as they can have falling or rising intonation as appropriate. Usually the tag question reflects the main verb and its subject: *You think I'll fail the exam, don't you?*; *He can't see the clock from where he's sitting, can he?* and in sentences with TRANSFERRED NEGATION (**NEGATION OF VERBS*), we have: *You don't think I'll pass the exam, do you?* However, when the subject is in the first person: *I don't think he'll pass the exam, will he?* the tag question reflects the subordinate clause but is not negative as the transferred negation gives a negative implication to the subordinate clause.

After *let's* the tag question is *shall we?*
Let's go home, ↗*shall we?*
Let's finish now, ↗*shall we?*

The use of the correct auxiliary verb comes naturally to native speakers, even in long sentences: *He'd never have had the consideration to tell you that he was thinking of resigning and getting a new job, would he?*; *You'll just have to deal with the situation as it arises and do the best you can, won't you?*

talisman
This is not a compound of *-man*. The plural is *talismans*.

Taoiseach
This is the Irish title of the Prime Minister of the Irish Republic. It is pronounced /ˈtiːʃəx/.
See CELTIC LANGUAGES.

tasty & tasteful
Tasty refers to food that tastes good or pleasant.
Tasteful refers to taste in aesthetic or other similar matters.
Tasteless is the antonym of both.

tax
Tax on personal income is *income tax*; tax on a company's profits is *company tax* or *corporation tax*.
Capital gains tax is a tax payable on the profit made from selling property or an investment.
Inheritance tax is paid on the value of an ESTATE that is inherited, and *council tax* (formerly *rates*) is a local tax related to the value of a property. See POLL. *Value added tax* (*VAT*) is a percentage (*ad valorem*) tax charged at each stage of production and at the final point of sale.
Customs or *import duty* is charged on goods that are imported (HENCE the sale of *duty-free* goods at airports).
A *toll* is a charge for using a bridge, tunnel or motorway.
The money that motorists pay to enter central London is called a *congestion charge*.

tea
Tea is the drink made from the leaves of *Camellia sinensis*. The name is also used for other infusions such as mint, camomile or other leaves. *Beef tea* is a stewed beef extract for feeding INVALIDS.

teenager
A *teenager* is effectively an adolescent but as the word derives from the numbers ending in *-teen* it is refers specifically to someone aged from *thirteen* to *nineteen* inclusive.

telephone language
Speaking on the telephone in a foreign language can be a difficult experience, partly because of the absence of visual response from the other person, but also because of the difference in language use.

T

In Britain, when people pick up the phone they usually give their phone number, name or company name. Third person expressions with *it, this*, and *that* are used in establishing identification. Telephone numbers are usually spoken individually; *0* is spoken as the letter *O* (see NUMBERS). Numbers with four or six digits are broken into groups of two or three respectively with a slight pause between them. The first group has a rising intonation and the intonation falls on the second group.

452 7106 four five two, ↗ *seven one* ↘ *o six.*
0987 567432 o nine eight seven, ↗ *five six seven* ↘ *four three two.*

Some people now break six-digit numbers into three groups of two: *fifty-six, seventy-four, thirty-two* with no particular intonation. As the form of telephone numbers changes and with the increasing use of mobile phones, the way of speaking the numbers is changing.

Call, ring and *phone* all have the same meaning as verbs and can be used indiscriminately; *call* is the only one of these three words that can be used as a noun: *I am waiting for a call from ...*

A typical conversation between friends:
452 7106 (Four five two - seven one o six.)
HELLO. *Is that Mary?*
No, it isn't. It's Jane. Do you want to speak to her?
Yes please.
Is that Bill?
Yes, it is.
OK. I'll get her for you now.
(Pause - heard in background: *It's for you. – Who is it? – (It's) Bill.*)
Hi, Bill.
Hello Mary. I'm phoning to ask you...

See CALL & CALL ON.

a typical business phone call:

Hill, Dale and Moore. Can I help you?		
Can I/Could I/I'd like to speak to Mr Heath please?		
Who's speaking, please?		
Chris Rivers of Avon Environmental plc.		
I'll connect you/put you through now.		
Thank you.		
Heath speaking. *Ahh, good morning Eddy. This is Chris here. I was wondering...*	*I'm sorry.*	*I'm sorry. He's in a meeting. Would you like to call back later?* *Yes I will.* *Thank you.*
	His phone's busy/engaged.	*He's on the other line.*
	Would you like to/Will you wait? No. I'll ring back in a few minutes.	
Goodbye.		
Goodbye.		

other typical expressions

'*Can I speak to Mr Moore please?*' '*Speaking.*' (Mr Moore identifies himself as the speaker.)
You've got the wrong number.
This is a bad connection.
Your signal's breaking up.
I was out of cover.
We were cut off.

➤

T

Numbers in the British national network (except local calls) have 0 as the first digit. The international access code from the UK is 00 (the code for dialling to the UK is 44). The main cities with their surrounding areas have the codes shown here. With the exception of London they are followed by a group of three and then a group of four: 0151 234 5678. The city codes are not used in dialling a number with the same code area. Telephone numbers in London BEGIN with the code 020 followed by two groups of four numbers: 020 7123 4567 is in central London and 020 8123 4567 is in outer London (7 for the central area and 8 for the outer area). The initial 0 is not used when dialling from outside the UK: 0044 20 1234 5678.

020	London
0121	Birmingham
0131	Glasgow
0141	EDINBURGH
0151	Liverpool
0161	Manchester
0191	Newcastle-upon-Tyne

temperature

In Britain many people still use the Fahrenheit system for temperatures.

Water freezes at 32° F and boils at 212° F. For the weather the Fahrenheit system has the advantage that 0° F is very cold (-18° C) and 100° F is very hot (38° C), thus giving in practice a scale which runs from 0 to 100. The *C* in 38° C can stand for either *Celsius* or *Centigrade*. Weather forecasts and reports now use both systems simultaneously. In the USA only the Fahrenheit system is used outside the scientific world.

To convert Celsius to Fahrenheit multiply by 1.8 and add 32:
20 x 1.8 = 36
36 + 32 = 68
So 20° C = 68° F

To convert Fahrenheit to Celsius, deduct 32, multiply by 5, and divide by 9:
68 – 32 = 36
36 x 5 = 180
180 ÷ 9 = 20
So 68° F = 20° C.

See MATHEMATICAL TERMS.

I've got a temperature means that I am ill because my body temperature is above normal.

tense & time

It is extremely important to realise that grammatical tense and chronological time are different concepts. On many occasions the name of the tense and the time of the action do not coincide. For example, *I read a newspaper every day* is in the PRESENT SIMPLE *(*PRESENT TENSES)* tense although the speaker is not usually reading a newspaper at the moment of speaking, which would be *I am reading a newspaper*; on the other hand *I'm flying to Barcelona* almost always refers to a future plan rather than a current action. In *I will ask him when he arrives*, the time is future although the tense is present.

All subordinate time CLAUSES that refer to future time use a present tense:
Once/as soon as/when he arrives I'll ask him what to do.
Once/as soon as/when he has arrived I'll ask him what to do.

I have seen the Taj Mahal refers to an event in the past, though the tense is PRESENT PERFECT *(*PERFECT ASPECT)*, and this tense is used even more surprisingly for a future event in *It will be the first time I have seen my cousin's daughter*.

Some modal verbs used in the present or past tense refer to the future time: *It may/might rain later; I must phone my mother this evening; You should work harder; He should pass the exam.*

The PAST SIMPLE is used in hypothetical statements that refer to the present or future:
I WISH I had more money. (Present time.)
I wish it would stop raining. (Future time.)
If I won the lottery I would buy a car. (Future time.)
See CONDITIONAL SENTENCES.

terror

Terrible means *very bad* and is a SYNONYM of *horrible, awful* etc.: *He was wearing that terrible old coat; That's a terrible idea.*

Terribly means *very*: *She's terribly intelligent; That's a terribly good/bad idea.*

Terrific means *very good* and is a synonym of *fantastic, great* etc.: *I went to a terrific party yesterday; That's a terrific idea.*

Terrifying means *inspiring terror*: *I had a terrifying experience last night; The noise of the thunder was terrifying.*

Terrorists are people who use *terror* to achieve their political aims.

Films about ghosts, monsters and the supernatural are called *horror films* in English.

text

This word is used as a verb meaning *send a text message* from a mobile phone: *I'll text you his address tomorrow* and as a noun: *I'll send you a text with his address.*

thanking

Thank you elliptically represents the words *I/we thank you* and is usually written as two words, though there is a tendency to write it as one: *thankyou*. In a *thank-you letter* it should have a hyphen.

Sometimes people say *Many thanks*, which seems to be a plural form but there is no singular form ~~a thank~~.

Thanks is used informally or when no great degree of thanking is required. *Thanks (a lot/very much/awfully)* is stronger. These are also used ironically to acknowledge receipt of something unpleasant. *Thank you (so much/very much)* is emphatic and polite.

The associated preposition is *for*: *I am writing to thank you for the present you sent me; Thanks/Thank you for telling me that.*

CHEERS is used informally to mean *thank you*. *Ta* /tɑː/ (*very much*) is very informal and familiar.

Responses to thanks are *Not at all; It doesn't matter; Don't mention it* or (especially American English) *You're welcome*.

that (omission of conjunction)

In sentences introduced by verbs such as *think, believe, suppose, expect*, the conjunction *that* can be omitted, even in formal writing. *I think (that) his wife's Japanese; I suppose (that) they'll be late as usual.*

See RELATIVE CLAUSES.

that (pronunciation)

As a demonstrative adjective or pronoun, *that* has a strong pronunciation /ðæt/: *For that reason...; And that is the reason why...; That is satisfactory*. As a conjunction or relative pronoun it is weak /ðət/: *I know that the answer is 42; He is not the man that I spoke to*. The two words can come together with their different pronunciations: *I hope that that* /ðət'ðæt/ *is satisfactory*.

the

Like A & AN, the word *the* has two pronunciations. They depend on the following sound, not the letter of the alphabet.

Before consonant sounds it is pronounced /ðə/: *the banana, the pencil, the university, the European*.

➤

T

Before vowel sounds it is pronounced /ði/: *the apple, the end, the honour, the hour.*

When it is emphasised, it is pronounced /ðiː/: *That is **the** book to read on the subject* (i.e. the best, the most useful, appropriate).

theatre

Members of the *audience* buy their *tickets* at the *box office*; they might also buy a *programme* with information about the *play*. Seats in the *auditorium* could be in the *stalls* (on the ground floor) on one side or other of the AISLE /aɪl/, or upstairs in the *gallery*; the gallery, especially its highest point, is sometimes informally called the *gods*. Some people have a private area at the side of the auditorium called a *box* (HENCE the name of the box office). They wait for the *curtain* to rise for the start of the show, and when it falls at the end of the first *act*, there is an *interval*. The audience usually *applaud* by *clapping* their hands, and if a particular act in a variety show has been very popular they might shout *bravo* or *encore* /ˈɒŋkɔː/. But if the audience are unhappy, they might *boo* or *hiss*.

Before the show can have its *first night* or *première* /ˈpremɪeː/ the *producer* must provide the money and the administrative support and there must be *rehearsals*, at which the *director* explains how he wants the artistic presentation to appear and ensures that his/her instructions are followed by the *cast* (the actors) and the *stage crew*, who are responsible under the *stage manager* for building the *set* (the *scenery* that is on stage) and for providing the *props* (properties, the things that that actors carry on and off stage, and use).

Backstage, where the audience do not see them, the actors have *dressing rooms* where they change into their *costumes* and a *green room* where they wait before they have to appear onstage.

The *wings* are the areas at the side of the *stage* where actors wait to *make an entrance* and where they go when they *exit*; the wings are also used for storing props and if an actor onstage forgets his lines he can look to the wing for a *prompt* to help him remember what he has to say next.

Also, the room in which a LECTURE is given is called a *lecture theatre* and the place in a hospital where operations are performed is the *operating theatre*, or simply the *theatre*. The reason for this name goes back to the origins of SURGERY and dissection, when operations were unusual and were performed in a place where the students could all watch the surgeon at work.

their, there & they're

Their is the possessive CASE of the PRONOUN *they*; the *i* in *their* corresponds to the *y* in *they*.

There is an adverb, the opposite of *here*.

They're is the CONTRACTION of *they are*.

All three words are pronounced /ðeə/. Native speakers sometimes confuse them in writing but they should always be used correctly.

there is

This construction can be used with every possible tense and form of the verb *be* including the infinitive: *There will be; there should not have been; there must be; there ought to be; there seem(s) to be; I expect there to be*; and the -ING FORM: *There is no money available, and there is no likelihood of there being; There being no further business, the meeting was closed*. It is used in short answers *(Yes, there is/are)* and tag questions *(There's no money, is there?)*.

It varies for SINGULAR AND PLURAL in the present: *there is/are*; past: *there was/were*; and present perfect: *there has/have been*.

In *There are a lot of cars in the streets* and *There are a large number of mistakes in this work* the COMPLEMENT is taken logically as *cars* and *mistakes* and the verb is plural. In colloquial speech native speakers sometimes use *there is* with a plural complement: *There's four people waiting to see you.*

the ... the ...

Used with two comparative forms of ADJECTIVES or ADVERBS this refers to two things that are changing in proportion:
The harder you work the happier you will be.
The faster she spoke, the more difficult it was to understand her.
The later it got, the more we wanted to go home.
The less you say, the better it will be for all of us.

When the meaning is clear from the context, one or both verbs can be omitted: *The less you say, the better; 'Would you like it bigger, if possible?' 'Oh yes, the bigger the better.'*

The fixed expression *the more the merrier* is a way of saying that more people are welcome in a situation.

thing

The word *thing* is used as a completely general noun in sentences such as *The thing that I forgot to say is...; The good/important/interesting* (etc.) *thing is...; The thing (point, problem, difficulty* etc.*) is that...*

See ONE REPRESENTING A NOUN.

thing & think

Do not confuse these words.

think

The word *think* has two meanings: *consider* or *contemplate*, and *have an opinion*. The FORMER is DYNAMIC and has a continuous form; its associated PREPOSITION is usually *about*: *'What are you thinking about?' 'I was thinking about next week's meeting.'* The latter is stative and does not have a continuous form; its associated preposition is usually *of*: *I think (THAT) it will rain; What do you think of his new film?*

this & these

This /ðɪs/ is singular. *These* /ðiːz/ is plural. There is an important difference in pronunciation, both in the vowel and in the final consonant.

thou etc.

Thou, thee, thy, thine, thyself (all pronounced with /ð/) are the English forms of the familiar second person singular pronoun (corresponding in case and usage to the first person *I, me, my, mine, myself* respectively).

This has now been totally replaced by *you, your, yours* in modern standard English but is found in some dialects and is still used by members of the Quaker religion, who use *thee* as the subject. It is common in SHAKESPEARE and in the Authorised Version of the BIBLE. After *thou* verbs have the inflection *-st* except for *art* (be), *hast* (have), *dost* (do), *shalt* (shall) and *wilt* (will).

See YE.

three & tree

Do not confuse these words. They are pronounced /θriː/ and /triː/ respectively.

through & until

The American usage *Monday through Friday; July through September* makes it absolutely clear that the time period is inclusive. The British equivalent with *till/until* or *to*: *Monday till/until Friday; July to September* could be unclear: is it to the beginning or end of September? The American form is recognised in British English but is not comfortably used. For the American spelling *thru* see DEVIANT SPELLING.

T

thug

The original thugs were professional robbers in India who murdered their victims. Now the word is used for any person who threatens or uses violence against others.

tilde

The symbol ~ is commonly called a *tilde* in English from the Spanish name for an accent, in this case the symbol that forms part of the letter ñ, Ñ. In English punctuation it is called a *swung dash*.

time

Time is countable when it means *occasion*: *I spoke to him five times; How many times have I told you not to do that?* (For its use in multiplication see MATHEMATICAL TERMS.)

Time is uncountable when it refers to chronological time: *I have very little time; How much time will you need?*

Long and *short* are used with time; *a long time, a short time*. For *long* as an adverb in time expressions see LONG. *Short* cannot be used as an adverb.

The exact hour is *one O'CLOCK, two o'clock* etc. *O'clock* is often omitted: *I'll meet you at two; The shop shuts at seven*. The five minute intervals are *five past, ten past, (a) quarter past, twenty past, twenty-five past* and *half past*, then *twenty-five to, twenty to, (a) quarter to, ten to, five to*. So: *ten past six, half past four, (a) quarter to ten*. The hour is not always stated if it is clear from the context: *The train leaves at ten past; The film starts at twenty-five to*. With more precise times the word *minutes* is always used: *The train leaves at twelve minutes past (six)* or more precisely *The PROGRAMME started at fifteen minutes and twenty-seven seconds past (ten)*. The time can be spoken as the numbers: 7.40 *seven forty*, 1.30 *one thirty*, 3.15 *three fifteen*. This is very common but often seems more formal. The twenty-four hour clock is used in Britain, especially for public transport timetables, but its use is far from universal. It is spoken as *thirteen hours, twenty-two forty-seven* etc.

On time means *at the correct/expected time*. *In time* means *sufficiently early for something*. If a train is due to leave at four o'clock and it actually leaves at four o'clock, it leaves *on time*. If you arrive at the station at 3.45, you arrive *in time*. If you arrive at 3.55, you arrive *just in time* or *in the nick of time*.

calendar expressions

M	T	W	T	F	S	S
1	2	3	4	5	6	7
8	9	**10**	11	12	13	14
15	16	17	18	19	20	21
22	23	24	25	26	27	28
29	30	31				

Today is *Wednesday the tenth of* the month. Yesterday was *Tuesday the ninth*. *On Sunday* (7) I washed my car. *Last Monday* (1, i.e. last week, not the immediately preceding Monday) I went to the cinema. Tomorrow is *Thursday 11*. *On Saturday* (13) I am going on holiday and I'm coming back *next Sunday* (or *Sunday week* or *a week on Sunday*). My boyfriend's birthday is *a fortnight today* (or *today fortnight*) (24) and we're getting married *eighteen weeks on Saturday*. For writing and saying dates, see DATES.

A *week* is seven days; a FORTNIGHT is two weeks or fourteen days. *Fifteen days* is two weeks and one day; it is not a synonym of a fortnight. A *quarter* is a three-month period especially for accounting and financial purposes.

See QUARTER, TERM & TRIMESTER; SEMESTER.

time prepositions

The prepositions *in, on, at* and *by* are used as follows:

in

Parts of days: *in the morning, afternoon, evening*.

Months, seasons, years etc.: *In February; in winter; in 1951; in 68; in the second quarter; in the first half of August; in the holidays*.

on

Days and dates: *on Tuesday, on Thursday morning, on 10 June, on my birthday, on CHRISTMAS Day*.

at
Clock time: *at ten o'clock; at half past seven; at 10.32; at about six in the morning.*

Night: *at night* (cf *in the morning* etc.)

Holiday periods: *at Christmas; at Easter* (During the holiday period but not necessarily on any special day.)

by
By sets a limit: *I'll be here by ten o'clock* means that at ten o'clock at the latest I will be here. I will probably arrive earlier. *You must have that report ready by ten o'clock on Thursday* sets the deadline, the latest acceptable time as the report is to be presented to a meeting later that morning. *By* is not the same as *about* or *approximately*. See FUTURE | FUTURE PERFECT.

till and until
These words have the same meaning but *until* is in some cases more formal. At the beginning of a sentence only *until* is used: *Until he told me, I didn't know he was a writer.* Note that *until* has one *l* and *till* has two. *Till* is not short for *until*. Some people assume that it is and write it as *'til* with an apostrophe. There is no reason to do so.

-tion & -xion
Despite its origin as Latin *connexion-*, *connection* is now written thus in line with the verb *connect* and the influence of other words such as *correction*. Similarly *inflection* and *reflection* are more common than *inflexion* and *reflexion*. *Complexion* and CRUCI*fi*XION are the only common words always written with *-xion*.

titles of films etc.
Titles of films especially, and also other works of art, are often translated into other languages in forms that are quite different from the original. This is because the original title is often designed to have a special impact or appeal, or to make a cultural reference that cannot be translated.

to with -ing
Some PREPOSITIONAL VERBS *(*MULTI-WORD VERBS)* have *to* as the preposition:
I'm looking forward to the weekend.
That will contribute to pollution.
I object to the price.
They devoted their lives to education.
I'm used to hard work.

In these examples *to* is followed by a noun: *the weekend, the price* etc.

If it is followed by a verb, the verb is in the -ING FORM.
I'm looking forward to going away.
That will contribute to polluting the environment.
I object to paying so much.
They devoted their lives to teaching deaf children.
I'm used to working hard.

Not ~~*I'm looking forward to go away*~~ etc. This is a preposition followed by a gerund, not an INFINITIVE WITH TO.

See USED TO.

to & towards
If you *go to* a place, you reach it, or intend to do so. If you *go towards* a place, you are going in the direction of a place but have not reached it and might not ever reach it.

tongue-twisters
Tongue-twisters are phrases that are difficult to pronounce quickly or repeatedly. Some examples are: ➤

T

She sells seashells on the seashore,
The shells that she sells are seashells, I'm sure,
For if she sells sea-shells on the seashore,
Then I'm sure she sells seashore shells.
This plays on the HOMOPHONES *(*HOMONYMS)* shore *and* sure.

What annoys a noisy oyster? A noisy noise annoys a noisy oyster.
Red leather, yellow leather (repeated).
The sixth sheikh's sixth sheep's sick.
I can think of six thin things and six thick things too.
Mixed BISCUITS (repeated).

to, too & two

To is the preposition; it is also sometimes found with the infinitive of the verb. It is pronounced /tʊ/ or /tə/ before a vowel, /tə/ before a consonant, and /tuː/ when it is emphasised (strong pronunciation).

Too is an adverb. It means a) *excessively*, and b) *also*. It is pronounced /tuː/.

Two is the number 2. It is pronounced /tuː/.

touristic

This word appears in dictionaries and is used in English in non-English-speaking countries but is not in common current use in the UK; it is preferable to use *tourist* as an adjective in collocations such as *tourist class, attraction, bus, hotel, resort, shop* etc.

See DICTIONARY WORDS.

travel etc.

Travel: This is a verb (with the exception noted below*)*: *He spent a month travelling; I have to travel to Germany next month.*

nouns

Journey is the usual word for the act of travelling. *Have a good journey; a ten-minute bus journey; a book to read on the journey.*

Trip is a return journey and covers all the time you are away. *A three-day trip* does not mean three days' constant travelling.

An ***excursion*** is a short journey, maybe half a day or a full day, for pleasure. Often it is part of a longer holiday. *A day trip* could be an *excursion.* A *flight* is a journey in an aeroplane or other aircraft. A *drive* is a journey in a car. A *voyage* is a journey in a SHIP. These nouns are all countable.

Travel can be used as an uncountable noun: *Travel is an important part of education.* It can also be a countable noun in the plural: *During his travels in Africa. Gulliver's Travels* and *Travels With My Aunt* are books by Jonathan Swift and Graham Greene respectively. This sense implies long, adventurous travel. Its countable form is never used: *A travel in the Amazon jungle; He made three travels in Central Africa. Expedition* is the word to use here.

Travel cannot be used as a countable noun meaning *journey*: *My travel to work; A six-hour travel.*

travesty & transvestite

A ***travesty*** is a CARICATURE or great misrepresentation of something: *A travesty of his words*; *A travesty of justice.*

A ***transvestite*** is a person who dresses in the clothes of the other sex.

treason

Treason is specifically the crime of betraying one's country. A person who does so is a ***traitor***; such behaviour is ***traitorous***.

Betray itself is a more general word: you can *betray a friend* or *betray his trust in you* by being disloyal; your facial expression or body language can *betray* your emotions.

The nouns *betrayal* and *treachery* are SYNONYMS.

The adjective **treacherous** can describe behaviour involving betrayal, and can mean *unreliable, perhaps dangerous*: *The ice made the roads treacherous; The old wooden bridge looked treacherous.*

Treasury

The Treasury is the name given to the UK's finance ministry. It is headed by the *Chancellor of the Exchequer*, sometimes known simply as the *Chancellor*, who is the finance minister.

treat and treatment

A *treat* is something unusual and pleasant which someone does for you, like taking you somewhere special on your birthday.

As a verb it can correspond to the above noun meaning: *I'll treat you to dinner because it's your birthday* or it can refer to the way of handling a person or situation: *Treat her kindly*; *He treated the subject* HISTORICALLY. An injury or disease is *treated*.

Treatment is the noun.

A written discussion can be called a *treatise*.

A *treaty* is a legal agreement between two or more countries.

trek

This word means *a long, tiring, difficult journey* or, as a verb, *to make such a journey*; it is often used ironically: *Trekking round the shops*. *Pony-trekking* is the leisure activity of travelling on a pony in rural areas. The word is Afrikaans in origin, which explains why it ends with *-k* rather than the regular English *-ck*. Irregularly for an English word it makes the forms *trekking*, *trekked* and *trekker*.

troop & troupe

Troop is a word used to describe a group of soldiers; *troops* are military personnel of all kinds. A *troupe* is a group of actors or other performers. Both are pronounced /truːp/.

try

In *I'll try to have the answer tomorrow* and *I'll try and have the answer tomorrow* the meaning is the same but the second is more informal. However, the second is only possible with the uninflected word *try*: *Try and remember his name* is good but *I tried and remembered his name* is not; or RATHER, it means that I tried to remember his name and succeeded in doing so.

To try to do something means to make an attempt, not knowing if it will be successful.

To try doing something means to do it as an experiment to see if it produces the required result: *Try putting less salt in it next time!*

See INFINITIVE OR -ING?

tummy

A childish form of *stomach*.

See BELLY.

-ture

Words that end with *-ture*, *future*, *nature*, *caricature* etc., are pronounced /-tʃə/.

See T, T.

two

The *w* is not pronounced in *two* /tuː/, but it is pronounced in the words *twice* and *between*; it is also pronounced in the archaic words *betwixt* (= *between*) and *twain* (*two*).

See AMONG & BETWEEN.

U

u, U /juː/

The twenty-first letter of the alphabet.

It is normally pronounced /ʌ/: *but, cut, gun, mug.*

In some words it is pronounced /ʊ/ e.g.: *bull, bullet, bush, butcher, cushion, full, pudding, pulley, push, put.*

Its long pronunciation is /juː/: *tube, computer, cute.* After *l, r* and *s* it is /uː/: *blue, lunar, rule, sue, suit, supreme,* but *assume, presume, resume* have /juː/.

For more details on the pronunciations /ʌ/ and /juː/, see DOUBLE CONSONANTS.

U and non-U

In 1954 an article appeared in a Finnish philological journal describing the ways in which different social classes in Britain used words. The following year the writer Nancy Mitford wrote a magazine article in which she used the terms *U* and *non-U* to describe upper class and other speech respectively. *U* terms are *lavatory, napkin,* and *knave* (PLAYING CARDS) and the *non-U* equivalents are *toilet, serviette,* and *jack.* The distinction now is far from being as strong as it used to be, but choice of vocabulary is still often an indicator of social background among British people.

Uncle Sam

Uncle Sam, whose initials are US, is a figure representing the government or people of the United States. He is shown as a tall thin nineteenth-century character with a top hat. His clothes have the pattern of the American flag.

underground railways

In London two names are used, *underground* and *tube,* although strictly the tubes are the deep lines that were built as circular tunnels rather than the shallow cut-and-cover lines. In non-English-speaking cities the local name is used in speaking English: *Metro, U-Bahn* etc.

undertaking & undertaker

The verb *undertake* can be intransitive or transitive. You can *undertake* (promise) *to do something* or *undertake* a project. An *undertaking* is a project, enterprise or a promise, a commitment. However, it is important to note that an *undertaker* is specifically a person who organises funerals; the word is rarely used in any other sense.

universities

A basic university (colloquial *uni* /juːni/) course in Britain requires three years of full-time study and it is usual for students to go away to university rather than study at a local university. Many students take a *gap year* between school and university in which they travel and/or work. The university year starts in October and has three terms with *vacations* (*vacs*) for CHRISTMAS and Easter, and in the summer (the *long vac*). Universities often provide accommodation for students in COLLEGES or *halls of residence.*

After three years, a successful student receives a *bachelor's degree*; this probably gives the title of *Bachelor of Arts* (*BA*) or *Bachelor of Science* (*BSc*), though universities can give whatever names they like to their degrees; *B.Econ.* (economics) and *Ll.B.* (LAW) are common. *Arts* here refers to the humanities, not only fine art. These degrees are given in three classes: first, second and third, the second class being divided into two parts: *upper* and *lower second* or *2.1* and *2.2* (*two one* and *two two*). One class of degree is given for all the subjects together, and marks or classes for individual subjects are not usually given.

A student who wishes to continue with further study does a *master's* degree (*MA, MSc* etc.); the degree of *Master of Business Administration* (*MBA*) is one well-known example of this. Further research leads to a *doctorate,* with the title *PhD,* for a thesis containing original work. University teachers are known as LECTURERS or *dons*; a *professor* is the head of a *department* or *faculty.*

Access to university is provided by results in the *A-level* (advanced level) exams. These are taken at the age of eighteen after a two-year preparation course. Students usually take three or four subjects, and a grade is given for each subject separately, so someone looking for a university place may have physics B, technology B, mathematics C; or English A, history A, French B, economics B (A, B, C, D, and E are all pass grades). There are no compulsory subjects for all students; specialisation starts comparatively early. There is a process for administering entry to university by which students can receive places on condition that they achieve specified A-level results. A student who fails to do so, or who wants to change university, can approach other universities to find one that will provide a place in the light of the exam results. The custom of going away from home to university makes this process more flexible.

The oldest university in England is Oxford, which dates from the MIDDLE AGES; the first college, University College, was founded in 1249. In 1209 some scholars who were threatened by the people of Oxford moved to Cambridge and founded a university there. Peterhouse, the oldest college in Cambridge University, was founded in 1284. For many years these two universities dominated the intellectual life of the country while developing different characters, Oxford being more philosophical and abstract, Cambridge being more practical and realistic. Oxford supported the King in the Civil War (1642-1651) and was the Royalist capital, while Cambridge was for Parliament and Cromwell. While both universities provide excellent teaching and research in all subjects, it is hardly surprising that the great theological debates of the nineteenth century took place in Oxford while Cambridge has seen the scientific achievements of Newton (gravity), Rutherford (splitting the atom), and Crick and Watson (DNA).

The nineteenth century saw the founding of the first English universities since the Middle Ages in Durham (1832) and London (1836). These were followed by the establishment of universities in the fast-growing industrial cities, known as redbrick universities because of the typical building material of the time. The 1970s saw a further expansion of universities, mostly on the outskirts of towns and cities. In 1992 the polytechnic colleges, which had previously been under the control of local authorities, were given the status of universities.

Scotland has four medieval universities: St Andrews (sic, without apostrophe) (1411), Glasgow (1451), Aberdeen (1495) and EDINBURGH (1582) as well as a number of more modern ones. Trinity College Dublin was founded in 1592. The University of Wales was established by charter in 1893, although its first college in Aberystwyth had been preparing students for London University degrees since 1872. This university had campuses throughout the country but in 2007 those in Aberystwyth, Swansea and Lampeter became separate universities.

The Open University took its first students in 1971. Its courses are mostly taught by correspondence, video and DVD material, and the INTERNET, though there are personal tutorial sessions and short residential schools. The OU is open to anyone who wishes to apply; there is no requirement to have A-levels and students are of all ages. About 70% of undergraduates are in full-time employment and many see the opportunity to take a degree as a means of advancing their careers; the OU is increasing its international presence. The structure of the courses is more flexible than at a conventional university and students typically take six years to gain a first (bachelor's) degree. Open University degrees are recognised as equivalent to degrees from conventional universities.

All these universities receive their funds from the state. There are five private universities in the UK. The UK has a total of around 130 universities (September 2016).

up

Many people talk of going *up to London* or *down from London*. The railways have *up trains* (to London) and *down trains* (from London) on the *up* and *down lines* respectively.

use

The noun is pronounced /juːs/. The verb is pronounced /juːz/.

See USED TO.

U

used to, would & accustomed to
auxiliary verb

Used to is pronounced /'juːstə/ or /'juːstu/ before a vowel or when it stands before an ELLIPSIS, for example: *Does he smoke? Not now but he used to.* It is pronounced /'juːstə/ before a consonant. See TO, TOO & TWO.

It expresses an action or state in the past (with DYNAMIC OR STATIVE verbs respectively) that was repeated or that lasted for a considerable time and took place a fairly long time in the past: *I used to play football a lot; I used to live in Frankfurt.*

It is only used in the past; in the present adverbs must be used: *I often/regularly/play football; I play football on Saturdays/twice a week/in the winter.* ~~I use to play football on Saturdays~~ is not used as it is impossible to distinguish the pronunciation from *I used to ...*

There is uncertainty regarding the questions and negatives; the recommended forms are *Did you use to play football?* and *I didn't use to play football* but *I used not to play football* is also found. ~~Did you used to play football?~~ and ~~I didn't used to play football~~ are also found but are regarded as non-standard.

The TAG QUESTION is *You used to play football, didn't you?*

would

This can also mean that an action was habitual. It is more formal than *used to*, it must be associated with time reference, and is only used with DYNAMIC verbs: *When I was young I would play football every Saturday* but not ~~I would live in Frankfurt in the 1970s.~~

accustomed to

Used to (pronounced as above) means *accustomed to*: *I'm used to/accustomed to life in a big city; I'm used to/accustomed to living in a big city.* In *I'm used to living in a big city* the *to* is a preposition followed by the gerund or -ING FORM of the verb: ~~I'm used to live in a big city~~ is incorrect. See TO WITH -ING. This can be used in all tenses: *I was used to living in a big city; I have always been used to living in a big city; I'll never be used to living in a big city.*

While *be used to* describes the state, *get used to* describes the process of reaching that state, i.e. the process of *becoming used to it* (see PASSIVE VOICE with *get*): *I suppose I'll get used to living in a big city; I got used to living in a big city surprisingly easily.*

When it is a passive of the verb, *use* is followed by an infinitive, e.g. *A computer was used to calculate the answer.* The pronunciation is /'juːzdtʊ/ or /'juːzdtə/.

V

v, V /viː/

The twenty-second letter of the alphabet. It is pronounced /v/ (with the upper teeth touching the inside of the lower lip).

When it is the final sound of a word, it is followed by a silent *e*: *active, achieve, behave.* Exceptions are:

chav (pejorative, a lower class person with poor taste in clothes and lifestyle)

guv /gʌv/ (slang for *boss*, from *governor*)

rev (revolution per minute, e.g. *3,000 revs*; to *rev* an engine is to run it quickly; *rev* is not used for a political or any other kind of revolution)

Slav

spiv (a black-market operator).

It is rarely doubled, even after a short vowel: *giver* /gɪvə/, *living* /lɪvɪŋ/, *having, never* (not ~~givver~~ etc.) The exceptions are the verb *rev* (above), which is regular and has *revving, revved,* and a few words ending in *-vvy,* e.g. *bevvy* (a drink, from beverage) and *luvvy* (an informal word for an actor, from *love*).

vacation & vacancy

Vacation is the usual American word for a holiday. It is used in British English, often abbreviated to *vac.*, for the periods between university terms; however, schools have *holidays*.

A *vacancy* is a position or job that is not filled: *There are two vacancies for English teachers*; or available rooms in a hotel.

vain, vein & vane

As an adjective *vain* means *proud*. A *vain* person is one who is very proud of his/her appearance or achievement. A *vain boast*, a *vain hope*, is one that has no substance. If something is done *in vain* an attempt is made but it is unsuccessful: *I have tried in vain to find her phone number.*

A *vein* /veɪn/ is a blood vessel that returns blood to the heart.

A *vane* is a blade of a propeller or turbine. A *weathervane* is a device on the roof of a building that indicates wind direction.

These three words are HOMOPHONES *(*HOMONYMS)*.

venal & venial

A *venal* person is one who is corrupt, who is willing to accept bribes. In Christian theology a *venial* sin is one that does not deprive the soul of divine grace. The word is used colloquially for a minor mistake or offence that can be forgiven.

verbal & oral

Verbal is often used to mean *spoken, not in writing* as in *verbal agreement, verbal communication, verbal contract*. However, this use, which is well established and is more than 400 years old, is ODD since *verbal* means to do with words rather than with speech.

Oral seems more appropriate to describe spoken language and is always used for the *oral tradition* of early Greek or other poetry that has been passed from generation to generation orally rather than in writing; *oral history* is history that is recorded from speech of people who have personal experience of the events. An *oral* is an oral examination.

visa

A visa is special permission that is sometimes required in order to enter a country. The credit card takes its name from this.

V

voiced and unvoiced consonants

Voiced consonants are those that are made with vibration of the vocal cords in the larynx; *unvoiced* (also known as *voiceless*) consonants are made with no such vibration. The difference can be observed by placing a finger on the larynx while pronouncing the consonant. If a vibration is felt, the consonant is voiced. A list of voiced and unvoiced consonants can be found in PHONETIC SYMBOLS. For the pronunciation of *-ed* in past tense forms, see -ED & -ES, PRONUNCIATION.

Vowels are voiced by definition.

W

w, W /ˈdʌbljuː/

The twenty-third letter of the alphabet. Its name is correctly pronounced /ˈdʌbljuː/, though /ˈdʌbəjuː/ is common, especially in *www* for websites.

It is silent before *r*: *write, wrong, wrestle* etc.; it is silent in *TWO* and *answer* /ˈɑːnsə/.

w- and wh-

There is no difference in Standard English pronunciation between words that begin with *w-* and *wh-*, but in Scotland, Ireland and parts of the north of England *wh-* is pronounced with the aspiration of a slight /h/ sound before the /w/. The large majority of English words which begin with the letter *w* do not have an *h* following it.

Question words have *wh-*: *what, when, whence, where, whether, whither, which, who/whom/whose* and *why*, as do their compounds: *whatever* etc.

Many onomatopoeic words have *wh-*: *whack, wham, whee, wheeze, whew, whiz, whine, whine, whinge, whinny, whir, whoa, whoop, whoopee,* and *whoosh*.

The following is a list of words which begin with *wh-*. It does not include proper nouns and a few other words which are extremely rare: *whale, wharf, whatnot, wheat, wheel, whelk, whet* (different from *WET*), *Whig* (different from *wig*), *while, whim, whimper, whip, whirl, whisk, whisky, whisper, whist, whistle, whit* (different from *WIT (*CLEVER)*), *white, Whitsun, whittle, who, WHODUNNIT, whole, whore* and *whorl*.

In the words *who, whole* and *whore* the *w* is not pronounced: /huː/, /həʊl/, /hɔə/.

wait

Wait can be intransitive: *I waited until he came; Wait there*. When it is transitive it has the preposition *for*: *Wait for me*. It is not used with a direct object: ~~Wait me~~; ~~I waited the bus~~.

To wait on someone was to *serve them* (from the idea of attending and waiting for orders); nowadays this is found only in the expression *to wait on someone hand and foot*, often used ironically: *Do you expect me to wait on you hand and foot?* It is this meaning that has given the word *waiter* for someone who serves at table.

The transitive verb *await* is not used in the colloquial sense of *wait for*: ~~I'll await you outside the cinema; I awaited the bus in the rain~~. It is used more in the sense of *expect*: *I await your reply with interest; We are awaiting the judge's decision* or that something is ready, prepared or waiting: *A surprise awaits you; Who knows what will await us when we arrive?*

Wait and see means *to wait until a situation becomes clear*; *We'll just have to wait and see what time they arrive*.

Wait for it! means *Don't anticipate something*, a signal or order for example.

Wait up means *to stay up, not to go to bed*: *I'll be late tonight. Don't wait up for me.*

That can wait means that it is not urgent and can be dealt with later.

(Just) you wait is a threat or warning of a punishment or some other unpleasant consequences.

waive & wave

To **waive** a right is to decide not to use it. *In this case I will waive my right to compensation; I am not able to waive the rule that you must be a resident of the city.*

To **wave** something is to move it in one's hand: *Survivors were waving white CLOTHS to attract attention*. You *wave your hand* to attract somebody's attention or as a sign of goodbye. It can be intransitive: *flags, tree branches* etc. can *wave* in a breeze.

wake etc.

Wake, woke, woken is the commonest of these verbs in colloquial use, transitive and intransitive. It is often used with *up*, with no difference in meaning. ***Awake, awoke, awoken*** (without *up*) has the

W

same meaning but is more literary. *(A)waken* (regular and without *up*) can be used in the same way but is less common.
The thunder woke me (up) / awoke me / (a)wakened me.
I was woken (up) / awoken / (a)wakened by the thunder.
I woke (up) / awoke / (a)wakened at seven o'clock.

Only **awake** can have the intransitive meaning *to become fully aware of something*: *He awoke to the difficulty/danger involved.*

The regular **awaken** has the transitive use of *make someone AWARE of something*: *Her comment awakened me to the possibility.*

Awake is a predicative ADJECTIVE: *Are you awake?* For emphasis we say *wide awake* not ~~very awake~~. See A- ADJECTIVES.

A *wake* is a vigil held over a dead body before burial, especially in IRELAND.

The entirely different word *wake*, a HOMONYM, is the trail left on the water by a SHIP.

Wales, a brief history

See the note for history articles on page xv.

When the Romans occupied Britain in the second half of the first century AD, the native Celtic population spoke a language that is the ancestor of modern Welsh. When the Romans withdrew in the fifth century, the Germanic tribes that invaded England did not extend into Wales and the ancient culture remained alive there. Wales, with remote parts of the north of England and Scotland, preserved the Christianity of the Roman Empire. During the Middle Ages four main Welsh kingdoms developed but no united Welsh nation ever appeared, perhaps for geographical reasons; the mountainous nature of the country makes internal communication between north and south difficult even today.

The Norman invasion of England extended into Wales, with the building of castles to maintain Norman power in the land they had conquered. With time, these new Norman landowners became accepted by the Welsh people and alliances and marriages became more frequent. Resistance to Norman occupation continued however. Llewelyn Olaf (Llewelyn the Last; for pronunciation of Welsh *ll* see L, L) was recognised by England as Prince of Wales, but in 1282 Edward I declared him a rebel and defeated and killed him in battle. In 1284 all Welshmen were declared subjects of the English Crown; many more castles were built to maintain the occupation. These castles and fortified towns established the pattern, which can be found even today, that Welsh language and culture survive in rural areas while the commercial towns are more English in character. In 1404 Owain Glyndwr had united the Welsh people under his leadership and he drove the English out of much of Wales. He planned to establish a Welsh nation with a university. But he failed; his capital Harlech fell in 1409 and he became a fugitive. There is no record of his death. Welsh customs and laws were abolished by the English and in 1536 Henry VIII of England (whose own family, the Tudors, were Welsh in origin) signed an Act of Union making Wales entirely subject to English law. This incorporated Wales into England more comprehensively than the Act of Union with Scotland.

Although Wales maintained a separate cultural identity, its political history since 1536 has been that of England. The Reformation led to a more Protestant religion in Wales than in England, with a stronger puritan disapproval of alcohol, tobacco and FUN. Wales remained largely agricultural, but in the nineteenth century coal mining and steel developed as important industries in South Wales although they were usually owned and managed by Englishmen. Welsh nationalism developed in the nineteenth century as the use of the Welsh language decreased, partly as a result of political pressure to use English. The UNIVERSITY of Wales opened in 1872. In the twentieth century Plaid Cymru /plaɪd'kʌmri/, the Welsh nationalist party, increased in strength. In 1999 a Welsh Assembly opened in Cardiff, the capital.

See CELTS AND CELTIC; ENGLAND, A BRIEF HISTORY; IRELAND, A BRIEF HISTORY; PERSONAL NAMES; PLACE NAMES; SCOTLAND, A BRIEF HISTORY; WELSH.

W

want

This word is pronounced /wɒnt/ and is both a noun and a verb. Its most common use is as a verb indicating desire: *I want to go home*; *She wanted a different colour*. However, the original meaning of the word was related to *lack* or *absence*; the present meaning arose because people often desire and wish to have what they lack. The word is no longer used with this meaning as a verb, though in nineteenth and early twentieth-century literature it is found in time expressions such as *it wanted twenty minutes to eight*; the PROVERB *waste not, want not* uses this meaning of the verb.

Wanted in a poster means that someone is looking for a person or thing: *Wanted – £10,000 reward* for a criminal, or *Wanted* in ADVERTISEMENTS for employment or for things to buy.

When used as a noun, *want* can mean a lack or a desire. Franklin D. Roosevelt spoke of *freedom from want*, Jane Austen wrote that *a single man in possession of a good fortune, must be in want of a wife*, and Benjamin Franklin wrote *for want of a nail, the shoe was lost; for want of a shoe the horse was lost; and for want of a horse the rider was lost*. The common expression *for want of anything better/more interesting* etc. means *in the absence of*. A *long-felt want* is a desire that has been felt for a long time; to *satisfy someone's wants* means to satisfy their desires or needs.

Want /wɒnt/ should not be confused with WONT /wəʊnt/ meaning custom or habit.

-wards

This is a suffix meaning in a certain direction; it is pronounced /wədz/. If you travel *northwards* you are travelling towards the north. Words that can combine with *-wards* are *north, south, east, west; in, out; up, down; on, to; home*; other forms can be made as required: *landwards, citywards, polewards*. When these words are used as adjectives, or as adverbs directly before a verb, the *s* is not present: *inward movement, southward migration; homeward bound*. See BIND & BOUND. *Forwards* is only used with a very clear sense of direction: *backwards and forwards, take two steps forwards*. In other cases *forward* is the usual adverb: *from this time forward, lean forward, look forward to something*; and *forward* as an adverb is becoming more common. In American English it is standard to use the *-ward* form as the adverb in all cases. To *forward* a LETTER or EMAIL means to send one that you have received to another address or to someone else.

wash

The commonest use of *wash* relates to cleaning by the use of water. However, in the wider use of the word the presence and action of water is more important than the idea of cleaning. Cars and bridges can be *washed away* by rain or flood water. Objects from the sea can be *washed up/ashore* on the coast by the tide; objects or people from a SHIP can be *washed overboard* by the waves.

To *wash up* means to wash the things that have been used in the preparation and eating of a meal. In American English it means *to wash oneself*. A *washing-up machine* or *dishwasher* washes the dishes; it does the *washing-up*. A *washing machine* washes clothes.

The expression *that won't wash* means that an argument or proposal is unacceptable.

Whitewash is a solution of quicklime (calcium oxide, CaO) in water, used for covering walls etc. Colloquially a *whitewash* is an attempt to cover up a mistake or a scandal.

To *brainwash* a person means to subject him/her to a psychological process designed to force acceptance of and belief in ideas that would not normally be held.

way

Originally, *way* meant *road* or *path*. It no longer has this sense; we do not say ~~He bought a house in the next way~~. However, this meaning has survived in *highway, gangway, runway, slipway*, and a number of idiomatic expressions.

Can you tell me the way to the station?
You've gone the right/wrong way.
Right of way.
In the way.
On the way.

➤

W

Go out of one's way. (Literal and metaphorical.)
Fall by the wayside. (Drop out of a project before it is completed.)
To be waylaid. (Attacked by surprise.)
WayFAREr (= traveller.)
The way must be open to legal action.

By extension from this it means *manner, method*: *Can you show me the way you make a pasta salad?; What's the best way to fry an egg?*

Under way is a phrase that describes a BOAT or SHIP moving through the water. It is also used in other metaphorical senses to mean *making progress*.

wear

The commonest use of this verb refers to clothes: *She wore a white dress; I'm wearing a grey sweater* but it can also be used for people wearing make-up, perfume, jewellery, glasses, watches, wigs or beards. By extension from this meaning it refers to the way in which clothes gradually lose quality or become damaged as they are worn. It can be transitive *I've worn a hole in the elbow of my sweater* or intransitive *These shoes have worn well* (i.e. have kept their shape, colour, quality etc. well).

This meaning is not confined to clothes, and an adverb is often added to create a MULTI-WORD VERB. If something has *worn out*, it has become useless and must be replaced. If someone says *I'm worn out*, he/she is very tired. If something has *worn through*, a hole has appeared in it. If something has *worn down*, it is not as tall as it was (e.g. the tread on a bicycle or car tyre *wears down* with use) and something that has *worn away* has disappeared wholly or partly with use. It can be followed by adjectives (stones can be *worn smooth* by the action of water) and other expressions: *I've worn my fingers to the bone* means that I have done a lot of work with my hands. These expressions can be transitive: *wear something out, through, away* etc. With relation to clothes, the verb can be followed by a colour: *Why are you wearing black?*

Wear can also mean *accept, tolerate*: *I asked him to lend me £100 but he wouldn't wear it.*

Wednesday

The first *d* and the second *e* are not pronounced: /'wenzdeɪ/.

weekend

The *weekend* is Saturday and Sunday. *The end of the week* is Friday afternoon: *I'll give it to you BY (*TIME) the end of the week.*

weigh & weight

Weigh is a verb: *Will you weigh it for me?; It weighs 100 kg.*

Weight is a noun: *Its weight is 100 kg.* However, *weight* can also be used as a verb in statistics meaning that a certain value is attached to a certain factor to reflect its importance. A *weighted average* is one that gives exceptional importance to certain factors. A *weighting* is an extra payment added to a salary for a special reason: a *London weighting* is a reflection of the higher cost of living in London than in other places.

weights and measures

The metric system is not widely used in Britain outside the world of science and technology, though food shops now sell goods in metric units. In normal conversation, in shops and in road signs the traditional imperial system of weights and measures is commonly used. The following are **approximate** equivalents; for precise equivalents, consult a conversion table.

linear measure

1 *inch* (1 in. or 1") is 2½ cm. One *foot* (1 ft or 1') is 30 cm. One *yard* (1 yd) is 90 cm. One metre is 1.1 yards or 3.33 feet but for many practical purposes the metre and the yard are the same: *Turn right and it's 200 yards/metres on the right.* A *mile* is 1,760 yards or 1.6 km. A kilometre is ⅝ mile. Common speed limits on British roads are 30 mph (50 kph), 50 mph (80 kph) and 70 mph (110 kph).

W

A *nautical mile* is 1.85 km. Vertical distances, including heights of mountains and altitudes of aeroplanes, are always measured in feet; horizontal distances are measured in yards or miles. A *fathom* is a unit used in measuring the depth of water; it is six feet.

square measure
One *square foot* (1 sq ft or 1 ft^2) is about 0.1 m^2. Land is measured by the *acre*: 1 acre is 0.4 hectares and 1 hectare is 2½ acres. One *square mile* is 2½ square kilometres and 1 sq. km. is 0.4 sq. m.

weight
One *ounce* (1 oz) is 28 gm. Sixteen oz make 1 *pound* (1 lb), which is 454 gm. One kg. is 2.2 lb. Cheese and cooked meat are normally sold by the *quarter* (qtr), which is a quarter of a pound, 110 gm. People's weights are normally given in stones and pounds. One *stone* (1 st) is 14 pounds and is therefore about 6⅓ kg. In the USA the stone is not used, and people's weights are given in pounds only. A *hundredweight* (1 cwt) is, confusingly, 112 lb. (8 st) equivalent to 50 kg and, surprisingly, the *ton* (20 cwt, or 2,240 lb) is almost precisely the same as the *metric tonne* (2,205 lb) (note the difference in spelling). The American hundredweight has 100 lb and twenty American hundredweights make a *short ton* of 2,000 lb.

liquid measure
A *pint* /paɪnt/ is 20 oz of water (the *fluid ounce* is a unit of volume not of mass), which is equivalent to 56 cl. A *gill* /dʒɪl/ is legally defined as a quarter of a pint, but in some places a gill of beer is colloquially half a pint. A *quart* is two pints. A *gallon* is 8 pints or 4½ litres. One *litre* is 1¾ pints. In the USA the pint is 16 oz of water (475 cl, not 448 cl as it would be in the UK, owing to a slight difference in the definition of the fluid ounce on the two sides of the Atlantic Ocean); the AMERICAN gallon is correspondingly smaller, about 3.8 litres.

circular measure
Britain uses the same system of degrees, minutes and seconds as is used in other countries.

See MONEY.

well
Well is the adverb corresponding to the adjective *good*: *She works well*/*She is a good worker*.

It can also be used as a predicative ADJECTIVE. *I am well*, means *I am healthy*. The comparative is *better*: *I am/feel better than I did yesterday*. Sometimes it is used ATTRIBUTIVELY: *He's not a well man*, but this is unusual. See ILL.

I am *well in with* him means that I am on good terms with him or in his favour.

They are well off means they are rich or at least not short of money. This can be used attributively: *a well-off businessman*.

It is (just) as well that means that otherwise things would have developed badly: *It's (just) as well (THAT) you told me that* (the same as *It's a good thing (that) you told me that*).

All's well that ends well is a PROVERB.

To *leave well alone* means not to try to improve something that is already in a satisfactory state.

It's all very well means that something is fine and satisfactory in certain situations, and is often followed by an objection or contradiction: *Becoming a monk is all very well but what would happen if everyone became a monk?*; *It's all well and good wanting to become a monk, but...*

That's all well and good, but ... means that something is satisfactory as far as it goes but is not complete.

A *well* is a hole in the ground from which water, oil or gas is obtained.

Welsh
This is the adjective relating to WALES. It comes from a Saxon word meaning *foreign, strange* and is related to the *Walach*, the name for an ethnic group in Romania and also to the first syllable of *walnut* as the nut came from Roman lands. As a surname it is often spelled *Welch*, and this form is found in the name of the British army regiment the *Royal Welch Fusiliers*. ▸

W

As a verb *to welsh* or *welch* (with a small *w*) *on an agreement* means to fail to carry it out; it is especially used with a failure to pay money due for a bet *(to welsh on a bet)*. The exact origin of the word is not known. It may have originated with a BOOKMAKER called *Welch*, but it is understandable that Welsh people do not like its use and are offended by the word.
See CELTS AND CELTIC.

wet
Wet is a general word that can apply to various degrees of wetness.

damp & moist
These both mean slightly wet, as in a cloth that is used for cleaning things or as in earth or leaves after rain or dew. *Damp*, however, tends to suggest unpleasantness; the air in winter may be cold and damp; *damp* sheets should not be slept in and *damp* clothes should not be worn. *Damp* (as a noun) is a problem or danger if it is found in the walls of a house or in the air. *Dampness* is the state of being damp: *The dampness of the ground was a surprise. Damp*, unlike *moist*, can refer to something that is temporary or casual.

humid
This is not so common as *damp* and *moist* and is not used to refer to CLOTHS, clothes, earth, walls etc. It is used to describe the air in hot countries when it contains a high proportion of water vapour. *Relative humidity* is the meteorological term to describe the air's content of water vapour.

soggy
Something that is *soggy* is completely soaked and has no strength. Overcooked vegetables are *soggy*.

what & which
Which is used when the range of possibilities is limited: *Which political party do you support?; Tell me which text book you use; Which (of these cars) is yours?*

What is used when the choice is unlimited: *What's your phone number?; What news have you heard?; No-one knows at what time he returned.*

So *Which wine is this?* is the question when there are a limited number of possibilities and you know what they are. *What wine is this?* is the question when you have no idea of what it might be.

what is ... like? & how is ...?
What is ... like? is asking for a description: *'What is her house like?' 'It's big and old.'; 'What is your brother like?' 'He's 28, 1.81m, with dark hair.'* (physical description) or *'What is your brother like?' 'He talks a lot and he has a good sense of humour.'* (description of character.)

How is ...? is the question used for asking about health: *'How is your brother?' 'He's much better now, thank you.'* In greetings this is usually almost a formality:

'How are you?' *'Fine thank you. And you?'*
            'I'm OK. How's your wife?'

It is sometimes used to ask about the status of something: *'How's your car?' 'I got it back from the GARAGE yesterday and it seems to be OK.'*

'How was your holiday?' is asking for an opinion, a JUDGEMENT: *'Good, pleasant, unsatisfactory, horrible.'*

'What was your holiday like?' is asking for a longer description.
See LIKE.

while = although
In addition to its normal meaning as a conjunction, *while* also means *although, whereas*: *While I don't think he's stupid, he's not exactly intelligent; Apples have become more expensive, while the price of pears has fallen.*

whisky

Whisky is the Scottish and Canadian spelling; in IRELAND and the USA the spelling is w*hiskey*.

In SCOTLAND and IRELAND the main ingredient is barley, while in the USA maize and rye are used.

who and whom

Whom is the object of the pronoun *who*. It seems to be dropping out of use in modern English, but it is still found in certain circumstances: *Whom did you see?*; *Whom did you speak to?* are certainly correct, but are now found mainly in extremely formal style.

In cases where it immediately follows a PREPOSITION however, *whom* must be used: *To whom did you speak?*; *For whom are you buying that? Who(m) are you buying that for?* is unusual. See PREPOSITIONS AT THE END (DEFERRED PREPOSITIONS).

Similarly in RELATIVE CLAUSES: *The man from whom I bought it ...*

whodunnit

This is a popular name for a crime mystery book or play. It comes from the popular but non-standard *Who done it?* for *Who did it?*

who's & whose

Who's is the CONTRACTION of *who is* or *who has*. *Whose* is the possessive of *who*.

wh- questions

These are questions with the question words WHO, WHOM, *whose/what*, *which*, *when*, *where*, *how*, *why*. *Who*, *whom*, *whose*, *what* and *which* can be the subject or object of a sentence (*whom* is object only).

Compare the following subject and object forms:

subject	object
Who saw you?	*Who(m) did you see?*
Whose car won the race?	*Whose car did you see?*
What made the noise?	*What did you hear?*
Which book won the prize?	*Which book did you buy?*

In each of these pairs of sentences the first question has the *wh-* word as the subject and the verb follows the subject in the order *subject - verb - object* as in an affirmative statement. In the second question of each pair the *wh-* word is the object and the word order of the question is *object - auxiliary verb - subject - main verb*, the usual order for simple questions.

The other *wh-* words are adverbs and always have the usual construction and word order for questions: *When did she arrive?*; *Where did you buy it?*; *Why did you say that? How do you know?*

See QUESTIONS; WHAT & WHICH; WHO AND WHOM.

widget

This word has no precise meaning but is used in business and economics as a generic term to describe a small gadget or mechanical device: *Britain has fewer widget-making factories than it had thirty years ago.* In computing it is a component of a user interface that has a particular function.

wish

Wish is followed by verbs in the PAST SIMPLE when the wish refers to a present time: *I wish I had more money* (now); *I wish he would stop talking* (now); *I wish he were here* (now); *I wish it didn't rain so much here* (always).

Notes: For grammatical purposes *would* is the past of *will* (see TENSE & TIME). *He were* is the past SUBJUNCTIVE. Informally people often say *I wish he was here.*

When the wish refers to an event in the past, the PAST PERFECT is used: *I wish you hadn't said that* (but you did); *I wish he'd told me that yesterday* (but he didn't). There is an analogy between the way in which verb tenses are used with *wish* and in the second and third CONDITIONAL sentences.

W

without

This is the opposite of *with*. In origin it is the opposite of *within* (meaning *inside*) and meant *outside*. It is not generally used now with this meaning but is still occasionally found in the expression *within and/or without*. *Outwith* is in common use in Scotland meaning *outside*.

won't & wont

Both words are pronounced /wəʊnt/.

Won't is the CONTRACTION of *will not*.

Wont is a predicative ADJECTIVE: *to be wont to do something* means to be used to doing something or be in the habit of doing something: *He was wont to sit in the corner* and a noun: *He sat in the corner as was his wont*. There is an adjective (*un*)*wonted*: *He sat in his wonted corner seat*; *He was sitting unwontedly at the table*. These forms are rarely used in modern English except humorously.

work

As a verb *work* is used with reference to machines, meaning *function* or *operate*: *The telephone doesn't work; I don't know how to work the DVD recorder*.

Work is regular (*work, worked, worked*), but this developed in the fifteenth century. Before that it was an IRREGULAR VERB: *work, wrought, wrought; wrought* is now used only for *wrought iron* and is also found in the word *overwrought*, meaning *nervously excited or anxious*. *Overworked* describes a person who has an excessive amount of work to DO.

As a noun in its usual meaning *work* is uncountable: *I've got a lot of work; His work is always satisfactory*. It is countable when it refers to collected literary production: *The Complete Works of William Shakespeare* or to civil engineering: *road works*. *Good works* are charitable activities. In compounds it also refers to industrial premises: *steelworks, waterworks; the works* can be a synonym for a factory. *Waterworks* is also a colloquial expression for crying (*stop/start the waterworks*) and for the urinary system (*trouble with the waterworks*).

worth, worthwhile & worthy

worth

This is a noun with a meaning similar to *value*: *a jewel of great worth*, and to describe the value in money of something: *ten pounds' worth of petrol*. It is also a predicative ADJECTIVE: *It is worth £500*. It is not only used with money: *It is not worth the effort; It's well worth reserving seats in advance* (*worth* is intensified with the adverb *well*, not *very*).

In the second example the meaning is similar to *It's a good idea to reserve in advance*. It could be understood as *It's worth the trouble of reserving seats in advance*.

He was running for all he was worth means that he was making the greatest possible effort, running as fast as he could.

For what it's worth means that there is no guarantee of the truth, accuracy or relevance of a statement: *For what it's worth, John says that Mary's looking for a new job; For what it's worth, I paid £3,000, but that was five years ago*.

Someone who is *worth his/her salt* is worth employing, and by extension is reliable in his/her position: *Any philosopher worth his salt can discuss Kant*.

worthless

This is a synonym of VALUELESS *(*PRICELESS)*; something that is *worthless* has no worth or value: *That painting is worthless, a worthless suggestion*.

See INVALUABLE *(*PRICELESS)*.

worth while

Another way of saying that it is worth the effort of doing something is that it is *worth while*: *It's worth (your) while asking John if he knows; I thought of asking John but decided it wasn't worth (my) while (to do so); I didn't think it was worth while to ring the police; I'll make it worth your*

W

while. (I will pay you or give you some other compensation.) If the possessive is not used in these examples, *worth while* can be written as one word or two: *It's worthwhile asking John if he knows* etc.

When *worthwhile* is used as an attributive ADJECTIVE it is written as one word: *a worthwhile proposal.*

Worthy is used to describe people or things that deserve respect: *that worthy man, a worthy attempt, a worthy winner.* In these examples *An opinion worthy of respect* and *He's worthy of consideration for the job* the meaning is that of *deserves*: *An opinion that deserves respect; He deserves consideration for the job.* In *A speech worthy of the occasion; That comment is not worthy of you* it means that something is suitable to the dignity of an occasion or person.

As a noun, *a worthy* means a worthy person: *All the local worthies were at the ceremony.*

-worthy

This is a suffix meaning
1. *deserving of*: *blameworthy, creditworthy, noteworthy, praiseworthy,* TRUSTworthy *(*RELY & TRUST).*
2. *suitable, appropriate for*: *airworthy, roadworthy, seaworthy.* A *roadworthy car* is one that is in a suitable state of repair to be operated on a road.

write

In British English, you *write to someone*; in American English you *write someone.*

wrong(ly)

The adverb *wrong* means *in a wrong manner* or *direction; with an incorrect result.* If things *go wrong* they do not go as planned; if you *guess wrong* you have the wrong answer; if you *get something wrong* you make a mistake in doing it or understanding it.

Wrongly means *unsustainably or in the wrong way*: *Wrongly, he decided that I had gone home; He acted wrongly; He was found guilty, but wrongly so; I thought, rightly or wrongly, that he was mad.* It is often used with a past participle: *He was wrongly described, condemned, promoted* etc.

See RIGHT(LY).

X

X

x, X /eks/

The twenty-fourth letter of the alphabet. It is pronounced /ks/ except in many cases when the prefix *ex-* is followed immediately by a vowel: *example, executive, exit, exotic, exuberant* /egz/.

In the few words in English which begin with *x-* it is pronounced /z/: *xenophobia, Xerox, xylophone*.

A lower case *x* is the MATHEMATICAL symbol for multiplication. Thus it is used to give dimensions; a room might be *4m x 3m* (four metres by three metres) in size. It is also used to avoid ambiguity in writing numbers that are separate but come together: *2 x 1000 kVA transformers* means two transformers each of 1000 kVA.

It is often used in personal correspondence to symbolise a kiss: *Lots of love, Mary. XXXXX.*

X-ray

As well as being the actual electromagnetic rays, an *X-ray* can be the image that they produce: *The doctor examined the X-rays*. It can be a verb: *The doctor X-rayed my foot*.

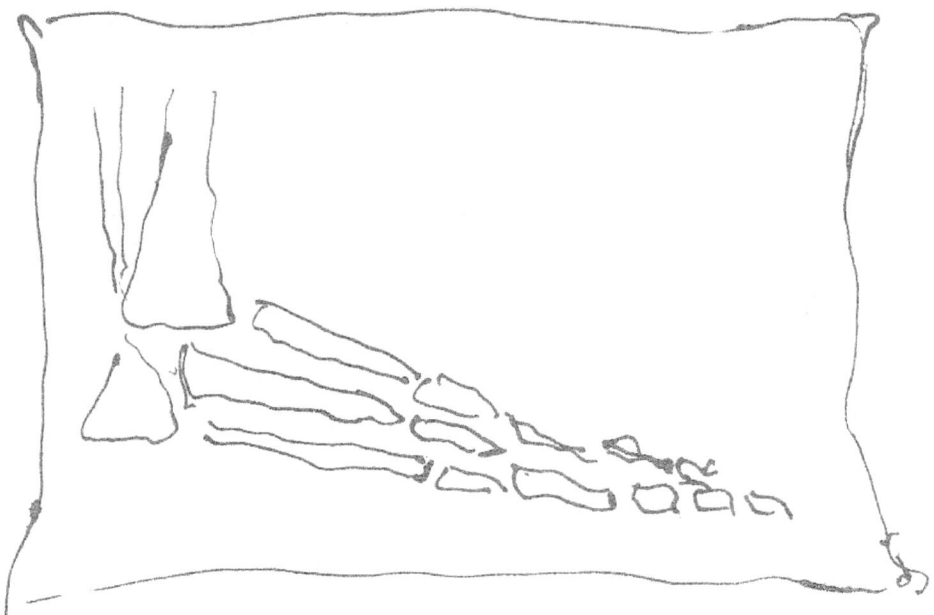

Y

y, Y /waɪ/

The twenty-fifth letter of the alphabet. It can be either a vowel or a consonant.

It is pronounced /j/ at the beginning of a word: *yet, young*; and /ɪ/ at the end of words: *easy, carry, lady*; except in monosyllables where *y* is the only vowel /aɪ/: *by, cry, dry, fly, fry, my, pry, sly, sty, try, why, wry.*

It is found in diphthongs:
-ay /eɪ/
-oy /ɔɪ/
-uy /aɪ/ (*buy, guy*)

As a vowel between consonants it is pronounced, and behaves, exactly like the letter *i*: *hymn* /hɪm/, *Olympic* /əˈlɪmpɪk/, *rhyme* /raɪm/.

As a consonant it is pronounced /j/.

For cases where *y* changes to *i*, see *i* and *y* under I, I.

-y

Very many English adjectives end with *-y*. Some are formed from nouns to say that something has the quality of the noun: *airy, curly, flowery, rubbery, watery.*

Some are made from verbs and mean *liable to do the action of the verb*: *bendy, sticky.*

This is not a free formation and of course there are very many words that end with *-y* but are not adjectives.

See EASE & EASY.

Yank and Yankee

In Britain these words are often used to refer to the USA; A *Yank(ee)* is an AMERICAN, a citizen of the USA. In the USA itself, they are used only of the inhabitants of New England in the north-east of the country.

ye

When THOU was used as a familiar form of *you*, *ye* was its plural; it was also used as a polite singular. It is never used nowadays.

It is also used with the meaning of *the* in the deliberate archaism *Ye Olde Englishe...*; although this is still occasionally seen, it is a cliché that should be avoided. It arises from the similarity of a written *y* to the old English letter *thorn Þ, þ*, which was pronounced /θ/ or /ð/ and was the first letter of the word *the*. It was abandoned in favour of *th* with the introduction of printing to England.

yeah

This is a common colloquial pronunciation of *yes*. *Oh yeah* is often used ironically to express disbelief.

youth

As a countable noun a *youth* is *a young person*, almost always a young male, but a *group of youths* could consist of both sexes. As an uncountable noun *youth* means young people in general as in *The youth of today are our future* (always with a plural verb) and the time when one is young, especially adolescence: *In my youth.*

Z

Z

z, Z /zed/ (American /ziː/)

The twenty-sixth letter of the alphabet. It is pronounced /z/.

For *Mozart* and *Nazi* see FOREIGN WORDS AND NAMES.

At the end of a word it is written -*zz* except in *fez, quiz, showbiz* (show business), and *topaz*.

Some Scottish names have the letter *z* in them: *Dalziel* (also written *Dalyell*) /dɪˈjel/ and *Menzies* /ˈmɪŋɡɪs/. This is because when printing was first introduced, Scottish printers used *z* to represent the old English letter *yogh* (ȝ, Ȝ), which they did not have.

See GH, GH *(*G, G)*.

zh, ZH

This is sometimes used to represent the sound /ʒ/, in Russian transliteration for example.

zodiac

The English names of the signs of the zodiac are *Aries*, ram; *Taurus*, bull; *Gemini*, twins; *Cancer*, crab; *Leo*, lion; *Virgo*, virgin; *Libra*, scale; *Scorpio*, scorpion; *Sagittarius*, archer; *Capricorn*, goat; *Aquarius*, water BEARER; *Pisces*, fish.

index

This index lists incidental references. A word listed here with a reference to another entry may have its own full entry as well. For example, *pepper* is referenced here to *corn* but it also has its own article under its own name.

This index does not contain any cross-references to these articles: *abbreviations*; *American English; anger, surprise insults and taboo words; countries and nationalities; irregular verbs; personal names; prepositions; proverbs.*

A

abdomen	belly
ability	modal auxiliary verbs
abreast	breast
accent	stress differences
accustomed	used to, would & accustomed to
acre	weights and measures
actual(ly)	false friends
addict	stress differences
adopt	adapt
advertise	-ise &-ize
advise	-ise &-ize
afraid	a- adjective
aft	ship
again(st)	amid(st)
agenda	plural
agent	passive voice
all right	already
always	ever & always
altogether	already
among(st)	amid(st)
Anglican	catholic; Church of England; clerk; dog collar
antenna	aerial
Anthony	notes for personal names
antique	ancient
antonym	synonym
anxiety	-iety
apostrophe	punctuation
apprise	-ise &-ize
architectonic	dictionary words
arise	-ise &-ize; rise
arouse	rouse
arrive	get
at	in & on (including at); time
attribute	stress differences
audience	theatre
avenue	road
awake(n)	wake etc.
award	prize

B

backslash	punctuation
bacteria	plural
Balkan peninsula	East
ballot	elections
bang	hit
bank holiday	holidays
banknotes	money
Baptist	Dissenter and Nonconformist
barley	corn
barrister	law
bash	hit
bat	cricket
batter	hit
BBC	media
beam	ship
bear	bare
beard	bare
beat	hit
become	get
bedstead	instead
beer	ale; bare
belt	hit
betray	treason
between	among
betwixt	among
billion	numbers
bird	bare
bishop	chess
blacken	-en verb suffix
bloke	chap
blood	examination & test
boast	say
bob	money
bold	bald
boob	breast
bosom	breast
bound	jump
bow	ship
bowl	cricket
bowsprit	ship
box	theatre
boxing	days with special names
Boxing Day	etymology
bracket	punctuation

index

bravo	theatre
breakfast	meals
breath	examination & test
breathalyser	blend
brethren	plural forms
bridge	ship
brief	case
bright	clever
brighten	-en verb suffix
brilliant	clever
Brit	Briton
broaden	-en verb suffix
brunch	meals
Buckingham Palace	constitution
bump	hit
burgle	back-formation
bust	breast
butt	hit
buttocks	backside

C

Cabinet	constitution
cannon	plural forms
Canterbury	Church of England
carsick	ill
carve	cut
cast	theatre
castle	chess
century	cricket
chairman	inclusive language
chance	odds
Chancellor	Treasury
chastise	-ise & -ize
cheapen	-en verb suffix
checkmate	chess
children's	childish
chop	cut
Christmas	days with special names
circumcise	-ise & -ize
City of London	police
clipper	ship
coarsen	-en verb suffix
coast	beach
coffin	death
cold	adjective
colon	punctuation
combine	stress differences
comma	punctuation
commander	police
commissioner	police
Commons	constitution
community	-arian
compact	noun & adjective
company	enterprises
complete	cease
compound	stress differences
comprise	-ise & -ize
compromise	-ise & -ize
conduct	stress differences
conflict	stress differences
Congregationalist	Dissenter and Nonconformist
conscript	stress differences
console	stress differences
constable	police
constabulary	police
constituency	elections
content	stress differences
contest	stress differences
contract	stress differences
contrast	stress differences
converse	stress differences
convert	stress differences
convict	stress differences
cooking	meals
coroner	death
costume	custom
costume	theatre
countable nouns	nouns
court-card	playing cards
couth	back-formation
craft	plural forms
cremate	death
croquet	cricket
Crown	constitution
crown	money
cruise	ship
cul-de-sac	road
currently	present & presently
curtain	theatre

D

daily	dairy
dampen	-en verb suffix
dance	ball
Dark Ages	England; Ireland; Roman influence in Britain
darken	-en verb suffix
dash	hit; punctuation
data	plural
deaden	-en verb suffix
deafen	-en verb suffix
deceased	death
decrease	stress differences
deepen	-en verb suffix
defect	stress differences

index

defendant .... law
deferred prepositions .... prepositions at the end
demise .... -ise &-ize
deposit .... elections
descendant/ent .... dependant/ dependent
desert .... stress differences
despise .... -ise &-ize
despite .... although
destination .... doom
destiny .... doom
devise .... -ise &-ize
dhow .... ship
diagnose .... back-formation
diary .... dairy
dictate .... stress differences
dim .... dark
diminutives .... -let
dinner .... meals
director .... theatre
discount .... stress differences
dis(en)franchise .... -ise &-ize
disguise .... -ise &-ize
dishonest .... compound nouns
disinterested .... interest
Disney .... lemming
donkey .... say
double .... single
doublespeak .... say
dove .... pigeons
Downing Street .... constitution
draft/draught .... draw
draught .... ship
drive .... travel
driving .... examination & test
dug .... breast
dull .... dark
duty .... tax

E

earn .... gain
Easter .... days with special names
Economist .... media
edit .... back-formation
effect .... affect
elderly .... ancient
elevenses .... meals
encore .... theatre
end .... cease
enfranchise .... -ise &-ize
ensure .... assure etc.
enterprise .... -ise &-ize
escort .... stress differences

euro .... money
every .... each
evil .... devil & evil
excise .... -ise &-ize
exclamation mark .... punctuation
excursion .... travel
exercise .... -ise &-ize
expertise .... -ise &-ize
exploit .... stress differences
export .... stress differences
Express .... media
exterior .... inner
external .... inner
extract .... stress differences
eyebrow .... brow

F

fall .... drop
fanfare .... fare
Far East .... East
farewell .... fare
farmstead .... instead
farthing .... money
fasten .... -en verb suffix
fate .... doom
fathom .... weights and measures
fatten .... -en verb suffix
fellow .... chap
ferry .... ship
figurehead .... ship
finalise .... cease
finance .... City of London; stress differences
finish .... cease
fire .... dismiss
fireman .... inclusive language
fish .... plural forms
flatten .... -en verb suffix
flight .... travel
flog .... hit
florin .... money
foot .... weights and measures
foothill .... compound nouns
fore .... ship
found .... find
founder .... find
foundry .... find
franchise .... -ise &-ize
Free Church .... Dissenter and Nonconformist
freshen .... -en verb suffix
full stop .... punctuation
funeral .... death

index

future perfect............perfect aspect

G
gallery......................theatre
galley.......................ship
gallon......................weights and measures
garment..................clothes
gay..........................etymology
gaze.........................see
genitive...................possessive
gestate....................back-formation
gill............................weights and measures
ginger......................ale and beer
gipsy........................gypsy
give rise to...............rise
gladden....................-en verb suffix
glance......................see
glimpse....................see
gloomy....................dark
glottal stop..............Estuary English; pronunciation
gods.........................theatre
going to..................future
Good.......................days with special names
grasshopper.............jump
great-......................family relationships
greed.......................back-formation
Greek......................plural
greyhound...............etymology
Guardian.................media
guinea.....................money
guy..........................chap

H
hack........................cut
hamlet....................city
harden....................-en verb suffix
hat..........................say
hawk......................pigeons
hearse....................death
heaven...................capital letters; haven &heaven
Hebrew..................Jew; plural
hectare...................weights and measures
hell..........................capital letters
helm.......................ship
hold........................ship
home......................house
Home Secretary........Home Office; police
homestead..............instead
hop.........................jump
hope.......................expect
Hope, Anthony........Ruritania
hot..........................adjective

hundredweight.........weights and measures
hungry.....................adjective
hypercorrection........case, grammatical
hyphen....................prefixes; punctuation

I
i.e............................e.g.
implicit...................imply
import....................stress differences
improvise...............-ise &-ize
incense...................stress differences
inch........................weights and measures
incise......................-ise &-ize
incline....................stress differences
increase..................stress differences
Independent............media
independent schools...........public schools
infantile.................childish
infer........................imply
inference...............modal auxiliary verbs
in front of..............before; opposite
-in-law...................family relationships
inquest...................death
inspector................police
insult......................stress differences
insure.....................assure etc.
intelligence............examination & test
intelligent..............clever
interior...................inner
internal...................inner
interval...................theatre
invalid....................noun & adjective
invaluable..............priceless
invent.....................discover
inverted comma......punctuation
Israel......................Jew
ITV.........................media

J
Jacobin...................Jacobean
Jacobite..................Jacobean
James.....................Jacobean
jealousy.................envy
journey..................travel
Judaism..................Jew
judge......................law
junk........................ship
jury.........................law
juvenile..................childish

K
kick........................hit
kin..........................kith & kin

index

king	chess
Kirk	Church of Scotland
knight	chess
knock	hit
knot	ship

L

lad	chap
lane	road
lass	chap
Latin	plural
latter	former
lawful	legal
lawn	grass
lay	lie
leap	jump
lease	hire
legitimate	legal
lessen	-en verb suffix
let	hire
liaise	back-formation
licit	legal
lift	stairs & steps
lighten	-en verb suffix
liken	-en verb suffix
liner	ship
listen	hear
London	City of London; police
look	see
loose	lose
loosen	-en verb suffix
lord etc.	honours and titles
Lords	constitution
loudspeaker	say
lough	loch
love	make love
lower case	case
lunch	meals

M

machine gun	gun
macho	female
madam	honours and titles
madden	-en verb suffix
Mail	media
maize	corn
majority	-arian; elections
make	do & make
male	female
mankind	inclusive language
many	lot
marmalade	jam
masculine	female
Maundy	days with special names
mayor	major
meanings, change in	semantic change
meat	flesh
media	plural
merchandise	-ise & -ize
Methodist	Dissenter and Nonconformist
metre	weights and measures
metropolitan	police
Middle East	East
mid, middle	centre
mile	weights and measures
milliard	dictionary words; numbers
mincemeat	flesh
Mirror	media
miscarriage	abortion & miscarriage
mishap	compound nouns
mistress	master
mizzen	ship
moisten	-en verb suffix
mongoose	plural forms
motel	blend
motorway	road
mourn	death
much	lot
murky	dark
Muslim	Islam

N

name	personal names; place names
nay	aye
Near East	East
necessity	modal auxiliary verbs
negotiations	say
newspeak	say
nice	etymology
nipple	breast
Nonconformist	Dissenter and Nonconformist
notoriety	-iety

O

oar	ship
oats	corn
object	stress differences
obligation	modal auxiliary verbs
obtain	get
occidental	dictionary words
on, onto	in; time
only	single
orient	East
ounce	weights and measures

index

out	away
outer	inner
over	cricket
overflow	stress differences
Oxbridge	blend

P

p	money
pall-bearer	death
paratroops	blend
pardon	forgive
Parliament	constitution
past perfect	perfect aspect
pawn	chess
peddle	back-formation
pence, penny	money
people	person and people
pepper	corn
perfect	stress differences
performance	examination & test
period	punctuation
permission	modal auxiliary verbs
permit	stress differences
personage	character
personality	character
personnel	personal
phantom	ghost
pharmacy	chemist
phone	call
phrasal verbs	multi-word verbs
pint	weights and measures
pistol	gun
plain clothes	police
plaintiff	law
policeman	inclusive language
polite	policy
politics	policy
poll	elections
poorly	ill
popcorn	corn
portmanteau word	blend
posh	etymology
possibility	modal auxiliary verbs
pound	hit; money; weights and measures
prediction	modal auxiliary verbs
pregnancy	examination & test
première	theatre
premise	-ise &-ize
prepositional verbs	multi-word verbs
prepositions	time
prescriptive	grammar
present	stress differences
present(ly)	current(ly)
present perfect	perfect aspect
prise (force open)	-ise &-ize
Prisoner of Zenda	Ruritania
Private Eye	media
Privy Council	Commonwealth; constitution
produce	stress differences
producer	theatre
programme	theatre
progress	stress differences
progressive	continuous aspect
promise	-ise &-ize
prompt	theatre
propriety	-iety
props	theatre
prospect	stress differences
protest	stress differences
public	company
puerile	childish
pun	homonym
punch	hit

Q

quadrillion	numbers
quarter	quarter, term & trimester; weights and measures
quarterdeck	ship
queen	chess
Queen's Counsel	law
question mark	punctuation
quicken	-en verb suffix
quieten	-en verb suffix
quintillion	numbers
quit	cease
quotation mark	punctuation

R

raise	rest
reach	get
reassure	assure etc.
rebel	stress differences
received pronunciation	BBC English
record	stress differences
redden	-en verb suffix
refund	stress differences
refusal	modal auxiliary verbs	will & would
refuse	stress differences
rehearse	theatre
reject	stress differences
rent	hire
reported speech	indirect speech; punctuation

index

reprise .... -ise & -ize
resurrect .... back-formation
revise .... -ise & -ize
revolver .... gun
reward .... prize
rhyming slang .... cockney
rifle .... gun
right .... adjective
ripen .... -en verb suffix
Roman .... Arabic numerals
romantic .... Roman
rook .... chess
roughen .... -en verb suffix
rudder .... ship
rugby .... football
rumour or gossip ..... say
run .... cricket
rye .... corn

S

Sabbath .... days with special names
sabbatical .... days with special names
sack .... dismiss
sadden .... -en verb suffix
safety .... abstract nouns
sail .... ship
sane .... healthy
sanitary .... healthy
scavenge .... back-formation
Scotland Yard .... police
seafarer .... fare
seasick ill
seat .... theatre
security .... safety
seem .... sense verbs
-self .... same
semicolon .... punctuation
sense verbs .... infinitive | bare infinitive
sentence .... law
sergeant .... police
sex .... gender & sex
sharpen .... -en verb suffix
shepherd .... compound nouns
shilling .... money
shirt .... skirt
shop .... say
shore .... beach
shorten .... -en verb suffix
shotgun .... gun
should .... could
sick ill
sicken .... -en verb suffix
silk .... law

silly .... etymology
sir .... honours and titles; letters
skip .... jump
slacken .... -en verb suffix
slap .... hit
slash .... cut; punctuation
slice .... cut
smack .... hit
small .... little
smarten .... -en verb suffix
smoke .... fumes
smoothen .... -en verb suffix
snob .... etymology
society .... -iety
soften .... -en verb suffix
sole .... single
solicitor .... law
some .... any
sooner .... would rather
sore .... etymology
sorry .... etymology
sovereign .... money
speak .... say
speakeasy .... say
Speaker .... constitution; say
special branch .... police
Spectator .... media
speech or lecture ...... say
spirit .... ghost
spokesman etc. .... say | speak
spook .... ghost
spouse .... family relationships
spring .... jump
stage .... theatre
stalemate .... chess
stall .... theatre
stamina .... plural
starboard .... port
stare .... see
Stars and Stripes ...... flags
start .... begin
Statesman .... media
stative .... dynamic
steal .... rob
steam .... fumes
step- .... family relationships
stern .... ship
stiffen .... -en verb suffix
still .... already, yet & still
stomach .... belly
stone .... weights and measures
stop .... cease
stouten .... -en verb suffix

index

straighten.................-en verb suffix
strait ....straight & strait
street..........................road
strike ....hit
stroke.........................hit; punctuation
stump.........................cricket
stupid.........................dumb
subject ....stress differences
submarine.................ship
successful ....adjective
such as.......................like
sue ....law
Sun ....media
superintendent.........police
supervise ....-ise &-ize
supper........................meals
sure.............................certain
surmise ....-ise &-ize
surprise......................-ise &-ize
survey........................stress differences
suspect.......................stress differences
sweeten ....-en verb suffix
sweetmeat ....flesh
syllabus ....curriculum

T

talk ....say
tauten.........................-en verb suffix
taxi ....cab
teat..............................breast
Telegraph ....media
televise ....back-formation; -ise &-ize
tell ....say
Thames......................t, T | th, TH
thence ....hence
there- ....here-
Theresa......................personal names
they (singular)..........inclusive language
thicken.......................-en verb suffix
thirsty ....adjective
Thomas ....notes for personal names
thorn..........................ye
thorough ....although
thoroughfare.............fare
thought ....although
thrash.........................hit
through ....although; road
throughout................although
thump ....hit
tighten ....-en verb suffix
Times ....media
tit................................breast
ton, tonne ....weights and measures

torment.....................stress differences
tough ....although
toughen ....-en verb suffix
town ....city
traffic warden ....police
transfer ....stress differences
transferred negation .negation of verbs
transport ....stress differences
trillion ....numbers
trip.............................travel
trough ....although
tummy ....belly

U

udder ....breast
umpire ....cricket
uncountable nouns ...nouns
uncover ....discover
underscore...............score
undertaker ....death
unique ....single
university ....-arian
unrest........................rest
unsafeness ....abstract nouns
upon ....on and upon
upper case ....case
upset..........................stress differences
urn ....death

V

valueless...................priceless
vapour ....fumes
variety ....-iety
vein ....vain
verdict ....law
very ....same
village ....city
voyage......................travel

W

wait for.....................expect
warfare ....fare
watch.........................see
weaken ....-en verb suffix
weathervane ....vain
wedding...................marriage
weep..........................cry
welfare ....fare
Westminster ....constitution
wheat........................corn
where- ....here-
whether ....if
while (whilst) ....amid(st)
Whitehall.................constitution

index

whiten	-en verb suffix
wicket	cricket
wide	broad
widen	-en verb suffix
wild animals	plural forms
win	gain
wings	theatre
wise	clever
witty	clever
worsen	-en verb suffix
worthless	priceless
would	could; used to, would & accustomed to
wrong	adjectives

Y

y	I | i & y
yard	weights and measures
Yeats	Keats and Yeats
yet	already, yet & still
yogh	gh, GH; z, Z
York	Church of England
youthful	childish

Also by Peter Harvey

Great English Mistakes
made by Spanish-speakers
(with a few Catalan specials)

An easy-to-read and user-friendly book … grammar receives careful attention … may benefit both intermediate and advanced students of English … Teachers of English may also find it useful.

TESOL Spain Newsletter

While [this book] is clearly aimed at the Spanish-speaking learner of English it is also valuable for the teacher of English working in a Spanish-speaking environment … [it highlights] many of the false friends which exist … Translations show the learner what words do, and, equally importantly, do not mean … with a wealth of real-life examples which are sometimes humorous, the book is very readable … There is certainly a gap in the market for such a book … of all the many English language books I have on my bookshelf, this is the only one that has a long waiting list of Spanish-speaking friends wanting to borrow it.

Modern English Teacher

Pearls of the English Language

As the name suggests, Lavengro Books Pearls are concentrated units of concise information averaging about 75 words each, intended for people learning English.

Each Pearl contains a point about the English language in a short form that is easy to assimilate and remember. The Pearls contrast with and complement the detailed descriptions contained in A Guide to English Language Usage.

For information about Lavengro Books
including full reviews and samples go to
www.lavengrobooks.com

Lavengro Books

English language usage made plain

www.ingramcontent.com/pod-product-compliance
Lightning Source LLC
Chambersburg PA
CBHW081208230426
43666CB00015B/2679